KU-451-096

NEWNES'
PICTORIAL KNOWLEDGE

VOLUME EIGHT

NEWNES'

PICTORIAL KNOWLEDGE

General Editors

R. H. POOLE

PETER FINCH, M.A.

WALTER SHEPHERD

Art Editor

A. H. J. HUMPHREYS

VOLUME 8

GEORGE NEWNES LIMITED

CARLTON HOUSE, GREAT QUEEN STREET,

LONDON, W.C.2

PRINTED IN GREAT BRITAIN
BY THE WHITEFRIARS PRESS LTD., LONDON AND TONBRIDGE, AND
BOUND BY HAZELL, WATSON & VINEY LTD., AYLESBURY AND LONDON
N.P.K. 7055. W.P. 5316

CONTENTS OF VOLUME EIGHT

Colour Plates

Special Colour Supplements

Photo-tone Supplements

The Long Hard Fight for the Freedom of the Seas

The Story of our Ships and the Sailors Who Man Them

RECORDS OF THE ROYAL NAVY

THERE had been one or two kings before Alfred who made use of ships to help them in their battles. But it is to King Alfred that the main credit must be given as the founder of the Royal Navy. Danish vessels at that time were in the habit of ravaging the coasts of England and were able to land their men at will. Alfred determined to put a stop to this form of amusement.

His biggest naval battle off the Devonshire coast was fought with nine of the new ships he had built specially for the task. It must have been a tough fight, with stranded vessels being attacked by parties of men who waded from their own ships to board the enemy craft, or with one ship getting alongside another and beginning a fight which was literally "to the death." Three of the Danish ships managed to get away but, owing to lack of men after the fierce battle, two of them were wrecked and the sole survivor was captured.

This was in 892, and for the rest of his reign Alfred had no more trouble with the Danes. These ships of Alfred's Navy were big for their time. They carried a single mast and some of them had as many as sixty oars. It was a long time before the Danes ventured across the sea again and they had learned the lesson of a big Navy. Having established themselves in England in 1013 they kept a strong fleet in readiness to guard the shores.

Harold, who came to the throne in 1066, might have commanded a fair-sized fleet but was busily occupied in fighting the invaders from Norway and failed to use his ships when the Normans crossed the Channel. Harold lost his life and William the Conqueror made full use of the ships both for defence and trade. William's successors followed the same way and Henry de Burgh in 1217 won a great naval victory over the French off Dover. When Richard Cœur de Lion set off on the Crusades he took the first English Navy overseas expedition, some of his ships carrying forty knights and their horses, with forty foot soldiers and a number of servants as well as fifteen seamen. The stores aboard were sufficient to last them for twelve months.

The men themselves were armed with bows and arrows, pikes, lances and swords, and had cumbersome weapons for throwing heavy stones, but most of the fighting that took place was of necessity hand-to-hand conflict. Yet the Navy was not, strictly speaking, the Royal Navy, nor were the vessels warships. They could trade or they could fight, but they were mostly private ships called on to serve the king. The Cinque Ports were required to furnish a certain number of galleys when demanded and the king paid for their use. It was not always easy to muster the ships and the ports often did their utmost to avoid the service, while the seamen preferred to carry on their own private wars against their neighbours on the other side of the Channel.

The first time the word "admiral" was used was about 1297 when William de Leybourne was made "Admiral of the Sea of the King of England." In 1340 Edward III was able to collect a fleet of some 200 vessels in all to attack a French fleet preparing to settle finally Edward's claim to be King of France. Edward's fleet crossed the sea and attacked the French at their anchorage. The result was the almost complete destruction of the French fleet. Ten years later the Navy of Edward III fought another great battle off Winchelsea against a Spanish freebooter Carlos de la Cerda, whose forty large ships had captured many English merchant ships. The English won a complete victory and for a short time the freedom of the seas was theirs.

Guns were first used around 1338 and in the time of Henry VII "the King's ships" came into being. One of them, the *Regent*, had four masts and was armed with 225 small guns known as serpentines. These ships of the *Regent* class were built for both war and trade; the

Specially drawn for this work.

HOW THE NAVY BEGAN

King Alfred is regarded as the real founder of the Royal Navy and the ships he built were big for their time. Our picture shows a ship of the type that protected England's shores in Alfred's reign and kept the Danes away for a full century after his death.

Specially drawn for this work.

THE CRUSADERS SET SAIL

Our first Overseas Naval Expedition sailed from English ports when Richard Cœur de Lion set forth on the Crusades to help in recapturing the Holy Land from the Saracens for the Christian countries of Europe. The ships carried sufficient stores aboard to last them for twelve months.

holds carried wool from England and brought back wine and other products of sunnier lands. A great part of the world's sea trade then was between the Mediterranean and the Baltic.

Sailors of Queen Bess

The Cinque Ports silted up and Portsmouth and Plymouth grew in importance. There were dockyards at Portsmouth, Woolwich and Deptford. Henry VIII succeeded his father and inherited the wealth gained by trade over the seas. One of the ships Henry VIII had built was *Henry Grace à Dieu*, or the *Great Harry*, a vessel of 1,000 tons, carrying over 150 brass or iron guns and 100 smaller guns. It was a show-piece, however, rather badly designed, but all told Henry had a navy of seventy-one ships, and there were many privateers, seeking fortunes but available for the king when necessary. Henry also brought in foreigners to help in the making of cannon, demi-cannon and culverins with which to arm his ships.

Spain had discovered the New World while Portugal opened up the sea routes to the East. Pope Alexander VI allotted the Western World to Spain and the Eastern to Portugal. England was left out, but her sailors had already begun to explore other parts of the Western world where the Spaniards had not encroached. There was tough John Hawkins, merchant, sailor, Member of Parliament, shipbuilder, and later a rear-admiral, in command of one of his own ships, the *Victory*, when the Armada came. Twice Hawkins sailed to the West Indies without encountering much trouble, but on the third occasion the Spaniards lured him almost to his doom. His ship was sunk, but he managed to board another, the *Minion*, and in the company of the *Judith*, commanded by a young Devon captain, Francis Drake, they sailed back to England, hating the Spaniards and with a fierce determination to open up the New World to British ships.

It was the beginning of a long war, unofficial but deadly in its intensity. Hawkins and Drake harried the Spanish merchantmen and captured immense treasure. Spain protested to England with whom she was at peace. British mariners who fell into Spanish hands were branded and burnt, and British ships were denied the right to sail the Western seas. Drake himself left a message with the envoys of Spain, asserting the right of Englishmen to sail wherever their merchandise was desired. Queen Elizabeth sent Drake on an expedition to find out what preparations the Spaniards were making. Right into the harbour at Cadiz, Drake sailed with four ships and burnt or sank about a hundred Spanish vessels. He had " singed the King of Spain's beard," in his own words, and then

Specially drawn for this work.

FOR WAR OR PEACEFUL TRADING

Henry VII developed overseas trade and built ships of the *Regent* class, as depicted above, suitable for both war and trade. These ships carried four masts and were armed with 225 small guns. The holds carried wool from England and brought back wine and other products.

Specially drawn for this work.

A DOCKYARD IN THE DAYS OF PEPYS

The first dockyard in British naval history was built at Woolwich about the time of Henry VIII for the king's ships. Other dockyards were built at Portsmouth, Deptford, Chatham and Sheerness. The famous diarist, Samuel Pepys, was Secretary of the Admiralty in the time of Charles II and our picture shows one of the dockyards at that time.

sailed the Spanish coasts, destroying or capturing other vessels.

Spain was preparing her great Armada to settle once and for all this claim of English sailors to the freedom of the seas and to avenge the acts of violence English ships had committed against the merchantmen of Spain. Drake's exploits at Cadiz and other interferences postponed the sailing of the Armada for two or three years, while in the Netherlands a large

Specially drawn for this work.

A SEVENTEENTH CENTURY FIRST-RATE

Towards the end of the seventeenth century the British Navy had become a fine fighting force and warships such as the "first-rate" shown above utterly destroyed the French fleet and all hopes of a successful invasion by the armies of Louis XIV.

Spanish army under the Duke of Parma lay waiting to be transported to England for the great invasion, once the Armada had cleared the seas of English ships. The English Commanders too were waiting, planning to break the Spanish fleet before ever it reached the Netherlands.

The English Navy, that is the "Queen's ships," only numbered thirty-four, but these were reinforced by the impressed ships, galleons, pinnaces, barks and galliots, all merchantmen owned and manned by men of the southern ports, and all ready to fight. Altogether Elizabeth's Navy numbered 197, most of them quite small craft, and on July 19th, 1588, the word came that the Spanish ships were in sight. The main English fleet was at Plymouth, under the command of Lord Howard of Effingham, with Drake, Frobisher and Hawkins as his chief officers, and that same night they put to sea.

The battle, or series of battles, lasted from July 21st to July 29th. The great Spanish fleet was badly handled; the smaller English ships were well manœuvred. Almost from the beginning of the fight the Spanish leaders were paralysed by the English methods of attack. Even so, the English could not get the upper hand. They could cling on to the enemy's heels and harry his ships without really bringing them to action. Then, as the wind freshened, the Spanish fleet came to anchor off Calais. Howard hastily prepared fireships and sent them drifting with wind and tide among the Spanish ships. In panic the Spaniards cut their cables and tried to sail away, and again the English ships attacked, but still had to keep out of range of the Spanish guns, though they drove them to the North, away from the waiting army in the Netherlands. Most of the English ships were short of ammunition by this time and put back to harbour for supplies.

The Spanish fleet was battered and beaten but was not destroyed entirely; it was the storm that completed the work that the English guns and fireships had begun. As the remnants of the Armada sought escape round the north of Scotland and down the coast of Ireland, one after another was driven on to the rocks before the fury of the gale, and the wrecks of the great Armada were piled up on the coasts of Scotland and Ireland. "The Lord sent His wind and scattered them" was the inscription in Latin on the medal struck to commemorate the complete overthrow of Spain's mighty Armada.

The untrained army of Elizabeth gathered at Tilbury that summer in 1588 to fight against the invaders from across the water was not unlike another citizen army that was enrolled as a Home Guard 352 years later in readiness for another expected

Specially drawn for this work.

OVER A CENTURY AGO

It was not until 1857 that a regular uniform for men of the Royal Navy became official, though the captains for years past had arranged for their men to buy "slop-clothes," as they were called, through pursers. Our picture shows a sailor in the dress generally worn about 1845.

invasion that failed to arrive just as the Duke of Parma's army had failed. The Navy of Queen Elizabeth established the freedom of the seas and broke the arrogant claims of Spain to restrain other ships from sailing wheresoever they wished.

Yet for a time after Elizabeth had died the Navy was allowed to decline. Cromwell revived it and organised a new merchant navy as well as a fighting navy. Under the command of one of the outstanding admirals in English history, Robert Blake, Britain waged war against the Dutch and again established her right to trade on the seas by final victory off the Thames in 1653. Nor did the Navy suffer again when Charles II was restored to the throne his father had lost. The Navy was directed by a board composed of men of experience such as Sir George Carteret, Sir Robert Slingsby, and others, with the famous diarist, Samuel Pepys, as secretary of the Admiralty.

Great Names in Naval History

In the reign of James II the Navy possessed 173 vessels, and when James gave way to William of Orange and his Queen, Mary, this fleet was ready to defend the shores of Britain against another invasion. It was the French under Louis XIV who prepared a great army for this purpose. The French fleet was powerful and at the chosen time it was ordered to attack and clear the Channel of all British ships. In May, 1692, two battles were fought, one at Barfleur and the other at La Hogue. The outcome was the utter destruction of the French fleet and once again the waiting armies across the Channel never had the chance to make history on English soil.

For a time the British Navy was supreme and the country's trade spread to the far corners of the world. Then for some years in the eighteenth century the Navy became weak till Anson rose to a position of authority. The story of this great admiral's voyage round the world (1740–44) is told elsewhere in these volumes; his ships became a school for seamen and his officers were men such as Hawke, Boscawen, Rodney, Howe and Keppel, names still honoured in the Royal Navy of to-day. The building of warships was improved, too, though conditions for men at sea were primitive and the food often revolting even to the tough men who could stand up to the hardships inseparable from the life of a sailor in those days.

From Cabin-boy to Admiral

It is to Nelson that many improvements aboard the ships of the Royal Navy were due. " These things are for the Commander-in-Chief to look to," he wrote in 1803 when explaining some of the steps he had taken on his own ships. He believed in the virtues of onions for seamen, good mutton for the sick, and plenty of fresh water for all on board. Lime-juice became a regular issue in Nelson's day. Yet the sailors of the Royal Navy had no official uniform at that time, though efforts were made in that direction by the supply of " slop-clothes " to be bought by the men from the pursers. Actually it was not until 1857 that a regular uniform for men of the Royal Navy became official.

Naval officers had official uniform a century before this. They began their training early. Drake went to sea at twelve and so did Nelson, Rodney, and many other famous sailors. The " cabin-boy " or captain's servant, as he was sometimes called, was generally a youngster known to the captain and taken to sea under his care to learn seamanship. Nelson was a " captain's servant " on his uncle's ship. The rule for many years was that a seven-years' apprenticeship had to be served before a boy became a midshipman. Often enough, however, the captains had the power to promote their protégés in a shorter time. A system of examinations had begun as long ago as 1728 and a Naval Academy was opened in that year at Portsmouth. The cabin-boy method, however, went on until 1859, when the *Britannia* became the training-school of all naval cadets.

There was nothing in the way of training or inducements for the men who manned the ships. From 1355 in Edward III's reign down to 1815 the press-gang was the authorised method of recruiting men when ships were short-handed. The "takers," as they were called in Elizabeth's days, were bodies of men who "impressed" or seized men in seafaring towns and forcibly took them aboard a warship to become sailors whether they liked it or not. There were certain rules governing the press-gang but they amounted to very little. Even merchant seamen returning from a long voyage overseas were taken and had no redress. Some of the local authorities had to supply men under a quota system, and usually did it by releasing prisoners from the gaol so that they would fall into the hands of the press-gang.

Specially drawn for this work.

THE PRESS-GANG AT WORK

From 1315 right down to 1815 the Navy gained new recruits when volunteers were lacking by means of the press-gang. Men were forcibly seized in towns by the sea and taken aboard a warship to become sailors whether they liked it or not.

It was neither an efficient nor a reliable system and the wonder is that the country tolerated it so long. Captains had grounds for complaint, too, since men were brought aboard who were totally unfitted for life at sea. It is equally remarkable that these pressed men, despite the injustice and hardships, made the British Navy mistress of the seas. In 1815 the press-gang method of recruiting for the Navy came to an end, though the right of impressing men was never properly abolished.

There were many other grievances in the Navy which lasted far too long. Brutal treatment, wretched living conditions, bad food and little enough of it at that, and lack of pay were the chief. No wonder there were desertions and mutinies. It was not merely the ships' officers who were to blame ; in a good many cases conditions were not so very much better for them on half-rotten ships and poor quarters. Much of the fault lay with those on land whose duty it was to see that the Navy was properly provisioned and that corruption and jobbery on the part of officers and their clerks was made impossible.

Yet reforms did come, and men such as Anson, Nelson, Howe, and John Jervis, when as Earl St. Vincent he became first Lord of the Admiralty in 1801, are outstanding names in naval history not only for their seamanship and battle records but also for the great work they did in improving conditions in the Navy.

The Glorious First of June

When the Seven Years' War broke out in 1756 the press-gang as well as the offer of bounties were both needed badly. The Navy was not prepared. Yet by 1759 the French fleet had been beaten in several minor battles and then at Quiberon Bay in the same year Hawke gained a decisive victory. The British fleet was free to go wherever it wished and the outcome of the war was no longer in doubt.

War came again with France in 1793, the beginning of that struggle which developed into the Napoleonic wars. One of the greatest victories in the history of the Royal Navy was the battle which came to an end on the "glorious first of June," 1794, when after four days' fighting the fleet under Lord Howe completely defeated and almost destroyed the French fleet off Ushant. It was followed by other victories off Cape St. Vincent in 1797 and the destruction of the Dutch fleet in the same year. The great plans for the invasion of Britain had once more been temporarily banished.

Yet twice during this year of 1797 there were serious mutinies in the Navy. The first was at Spithead and was well-organised and disciplined; the sailors put many of their officers ashore and refused to sail until their grievances were put right. The Admiralty gave in; pay was raised, some hundred or so officers were dismissed for brutality and jobbery, and the mutineers were pardoned.

The mutiny at the Nore did not end so happily. The ringleader, Parker, was eventually handed over to the authorities and hanged, and the outbreak was sternly suppressed. Yet it was one of several warnings to those in authority and efforts were made to improve conditions in the Navy.

A bigger threat against England was looming up across the Channel. Napoleon Bonaparte's great schemes of domination began to take shape, not only in Europe but towards the East as well. The British Navy under Nelson called a halt to his Eastern plans by the decisive defeat of the French at the Battle of the Nile in 1798. In 1802 came a peace that was merely a temporary truce, and the Navy was kept prepared for the war which threatened almost before the peace treaty was signed.

'Twas in Trafalgar's Bay

It came in 1803 and in the following year Spain joined France. Their combined fleets eventually put to sea in January, 1805, on Napoleon's orders. For two years he had made extensive plans for the invasion of England and the preparations were almost complete. But it was not until October that Nelson was able to bring the enemy to battle. On the 21st of that month the most famous sea battle in English history took place off Cape Trafalgar on the south-west coast of Spain. It was a short but fierce fight. Not until noon was the first shot fired, but by 1.30 the battle was at its height and it was shortly before this that Nelson was fatally wounded on board his flagship the *Victory*. At half-past four

AT THE BATTLE OF THE NILE

Specially drawn for this work.

One of Nelson's great victories was at the Nile on August 1st, 1798. The French admiral's ship blew up, and to save as many of the enemy as possible Nelson ordered the boats away and every exertion was made. As a result about seventy French sailors were saved.

that afternoon the great admiral died with the knowledge that overwhelming victory had crowned his last and greatest battle.

Fifteen enemy ships were taken or destroyed, and of the eighteen that escaped two were wrecked and four others captured later. No British ships were lost. Trafalgar established the supremacy of the British Navy on the seas of the world, a supremacy that was never really challenged for more than a hundred years. In that time great changes took place. The wooden sailing ships of Trafalgar made their last voyages; steam took the place of sails, and iron and steel replaced the wooden walls. Guns were improved and the old solid cannon balls, the grape-shot and chain-shot were ousted by the new explosive shells. Whitehead invented the torpedo in 1870.

Another menace to the big ships came in the last ten years of the nineteenth century. The submarine vessel was not altogether a new idea, but until the motor-engine was devised it was not a very practical proposition to build an underwater craft. Submarines armed with torpedoes were launched and according to some experts their development spelt the death knell of big battleships. Britain was one of the last countries to become really interested in this kind of ship but, having made a start about 1900, she quickly made up the leeway.

The Submarine in War

Then war came again in 1914. The German submarines, known as U-boats, only came into action step by step, though the first attack on a merchantman was made in October, 1914, when the *Glitra*, a steamer of under 1,000 tons, was sunk off Norway after her crew had been given time to get away in boats. Until the Germans proclaimed their disregard for all the rules previously made about attacks on merchantmen, it was laid down by international law that while a warship could capture a merchantman, and, in certain circumstances, sink it, full provision must be made for the safety of all on board, who were of course non-combatants.

In 1915 the Germans proclaimed that the waters round Great Britain and Ireland were a war zone and any merchantmen in those waters would be sunk. Within a year some 1,724 ships of over 1,000 tons were lost. Then early in 1917 an unrestricted submarine campaign was launched and sinkings rapidly increased. The British and American navies concentrated all their ingenuity on efforts to defeat this form of warfare. Convoys, guarded by escorts from the Navy, lessened the sinkings; Q-boats, which looked like harmless merchantmen but were really fully-armed fighting ships, lured the submarines to their doom. Other anti-submarine devices were devised and the U-boat warfare, if not completely mastered, was rendered ineffective.

At the Battle of Jutland

There were no spectacular sea-battles comparable with the Armada, Quiberon, the Nile or Trafalgar, but the battle of Jutland saw a larger number of warships opposed to each other than ever known before. It began on May 31st, 1916, and continued into the next day. Mist, and the excellent use of smoke-screens by the enemy, brought about an indecisive result. The Germans indeed made a weak claim that the victory was theirs since the British losses in ships were rather heavier than the German. On the British side victory could be claimed on stronger grounds. The Germans had tried to avoid action; the British had taken risks to force the enemy to fight and they were left in undisputed possession of the sea with the German fleet forced into hiding from which it never dared emerge again until the day when it sailed out to surrender at the end of the war.

Most of the German ships were

scuttled by their own crews after that surrender at Scapa Flow in June, 1919. Once the war was over even the victorious nations desired nothing better than a rest from all the strenuous shipbuilding programmes they had laid down. At the Washington Conference in 1921 the leading nations agreed to limit their navies and enjoy a kind of naval holiday for ten years. It was not altogether a success but it gave time to think about the whole question of what naval warfare might mean in the future.

Aircraft for the Navy

Aeroplanes had developed rapidly though their possibilities in naval co-operation had not been tested to any extent. Their development in naval warfare might render the big battleships useless. Ideas and opinions differed very widely, particularly on the question of aircraft carriers. The flying-off deck of such a vessel would be an admirable target for enemy bombers, and once that was damaged the usefulness of the carrier had gone. Nevertheless aircraft carriers seemed necessary. Warships were fitted with catapults to launch aeroplanes, and the Fleet Air Arm experimented with many ideas and with several different types of aircraft.

Then came the war of 1939–45 and the value of aeroplanes to the Navy was quickly demonstrated. Some hard lessons were learned, too, particularly when the Japanese launched their attacks by carrier-borne aircraft on the American Navy at Pearl Harbour in December, 1941.

This sensational start crippled the American fleet for the time being. Two U.S. battleships were sunk, three disabled, three heavily damaged, while

Specially drawn for this work.

THE FIRST BRITISH IRONCLAD

There was long argument before the first British ironclad warship was built, but in 1860 the *Warrior* was completed at Blackwall, and the long and glorious reign of the wooden fighting-ship was over. In time wrought-iron gave way to specially hardened steel plates.

extensive damage or destruction of cruisers, destroyers and aircraft occurred. Three days later the British battleship *Prince of Wales* and the cruiser *Repulse* sailed into the Gulf of Siam without the protection of fighter aircraft and were ignominiously sunk by Japanese bombers. For a short time Japan held naval supremacy.

The entry of America into the war extended the scope of naval operations and it was followed by a steep rise in submarine sinkings of our merchant ships as the U-boats pressed into new and undefended waters such as the Gulf of Mexico and the Caribbean Sea.

It was for a time a bad patch for the Allies, especially in the East, where for various reasons it had been impossible for Britain to have her fleet at full strength. There had been other more urgent demands on the Navy in the Western hemisphere. When war broke out in 1939 the powerful French fleet shared with Britain the task of guarding the sea-routes of the world. In the Mediterranean the British fleet had bases at Gibraltar, Alexandria and Malta and was also able to use French bases when necessary. Italy was neutral and the Mediterranean was completely under Allied control.

In June, 1940, Italy declared war, France fell, and within a short time the coastline of Europe from Norway to the South of France was largely in German hands. The French Navy was no longer with Britain and there was a possibility that it would be used against us. The narrow seas of the Mediterranean could now be largely controlled by the enemy aircraft bases in Sicily, Sardinia, and the Italian mainland, while the Italian fleet from its base at Taranto was presumably ready to deal with the comparatively small British Mediterranean fleet. An

Planet News.

ANTI-SUBMARINE HOVERPLANES

The first anti-submarine helicopter squadron went into operational service with the Royal Navy in 1954, and here the " hoverplanes " are seen flying over shipping in the Solent. They are powered by Wright Cyclone engines and are known in the Navy as Whirlwinds.

THE COST OF KEEPING THE SEAS

Specially drawn for this work.

By air and submarine attack the enemy did his utmost to prevent the convoys bringing supplies to Britain from reaching our ports. Ships of the Navy protected the convoys, and in the picture above an incident of this ceaseless battle is shown: an H class destroyer has received a mortal wound and the end is near.

MOTOR GUNBOATS AND "JOLLIES"

Manned by the young men of the Coastal Forces, the Motor Torpedo Boats and Motor Gunboats, "flyweight terrors" of the Navy, carried out hard-hitting raids on enemy shipping during the war years. They operated mainly on the east and south coasts from bases seventy-five to 100 miles from enemy shores.

Photos : Crown Copyright.

Soldiers and sailors, too, are the Royal Marines, a regiment whose history goes back to 1664, when the Admiralty of that day decided to train their own soldiers for service on board ship. Our photograph shows a Royal Marine crew manning the pom-pom gun of a battleship at sea. Their nickname of the "Jollies" is almost as old as the regiment itself.

BRITAIN'S LATEST DESTROYER

Keystone.

One of the largest destroyers ever ordered by the Royal Navy, H.M.S. *Daring* was the first of her class to be built and after completion joined the Mediterranean Fleet. She is fitted with electrical cooking apparatus and many mechanical and labour-saving devices for cleaning ship. Her displacement is 3,500 tons and her armament includes twelve guns.

Topical Press.

H.M.S. *Daring* was nicknamed " Ugly Duckling " because of her odd appearance, but she is fitted with the most modern radar and other devices. This photograph shows naval ratings aboard the *Daring* loading a " squid," an anti-submarine weapon. This is a type of mortar now carried by many destroyers and frigates. The " squid " fires a pattern of charges ahead of the ship.

Italian picture put out just after they declared war showed the British fleet cornered and helpless against the overwhelming Italian sea and air power.

Yet the British Mediterranean fleet under Admiral Cunningham put to sea on the day after the Italian declaration of war and swept the Central Mediterranean. Another force under Admiral Somerville assembled at Gibraltar to defend the Western end and to make attacks in the Atlantic if necessary. The French fleet at Oran on the North African coast suddenly became a dangerous threat and Admiral Somerville was compelled to sink or damage some of the French ships. At Alexandria the French ships agreed to disarm.

In the Mediterranean

When the Italian fleet did at last venture out they were promptly attacked, and just as promptly they turned away and raced back to port again. In July there was another clash and an Italian cruiser was sunk; the Swordfish of the Fleet Air Arm were also busy whenever opportunity offered and sank submarines, destroyers and depot-ships. Our own submarines were also engaged on many hazardous tasks, while destroyers carried out surprise night bombardments until the Australian officer in charge of the flotilla had to report: "All targets driven inland, leaving practically nothing to be engaged from seaward."

The Italian fleet refused to be drawn from its safe hiding-place in the harbour at Taranto. The aircraft carrier *Illustrious* took up a position 170 miles from Taranto on November 11th, 1940, and from there her torpedo-carrying planes attacked the Italian ships. Half the Italian fleet was put out of action that night and the oil-storage depot was successfully bombed by the flare-carrying planes after they had lighted the target for the torpedo-carrying planes. Photographs taken by reconnaissance aircraft the next day confirmed the airmen's belief that tremendous damage

Central Press.

A GAS TURBINE WARSHIP ON PATROL

This patrol boat *Bold Pioneer* is the first operational warship powered by gas-turbine engines to come into service with the Royal Navy. With her sister-ship *Bold Pathfinder* they are the first of a new class of light warship. They are 121 ft. long, with a beam of 25 ft. 6 ins., and carry a crew of two officers and sixteen ratings.

Central Press.

BRITAIN'S LARGEST AIRCRAFT CARRIER

One of the largest and newest aircraft carriers, H.M.S. *Eagle*, 36,800 tons, is seen here. Built by Harland & Wolff at their Belfast yards, she was the first in any Navy designed to operate jet aircraft, and is able to launch one every twenty seconds from her flight decks, which cover more than two acres. H.M.S. *Eagle* is the twenty-first British warship of her name.

had been done. The night's work made the British Fleet the master for the time being of the Mediterranean.

Greece had entered the war when Italy invaded the country in October 1940. Fresh responsibilities were laid upon Admiral Cunningham's fleet. Troops had to be safely transported from North Africa to help the Greeks in their desperate struggle. The Italians were beaten back, but the German Luftwaffe appeared on the scene. Against them the British had little or no fighter opposition to put up.

The Spirit of Tenacity

Towards the end of March, 1941, the Italian fleet decided to come out. Overwhelming odds on land and in the air had driven the British army in Greece into desperate straits. The Italians were in a position now to upset any plans the British fleet might have in connection with evacuating the Army from Greece and Crete. The result was the brilliant night victory off Matapan when the British fleet sank at least three 10,000-ton cruisers and two destroyers, and crippled the flagship of the Italian fleet as well as seriously damaging other enemy ships. The rest of the Italian fleet made no further attempts to interfere with the work of the Navy but left it to the Luftwaffe. With little to oppose them the German planes made the position of the British forces on Crete a hopeless one.

Aircraft and gliders brought over the German land forces. The attempts of the Germans to take troops across from the mainland by sea were frustrated by the British Navy. On one night alone, that of May 21st, 1941, an enemy convoy carrying 4,000 German soldiers to Crete was completely destroyed.

The Germans did their utmost to exact a full revenge by air attacks on the fleet, and the damage they did was heavy. Nevertheless, despite the severe strain both men and ships sustained,

Planet News, Ltd.

MIGHTIEST BATTLESHIP AND LARGEST LINER

In this photograph is seen Britain's mightiest battleship, the 42,500 ton H.M.S. *Vanguard* as she sails down the Clyde and passes quite near to the biggest ship in the world, the 85,000 ton liner *Queen Elizabeth*.

the task was accomplished ; the Army was safely brought back from Greece and Crete though the German hordes took possession of the land. At the end of his dispatch the Commander-in-Chief wrote " There is rightly little credit or glory to be expected in these operations of retreat, but I feel that the spirit of tenacity shown by those who took part should not go unrecorded."

Romance and Drudgery

That same spirit of tenacity was shown by the Royal Navy on all the Seven Seas. Whether guarding the convoys across the Atlantic, to Malta, to North Africa, through the Arctic to take much-needed supplies to Russia, across the equator to India and Burma or still farther, to the Pacific where the Japanese fleet was for just a short time triumphantly dominant, or whatever other task they were called upon to do, the Navy carried it through.

To-day the Royal Navy is made up of many types of ships from mighty battleships to midget submarines. There are great aircraft-carriers, battle-cruisers, destroyers, corvettes, frigates, scout and patrol vessels, mine-layers and minesweepers, fast-moving motor gunboats and motor torpedo-boats.

Each type made its own special contribution to naval supremacy, and most of them would require volumes to themselves to give their story adequately. Stories of the submarines and the aircraft-carriers make thrilling reading, but there are other craft that scarcely seem to offer much in the way of romance but a great deal of hard drudgery with even a bigger share of dangerous risks.

There are the minesweepers, for instance, many of them in peace-time doing their job as fishing trawlers. In war-time they changed over from fishing for herrings to the more dangerous task of fishing for the deadliest ship-wrecking devices German scientists could devise. They kept the channels to our ports clear of the dreaded mines. With mine-laying submarines and aeroplanes the enemy hoped to make every port in Britain impossible to enter or leave. Mine-sweeping demands courage of the highest order as well as precise navigation. The work was often done in the face of air attack and with quite a big possibility that

SOME BADGES WORN BY NAVAL RATINGS

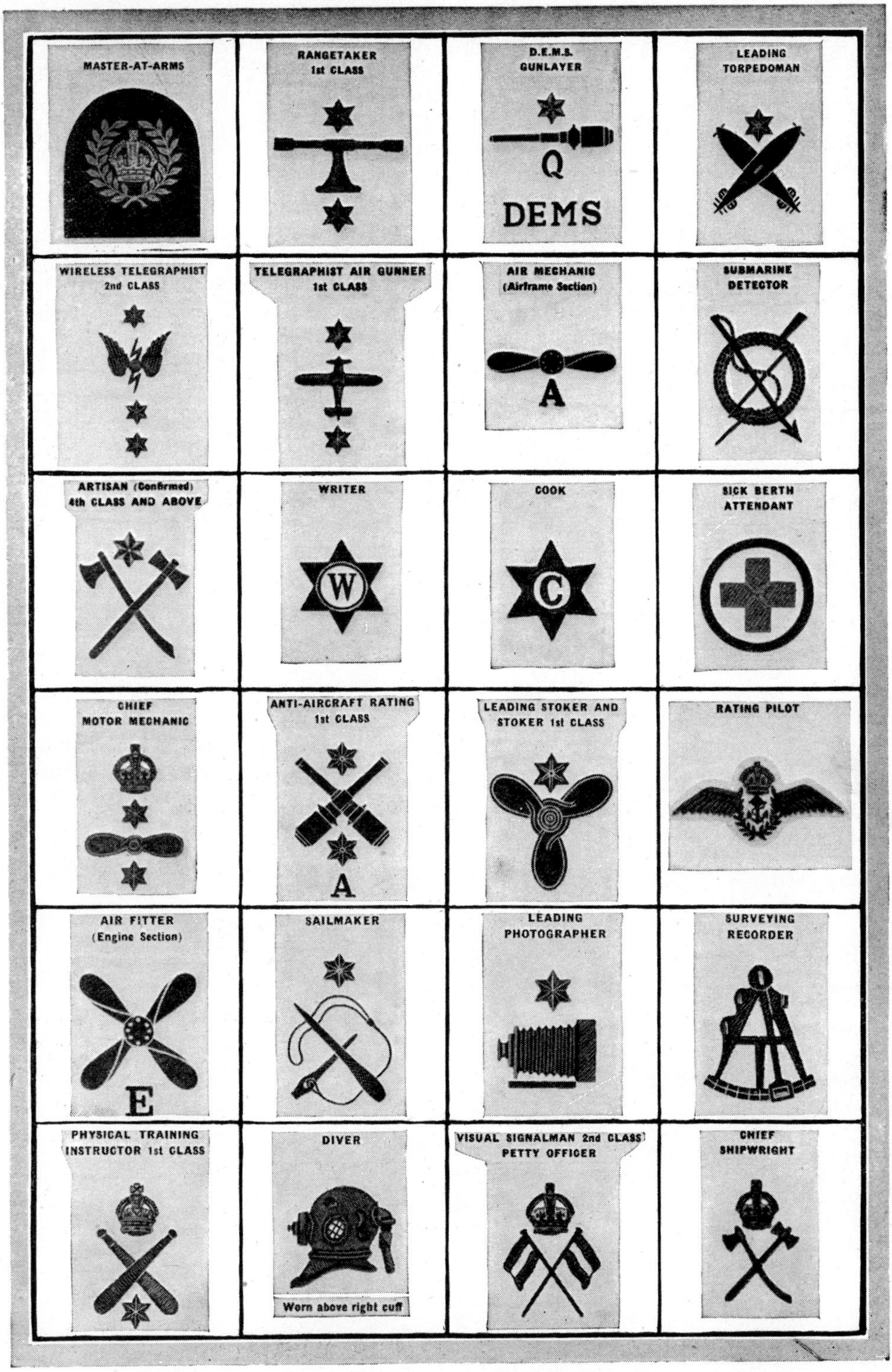

MASTER-AT-ARMS	RANGETAKER 1st CLASS	D.E.M.S. GUNLAYER	LEADING TORPEDOMAN
WIRELESS TELEGRAPHIST 2nd CLASS	TELEGRAPHIST AIR GUNNER 1st CLASS	AIR MECHANIC (Airframe Section)	SUBMARINE DETECTOR
ARTISAN (Confirmed) 4th CLASS AND ABOVE	WRITER	COOK	SICK BERTH ATTENDANT
CHIEF MOTOR MECHANIC	ANTI-AIRCRAFT RATING 1st CLASS	LEADING STOKER AND STOKER 1st CLASS	RATING PILOT
AIR FITTER (Engine Section)	SAILMAKER	LEADING PHOTOGRAPHER	SURVEYING RECORDER
PHYSICAL TRAINING INSTRUCTOR 1st CLASS	DIVER — Worn above right cuff	VISUAL SIGNALMAN 2nd CLASS PETTY OFFICER	CHIEF SHIPWRIGHT

the vessel would itself be mined. Many minesweepers were lost, but the work went on unceasingly.

One of the Secret Weapons

There was one particular type of mine, however, that beat even the minesweepers for a time and threatened to accomplish the enemy's highest hopes. This was the magnetic mine, the first of Hitler's secret weapons, though the idea was not entirely new by any means. The ordinary moored mine, constructed with sufficient buoyancy to float just below the surface of the sea, exploded only if one of the sensitive horns was broken by the impact of the hull of a ship. The magnetic mine lay on the bottom in comparatively shallow water. Its firing mechanism was actuated by the magnetic field of a ship passing above it.

The recovery intact of the first magnetic mine for the naval scientists to examine is one of the greatest stories of British seamen's gallantry during the war. Once the scientists had it in their hands the remedy was soon found. Magnetic minesweepers were produced and, in addition, all merchant ships were fitted as soon as possible with a de-gaussing girdle which neutralised the ship's magnetic field and left the mine over which it passed as harmless as a chunk of old iron at the bottom of the sea.

The acoustic mine was another secret weapon. Its existence was suspected and an unexploded mine recovered, rendered harmless, then dissected and examined by the naval scientists. In this case the firing mechanism was operated by the sound waves transmitted through the water from the

Radio Times.

AT SEA WITH THE FLEET

Exercises under conditions such as those which would be encountered in wartime are regularly carried out by ships of the Royal Navy. In this drawing by C. E. Turner an impression of such an exercise while it was taking place in the English Channel is depicted. The aircraft carrier H.M.S. *Illustrious* is escorted by a destroyer and an " enemy " submarine can be seen on the right, while both defending and attacking aircraft are coming into action.

TRAINING THE FROGMEN

During the last war specially-trained volunteers carried out daring underwater raids, attaching limpets and other explosive charges to enemy shipping. To-day the " fiogmen " are trained at the Royal Marines Amphibian School and here a canoeist is taking a frogman to a selected spot.

Photos : Central Press.

Methods of entering the water are being practised here. Afterwards the rescue of the frogman will be carried out. The canoeist in the top picture may wait for his companion, or in other cases rescue may be effected from a dinghy by means of a rope loop through which the floundering frogman thrusts his arms.

ship's engines. The answer was found, and remained a secret, but the acoustic mine joined the magnetic mine as a weapon which failed to explode.

The Battle of Scientists

In naval warfare it is to-day as much a battle of wits between scientists on each side as it is between the skill and courage of the men on board the ships on either side. At Trafalgar one of the French ships opened fire on the *Victory* at $1\frac{1}{4}$ miles range, to which Nelson's ship made no reply until within 30 feet, and then every gun on the broadside came into action.

At the Battle of Midway Island in June, 1942, when the American Navy inflicted heavy damage on the Japanese fleet, the battle opened when the opposing fleets were 700 miles apart. All the casualties, including four aircraft-carriers lost by the Japanese and one by the United States Navy, were caused by naval aircraft flying many hundreds of miles from their carriers during a four-day battle.

Conditions of naval warfare have undergone remarkable changes within the last few years, and difficult problems will face those in charge of our Navy during the next few years. The new weapons, and in particular the range, speed, and capacity of modern aircraft, have brought in tremendous new factors. Even the biggest and most heavily armoured battleship can be sunk by aircraft. The only protection is adequate fighter cover to drive off the attacking planes. That means more aircraft-carriers and perhaps fewer mighty battleships. The Fleet Air Arm to-day is probably the most essential branch of the Navy.

In Australia and Canada

Britain's naval power is not confined to the fleets based on United Kingdom ports. The Royal Canadian Navy and the Royal Australian Navy form an important part of the mighty sea defences which protect the citizens of the great British Commonwealth. The Royal Canadian Navy is planned mainly as an anti-submarine fleet and is designed for speedy expansion in any emergency.

At present the flagship of the Royal Australian Navy is the aircraft-carrier *Vengeance*, on loan from Britain while *H.M.A.S. Melbourne* is being built in Britain to join the aircraft-carrier *Sydney*. In addition the Royal Australian Navy has a number of destroyers, frigates, mine-sweepers, and other craft, as well as ships in reserve. Four of the new *Daring* class destroyers are being built in Australia, the first having been launched in Sydney in 1952.

Other Commonwealth countries can make their naval contributions to the strength of the forces ready to defend all parts of the Commonwealth, should the necessity arise. In every part of the Commonwealth men will be found whose pride it is that they have served in the Royal Navy.

The Navy Will Be There

Whatever new types of warship may be evolved, or whatever new trades or professions may be added to the long list already practised by our modern sailors, one fact stands firm. The Navy will be there, as it always has been, and the great traditions built up through long years by British seamen will be carried on. Old Tom Bowling has gone below and the great sails have given place to turbine engines; electricians and mechanics, wireless and radar operators, engineers and photographers, all form part of the big ship's company to-day, but the skilled sailmaker has not vanished, though his job to-day is to repair the canvas of gun coverings and awnings.

Drake is in his hammock, sleeping his last long sleep in Nombre Dios Bay but his spirit is still alive in the Royal Navy of to-day. That spirit has been shown a thousand times since the days when the sailors of Britain established their right to the freedom of the seas.

The Ships that Carry British Merchandise Across the Seas—

And the Men who Bring Back the Food To Our Home Ports

THE MERCHANT NAVY

FOR long centuries Britain has been a seafaring nation, and the Royal Navy dates its beginning from the closing years of the ninth century when King Alfred built his long-boats to ward off invasion. No one can be so definite about the beginning of the Merchant Navy; from little boats that ventured on perilous voyages between one coastal settlement and another, and carried on some form of barter, the Merchant Service slowly developed. To-day the carrying of merchandise and passengers in ships sailing to and from all parts of the world has become one of Britain's greatest industries.

The first shipping code was drawn up in the reign of Richard I (Cœur de Lion) who reigned from 1189 to 1199. Richard needed many ships to transport his fighting men to the East on his great Crusade. The Crusades, indeed, began an era of travel in Western Europe and opened up the possibilities of trade by means of shipping. In Magna Carta (1215) it states in the 41st Article that "all merchants shall have safe conduct to go out or come into England and to stay there; to pass either by land or water and to buy and sell by the ancient allowed customs without any civil tolls."

Trade with the Continent began to grow, and the history of the Navy is mixed up with that of the merchants' ships, which were liable to be called upon to serve the king in defence of the realm at any time. Edward III (1322-77) was the first English ruler who directed his policy towards the expansion of trade. He fought wars against France in order to make the English merchants' trade with Flanders more secure.

It was in this reign, too, that the Merchant Adventurers came into prominence. They were a body of leading merchants chiefly concerned with the export of cloth to the Continent where their great trading centre was Bruges. Similar companies were formed later in Bristol and York. Not very much is known about the ships which were used for this Continental trade in the fourteenth and fifteenth centuries, but it is probable they were under 100 feet long and by modern standards no more than 200 tons burden. They carried one sail and were fitted with a rudder hung on the stern-post. Before this period vessels were steered with a rudder lashed to the starboard quarter.

Bigger ships were built and the Portuguese began to take a lead in shipbuilding, though the shipbuilders in Venice and Genoa were also well known. In England naval architecture developed during the reign of Henry V, but the merchant service suffered for it. The Portuguese, on the other hand, designed ships to withstand the gales of the Atlantic and it was her navigators who began that great era of exploration when the vast continent of North and South America was discovered, the coasts of Africa were explored, and both the East and West Indies became known.

A great deal is owed to a Portuguese prince, Henry the Navigator, son of an English mother and a grandson of John of Gaunt. Maritime exploration and scientific navigation were the objects to which he devoted the greater part of his life. To a very considerable extent it was these studies of Prince Henry and the improved instruments for navigation he devised, as well as his methods of charting, that made longer voyages possible.

Specially drawn for this work.

A SHIP OF THE 15th CENTURY

In the earlier years of shipbuilding in this country a vessel was designed for both trade and war. The ship depicted above was known as a carrack and with its bluff bows is typical of the 15th century. Usually these vessels were about 600 tons burden.

The compass had been known long before his time and was steadily improved. The astrolabe enabled the sailor to calculate latitude and to take altitudes. It was superseded in the eighteenth century by the quadrant and then by the sextant. For a long time the hour-glass was the only means of telling time, while the actual speed of the vessel was largely a matter of guesswork.

Christopher Columbus in his *Santa Maria* was the first to touch the fringes of America when he landed on the Bahamas, but John Cabot, born in Genoa as Columbus was, is entitled to

Specially drawn for this work.

A BINNACLE OF THE 17th CENTURY

In the ships of the 17th and 18th centuries the half-minute glass, compass, long-board, etc., were stored in the binnacle, or bittacle as it was then spelt, and in the picture above is shown one of these old-time essentials for navigation.

claim to be the first to have set foot on the mainland. Cabot made his home in Bristol, and in 1496 received from Henry VII an authority to "seek out, discover and find" all hitherto unknown lands. Bristol already had a considerable trade with Iceland and Cabot decided to explore Greenland. After that he turned south and eventually touched the coast of Canada in the region of Quebec. The inhabitants had only fish, furs and timber to offer. To-day these are valuable enough, but they were not the kind of merchandise Cabot had set out to find and he returned with little to show for his venture.

Gradually the Spaniards and the Portuguese established important trade routes to America and India, and, with the backing of the Pope, they claimed exclusive rights to all the vast wealth opened up to them by these early navigators. Magellan, who renounced his Portuguese nationality owing to a quarrel with the king, offered his services to Spain. He was the first to cross the Pacific, and though he himself was killed in a fray with the natives of the Philippine Islands in April, 1521, his ship, the *Vittoria*, under its captain, Sebastian del Cano, reached Seville in September, 1522, after a three years' voyage. They had sailed more than 40,000 miles and circumnavigated the world.

Francis Drake was the next to sail round the world in 1577–80. He was followed in 1586–88 by Thomas Cavendish who brought back much valuable information. This led a few years later to the founding of the famous East India Company and British trade with the East was opened up.

There were other navigators who brought back knowledge and valuable information. Merchants anxious for trade and fortune took big risks. A ship was bought and a captain and crew were gathered. The merchant probably staked his whole fortune in the ship and cargo she carried. The sailors staked their lives, yet volunteers were never lacking. There was the prospect of adventure and of a fair reward, even the gambling chance of picking up something of very considerable value on one's own account, since much of the trade in these early days was by barter.

The East India Company, otherwise

Specially drawn for this work.

THE SAILOR'S SAND-GLASS

The old navigators kept time by the sand-glass, or sez-clock, which indicated the half-hour. Eight times in his four-hour watch the man at the wheel turned the glass and marked the time by striking upon a small bell near him.

"the company of the merchants of London trading to the East Indies," received its charter from Queen Elizabeth on December 31st, 1600. It was largely concerned with the establishment of trading stations or factories in India. Although it was purely a trading concern it was highly necessary to arm many of its ships and the East Indiamen became the most famous sailing-ships of the seventeenth and eighteenth centuries. A rival company was sanctioned later, but the two were amalgamated in 1701 and became the Honourable East India Company.

The East Indiamen usually sailed in convoy and were ready to give battle to any of the foreign privateers lying in wait for such rich prizes. If an East Indiamen fell a prize on rare occasion to some French privateer, it can also be said that more often than not it was the privateer that had the worst of the battle. In due course the East India Company built their own East India Dock in 1804 to enable larger vessels to be docked nearer the heart of the City.

Life on board an East Indiaman was in many ways better for both crew and passengers than in any other ships sailing the seas at that time. But it was very poor compared with the accommodation aboard ships after sails had given way to steam. A cabin passenger on an East Indiaman had to bring many of his own supplies, such as bedding, wine and servant, but his free luggage was from 1½ to 3½ tons. The food would seem to have been good, though this depended largely on the honesty of those in command. Live cattle and poultry were carried to last the voyage which usually took some seven months.

Speed was not then regarded as anything of great importance as there was no competition between rivals. British ports since Cromwell's day had been open only to British ships. It was not until 1849 that the Cromwell Acts were repealed. Similar conditions obtained in several other countries, including the

U.S.A. after they had their own ships, but all these restrictive laws were eventually abolished almost universally.

Specially drawn for this work.

TAKING HIS SIGHTS

Here we see the master of a ship in the year 1590 using his cross-staff to observe the position of the sun. The staff had a sliding-piece which was moved up and down until the upper end was in line with the sun. Columbus, Drake and other great mariners used the cross-staff.

Most famous of the sailing ships were the clippers, a name applied to a particular type built for speed and to carry a special type of cargo. Until about 1850 only those ships engaged in such occupations as privateering (or what really amounted to piracy) or in slave-trading, or smuggling, were much concerned about speed. Then, from one cause or another, the monopolists, such as the East India Company, had to face competition on both the India and China trade routes.

Tea at this period was a valuable and expensive cargo and the earliest consignments commanded high prices. Large quantities can be stored in a fairly small space and clipper-built schooners were ideal for the China tea trade. The first record-breaker was the American *Oriental*, one of the first vessels to take advantage of the opening of British ports to all ships. She did the voyage from Hong Kong to London in ninety-seven days,

British ship-owners soon took up the challenge and the sailing-ship record still stands to the credit of the *Ariel*. This British ship only ran for seven years, but took part in several Clipper races from China. She made the record of seventy-nine days twenty-one hours for the voyage between London and Hong Kong.

The *Ariel* was lost on her first trip to Australia in 1872 through carrying too much sail. A heavy wind plunged her bows under water and she went to the bottom.

As merchant ships the clippers had their faults and life aboard them in rough weather was often desperately hard, but they were splendid in their beauty, and even the pictures of them bring to mind all the romance and wonder of the sea. It is scarcely surprising that the men who learned their seamanship aboard such ships looked down with a certain amount of contempt on those who sailed aboard ships without sails and never climbed high above deck to set sail on a swaying yard.

Most famous of all British clippers was the *Cutty Sark*, though she was not built till 1870, when the days of the clippers and of most of the merchant sailing-ships were nearing their end. The *Cutty Sark* took part in several races and put up some splendid times, on one occasion covering 363 miles in one day on the China run.

The Suez Canal was opened in 1869, and steamships able to use this route had a tremendous advantage over the sailing-ship. The *Cutty Sark*, the *Thermopylæ*, and other well-known clippers went on the Australian run, bringing home cargoes of wool. Both these vessels were eventually bought by the Portuguese Government. Later the *Cutty Sark* was bought again by an English captain and finally came to rest in Falmouth Harbour as a training-ship.

Steam had been used to propel a vessel as long ago as 1801 when the *Charlotte Dundas* was used as a tug on the Forth-Clyde Canal, but owing to damage caused by the wash from her paddle-wheel she was put out of business. In America, the *Clermont*, using engines supplied by Boulton and Watt,

Specially drawn for this work.

AN EAST INDIAMAN OF 1700

In the reign of Queen Elizabeth the company which later became known as the Honourable East India Company was founded and its ships became the most famous of their time. They were ready to give battle to privateer or pirate who dared to attack them, while life on board was more comfortable for both passengers and crew than in any ships afloat in those days.

Specially drawn for this work.

OUT OF THE STORM

Life on the old windjammers especially in rough weather was often desperately hard. In the picture above the artist has depicted the plight of a Clipper after rounding the Horn in a hurricane. A mass of tangled cordage and splintered spars, the weather-beaten craft steers for the nearest port under such rig as she can manage.

carried passengers on the Hudson River in 1807, but it was not till 1827 that an all-steam crossing of the Atlantic was made by the Dutch steamer *Curaçao*. Before this, however, the *Susannah*, which had an auxiliary paddle-wheel, crossed in 1819, taking thirty-five days for the passage, but using her engines on only eighteen of these days.

The first British steamer to do the crossing was the *Sirius* of 703 tons. She left Queenstown and took nineteen days for the trip to New York. This was in April, 1838, and some hours after the *Sirius* had reached port the *Great Western* also arrived in New York, having taken three days less than the *Sirius* to do the crossing.

Another revolutionary idea came to the stage of practical test about this time. Iron, instead of oak, had been tried in shipbuilding, but was strongly opposed, particularly by the Admiralty. When it was found that iron ships did not sink there was still an objection that cannon shots would pierce iron more easily than the stout timbers of a wooden man-o'-war. It took many years to convince the Admiralty that iron had any advantages over wood.

The builders of merchant ships had no such doubts, though it was a long time before iron and steel really displaced wood, just as the sailing-ship did not by any means vanish as soon as the steamer appeared on the sea.

One famous windjammer was the *Herzogin Cecile* built in 1902, which ran on the rocks off the Devon coast in 1936 when homeward bound from Australia. She was refloated, but broke her back later and so ended her career.

It was in 1843 that the first big transatlantic steamer was built at Bristol. This was the *Great Britain*, a vessel of 3,270 tons, measuring 323 feet long, 48 feet broad, and 31½ feet deep. She was fitted with engines of 1,500 horsepower, and her voyages across the Atlantic were quite successful. Unfortunately she ran ashore off the Irish coast in 1846 and lay there stranded for nearly a year, defying the waves to break her up. Finally she was refloated and sailed the seas again, though she ended her days as a full-rigged sailing-ship.

Famous Names in Shipping

The great names of the big shipping companies begin to appear from 1830 onwards. The P. & O. began as the Peninsular Steam Company about 1835 when Arthur Anderson and Brodie Wilcox bought the *William Fawcett*, a paddle-steamer of 209 tons. Later they obtained a contract for carrying the mail weekly from Falmouth to Gibraltar, calling at Vigo, Oporto, Lisbon and Cadiz. The name was afterwards changed to Peninsular and Oriental Steam Navigation Company, and Anderson lived long enough to see P. & O. ships sailing regularly to India and China, with their own repair depots at many ports between.

Another great name in shipping history is that of Samuel Cunard, owner of whalers at Halifax, Nova Scotia. He was past fifty when he came to England in 1838 to found a shipping company in partnership with George Burns and David McIver of Liverpool. This was known as the British and North American Royal Mail Steam Packet Co. as they had been successful in obtaining a valuable contract to carry mails. The first Cunard vessel crossed the Atlantic from Liverpool to Boston in 1840, taking fourteen days eight hours for the voyage.

Later the company became the Cunard Line and, since the amalgamation with another company, has been known as the Cunard White Star Line. The White Star Company was formed in 1871 by T. H. Ismay, who had been head of a line of clippers as well as a director of the National Steam Navigation Co. formed in 1863.

Donald Currie began his career in the Cunard Line, but left them to found the Castle Line in 1862, not as rivals in any way to the Cunard Line, but to run a service from Liverpool to Calcutta and later to South Africa. In 1900 the Castle Line was amalgamated with the Union Steamship Company to become the Union Castle Line.

There was James MacQueen, a Scottish journalist, whose passion was the sea and travel. He submitted plans to the Government for steam packet service to carry mails to the West Indies, North America and the Far East. After a good deal of struggle he succeeded in obtaining a contract. For this purpose the Royal Mail Steam Packet Company was founded and received its charter in 1839.

Tramps and Food Ships

It was in this way that most of the great shipping companies were formed. There were other men who made their names and fortunes as shipowners, but in a rather different class. Ocean-going ships can be divided into three kinds: the great passenger lines, of which such a company as the Cunard White Star is an example. These carry a certain amount of cargo besides a large number of passengers. Next, the cargo liners which have fixed runs and a regular schedule showing the ports of call and dates of arrival and departure.

Then there is the tramp ship which has no regular schedule; the tramp is not necessarily a small ship, but whatever her size she is prepared to go to

Specially painted for this work by Ellis Silas.

A CLIPPER ON THE HOMEWARD RUN

Most famous as well as most graceful of all sailing-ships were the Clippers, a special type of sharp-bowed vessel built for quick sailing and chiefly employed in the China tea trade. The days of their great races to be first home with the season's new tea were between 1850 and 1870, and the record for the run between Hong Kong and London was just under 80 days. With the opening of the Suez Canal the era of the Clippers passed away.

Specially painted for this work by Ellis Silas.

DRAKE DESTROYS THE SPANISH FLEET AT CADIZ

One of the most valiant exploits of that great sailor, Sir Francis Drake, took place in 1587 during the war against Spain. The Spanish fleet lay at Cadiz, almost ready for its attack on England. With four of his ships, Drake sailed right into the harbour and burnt or sank thirty-three of the enemy vessels. Drake's own characteristic summary of this daring raid was that he had "singed the King of Spain's beard." The practical result was that the sailing of the great Spanish Armada was postponed for another full year.

any part of the world and to pick up a cargo from any port. Broadly, in normal times, the tramp's main cargoes from England are coal while the imports which she brings back are timber, grain or iron ore. Nearly all the tramp shipping companies were formed by men who were seamen or employed in shipping offices. Runciman, Nicholl, Reardon-Smith, and Hain were among shipowners who began life as lads before the mast.

There are the special ships, too, such as the oil-tanker which may carry up to 20,000 tons of oil, and the foodstuff carriers, fitted with elaborate refrigerating devices. Frozen meat has become a highly important cargo now that the greater part of our population is fed on meat brought from Australia, New Zealand or South America. It was in 1880 that the very first cargo of frozen meat was brought to this country from Australia.

Specially drawn for this work.

MOST FAMOUS OF BRITISH CLIPPERS

Although not built till 1870, when the days of the fast sailing-ships engaged on the China run were drawing to a close, the *Cutty Sark* took pride of place among all British Clippers. She took part in several races from Hong Kong to this country and on one occasion covered 363 miles in one day.

Specially drawn for this work.

THE FIRST PRACTICAL STEAM-BOAT

In 1801 the *Charlotte Dundas*, a steam-boat built by William Symington, was used as a tug on the Forth-Clyde Canal and towed two heavily-loaded barges. Protests were made and eventually the *Charlotte Dundas* had to be taken off the water because of the damage caused by the wash from her paddle-wheel.

For some sixty years before the Great War of 1914–18 the British merchant ships did very well, while British seamen were known in every port in the world. During the Great War, however, the enemy did all in his power to prevent our ships bringing their cargoes of food and raw materials to British ports. It was then that the country realised to the full just what the Merchant Navy meant to us in our island home.

In the old days life at sea on board a tramp was pretty grim and there were owners who neglected to spend money on necessary repairs, or insisted on having their ships loaded to a dangerous degree. One man, Samuel Plimsoll, spent the greater part of his life in calling attention to the scandal of what he called "coffin ships."

A Royal Commission was appointed and eventually the Merchant Shipping Act of 1876 was passed. As a result of that Act all our merchant ships are compulsorily marked with a circle, having a horizontal line drawn through it, to indicate the maximum depth to which the vessel can be loaded. The Plimsoll Mark, or Load Line, is a testimony to the efforts of Samuel Plimsoll to secure safer conditions for the merchant service.

There are other precautions taken now to ensure that every British ship is seaworthy. Lloyd's Register classifies each ship, and, even when it is building, the Lloyd's surveyor watches the progress and sees that everything on board is up to standard requirement. Not until he is satisfied is the ship given her letters and figures which form her passport for insurance and chartering. A first-class steamer is marked 100 A1. A steamer marked merely A1 is generally one that has been built to the surveyor's satisfaction for some special purpose. All vessels must be surveyed every four years. *Lloyd's Register of Shipping* gives the list of every ship in every country (except certain Japanese and Chinese sailing vessels) of over 100 tons gross.

It should be noted that *Lloyd's Register* is a separate institution from Lloyd's, the great corporation of marine underwriters who insure ships and cargoes as well as risks of other kinds. The members of Lloyd's, whose home is in Leadenhall Street, London, deal in marine insurance and are governed by a committee elected by themselves. *Lloyd's Register*, with headquarters at Fenchurch Street, London, classifies all ships and has surveyors in almost every port in the world; it is controlled by a committee of shipowners and others concerned with the seaworthiness of vessels, and issues regular lists of ships, showing their movements as well as giving other information.

After the war of 1914–18 British shipping, which had performed such magnificent services despite all threats from submarines and mines, drifted into the doldrums, to use the term the old sailors employed when a sailing-ship lay becalmed and helpless. One-third of our ships had been lost and those built hastily to replace losses were not up to standard. Other countries which had relied on British shipping had been compelled to build their own vessels while British shipping trade for countries other than our own had ceased to exist. In 1935 the British

Specially drawn for this work.

FIRST BRITISH STEAMER TO CROSS THE ATLANTIC

In April, 1838, the *Sirius*, a paddle-steamer of 703 tons, did the Atlantic crossing under steam from Queenstown to New York in 19 days. A Dutch steamer made the first crossing 11 years earlier, while the *Great Western* reached New York a few hours after the *Sirius*.

Specially drawn for this work.

THE FIRST CUNARD LINER

Samuel Cunard founded in 1838 the line that still bears his name and in 1840 the first liner of the new company, the *Britannia*, accommodating 115 passengers and 200 tons cargo, made her maiden voyage across the Atlantic in 14 days, 8 hours from Liverpool to Boston. She was a paddle-steamer, 207 feet long, with engines developing 740 h.p.

Shipping (Assistance) Act was passed and a subsidy of £2,000,000 was granted to tramp shipping. With this aid and general reorganisation shipping improved to some extent, but when war came again in 1939 there was a sudden great need for merchant ships and for the men to sail them.

Then, too, when war broke out quite a large number of merchant officers and seamen went immediately into the Royal Navy, either because they were in the Royal Naval Reserve or were serving in vessels which became armed merchant cruisers, such as, for instance, the *Jervis Bay*. Moreover, during the years of peace before 1939 many men had left the Merchant Service. Ships had lain idle, out of work, as were the men who had manned them. In many cases marine engineers found jobs ashore, but deck officers had not the same openings and in some cases took jobs as ordinary hands aboard ship again. Roughly some 15,000 men left the sea each year and replacements were few.

What this meant when war came can be understood if we bear in mind that at normal times at least one-third of Britain's food in weight comes to us from overseas. Most of our meat, butter, cheese and wheat is brought to us in ships, whether British or foreign. In time of war we need all that, but we also need the munitions of war, raw materials, petrol for aircraft on an ever-increasing scale. One bomber raid on

Germany with 500 planes took 750,000 gallons of oil. All of it comes to Britain by sea.

Ships were needed to take men overseas or to bring others to this country. Ships and more ships were wanted—and the men to sail them. They came. The first call was for those who had served on ships since 1936, and by 1941 nearly 60,000 officers and men had registered. There were other volunteers, too : in the list is a cabin boy of fifteen and a half (they don't take boys under sixteen, but this Scots boy was there); a bos'n of twenty-eight with 100 men under him ; engineers of sixty,

Specially drawn for this work.

A DEEP-SEA FISHING TRAWLER

In peace-time the trawler plays a big part in supplying this country with fish ; in war-time the same vessels did valiant work in mine-sweeping as well as in many other hazardous tasks. The trawler is larger than the drifter and drags its large nets, known as trawls, along the bottom of the sea.

and a greaser whose age was seventy-five! The second mate of one big ship was a J.P. who had left the sea twenty years before, while an able seaman who came back owned hunters, flew his own plane, and sailed his own yacht. A junior engineer was Maths. master at a big school.

Not all the seamen on British ships belonged to these islands. There were more than 45,000 Indians, besides Chinese and Arab firemen. Asiatic sailors are usually known as Lascars or "Indian seamen," and cause much less trouble than some of the Chinese. Stories of Lascar bravery and devotion to duty are certainly not wanting and their services were invaluable in war time.

The Call of the Sea

It is on record, too, that the young seamen of to-day are not behind the older men in anything but experience, and in some ways they begin with a flying start. Education gives them an advantage many of the older men never possessed. The newcomer can set a course by the stars and judge wind direction by cloud formations and weather reports. And the records have many stories of youngsters who took charge of a boatload of survivors after their ship had been sunk, and they proved themselves as coolly efficient as any older man would have done. Moreover, despite the stories of sinkings and the dangers of life at sea in war-time, there were more applications from boys anxious to go to sea than at any previous time in history.

In war-time the ships sail in convoy, fifty or sixty, or even more ships. A Commodore is in charge of them all and his job is to keep the ships together as a fleet, take all necessary steps to ward off attack from submarines or aircraft, to see that no chink of light shows from the ships at night, and to keep up the stragglers, whether they are falling behind, or, as may happen, getting too far ahead of the rest of the convoy. There are many other details on which the Commodore advises the captains at the conference before the convoy sails. Lifejackets must be examined to see that their lights are in good order. Coloured sails for the ships' boats are important as they enable rescuers to see the boats more easily.

There are scramble nets on the Commodore's ship to prevent wrecked men from drifting helplessly past. Other points are explained on the subject of what must be done if a ship is unlucky and falls a victim to the submarines. "Believe me, you won't be left," the Commodore assures them, and wherever it was humanly possible the helpless men were rescued after their ship had gone down. It was a long and bitter struggle against the U-boats, but the merchant ships never failed to sail, and gradually, as one device after another was brought into operation, the peril of the U-boat packs was overcome to a very considerable extent, though it never ceased to exist till the war ended.

For Courage and Endurance

Aircraft played a great part, too, in rescue work. In one instance aeroplanes flew some 25,000 miles before their search was rewarded and they were able to drop a message to tell the helpless occupants of a solitary ship's boat that rescue was near at hand. Stories of individual heroism on the part of merchant seamen are legion. Even the record of the many awards for courage and endurance in the face of incredible difficulties can only tell of a fraction of the truly great deeds the merchant sailors performed. Men lived on flying-fish or dived overboard to scrape weeds from the bottom of their boat; they collected rain in small tins, and tried every device possible to keep alive till rescue came. One officer kept a log in tiny writing on the back of labels from condensed milk tins.

Ship's boats and rafts were eventually fitted with water-distilling apparatus.

A solid fuel that can be saturated with seawater without harming it is part of the apparatus. All boats and rafts were equipped with buoyant self-igniting electric lights which come into operation when the craft reaches the sea. Early in the war a buoyant waistcoat or lifejacket was devised which could be worn even when at work.

It was a civil servant who devised a clip-on red light which could be switched on or off as necessary. This was fitted to all lifejackets and saved many hundreds of lives. Another civil servant designed the protective suit, weighing only 3 pounds 6 ounces, yet windproof and waterproof, for wear in open boats and rafts. Another idea which came into use was a simple wireless transmitter which sent out an automatic signal from the lifeboat. Few of these were in use when war began, but determined efforts were made in every direction to find means of lessening the risks and hardships following the sinking of a ship.

Perhaps the most famous of all convoys were some of those which made the run to Malta after Italy had joined Germany. Mussolini announced his intention of clearing all British ships from the Mediterranean. It didn't quite work like that, of course, but German and Italian aircraft, flying from bases in Sicily and Southern Italy had every chance, it seemed, of preventing any supplies getting through the narrow seas to the little island of Malta. Once supplies were stopped there would be little hope for the island, "the unsinkable aircraft carrier," as it had been called.

Yet the convoys, battered and damaged, with a record of ships sunk, carried out the message sent by Vice-Admiral Somerville to every ship's master in one of the convoys. "Remember, everyone, that the watchword is THE CONVOY MUST GO THROUGH."

The cargoes aboard the ships were vital to the island: fighter aircraft and parts, guns, shells, ammunition;

Central Press.

A FAMOUS WINDJAMMER

It was long after the coming of steam before the merchant sailing-ships disappeared. Our picture shows the *Herzogin Cecile* which was built in 1902 and sailed the seas till 1936.

thousands of tons of aviation spirit in 4-gallon tins ; maize, wheat, flour, corned beef and mutton ; cloth, cement, cigarettes and tobacco. There were other necessities without which Malta could not have continued its heroic defence against the continual attacks from the air. As a token of the admiration of Britain for the fortitude and courage of the Maltese people, the island was awarded the George Cross.

Not only aeroplanes, but fast-moving motor gun-boats, the German E-boats, slipped out at night to attack the convoys. They claimed their victims, yet in some way supplies got through. The famous tanker *Ohio*, carrying aviation spirit and petrol in cases and drums, had her full share of enemy fury. On one August convoy she was torpedoed, lamed, and set on fire ; the tail of a dive-bomber fell on her decks; her boilers blew up and her engines failed. Yet, taken in tow by two escort ships, she reached Malta, two days late, but with her precious cargo safe.

There were convoys across the Atlantic and through the icy Arctic seas to Russia. Troops and supplies were sent to the desert army in North Africa. Voyages to the Middle East

Specially drawn for this work.

HEROES OF THE " SAN DEMETRIO "

Sailing in convoy the oil tanker *San Demetrio* was shelled by an enemy pocket battleship and set on fire. Her crew were forced to abandon the ship but later a few men, adrift in a life-boat, boarded her again, put out the flames, got the engines going, and brought the tanker safely across the Atlantic to the Clyde.

THE "JERVIS BAY" SAVES THE CONVOY

Specially drawn for this work.

On the evening of November 5th, 1940, as the convoy sailed into the gathering dusk, an enemy warship was sighted. The *Jervis Bay*, a light armed merchantman, went ahead to give battle while the convoy sought cover of darkness. Fighting against overwhelming odds the *Jervis Bay* went down at last, but the convoy was safe.

Specially drawn for this work.

SAFE HOME IN PORT

The big merchant steamer has come to the end of her long voyage and has been safely docked. In the picture above our artist depicts a scene at the Port of London where the ship has been tied up and is ready to discharge her cargo.

had as big a variety of hazards as any other route. Never had such armadas of ships left Britain's shores as those which sailed to North Africa in 1942. In addition to the First Army and its reinforcements, these ships took 394 aircraft, 63,784 vehicles, 900 tanks, 3,677 guns, and six locomotives and tenders. Petrol, oil and coal, and hundreds of thousands of tons of stores and equipment were carried. In addition, 1,416 aircraft were taken to Gibraltar during this period and then the planes were flown onwards to their various landing-grounds.

Then came the great D-Day of June 6th, 1944. The merchant ships had their full share in this tremendous undertaking, and in particular the little ships of coastal waters. Preparations had begun two years before. Cross-channel ships that had taken holiday travellers to the Continent in peace days were making the trip again, but this time they were fitted as infantry assault ships. Coasters which had carried coal and potatoes between Liverpool and Ireland were overhauled and made ready for the great day. There were many hundreds of them and the short sea voyage allowed these little ships to carry men and tanks in great convoys across the Channel, and then go back for the next shipment.

There were deep-sea vessels, too, carrying special landing craft to take the troops on board from ship to shore. Many of them came under heavy fire from the shore batteries and there was bombing from the air by night. But the landings were made, stores and equipment put ashore, repair shops erected and airfields quickly in use. The weather was not particularly kind, and on June 20th tugs had to be sent post-haste to deal with ships being driven ashore in a full gale that lasted almost without a break for six full days. Only heroic efforts on the part of the crews enabled the unloading to go on as soon as the storm abated.

When Victory Came

"We are seamen and soldiers and dockers, too," one chief officer said, and that was true enough. As the invading forces became firmly established and armies and supplies increased, so did the number of ships grow. The task went on as other ports were opened; always the armies were kept supplied. The Merchant Navy played its very full part in all the hard and often heroic work that eventually brought the day of victory in May, 1945.

Peace brought no relief so far as the merchant ships were concerned except the fact that enemy attacks by aircraft and U-boats were no longer to be feared. That was an important factor, but the tasks of the ships became more urgent than ever. There were millions of men, women and children in Europe who were on the verge of starvation and with no hope of relief except by the food the United Nations could bring them. The burden in the main was bound to fall on Britain, still free, still powerful, still possessing a great Merchant Navy, despite all the efforts of enemy U-boats.

Facing Further Cuts

Britain herself had cut down her food rations to the lowest level on which the workers could remain fit and strong. Stocks had gradually been reduced in those months when everything was concentrated on the final supreme effort to win the war at the earliest moment. The people of this country were justified in thinking that the end of the fighting would mean a

AN HISTORIC PICTURE OF A MIGHTY CONVOY

One of the greatest convoys that ever left our shores was that which took a great army with all its machines of war to land in North Africa in November, 1942. The Merchant Navy carried this army and the Royal Navy escorted it while British and American Air Forces maintained constant patrol to ward off enemy bomber attacks.

BRITAIN CAN MAKE IT

Fox Photos.

Napoleon once described this country as a nation of shopkeepers and it is upon our capacity to supply the world with the products of British factories that our prosperity depends. In this photograph, we see a fleet of motor-buses, made in Britain, being shipped aboard a steamer for an East African port.

P. N. Ltd.

Big ships require big tackle and some idea of the size and weight of the ropes for the *Queen Mary* can be gathered from the photograph above which shows a huge coil of rope being rolled along the dock-side at Southampton to be taken on board.

SHIPS AT TILBURY

Fox Photos.

Though not the largest of all the big docks that make London the greatest port in the world, those at Tilbury have always been highly important. They are some twenty-one miles down the river from London and have a water area of 90 acres. Our photograph gives a typical view of what Tilbury Docks are like on any day throughout the year.

gradual improvement in their food difficulties.

Instead, they had to face further small cuts in their meagre supplies. The harvests of the world had been bad. On the Continent whole sections of the people would starve unless they had bread. Nearly a year after Victory Day in Europe there was an urgent call to the British people to save bread, while other foods, instead of becoming more plentiful, were in some cases slightly reduced. Bread was rationed eventually to conserve our stocks, pending the results of the 1946 harvest in the great wheat-producing countries. And still the cry from the devastated lands of Europe was " Send us food! "

Back to the Homeland

Ships were wanted to bring food; ships were urgently needed to bring home men from the East and Middle East, the prisoners of war and internees in Japanese prison camps, and to bring home, too, some of the fighting-men who had been away from their homeland for more than three or four years. Still more ships were required to take back American, Canadian, New Zealand and other overseas troops who had been in this country or on the Continent with the armies.

Our two biggest liners were among the ships engaged in work of this kind. During the war and up to March, 1946, when she ceased her war work, the *Queen Elizabeth* steamed about a million miles and carried some 800,000 troops across thousands of miles of ocean. The *Queen Mary* had a similar record across the Atlantic and the Pacific and was then engaged in taking the English brides of American soldiers to join their husbands in the U.S.A.

Still Sailing the Seas

Not until these post-war tasks had been carried through were these two great ships released from service. Gradually our Merchant Navy began its urgent peace-time work of taking British goods to all the countries of the world, anxious to buy our merchandise after several years during which Britain had little to sell and her export trade almost ceased to exist.

Britain's great need after the lean years of war was for more imports of food and raw materials for civilian manufactures. It was even more important that her export trade should be bigger than ever in her history. We cannot buy goods in other countries without supplying them with other goods in return. British workers must have their products sold in the markets of the world and British ships must sail to every country taking those goods.

They are doing it now, and the call of the sea is still as strong as ever to the men and boys of this sea-girt island. From the fishing fleets to the great ocean trawlers, the coasters, the tankers, the big food ships that carry the meat from Australia or South America, the fruit ships, and the vessels laden with ore from Spain or with sugar from the Indies, all are needed.

Brought to us Daily

They are sailing the Seven Seas from British ports to take our goods to other lands and to bring back the many things we need in this country. As Rudyard Kipling wrote years ago:—

For the bread that you eat and the biscuits you nibble,
The sweets that you suck and the joints that you carve,
They are brought to you daily by all us Big Steamers—
And if anyone hinders our coming you'll starve.

Centuries ago Francis Drake and many another great English sailor fought for the right of British sailors to take their ships wherever their merchandise was desired. The British Navy has maintained that right ever since, despite all threats of mines, torpedoes, guns and bombs, while the Merchant Navy, no matter what the risks, has never ceased to carry on its business across the deep waters of the world.

Tales of Mystery and Superstition, Smugglers, Pirates, Records and Wrecks

And Other Aspects of the Work of Ships and their Crews

ROMANCE OF THE SEA

WE have no record of the first man who shaped for himself some kind of sailing-craft and adventured forth on the great waters beyond the dry land. There must have been a beginning to the building of boats and ships, and from the dawn of recorded history the story of man's battles with the sea has held an abiding fascination for all the human race.

At best, however, man's mastery of the sea remains a strictly limited one. Every now and again the mighty ocean exerts her power to show how puny are man's strength and invention against the illimitable forces of the great waters. It is scarcely surprising, therefore, that a wonderful lore of superstition and mystery, of strange adventures and great fortunes, as well as of tragedies and evil deeds, should have gathered round the long story of the sea.

Signs and Omens

The men who went down to the sea in ships and risked their lives long before anyone had dreamt of steam-power and wireless communication were almost bound to be superstitious and to have regard for signs and omens. Luck played its part so far as the elements were concerned, and luck, good or bad, might be greatly influenced by chance happenings.

Friday was always regarded as an unlucky day on which to begin a voyage, except among the Spaniards. Did not Columbus begin his voyage to the New World on Friday, August 3rd, 1492? Not many sailors object to sailing on a Friday in these days, but to have too many clergymen aboard as passengers is still regarded as unlucky. Nor is the presence of a lawyer on board regarded as a lucky sign. Among certain nationalities, particularly the hardy Bretons, a tailor on board is certain to bring bad luck. Nor is it wise to make or mend clothes, or to have a hair-cut, during stormy weather.

To drop a bucket overboard was a sure sign of trouble, although if a sailor carried salt in his pocket he stood an excellent chance of averting evil and attracting good fortune. Finns are supposed to have control of the winds and are accordingly treated with respect. Cats are unlucky, and even a horse aboard worried some seamen of the old school, while a live hare on board was a certain method of sending any ship to the bottom. Even rabbits were not mentioned on board ship at one time.

The albatross was regarded rather as a protective spirit. Rats, too, were looked upon in a friendly way as they gave warning when disaster threatened. " Rats always desert a sinking ship," and usually long before there is any hint of coming disaster apparent to the seamen. Old-time sailors were fond of a female figurehead on their ship as that brought good fortune, but it was just sheer bad luck to meet a woman on the way to join a vessel or to have a woman on board. " Whistling for the wind " was quite a sound practice when a ship lay becalmed, but at other times whistling on board was a dangerous amusement.

An Omen of Disaster

Then there are strange stories of ghost ships such as the one commanded by the old Dutch captain, Vanderdecken, who was trying to round the Cape of Good Hope. He swore with many a dreadful oath that he would not put back into harbour till he had succeeded. Providence, becoming impatient with him, condemned him to continue his efforts till the end of time. Few seamen believe such yarns in these days of wireless and aircraft, but for a few centuries the old Flying Dutchman, Vanderdecken, was regarded as an omen of dreadful disaster.

Modern invention has robbed many of the old superstitions of their former power, and the marvels of wireless are more real than ancient ghost-ships or imaginary spirits of ill omen. It was a White Star liner, the *Republic*, which was the first to use wireless to call other ships to her aid. Badly injured in a collision at sea she sent out radio signals, and receiving ships arrived in time to take off every person on board in safety.

Radar has already proved itself an equally valuable aid when fog cuts out all visibility. When eventually all ocean-going ships are fitted with Radar as they are with wireless the dangers and perils to which voyagers have always been exposed will be reduced to a minimum. Tragedies such as the loss of the *Titanic* might very easily have been avoided if Radar had been known at that time. Wireless had begun to form part of the equipment of most big ships at that time and it played a part in this case in bringing about the rescue of nearly a third of those on board the ill-fated liner.

The *Titanic*, greatest and most luxurious liner of her day, so well built that she was regarded as unsinkable, left Southampton on her maiden voyage on April 10th, 1912. On the following Sunday night everything was well, but a quarter of an hour before midnight something caused the ship to heave. There was nothing startling in that first shock, but the *Titanic* had struck an iceberg, cutting through the bottom of the ship and smashing many of her watertight compartments.

Birth of a Great Tradition

There was no panic. Few indeed realised fully the danger that threatened and developed with such dreadful swiftness. Wireless messages were sent out and the sixteen lifeboats were manned and lowered. Women and children were ordered into them first and not till then were any men allowed in the lifeboats. The ship's band came on deck and played till the end. At 2.30 a.m. the *Titanic* stood on end and slowly slipped down into the dark waters of the Atlantic.

Right to the end the wireless operator sent out the distress signal and kept in touch with all possible rescuers. In so doing he created a tradition for a service then in its infancy, and his fine example has been followed whenever the necessity has arisen. Seven ships answered the call, but the ice hampered them. The *Carpathia*, 70 miles away when the S.O.S. came,

Specially painted for this work by Ellis Silas.

MORGAN LEAVES HIS SHIP TO BOARD A PRIZE

Most notorious of all the pirates that sailed the Spanish Main was Captain Henry Morgan. After working as a slave in Jamaica he joined the pirates and rose to command twelve vessels with 700 men under him. His greatest exploit was the sack of the Spanish city of Panama, which was pillaged and burnt. Eventually Morgan was brought for trial to England but was acquitted and later knighted by Charles II who sent him back to Jamaica as Lieutenant-Governor. He fell into disgrace later, and died in obscurity.

Specially painted for this work by Ellis Silas.

A NAVAL INCIDENT IN WAR TIME

In this picture a naval incident that was often repeated has been recorded by our artist. A merchant ship has been attacked while in convoy; the damage to the ship can be repaired by her own crew, but there have been serious casualties among the men, some of them beyond the limited skill of the captain. From the light cruiser in the background a naval surgeon is being sent across the fairly rough sea in the Service whaler which is here seen pulling in close to the merchant ship. The lives of several gallant sailors are at stake, and the knowledge and skill of the Royal Navy surgeon will make all the difference to their chances of seeing their home port once more.

THE FLYING DUTCHMAN

Specially drawn for this work.

Of all the many superstitions connected with the sea, few held their place so long and firmly as that concerned with the ghostly ship commanded by the old captain Vanderdecken. Beaten by storms in his efforts to round the Cape of Good Hope, he swore to persist if need be till Doomsday. To have even a glimpse of this ghost-ship was regarded as an omen of disaster.

Specially drawn for this work.

THE LOSS OF THE "WARATAH"

On July 26th, 1909, the *Waratah* left Durban for Cape Town and exchanged signals with another ship the next day. She was never heard of again. The artist who drew the above picture was aboard another ship that went through the same hurricane and was in the vicinity of the spot where it was assumed the *Waratah* went down in the tremendous seas that raged for more than a week.

steamed to the scene as quickly as possible. All those in the lifeboats were eventually found and taken on board, but they numbered in all only 711. More than twice that number, 1,513 persons, went down with the ship.

One of the blackest incidents of the war of 1914–18 was the sinking of the Cunard liner *Lusitania* off the Irish coast on May 7th, 1915. At that time, despite German threats of ruthlessness, there were certain rules of warfare which it was assumed even Germany would respect. The *Lusitania* was a passenger liner, carrying no munitions of war, and on board were a large number of passengers, including 218 Americans. Without any warning a German U-boat fired two torpedoes and within forty minutes the *Lusitania* had gone to the bottom. Nearly 1,200 people were drowned and of the Americans aboard only 79 were saved. Although America did not enter the war immediately after this tragedy there is no doubt that it was one of the important factors that eventually determined America's entry into the war in 1917.

Vanished Without Trace

Many of the mysteries of the sea which have never been solved would in all probability not have been mysteries at all if wireless had been available. How many fine ships have sailed from port in the days gone by and disappeared without trace? There was the *Pacific*, for instance, which sailed from Liverpool for America in 1856 and was never heard of again. More than half a century later the *Waratah*, a new liner of 16,000 tons, left Durban for Cape Town on July 26th, 1909. On the evening of the following day she exchanged signals with the *Clan MacIntyre* as she overhauled her. That was the last ever known of the *Waratah*. There had been heavy seas and a hurricane, and the only conclusion is that the *Waratah* capsized and there was never a hope of any small boat surviving in the storm. Nor was the *Waratah* fitted with wireless, although round about that time many vessels had begun to fit the new equipment.

One of the most extraordinary of sea mysteries about which discussions have been carried on and books written over many years is the case of the *Marie Celeste*. She was a small vessel well under 1,000 tons and sailed from New York for Genoa in the latter part of 1872. She carried a crew of six, under Captain Briggs, who had his wife and child on board with him. On December 5th she was sighted by the British *Dei Gratia*. Something about the vessel impelled the *Dei Gratia* captain to send a boat across to investigate.

An Unsolved Mystery

They found the ship in perfect condition and there were signs of an unfinished meal. On a table was a partially-written letter; money and personal possessions were found on board.

Specially drawn for this work.

MYSTERY OF THE "MARIE CELESTE"

In 1872, the *Marie Celeste* was found off Gibraltar without a soul on board, and yet in perfect condition. Nothing was ever heard of her crew and the mystery of why they abandoned the ship in calm seas has never been solved, and after the lapse of years, is never likely to be.

Specially drawn for this work.

THE BARBARY PIRATES

During many centuries the pirates of the Barbary coast, North Africa, made the Mediterranean a sea of danger and peril. Many countries at different times tried to wipe them out, but they persisted till 1830, when they were finally driven out of business. Our picture shows the pirates closing in on a ship that is lying becalmed and helpless.

The log was written up to November 24th but the slate log had been entered up at 8 a.m. on the following day. There was no sign of any collision or anything at all to account for what had obviously been a sudden abandonment of the vessel since there was not a soul on board. Why ? What had happened to the captain and his company ?

Theories have been put forward and on one occasion at all events a man who professed to have been a member of the crew left behind him his story of what had happened. Unfortunately some of his details did not fit the facts and there was no member of the crew bearing his name among those who sailed with her. He merely added to the mystery. Why, as his story did not reflect on anyone, did he not tell it while he was alive ? There was no answer to that query, or to several others that arose, and the full truth about the *Marie Celeste* is never likely to be revealed after all these years.

Pirates and Privateers

The passage of time often adds a false atmosphere of romance to things which were utterly brutal and sordid.

Thus the pirate and his flag bearing the skull and crossbones have acquired through the years something of the air of a gentleman adventurer of the sea. Some pirates, it is true, were magnificent sailors with a courage that dared all risks and dangers, whether from the sea or from men.

The pirate appeared on the scene almost as soon as trading vessels first put out to sea. Homer and Herodotus wrote of them, and in the days when Rome was paramount the pirates flourished. Julius Cæsar, in his earlier years, was captured and held to ransom by them. Released when his ransom was paid, Cæsar made his plans, returned to the pirates' lair and captured the lot, numbering nearly 400. In due course every one of them was executed.

In the Mediterranean the Barbary corsairs have at different times during many centuries made piracy into a very popular and paying profession. Not only natives of those shores, but adventurers from England and other European countries joined with the pirates of North Africa to plunder ships and to take men and women as slaves, or hold them to ransom. Cromwell sent an expedition against them in 1655, and right down to the nineteenth century the English, French, Dutch, and later the United States of America, fought against them. In 1816 Lord Exmouth bombarded Algiers and was able to release hundreds of captives. It was bombarded again in 1824, but in 1830 the French conquered Algeria and the days of the Barbary Pirates were over.

On the Spanish Main both piracy and privateering flourished, especially in the days of Queen Elizabeth. The pirate made no claim to patriotism, but robbed any ship for his own gain ; the privateer carried on his work much as the pirate did, but only against ships belonging to a country with which his own country was at war. Drake, for example, with some of his companions, held "Letters of Marque," a Royal commission to attack the merchantmen belonging to the enemy. Queen Elizabeth I used some of her money to

Specially drawn for this work.

A PRIVATEER CHASES ITS PREY

Often enough a privateer was little better than a pirate, but he held authority in some form from his country to attack all merchantmen of any country then at war with his own. Here we see a "private" warship giving chase to an enemy merchantman in the hope of valuable booty.

fit out Drake's ships and drew her share of the plunder.

Morgan of the Spanish Main

When the Spaniards protested to her against "El Draque," the terror of the seas, and demanded that he should be hanged, Elizabeth gave her answer by knighting him. Another man who gained a knighthood after earning fame as a pirate was the bold Harry Morgan (1635–88), who sacked Porto Bello and later Panama. England was not at war with Spain, and, quite reasonably, there were strong protests from the Spaniards about Morgan's conduct. The result was that Morgan was in due course sent home for trial. Charles II took a strong liking for him, made him Sir Henry Morgan, and sent him back as lieutenant-governor of Jamaica, where he did his best to suppress piracy.

Long Ben and Captain Kidd

Another famous pirate was Captain John Avery, who was second-in-command of a merchant ship in 1794. "Long Ben" became a pirate by way of protest against his Spanish employers who failed to pay the crew's wages. Avery took the ship and made his headquarters in Madagascar. His victims were mainly those ships taking Mohammedans from India to Mecca, and among his prizes was the Great Mogul's own ship. Having acquired sufficient treasure Avery retired to England, but discovered too late that there were sharper pirates on land than there were at sea, and they succeeded in relieving him of all his ill-gotten wealth. Eventually the bold buccaneer died in poverty.

There were other pirates such as Captain Edward Teach and Captain William Kidd. There was little of the hero about Kidd nor does he appear to have been a very successful pirate. Eventually he was captured, tried and executed in 1701.

Except for a certain amount of business in the China seas the buccaneer and pirate died out completely with the coming of the steamship. But the stories of pirates' hidden hoards of treasure lived on much longer. Captain Kidd was reputed to have buried several fortunes on lonely islands, but only one of these fortunes was ever found and that was recovered almost immediately. True, there were gold and jewels, calico, canvas and bags of sugar. From this the lawyers and others were paid and the rest went to Greenwich Hospital.

Treasure in Deep Waters

There has been, and still is, buried and sunken treasure. H.M.S. *Lutine*, laden with gold and silver bullion worth over a million pounds, went down in 1799 off the Dutch coast. At different times a fair amount was recovered, but the last effort in 1911 showed that the wreck was embedded deep down in the sand and work was impossible. One relic was recovered round about 1859 and is well known to-day. The *Lutine* ship's bell is now used at Lloyd's to warn underwriters that important news of ships is about to be announced. Altogether bullion to the value of about £100,000 had been recovered by 1861, but later efforts have been unsuccessful.

One of the most famous sea treasures is the Armada galleon, sunk in Tobermory Bay. The name is now generally believed to be the *Florencia*, pay ship of the Armada. The value of the treasure on board has been estimated at different times at sums ranging from £300,000 to £30 million. Guns, goblets and coins have been recovered, and special expeditions have attempted to get through the silt in which the wreck is now deeply buried. Then in March, 1950, the Duke of Argyll enlisted the aid of the Admiralty and naval divers went down. The wreck was located but it was so deeply embedded in the sand that the task was abandoned. With new diving equipment hopes were again raised and in 1954 another attempt was planned.

The story of the Cocos Island trea-

THE TREASURE OF COCOS ISLAND

Specially drawn for this work.

In 1818, a British pirate, Bennet Graham, or Benito Bonita, as he preferred to call himself, buried loot taken from Peruvian churches on Cocos Island. More wealth was added later by Graham's partner, Thompson. Both men died before they could recover the treasure, and since then, right down to 1946, expeditions have gone to Cocos in the hope of finding the buried treasure.

Specially drawn for this work.

A REVENUE CUTTER OVERHAULS A SMUGGLER

For more than a century from 1730 onwards, smuggling was a flourishing business along our Southern coastline. The efforts made to prevent this illegal trade were often too weak to stop the smugglers, but occasionally one of the Government Revenue cutters seized a chance and captured the vessel carrying contraband to the smuggling band ashore.

sure dump begins about the year 1818 when a British pirate, Bennet Graham, or Benito Bonita as he preferred to call himself, brought the loot from Peruvian churches and merchant ships to be buried on Cocos Island until he could collect it later. It is fairly certain that more wealth was added to this dump later.

Fortunes from Spanish Grandees

With Bonita was William Thompson who turned up at Cocos Island again in 1821. The Spaniards had managed to get away much of their treasure from Lima when Peru was in revolt against the rule of Spain. Lord Cochrane, then in command of the Chilean Navy and giving help to Peru, went to the port of Callao, to which the treasure had gone, and demanded two-thirds of the money with which to pay his men. On the scene appeared Thompson, now in command of a trading brig *Mary Read*. He arranged to take off some of the Spanish grandees with their enormous fortune and avoid Lord Cochrane's attentions. What had happened to Bennet Graham nobody apparently knew.

As soon as the *Mary Read* with the escaping Spaniards and their wealth was well clear of the port the helpful Captain Thompson killed the Spaniards and flung them overboard, then set sail for Cocos Island to bury his share of this additional loot. Unfortunately it was many years before Thompson had a chance of returning to collect his vast wealth. When he did at last manage the return voyage he took a partner with him and discovered that both the treasure of Bonita (Graham) and Thompson's own were untouched. It was too risky to take away just then and Thompson and his partner, Doig, made careful preparations for another voyage.

Thompson died without ever seeing his treasure again, but in due course some years later, his partner, Doig, with his son, went out to Cocos once more, all prepared to bring home their great fortune. Unfortunately a landslide had occurred and made the recovery of the treasure a serious engineering task. They were totally unprepared for anything of that sort and had to return home to consider their plans.

Treasure Trove and Salvage

The elder Doig died and the son never had a chance of going out again, but he left clear directions regarding the location of the treasure hoards. Many expeditions have been made and a few coins and ornaments have been found in circumstances which certainly help to confirm the story. Most of the

Specially drawn for this work.

THE FIRST ATLANTIC CROSSING

In 1492, three little ships, *Santa Maria, Pinta* and *Nina,* under the command of Christopher Columbus, made the first crossing of the Atlantic in 70 days. Many thousands of crossings have been made since then and many ships have held the record for a time. In 1952 the American liner *United States* did the crossing in 3 days, 10 hours, 40 minutes.

seekers, however, have done just as much to obliterate helpful landmarks as have the storms and natural changes through the long years which have elapsed since Thompson buried his loot.

Yet there are reasonable grounds for the belief that there is still a very considerable fortune buried somewhere on Cocos Island, but the modern treasure-hunter would need to be equipped with excavators and other engineering machinery and to have plenty of time to spend on the task. There have been several attempts in comparatively recent years, usually in a fairly light-hearted spirit, with a limit on both the time and money to be expended on the task. Quite possibly it would take more money to recover the treasure than it would be worth if and when it was finally unearthed.

Commercially the salvaging of sunken treasure from ships that have gone to the bottom when carrying known wealth, such as the *Lutine* already mentioned, is a task for experienced divers, armed with scientific equipment and assisted by skilled technicians. Some truly remarkable jobs have been carried out by skilled salvage companies, but this is essentially a business undertaking in which the actual cost of carrying through the necessary work is carefully estimated and balanced against the certain known value of the completed task.

Planet.

THE "LUTINE" BELL AT LLOYD'S

Our photograph shows the Rostrum at Lloyd's with the caller ringing the *Lutine* bell. One stroke is the signal that bad news is about to be announced while two strokes indicate good news is coming. The bell was recovered in 1859 from H.M.S. *Lutine*, wrecked off the Dutch coast in 1799.

When Smugglers Flourished

Salvaging is a modern business to some extent, but there was one flourishing business connected with the sea which, like piracy, has acquired an atmosphere of romance with the passage of time. For more than 100 years, from 1730 onwards until well into Queen Victoria's reign, the business of smuggling could fairly be classed as one of Britain's industries.

At one time, round about 1740, it was calculated that only

A MODERN CAR FERRY

Cars and double-decker buses can be carried comfortably on board the newest and biggest car ferry vessel, the *Lord Warden*, which went into service between Dover and Boulogne in the summer of 1952. It can carry 1,000 passengers and 120 cars, and in the ship's garage is a turntable so that the cars can be swung round ready to drive off.

In this picture the first cars are seen running down the ramp to pass through the steel doors at the stern when boarding the vessel for the cross-Channel trip.

Photos : Central Press.

" First on, first off " is the principle on board the *Lord Warden*, and the first car is seen here as it was driven off the ship on to the special ramp at Boulogne.

one-fifth of the four million pounds of tea which came into this country paid its fair share of duty. One fleet of five fast cutters running contraband between France and the South-East coast were believed to bring in some six tons of tea and 8,000 gallons of brandy every week. There were men in several of the Southern seaboard counties who built up big fortunes as smugglers and were regarded as comparatively respectable citizens.

A Battle for Tea

Some of the smugglers, particularly in the Western counties, most certainly did not regard themselves as criminals, but as members of a straightforward profession who were merely concerned with outwitting, or possibly, bribing, the preventive men, whose unenviable task it was to stop the smugglers if they could. Usually, however, the forces employed by the Government for this purpose were utterly inadequate for the task. Sometimes the preventive men were supported by Dragoons, and occasionally pitched battles took place in which the Government forces were as often as not utterly routed.

The most infamous of all smugglers were undoubtedly the members of the Hawkhurst gang. They were led by a couple of out-and-out scoundrels, Kingsmill and Fairall. Usually the smuggling fraternity kept on the best of terms with local residents who often received some benefit. The Hawkhurst gang terrorised a whole district after their first notorious affair in 1744 when they captured a revenue patrol of four men, two of whom were released eventually after being badly beaten. What happened to the other two was never known, but it was said that these two had originally been members of the gang and had then deserted.

One of the Hawkhurst gang's most daring outrages was the capture of Poole Custom-house in October, 1747, to take a quantity of smuggled tea which had been captured by the authorities. Sixty armed men took part in the attack and removed the tea. As the proceeds of this affair amounted to only 27 lbs. of tea per man, it scarcely seems to have been worth while.

Their outrages included the killing of a number of persons, and finally the authorities were compelled to make a determined effort to break up the gang and capture the ringleaders. It was a fairly long struggle, but at last, in April, 1749, Kingsmill and Fairall were captured and paid the penalty of their crimes.

Not all smugglers were in the Hawkhurst gang class, but there were few people willing to turn informer in any case. Rudyard Kipling, in one of his poems, sums up the general attitude in the advice: " Don't go drawing back the blind or looking in the street." And again:

" *Five and twenty ponies, trotting through the dark—*
Brandy for the Parson, 'baccy for the Clerk;
Laces for a lady, letters for a spy,
And watch the wall, my darling, while the Gentlemen go by! "

In some parts of the country a farmer would be warned to leave his stables and cart-sheds unlocked on a certain evening. The wisest course was to obey; if he refused there was more than a chance that his ricks would be fired and cattle maimed, just by way of a lesson to teach him better manners. If he complied—the horses would be in their stables next morning, a little the worse for a hard night's work perhaps, while in the cart-shed, somewhere near the carts which had been used, there would probably be a tub of spirits or bag of tea.

Aid from Parson and Ploughman

It was obviously better to fall in with the smugglers' ideas of friendly aid even though the farmers objected to smuggling on several grounds, chief of which was that the trade attracted too many of their labourers. It was a temptation to many an honest ploughman, who

TRAINING FOR LIFE AFLOAT

Fox Photos.

In the old days a boy learnt the art and science of seamanship in the hard way by practical experience at sea. To-day he goes through a properly-planned course of training both ashore and afloat before he is signed on as a member of a merchant ship's crew or becomes a Royal Navy rating. Here we have two classes in such a training-school for seamen. In the foreground the way to hitch a rope round a barrel for unloading is being taught, while beyond can be seen a group engaged in the task of lowering a ship's boat over the side.

Planet.

TIMBER COMES TO BRITAIN UNDER SAIL

Few sailing-ships are employed in overseas trade to-day but they have not entirely disappeared. Our picture shows the Swedish 4-masted schooner *Albatross*, used in recent years as a training-ship, back at work again after the end of the last war. Her cargo was much-needed timber for Britain's housing drive, and she is here seen entering Lowestoft harbour to unload.

earned sixpence a day, to become a rider for the smugglers at half-a-guinea a journey, with probably enough tea as a little extra present to enable him to make a pound or so.

Some of the magistrates were hand in glove with the smugglers, and not a few clergymen gave useful assistance, as did the sexton and the clerk in suitable parishes where it was convenient to use the crypts as temporary store-houses for smuggled tubs of brandy and bags of tea.

Even the Navy took a hand during the early years of the nineteenth century in trying to prevent smuggling. Britain was at war with France, but those engaged in the smuggling business on both sides of the Channel ignored the question of enemy nationals. British smugglers were welcome enough in certain French districts where the goods they collected for running across the Channel were paid for in gold.

This gold was quite useful to France, but was a real loss to Britain. There was no reason whatever why the French police should interfere, nor why the French Army should worry about British smugglers who were often very useful in taking secret letters to their spies in England. Eventually coastguards were established and became a highly efficient and useful body of men.

Other steps were taken in addition, and the coming of steamships was a last nail in the coffin of the dying profession of smuggling. It had ceased to be quite such a profitable game before then and the rewards were inadequate compared with the increased risks. There has, of course, been some little revival of smuggling in a new form in our own day, and aircraft have taken the place of the fast-sailing cutters slipping across Channel before a favourable wind. But smuggling by air is an exceedingly risky business and the penalties extremely heavy. The records so far indicate very definitely that there is no future in it!

Blue Riband of the Atlantic

In recent times there has been a revival of the old-time rivalry to lower the record for the crossing of the Atlantic. Until 1952 " the Blue Riband of the Atlantic " was held by that fine ship the *Queen Mary*. In August, 1938, she beat her own previous record by making the crossing in three days, twenty hours and forty-two minutes. Then the fourteen-year-old record was beaten by the American liner *United States* on her maiden voyage in July, 1952, with a record for the 2,938 miles from Bishop Rock Lighthouse off the Scillies to the Ambrose lightship in New York Bay, of three days, ten hours, forty minutes.

That first historic voyage by Christopher Columbus in 1492 took seventy days. The marvel then was not so much the time as the fact that he had managed to get across—and to return again. It was not till the middle of the nineteenth century that anybody really began to trouble about speeds and records. In July, 1840, the *Britannia*, owned by the newly-formed Cunard Company, made the voyage from Liverpool to Halifax in a little under

International News.

A GALLANT SHIP GOES DOWN

A stirring story of the sea was recorded in January, 1952, when Captain Carlsen of the *Flying Enterprise* ordered his passengers and crew to abandon ship. The captain remained on board, despite the hazardous list. An Admiralty tug reached him, and the mate, Mr. R. K. Dancy, managed to swing aboard. Despite all efforts, however, Captain Carlsen and Mr. Dancy had eventually to leave the ship only a very short time before she went down off Land's End.

twelve and a half days. This beat the *Great Western's* record, made two years earlier, of fifteen days for the outward crossing.

Some of the old sailing-ships had put up remarkable records, but the steamships drove them out of business. For some years the real contest for supremacy lay between two British shipping companies, the Cunard and the White Star, which were then separate companies. In 1850 the Cunarder *Asia* did the voyage in 8 days 17 hours.

The Battle for Honours

For the next thirty years or more there was continual competition to hold the record for this particular crossing, which eventually became known as the Blue Riband of the Atlantic, though there was no ribbon and no prize at stake. The White Star sister ships, *Teutonic* and *Majestic*, shared the honours in 1891, but were beaten by the Cunard *Campania* and *Lucania* two years later. German shipping companies then entered the contest, and in 1897 the *Kaiser Wilhelm der Grosse* crossed from Southampton to New York at an average of 21·39 knots, and on the return voyage at 21·95 knots.

Other German ships that maintained the supremacy were the *Deutschland*, *Kronprinz Wilhelm* and *Kaiser Wilhelm II*. Then came the ever-famous *Mauretania* in 1909, which did the Queenstown to New York trip in four days ten hours at an average speed of 26·06 knots. The *Titanic* was expected to wrest the honour from the Cunarder, but the tragic ending of her maiden voyage not merely finished such hopes, but for a time raised doubts about the wisdom of this attempt to knock a few hours off the record.

The Great War of 1914–18 came and the *Mauretania* record remained unbroken until 1929 when the *Bremen* took the honours for Germany, averaging 28·51 knots, followed in 1933 by the Italian liner *Rex*, which averaged 28·92 knots on her 3,188 miles run from Gibraltar to New York. In May, 1935, France took pride of place when the *Normandie* made a new record on her maiden voyage by crossing in three days twenty-one hours forty-five minutes at an average speed of 30·1 knots, increased to 30·31 knots on her return voyage.

It was in August, 1938, that the Cunard White Star liner *Queen Mary* did the run in three days twenty hours forty-two minutes, and the Blue Riband was held by Britain again for fourteen years. The World War temporarily ended all efforts to lower this record. There was more arduous and dangerous work for the *Queen Mary* to do. Six years of war service stood to her credit when in August, 1945, she came back for overhaul and refitting at Southampton Docks. Her record was eventually beaten by ten hours by the American liner *United States*, as already mentioned, at an average speed of 35½ knots.

Superstitions Pass but Courage Remains

The old superstitions are dying, the pirate and the smugglers have gone ; the wooden walls and the graceful clippers have given place to more solid-looking ships of steel and iron, with great funnels leaving a long trail of smoke behind them, while the masts carry wireless aerials but no sails. The sea shanties are sung by land-lubbers and the sailor a thousand miles from land listens-in to the latest news from London.

But the sea itself is unchanging and its perils have not been utterly banished. Nor has the spirit of the men who sail from our ports changed since the days of Drake and Hawkins. The long traditions of courage shown by British sailors have not been tarnished during those recent years of direst peril when our ships were the lifeline of this country. Our sea-girt isle still stands impregnable and for that great blessing the chief credit goes to the men of the Royal Navy and their brothers in the Merchant Navy.

LIFE-BOATS AND THEIR CREWS

Topical.

A LIFE-BOAT ON THE CORNISH COAST

Probably no part of the British coast-line has seen more wrecks than Cornwall, and in modern times its life-boats have earned well-deserved fame. In this photograph we see the 8-ton life-boat *Edgar George Orlando and Eva Child,* stationed at St. Ives. This vessel is fitted with the most up-to-date equipment and can travel 100 miles at seven knots without re-fuelling.

ANY work dealing with ships and seafaring matters would be sadly incomplete without some reference to the work of the Royal National Life-boat Institution, its boats and their heroic crews. From the little fishing coble to the great liner, and even to the ships of the Royal Navy, there is no class of sea-going craft that has not at some time or other been helped by the lifeboatmen.

A life-boat is, of course, a specially-designed craft for saving life from shipwreck and must be able to weather storms in which other boats would founder. One or two attempts had been made to design such a craft before three Englishmen, Lionel Lukin, William Wouldhave and Henry Greathead, all tackled the problem about the same time. Each of them contributed something to the building of the first life-boat which was launched at Newcastle-on-Tyne in 1789. For thirty years this first life-boat was in use and saved hundreds of lives.

What is the difference between a life-boat and any ordinary boat? In the first place the life-boat is very much stronger in build. For the stem, stern and framing, English Oak is used entirely, and for the planking there is African mahogany. Burma supplies the teak for the keel, while from Canada comes the Western Red Cedar used for the air-cases.

To Ensure Buoyancy

This brings in the second important difference: the life-boat is fitted with air-cases and chambers to make her specially buoyant and she is able to free herself quickly of water through valves or scuppers fitted in the bottom or sides. These valves are so made that they empty the water in a few seconds but allow none to return. If you were to fill the deck of a life-boat with water right up to the thwarts she would empty herself in twelve seconds.

There may be from seven to fourteen water-tight compartments and this means that, should the vessel be damaged, only a small part of the craft can become flooded. There are from 70 to 160 air-cases, and these make her practically unsinkable. A life-boat can be kept afloat by her air-cases even if every water-tight compartment is badly damaged and wide-open to the sea.

STERN WORK FOR THE LIFE-BOAT'S CREW

Here is a line-throwing gun about to be fired. The photo was taken on board the Yarmouth, Isle of Wight, life-boat and you see how the line is coiled in a case.

On many a winter's night sheer darkness may interfere with the work of rescue. Modern life-boats are therefore equipped with searchlights.

Graphic Photo Union.

During a storm and in the dark hours of the night the Greek steamer *Varvassi* was driven on to the rocky Needles off the Isle of Wight. With heavy seas pouring over her the ship was in danger of total destruction. The Yarmouth (I.O.W.) life-boat put out and rescued the thirty-five members of the crew on board

"FOR THOSE IN PERIL——"

R.N.L.I.

All life-boats are now being built with two engines and twin screws and are entirely independent of sail on which they relied for so long. The last of the sailing-boats was replaced by a motor-boat in 1948. To-day there are over 150 motor life-boats stationed round our coasts. These life-boats usually carry a crew of eight and can carry from 30 to 100 people when required.

Daily Telegraph.

It is from a photograph such as this that some idea of the tremendous power of heavy seas can be gained. Here we see the *Northeastern Victory*, broken in two, as she lay helpless on the Goodwins. The vessel could not be saved, but the life-boat came to the rescue of those on board and brought them safely ashore.

Shields Evening News.

It was on the River Tyne in 1789, at Newcastle, that the first specially-constructed vessel for saving life at sea was launched. In its thirty years this first life-boat saved hundreds of lives off the rocky Northumberland coast. Many improvements in design have been made since then, and this photograph shows a motor life-boat being launched at Tynemouth in recent times.

Elsam, Mann & Cooper.

The adaptation of radio-telephony apparatus for use on the modern life-boat was not a simple task, but the special designs now in use ensure that the instruments are fully protected from all risk of being rendered useless owing to damage by water. Here we see the wireless operator in the cabin of a motor life-boat which is now in service.

One of the two main types of life-boat is the self-righting class. If such a vessel had a full crew on board and all the sails she carried were set, she could be turned over completely but would come the right way up and empty out all the water in about twenty-five seconds. This property was given to the boat by a heavy keel and by end-boxes, one in the bow and the other in the stern, which were really air chambers.

The Passing of Sails

For a time steam engines were used in some life-boats but the coming of the petrol engine provided just the right motive power for a vessel of this type, whether of the self-righter type or the non-self-righter. The latter kind of life-boat relies on her greater beam and general construction to avoid the risk of being capsized.

The first experimental motor was installed in a pulling and sailing life-boat in 1904. Now there are over 150 motor life-boats, and the last of the sailing-boats was replaced by a motor life-boat in 1948. All life-boats, small as well as large, are now being built with two engines and twin screws so that they will be entirely independent of sail, and heavy oil engines are replacing the petrol engines. This means a great increase in range of action as well as a great decrease in the risk of fire.

The chief problem with all mechanical things used on a life-boat is to make them water-tight. She is a small boat that has to do her work in the worst of weather, to travel smothered in the seas, her decks awash, her cockpits filled, and it may be, if she is damaged, with her engine-room flooded. So her engine must be able to work even when it is under water. Her searchlight will go on burning even if it is dropped to the bottom of the sea. The launching tractor can drive out into the surf pounding the sea shore without fear of the water damaging the magneto or dynamo, the sparking plugs or the carburettor.

Because of this need to make every-

Graphic Photo Union.

WHEN THE LIGHT OF MORNING CAME

Here is another scene of shipwreck on the Goodwins in which the life-boat had played its part before morning came to reveal the fate of the ship. On an average, eleven lives have been saved every week since the Royal National Life-boat Institution was founded in 1824.

thing water-tight the most difficult invention of all to adapt to life-boat work was the wireless apparatus, obviously a highly important addition in modern times. For a long time it had to be confined to boats with cabins in which the apparatus could be fully protected from the sea. Now, however, the Service has a special design of radio-telephony sets which can be used in all life-boats without fear of damage by water. These sets also work a loud hailer; the wireless operator, by pressing a switch, can pass from talking by radio to the shore to calling direct to the wrecked vessel by means of the loud hailer.

The Royal National Life-boat Institution was founded in 1824, and since that date its fleet of life-boats with their gallant crews have been responsible for saving some 76,000 lives. This means that on an average eleven lives have been rescued from the sea every week. If you can imagine a large football crowd of 76,000 people it will give the right impression of the number of persons saved from death by shipwreck by our life-boatmen.

Fine fellows are the coxwains of the life-boats. They and their crews guard 5,000 miles of our storm-swept coast. All of them are volunteers and the work is organised and financed by the Royal National Life-boat Institution. To maintain its services and carry on with the great work the Institution needs over £800,000 a year. It does not seem an extravagant amount when one considers the wonderful work which has been and will continue to be done to save those in peril on the seas around our coasts.

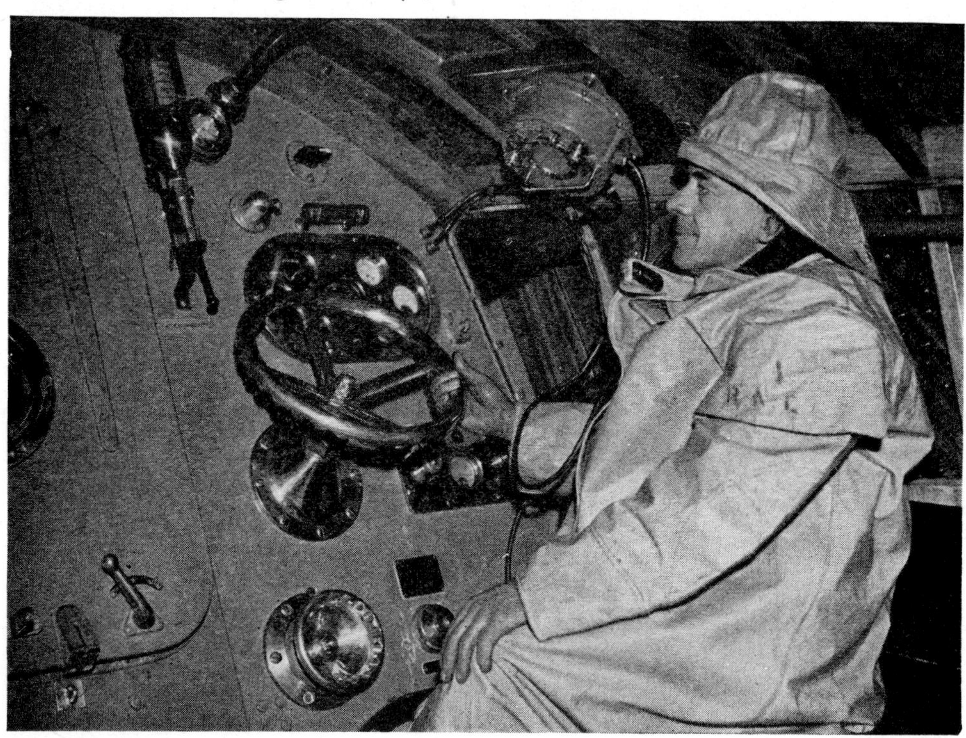

J. H. Cleat.

THE MAN IN THE CABIN

The equipment fitted to the latest motor life-boats varies according to the particular type of craft. In this picture we see the man under the canopy of the cabin where he is able to communicate by wireless with those on shore, or, by pressing a switch, can pass from radio to the loud hailer and so call direct to the wrecked vessel.

WITH THE FISHING FLEETS

Fox Photos

THE DRIFTERS MAKE FOR PORT

Sturdy little vessels are the Scottish drifters seen above. They have been at sea a full week in search of the herring harvest and are now making as fast as their engines can drive them for Great Yarmouth. East Anglia is the chief herring centre, and girls from Scotland gather here in the late summer to give deft and willing aid in the cleaning and packing of the fish.

AMONG the most resolute, fearless and also enterprising of our British seagoing fraternity are the brave men who go forth in the least sizable of vessels to catch for us our harvest of fish, the flesh of which forms such a welcome part of our daily diet. Year in and year out, by day and night, through storm, icy cold or paralysing fog they carry on their hazardous work whilst we ashore accept the good food brought to us often without knowing the first thing about the stern routine of fishing for a living.

The Master Fisherman

Let us therefore consider some of the main aspects of deep sea fishing, never imagining for a moment that any fleet sets sail and casts its nets haphazardly. Such a simple plan as this would bring nothing but disaster, for fish are found only where the water is of the right depth, where the sea bed is suitable to their habits and where their natural food is abundant. Moreover, fish visit certain well-defined parts of the sea at particular times of year and where there is first-class fishing say in September there may be nothing worth the catching in April. These are a few of the lessons every master fisherman must learn, quite apart from navigation, seamanship and the lore of the tides and weather. He has, indeed, to know his fishing grounds as you know the way between home and school.

Has it ever struck you how much the sea, despite its uniformly level surface, is in a fishery sense to be compared to the land? You can think of high rolling downs where the soil is so thin and the herbage so scanty that there is scarcely any food for the creatures of the earth. In the sea, there are cavernous hollows corresponding to the hills. No light reaches deep water, there is no plant life upon which the fish can feed and consequently no fishing.

Thus, our fisherman has a chart which shows him where there are fathomless holes, the position of sand-

Fox Photos.

SEINE-NET FISHING

From many a port round our coasts fishermen set forth by day and night to make catches with their nets. Above, the Seine-net is being cleared of its herrings.

banks, the set of the tides, the location of a rocky sea bed that would rip his nets, and all such matters. The chart is his map of fishing territory, but whether there are fish or not depends upon the season, perhaps on the moon and winds and to some extent on chance or luck.

Plant Life in the Sea

You may wonder, possibly, at the reference made above to plant life, but this was no mistake. The surface of the sea and the water for several feet down is literally alive with tiny growths, some like miniature plants and others in the nature of microscopic animals. Many of the little objects you could not see at all with the naked eye, and there would be added to your difficulty in this respect the fact that some of them are quite transparent.

The term for this layer, which floats and drifts about, is plankton. Most of the particles are just carried along in the water, but some of them possess the power of movement. The vegetable plankton (the word means merely something that drifts) is more plentiful as a rule than the animal sort, but the latter include diatoms, copepods (sometimes called water fleas, though they are not fleas at all) and flagellates, which can swim. Plankton is the material that in some way or other brings food and nourishment to all the creatures of the sea and there is mingled with it eggs and spores to produce further generations and the very small fry of fish as well; fry, as you know, being the word we use to denote baby fishes that have just been spawned. Among the plankton too we might find curious worms, wee shell fish and other strange forms of life, for the entire mass is very much alive, drawing its sustenance largely from salts and matter in the water around it.

Very likely you have often wondered upon what fish feed, but you will know now that plankton is the basic food of the fish world, what may be termed the lowest link in the food chain. Large

Fox Photos.

ON THE SLAB

This fishmonger has been to market early and bought his stock for the day. Now he is arranging the fish so that customers can make their choice.

THE FISH-QUAY AT LOWESTOFT

The ports of East Anglia are noted as the centre of the herring industry, and in this photograph, taken on the quayside at Lowestoft, some idea is given of what happens when the drifters come in and unload their catches. "Drifter" is the name given to a type of vessel, smaller than a trawler, used in drift net fishing.

Photos: Topical.

This photograph shows the scene after the catches have all been unloaded. The crews of the drifters now turn their attention to their vessels and the equipment which has been in use at sea. In the foreground a net is being unloaded for repair, and everything is being cleaned up and made shipshape before the fishermen go ashore.

Topical.

PREPARED FOR MARKET

From the quayside the fish are quickly transferred to the gutting shed where they are dealt with by girls who are experts in preparing them for the markets.

fish may not take much plankton but live mainly on small fish (perhaps even the young of their own kind), but the small fish will be plankton-fed. Strangely enough, some of the very biggest sea creatures derive their living solely from plankton, sieving it against plates from the great stream of water they pass into their mouths and then through the slits of their gills.

Now it often happens that there is more plankton in a particular part of the sea at one season of the year than another. Where there is a great abundance we can carry the comparison between sea and shore one stage farther and say that a rich pasture land has been formed for the floating population. Thus, the fish concentrate in the region of this pasture and there the knowing fisherman goes to catch them. Indeed, on many fishing craft, appliances are carried with which samples of surface water are taken so that the plankton it contains can be examined, largely because certain fish will avoid particular types of plankton and be attracted to others.

Though the most fascinating of fishermen are those who go far out to sea in drifters and trawlers, clever craftsmen about whom we shall read later, we must not forget the ones who carry on very valuable work much nearer to the shore. They are known as inshore fishermen and ply their calling, chiefly by night, from at least a hundred ports all round our coasts, mostly in motor-propelled boats. At certain times they may make use of drift nets, but you will find them working mainly with strong lines, every line furnished with about 800 hooks. The hooks are not attached directly to the line, but each is fastened at the end of a short length known as a snood secured at regular intervals to the line.

How Women Help

The hooks are baited with mussels and there may be three fishermen to one boat and as many as six lines, each tied end to end. Very often the women bait the lines, which are built up in neat handy coils so that they can be shot deftly into the sea without becoming tangled or fouling the boat's gear.

The station one of these fishing boats takes up on the sea is known as its berth and there are buoys made of canvas to keep the lines, each some hundreds of yards in length, at the correct depth, and an anchor to hold the end fast. Once the lines are shot the boat is kept just moving facing the tide; and, when about a couple of hours have passed, slowly enough one may be sure to the waiting men tossed about perhaps on a restless sea, the buoy and anchor are found and the work of hauling in begins.

It is hard toil indeed, especially when some part of the line fouls an unseen ledge of rock, but there is all the excitement that goes with every type of fishing. Though extremely unlikely, there may be a fish on every hook, but quite possibly only one hook in a dozen will hold a cod, a haddock or some other captive, the creatures being taken from the hooks as the line is carefully re-coiled. Then, as soon as the lines are inboard, the boat sets off for its harbour and there is deliciously fresh fish available in the market—or it may be sold on the beach exactly as landed.

Though this line-fishing fills in much of the time of an inshore crew they also at favourable seasons catch flat fish with what is known as a seine. This is really a wide net with long ropes at either end. The net is set with the aid of boats, and the ropes or warps may then be drawn in by men on the beach. You have perhaps watched this sort of fishing during summer holidays at the seaside, when the net becomes smaller and smaller as it is drawn in. Sometimes there is a bag made of netting at the rear of the net and when its mouth is drawn over the sea bed flat fish are swept into it. Seine fishing is carried out by fishing boats, much the same methods being followed as when the net is dragged in to the beach.

From our inshore fishermen we should proceed to those who form the crews of trawlers, these ships being propelled by steam. The newer vessels will travel at 16 knots (a knot is a sea mile of 6,080 feet) and may carry more than a score of hands. The crews are away from their home ports sometimes

John Topham.

ON BOARD A TRAWLER IN THE NORTH SEA

Much of the fish caught for British markets is brought in by the trawlers. In trawling, a bag-shaped net, the mouth of which is kept open by heavy wooden frames, sweeps along the bed of the sea. The large trawl net is hauled on board by steam winch and the catch emptied on the deck plates. In this photograph the men aboard an Aberdeen trawler out in the North Sea are emptying the catch from the trawl.

Fox Photos.

PACKING OYSTERS FOR MARKET

This picture comes from the famous Royal Whitstable Oyster Beds and we see two experienced men packing the shell-fish just as they have been dredged up at this Kentish seaport.

for three weeks at a stretch, and it is because of the trawlers' speed and the ice carried that they can get their catches home in good condition for market, some of the larger ships bringing in 200 tons at a time if they have been fortunate.

What is the purpose of trawling? It is, briefly, to draw a bag-shaped net by means of a fishing vessel so that it sweeps along the bed of the sea. The mouth of the net is kept in an extended position by heavy frames of wood filled in with spars like slats. These wooden parts are fixed by wire hawsers some distance from the trawl mouth. Beyond them come two stout ropes known as warps secured to the vessel, one forrard and the other aft. It is only because steam winches are available that this large otter trawl can be used at all. In the days of sailing trawlers and man power only a comparatively small beam trawl was feasible.

Even now, on the most up-to-date trawlers, with echo-sounding apparatus to tell the depth of water beneath the ship and all such modern gear, it is an exacting task to get the trawl net into the water, and in the correct position. Thus, when the net has been favourably cast, the ship steams slowly forward, it may be for a couple of hours. At the end of that time, a signal is given, machinery gets to work and the trawl is dragged in, the upper part of the net being hauled well up the foremast so that what is known as the cod end has its mouth immediately over the deck just in front of the bridge.

Stowing the Catch

Another moment and we might see a deck hand untie this cod end so that a perfect cascade of fish (if the cast has proved a lucky one) comes tumbling to the deck plates so much all-alive-o that the flapping of tails and jumping movements tell only of living fish. There may be cod, haddocks, and flatfish, and very likely other denizens of the deep for which no market is available so that they must be flung overboard to the delight of the flock of noisy gulls that has been wheeling overhead. Then, at another order, outwards goes the trawl again for a further spell of duty.

In the meantime, the fish just caught must be packed in ice in the thick wooden boxes you will so often have seen and stored away in the hold. For perhaps seven days, provided the weather is propitious, this trawling will continue, according to the size of the catches. In due time, when the hold is full, back will go the trawler to her home port, piling on every ounce of speed in her haste to catch the market. In all probability the vessel will be at sea again within twenty-four hours, for there is little rest for trawler crews at the height of the fishing season.

We have fishing fleets at Milford Haven, Aberdeen, Fleetwood, North Shields, Cardiff and other places, whilst there are groups of hardy fisher folk at almost all our ports and harbours. Hull and Grimsby are, however, the great centres of the steam trawling industry, and their well-found craft scour not only the North Sea but the waters of the White Sea and Arctic Ocean, their efforts taking them to the Faroe Islands and to Iceland. It should be noted, however, that foreign fishermen are not allowed to operate within a three-mile limit of a country's coasts.

We will consider next the romantic story of the herring, one of the fish that lives almost entirely on plankton. It is called a migrant because it moves from place to place in the different seasons. Thus, it approaches our shores from the direction of the Atlantic and may be found off Scotland during the months of summer. As autumn draws on, Yarmouth is the chief herring centre, girls travelling down from Scotland to handle the huge catches, deftly cleaning the fish and packing them in barrels for export.

Because herrings in almost untold numbers move from one part of the sea to another, the fishing fleet follows them, the vessels being for the most part steam or motor - propelled drifters which still find a small sail most helpful in their work. What is called a drift net is some 40 yards in length and at least 30 feet deep. A single drifter may have upwards of a hundred of these nets which hang in the water just like so many curtains supported at the top by buoys and cork floats, with the upper edge of the net nearly 20 feet below the water surface. The nets are fastened together at their top and bottom corners to form a continuous line.

Let us consider that herrings are not caught in the bag of a net, as other fish are captured in a trawl net. Drift net work is carried out at night when the fish rise from the sea bed, partly because plankton is then nearer to the surface. Each opening or mesh in the net is diamond-shaped, its sides about 1 inch in length, and what happens is that the fish are actually caught in the meshes.

Gleaming, Silvery Herrings

When morning comes, the winches clank and clatter and the nets are hauled in one after another, silvered with gleaming, glittering fish. If the catch is a good one, the fishermen have merely to tauten the net and shake it, when the herrings fall to the deck. In favourable circumstances a drifter may take 10,000 fish at a time, or over twenty times that number if fortune is exceptionally kind. The measure of capacity for herrings is a basket or

P. Thornton.

PACKING HERRINGS AT THE QUAYSIDE

From ports all round our long coastline the fishing fleets go out, and their catches are packed at the quayside. Here we see the fisher-girls at Mallaig packing herrings in barrels.

P. Thornton.

SHIPPING HERRINGS AT MALLAIG

By rail and by sea the barrels of herrings are taken from the ports to the distribution centres. Here we see the barrels of herrings being shipped at the Scottish port of Mallaig.

cran, which usually holds some 750 fish.

Strangely enough, the best fishing grounds are sometimes found completely empty of herrings and no one can say for certain where the finest harvests of this wayward fish will be gathered. When salted and partly dried a herring becomes a bloater, and it is a kipper if smoked. A member of the same family as the sprat and pilchard, the herring is one of the most valuable of our food fish, and enormous quantities are exported to other countries.

There is a lot more that could be told about our fisher folk. In the time of your grandparents there were parts of the countryside where the people scarcely ever saw fish at table from one year's end to another, unless it was cured or tinned. This is all changed in these days of motors and other speedy transport, and there are very few homes indeed where fresh salt-water fish is not available two or three times a week.

How is this brought about? Let us imagine we are standing on the fish-quay, say at Grimsby. It is bitterly cold, being scarcely four o'clock in the morning, but a trawler fleet came in on the midnight tide and the men we see moving about in the darkness are the crews of these vessels, their task being to bring the fish from the holds and dump them on the quay.

Thereupon experts known as packers come along and divide up the fish according to their individual sizes. Very large specimens may be set in piles and others placed with ice in boxes. Long before the workaday world has had its breakfast, buyers begin to appear, looking over the fish with critical eyes. They know exactly what is needed in the markets of the country because they telephoned here and there late the previous night and now they see what fish has been brought in to meet requirements.

Presently the salesmen (representing the trawler owners) arrive and very quickly indeed the cargoes are transferred in lots to buyers, who label what they purchase. Meanwhile, on sidings near the fish docks, special trains are being loaded, or else long refrigerator vans to be attached to passenger expresses. Everything is carried out in orderly haste and soon this consignment of precious fish, the harvest of far-off seas, will be on its way as rapidly as it can be carried to markets all over the country.

Even the fishmongers must be astir whilst other people are still sleeping for they visit the local market or wholesalers where there will be fish of every type derived from many sources and brought together at centres like these for distribution. Meanwhile, the fleet has probably sailed again, its crews spending little more than a few hours at a time at home.

The Sweep Net

You will have heard how salmon ascend certain of our rivers at spawning time and even make their way past little waterfalls and rapids in the stream. In some of our rivers these royal fish are caught with a sweep net. One end of such a net is made fast on the shore and the other end taken out in a rowing boat, which returns in a semi-circle pretty much to the place from which it started. The upper edge of the net is supported by cork floats and it is a simple matter for men in waders to start at the two ends and slowly pull in this sweep net, so securing any fish that may have been entrapped. In other parts of the country wooden stakes are set up across the river and a net tightly stretched from stake to stake. Here the size and shape is so arranged that the fish are caught in the meshes.

Lobster pots or creels you may have seen at the seaside. They are made of basketwork; and, like so many other traps, have an entry that is large and alluring from the outside, but an exit so small as to prevent the escape of a captive from inside. Lobster pots vary in design in different parts of the coast, but the bait is almost invariably a tempting piece of fish. A lobster pot is weighted and dropped into the sea from a boat, its position being indicated by an attached length of rope, to the upper end of which a bundle of corks is secured. Crabs for market are also caught in pots.

Topical

HERRINGS, BLOATERS, RED HERRINGS AND KIPPERS

Herrings, seen in this picture, are among the most popular of fish, and about a million tons are taken from the North Sea alone each year. Some 70 per cent. are cured in one way or another. Lightly salted and smoke-cured they are called " bloaters "; split down the back and more heavily salted and strongly smoked they are " red herrings "; split, slightly salted and smoked they are " kippers."

Oysters, of course, have to be dredged from the bed on which they rest and one can see the oyster bed marked by a series of tall wooden poles. Shrimps, which form the food of many flat fish, are caught in a large net attached to a T-shaped handle by a fisherman who wades in the water and passes his net along the top crust of the wet sand. Cockles are dug from sand at low tide, whilst mussels are taken from the beds they form, often at river mouths.

To-day our fisher folk have the invaluable support of scientific research workers and naturalists. Efforts are being made all the time to find out more about the habits of fish, exactly what the creatures feed on, how they breed and why they are discovered more extensively on one fishing ground than another. It is said that some classes of fish are smaller in size and found in lesser numbers than was the case only twenty years ago. Specimens of fish are caught and marked and sometimes, when they fall again into man's hands, it is possible to say just how far they have travelled.

The demand for fish is increasing, but it cannot be said there are more fish in the sea. Many nations fish the North Sea and the harvest of these waters is not so bountiful as it once was, so that our fleets must tend to go farther and farther afield. As for maintaining the supply, we must use nets with larger meshes, return all undersized fish to their natural element and do all we can to conserve the fish population. Perhaps one day we shall breed fish on a colossal scale and thus artificially re-stock the depleted fishing grounds.

Central Press.

SALMON FISHING IN SCOTLAND

That royal fish the salmon comes in from the open sea and ascends some of our rivers at spawning time, being able even to pass the weirs. It is caught by means of nets erected on stout poles in some streams and the above photograph was taken on the River Cree. In other rivers a sweep net is used.

THE WORK OF THE DREDGER

By Courtesy of the Tilbury Contracting and Dredging Co. Ltd.

A HOUSEMAID OF LONDON'S RIVER

This is the largest type of dredger used in the Thames. She is 216 feet in length and the ladder up which the buckets pass is 28 feet high. These big vessels work day and night all the year round to scour the bed of the river and ensure a safe way to and from the Port of London for the ships of every nation. Dredgers of this type have neither paddles nor propellers.

THOUGH it cannot be claimed that dredgers are beautiful vessels, they serve a most important purpose and without them our rivers, canals, harbours, docks and other areas of water would soon be rendered useless to navigation by the accumulation of mud, sand and silt. In a sense, they are housemaids to the craft using the water, simply because they scour and clean, but their main aim is to ensure a channel sufficiently deep for the use of any ship likely to pass that way.

There are many types of dredger, for such craft must be designed and built according to the work they have to carry out. For instance, where the sea bed is composed of sand, an hydraulic suction pump system of dredging may be capable of raising many thousands of tons of matter in the course of an hour, the silt being drawn up through monster pipes. In a dock a grab dredger may be employed, the grab having jaws which open and close as it is lowered and raised by means of a powerful crane so that even corners can be cleared. To remove mud from the entrance to a dock a terrific jet of water may be directed to the deposit, to stir it up so that the current can carry it down stream. Dipper dredgers belong to yet another group, performing their work with huge scoops.

In this country, though, the dredgers mostly in use are of the bucket and ladder type, and such appliances can perhaps best be seen at their unending task of scouring the bed of Old Father Thames. Here, they are owned and directed by the Port of London Authority, which controls London's river, dredging from the Nore light-ship to Teddington, a distance of 69 miles.

Now just suppose the P.L.A. has kindly given us permission to go aboard one of the big Thames dredgers and find out for ourselves exactly how it works. The prospect is full of interest if not of adventure and we must wear our oldest clothes because dredging is a messy job especially when a choppy cross-wind sends muddy spray flying to and fro. When the time comes, our excursion will probably begin at some well-worn landing steps on the river's bank where we shall clamber aboard a steam tug.

In a New World

Threading our way through the busy traffic of the stream we shall presently draw alongside the dredger and find ourselves on her steel deck in a world of clamorous din, ponderous machinery keeping up a continuous clatter. The captain, who has been expecting us, offers a cheery greeting and we are astonished when he tells us he carries a chief engineer, two mates, two second engineers, one steward, six winchmen, four deck-hands and four greasers or firemen—a crew of twenty-one in all.

Right through the week, from Monday morning till Friday evening, the dredger keeps on working by day and night, half the crew being on duty and the other half resting. Strangely enough, the men sleep soundly through all the clanking racket of ever-moving buckets and rouse only if the engines should, for some untoward reason, stop. At the week-end, three watchmen come aboard, leaving the other men free to return to their homes.

You will marvel first of all at the size of this dredger. In length she is 216 feet, her beam or width being 42 feet. From her keel to the upper edge of the deck or gunwale she is 12 feet 6 inches; and, from the deck to the top platform of the ladder up which the buckets pass, 28 feet. If we walk to the stern we see it is rounded. Then, as we get for'ard to examine the bows, we find them different from those of any other type of ship. Thus, they are divided into two separate parts, and it may even strike you that these parts can be likened to a pair of boats, each facing the same way but with water in between.

As we are obviously a little puzzled, the captain explains that this is the well of the dredger, in which the ladder supporting the buckets is raised and lowered. He may point out that on some smaller dredgers the well is an opening right in the centre of the ship and that one can walk round it on all four sides.

In the case of this particular dredger the bottom end of the ladder can be raised with a derrick to deck level when the ship is at rest. At present, during the working period, the ladder passes down through the well at such an angle that the lowest part is in the correct position on the river bed.

From where we

By Courtesy of the Tilbury Contracting and Dredging Co. Ltd.

BOTH DREDGING AND BANK BUILDING

The dredger here illustrated is named *Prince Farouk*. She is at work on a canal in Egypt sucking up sand and discharging it through a pipe so that it builds the canal bank afresh.

stand, we can see the buckets, one after another, emerge from the water and go clanking up the ladder, spilling liquid mud all the while. You, who have travelled so often on the London tube railways, may now be thinking of the moving staircases at stations, for there is something about the buckets and ladder very reminiscent of an escalator. In the latter case, hinged wooden steps, running on wheels, pass up a steel slope, over the top and then down again out of sight, to reappear once more at the base of the incline.

F. C. Ivory.

AN UP-STREAM THAMES DREDGER

This is a small bucket type of dredger as used on canals and narrow rivers. The Port of London Authority controls the Thames from the Nore to Teddington and uses such a dredger in the higher reaches.

This is pretty much what occurs to the buckets of a dredger, but there are no other buckets quite like them and the word is really inadequate. To begin with, they have flat backs and rounded fronts with a top like the broadened lip of a jug, bevelled after the manner of a chisel and made of one of the toughest metals known, manganese steel. Cast-steel forms the back of the buckets, whilst the body consists of armour plates riveted round a sturdy framework. The skipper tells us that each of these buckets brings up a load of one ton and an eighth, and that an empty receptacle weighs 2 tons 3 hundredweight. As it requires forty-two of these buckets to complete the chain, one is not surprised to hear that the ladder, gear and buckets weigh 276 tons. The massive links which couple the buckets together would each tip the scales at 7½ hundredweight, and even the pins securing the buckets to the links weigh 96 pounds apiece.

A Floating Giant

With these figures in our minds, we decide at once that the dredger is a veritable giant and it may have struck you during our brief first inspection that she possesses neither propeller nor paddle wheels. Very likely you wonder how the vessel can move at all without any of the usual means of driving herself through the water, but the dredger-master has anticipated this question, for he takes us to a good vantage point and explains how so massive a vessel is kept under control and made to do her work.

In this way we learn that in the water ahead, holding fast to the river bed, is a 3-ton anchor with another of the same bulk astern. These two anchors are connected with the dredger by 600 fathoms (a fathom is 6 feet, you know) of 2-inch chain and 1,000 feet of thick steel cable. In addition, there are four smaller anchors, two on either side, to which the ship is secured with chains and cables.

It is next described to us how the vessel is moved by means of these anchors. Thus, the winchmen haul on one set of chains and cables and slacken off the hold on corresponding hawsers on the opposite side. This makes sideways movement or traversing possible whilst the ship can go ahead by hauling on the forward anchor and letting go from the stern anchor. When no further forward movement is possible by this method, an attendant tug comes along and shifts the set of anchors to new positions. Once in about two years, when the dredger requires overhaul and painting, she must be towed into dry dock.

Marine Surveyors

If you have ever thought at all about a dredger you may have formed an opinion that so long as a deep channel is cut in mid-stream all will be well. Such a plan, however, would not be satisfactory simply because the bed of a river is seldom level. Round the inner side of a sharp bend the bed is cut deeply by rushing, swirling waters; but, on the outer or opposite curve, mud and sand may be silted up to form a considerable bank.

What actually takes place is that marine surveyors come along, make frequent soundings to discover the depth of water and then prepare a chart, drawn in the form of oblong spaces, and such a chart becomes the sailing orders of the dredger-master. With the lips of his buckets he makes a perfectly straight cut 6 feet across from one bank to the other bank. The dredger is moved forward 6 feet and the next cut is made in the opposite direction. When instructions have been carried out, surveyors appear again to check the work by further soundings. As for the dredger's position in the river, the captain fixes this to within a foot or two by using his sextant, just as though he were at sea, sighting his instrument on prominent buildings instead of on the sun.

In the Chart Room

By this time we have been taken to the chart room so that we may the better understand this phase of the task, and are shown the working chart spread out upon the table. Now, as the captain is busy, the chief engineer takes us over, giving each of us a lump of cotton waste with which to wipe our hands because we are going where even the rails may be oily. Like so many seafaring engineers, our new friend is a broad Scot and a man of few words, but he makes our trip below extremely fascinating all the same.

In this way we discover that the big dredger possesses an ordinary triple-expansion marine engine with two main boilers and half a dozen furnaces capable between them of using 15 hundredweight of coal in an hour's working. Here, however, the motive power is not coupled to a propeller shaft or to the cranks of a paddle shaft but is applied by means of gearing to the very top of the ladder, 40 feet above water level. There is one short shaft in a horizontal position and then an upright shaft, like a stout steel pillar. When this pillar revolves it turns a tumbler at the top of the ladder and the endless chain of buckets is set in motion.

From the Depths

We thank the engineer at this stage and proceed to the deck, walking forward until we are standing abaft the well. A dripping, slopping bucket is just emerging from the water and we watch its passage up the ladder. Then, at the top, it meets the 9-ton manganese steel tumbler to be turned completely upside down so that its watery contents are caught by a chute and go slithering down, splashing into the hold of a barge that is tied alongside.

A deck-hand is on duty beside us, watching to see there is nothing untoward to hinder the work or anything unusual coming up in the buckets. He is grizzled and weather-beaten and tells us that strange things are sometimes dredged from the depths. In his experience, he has seen lost anchors brought to the surface hooked in the

A GUN FROM A GALLEON

Fox Photos.

Many and strange are the objects brought to the surface by dredgers. Anchors lost from ships are sometimes raised by the buckets, and the old gun seen above, which may have come from a galleon of other days, was recovered from the bed of the Thames. Fragments of wreckage are often found.

By Courtesy of the Tilbury Contracting and Dredging Co. Ltd.

Suction dredgers operate on quite a different system from those equipped with buckets. They are, in effect, enormous hydraulic pumps, and when working on a sandy sea-bed can raise thousands of tons in a short while. Above is a discharge pipe from one of these dredgers sending out 500 tons of matter an hour. An old dock is being filled in and an adjacent dock deepened in one operation.

F. C. Ivory.

THE ALL-CLEAR SIGNAL

The steam hopper seen above has dumped her cargo of dredgings out in the North Sea. The flags are a signal to a light-ship that the load has been disposed of.

buckets, old guns from the days of galleons, fragments of wreckage, often from the ships of long ago, and similar bits of jetsam.

How deeply does a dredger work? It is possible for this big vessel to break up the river bed, even if it be rock, at 55 feet below water level. Seldom however, is a ladder in the Thames set at 50 feet and more usually the depth is 30 feet or thereabouts with a bed of chalk, gravel or mud below.

A Staff of Servants

Now we walk astern, keeping out of the way of muddy, flying spray from the ladder-top and chute, so far as we can, wondering what becomes of all the material dredged up. Here the captain joins us again to say that his ship can raise 60,000 tons of the silt in the course of a week's work.

We hear next that the dredger has its own staff of servants, no fewer than nine of them. Four of these attendants are 2,000-ton "dumb" hopper barges, which have no motive power and so must be towed; three steam hoppers, each of about 750 tons; and a couple of steam tugs.

Thus, so long as the buckets are working, there must always be a hopper alongside the chute, the barge being filled until its hold is solid with mud and all the water possible has poured over the side and made its way back to the river.

To the Black Deeps

We find that one dumb hopper can be filled every three hours and that such a vessel carries a crew of eight, who live on board all through the week. As for the disposal of the dredgings, we learn of a bottomless pit away out in the North Sea, fifty miles from Thamesmouth, a place known as Black Deeps. Here the scourings of the river are taken, the barges having along their bottoms fittings like enormous hinged doors which can be opened downwards, releasing the cargo and allowing water to come swirling in to wash the grimy plates. The hopper does not sink because of watertight compartments and there are chains and a steam donkey engine for the closing of the underwater shutters when required.

A dirty job, especially now that Thames mud is charged with oil from the ships of all the nations, but yet a task that renders possible the passage of ocean-going vessels to and from our premier port. It has been an interesting and instructive trip; and, as we thank the captain and leave the dredger he tells us that he has heard that the material taken from London's river in a period of twenty years would build a wall 1 foot thick and 10 feet high all round the Equator, or form a mountain at least half the height of Snowdon. On the other hand, it could be set up in twelve separate masses and each of them would be an equivalent to the Great Pyramid of Egypt.

A VISIT TO LONDON'S DOCKS

P. L. A.

HEADQUARTERS OF THE PORT OF LONDON AUTHORITY

London was a port before it became a city. Even before the Romans came to Britain there was sea-borne trade from the settlement on the Thames. Under the Romans the shipping developed and it has continued to expand. In 1908 all the dock companies were transferred to a new body called the Port of London Authority. Our photograph shows the head office of the P.L.A. in Trinity Square near the Thames and the Tower.

LONDON was a port before it became a great city and the capital of England. Before the Romans came the inhabitants of the south-eastern part of Britain had attained a fair standard of civilisation and carried on trade with the Continent mainly through the old south coast ports of Richborough, Lympne and two or three other little places which have long ago lost their importance.

The shortest route for those who brought the goods from the rich agricultural areas of East Anglia to these ports was by way of the ford a little below where London Bridge now stands. This ford became the focus of many trackways where traders met, and gradually a settlement was established. The name London by which this settlement came to be known springs from an old Celtic word.

When the Romans came they very quickly developed British exports to the Continent. Apart from slaves these exports included skins, hunting-dogs, corn, cattle, metal, iron, silver and even gold, and these were exchanged for ivory, amber, jewellery, glassware, pottery and household articles. The estuary of the Thames is directly opposite the mouths of the three great Continental rivers, the Elbe, Scheldt and the Rhine, and so the Roman Londinium grew in importance. Tacitus, the Roman historian, writing of it in A.D. 61 says that it "was much frequented by a number of merchants and trading vessels."

"The Mart of Many Nations"

By the end of the second century London was "a great and wealthy city," and in the year A.D. 359 some 800 cargoes of grain were exported to the Roman storehouses on the Rhine. When the Romans left half-a-century or so later their departure must have had its effect on this trade, but there are few records of its development during the next century. Yet in A.D. 604 the City had its own Bishop, and about this time the Venerable Bede speaks of London as "the metropolis of the East Saxons" and "the mart of many nations resorting to it by sea and land."

London became strongly fortified and it was sufficiently far inland to present great difficulties to the Danish invaders who harried our shores. King Alfred gave some land to Archbishop Ethelred who made a "hithe" (meaning a wharf or landing-place) which later became known as Queenhithe. Billingsgate was probably the very first "hithe" to be constructed on the river front, and there are records of the tolls charged towards the end of the tenth century in respect of vessels from Normandy, France, Liége and other Continental places.

When William, the Norman Conqueror, came to London he bargained with the people and granted them their first Charter. It was during this period too, that many foreign merchants came to London from Normandy, Flanders, Italy, Spain and many other countries as they found the city "fitted for their trading and better stored with merchandise in which they were wont to traffic."

The story of the growth of the Port of London since those days is one of enterprise, romance, and high adventure. The merchants and shipowners of

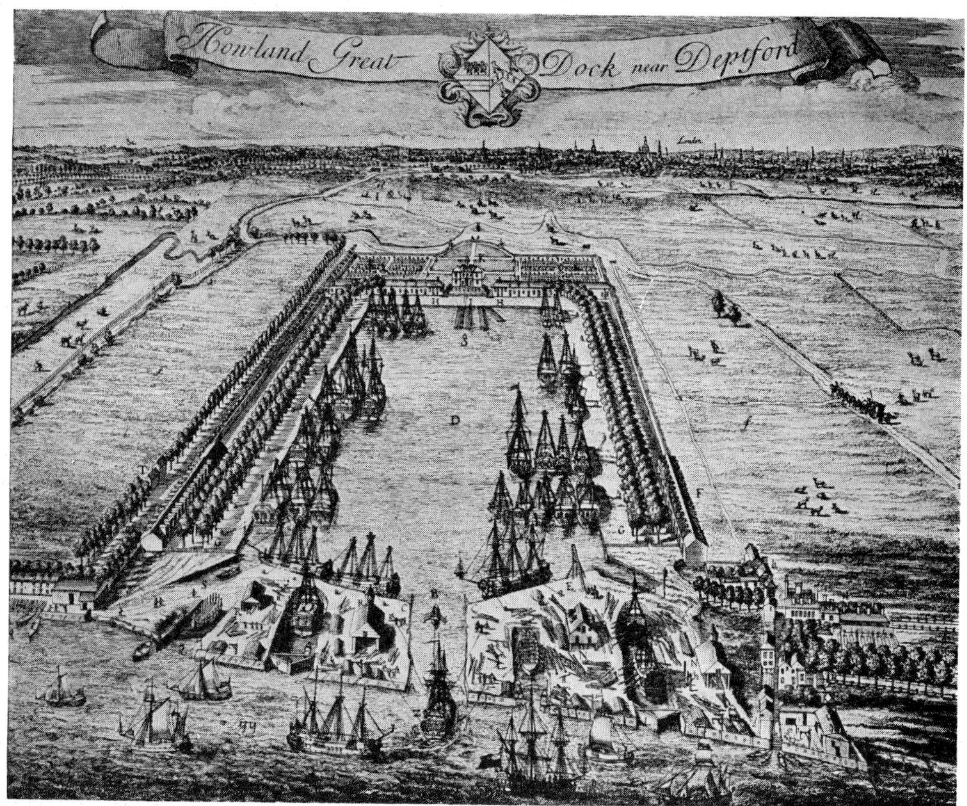

ONE OF LONDON'S FIRST DOCKS

Docks as we know them to-day are a comparatively modern development. One of the first wet docks to be constructed was at Blackwall, and Samuel Pepys visited it in 1671. What was really the first of London's docks was the Howland Great Dock which could harbour 120 merchantmen when it was opened in 1700. Our photograph from an old print shows how it appeared in those days.

Aerofilms Ltd.

LONDON'S ROYAL DOCKS FROM THE AIR

The Royal Victoria Dock was opened in 1855 and was the first to be connected with the country's railway system, while the Royal Albert Dock, opened 25 years later, was the first to be equipped with electric light for night work. With King George V Dock these "Royal Docks" are the largest enclosed docks in the world, and are interconnected by waterway passages. King George V Dock is in the centre; parallel, on the right, is the Royal Albert, and at the top the Royal Victoria Dock.

London did not sit in their offices and wait for trade to come to them. They took great risks and there was no lack of fine sailors and brave adventurers willing to share those risks. You will read in Volume II of Sir Hugh Willoughby and Richard Chancellor who sailed from Deptford in 1553 to open up trade with Russia. The Russian Company, which was the outcome of this, was one of the most successful of the early maritime companies. Other Merchant Companies were formed, among them the East India Company whose first fleet sailed from Woolwich in 1601. Five vessels there were and they returned two and a half years later with over a million pounds of pepper.

An Early Link With Canada

This broke the Dutch monopoly of the spice trade and not before it was time. The price of pepper had gone up in 1599 from 3s. to 8s. a pound, and at that time there was great need for pepper and other spices to make the coarse food of most people more palatable. The East India Company quickly became soundly established after its first successful venture and the trade with India has ever since been closely associated with the Port of London. There was, too, the foundation of the Hudson's Bay Company in 1668, and the connection then formed between Canada and the Port of London has remained unbroken.

With the East India Company's trade developing, larger vessels were built. There were no docks as we know them to-day. The big ships were moored in the stream and their cargoes transferred to and from shore in small boats. The East Indiamen anchored off Blackwall, their cargoes being transferred to the legal quays in the Pool in the only covered barges used in the Port. About the middle of the seventeenth century the Company constructed a small wet dock at Blackwall for fitting out their vessels after launching from the nearby shipyards. This dock was the first on the Thames to be fitted with gates, but it was not used for handling goods. Samuel Pepys records in his diary that he went to see this dock in 1661. In due course it became part of the Brunswick Dock, which in turn was absorbed by the East India Dock of to-day.

In the year 1700 the Howland wet dock was opened at Rotherhithe on the south side of the river, about three miles below the present Tower Bridge. This was really the first of the London docks and it had room for 120 of the largest merchantmen of the day. Trees were planted round the dock as a protection against the wind and it became very popular after the great storm in 1703 which wrought havoc among the shipping moored in the river. This Howland Dock was the nucleus of the present Surrey Commercial Docks system.

River Pirates and Mud Larks

Howland Dock was intended only as a safe anchorage and had no facilities for loading and unloading cargo. For a century it was the only dock and gradually became the headquarters of the Greenland whale fishery trade; its site to-day is occupied by the Greenland Dock, part of the Surrey Commercial

P. L. A.

NEAREST TO THE SEA

Twenty miles down the river are the Tilbury Docks and these are much nearer the open sea than any of the others. To Tilbury come many liners of the famous shipping companies and here passengers are landed and cargo is unloaded. At Tilbury, too, are two of the ten dry docks owned by the Port of London Authority, and repairs to the largest vessels can be carried out here. Our photograph shows shipping in the Centre Branch Dock at Tilbury.

Docks system. Writing of the Howland Dock in 1790, Thomas Pennant mentioned the fact that the Greenland ships discharged their cargoes here "and at this place the blubber is boiled at a fit distance from the capital." To-day London has not merely reached Rotherhithe but stretches far eastwards of it.

TO LIFT 150 TONS *P. L. A*

The largest of all the floating cranes in the London Docks is the "London Mammoth" seen in the photograph above. It has a lifting capacity of some 150 tons and can be moved in and out of the docks to tackle whatever heavy job may be required of it.

Some idea of the congestion that existed in the river about this time may be gathered from the fact that in the Upper Pool 1,775 vessels were allowed to moor simultaneously in a space adapted for about 545. It must be remembered that a ship of 500 tons was spoken of at this time as being of exceptional size. The position was aggravated by the large number of craft, probably about 3,500, employed to carry the cargoes from the moorings to the wharves. The extent of these wharves was wholly inadequate and goods remained for weeks at a time in lighters before they could be dealt with. They lay exposed to the weather and to the mercies of the river thieves who carried on a well-organised and highly profitable business. The several classes of thieves were known by the type of work they carried out: there were River Pirates, Night Plunderers, Light Horsemen, Heavy Horsemen and Mud Larks.

Parliament was moved to act at last and a Bill, promoted by the West India Merchants and the Corporation of London, was passed in 1799. Two docks were built with a range of splendid five-storey warehouses. High walls and a wide ditch surrounded the premises and an armed watch of 100 men and officers, supplemented by 100 special constables, kept safe guard.

Australia's First Cargo of Meat

During the nineteenth century many

SHIPPING IN THE POOL

Stanley.

One of the busiest parts of London's river is just below Tower Bridge on the stretch of water known as the Pool of London. The headquarters of the Port of London Authority almost overlook the Pool and here may be seen shipping from every port in the world, with tugs, barges, cranes and their operators all busily employed in the big task of manœuvring the ships, or in unloading or loading cargoes.

steps were taken to increase the Port's facilities, and, as the size of vessels increased, additions were made to meet the changing circumstances. The steamship made its first appearance on the Thames in 1815, but it was not until 1875 that sail definitely took second place to steam in the tonnage of vessels using the Port.

London has played a specially important part in the commercial development of Commonwealth countries. The first exports of wool, meat, butter, cheese and other products from Australia and New Zealand were sent to London and sold on the London Market. The first consignment of frozen meat and butter from Australia arrived in the Thames in 1880. New Zealand's first meat shipment came to the Port in 1882 by the sailing ship *Dunedin*, an historic event that may be said to have laid the foundations of New Zealand's economic progress.

At this stage the docks were owned by private companies. Financial and other difficulties arose and eventually in 1908 all the docks of the Port of London were taken over by a public body named the Port of London Authority, which paid the owners some £32 million for them. The "P.L.A.," as it is familiarly called, levies dues on all ships entering the river, and "dock rates on all ships using the docks as well as charges for any services rendered." Any profits made are used to improve conditions in the port itself.

Rather more than a century and a quarter ago the tonnage of ships entering and leaving the Port of London, which is that part of the Thames between Teddington and the Nore, totalled 2½ million. In the peak year of 1937 it was over 62 million net registered tons. To accommodate the steady increase in the volume of shipping, great groups of docks have been built.

The Groups of London Docks

Starting from the Tower Bridge and working down along the north bank we come first to the St. Katharine and London Docks. A few miles eastwards are the West India Docks and Millwall Dock in the Isle of Dogs, and then East India Dock. Further down the stream we reach the "Royal" group of docks —the Royal Victoria, Royal Albert and King George V—and finally at Tilbury, which is well outside London but still in the Port of London, is the group nearest the sea.

On the south side of the Thames we find a single group, the Surrey Commercial Docks, in the bend which the river makes northwards between Rotherhithe and Deptford. These include the Greenland Dock already mentioned.

As one travels by water down the river all that one sees of the docks from near water-level are the wall-like gates of their entrances. But for the hulls, funnels and masts of great ships rising high and unexpectedly above the surrounding buildings, the presence of great sheets of still water so near the tidal waters of the Thames would never be suspected.

The docks represent a great amount of human labour and planning. A wet dock is usually formed by cutting deep trenches all round the site, building in them the massive walls which will act as quays, and then removing all the earth enclosed by the walls to the required depth—thirty or forty feet as the case may be. If all the docks of the Port of London were merged into a single sheet of water it would be more than a mile square.

But a dock is far more than a sheet of water confined by great walls of masonry or concrete. The water is merely the counterpart of the sidings of a big railway goods yard. A ship is earning money only while she is carrying cargo and it is therefore important that the operations of loading and unloading shall be made as brief as possible. So a dock must be equipped with machinery and have sheds and stores, called warehouses, for holding goods, as well as roads and railway tracks for moving them. Every day that a ship can save in loading or clearing out her cargo may mean hundreds and even thousands of pounds to her owners.

Our Imports and Exports

In normal times the annual value of the Port's overseas trade, exclusive of coastwise trade, was £593 million, *i.e.* one-third of the overseas trade of the United Kingdom. The volume of goods handled each year was approximately 42 million tons. As a result of the disturbed state of post-war international trade, the latest figures show some diminution in these totals, but this drop is approximately the same as the lower trade levels in most British ports. More than a hundred shipping companies operate regular direct services from the Port of London to over 300 ports throughout the world, and more than 700 ships on regular services leave London every month.

Here are a few items out of a very large number which will give you some idea of the quantities which have to be dealt with: Cheese, 80,000 tons; eggs, 31,000 tons; spices, 11,000 tons; sugar, 832,000 tons; tea, 127,000 tons; wine, 30,000 tons; tobacco, 35,000 tons; wool, 191,000 tons; paper, 134,000 tons; rubber, 90,000 tons; frozen and chilled meat, 554,000 tons; wheat and flour, 1,323,000 tons. These are round figures for a post-war year.

Then there are exported goods of enormous value to be put aboard the

P. L. A.

GRAPEFRUIT FOR BRITISH TABLES

This photograph shows a cargo of 57,000 cases of grapefruit arriving in the Surrey Commercial Docks by the steamship *Corrales*. The " set " is being manœuvred into position as it is lowered to the quayside on to a waiting electric truck. Some 26,000 transport workers are directly employed in handling cargo in the Port of London.

outgoing ships. These include some millions of pounds' worth of goods brought in to be exported again to other countries, for London is the great market of the world in certain commodities such as tea, rubber, wool and tobacco, collected from all parts of the globe.

IN THE DRY DOCK AT TILBURY *P. L. A.*

Only by the use of a dry dock can the hulls of ships be examined, repaired and painted. This dry dock at Tilbury has the most modern equipment of any dock in the world and will accommodate the largest ocean liners. In this photograph the *City of Agra* has been safely settled, the water has been pumped out, and the ship is ready for examination and whatever repairs to the hull may be necessary.

Passengers, Mail and Mixed Cargoes

Though all the docks are now under the one control of the London Port Authority, the various groups still specialise in certain cargoes. The London Docks (which must not be confused with the docks in the London area generally) are the great wool docks. Normally at the Surrey Commercial Docks more than half a million tons of sawn timber are unloaded annually, and many piles of it are always to be seen in the open or under cover. A considerable amount of general cargo is also dealt with at this dock.

The West India Docks are the great sugar centre, and there you may find 100,000 tons of it in store ; while at the " Royal " Docks most of the frozen and chilled meat and tobacco comes ashore. But some of the docks handle all sorts of commodities as they are the headquarters of different lines of steamship companies which combine passenger and mail carrying with the transport of " mixed " cargoes.

Dockland is, generally speaking, not at all beautiful, but it is the centre of London's wealth, and, to anyone who loves ships and the bustle of commerce, it is full of romance and interest. It is a land of curious sights. Spires and masts are mixed up together. Ships' funnels appear to project from the tops of buildings ; factory buildings sometimes appear to have been fitted up with spars and rigging.

On reaching a dock one finds oneself blundering over railway tracks, dodging wagons and crane loads, and, as likely as not, cut off for a time by the raising of a bridge to let a vessel pass. But any slight inconvenience is amply repaid when at last the visitor is at the quay where one of the thousand ships that pass up and down the Thames is being discharged.

To ensure the prompt discharge and loading of ships hundreds of quay cranes, fixed and mobile, of varying capacities, are provided, while for awkward and heavy lifts a fleet of floating cranes is available, the largest of which is the "London Mammoth" with a lifting capacity up to 150 tons. These, however, do only part of the work since the ships' own tackles are busy discharging or loading cargo as fast as they can. Other equipment for handling cargo includes rail shunting cranes, petrol shunting trucks for the dock railways, fork-lift and electric runabout trucks.

Besides all this apparatus many strange devices for unloading are used. Grain is sucked out of a ship's hold by great pipes with large nozzles on the end acting on the same principle as a vacuum-cleaner. Many other types of mechanical labour-aids have been introduced into the Port of London while others are being tested for their suitability on different types of work.

In the Bonded Warehouse

As the cargo leaves the ship it may be loaded straight into waiting wagons, or on to the quay, or into the "transit" sheds running parallel to the quay's edge. Once in the sheds, the goods are protected from the weather while being sorted for delivery to railway wagons or lorries which carry them away to their purchasers or to one of the many large warehouses belonging to the Port of London Authorities.

All dutiable goods, such as tea, tobacco, wines and spirits, come under the care of the Customs authorities immediately they land and go into bonded warehouses. They cannot be taken from these warehouses for sale in the country till the duty has been paid on them. While in the care of the Customs—and they may be there for a long time—experts look after the goods, carrying out various operations for the importers. For instance, the tobacco, of which there may be 40,000 to 50,000 tons "in bond," is sorted out; damaged or useless leaves are burnt in the "Queen's Pipe" which is a furnace in a small building used only for destroying condemned cargo. The tobacco is worth taking care of, as can be imagined, since the duty payable on it in these days is so enormous.

Among the Treasure Houses

A visitor to Dockland would hardly suspect how immense a quantity of valuable goods is stored within its somewhat dingy area. The rapid unloading and loading of ships makes it necessary that there should be large premises handy to the quay where goods can be stored.

Importers and exporters also find it much cheaper to hire warehouse space from the P.L.A. than to construct or rent huge buildings of their own outside the dock areas. For these two reasons there are, within easy reach of the dock quays, buildings of great size crowded with goods of all kinds, other than those liable to duty. In this area there are nearly 24 acres of floor space piled with great bales of wool—more than 10,000 tons of it usually. In another building are thousands of tons of rubber. In that gaunt pile over there is a cold store in which over a quarter of a million carcases of lamb or mutton can be kept in good condition indefinitely. Beyond this is another building given up entirely to fruit.

Possibly more interesting than these are the warehouses set apart for Oriental goods—carpets, spices, drugs, antiques, and so on. Nor must we forget the ivory warehouse, with its many tons of ivory in the tusk worth £1,500 a ton, to buy which people come from every part of the world!

GUARDIANS OF THE SEAS

Keystone

"It is upon the Navy, under the good Providence of God, that the wealth, safety and strength of the Kingdom do chiefly depend." That has been true for many centuries down to our own times, when in two World Wars attempts were made to starve Britain into submission. It was the Navies of the British Commonwealth which to a large extent kept the seas open to the ships of the Allies during those years of peril. In this photograph, taken from H.M.S. *Agincourt*, can be seen *Dunkirk*, *Corunna* and *Jutland*, forming in line ahead, while in the distance *Loch Veyatie*, leader of frigate, is turning into line.

In the reign of Charles I the Royal Navy had a three-decker man-o'-war. This vessel, shown above, carried no fewer than 104 guns and was the finest battleship of her day.

Probably no vessel in the world is better known than H.M.S. *Victory*, Lord Nelson's flagship at Trafalgar. She has been restored to her original state and is now at Portsmouth.

Drawings specially prepared for this work

Commissioned in 1867, H.M.S. *Minotaur* was one of three sister ships, the largest single-screw warships ever built, and among the very earliest ironclads of the Royal Navy. The three sisters, *Minotaur*, *Agincourt* and *Northumberland*, each had five masts as they could only carry 750 tons of coal, and a large spread of canvas was necessary owing to their small range of action and slowness under steam.

PORT AFTER STORMY SEAS

Central Press

In this fine aerial photograph of the famous battleship H.M.S. *King George V*, the crew are lining the decks in traditional manner as she sails into Portsmouth Harbour after duty at sea. During the war *King George V* sank the *Bismarck*, and later, as flagship of Vice-Admiral Rawlings in the Pacific, took part in many operations until the end, when she was present at the Japanese surrender.

Central News

Cruisers are smaller, faster, and more lightly armed war vessels than the battleships. Formerly the place of the cruisers was right ahead of the main battle-fleet, but they are now used more on important convoy work, or as squadrons in distant waters. Some may be fitted with A.A. guns for defence of the fleet. Our picture shows the cruiser *Superb*, a vessel of 8,000 tons, capable of 31.5 knots.

BATTLESHIP, SUBMARINE AND SPEED-BOAT

Central Press

In this photograph is seen H.M.S. *Howe* engaged on exercises. Some idea of the formidable power of such a ship is indicated by the size of the guns in the forward part of the vessel.

Central Press

Midget submarines played an important part in the last war. In this photograph we have one of the latest XE class returning to Tower Pier on the Thames after taking part in naval exercises.

Central Press

Revolutionary in build and design, the *Celerity* was the first vessel to be fitted with air-cooled aero-engines (Bristol Hercules XVII radial air engines) which drive variable-pitch propellers. Her superstructure and practically all her fitments are made of a light alloy. *Celerity* has a maximum speed of 40 knots, and our picture shows her travelling at speed when at sea.

Fox Photos

The Commonwealth of Australia has its own Defence Forces: Navy, Army and Air. In this photograph is seen H.M.A.S. *Vengeance*, an aircraft carrier which took the place of the heavy cruiser, H.M.A.S. *Australia*, as flagship of the Australian Navy in 1954. Before her retirement the *Australia* had seen more than a quarter of a century of active service.

Fox Photos

Canada, the oldest Dominion of the British Commonwealth, has a proud record of gallantry during the years when her armed forces, naval, military and air, fought in many parts of the world alongside those of the Allied Nations. The largest vessel in Canada's present-day Navy is H.M.C.S. *Magnificent*, a Fleet aircraft carrier of 18,000 tons, carrying thirty-five aircraft and the men to fly and service them.

MODERN DESTROYER AND AIRCRAFT CARRIER

Two of the Royal Navy's latest and most powerful destroyers are the *Crossbow* and *Battleaxe*, which in many aspects are regarded as the most modern fighting ships afloat today. Destroyers, which is an abbreviation of their earlier name of torpedo-boat destroyers, were first designed in 1893, and have since played an important part in naval warfare. Our photograph shows H.M.S. *Crossbow* at sea.

Topical

One of the most famous names in the records of the Royal Navy is *Ark Royal*, and the name is being perpetuated in the most recent class of aircraft carriers. In this photograph H.M.S. *Ark Royal*, 36,800 tons, which has taken eleven years to build, is seen as she left the shipyard at Birkenhead for her first short voyage in 1954 before her official trial and final adjustments.

ALL AT FULL SPEED AHEAD

Central Press

Motor torpedo boats (MTB) of the Light Coastal Forces carried out amazing exploits in war-time. In this picture an MTB of the 71 ft. 6 in. type is seen at speed in heavy weather.

Charles E. Brown

Next in size to the battleships and aircraft carriers of the Navy come the cruisers. Our photograph shows one of the County class cruisers, H.M.S. *Devonshire*, a fighting ship of 9,850 tons.

Central Press

Although underwater craft had been used experimentally before this century began it was not until 1901 that the Royal Navy ordered its first submarines. The 1914-18 war gave this type of craft an important place in warfare and since then many improvements have been made. In this photograph the submarine *Seraph*, stripped for special exercises, is seen passing the destroyer *Battleaxe*.

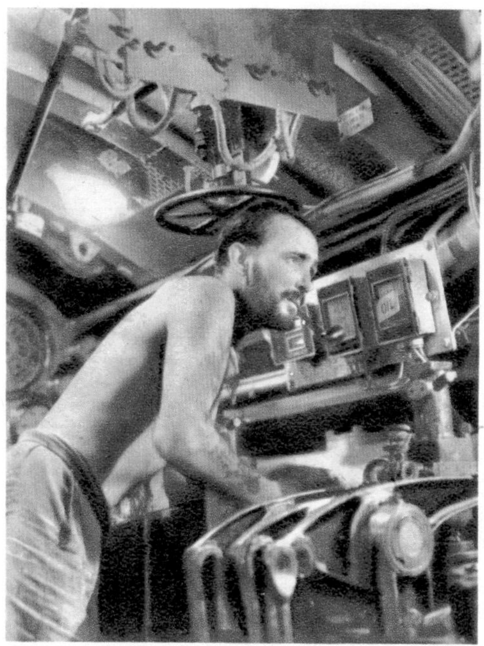

P.N.A.

Men selected for submarine crews are of high physical and mental standard. Our photograph shows a leading stoker making adjustments in the engine room at the end of a patrol.

Fox Photos

The periscope is the eye of the submarine when just below surface, and here we see an officer on the look-out for other craft during exercises while at sea.

Fox Photos

In this photograph we see the final preparations being made aboard a submarine before the vessel sets out for whatever task or exercise it has been allotted. Torpedoes are the main weapons carried, and here we see two members of the crew helping to load the tin "fish" which, in peace-time, are recoverable after the exercise, while in war-time they may mean the end of some great ship.

DOCKING AT THE END OF THE VOYAGE

Stanley.

King George V Dock is one of the latest and most up-to-date in the world. It was opened in 1921 and has every facility for dealing with the loading and unloading of cargoes as well as for reconditioning ships in dry dock. In this photograph a tug is seen towing a large cargo ship, part of which can be seen on the right-hand side of the picture, through the entrance lock of the King George V Dock.

BROUGHT BY THE BIG STEAMERS

" For the bread that you eat . . . and the joints that you carve . . . are brought to you daily by all us Big Steamers," wrote Rudyard Kipling in one of his poems. In the two pictures on this page is evidence of the truth of these claims for the big ships that bring us our daily food. Here we see grain being discharged by pneumatic elevators from the big cargo vessel into the barges alongside.

Photos: P.L.A.

Here in this photograph are " the joints that we carve," as Kipling puts it. The cargo has been safely landed at the Royal Docks after its voyage in the refrigerated holds of the meat ship running between London and New Zealand. Electric trucks and smaller barrows are busily employed carrying the different consignments from ship to store rooms to await distribution to all parts of the country.

PACKED AND READY FOR EXPORT

Stanley.

Every hour of the day goods packed for export to a thousand different places overseas come pouring into the London Docks. Here they are sorted and arranged in great transit sheds, awaiting their turn to be taken by truck to the quayside when the cranes will lift the heavy packages seen in this photograph, swing them aboard and lower them into the holds of the different ships for which they have been marked.

P.L.A.

This photograph with its glimpse of the river through the forest of cranes gives a good idea of the work that is handled in the Royal Docks of the Port of London. Once a cargo has reached port the next thing is to transport it to its final destination, and, as seen here, the railway and the road run alongside the dock and the task of transferring cargo from water to land transport is facilitated.

A BARGE IN THE LOWER REACHES

Stanley.

In this picture we are in the lower reaches of the Thames and have a view which is in contrast with the river as seen in the neighbourhood of London Bridge. Our picture shows a Thames spritsail barge flying light and bound up Northfleet Hope in the lower Thames. These barges are slowly becoming fewer in number as the competition of powered craft gradually forces them into retirement.

Going into Dry Dock

The depth of the Thames decreases from the estuary inland and the distances which ships can steam up the river are limited by their draught. But even from London Bridge one may see ships of 6,000 or 7,000 tons unloading at one of the many riverside wharves.

As one sails down the river the really big ships of many well-known passenger and cargo liner companies can be seen. These great vessels link London with all parts of the world and make use of the Port of London Docks. Some of these fine ships have a registered tonnage up to 35,000 tons, and it is interesting to watch them being worked in or out through the narrow entrance of a dock by the special pilots entrusted with this duty.

P.L.A.

A GIANT FLOATING CRANE

Mechanisation in all our great ports enables cargoes to be handled speedily. Pneumatic elevators for grain and specially designed conveyors for unloading meat and fruit are in constant use. In this photograph is seen one of the huge floating cranes, the " Titan," passing down the Royal Victoria Dock to help in unloading heavy cargo.

Any ship using the docks can be put in dry dock to have her hull examined and repaired, or cleaned and painted. The P.L.A. owns ten dry docks of various sizes, the largest of them in the Tilbury Docks being 750 feet long and 1,000 feet wide.

When empty a dry dock is seen to be a long cavernous pit, enclosed on the sides and at one end by walls sloping back in a series of great steps. Along the centre of the bottom is a row of keel blocks. If a ship is to be docked, water is let in till level with the water outside, then the gates, or " caissons " as they are called, at one end are opened and the ship manœuvred in by means of tug-boats. Great pumps then get to work and in a couple of hours or so the whole of her hull is bare and all the parts of the ship which have for so long been unreachable are exposed.

In many respects the equipment of the Tilbury dry docks is in advance of any other in the world. Mechanical bilge blocks obviate the use of the usual wood shores, and a " leading-in-girder " automatically ensures the centralising of a vessel when floating in and being lowered on to the keel blocks.

How Swimmers Discover a World Under the Sea

Modern Invention Aids a New Form of Adventure

Photos by courtesy of Messrs. Hamish Hamilton, Ltd., from "The Silent World," by J.-Y. Cousteau.

USING AN AQUALUNG

This underwater explorer swims freely and confidently below the surface with the help of an Aqualung. This breathing apparatus was invented by two Frenchmen, Capt. Jacques-Yves Cousteau and Emile Gagnan. Compressed air from tanks strapped upon his back is fed to the swimmer in carefully regulated quantities so that the pressure within his body is equal to that of the sea surrounding him.

UNDERWATER EXPLORATION

HAVE you read the famous book by Jules Verne, "20,000 Leagues Under the Sea"? It is the story of the submarine *Nautilus* and her crew, and of their adventures in the depths of the ocean. Although Verne's book was first published in 1869, it is still popular and has, in fact, recently been made into a Cinemascope film.

The book sprang, of course, from Verne's wonderful imagination. He had that strange power to think and write of many things long before they were actually invented or became possible. To-day, his story does not seem nearly so fantastic, because our ocean explorers have found ways of sending their instruments down to great depths and, indeed, of making deep descents themselves. The use of special breathing apparatus now permits many a swimmer to explore the shallower regions for himself, and underwater swimming has now become a popular sport in many countries. You may well have done it yourself.

Venturing through Neptune's Realm

Let's do some underwater swimming, or "skin diving" as it is sometimes called. Provided that he or she is healthy enough, anyone can do it. It is not necessary to be extremely strong, or to be an expert diver or swimmer—although strength and skill will be advantages, of course.

What we shall need is some underwater equipment—special goggles, a snorkel or breathing tube, and long rubber flippers for our feet. The whole outfit will probably cost something less than four pounds.

If we want to shoot fish during our underwater ventures, we shall also need a special gun, powered by a large rubber band and with a range of about nine feet. We could buy one for about eight pounds, but many people make their own, using rubber strips cut from old car tyres. Swimmers hunting small fish often use a trident, very like the one that Father Neptune himself is supposed to carry.

There are several other types of gun, including a powerful compressed-air weapon used recently off the Brazilian coast to spear a fish weighing 628 pounds. This catch is said to be the largest made by an underwater swimmer.

Along Britain's Coasts

Where shall we go for our expedition? France and Italy, where underwater swimming as a sport began, are rather far away; and the tropical waters of Australia and Brazil, where skin diving is very popular, are farther still. But there is really no reason for us to hanker after these faraway places. Many parts of our own coastline are quite suitable and will provide all the fun and excitement we want.

In the summer, our coastal waters are quite warm enough for underwater swimming; in winter, we could still swim, if we equipped ourselves with special lined rubber suits to keep us warm. Our clearest coastal waters are off Devon and Cornwall, some parts of Wales and Scotland, and off the Channel Islands and the Isles of Scilly. If we want expert information about the best localities, we shall probably join one of the underwater swimming clubs which have been formed in this country.

At last we are ready. Our equipment

RETURNING FROM A TRIP TO A STRANGE NEW WORLD

Philippe Tailliez, a member of the Undersea Research Group founded by Capt. Cousteau, returns from an exciting descent off the coast of Tunisia. He has removed his mouthpiece and is telling his comrades of the ancient Greek galley he has found 130 feet below the surface. More than one thrilling discovery of this kind has been made by underwater explorers.

is to hand and we are sitting on the shore, putting on the long rubber flippers that are just like those used by the frogmen during the last war. We adjust our goggles, or face mask with its glass window, and with our gun and breathing tube, we enter the water.

One end of the breathing tube goes into our mouth ; the other will remain above the water, like the periscope of a submarine, and provide us with air while we leisurely swim along about 6 inches below the surface. In clear water, this is quite deep enough for us to see the beauties of Neptune's realm.

Are you ready ? Then off we go ! It is a strangely quiet world that we are watching. The sand, rocks and seaweed look far more beautiful in their natural element than when we see them high and dry on the shore ; and if we do not scare them by splashing, the fish will take little notice of us.

Presently we see a likely target for our underwater gun. Taking a deep breath, we dive down gently. For the time being, we must forget about the breathing tube and rely on the air in our lungs. We get within range, aim and fire—and then return triumphantly to the surface with our catch.

For the More Venturesome

Some underwater swimmers use advanced equipment that allows them to go into deeper water and remain under the surface for about one hour. These more venturesome skin divers wear the usual goggles and flippers, but also have weighted belts, which help to keep them below the surface, and cylinders of compressed air, with mouth-tubes attached. They carry the cylinders on their backs, drawing in air through the feed-tube and mouthpiece, and breathing out through their noses. Other equipment carried may include a depth gauge, a waterproof watch and a compass.

Underwater swimming can be dangerous, especially if the deeper regions are sought. Divers who descend below a certain depth may become victims of nitrogen narcosis. This simply means that they become dazed and unaware of what they are doing through too much nitrogen.

"Rapture of the Depths"

Nitrogen narcosis has been called "the rapture of the depths." A famous French expert, Capt. J. Y. Cousteau, has likened it to intoxication : "With some divers this intoxication begins to occur as early as 120 feet down ; with others, not until 180 or 200. Mild elation grows into ecstasy ; danger reactions tend to fade. Below 330 feet the diver may pass out, lose his mouthpiece, and drown." It has also been suggested that another cause of the danger is the build-up of carbon dioxide within the diver, who, being under high pressure, cannot properly expel this gas with each exhalation.

Another danger is known as "the bends." What happens is this : a diver using compressed air gets a lot of nitrogen into the blood stream under pressure. When he starts to ascend, he passes into a zone of lighter pressure. For example, at 132 feet below the surface, the atmospheric pressure on the body is about 73½ pounds per square inch. At lesser depths, the atmospheric pressure is lower ; at greater depths more.

If the diver ascends too rapidly, the pressure changes so suddenly that the nitrogen rushes through the circulation system, causing intense nerve pain and doubling the diver up in a helpless position. To swim upwards in safety, the diver must halt at certain levels for specified periods of time, so that his system can adjust itself to the change in pressure. This process is known as "stage decompression."

The Admiralty has tables showing how long a diver must halt at each stage if he is to avoid an agonising, and perhaps fatal attack of "the bends" (caisson disease). If proper heed is taken, there is no danger.

It is said that underwater swimming

AN UNUSUAL FAMILY OUTING

Captain Cousteau, his wife and their two sons, aged twelve and thirteen, on one of their regular under-water trips. They move along leisurely, propelling themselves by kicking out with their feet, to which are attached large rubber flippers. Goggles enable them to see clearly the many beauties of the undersea world. Heavy equipment is not needed. Air is provided by the Aqualung and the weight of this apparatus is hardly felt in the water.

began one day in 1932, when Japanese divers at Capri surprised people on the beach by their skill at spearing fish underwater. From here the sport soon spread to France and America.

France has produced some of the most notable figures in underwater exploration. It was a French naval officer, Commander Yves LePrieur, who designed the first practical breathing apparatus for deep swimming and the first specially-heated swimming suit. He was also responsible for the first colour film of underwater life and was the founder of the first club for this exciting sport.

One of the leading figures in modern underwater research is another French officer, Capt. Jacques-Yves Cousteau, who, with a French engineer named Emile Gagnan, designed the Aqualung, one of the most widely used breathing equipments for deep underwater swimming.

Capt. Cousteau began his adventurous work with no more than a pair of goggles, but it was not long before he craved for the deeper waters and the longer stay below the surface. With the help of two friends, Frédéric Dumas and Philippe Tailliez, he set about designing suitable breathing apparatus. His experiments, and the help of the engineer Gagnan, eventually produced the automatic breathing apparatus known as the Aqualung, which underwent its first trials in 1943.

After France had been liberated, the French Navy asked Capt. Cousteau to set up an Undersea Research Group and this he did, with the help of his friends. It was not long before the team he had trained was employed to clear German mines from the entrance to a port in southern France. Later, he acquired an old mine sweeper, which he converted into a floating base and laboratory. It was in this ship, the *Calypso*, that he and his team carried out underwater exploration in the Mediterranean and Red Seas (1951–2).

Cameras below the Surface

You may have seen some of the remarkable films and photographs taken by the Cousteau Expedition below the surface of the sea. It is dark in the depths, and extremely powerful flash bulbs have to be used to light the scene for the special camera. These bulbs require watertight reflectors and small Aqualungs. The latter equalise the pressures so that the housing of the equipment does not collapse. The

EQUIPPED FOR UNDERWATER PHOTOGRAPHY

Captain Cousteau is seen here with one of his cameras. It has its own miniature Aqualung attached and is mounted on a special shaft. Two pistol grips on the shaft enable the swimmer to regulate focus and aperture. The flashlights are carried by other swimmers.

EXPLORING A TORPEDOED SHIP

A member of the Undersea Research Group swims through a jagged hole torn in the side of a ship by a torpedo during the Second World War. This was one of several wrecks in the waters near Marseilles which were explored by the Group. Over a period of fifteen years Capt. Cousteau and other members of the Group made about five thousand dives.

camera also has its own Aqualung and special pistol grips by which the diver can adjust aperture and focus.

Adventures and Discoveries

Many strange adventures have befallen these intrepid divers and many interesting discoveries have been theirs.

Take, for example, the encounter Capt. Cousteau and his friend Dumas had with two blue sharks during an expedition off the Cape Verde Islands. The divers knew from experience that sharks are most dangerous in shallow water. They will swoop suddenly at a diver : but if he swims towards them, they will turn away, giving him time to get out of the water before they return. In deeper water, they remain curious, but are not prone to attack.

When the Captain and his friend were swimming at fifty feet off the Cape Verde Islands, however, two blue sharks, with pilot fish and shark suckers in attendance, suddenly appeared and displayed an alarming interest in the divers. The Captain turned one away by hitting it on the nose, and then he and his companion kept them at bay for several minutes, continually swimming head on at them until help arrived.

On another occasion, the divers investigated the wreck of an ancient Roman trading vessel off Marseilles. They found her more than 100 feet below the surface under a mound made of mud in which were embedded pots and amphorae (wine jars) that had been the vessel's cargo.

The divers were able to clear away the slime and debris from her main deck—miraculously the ship was almost intact under its strange submarine burial mound—and examination of the many prizes they got to the surface showed that the ship probably made its last voyage about the year 230 B.C. They were even able to taste wine more than

A STRANGE FISHERMAN AND HIS PREY

The large black shape, partly hidden in marine vegetation, is a fish called a grouper. Sensing danger, it bristles the spines upon its back. Poised almost above the fish is an Aqualung swimmer, his arm outstretched and his knife ready. But perhaps the grouper will be too quick for him.

2,000 years old. Tightly-sealed in an amphora, it had not been affected by the salt water, although it had long lost its true flavour.

Seals found impressed on the lips of undamaged amphorae bore the letters " SES " and the sign of an anchor. A similar sign can be seen worked in mosaic in Roman ruins on the Greek island of Delos. We know that a wealthy Roman trader named Marcus Sestius had his mansion here and it is therefore reasonable to suppose that the ship was one of his. A further pointer to this conclusion is that black pebbles found in the wreck are of the same volcanic origin as some found in the courtyard of the ruined house at Delos.

Some of the most beautiful photographs taken by divers show coral formations in the caves and grottoes below the surface. For all their beauty, some of these delicately fashioned and marvellously coloured formations have a place on the divers' danger list. For example, *millepora* coral is highly poisonous ; its spiky branches have but to touch a diver to set off a terrible rash. You can read about these perils and adventures in a book called "The Silent World," written by Capt. Cousteau himself.

In the Red Sea

Another explorer of the deep who has written an account of his adventures is Dr. Hans Hass, whose exploits have been shared by his wife, Lotte. One of his best-known expeditions was to the Red Sea, where he, too, had thrilling encounters with sharks and barracudas, and with that strange monster of the warm seas, the giant manta or Devil Ray.

In " Under the Red Sea," he tells of one of these creatures swimming straight at him, like a " giant butterfly." Large though they are (a giant manta may measure nearly 30 feet across) and fearsome though they seem, these Devil Rays are really quite harmless. Like whales, they feed on tiny marine life.

You can imagine how the exploits of these underwater swimmers have made it possible for us to add to our knowledge of the sea and its inhabitants. Ichthyologists (scientists who specialize in the study of marine life) are now able to go below the surface and observe fish in their natural habitat.

Some people earn their living as skin divers. Cargoes that would not be worth salvaging if heavy equipment had to be used are now brought up from wrecks with the help of the Aqualung, or similar apparatus. At some of the Mediterranean yachting ports, divers are ready to go down and scrape the barnacles off the keels, thereby saving the owners of the yachts the trouble and expense of taking their vessels into dry dock. Divers for pearls and pearl-shell in many parts of the world have found their work easier, safer and more profitable.

Deeper Still

What about the waters below those in which it is safe to skin dive with an Aqualung? They, too, have been entered by man in recent years.

One of the pioneers of descents into the extreme depths was Dr. William Beebe, a noted American ocean naturalist, who first used nets to bring up strange specimens from the very depths of the ocean. About 1929, he and a friend named Otis Barton set about designing a steel sphere in which they might go down themselves. They called their diving bell the Bathysphere, a combination of *Bathytroctes* (the name of a deep-sea fish) and the word sphere.

The Bathysphere was rather like a huge golf ball, but was made of steel and weighed 2 tons. On one side there was a heavy entrance door, with an observation window; on the other, a searchlight and other windows. Long cables were connected to the Bathysphere to provide electric light and telephone communication with the ship.

In this strange vessel, Dr. Beebe and Mr. Barton descended to a depth of over a quarter of a mile (June, 1930)

MAKING FRIENDS WITH A ROCKFISH

The Aqualung makes it possible for scientists to observe fish and other creatures in the waters that are their natural home. Such observation is much more valuable than the study of dead or captive specimens. In this picture we see a swimmer stretching out his hand to touch a Pei-qua, or Mediterranean rockfish.

NOT SO FEARSOME AFTER ALL !

Story-tellers would often like us to believe that the octopus is a terrifying and menacing monster of the deep. But those found by Capt. Cousteau and his companions in the Mediterranean were actually very timid creatures that did their utmost to avoid the interest of the underwater swimmers.

into the blackish-blue waters of Davy Jones' Locker. A searchlight in the Bathysphere enabled them to see many rare deep-water fish—the illuminated silver hatchetfish, strange luminous squids, orange-skins, and the transparent young of the avocet-billed eel.

Later, Dr. Beebe and his friend, Barton, made a record descent in the Bathysphere to a depth of 3,028 feet (August, 1934), in waters south-east of Bermuda. Among the denizens of the deep they encountered for the first time was a jagged-toothed monster, 6 feet long, which trailed from its body what seemed to be brilliantly coloured lights ; the tiny Three-starred Angler-fish, with lighted masts rising from its shoulders ; and the Black Swallower fish, which can eat a fish three times its own size.

And now the Bathyscaphe

The Bathysphere seems a very primitive deep-water craft when compared with the Bathyscaphe, which was developed after the Second World War. The Bathyscaphe owes its name to two Greek words : *bathy* (deep) and *scaphe* (boat). In its first form it was known as F.N.R.S.2, the initials standing for the Belgian National Scientific Fund, which provided money for the venture, and it was chiefly the work of Professor Auguste Piccard and Professor Max Cosyns.

This "deep-boat" was tested in 1948, and among those taking part was Capt. Cousteau who was also one of the technical advisors for a later model, the F.N.R.S.3. In this vessel, Capt. Cousteau descended to a depth of 4,000 feet in the Mediterranean in December, 1953.

What was this new "deep-boat" like ? Basically, it was the shape of a submarine, with a conning tower amidships and a strange observation and recording sphere protruding below the stabilizing keel. The sides of the sphere were 3½ inches thick and were designed to withstand pressures up to 9½ tons per square inch. Heavy iron weights, controlled by electro-magnets, helped the "deep-boat" to descend. The hull was really no more than a huge tank containing petrol, which is lighter than water and so gave the Bathyscaphe buoyancy below the surface.

In descent, the petrol contracted ; but sea-water brought in through an opening in the bottom of the hull kept

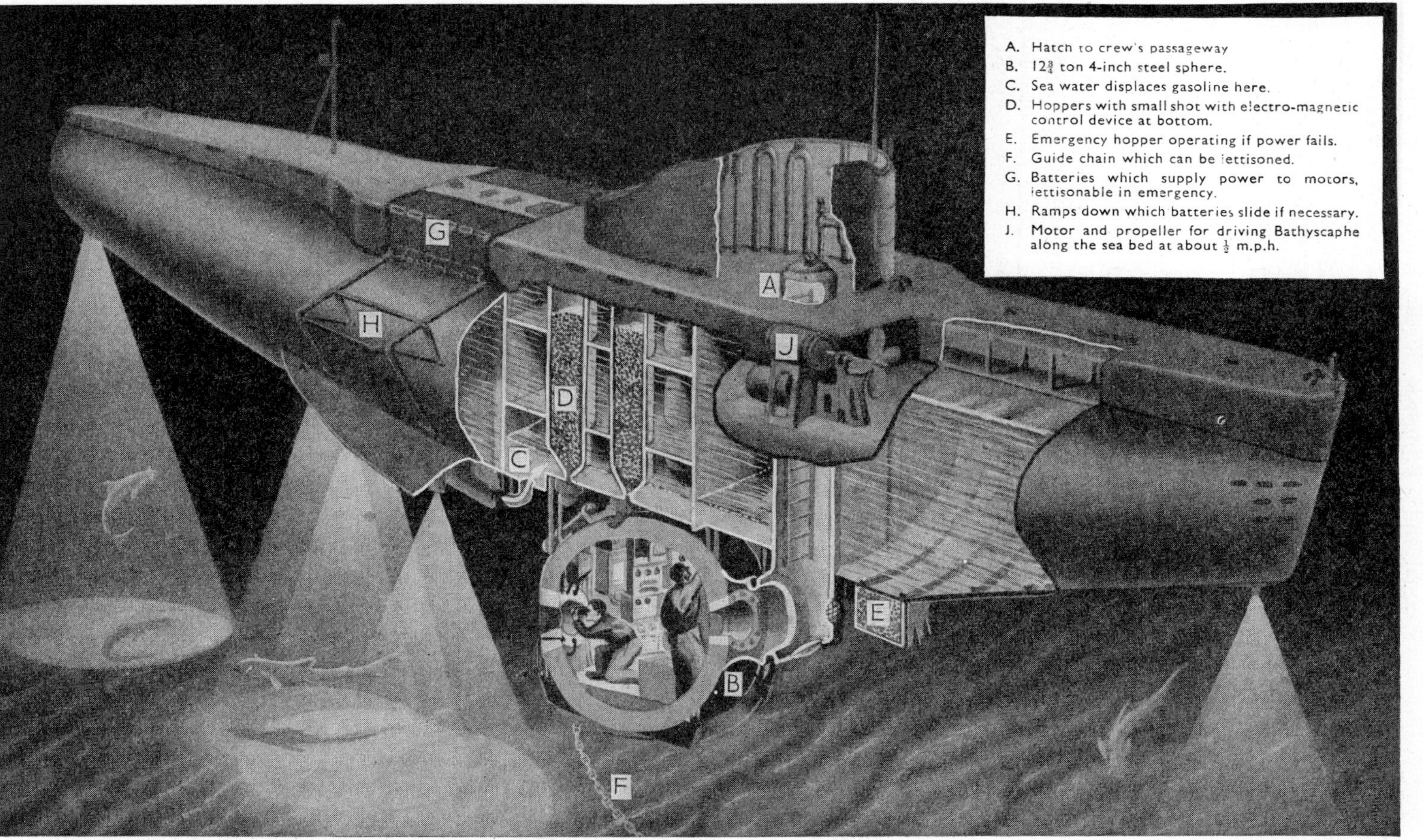

Specially drawn for this work.

THE BATHYSCAPHE WHICH HAS MADE A RECORD UNDERWATER DESCENT

This is a drawing of the Bathyscaphe in which Lieut.-Comd. Houot and Lieut. Willm made their record descent in February, 1954. The spherical observation chamber is made of solid steel nearly 4 inches thick and, because it is hollow, is subjected to immense pressure. The rest of the Bathyscaphe contains petrol and does not have to withstand such heavy pressure. A descent starts by admitting sea water to the crew's passageway. This adds weight to the Bathyscaphe, which therefore starts to sink. The rate of descent is controlled by releasing ballast shot from amidships. As the Bathyscaphe reaches the sea bed, a guide chain is lowered to lighten the vessel and keep it floating just clear of the bottom. This chain is cast off when the crew want to surface again.

inside and outside pressures equal and thus prevented the comparatively thin hull from buckling. Below the hull was suspended a guide chain, which served to keep the Bathyscaphe hovering about 10 to 15 feet from the ocean floor.

Searchlights, the special Edgerton electronic flash (for photography), depth recorders, radio-telephone, and other instruments completed the equipment of this, " the first independent diving apparatus without lines to the surface."

The Greatest Depth

In February, 1954, the Bathyscaphe was towed out of Dakar harbour, on the west coast of Africa. Manning the " deep-boat " were two French naval officers, Lieut.-Commander Georges S. Houot and Engineer Officer Pierre Willm. On February 15th, about 160 miles south-west of Dakar, the Bathyscaphe began its descent.

A little after noon on that day it had passed the record depth reached by Professor Piccard in his own bathyscaphe, the *Trieste*, in September, 1953—and it was still descending. When, at last, the droplights revealed the sea-bed, the instruments showed that they were at a depth of 2½ miles !

There was sand. There were beautiful sea anemones. There were peculiar bulbous-eyed sharks. And within the observation sphere, the two French officers watched, fascinated by the realization that they were the first humans to see marine life at this depth.

Their ascent came sooner than they really wished, but what a triumphant return to the surface it was ! Wrote Commander Houot later : " What mysteries of marine life will the Bathyscaphe yet probe ? What relics of our ancient past—buried wrecks, encrusted marbles, sunken cities—may she not stumble upon ? What curious new creatures will she perhaps discover in the vast, unknown continents that lie beneath our salty wastes ? "

AN ENCOUNTER WITH A SHARK

This picture was taken off the Cape Verde Islands at a depth of 50 feet and shows Frédéric Dumas swimming towards an 8-foot-long shark. Accompanying the shark are three pilot fish. Can you see the smallest of them ? It is swimming just in front of the shark's nose.

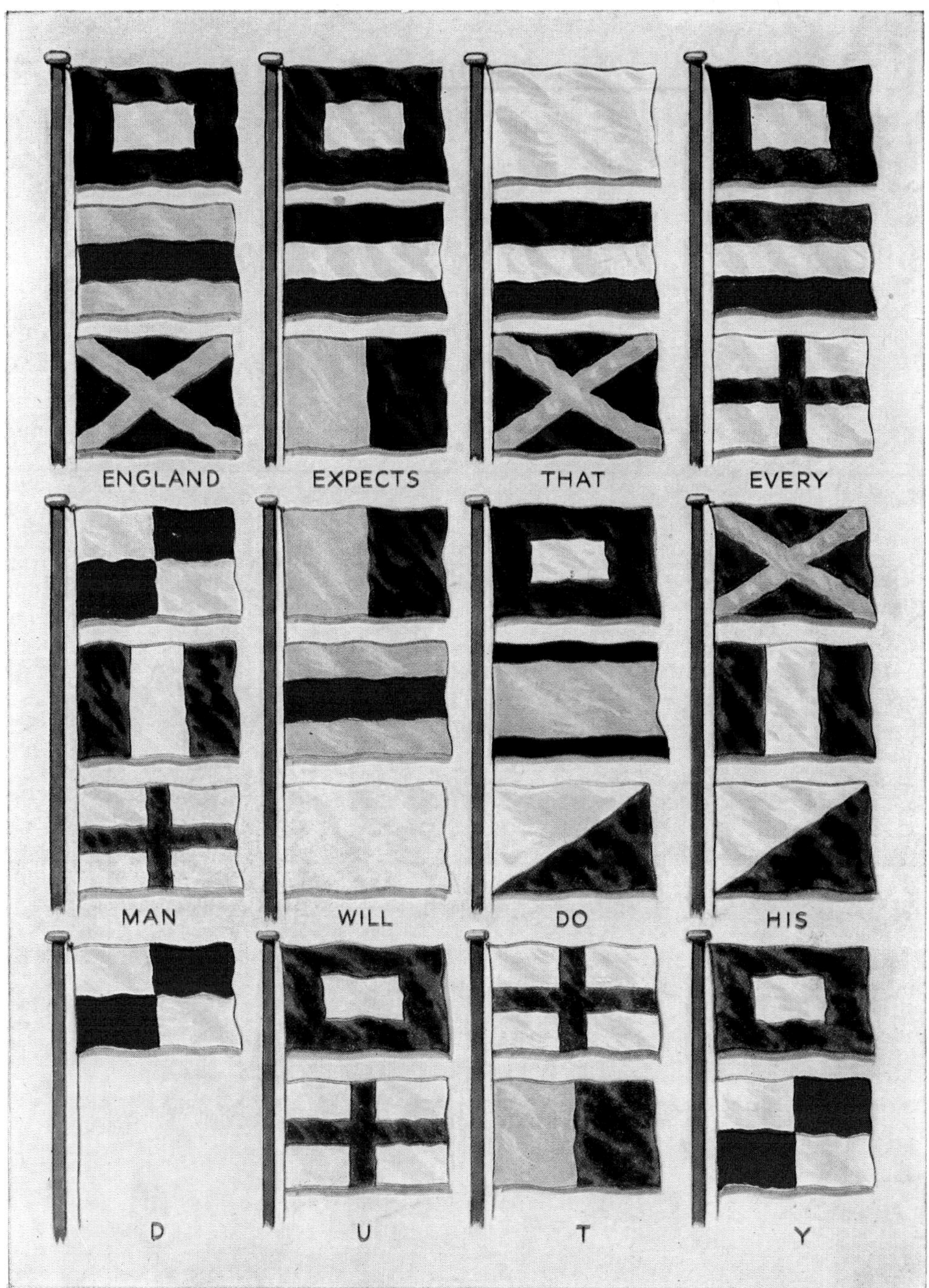

Specially painted for this work.

NELSON'S FAMOUS SIGNAL BEFORE TRAFALGAR

Signals by flags between ships have been in use at sea for some centuries, and even in these days of wireless the " bunting-tossers " remain an important branch aboard ships of the Royal Navy. Most famous of all flag signals was the one flown from the *Victory* on the morning of October 21st, 1805, when the French fleet came into sight off Cape Trafalgar. " England Expects That Every Man Will Do His Duty " was the message, and the flags flown to convey Nelson's inspiration to his fleet are shown in the picture above.

Specially painted for this work.

BRITAIN'S LARGEST BATTLESHIP — H.M.S. "VANGUARD"

It was on November 30th, 1944, that Princess Elizabeth, now Queen Elizabeth II, launched the Royal Navy's newest and largest battleship, H.M.S. *Vanguard*. The building and fitting-out was completed in 1946, and early in 1947 the late King George VI and Queen Elizabeth, now the Queen Mother, accompanied by the two Princesses, sailed on board this mighty battleship for their tour of South Africa. Their return voyage was made in the same ship. As a battleship *Vanguard's* main armament consists of eight 15 in. and sixteen 5.25 in. guns; displacement is 44,500–57,500 tons, and she has a speed of 30 knots.

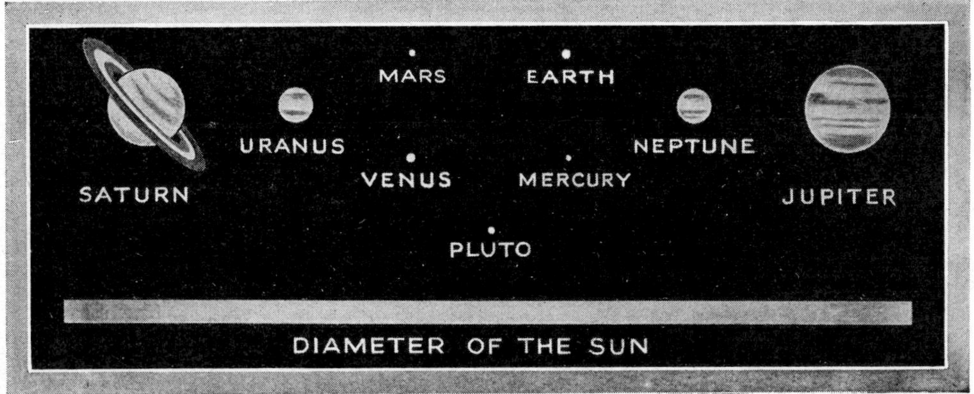

THE PLANETS AND THE SUN

The comparative sizes of the planets, showing also the huge diameter of the sun on the same scale. This would make a circle four and a half inches across !

THE SUN AND THE MOON

THE early astronomers, with the exception of a few ancient Greeks such as Aristarchus, believed that the Earth was the centre of the universe and that all the heavenly bodies revolved around it. This was taught by Ptolemy, who was born at Alexandria about A.D. 127, in his great work, the "Almagest."

The Copernican Theory

The Ptolemaic System, as it was called, held for over fourteen centuries after Ptolemy's death, no one having the courage or initiative to suggest an alternative. It was left to Nicholas Copernicus (1473–1543) to show that it held many difficulties. Copernicus realised that the stars must be situated at a tremendous distance and that if they did travel around the Earth, as Ptolemy had taught, then the speed at which they must move, in order to complete a revolution in twenty-four hours, was too great for the theory to be practicable.

Copernicus asserted that the daily movements of the stars could only be accounted for by supposing that the Earth rotated on its axis. He also showed that the movements of the planets could be accounted for by supposing them to revolve around the Sun, each in its own orbit. He believed that Mercury and Venus moved in paths that lay between the Earth and the Sun, and that the paths of the other planets were outside that of the Earth. The Copernican System was later improved by Kepler and it is the accepted theory to-day.

Galileo and Kepler

It was through supporting the Copernican theory that Galileo came into conflict with the Ecclesiastical authorities. Galileo, who was born in 1564 at Pisa, was the first to apply the telescope to a study of the heavenly bodies. When he saw the four principal satellites of Jupiter revolving

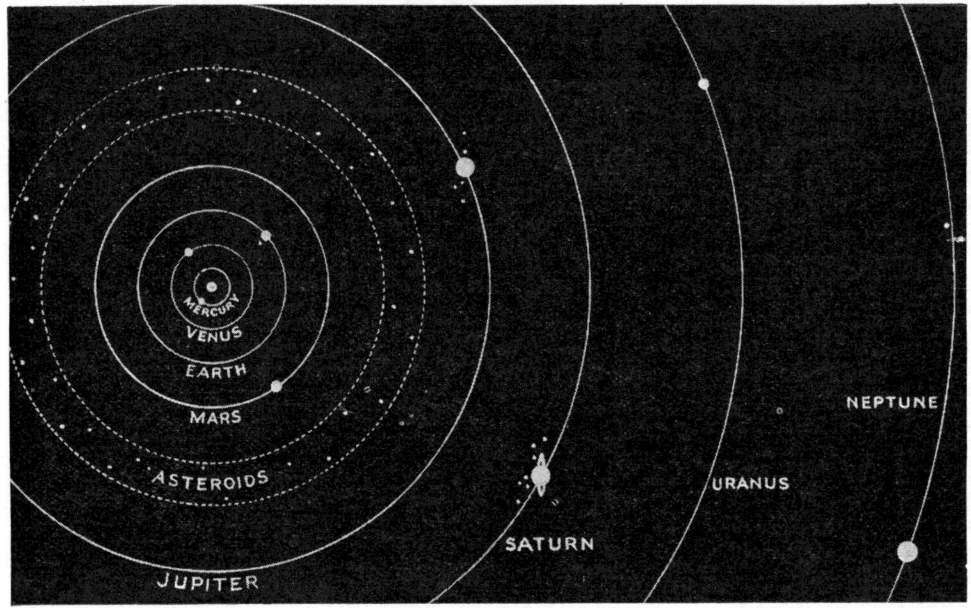

THE SOLAR SYSTEM

Although in this diagram Mercury looks amazingly close to the Sun, it takes 88 days to complete one journey around the Sun, while the year of Venus, the next planet, is 225 days. Beyond the orbit of the Earth is that of Mars, which revolves around the Sun in 687 days. Beyond Mars are the Asteroids, of which the largest is only about 500 miles in diameter. Giant Jupiter, 1,300 times larger than our Earth, comes next, then Saturn, Uranus, Neptune and, still further away, the most-recently discovered of all planets, Pluto, about which little is yet known.

around that planet, he realised that he was looking at what might be regarded as a model of the Solar System. As a result of his teachings he was summoned (in 1632) before the Inquisition and made to kneel and repeat a declaration that said, in effect, that he was entirely mistaken in his belief that the Earth travelled around the Sun.

Galileo died in 1642, and in the same year Sir Isaac Newton was born. Kepler had discovered the laws which govern the motions of the planets, but it was Sir Isaac Newton who first explained them. In 1687 he was able to show that they were all consequences of a single law of gravitation.

The Solar System

We know to-day that far from the Earth being the centre of the universe, as Ptolemy believed, it is not even the centre of that particular part of the universe to which it belongs. It is merely a planet—and a comparatively small one at that—circling round the Sun in company with eight other known planets, at least two of which are many hundred times larger than the Earth. The Sun, these nine " major " planets with their satellites or moons, the asteroids, most of the comets and all the meteors, make up the Solar System.

Names of the Planets

The planets and other bodies revolve around the Sun in paths that are known as orbits, to which they adhere year in and year out. The orbits are not perfect circles around the Sun, but are ellipses or " ovals," so that at certain times the planets are nearer to the Sun than they are at others.

The names of the nine planets in the order of their distance from the Sun are: Mercury, Venus, Earth, Mars, Jupiter, Saturn, Uranus, Neptune

WHAT THE ANCIENT GREEKS THOUGHT ABOUT ASTRONOMY

This picture represents the system of Astronomy as it was conceived by the Ancient Greeks and Egyptians. Notice that near the centre of the diagram the four elements of the ancients—Earth, Water, Air and Fire—are indicated. Then come the Heavens of the Moon, of Mercury, of Venus, of the Sun, of Mars, of Jupiter, and of Saturn. Outside these was supposed to be the Heaven of the Firmament in which the stars were fixed. The Moon, the planets and the stars were thought to be embedded in a series of hollow balls of crystal, fitting inside one another and revolving at different speeds.

E.N.A.

THE GREAT DOME

Being 7,000 feet above the sea, Mount Wilson Observatory is free from fogs and clouds. This domed building contains the great reflecting telescope. The dome, which is 100 feet across, was the largest in existence until the completion of that on Palomar Mountain.

TOWER TELESCOPE AT MOUNT WILSON

Mount Wilson Observatory was established by the Carnegie Institution. This photograph shows the tower telescope, with which the Sun is photographed each day. It gives an image of the Sun 16½ inches in diameter.

and Pluto. We can remember the order of the planets by memorising the following sentence: Men Very Easily Make Jugs Serve Useful Needs and Pleasures. The first letter of each word corresponds with the first letter in the name of each planet.

The planets nearest to the Sun have smaller orbits than those further away, and they revolve around it in shorter periods of time. None of the orbits intersects another and there seems to be a certain amount of regularity in the placing of the planets, as we shall see when we come to the asteroids.

A Model to Scale

If we desire to make a scale model

ONE OF THE GREATEST TELESCOPES

Ellison Hawks.

Mount Wilson's first telescope was a 60-inch reflector—that is, it possessed a concave silvered mirror 5 feet in diameter. This was followed by an even larger telescope, with a mirror 100 inches in diameter and no less than 12 in thickness. The grinding and polishing of this immense mirror was done in the Observatory's optical shop at Pasadena, a neighbouring town. The telescope, one of the largest of its kind in the world, is moved mechanically at a speed that exactly counteracts the movement caused by the rotation of the Earth.

of the Solar System, we should require a globe 9 feet in diameter to represent the Sun. On the same scale the Earth would be represented by a 1-inch ball at a distance of 325 yards, with the Moon a small pea 20 inches from the Earth. Jupiter would require an 11-inch globe a mile from the globe representing the Sun, while a 5-inch globe $5\frac{1}{2}$ miles distant would do for Neptune.

Each planet has some particular characteristic that makes it an object of special interest. Mercury is the smallest planet and the one nearest to the Sun. Venus—the planet nearest in size to the Earth—is sometimes called "the evening star," and is by far the brightest object in the heavens with the exception of the Sun and the Moon. Mars, the fourth planet in order of distance, has peculiar markings suggesting continents and oceans. Jupiter, the largest of the planets, has twelve satellites and a mysterious Red Spot. Saturn has nine satellites and a wonderful ring-system. Both Uranus and Neptune are the subject of interesting stories regarding their discovery. Pluto, the most distant, was the last major planet to be discovered (in 1930).

Density and Gravitation

Not only does the Sun provide light and heat for its family of planets, but it also holds them in their courses by the power known as gravitation. Most of you know how a magnet attracts light objects, and how a large magnet is able to lift larger objects than a small magnet. In a somewhat similar

H. J. Shepstone.

THE "BUSINESS END" OF A GREAT REFRACTOR

The huge telescope at Mount Wilson is a reflector. This picture shows the eye-piece end of another type of telescope called the refractor. This particular telescope, which is the second largest of its kind, is in the Lick Observatory at Mount Hamilton, California. Roughly speaking, the refractor is built like a sailor's telescope, but no refractor can be as large or as powerful as the largest reflector, owing to the difficulty in making very large object glasses.

H. J. Shepstone.

ENGLAND'S OBSERVATORY

This photograph shows part of the Royal Observatory at Greenwich. Its importance is world-wide as longitude is now universally measured from here and " Greenwich mean time " is known everywhere. Owing to deterioration in climatic conditions at Greenwich the Observatory has been removed to Hurstmonceux Castle in Sussex, but this will not entail any change in the prime meridian.

manner the Earth attracts objects to itself, but in this case the attraction is by gravitation, and not by magnetism. That is why objects thrown into the air fall to the ground again, and why everything has a certain " weight."

Gravitation depends solely upon the amount of matter in a body, or its " mass," so that we can compare the masses of two bodies simply by weighing them. Their size has nothing to do with it, for you can have a small heavy object, like a lead weight, and a much larger light one, like a block of wood. Galileo discovered the curious fact that all objects, however heavy, fall at the same rate ! A block of lead falls with more *force* than a block of wood, but it does not fall any more quickly.

The Earth is not the only body that attracts ; everything that exists has this power. We do not notice the attraction between small objects because their gravitation is so weak, but the force of gravity of a small house can be measured. The larger and more massive the object the more powerful is its force of gravity, and it is the enormous attractive force exerted by the Sun which keeps the Earth and other planets circling round their orbits instead of flying off into space.

Where Weights are Different

Since the planets are all different sizes, they all have different forces of gravity, and this means that any small object would have a different " weight " on each planet, and would weigh heaviest of all on the Sun.

For instance, let us suppose a 12-stone man is transported to the Sun. When he arrived there he would find that he weighed 2 tons, because everything on the Sun weighs twenty-seven times as much as it does on the Earth! The man's watch would weigh about 6 pounds, and the very act of lifting his arm would seem to him like moving an arm of solid lead. If he were unfortunate enough to fall down, he would not be able to rise, and if he once got into bed he would certainly never be able to get up again!

On the other hand, if we could visit the Moon we should find that things weigh only about one-sixth what they weigh on the Earth. It would be a comparatively easy matter for a boy to jump over a house; and a hunter that on the Earth can jump a five-barred gate would leap over a haystack on the Moon with the same amount of exertion. A fielder at a cricket match who can throw in from 100 yards would be able to throw in from 600 yards just as easily on the Moon. At football the players would have to be careful that they did not kick the ball off the field and over the housetops—an extra strong kick would send the ball soaring into the next parish!

HOW FAR IS THE SUN FROM THE EARTH?

We all know that the Sun is of the greatest importance to us, not only because it controls the movements of the Earth, but also because we depend upon it for light and heat. Even when the Sun is temporarily absent from the sky, as on a dull day, everyone seems to be affected by the absence of sunlight. Without the energy from the Sun's rays there could be no life on the Earth.

Although the Sun is to us the most

Topical Press.

THE NEW HOME OF THE ROYAL GREENWICH OBSERVATORY

It was about 1446 when Sir Roger Fiennes began to build Hurstmonceux Castle on Pevensey Level in Sussex. The material that he chose was red brick, for his castle was intended to be more country house than stronghold. To-day, the Castle with its 84-foot-high gate-towers is the home of the Royal Greenwich Observatory.

Topical Press.

THE SOLAR BUILDING AT HURSTMONCEUX

Greenwich, where King Charles II established the Royal Observatory in 1675, is now too near London to enjoy ideal observation conditions for astronomers. That is why the move to Hurstmonceux was made. The Castle, seen in the background in this picture, houses the library, instrument rooms and living quarters of the Royal Observatory. In the foreground is the new Solar building.

important of all the heavenly bodies, it is surprising to think how few people stop to consider its size, distance, or composition. Indeed, this applies not only to the Sun, but to the heavenly bodies in general, in spite of the great interest they hold for us.

Early Calculations

Mathematicians have devoted an enormous amount of time to measuring the Sun's distance, for this is one of the most difficult problems of Astronomy. Even at the present time the matter is not definitely settled and corrections are constantly being made.

Aristarchus of Samos, who lived in the third century B.C., was one of the first to attempt to solve the problem. He calculated that the distance of the Sun was some twenty times greater than the distance of the Moon, but his result was about twenty times too little. Other astronomers—including Ptolemy, Copernicus, and Kepler—devoted time to the problem, but their estimates were all incorrect. It was not until 1673 that Cassini obtained a result more in accordance with modern measurements, though he was still 6,000,000 miles out. The modern figure for the distance is about 92,900,000 miles—that is a little less than four hundred times the distance of the Moon from the Earth.

A Long Journey!

It is difficult for us to visualise such a distance, but we may get some idea of it by the following illustrations: If it were possible to lay a railway from the Earth to the Sun and to set off an express train, it would take that train over two hundred years to reach the

Sun, assuming it did not stop day or night. In other words, if King George III. had taken a ticket for the Sun he might not have arrived there yet!

Why it is Hot in Summer

It is strange to learn that, to us in the northern hemisphere, the Sun is nearer in the winter than it is in summer! Actually, it is nearest to the Earth about New Year's Day and at its greatest distance about the 2nd July. It is not the difference in distance, which at the two dates amounts to nearly 3,000,000 miles, that causes the alternation of summer and winter, but the difference in the tilt of the Earth's axis, which on 21st June is so placed that the North Pole is inclined about $23\frac{1}{2}°$ towards the Sun. At this season, the North Pole receives sunlight all day and all night—it is the "land of the midnight sun," and elsewhere in the northern hemisphere the day is longer than the night.

At mid-winter the conditions are reversed and the South Pole has sunshine all night while the North Pole has no sunlight at all for three months. In summer, too, the height of the noonday Sun in the sky is greater. This also has an important effect on the summer heat, for the more vertically the Sun's rays strike the Earth, the greater is the heat that they bring to each square yard of the surface.

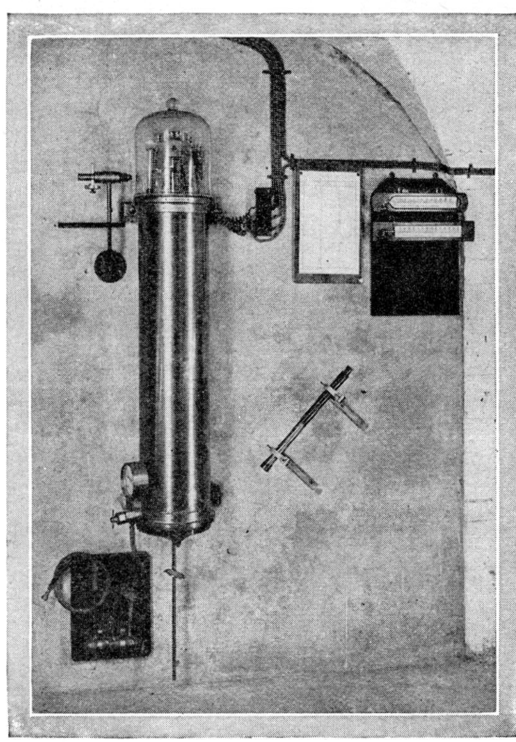

H. J. Shepstone.

A STAR CLOCK

This photograph shows the Standard Sidereal (or Star) Clock at Greenwich Observatory. This clock keeps accurate time and is regulated from observations of the stars. The chamber in which this clock is kept is maintained at a uniform temperature. In this clock a pendulum swings in a vacuum, but the most accurate of all time-keepers are controlled by the vibrations of an electrically-excited quartz crystal.

ABOUT THE SUN

THE Sun is a hot, self-luminous globe, composed of a mass of highly heated gas—chiefly hydrogen. Its diameter is about 864,100 miles, so that, in comparison with the Earth, it is enormous.

It is difficult for us to imagine the great size of the Sun, but we can obtain some rough idea from the following illustration. If we were to suppose the Sun to be a hollow sphere with the Earth at its centre, the surface of the sphere would be 432,000 miles distant from the Earth. As the Moon is about 239,000 miles from the Earth, we can see that the Sun is large enough easily to contain the path of the Moon.

If we wanted to make a "true-to-scale" model of the Sun and the Earth, we should require a globe 2 feet in diameter for the Sun, and a very small pea ($\frac{1}{5}$ inch in diameter) would represent the Earth. In other words, about 110 planets of the same size as the Earth, placed side by side and each touching, would be required to stretch from one side of the Sun to the other.

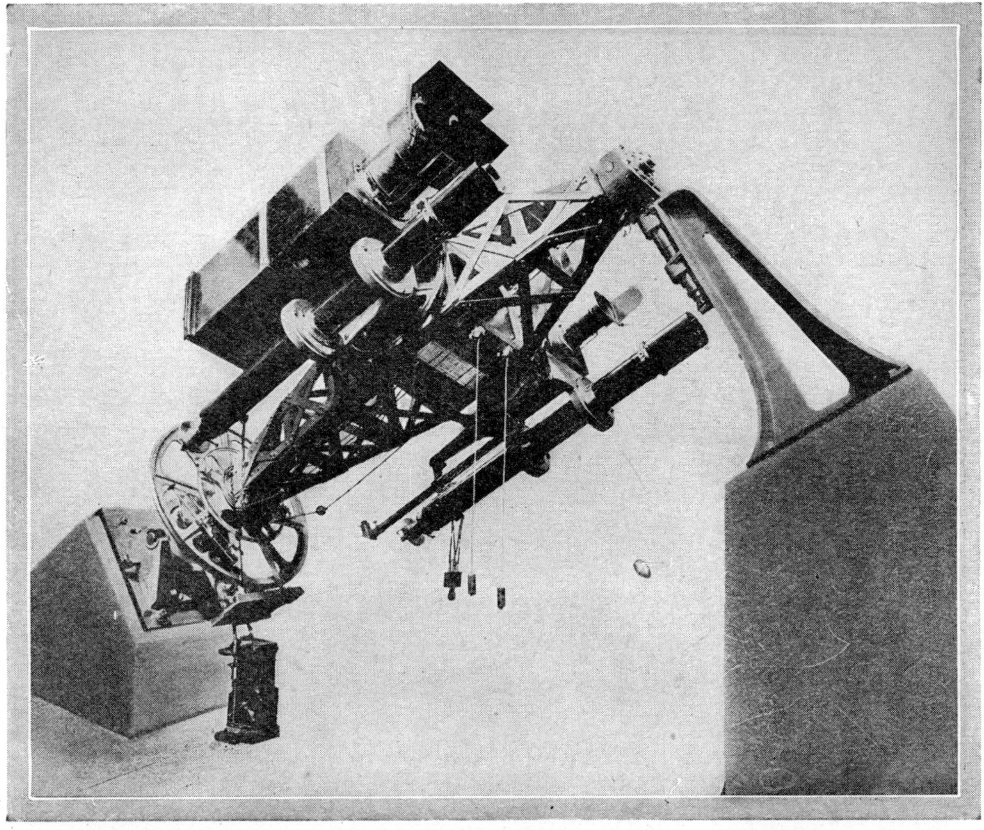

FOR PHOTOGRAPHING STARS

This strange-looking piece of machinery is a Franklin-Adams astrographic telescope. It is simply a camera combined with a telescope, and is used for charting the stars, for which work it is far more reliable than the human eye. Star-cameras are being used to make a chart of the whole sky.

Although the Sun is made of gas, and not of dense matter like rock, it is so large that it would weigh as much as 332,000 Earths ! In tons, this would be written as a 2 followed by twenty-seven noughts !

Brightness and Heat of the Sun

We all know that sunlight is very bright and that it is dangerous to look at the Sun without protecting our eyes with smoked glass or in some other way. Apart from the light of certain stars, and perhaps that of an atomic bomb, sunlight is the most intense light we know, being 146 times more brilliant than limelight. The brightest artificial light is that of the electric arc, but even this appears dark when compared with sunlight. Careful measurements show the Sun's light to be at least four times as bright as the electric arc.

The Sun's heat is no less intense, and it has been estimated that the temperature at the Sun's surface amounts to 10,000° F. This is about twice as hot as the hottest electric furnace. At the centre of the Sun the temperature is probably at least 40,000,000 degrees ! Experiments made by Sir John Herschel at the Cape of Good Hope caused him to conclude that the amount of heat received on the Earth's surface would melt an inch thickness of ice in about two hours and thirteen minutes.

How is the Heat and Light Maintained ?

You may wonder how it is possible

THE WONDERS OF THE HEAVENS

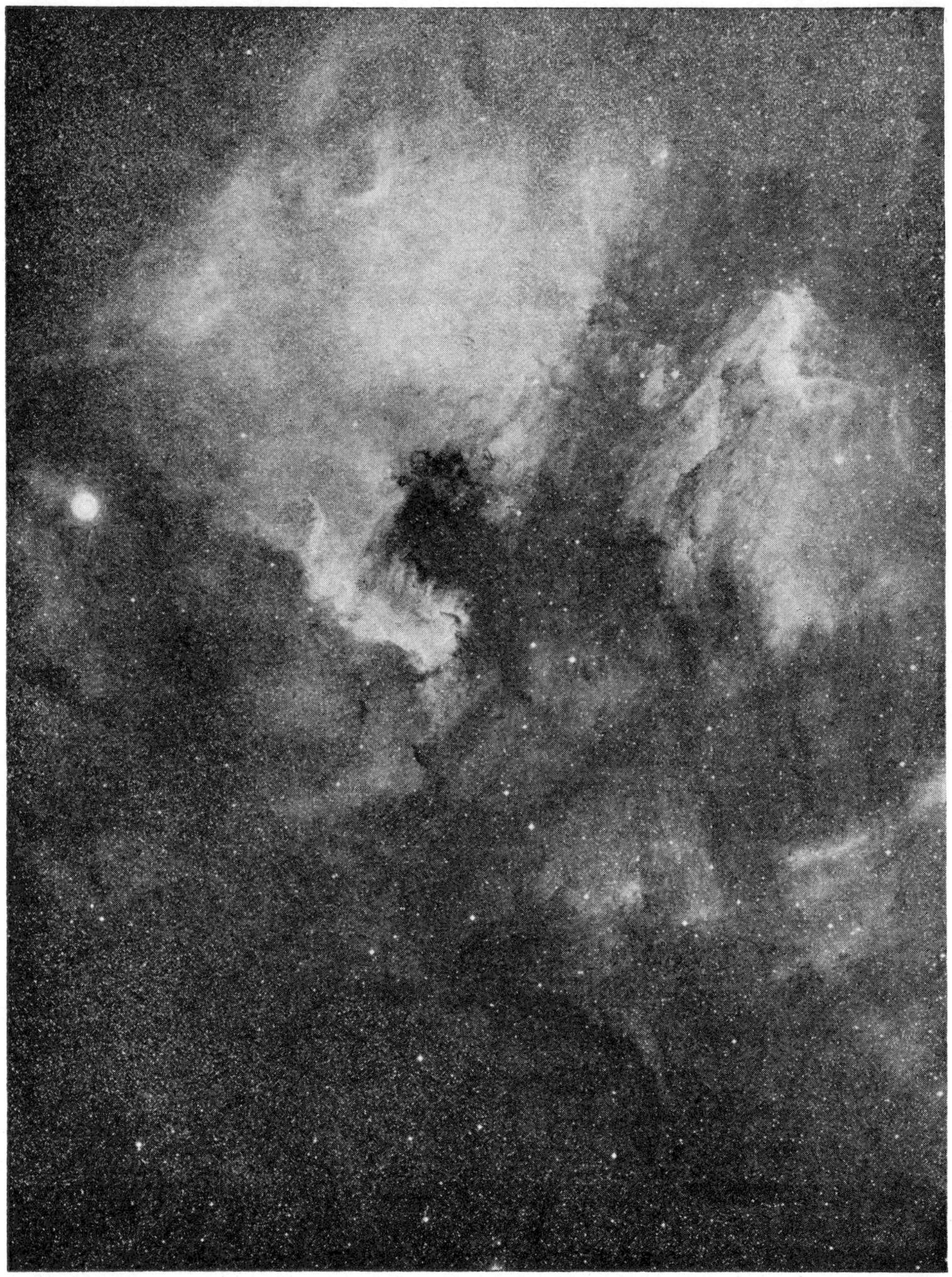

By courtesy of the National Geographical Society—Palomar Observatory Sky Survey.

The Palomar Observatory near San Diego, California, has built the largest telescope in the world and the wonderful Schmidt camera shown opposite. In 1949 the Observatory began to take a series of 2,000 photographs of the area of the sky visible from that latitude. This photograph, one of the first to be taken, shows the North American Nebula in the northern part of the Milky Way. The single bright star seen on the left is Xi Cygni, about 300 light years distant. One light year equals about six million million miles.

THE GREAT SCHMIDT CAMERA

Palomar Observatory.

This giant camera at Palomar Mountain, California, is known as " Big Schmidt." It weighs 36 tons, and its lens is a mirror 6 feet in diameter. Its tube is 24 feet long, and it is here seen pointing to the sky through the open slot in the observatory dome. One of its great advantages over the older types of camera is that it can include a larger area of the sky in the same photograph. It is connected to a small motor which turns it on its axis so as to follow the stars across the sky.

for the Sun to maintain its light and heat, the supply of which seems inexhaustible. It is now known that atomic energy is responsible, though exactly what happens remains a mystery. The conversion of hydrogen into helium, which is what happens when a hydrogen bomb explodes, is no doubt one of the chief causes of the Sun's light and heat.

THE SPOTS ON THE SUN

EVEN a small telescope will show spots on the Sun's surface, and occasionally very large spots may be seen by the unaided eye. Before examining the Sun, however, always protect the eyes by looking through a piece of glass that has been smoked in a candle-flame, or by using the dark part of an exposed photographic film.

To understand the cause of sunspots we must first learn something about the nature of the Sun itself. The luminous surface of the Sun that we see is called the " photosphere," a word which comes from the Greek meaning " light-sphere." It is a kind of envelope of highly heated gases surrounding the Sun in a somewhat similar manner to that in which the atmosphere surrounds the Earth. Seen through a low-powered telescope, the photosphere presents a mottled appearance not unlike that of rough drawing paper. When magnified the surface is seen to be covered with marks, called " rice-grains " from their appearance.

Australian Official Photograph.

IN THE SOUTHERN HEMISPHERE

This 74-inch reflecting telescope at the Australian Commonwealth Observatory photographs the spectra of stars in colour. The great mirror can be seen at the bottom of the telescope, while the dark oval object above it is a flat mirror set at an angle to throw the light-rays out to the camera at the side, which the observer is adjusting. The small telescopes on the left are " finders."

Topical Press.

PHOTOGRAPHING AN ECLIPSE OF THE SUN

This photograph shows the telescopic cameras in place and ready for action at Bocaivu, a remote place in Brazil where a total eclipse of the sun was visible in May, 1947. A large group of scientists journeyed to this lonely, wooded plateau to watch the eclipse. The weather was favourable and the observations and photographs taken at the time were excellent.

Great storms take place in the photosphere, and the bright surface of the Sun is ruptured and torn apart. Through the great hole that appears, we look into the depths of the Sun, which we see as a black spot. Although these depths appear dark they are not really so, being, in fact, brighter than molten steel and only appearing to be dark by way of contrast with the excessive brilliance of the photosphere.

How Big are Sunspots?

Sunspots vary in size from mere specks to great dark markings sufficiently large to be visible without optical aid. Even the spots that appear to be specks are some 500 miles in diameter, whilst the large ones may be 40,000 or 50,000 miles across. These large spots cover enormous areas, one having been estimated to measure over 3,500,000,000 square miles. One of the largest spots recorded, which was visible in February, 1905, was big enough to allow forty planets, each as large as the Earth, to pass through it without touching its sides. On this basis, assuming the Earth to be represented by a pea, the spot would be as large as a dinner plate.

As a rule, a sunspot is composed of two parts, the dark central part and a lighter fringe surrounding it. The dark part is called the *umbra* and the surrounding fringe the *penumbra*. Sometimes the *penumbra* entirely surrounds the spot, but at other times it may be broken and only be seen around part of it.

Sunspots are generally circular in shape, but they often take very beautiful and curious forms, with all manner of twists and turns. They change, too, from day to day or even hourly, and what may at first be a circular spot becomes distorted and mis-shapen as times goes on.

Sunspots may break out suddenly, or they may come into being slowly, in which case they are generally preceded by other disturbances. They may last for a matter of hours only, or for weeks—or even months in exceptional cases. In 1840 there was a remarkable spot that persisted for eighteen months. On an average, however, sunspots last only for from one to four days, during which time they undergo varied changes in appearance. They occur generally in particular latitudes of the Sun, the limit generally being between 5° and 40° north and south of the Sun's equator. Curiously enough, the spots have been found to be slightly more numerous in the southern hemisphere.

Because sunspots are seen to move across the face of the Sun each day, we know that the Sun revolves on its axis. In this it resembles the Earth, but whereas the Earth revolves in twenty-four hours, the Sun's equator requires about twenty-five days. Other parts of the Sun rotate more slowly, and near the poles the period may be as much as thirty-four days.

The Sunspot Cycle

In 1843 an amateur astronomer named Schwabe, who lived at Dessau, noticed that the number of spots varied greatly in different years. As a result of his observations, he discovered that the variation in the numbers was a regular one, increasing and decreasing through-

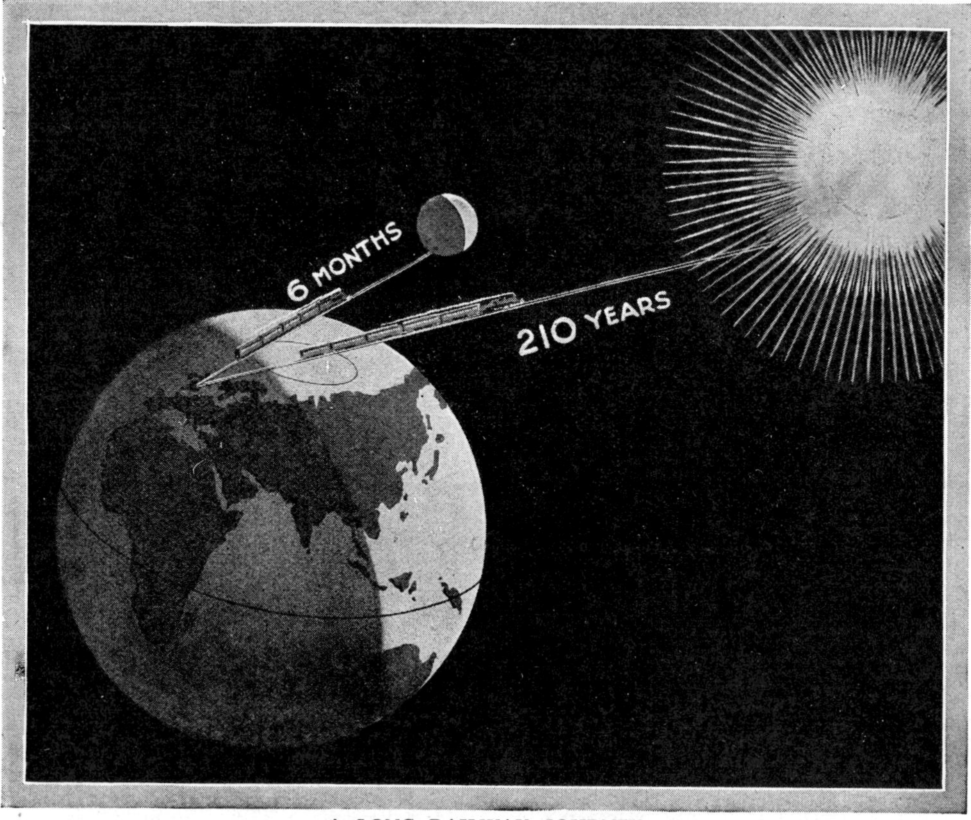

A LONG RAILWAY JOURNEY

It is easy to say that the Moon is 239,000 miles away and that the Sun is nearly 93 million miles distant, but figures mean very little to most people. This picture gives a much better idea of the distances between the Earth and the Moon and Sun. An express train leaving the Earth for the Moon and travelling night and day would reach the Moon in approximately six months, but the same train would require approximately 210 years in which to reach the Sun.

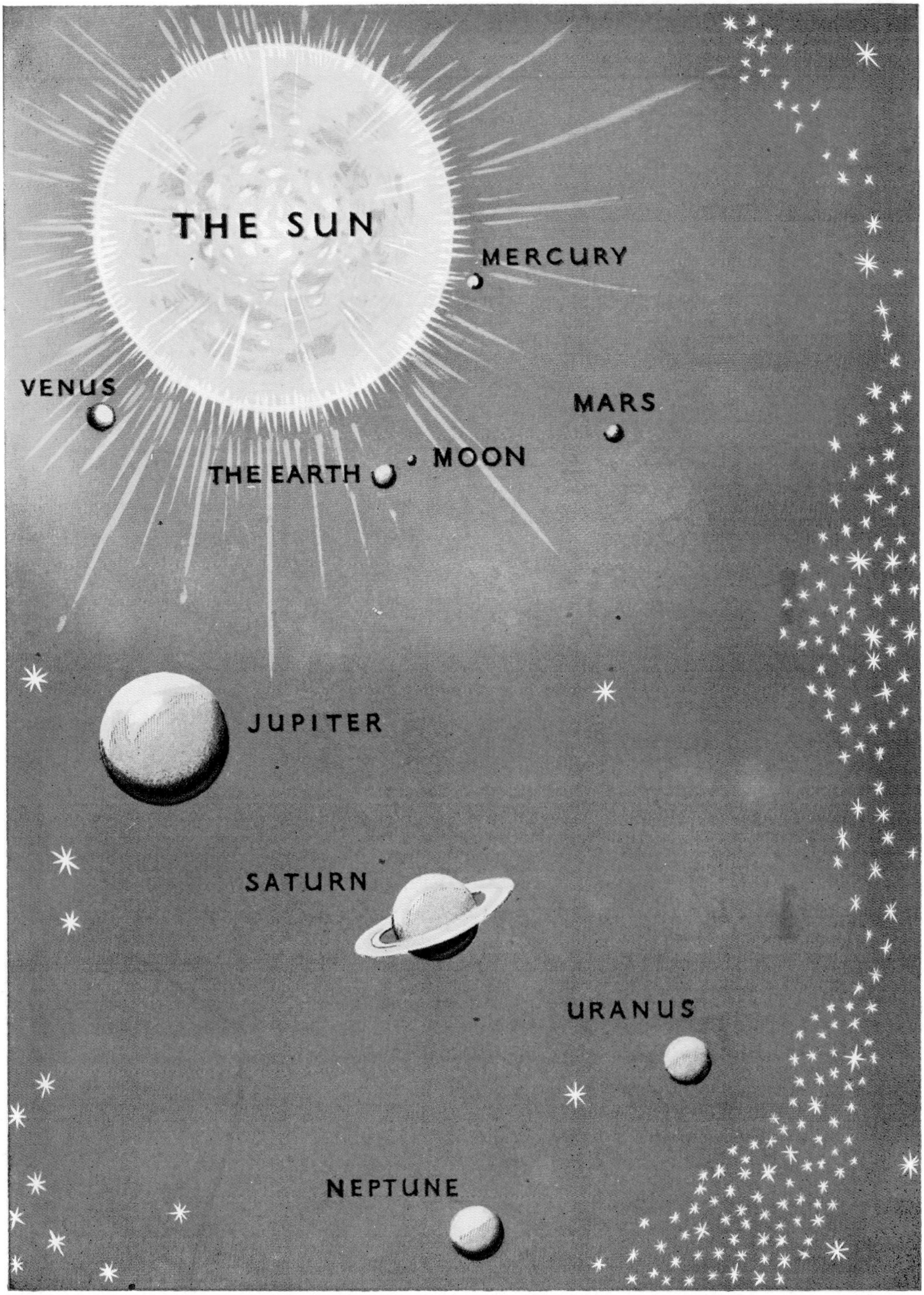

THE EARTH AS A PLANET AMONG OTHER PLANETS

The Solar System comprises the Sun, planets, satellites, comets, asteroids, meteors and the rings of Saturn. Our Earth is one of the planets, with the Moon as its satellite. Other planets are Mercury, Venus, Mars, Jupiter, Saturn, Uranus and Neptune, and their positions in relation to the Earth are shown in this picture. Another planet, named Pluto, was discovered in 1930, but little is known of it at present. Besides the one in which the Earth revolves there are of course many other solar systems, and all these form the Universe.

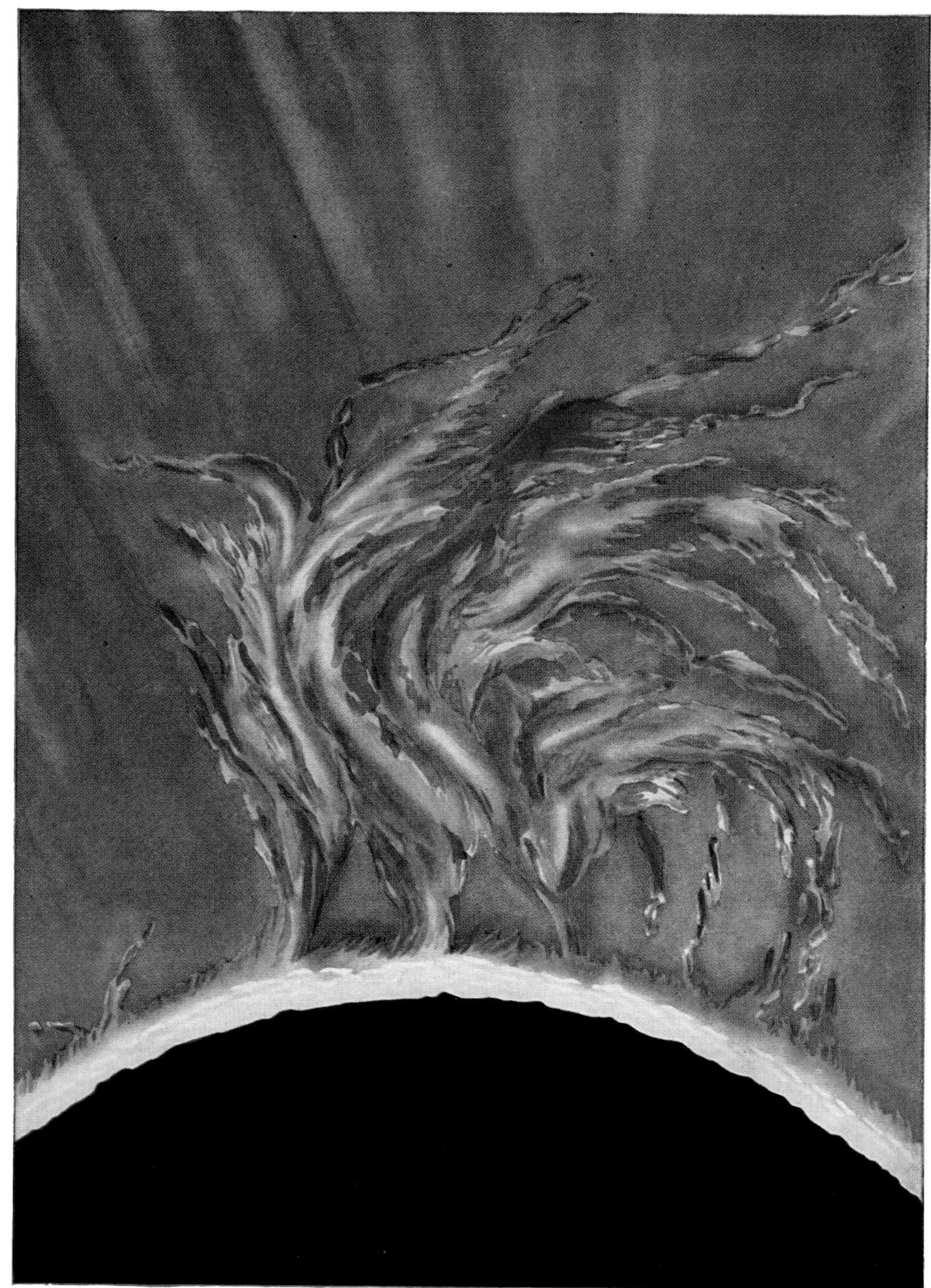

FLAMING OUTBURSTS FROM THE SUN

Of all the heavenly bodies the most important to mankind is the sun, and from earliest times men have recognised its beneficent power. Its grandeur and wonders have been realised more fully since the invention of the telescope enabled astronomers to study it more carefully from the earth, 92,900,000 miles away. Among the most notable features of the solar phenomena are the great scarlet prominences shown in the picture above. These are immense outbursts of flaming hydrogen rising sometimes to a height of 500,000 miles.

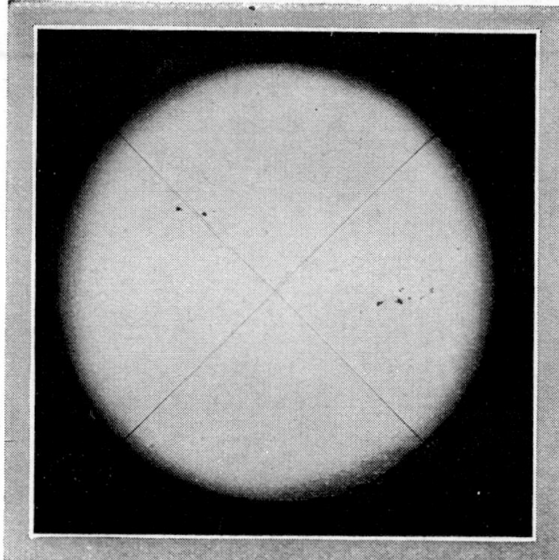

THE SUN AND ITS SPOTS

The Sun is about 864,100 miles in diameter and is the centre of our system. The tiny marks you see on his disc are sunspots. The lines crossing the Sun in the photograph are cross wires in the telescope, to help to determine the position of the sunspots.

discovered by Galileo when he turned his newly-invented telescope to the Sun over three hundred years ago. The famous astronomer was greatly surprised — and, indeed, perturbed — at what he saw, for up to that time the Sun had been regarded as a symbol of unblemished purity!

The "Northern Lights"

In addition to its dark spots the sun often shows brilliant outbursts of about the same size, and these are called "solar flares." These usually affect the Earth's magnetism and cause extraordinarily beautiful displays of the *aurora borealis*, which are seen in the sky at a height of about a hundred miles. These are due to the arrival of both electrons and electrified hydrogen atoms, shot out from the solar flares. They generate

out a period that he fixed at about eleven years. This period is now called the "sunspot cycle" and the time when the spots are most numerous is said to be the maximum, and the time when they are least the minimum.

It is interesting to know that Schwabe's discovery of the sunspot cycle was made with the use of a small telescope. He was a most assiduous observer, and for thirty years he never lost an opportunity of examining the Sun with his telescope. He made over 9,000 observations, in the course of which he recorded 4,700 groups of spots. Schwabe's work is an outstanding example of what an amateur can do even with only a small telescope, for he made discoveries that had eluded professional astronomers, with all their equipment, for two hundred years.

We may here mention, perhaps, that sunspots were first

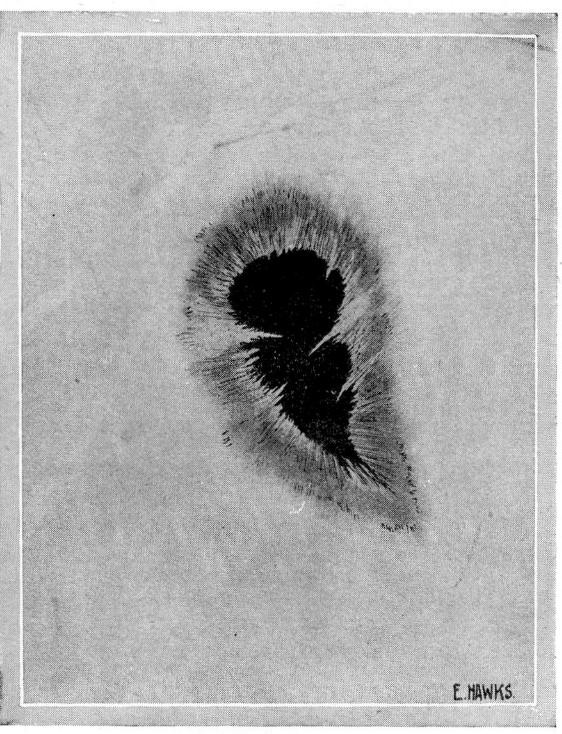

A SUN STORM (1)

The storms that rage on the Sun's surface are terrific beyond conception. They tear aside the white hot photosphere, or envelope of highly heated gas surrounding the Sun, and allow us to see the comparatively cooler regions below (*see illustration on next page*).

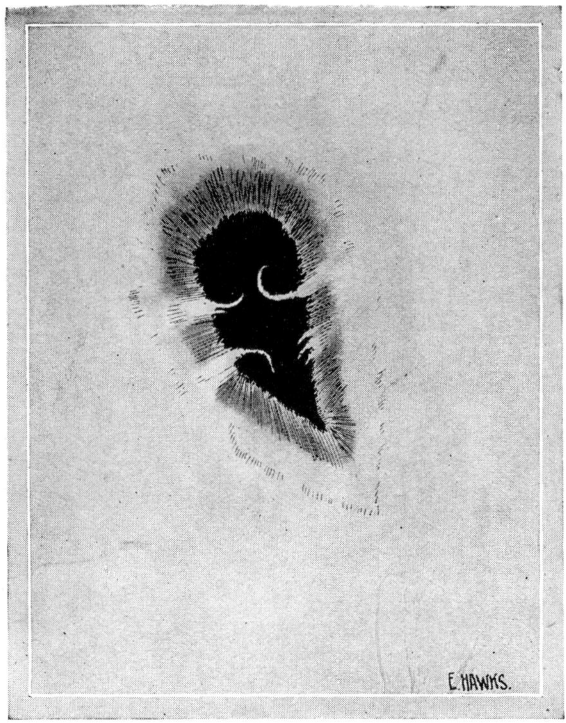

A SUN STORM (2)

Here is the same sunspot as it appeared a day later than in the previous illustration. The spike-like markings are flames of incandescent gas. Although they appear small, they are thousands of miles in length. They are constantly changing in appearance.

magnetic storms which are sometimes so violent as to change the direction in which ship's compasses point by 3° in as many minutes! They have also affected the telegraph service by interrupting its operation, one of the most remarkable of such instances occurring in 1909.

ECLIPSES OF THE SUN

IN the course of its revolutions around the Earth, the Moon sometimes comes between the Earth and the Sun, thus causing an eclipse. There are at least two eclipses of the Sun every year, and there may be as many as five. These eclipses may be partial, annular, or total.

A partial eclipse is one in which only part of the Sun is obscured. In an annular eclipse nearly the whole of the Sun is covered by the dark body of the Moon, but as the Moon appears slightly smaller than the Sun, an uneclipsed ring of sunlight remains.

Total eclipses are by far the most interesting, and astronomers will willingly journey to the opposite ends of the Earth to observe them. A total eclipse is perhaps the most magnificent and impressive sight that Nature affords us. Little by little the dark body of the Moon encroaches on the bright disc of the Sun, until at last it completely covers it. If the observer is favourably placed he may see the shadow of the Moon sweeping across the land with awe-inspiring speed. The Moon moves in its orbit at a speed of about 2,100 miles an hour, and the shadow it casts travels easterly over the Earth's surface.

At every place on which this shadow falls there occurs an eclipse of the Sun. The length of the shadow path may be anything up to about 8,000 miles, but the breadth is generally less than 100 miles at the widest part.

In addition to the motion of the Moon we must remember that the Earth is revolving on its axis at a speed of about 1,040 miles an hour. If we subtract this figure from the Moon's speed we find that the shadow will sweep across the Earth at a rate of about 1,060 miles an hour.

The Corona and the Prominences

When the Sun is totally eclipsed, the daylight becomes gradually less and a peculiar hush spreads over the land. The wind drops, and an appalling stillness makes it seem almost as though the universe is on the verge of some great catastrophe. When the last thin crescent of the Sun disappears, the black disc of the Moon is seen

SUNSPOTS AT CLOSE QUARTERS

Here we are shown what sunspots or Sun storms look like when seen through a powerful telescope. If you compare the size of our Earth, which you can see in the top left-hand corner of the picture, with the spots in the Sun's surface, you will gain some idea of the great size of the spots. These spots affect the Earth's magnetism and may sometimes cause ship's compasses to change the direction in which they point.

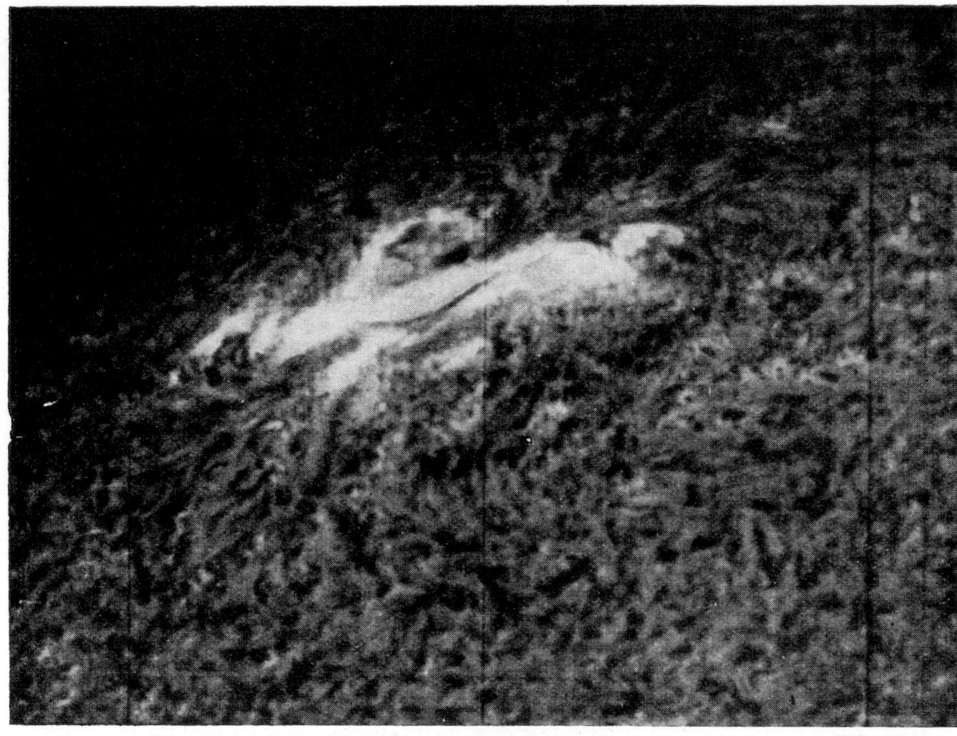

Walter Shepherd.

A SOLAR FLARE

This greatly enlarged photograph of the Sun showing a solar flare looks dark because it was taken with the light from one colour of the spectrum only. This is done by means of an instrument called a spectroheliograph, and it reveals details of the Sun's surface which are invisible in the full light. Solar flares cause great magnetic disturbances on the Earth, and are responsible for the " Northern Lights."

surrounded by a wonderful pearly halo.

This halo is called the corona, and it changes in form from year to year, varying with the sunspot cycle. At the time of the sunspot maximum short bright plumes are seen, but when the sunspots are fewest the corona throws off long streamers. Sometimes these streamers, which consist largely of incandescent gases, stretch for millions of miles into space.

In addition to the corona, there are often seen rose-coloured flames around the edge of the Moon. These projections, which are called the prominences, are really masses of luminous gas in the process of being ejected by the Sun. Prominences often reach a height of hundreds of thousands of miles above the photosphere, and by studying them it has been possible to learn a great deal about the physical constitution of the Sun.

The Mountains of the Moon

During an eclipse it is noticed that the edge of the Moon is irregular, an appearance that is due to the lunar mountains. This irregular edge accounts also for the fact that when the Moon has almost covered the Sun the last crescent of brightness does not suddenly disappear. Instead, it breaks into a number of tiny points of light called Baily's Beads, which are seen just before and just after totality. They are caused by the last remnants of sunshine peeping through the spaces between the peaks of the Moon mountains.

THE NORTHERN LIGHTS

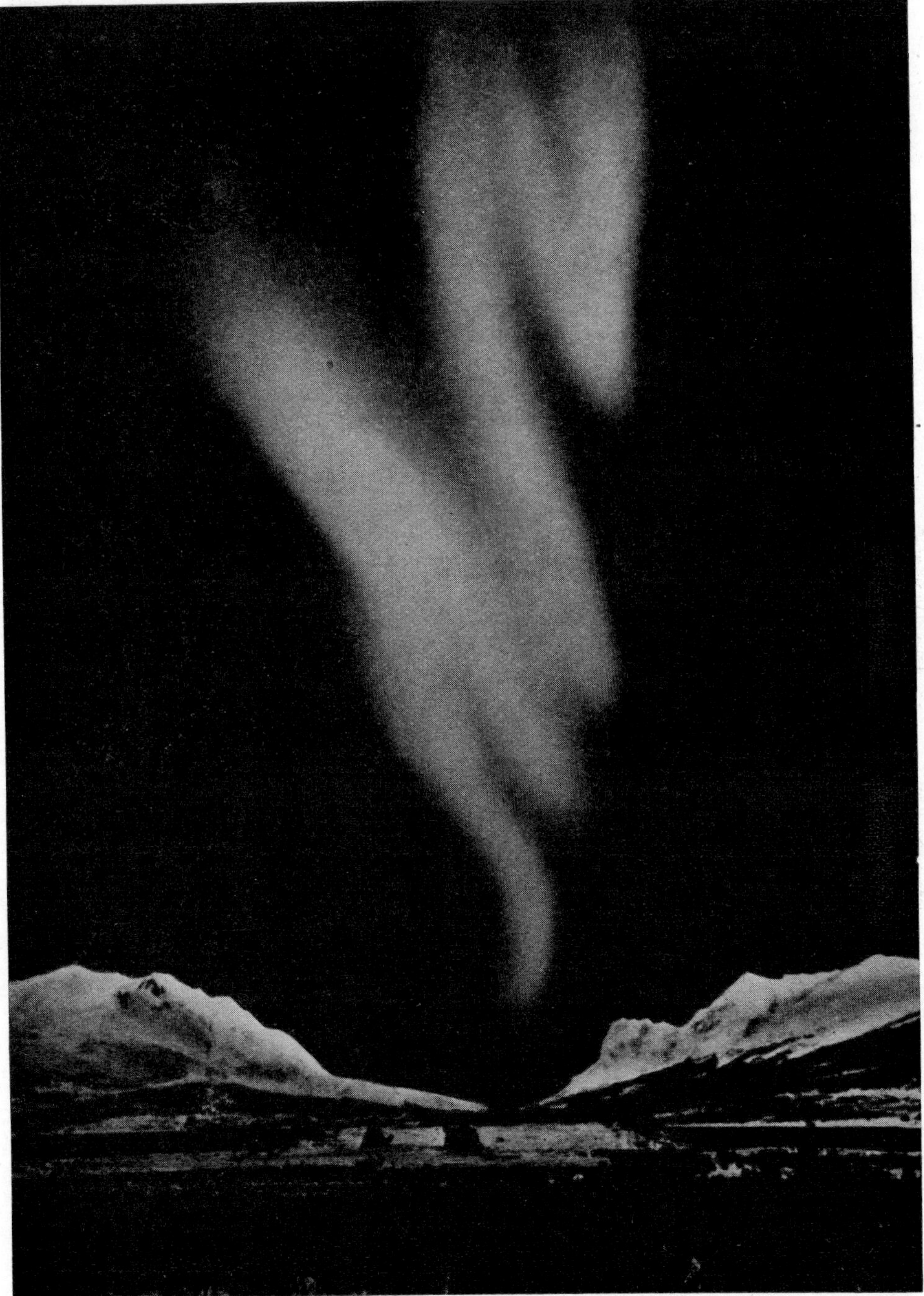

Dorien Leigh.

AURORA BOREALIS

This wonderful picture of the Northern Lights was taken in Norway, and the display is of the kind known as a " curtain " aurora. Other varieties exhibit darting rays of light, shimmering sheets, and brilliant flashes, all in the most delicate colours imaginable. Similar lights occur over the south polar regions, where they are known as the " aurora australis," and they are due to the arrival in the earth's magnetic field of electrified particles shot out from solar flares like the one shown opposite.

Historical Eclipses

Eclipses of the Sun have been observed from very early times. One of the earliest recorded is mentioned in the Chinese book "Chou-King," in which it is expressively written: "On the first day of the last month of Autumn the Sun and Moon did not meet harmoniously in Fang." It is believed that the eclipse referred to in this record occurred in either 2136 or 2128 B.C.

Both Greek and Latin historians recorded eclipses with particular care, because in those days their occurrence was supposed to foretell some disastrous happening. For instance, an eclipse that took place in 715 B.C. was thought to have been connected with the death of Romulus. In 585 B.C. there was an eclipse that has been of some service in helping historians to fix this year as the date of an important event.

Herodotus tells us that during a war between Lydians and the Medes, "just as the battle was growing warm, day was suddenly turned into night. . . . When the Lydians and the Medes observed the change they ceased fighting and were alike anxious to conclude peace." Curiously enough, there is no record of any eclipse having been observed in England until well into the sixth century. There are several records of eclipses in the Anglo-Saxon Chronicle, however, and here again we find that it was customary to associate these unusual events with misfortune.

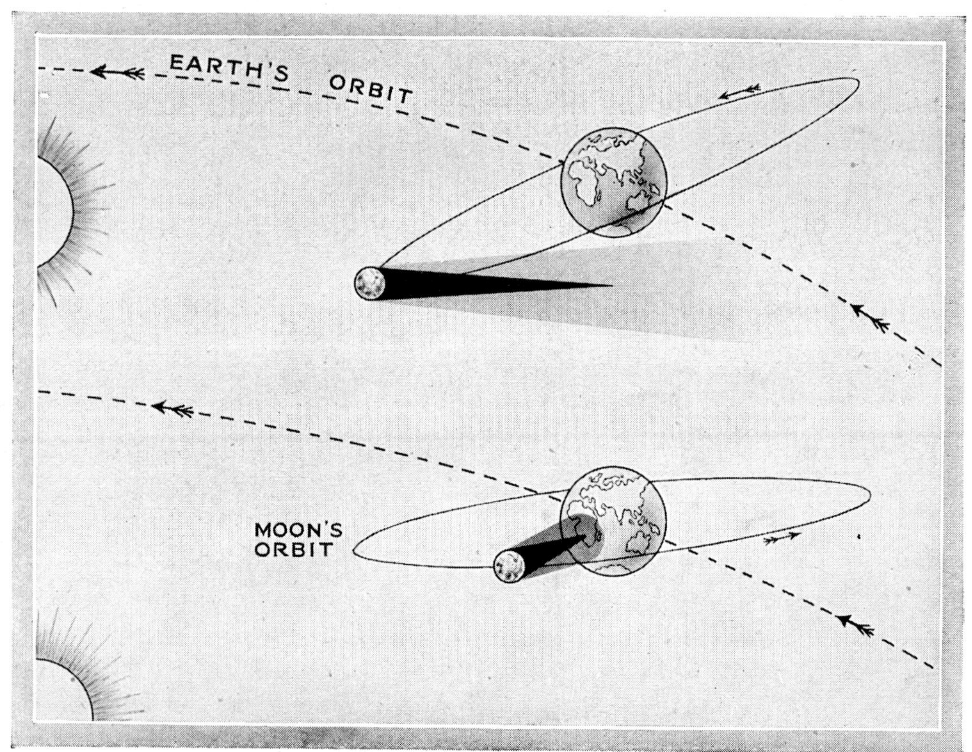

Ellison Hawks.

WHY A SOLAR ECLIPSE DOES NOT OCCUR EVERY MONTH

Solar eclipses are caused by the Moon passing between the Earth and the Sun. There is a time in each month when our satellite comes between us and the Sun, but this diagram makes it plain why a solar eclipse does not occur every month. The upper drawing shows that the shadow cast by the moon can miss the Earth altogether ; the lower drawing shows one of the comparatively rare cases when the shadow strikes our planet.

BAILY'S BEADS

BAILEY'S BEADS AS SEEN WITH THE NAKED EYE

BAILEY'S BEADS (HIGHLY MAGNIFIED) ARE CAUSED BY SUNLIGHT PIERCING THE LUNAR VALLEYS

IMAGES OF THE ECLIPSE PROJECTED UPON THE GROUND.
THE INTERSTICES BETWEEN THE LEAVES ACT AS A SORT OF PINHOLE CAMERA

During a total solar eclipse, when the Moon comes between us and the Sun, we see that the edge of our satellite is uneven. This rugged appearance is caused by the mountain ranges of the Moon appearing in profile. Sunlight coming through the mountain valleys causes the interesting phenomena known as " Baily's Beads." Below is seen a remarkable phenomenon that occurs during a total eclipse. The fact that the edge of the Moon shows so clearly when outlined against the Sun is proof that the Moon has no atmosphere. If there were air on the Moon its outline would be obscured by a bright halo due to the reflection of the Sun's rays. For the same reason, stars which pass behind the Moon disappear quite suddenly, whereas if the Moon had an atmosphere they would gradually fade from view.

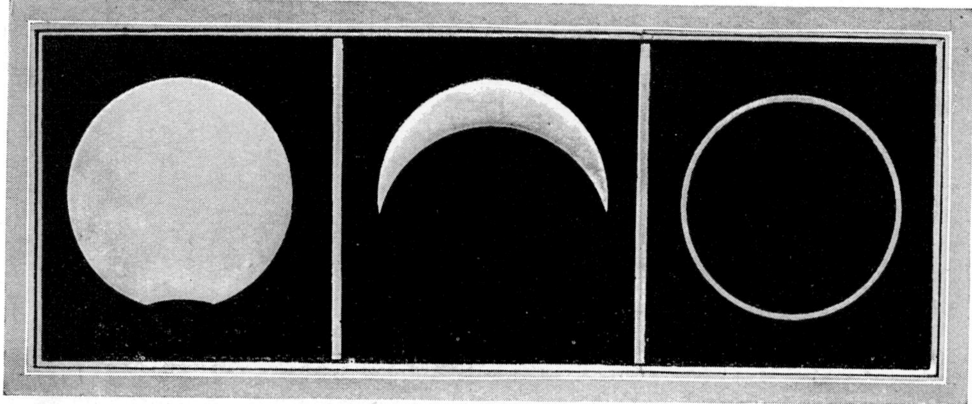

THREE FORMS OF SOLAR ECLIPSE

This diagram shows three different forms of eclipse, the first a small partial ; the second a large partial ; and the third an " annular." In this latter type of eclipse, the whole orb of the Sun is obscured except a narrow ring, for which the Latin name is " *annulus*." From this word is derived the name " annular." A " total " eclipse is shown on the opposite page.

ECLIPSES OF THE MOON

AN eclipse of the Moon is caused by our satellite passing through the Earth's shadow. This shadow stretches into space for some 859,000 miles, the length varying according to the distance of the Earth from the Sun. Although the Moon revolves around the Earth every month, it does not always enter the shadow, but may pass above or below it.

It is only when the Moon is in line, or nearly in line, with the centre of the Earth and the centre of the Sun that an eclipse can take place, and this seldom happens more than twice a year. There may be one or even two eclipses each year, or on the other hand there may be none. It is a very rare occurrence if there are three eclipses in one year, but this will occur in 1985, when all the eclipses will be total.

If we examine a shadow we notice that it consists of shadows of two kinds. The central dark part, called the umbra, is surrounded by a half shadow, called the penumbra, a word that comes from the Latin *pene*, " almost," and *umbra*, " a shade."

In the same way, the Earth's shadow is dived into umbra and penumbra. Sometimes the Moon does not enter the umbra, but passes only through the penumbra, resulting in what is called a penumbral eclipse. On other occasions the Moon only partly enters the umbra, passing to the north or south of its centre, when the eclipse is said to be partial. Partial eclipses are much more common than total ones.

The Earth's Shadow

The shadow cast by the Earth in space is cone-shaped. The duration of an eclipse varies according to the particular part of the shadow cone the Moon is passing through, depending on its distance from the Earth at the time of the eclipse. The Moon may remain totally eclipsed for about an hour and forty minutes whilst it passes through the shadow. It generally takes about two hours for the Moon to pass through the penumbra before entering and after leaving the umbra.

Whilst in the umbra the Moon does not entirely disappear, because the Earth's atmosphere refracts a certain amount of sunlight, bending the rays inwards towards the Moon and causing it to be fairly illuminated. The degree of this illumination varies according to the amount of light transmitted through our atmosphere, and this causes

Associated Press.

PROGRESS OF AN ECLIPSE OF THE SUN

A series of photographs taken at ten-minute intervals showing the passage of the Moon across the face of the Sun. At the bottom right-hand corner the Moon has already covered three-quarters of the Sun's disc. Ten minutes later only a crescent of the Sun remains visible. The next picture shows the Sun totally eclipsed, after which the Moon withdraws again from the face of the Sun.

the eclipsed Moon to have different appearances. Sometimes it is seen to be dull grey, whilst at others it is of a beautiful copper colour.

During an eclipse of the Moon it is interesting to see that the shadow of the Earth, as it creeps across the Moon, is distinctly curved. This was noticed even by ancient astronomers, two of whom—Manilius and Cleomedes, who lived some two thousand years ago—mentioned the fact to prove that the Earth was round. In those days, of course, telescopes were not known, and from this observation we can realise how keen must have been

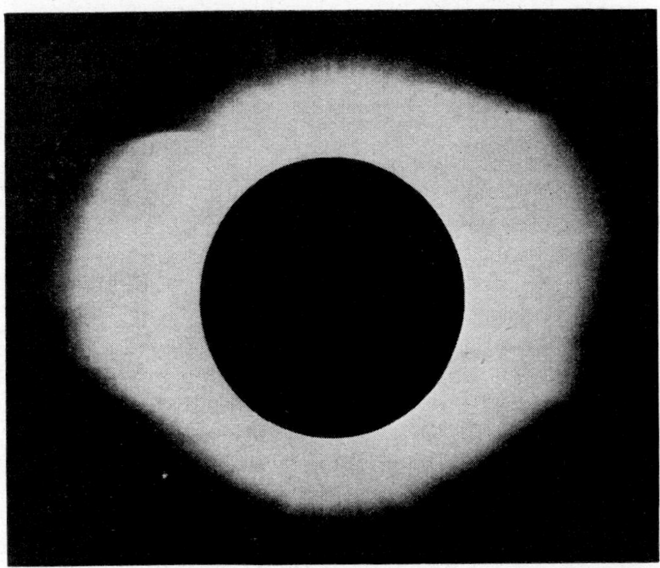

Planet News.

THE SUN'S CORONA

This is how the total eclipse of the Sun of 1954 appeared to observers in Sweden. The bright area of rarefied gases surrounding the Sun is known as the " corona," and it varies greatly in form.

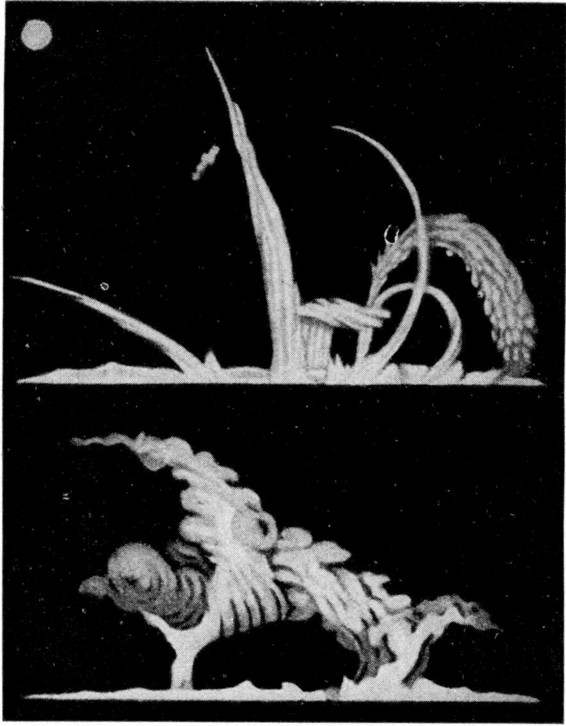

Ellison Hawks.

FANTASTIC FIRE CLOUDS

The upper picture looks like some strange plant and the lower resembles a very queer bird. Actually these are solar "prominences" or red flames observed during the eclipse of 1872. The "prominences" in the lower drawing stretched outwards to a distance of 70,000 miles, whilst those in the upper drawing extended 90,000 miles.

the sight of the ancient astronomers, and also the close attention they paid to detail.

Named by Chaldeans

The Chaldean astronomers discovered that eclipses repeat themselves in the same order after an interval of eighteen years, eleven days, eight hours. In this period, which the Chaldeans named the Saros, there occur twenty-nine eclipses of the Moon and forty-one eclipses of the Sun. The fact that eclipses repeat themselves enables us to say, for instance, that the eclipse of 1932 was a return of the eclipses of 1914, 1896, 1878, 1860, 1842, and so on. We can also predict that this particular eclipse will occur again in certain years.

The ancient astronomers watched and carefully recorded eclipses of the Moon. As in the case of the earliest record of a solar eclipse, the earliest record of the lunar eclipse was made by the Chinese. It relates to an eclipse that took place in 1136 B.C. Many records of lunar eclipses were left by Ptolemy and other ancient writers, but these eclipses are of little or no historical importance.

That knowledge of Astronomy may be of practical use was demonstrated by Columbus. In 1504 when at Jamaica, he had trouble with the natives who had refused to supply him with food. By predicting an eclipse of the Moon, Columbus gained a great reputation as a prophet. Commanding the respect that is accorded by natives to persons whom they believe to possess supernatural powers, he quickly found that the natives would obey him and he had no further difficulty in obtaining the supplies he required.

THE MOON, THE EARTH'S COMPANION

THE Moon is the Earth's satellite, a word that comes from the Latin *satelles*, meaning "an attendant." The moon is so named because it is the Earth's attendant in space. It revolves around the Earth in the same way that the Earth revolves around the Sun; and it is held in place by the same force that holds the Earth in its orbit—gravity. The Moon revolves around the Earth in a month, and, indeed, this is how the term "month" came to be used.

The diameter of the Moon is about 2,160 miles, so that it is rather more than a quarter of the diameter of the Earth. Its distance varies, and although at certain times it is nearer than at others, its mean distance from the Earth is about 239,000 miles. It

A TOTAL ECLIPSE OF THE SUN

This is a photograph of the total eclipse of the Sun taken at Alor Star on May 9th, 1929, at the moment of total eclipse. It clearly shows the corona—that is, the atmosphere of flaming gas surrounding the Sun, which extends outwards in great waves for thousands of miles. The wonderful " prominence," or crimson flame of hydrogen gas, seen at the top of the photograph is calculated to have been 180,000 miles long and 120,000 miles high. The corona can only be seen when the Sun is totally eclipsed.

THE SURFACE OF THE SUN

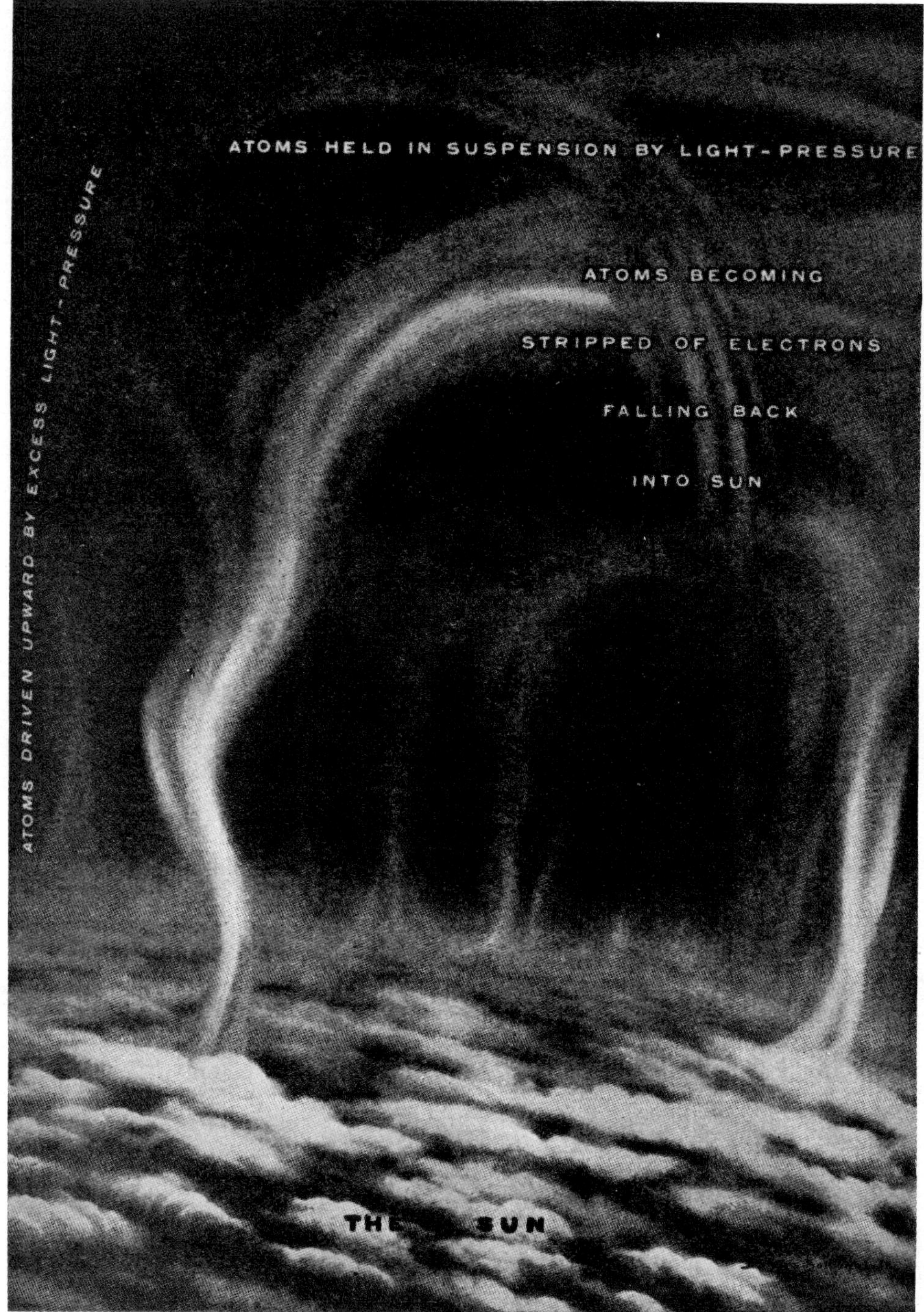

This drawing gives us some idea of what we might expect to see if we could get a "close-up" view of the Sun. From the incandescent masses of hydrogen, helium, sodium and calcium, atoms are driven up an enormous height by the pressure of light. The atoms rise until the pressure of light and the effect of gravity balance one another. In that neutral area the atoms remain until "ionised," or stripped of their electrons, and fall back into the Sun.

How different is the cold, solid surface of the Moon from the raging hot surface of the Sun, pictured opposite ! The mountains in the centre at the lower part of the photograph are the lunar Alps. The peculiar streak marked X is a great valley which may have been due to the fall of a huge meteorite that crashed through this mountain range, clearing all before it.

THE YOUNG MOON

The Moon, as we know, is dead, and has neither air nor water on its surface. This is a photograph of the Moon a few days old, and as it is taken with a telescope it is " upside down " as compared with the naked-eye view.

may recede to about 253,000 miles or approach to within 221,000 miles. If we were able to lay a railway from the Earth to the Moon, and to set off an express train, it would take the train over six months to reach its destination travelling day and night.

The changes in the appearance of the Moon from " new " to " full " troubled people in bygone times. Even to-day there are tens of thousands of educated people who could not give a correct explanation of the " phases," as they are called. The Babylonians thought that the Moon had a dark and a bright side, and that throughout the month she turned more and more of the bright side towards the Earth until at last the whole of it was seen.

Aristotle was the first to give the correct solution of the phases, which are due simply to the different positions from which we view the illuminated portion of the Moon's surface, during the time she is moving round the Earth.

The Moon's Phases

Like the Earth, the Moon is a dark body and is composed of similar materials to those that constitute the Earth. She does not possess any illuminating powers of her own, but shines only by reflected light from the Sun. On a clear night when we see the silvery Moon, it is difficult to believe that this is the case. We have only to remember, however, that at the time of a lunar eclipse, when the Moon passes through the Earth's shadow, the Moon no longer presents a bright disc, for then the sunlight is cut off.

When the Moon passes between the Earth and the Sun it is invisible, as all the sunlight falls on the part of her surface that is turned away from us. As she moves round her orbit, however,

ON THE WANE

In this photograph the Moon is just past " full "—that is, when the Sun's light illumines the whole of the side that is turned towards the Earth. Our telescopes tell us much about the surface of our satellite—we even know the height of the lunar mountains.

A MOUNTAIN OF THE MOON

This is a picture of one of the greatest lunar craters called Copernicus. The whole surface of the Moon is covered with thousands of craters, some of enormous size. If you stood on the rim of Copernicus you would look down over sheer cliffs thousands of feet high into a vast walled plain.

part of her surface that is visible to us becomes illuminated, and is seen as a crescent "new" Moon. Night by night this illuminated part increases until we get "half" moon. At the time of "full" moon the Earth is in line between the Sun and the Moon, and the whole of that hemisphere turned towards us is illuminated.

The Crater-rings in the Moon

The Moon is perhaps the most interesting of all the heavenly bodies; even in a small telescope with the naked eye we can see certain dark markings, and these have been likened to faces, figures, and animals. The "Man in the Moon," and the ancient legend that he was put there for gathering sticks on a Sunday, is familiar to everyone. The dusky markings that help to form such pictures were supposed by the ancients to be a reflection of the Earth's markings, for they imagined that the Moon was a great mirror hanging in the heavens.

Galileo saw that the markings were due to actual features on the surface of the Moon. Although he came to the conclusion that the markings must be seas, we now know that there is neither air nor water on the Moon. Perhaps these markings may be the beds of ancient seas, but to-day they are bare plains without water or vegetation.

Even with a pair of field glasses we can see numerous circular objects scattered over the Moon's surface. With the telescope these are seen to be crater-rings, of which there are many thousands. Each has its name, for the surface of the Moon has been so carefully mapped that we know its details better than we know those of some parts of the Earth. Altogether some 30,000 craters have been mapped, but this number forms only a small part of the whole, it having been estimated that there are something like 200,000 craters to be seen. In observing these crater-rings we must remember that we are obtaining a bird's-eye view of the Moon. If we imagine that we are hovering over the Moon in an aeroplane, and looking down upon its surface, we can understand more clearly what we see.

Sunrise in the Lunar Mountains

Most of the lunar craters have been carefully measured and many are found to be of huge size. One, for instance, named Ptolemæus is 115 miles across; another, Plato, is sixty miles across. A walled plain named Schickard has a diameter of 133 miles, while Grimaldi and Clavius are even larger, being 138 and 142 miles in diameter respectively.

In comparison with the size of the Moon the heights of the lunar mountains are relatively far greater than are the mountains of the Earth. For instance, the height of the Döerfel Mountains is 26,691 feet, which compares with the 29,000 feet, the height of the highest peak in the Himalayas. There are at least thirty-nine mountains each higher than Mont Blanc, the height of which (15,780 feet) is in several cases easily surpassed.

The Moon has been called a "dead world," but mysterious things happen on it. On the floor of one crater small grey patches which slowly move about have been observed, and in the centre of another a black dot—which may be a hole—sometimes appears. Altogether about twenty such unsolved mysteries are known.

One of the finest sights that can be seen through a telescope is to watch the sunrise on the lunar mountains. One can observe the light gradually spreading down the peaks into the valleys. Little by little they are illumined, until at length—at the time of full moon—the whole surface is bathed in sunlight.

IF YOU STOOD ON THE MOON

Here we have an artist's conception of the lunar scenery. There is no trace of vegetation as we know it on this dead world, and except possibly in the deepest valleys there is no atmosphere. During the lunar day, which is a month long, the temperature of the rocks rises to that of boiling water, while throughout the long night they are twice as cold as it is at the North Pole.

PLANETS, COMETS AND METEORS

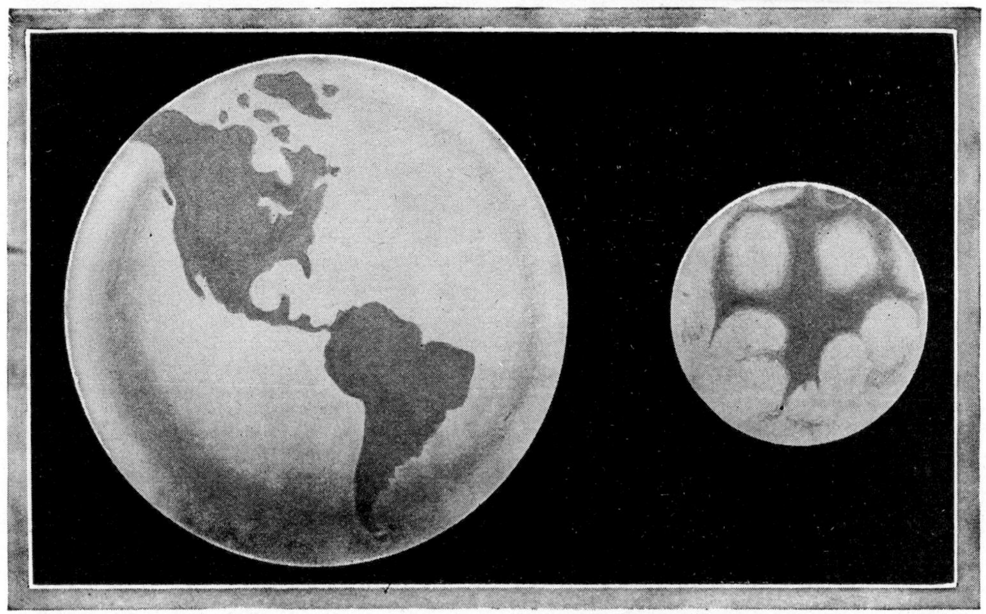

COMPARATIVE SIZES OF THE EARTH AND MARS

Mars is 4,215 miles in diameter, and is therefore approximately half the diameter of the Earth. It rotates on its axis in 24 hours 37 minutes and completes a revolution of the sun in 687 days. Its year is thus equal to nearly two of ours.

NOT only is Mercury the smallest planet but, so far as we know, it is the nearest planet to the Sun, receiving from it the greatest amount of light and heat. A hundred years ago astronomers believed that there might be another planet nearer to the Sun than Mercury, and in 1859 one of them stated that he had actually observed an object that he thought was this new planet. To it the name Vulcan was given, but, although observers once kept a keen look-out for it, no such planet has ever been seen and astronomers no longer believe it exists.

Nevertheless, a new planet *has* been discovered within the last fifty years. Until 1930 the number of known planets was eight, but in that year an astronomer at Lowell Observatory in the U.S.A. discovered one at a greater distance from the Sun than any of the others. It was not seen through a telescope, but was discovered as a tiny white dot on photographs taken of a certain part of the sky on different nights. The dot was known to be a planet because it changed its position in relation to the surrounding stars on each successive photograph. The new planet, which is only about one-tenth the size of the earth, was named Pluto.

The Greeks and Mercury

Mercury is a somewhat difficult object to see with the naked eye for two reasons—it is so small and it is so near to the Sun. The best time to look for it is either just before sunrise in September or October or just after sunset in March or April. At those times it is at a point in its orbit when we see it at its greatest distance from the Sun.

In spite of the fact that it is so difficult to observe, Mercury was well-known to the ancients. There is a record of its observation in 264 B.C., but even before this the astronomers of Nineveh allude to Mercury in a report that they made to Ashurbanipal, King of Assyria.

The Greeks did not know that Mercury could be seen either in the evening sky or in the morning sky, according to its position in its orbit. They thought that the two appearances were those of different planets and so they had two names for it—" Apollo," when it was a morning star, and " Mercury " when seen in the evening. Although Copernicus knew of the existence of Mercury it is said that he never actually saw it.

In the telescope Mercury is not a very interesting object, for it is practically devoid of markings. We know, however, that it has no atmosphere, and that water cannot exist on the surface which faces the Sun because the temperature there is far above the melting-point of lead.

There is reason to believe that Mercury always turns the same face towards the Sun, just as the Moon does towards the Earth, and if so, the dark side of Mercury is probably so cold that water could exist there as ice, though this seems unlikely. Its mean distance from the Sun is about 39,950,000 miles, but it has a very eccentric orbit and at times may be 7,400,000 miles nearer or further away. It revolves around the Sun in eighty-eight days and has a diameter of about 3,100 miles.

Phases of Mercury and Venus

We must mention that in a telescope both Mercury and Venus show phases exactly as the Moon does. They may be seen as crescents or at quarter, half, or full, and their phases depend entirely on the position of the planets in their orbits in regard to the Sun and the Earth.

When either Mercury or Venus is passing on our side of the Sun, and when the Earth, the planet, and the Sun are in line, the planet is said to be in " inferior conjunction." This situation is like that of a New Moon, and

THE SMALLEST PLANET

Mercury is a planet of which we know very little. In the first place it is the nearest to the Sun of all the family of planets; in the second it is very small, and in the third it is never above the horizon for more than two hours after sunset, or the same time before sunrise, and is therefore very difficult to observe. It shines with a rose-coloured light, has no markings and no moon. Here we see it crossing the disc of the Sun, or " in transit " as it is called.

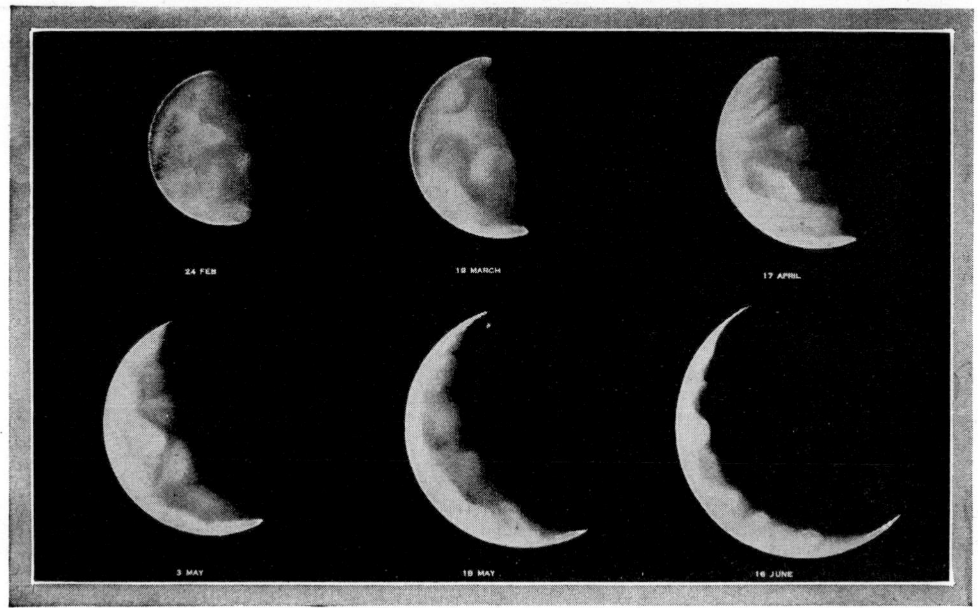

THE PHASES OF VENUS

While the Moon passes through its phases from " new " to " full " in 28 days, Venus passes through her phases much more slowly. A study of the dates printed under these drawings gives proof of this. The spectroscope shows us that the cloud surface of Venus rotates once in 20 days, but the clouds are very deep and it is possible that the planet itself revolves more rapidly.

occasionally the planet can be seen as a tiny black dot crossing the face of the Sun. Such transits, as they are called, are very rare, the planets usually passing just below or just above the Sun's disc.

Transits of Venus

Transits of Venus are more rare than those of Mercury, and they are of greater importance. In 1679 Halley pointed out that observations of the transits of 1761 and 1769 could be used to calculate the distance of the Sun. The transit of 1761 was observed from different parts of the world, but certain discrepancies in the observations caused the results to be unsatisfactory. The observations of the 1769 transit were of great value, however, the event being observed by several expeditions one of which was despatched by George the Third at his own expense to Haiti. The next transit of Venus will not take place until the year 2004.

When the planet is on the further side of the Sun, however, and in line with the Sun and the Earth, it is said to be in " superior conjunction." It is now fully illuminated (like a Full Moon), and while it may not be seen when it is actually behind the Sun, it appears " full " both before it is hidden and after it reappears.

VENUS—THE EARTH'S " SISTER PLANET "

VENUS is very different from Mercury in many ways. At times she is so brilliant that she may be seen by daylight, whilst when darkness falls she attracts the attention of everyone. When Venus appears in the evening sky after sunset she is sometimes called " the evening star." Should it so happen that she appears near Christmas time, there are generally " letters to the newspapers " from people who think they have seen the star of Bethlehem again!

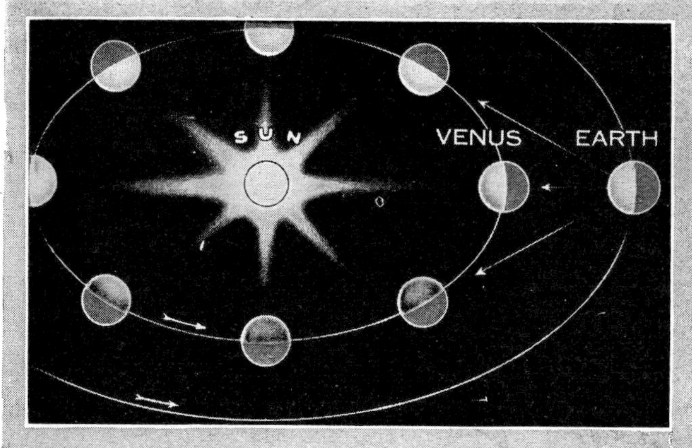

WHEN VENUS COMES NEAREST

Venus travels round the Sun at a distance of about 67 million miles, and at times its course brings it within 40 million miles of the Earth. Unfortunately when at its nearest point the planet turns its dark hemisphere towards us, so that we can see nothing of it.

The Greeks Knew Venus

Venus was known and admired in the earliest times and is supposed to be the " Mazzaroth " mentioned in the Book of Job. As in the case of Mercury, the Greeks had two names for Venus—" Phosphorus " for the morning star and " Hesperus " for the evening star. Pythagoras was the first to point out that the morning and evening appearances were not due to two planets but to the same planet in different positions in its orbit.

As we have already mentioned when dealing with Mercury, Venus shows herself in phases. Galileo was the first to discover these phases and announced his discovery in an anagram to his friend Kepler.

An anagram is a rearrangement of the letters in a given sentence. In those days this was a popular method of announcing discoveries, for after publication it allowed a certain amount of leisure in which the discovery might be verified before the clue to the interpretation was given. Should anyone else make the same discovery in the meantime it only became necessary for the original discoverer to translate his anagram to show that he was first in the field. Thus it came about that Galileo published this peculiar sentence in Latin: *Hæc immatura a me iam frustra leguntur: o.y.* Some months later by moving the letters to their correct places he gave the solution, which was: *Cynthiæ figuras æmulatur Mater Amorum*, meaning " Venus imitates the phases of the Moon."

Rotation Period

In the telescope, Venus is somewhat disappointing, for her great brilliance makes the detection of markings a somewhat difficult matter. Faint and badly defined spots and shadings have been seen, however, though their vagueness makes it difficult for us to learn how long Venus takes to rotate on her axis. It seems likely that the period is about two of our days, though it may be as long as a month.

Venus has a deep atmosphere which does not, however, consist of air. It is rich in carbon dioxide and probably contains nitrogen, but it is devoid of oxygen. No water-vapour has ever been detected on Venus, though there may be some liquid water on the surface of the planet. This is unfortunately concealed from view by the enormous clouds of dust which fill the atmosphere. It seems very unlikely that there is any life on Venus, though it is not impossible. If there *were* inhabitants of Venus they would see the Earth as a planet far brighter than Venus appears to us. They would see, too, our Moon close to the Earth and performing her monthly revolution—a beautiful and interesting spectacle.

The distance of Venus from the Sun is about 67,000,000 miles, and she receives almost double the amount of heat and light that the Earth does. She revolves around the Sun in 225 days, or nearly 7½ months, and her diameter is about 7,700 miles. She is therefore only a little less in size than the Earth, and for this reason is sometimes spoken of as being the Earth's "sister planet."

MARS, THE "RUDDY PLANET"

MARS, the fourth planet in order of distance from the Sun, is 4,215 miles in diameter. It completes a revolution of the Sun in 687 days, and rotates on its axis in twenty-four hours thirty-seven minutes. Consequently the seasons on Mars are about twice as long as on the Earth, but day and night on the planet are only a little longer.

Although Galileo examined Mars with his telescope he was unable to discover anything of importance. A Dutch astronomer named Huyghens who lived in the seventeenth century, was more fortunate, however, and saw dark markings. Since that time Mars has been closely studied by many astronomers, and so complete a knowledge has been gained of the planet's surface markings that maps and even globes have been constructed with each Martian feature depicted and named thereon.

The Polar Cap of Mars

Even to the naked eye Mars appears to shine with a ruddy hue, and the telescope shows that this is due to the fact that as a whole the planet is orange-coloured. It is as though we were looking at a great area of golden sand, and this is believed to be actually the case. At the poles there are patches of brilliant white, which do not remain of a uniform size. They increase as spring advances on the planet, and decrease until by the end of the Martian summer they have

A RARE AND BEAUTIFUL SIGHT

On March 14th, 1929, a sight of great interest to astronomers was seen in the western sky. Venus, Jupiter and Mars were all in conjunction with the Moon. Venus was at her brightest, shining with silvery brilliance. Jupiter, larger but less brilliant, had a primrose hue, while Mars, higher in the sky, shone with its familiar ruddy colour. The first magnitude star Aldebaran and the wonderful group the Pleiades were below Mars.

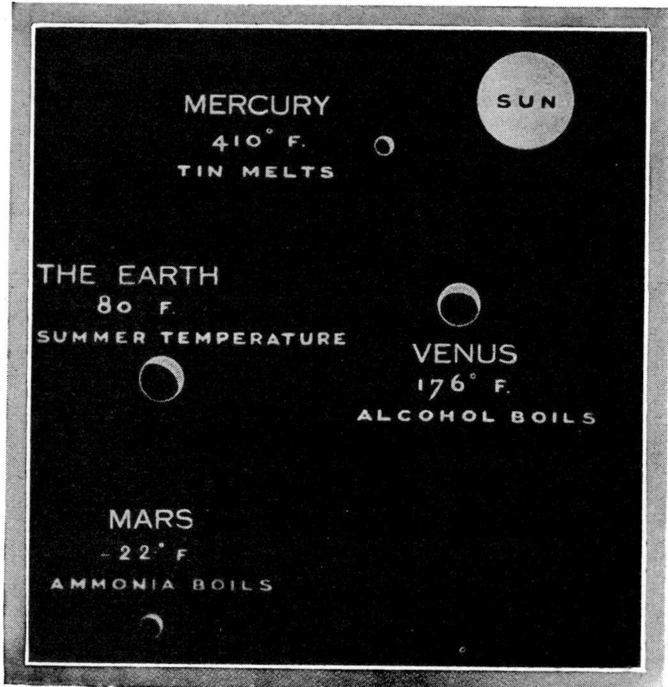

OUR NEIGHBOURS

This diagram suggests that the Earth may be the only planet on which life as we know it is likely to exist. Mercury and Venus are too hot, while Mars, with an average temperature of 10° below freezing point, is too cold. In the case of Venus, of course, these conditions may be mitigated to a certain extent by the envelope of clouds.

almost disappeared. These polar caps may be vast fields of hoar frost, an inch or two thick, surrounding the polar regions of Mars and corresponding with the Arctic and Antarctic regions on the Earth.

We have already mentioned certain dark markings, and at one time these were thought to be oceans or seas. It is now certain that they are not water, however, but they are probably areas of vegetation, which spring into life when the water from the melting polar caps reaches them.

Canals on Mars

In 1877 Schiaparelli of Milan announced that he had discovered a network of fine lines, some of which extended for hundreds of miles across the planet's surface. Although he called these lines "canals," Schiaparelli had no thought that they might be canals in the strict sense of the word—that is to say, artificial waterways made by intelligent beings. The peculiar markings have been seen by many other observers, and some have noticed that at places where they cross each other there are generally dark round spots, which are called "oases."

The late Professor Lowell, who erected an observatory in Arizona specially to study Mars, advanced a theory that the "canals" are actually artificial waterways constructed by the inhabitants of Mars. He pointed out that Mars has a very thin atmosphere and that clouds are rarely seen.

The absence of clouds means that there would be no rain, and no rain means no rivers. The question of water supply on Mars therefore is a very different thing from what it is on the Earth. If there is intelligent life there, Lowell argued, it is reasonable to suppose that the inhabitants exist on the produce of the land. Now, the only water available on the planet is locked up in the ice and snow of the polar caps. When the Martian summer advances and the ice and snow melts, the inhabitants bring the water from the polar regions to the desert areas by means of the canals that they have constructed.

The dark spots at the junction of the canals were believed by Lowell to be centres of habitation, their dark appearance being caused by the growth of vegetation watered by the canals. It is no longer believed that Lowell was right, though the true nature of many of the canals remains a mystery. It is known that some of them are optical illusions, however, and that many of the others are by no means as straight as they appear in small telescopes.

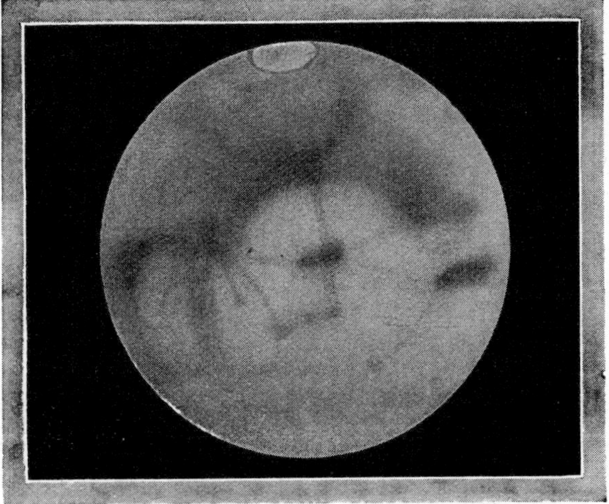

MARS THROUGH THE TELESCOPE

This is Mars seen through a fairly powerful telescope on October 12th, 1909. The white marking on the top of the disc is the South Polar Cap. Some of the so-called canals can also be seen. At the centre is an oasis named *Solis lacus*, or "Lake of the Sun."

The Satellites of Mars

Mars has two small satellites named Deimos and Phobos, which are the mythological names of the horses that drew the chariot of Mars. These two moons are very small, Deimos being only about 10 and Phobos about 35 miles in diameter. Their orbits are comparatively close to Mars, that of Deimos being 14,600 miles, and Phobos 5,826 miles distant from the planet. Deimos completes a revolution of Mars in 30 hours 18 minutes, whilst Phobos moves more rapidly, requiring only 7 hours and 39 minutes to complete a revolution.

In the case of Phobos, we have a curious state of affairs, for the satellite revolves around Mars in less time than it takes the planet to complete a revolution on its axis. As we have already seen, Mars requires 24 hours 37 minutes to complete one revolution, so that Phobos revolves around it more than three times in one Martian day! As it travels more quickly than the planet rotates, it will not rise in the east and set in the west as our Moon does but will rise in the west and cross the heavens 2½ times in a Martian day, setting each time in the east!

THE MINOR PLANETS

MERCURY, Venus, the Earth and Mars are sometimes called the "inferior planets," and the four planets beyond Mars—about which we shall read later—are called the "superior planets." The ancients knew only six planets; Uranus was not discovered until 1781, Neptune in 1846, and Pluto in 1930.

A Curious "Law" of Progression

Between the orbits of Mars and Jupiter is a space in which there are a large number of interesting little bodies—the Asteroids, or "star-like" planets. The discovery of these asteroids came about in a remarkable manner. In 1766, a German of Wittenberg named Titius noticed that a curious relationship existed between certain figures and the distances of the planets from the Sun. Another German, Bode, of Berlin, got hold of this and published it as his own discovery in 1772, and it has come to be called "Bode's Law." If we write down certain figures of which each but the first and second is double that of the number preceding it, we get:

0, 3, 6, 12, 24, 48, 96, 192, 384;

adding 4 to each number gives:

4, 7, 10, 16, 28, 52, 100, 196, 388.

It is strange to find that these latter numbers represent fairly accurately the distances of the planets from the Sun, expressed in ratio of the Earth's orbit. This is shown more clearly by the following table:

Planet.	True Distance from the Sun.	Distance as shown by "Bode's Law."
*Mercury	3·87	4
*Venus	7·23	7
*Earth	10·00	10
*Mars	15·23	16
Asteroids	27·66	28
*Jupiter	52·03	52
*Saturn	95·39	100
Uranus	191·83	196
Neptune	300·37	388

At the time Bode made his interesting discovery, only the planets marked * in the above table were known, but the discovery of Uranus in 1781, at a distance that corresponded to that shown by the "law," greatly strengthened belief in it. The blank between the orbits of Mars and Jupiter was noticed, and as Kepler had predicted that some small planets would be found in this zone, astronomers began seriously to consider the matter. In 1800, Baron von Zach called a conference at Lilienthal and each astronomer present agreed to combine with others in examining the sky, in the attempt to discover these small planets that were believed to exist. The astronomers named themselves the "celestial police," and they "patrolled their beats" each night with the aid of their telescopes.

The "Celestial Police" make Discoveries

At Palermo, in Sicily, is an observatory, the director of which at the time was Piazzi. He had actually been appointed one of the "celestial police," but he did not know the arrangements that had been made in this connection by the conference. Piazzi was engaged in making a catalogue of stars, and on the first night of the nineteenth century (January 1st, 1801) he charted the position of what he took to be a star. On several evenings he noted this object, but, much to his surprise, he saw that it was moving among the stars. At first he thought that the new body was a comet, but soon it became evident to him that a new planet had been found. When his observations were completed it was seen that this new planet revolved in an orbit that lay between Mars and Jupiter, and it therefore filled the blank space where—according to Bode—a planet should be found.

The new planet was named Ceres, after the patron goddess of Sicily. Although a very small object—it is only about 447 miles in diameter—it fulfilled the necessary conditions and once more the Solar System was regarded as being complete.

Ellison Hawks.

FROST OR SNOW AT THE POLES OF MARS

Here we see the South Polar cap, surrounded by a dark ring of moisture from the melting crown.

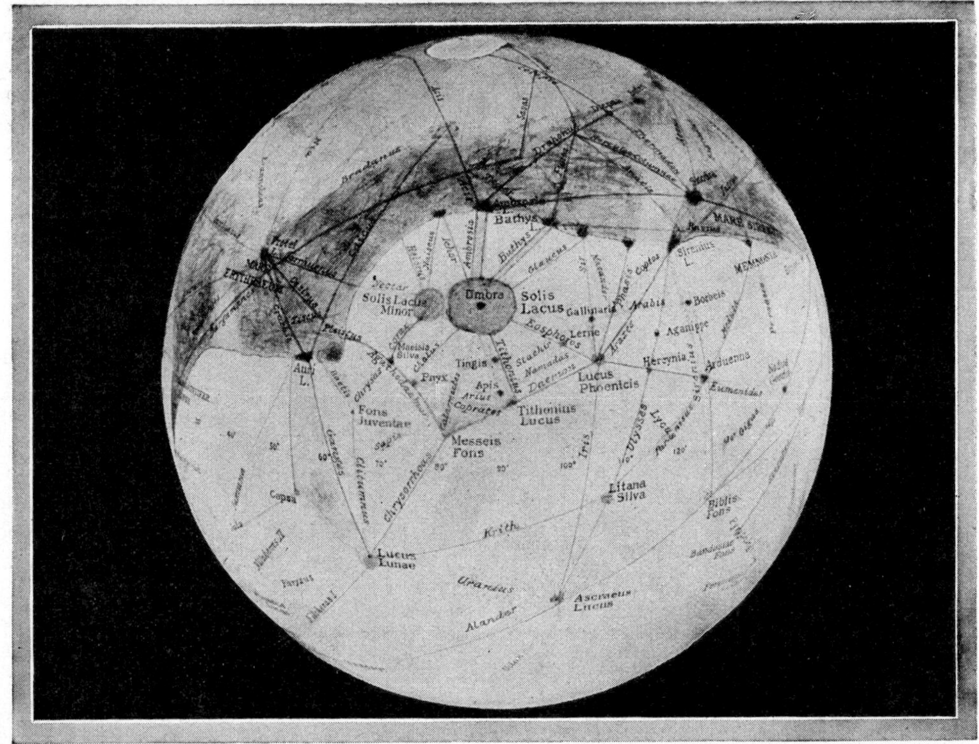

Ellison Hawks.

THE "CANALS" OF MARS

Some observers of Mars have claimed that the surface of the planet is covered with long straight lines which they have called "canals." There is some doubt about the existence of these, but there are many reasons why they cannot be water-channels irrigating the planet, as some have held. This is a photograph of a globe of Mars made by M. Wicks.

Shortly afterwards, however, Olbers, a German astronomer and another member of the "celestial police," discovered (in 1802) another small object. This turned out to be a second planet, and to it the name of Pallas was given. The discovery of this second planet caused much astonishment in the scientific world, and many theories were put forward to account for the two tiny planets. The "celestial police" became more enthusiastic than ever, thinking—doubtless—that if there were two of these tiny planets, there might easily be more. They "patrolled" the heavens more keenly than ever, and it was not long before their vigilance was rewarded, for two more planets were discovered—one in 1804 and the other in 1807.

It was suggested that these four planets were fragments of some larger planet that had at some remote date been blown to pieces. For many years this theory held the field, and although at one time it was supposed to be impossible, it has been revived in recent years, as we shall mention later.

The Amazing Number of Asteroids

Although the search was still carried on after the discovery of the fourth planet, it was abandoned in 1816, for no more discoveries had been made. Fourteen years later, however, a German amateur commenced a search, which he continued for fifteen years, when his patience was rewarded by the discovery (in 1845) of a fifth planet. Eighteen months later he found another, and two more were found in the same year (1847) by an English astronomer. Since that time there has been a continual record of discoveries, not a year having passed without from one to a hundred having been discovered. Now, well over 1,000 of these minor planets have been recorded and their orbits calculated.

The Importance of Eros

Of all the hundreds of asteroids, the most important and interesting is the one named Eros, which was discovered in 1898, and is probably only about 15 miles in diameter. Its special interest is due to the fact that the greater part of its orbit lies within that of Mars. At certain favourable times—once every thirty-seven years—it comes as close as within 13,840,000 miles of the Earth. With the exception of the Moon, therefore, Eros comes nearer to us than any other heavenly body.

JUPITER, THE GIANT PLANET

JUPITER is over 86,000 miles in diameter, and is therefore nearly eleven times as large as the Earth. Although in volume the giant planet is equal to about 1,312 Earths, its mass is so small that, were we to weigh it in a pair of huge scales, only 317 Earths would be required to balance it. Jupiter is situated some 483,000,000 miles away from the Sun, and it completes a revolution of the Sun in just under twelve years.

The Cloud Belts

Jupiter is a most fascinating object in the telescope, and even a small instrument will show much of interest. The planet itself is surrounded by a dense atmosphere, but this consists of hydrogen, marsh-gas and ammonia, instead of air! This poisonous atmosphere is packed with layer upon layer of thick clouds, so that we are not able to see below them, but the actual surface of the planet is believed to be covered with ice several thousand miles thick. Its temperature is about 200° *below* freezing.

What we see through a telescope are the clouds, which appear to lie in light and dark belts parallel to the planet's equator. The clouds are in a constant state of change—sometimes only two or three broad belts are to be seen while at others eight, ten, or even twelve narrow belts are visible. The clouds of which they are composed may remain in existence for days, weeks, or even months. As Jupiter rotates on its axis in less than ten hours, there is a constant panorama, as it were, moving before the eyes of the observer.

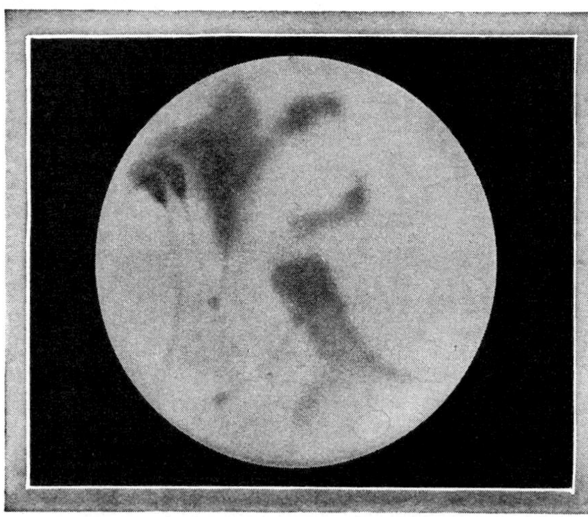

ANOTHER VIEW OF MARS

This drawing of Mars was made on March 30th, 1903. Here you see the North Polar Cap, and the dark markings which are possibly patches of vegetation in the Martian desert.

The Great Red Spot

Although the details of the cloud belts are in a constant state of change, there is one marking that seems to be of a more permanent nature. This is the Great Red Spot, an oval-shaped object to be seen in the southern hemisphere and situated in a kind of bay called the "Hollow."

It is believed that the Red Spot was observed in 1665, since which date it has sometimes faded or even disappeared, but always to re-appear at a later date. It appeared and vanished eight times between 1665 and 1708, after which it remained visible for five years. In 1878 it was described as being of a "full red brick colour," and was measured as being 30,000 miles in length and 7,000 miles in breadth. Four years later its colour began to fade, and since that date it has sometimes been so faint as to be scarcely visible; at other times it has been seen without difficulty even with comparatively small telescopes.

When the Red Spot was first seen it was suggested that it might be the mouth of some huge volcano on the surface of Jupiter, and that this volcano was so high that it reared above the dense envelope of clouds surrounding the planet. This theory was rejected after numerous observations had been made, however, for it was found that the rotation period of the spot changes, so that it must have a motion of its own and cannot therefore be attached to the planet beneath. It has been suggested that perhaps the Spot is a new satellite in the process of formation, but this is no more than a wild guess!

Fox Photos.

ENGLAND'S BIGGEST TELESCOPE

A notable telescope in England is the William Johnson Yapp reflector at Greenwich Observatory. Completed in 1933 at a cost of £15,000, it has a 36-inch mirror and weighs altogether some seven tons. This is the largest telescope that can be usefully employed in this country.

We have mentioned that the rotation period of Jupiter is under 10 hours. As a matter of fact, the different cloud belts have different rotation periods, some travelling faster than others. Generally speaking, the times are between 9 hours 55 minutes and 9 hours 50 minutes, the latter period relating to the clouds in the equatorial zone. These varying rotation periods result in an ever-changing appearance, for the quicker-moving clouds overtake others in another latitude, giving the interested observer plenty of work in charting and recording their movements.

Galileo and the Satellites

We have already mentioned that when (in 1610) Galileo turned his telescope to Jupiter he found the planet to be accompanied by four satellites. Their discovery occurred at a fortunate moment, for it helped to show that the Copernican theory might be correct. Galileo believed that Jupiter and his satellites

Planet News.

HOME OF THE WORLD'S BIGGEST TELESCOPE

The idea and plans for the greatest telescope ever made were put forward by the famous American astronomer, the late Dr. George Hale, and towards its cost £1,500,000 was granted by the Rockefeller Foundation. This photograph shows the exterior of the Hale Observatory at Palomar Mountain.

gave an unmistakable illustration of the Copernican teaching, and that the planet was, as it were, a model of the Solar System.

His contemporaries were not so easily convinced, however, and when Clavius—one of the leading astronomers of the day—was told of the discovery he said he would not believe it until he had seen it himself. When actually he did see it through the telescope, he expressed the opinion that the glass had been bewitched! Another philosopher—more prudent, perhaps, than Clavius and unwilling to be convinced—refused to look through the telescope lest he might really see the satellites! He died shortly after this incident, and Galileo sarcastically remarked: "I hope he saw the satellites whilst on his way to heaven!"

The four satellites discovered by Galileo can be seen with a small telescope—in fact, a pair of good field-glasses will sometimes show them to be present alongside the great planet. Although they have been named—Io, Europa, Ganymede, and Callisto—they are generally referred to by the numbers I., II., III. and IV. Europa is the smallest of the four, being about 2,000 miles in diameter, and Ganymede is the largest, 3,540 miles in diameter.

As in the case of the Earth and all opaque bodies, Jupiter casts a shadow. In the course of their revolutions around Jupiter the satellites sometimes pass through this shadow. When this occurs, they are eclipsed exactly as our Moon is when it passes through the Earth's shadow. The satellites also pass behind Jupiter, when they are said to be "occulted." When they pass in front of his disc they are seen "in transit," and their own tiny shadows are also seen on the cloud belts as little black dots.

In addition to the four Galilean satellites, Jupiter has eight others, making twelve in all, the last being discovered in 1951. Numbers VIII., IX. and XI. are remarkable in that they revolve in an opposite direction to that generally followed by the other satellites (and all the planets) in the Solar System.

A ROOM WITH A VIEW!

Planet News.

This photograph gives another aspect of the Observatory at Palomar Mountain. One of the workers stands on the skeleton tube of the 200-inch telescope during its last stages of completion in 1948. The revolving dome, through the aperture of which the man is looking, runs on rails built on the massive concrete walls well over 60 feet high. It is calculated that it will take many years to chart all the stars which the giant telescope has brought into vision.

SATURN, THE "PLANET WITH THE RINGS"

SATURN is the most beautiful of all the planets—indeed, it may be said that it is the most exquisite object to be seen in the heavens. The planet itself is surrounded by a great system of rings, and nothing like it has been found anywhere else in the universe.

Saturn Puzzles the Ancients

Saturn's rings are invisible to the naked eye, and their existence was unsuspected until Galileo turned his telescope to the planet. Even then their true nature could not be determined, and Galileo wrote to Kepler that: "Saturn has an oblong appearance, somewhat like an olive." Later observers, using imperfect telescopes,

THE GIANT EYE ON PALOMAR MOUNTAIN

Here we have a view of the massive tubular supports forming the electrically-controlled frame to hold the 200-in. telescope at the Hale Observatory, Palomar Mountain, California. At the base of the structure is the mounting for the great concave mirror. By way of contrast an observatory worker can be seen in the space below the giant framework, standing beside a standard 4-inch telescope.

THE GREATEST PLANET

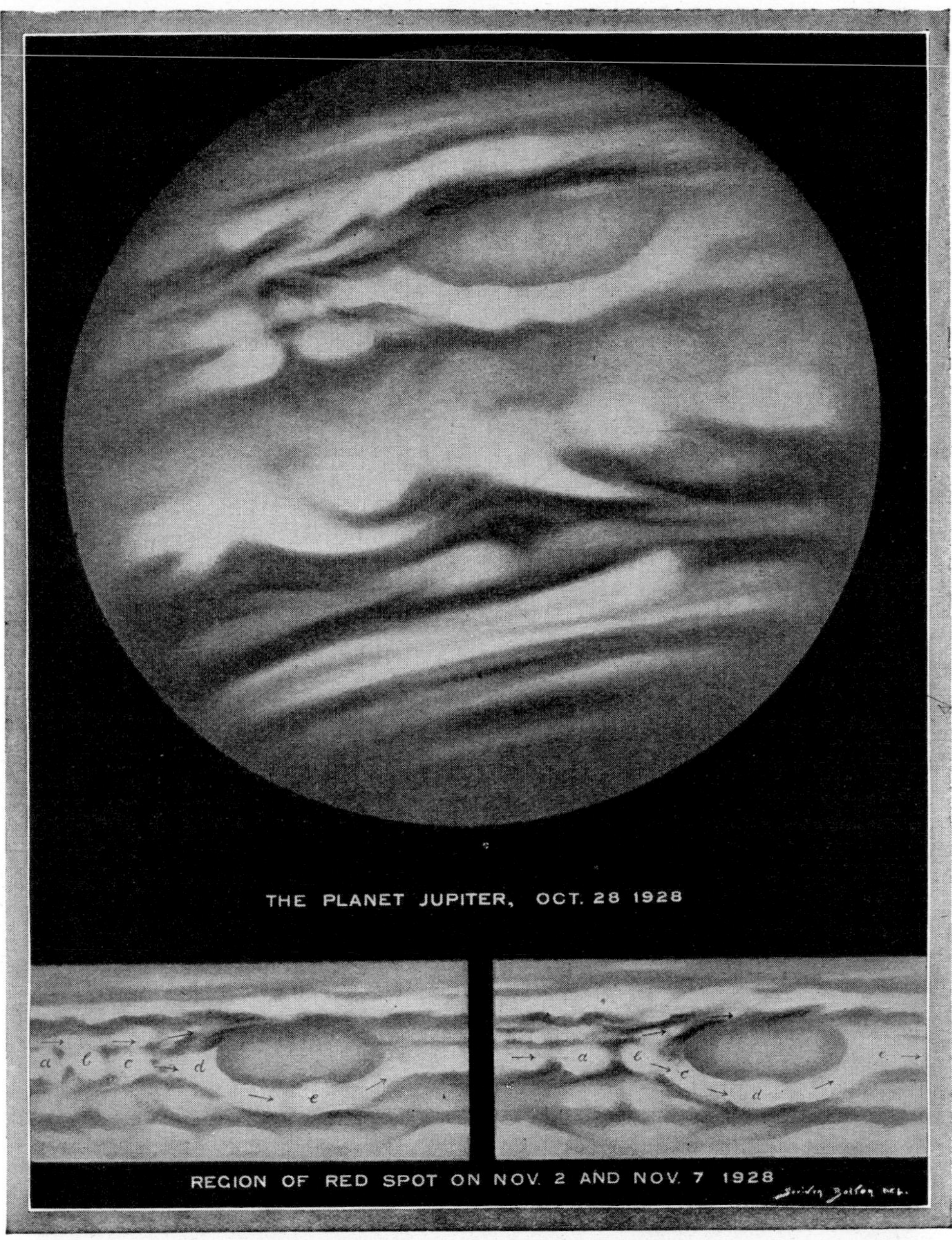

THE PLANET JUPITER, OCT. 28 1928

REGION OF RED SPOT ON NOV. 2 AND NOV. 7 1928

Although its size is 1,300 times that of Earth, the weight of Jupiter is only 300 times that of our planet. This shows that the Giant Planet is still in a nebulous (cloudy) condition, and that millions of years must elapse before it is in a similar condition to that of the Earth to-day. You will notice that Jupiter is flattened at the poles, owing, no doubt, to the speed at which it revolves on its own axis. The puzzle of Jupiter is the Great Red Spot, which has been visible for over 250 years. It is 30,000 miles long and 7,000 miles wide. The arrows in the small diagrams indicate the directions in which the clouds lettered *a*, *b*, *c*, *d* and *e* were observed to move. These motions show a circulation in the atmosphere of Jupiter, and the fact that the currents diverge to either side of the Red Spot suggests that this mysterious object is either solid or liquid.

came to the conclusion that Saturn was accompanied by two smaller planets, one on each side, and many curious drawings of the planet were made in those early days.

It was not until 1659 that Huyghens came to the conclusion that Saturn was surrounded by a ring, but being somewhat uncertain as to its exact form he announced his discovery in an anagram—a popular method in those days, as we have already mentioned. Three years later Huyghens confirmed his discovery and made known the solution of his anagram. The jumble of letters previously published were arranged to read: "Saturn is surrounded by a thin flat ring, nowhere touching . . ."

In 1675, Cassini, the French astronomer, found that the ring was divided by a dark rift, which to-day is known as the Cassini division. Another and similar rift in the outside ring was discovered in 1837 by Encke, and is also named after him. In the following year Galle noticed a faint ring lying between the bright rings and the globe of Saturn, and the ring is now called the "crape ring," because of its resemblance to that material.

Many measurements have been made of the rings, but it has been difficult to arrive at accurate results, owing to their extreme delicacy. The generally accepted figures are 171,000 miles for the diameter and 29,000 miles for the width. Their thickness is generally estimated to be about 50 miles.

Changes in the Rings

The rings vary in appearance year by year, owing to the difference in the angle at which we see them. They run through their cycle of changes in 29 years 167 days. When "edgeways" to us they are seen only as a thin needle of light on each side of the planet, whilst on occasion they completely disappear. As time goes on, however, they gradually open out again, until about seven years later they are seen at their widest opening. Once again they commence narrowing, and having passed through the "edgeways" stage open out so that we then see their under side, as it were.

What the Rings Are

There have been many speculations

JUPITER'S MOONS

Here is a drawing of Jupiter as it appears through a moderate-sized telescope, and with it are the four bright moons discovered by Galileo. They can be seen with ordinary field-glasses, and if watched on successive nights their motions may easily be seen. Altogether twelve moons have been found revolving about Jupiter, the last being discovered in 1951, but the other eight are too small and faint to be seen through small instruments.

SATURN, THE RINGED PLANET

Second in size to Jupiter, Saturn is 745 times greater than the Earth, but only 90 times heavier. Its disc carries cloud-belts, similar to those of Jupiter, but it has what no other planet possesses—an immense system of rings. In this drawing the rings are seen edgeways, and are so thin that from this aspect they are almost invisible.

as to the actual composition of the rings. It was proved that they could be neither solid nor liquid. Clerk Maxwell, the famous mathematician who predicted the discovery of the Hertzian waves, suggested that the rings could only consist of a multitude of small particles, and this has since been shown to be the fact.

By means of that wonderful instrument the spectroscope, Professor Keeler, of the Lick Observatory, showed that the rings are composed of numbers of tiny satellites, each revolving in its own orbit around Saturn. They are so small and so far away from us as to be indistinguishable from each other even in our largest telescopes. The dark rifts are caused by the absence of satellites in those particular regions, and the crape ring is accounted for by the fact that here the satellites are fewer in number.

Saturn has nine satellites in addition to the millions of tiny moons that form the rings. Each satellite is named, and the largest is Titan, which is about the size of Mercury. Phœbe, the outermost satellite of the system, also resembles Jupiter's eighth satellite in the fact that its movement around Saturn is retrograde—that is, opposite in direction to that of the other satellites in the Solar System. It requires 550 days to complete one revolution of Saturn.

Saturn's distance from the Sun is 885,900,000 miles, which varies by nearly 100,000,000 miles owing to the eccentricity of its orbit. At its nearest, it is 745,000,000 miles distant from the Earth. It requires 29½ years to complete a revolution of the Sun. The planet is 71,500 miles in diameter—just about nine times that of the Earth.

Like Jupiter, Saturn has a dense, cloud-laden, poisonous atmosphere, and the shell of ice beneath it must be even thicker than Jupiter's, for Saturn as a whole is lighter than water ! Its surface temperature is lower than that of Jupiter because it is 400,000,000 miles farther away from the Sun.

URANUS, HERSCHEL'S PLANET

TO the ancients, Saturn was the outermost planet, and until 1781 it was believed that the Solar System was complete with the six planets already known. But in that year a seventh planet was discovered by William Herschel, in circumstances that are as interesting as they are romantic.

A Musician Becomes an Astronomer

Herschel, who was born in Hanover

on November 15th 1738, was a member of the band of the Hanoverian Guards at the early age of fourteen. When the French invaded Hanover at the beginning of the Seven Years' War, Herschel's regiment was among the defeated at the Battle of Hastenbeck. Although not wounded, the fact that he had to spend a night in a ditch, together with other discomforts that invariably accompany campaigning, led Herschel to decide to change his profession. He deserted and escaped to England, where he arrived with only a French crown piece in his pocket.

He soon gained a reputation as a musician, however, and by 1766 he was a member of the Pump Room Orchestra at Bath. Later, he was appointed organist at the Octagon Chapel and became a concert director at Bath, which in those days was the resort of fashion, beauty and the talents.

Herschel was naturally of a studious disposition, and he spent every spare moment in endeavouring to learn more about music. He took up the study of mathematics in order to go further into the theory of music, following this with optics and astronomy, both of which subjects are closely connected with mathematics.

He was greatly interested in reading about the wonder of the heavens, and he made up his mind that he would have a telescope so that he might see these wonders for himself. He managed to procure a small telescope, and was so thrilled with what he saw with it that he determined to have a more powerful instrument. The price of such a telescope was more than he could afford, however, so he set to work to make one himself. He succeeded in making a large telescope that was of very good quality, and this was the first of many instruments that he made. Indeed, such was his mastery of the art that his name soon became known throughout the world as a maker of fine telescopes, and subsequently he received many orders from foreign potentates and princes.

Herschel Discovers a New Planet

He continued improving his instruments and making observations until 1781, when he commenced to review the heavens and to examine all the stars above a certain magnitude. On March 13th, 1781, he was engaged in these observations when he noticed an object that appeared to be quite different from the stars with which he was familiar. We must here explain that when seen through a telescope a planet shows a tiny disc, whilst a star is visible only as a point of light.

THE RINGS FULLY OPENED

Saturn's rings are believed to consist of an enormous number of small satellites revolving around the planet. Here they are seen opened to their full extent. Saturn also has no fewer than nine moons, the largest of which is almost equal in size to the planet Mars.

IN THE PLANET'S SHADOW

Here it will be noticed that Saturn has three rings, the two outermost (one of which is double) being bright, while the inner is dusky and is known as the Crape Ring ; it is visible here only where it crosses the planet's disc. Notice, too, the shadow of the planet on the rings, at the left-hand side of the globe and the shadow of the rings on the planet *below* them.

To a less careful observer, the object that had aroused Herschel's curiosity might easily have been mistaken for a star, but he saw at once that it presented a small but distinct disc.

At first he thought he had discovered a comet, but as he watched it night after night, and noticed how it changed its position in regard to the neighbouring stars, he was able to calculate its orbit and knew it could be nothing else but a new planet. We can imagine what great excitement there was when the discovery was announced. Herschel's name was in everyone's mouth, and he was commanded to appear before King George III to give an account of his work. His Majesty was so delighted that he appointed Herschel Astronomer Royal, so that he was no longer dependent on music for his living.

Although Herschel suggested that the new planet should be named the Georgian Star, as an honour to the King, it was eventually christened Uranus. It was certainly more consistent with the names of the other planets to choose Uranus, who was the mythological father of Saturn and grandfather of Jupiter, for Uranus comes next to Saturn and next but one to Jupiter in order of distance from the Sun.

Uranus is over 1,782,000,000 miles distant from the Sun, and requires 84 years to complete one revolution of its orbit. It is about 32,400 miles in diameter and rotates on its axis in 10¾ hours. It can only be seen by the naked eye on favourable occasions, and even in a powerful telescope it has little interest for the observer. It has five satellites, two of which were discovered by Herschel, the third and fourth being discovered in 1851, and the fifth in 1948. The satellites are remarkable for the fact that they revolve around Uranus in orbits at right angles to those of the satellites of the other planets of the Solar System. This is because the axis of Uranus itself is almost horizontal, so that the planet rolls round the Sun like a ball instead of spinning like a top.

NEPTUNE AND PLUTO

THE discovery of Neptune, the planet beyond Uranus and, until the discovery of Pluto, the outermost planet in the Solar System, was a veritable "triumph of mind over matter," for the planet was found on paper before it was ever seen with the telescope! To understand exactly how this was possible we must first explain about the various forces that affect a planet's movements.

Copyright.

SATURN

Saturn photographed through a telescope. The camera does not reveal the delicate details which the eye can see, but here the separate rings and belts of clouds can be distinguished.

The Effects of Gravitation

Kepler showed that the time required by a planet to complete a revolution of its orbit depends on its distance from the Sun. This was followed by Newton's proof that the movements of the planets were due to gravitation. He made it clear that every body of matter attracts every other body with a force that depends, firstly on the masses of the bodies, and secondly on the distance separating them.

Knowing this, we can quite understand that not only are the planets attracted by the Sun, but that they also attract one another. Of course, the Sun exercises an infinitely greater attraction on the planets because of his huge mass, but the fact remains that the planets themselves do exercise a measurable influence on each other.

Knowing the masses and the distances of the planets from the Sun, mathematicians are able to calculate exactly the positions where a planet should be at any given date. When required, these calculations can be made years ahead; and, in fact, every year there is published a kind of astronomical Bradshaw called "The Nautical Almanac," containing numerous details about the future position of the planets.

A Difficult Problem

After the discovery of Uranus its position was carefully measured, and some forty years after it was discovered, Bouvard, a French mathematician, published tables showing its movements. When the predicted positions came to be checked with the actual positions, however, it was found that they did not agree. These discrepancies caused Bouvard to suggest that perhaps an unknown planet was attracting Uranus and upsetting the calculations.

The difficult problem was to find the position of the unknown planet in the sky simply by the errors arising out of the position of Uranus. This was likely to take a very long time, but in 1843 J. C. Adams undertook the necessary calculations, and in October, 1845, took to the Astronomer Royal his calculated position of the theoretical planet. Unfortunately, the Astronomer Royal paid little attention, placed the papers in a drawer and forgot all about them.

Neptune Discovered

In the meantime a young French mathematician, named Leverrier, had also been working on the problem. Leverrier worked out the position of the supposed planet and wrote to Encke, the Director of the Berlin Observatory. When Encke received this letter he instructed one of his assistants to commence a search, and on the same evening (September 23rd, 1846) this observer found an object of about the eighth magnitude that was not shown on the star map. The same object was observed on subsequent evenings, and as it moved its position each night it was evident that it was the object of the search and a new planet.

When the Astronomer Royal at Greenwich received an account of Leverrier's work, he remembered the papers that Adams had left in his care nine months

THE STORY OF A METEOR

Every hour of the day and night the Earth is colliding with meteors. Although these, as a rule, are very small, the death rate would be fearful if we were not protected by our atmosphere against these celestial bullets. The terrific speed at which meteors strike into our atmosphere reduces all but the largest to powder before they reach the ground. The small diagram at the top gives the path of the swarm of Perseid meteors that the Earth meets at regular intervals.

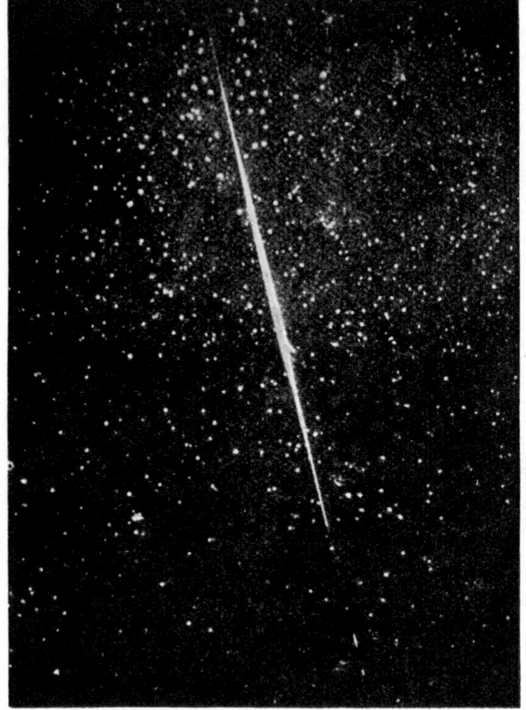

Copyright.

A SHOOTING-STAR

The camera was taking a time-exposure of the stars when a meteor or "shooting-star" flashed across the field of view. It left this track on the camera-plate. Observers watch every night for meteors. Two observations of the same meteor enable its height to be calculated.

before. On studying them, he was at once struck with the similarity in the results obtained by the two mathematicians. Remembering that both Adams and Leverrier had been working on the problem unknown to each other, he realised that there was something more than a mere coincidence in the success of the results. He asked Professor Challis, of Cambridge, to search for the new planet, and on September 28th Challis found the same object that had already been observed at Berlin a week before.

Neptune's Distance

Thus, Neptune was discovered in England and in France by the two mathematicians before it was seen in a telescope. As everyone knows, Neptune was the God of the Seas, and the name given to this outermost planet is certainly appropriate. Exactly as Neptune was thought to live in the gloom and darkness of the ocean depths, so is the planet that bears his name plunged in the gloom of space. It is over 2,794,000,000 miles distant from the Sun—so far away that details of its surface are invisible to us, but it is believed to rotate on its axis once every fifteen hours forty minutes. Its diameter is 31,000 miles—nearly four times that of the Earth—and it requires nearly 165 years to complete one revolution of its orbit.

Neptune is so far away from the Sun, that to anyone living on the planet the sun would appear no larger than Venus seems to us, although it certainly would appear immensely brighter. Mercury, Venus, the Earth and Mars would be invisible. So far as we know, Neptune has only two satellites, although there may be others that are invisible to us owing to their great distance.

Pluto, the outermost planet, is so far away that it is difficult to make accurate observation, but its size and mass are believed to fall between those of Mercury and Mars. Its mean distance from the Sun is about 3,700,000,000 miles, and one "year" on Pluto is equal to about 248 of ours.

SHOOTING STARS, METEORS AND FIREBALLS

OFTEN when we are out on a clear night we see a streak of light suddenly dash across the sky, to disappear as silently as it came. It seems almost as though a mighty star has fallen from its place in the heavens, but if we are anxious about it we can reassure ourselves, for a glance at the constellations shows us that each of our friends is in its accustomed place and none is missing. Few people other than astronomers can bring themselves to believe that these shooting stars are not stars at all, but such is the case, for they have a far more humble origin. As a matter of fact, a shooting star does not actually " shoot " in the heavens but in the Earth's atmosphere, and is only some 50 or 100 miles above our heads.

Fireballs and Meteors

To understand what a shooting star is we must realise that there are multitudes of small bodies circling through space, each in its own orbit, and that at some time or another these objects approach the Earth. These small bodies are travelling more than one hundred times as fast as a rifle bullet, and when they enter our atmosphere their speed is so great that they are heated to incandescence by the friction of their movement through the air. They vary in brilliance from being large enough to light up the landscape for miles around, to being but a faint streak. The brightest are known as fireballs; the next as meteors; and the faintest ones as shooting stars. It has been calculated that over 400,000,000 of these bodies are captured by the Earth every year. There are on an average about a hundred fireballs every year, and meteors and shooting stars may be seen on almost any clear night.

A Huge Meteorite

Occasionally a meteor is of sufficiently large size to withstand the terrific heat generated by its passage through the atmosphere, with the result that it does not burn away entirely, but part of it falls to Earth as a meteorite. One of the most famous meteorites fell in 1876 at Rowton, in Shropshire, and may now be seen in the South Kensington Museum, where there is a splendid collection of meteorites. Some are so large that they weigh several tons, and one of three brought from Greenland by the famous Arctic explorer, Peary, weighs 36½ tons and measures 11 ft. × 7 ft. × 5 ft. Most meteorites consist of iron and nickel, but some are stony and contain no metal.

Truly enormous meteorites fall to Earth on rare occasions, and the signs of their impact are awe-inspiring. The great Meteor Crater, in Arizona, is a bowl-shaped hollow nearly a mile across and 500 ft. deep, and this is believed to have been caused by a meteorite weighing some half a million tons. This meteorite lies buried 1,300 ft. below the floor of its crater, and has been reached by rock-drills.

The Arizona meteorite probably fell

Ellison Hawks.

A BRITISH METEORITE

This lump of mixed stone and iron fell near Scarborough, in Yorkshire, on December 13th, 1795. It is one of the largest meteorites that ever fell in England, and weighs 56 pounds. This photograph is one-third the natural size.

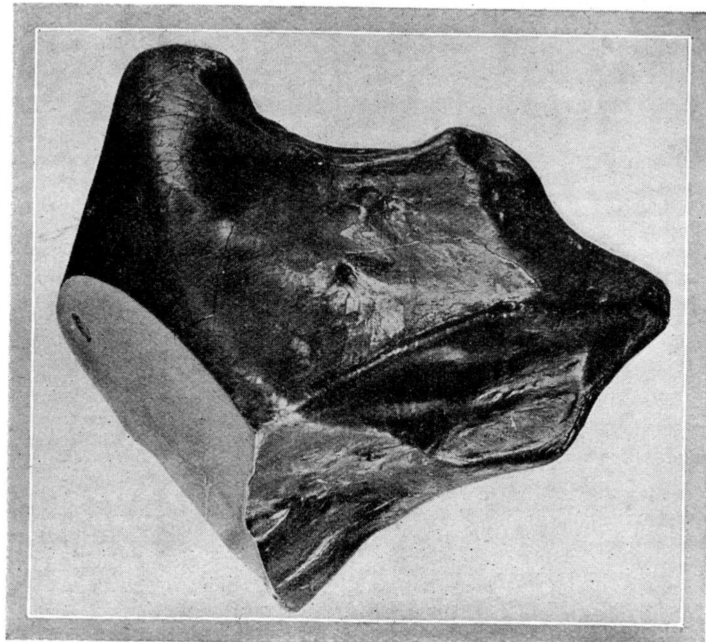

Ellison Hawks.

IRON FROM THE SKY

Meteorites nearly always contain a large amount of iron. This is a picture of a meteorite that fell at Rowton, near Wellington, Shropshire, on April 20th, 1876, and which is almost pure iron. The outer part has been fused by heat caused by a swift passage through the Earth's atmosphere.

about 5,000 years ago, and we can only guess what the fall must have looked like. It came down as a great, white-hot mass of iron at supersonic speed, flinging off lumps of hot iron as big as houses as it came. In front of it, a large volume of white-hot air was forced to the ground, where it mushroomed out to set fire to grass and trees in every direction for upwards of 100 miles. When the meteorite actually hit the ground and tore its way through the solid rock to a depth of a quarter of a mile, there must have been an earthquake shock equivalent to the explosion of several atomic bombs.

The Siberian Meteorite

Most of these things happened when the great Siberian meteorite fell in 1908, but on a smaller scale. Russian peasants, and others, witnessed this fall from various distances, and the sight and accompanying sounds were so terrifying, even at a distance of 300 miles, that trains on the Trans-Siberian railway were brought to a halt for fear they should be derailed. When the meteorite struck the ground a column of fire rose to a height of twelve miles, and then, suddenly, all the trees covering about 400 square miles of the dense forest-land were knocked flat and burst into flames. Five hours later, a great atmospheric wave passed over Britain, 3,500 miles away, and travelled twice round the world before dying away. Seismographs at Irkutsk, 1,000 miles away, recorded continuous earthquake shocks for an hour and a half.

A herd of 1,500 reindeer, and many whole families of peasants, were wiped right out, some at a distance of ten miles from the site of the impact. In all, as a result of blast and fires, this single meteorite destroyed 80 million trees over an area of nearly 2,000 square miles. Yet this meteorite was less than one-hundredth the size of the Arizona meteorite ! There is evidence that the greatest meteorite of all fell in Canada, but that was many thousands of years ago and we have no detailed knowledge of it.

Ordinary Meteorites

The majority of meteors and shooting stars are dissipated as they travel through the atmosphere, and their remains fall lightly to Earth in the form of a fine metallic dust. When this dust is examined with a microscope it is seen to consist of tiny rounded particles, from which the rough corners have been worn by friction with the atmosphere.

The appearance of a meteor cannot be predicted, because it is quite invisible until it enters our atmosphere. We can say, however, that on certain nights there will be more meteors than at ordinary times. This is because meteors travel around the Sun in swarms, and we know that on certain nights the Earth will cross the track of one or other of these swarms.

The Leonids

On the night of the 13th November, 1833, there occurred what was probably the finest display of meteors ever seen by man—it is estimated, indeed, that on that occasion something like 240,000 meteors were seen. After this wonderful display had taken place it was remembered that Humboldt had observed a similar shower about thirty-three years before.

Further inquiries resulted in the discovery that there had been showers of shooting stars every thirty-three years for at least a thousand years preceding. It was suggested, therefore, that these displays were caused by the same stream of meteors, and because the paths of the meteors of 1833 all seemed to commence at the constellation called Leo, these meteors were called the "Leonids." It was confidently predicted that as the Earth crossed this meteor stream about every thirty-three years, another display could be expected in 1866.

As the shower again duly appeared and was an impressive spectacle, astronomers had no hesitation in predicting a further display in 1899. Although hundreds of people in every town and city sat up to watch through the night, they were disappointed, for, remarkable to relate, the meteors did not put in an appearance! It was

E.N.A.

METEOR CRATER, ARIZONA

This enormous crater is nearly three miles in circumference and 500 feet deep. It was caused by an iron meteorite, weighing perhaps 500,000 tons, that fell in prehistoric times and buried itself a quarter of a mile underground, where it has been found by boring. Millions of tons of hard rock were thrown out to form the surrounding mounds. Some of these contain blocks of stone weighing hundreds of tons.

THE PATH OF A COMET

A comet does not circle the Sun as do the planets, but travels in a different kind of orbit. Its journey may carry it far into the depths of space and take many years to complete. Halley's comet requires 75 years to complete one revolution of its orbit.

apparent that something had happened to prevent their return, and it was suggested that the orbit of the meteors had probably been diverted by the attraction of the giant planet Jupiter.

COMETS, VISITORS FROM SPACE

FROM what we have read, we realise that there are certain definite facts known about the planets. In the first place, they may be regarded as being more or less solid objects; they move around the Sun in orbits that are almost circular, never travelling so far away as to be lost to our sight; and they are regular in their motions—that is to say, we can predict their positions with accuracy. We have now to consider an entirely different class of heavenly bodies—comets, which differ from planets in almost every respect.

Comets and their Tails

The name " comet " comes from the Latin *coma*, " a hair," and these objects are so called because they often carry a hair-like tail. Strange to say, we do not know what comets really are, nor what is their origin. For one thing, there have not been many bright comets that could be examined with modern instruments, the majority of those visible in recent times being comparatively small. There is no doubt, however, that comets are largely composed of gaseous matter, and they may also contain swarms of meteors held together by the mutual attraction of their particles.

A comet consists principally of two parts—the head, or nucleus, and the tail. Although the heads of different comets do not differ very much from each other except in their size and colour, there are considerable differences in their tails. Sometimes these are short, whilst at other times they are curved and long. Often there is more than one tail, and comets at a great distance from the Sun have no tails at all. This is because the tail of a comet is caused by the pressure of the rays streaming out from the Sun. The tail therefore always points away from the Sun, and a comet which is itself travelling away from the Sun goes tail foremost.

The Ellipse and the Parabola

Another point of difference between comets and planets is their movement through space. To understand this we must explain that there are two kinds of comets—the solar comets and the very much rarer interstellar comets. The former follow regular paths and belong to the Solar System, but the latter travel far out in the depths of space among the stars—as their name implies.

Those of you who have studied geometry know the difference between an ellipse and a parabola. The solar comets travel in elliptical (or closed) orbits in one of the foci of which the

Sun is situated. The interstellar comets travel in parabolic (or open) orbits that are quite different from the type of orbit pursued by the solar comets. A comet that travels in an elliptical orbit returns at regular periods, but as a parabola is an open curve with its two branches stretching away from each other and always getting further apart, a comet that travels in this type of orbit visits the Solar System only once. Some of the largest and brightest comets of history seem to have belonged to the interstellar comets which have come unexpectedly and are not subject to periodical returns.

Copyright.

A TELESCOPIC COMET

A time-exposure was required to photograph this comet through a telescope. While it was being taken the stars continued their journey across the sky, leaving the short tracks here seen.

Comets as Portents

It would seem that in past ages comets excited even more fear than total eclipses. Perhaps this was due to the fact that, although the ancients were able to predict eclipses, they were quite unable to give any idea as to when a comet would appear. It was thought that comets were signs sent by the gods as a warning of some coming disaster. Others associated comets with any extraordinary happening that might chance to occur at a convenient time. For instance, the Romans thought that a great comet that appeared in 43 B.C. was a chariot sent by the gods to transport the soul of Julius Cæsar, who had been assassinated shortly before.

William of Malmesbury, writing about the death in 1060 of Henry, King of France, said: " Soon after, a comet—denoting as they say, a change of kingdoms—appeared trailing its extended and fiery train along the sky. Wherefore a certain monk of our monastery, bowing down with terror at the sight of the brilliant star, exclaimed: ' Thou art come. . . . I have seen thee long since, but now I behold thee much more terrible, threatening to hurl destruction on this country.' " Later, the immortal Shakespeare voiced the general opinion when he wrote those celebrated lines in " Julius Cæsar ":

" When beggars die, there are no comets seen;
The heavens themselves blaze forth the death of princes."

It is rather fortunate for Astronomy that the ancients were so interested in comets, for their records—and particularly those of the Chinese—have been of the greatest assistance to us in tracing out the past appearances and history of certain comets.

Halley's Comet

A whole book could be written about the famous comets of history. As our space is limited, we can only briefly mention one that is of great interest. This is the comet named after the celebrated English astronomer, Halley, a great friend of Sir Isaac Newton, who in his famous " Principia " made the suggestion that comets revolve around the Sun as the planets do.

A COMET WITH MANY TAILS

This was the third comet of the year 1908 and is therefore known as 1908C. The comet was remarkable for the many different changes that occurred in its appearance.

Halley determined to investigate the orbits of certain bright comets, and he mapped out the orbits of twenty-four, which had appeared between 1337 and 1698. He noticed that there were three that followed orbits so remarkably similar that, it seemed, they could scarcely be three different comets but rather three different appearances of the same comet at intervals of seventy-five years. Going further back, Halley found that a bright comet had been seen on three previous dates separated by similar intervals to those that separated the three later appearances. This made six appearances in all, each separated by a period of seventy-five years.

Halley predicted that the comet would return again in the year 1757. He did not live to see the fulfilment of his prediction, for he died in 1742, eight years after his prediction had been made. His work was not forgotten, however, and as the year 1757 drew near, preparations were made by several astronomers to search for the comet. But all the professional observers were outdone, for the comet was discovered on Christmas night, 1758, by an amateur astronomer, named Palitzsch, with only a small telescope.

The fulfilment of the prediction definitely established the fact that some comets do return at regular intervals, and we shall always remember that we owe this discovery to Edmund Halley.

The Tail of the Comet

Although it is a long time since people regarded comets as warnings of fateful things to come, the more superstitious peoples of the world still show alarm when one of these fiery phenomena appears in the sky.

On the last appearance of Halley's Comet the Earth passed through its tail, but there was so little matter in the Comet that no effects were observed. In point of fact, the matter in a comet's tail is so rarefied that it could probably be packed comfortably into a large church.

Modern astronomers have noticed that comets seem to deteriorate. Each time they circle the Sun, there is a wasting away. In 1846 astronomers actually saw the destruction of Biela's Comet. The two parts into which it broke were seen, six years later, to be a million and a half miles apart, and that occasion was the last appearance of the comet.

In 1872, when Biela's comet should again have been seen, all that was observed was a particularly fine display of meteors.

THE STARS IN THE SKIES

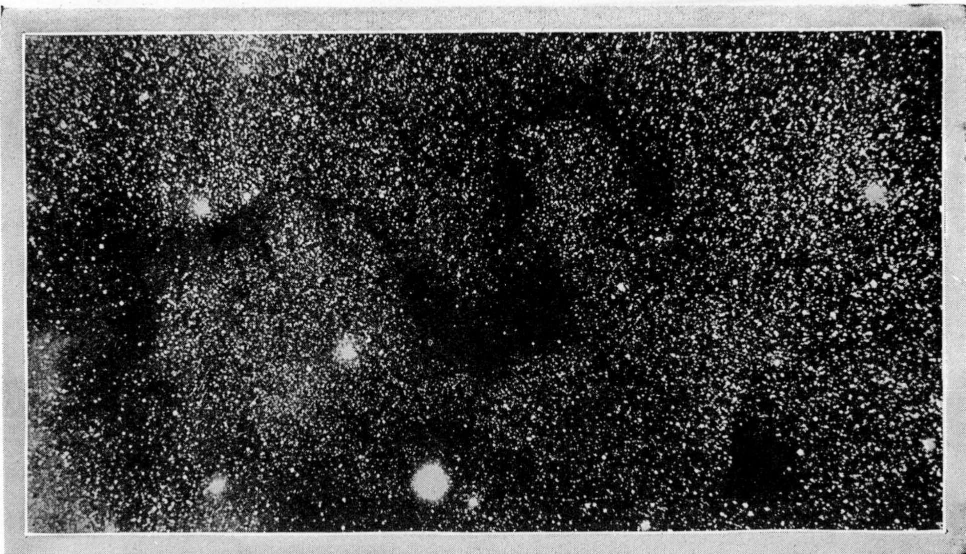

Ellison Hawks.

PART OF THE MILKY WAY IN THE CONSTELLATION OF OPHIUCHUS

The photograph clearly shows some of the remarkable " dark lanes," believed to be due to heavy gaseous clouds that blot out the stars behind.

THE objects that we have considered — planets, comets, and meteors—all belong to the Solar System, revolve around the Sun, and are governed by his gravitational powers. We are now to learn something of the stars themselves, which are vastly different from the planets.

In the first place, there is the difference in their appearance to which we referred when dealing with the discovery of Uranus. Even with the naked eye one can tell the difference between a planet and a star, for whereas a planet seldom twinkles, but shines with a steady light, a star twinkles almost unceasingly.

Then again if we look through the telescope a planet presents a definite disc, whereas a star is but a shining point of light no matter how powerful the telescope may be. But the greatest difference that we can observe is the fact that the stars never change their positions relative to one another, whilst night by night a planet moves its position among the stars. The name planet means " a wanderer," and it was given to these objects by the ancients. They had noticed that these objects moved about the sky.

As we have already seen, the planets are other worlds circling round the Sun in company with the Earth. We have now to learn that the Sun is a star, and the stars themselves are suns. Whether or not these other suns have planets circling around them—as our star has—we do not know, because they are so far away that even our most powerful telescopes could not show them.

Distances of the Stars

The distances of the stars are indeed enormous—Alpha Centauri, the nearest star, is over 25 billions of miles away from us. This is a number that we cannot be expected to understand, but let us try to gain some idea of what it means. If we were to commence counting, we should have to spend something like 300,000 years without

A STAR CLUSTER

This stupendous cluster of stars is in the constellation of Hercules. Our photograph, which was taken with the 60-inch telescope at Mount Wilson, was exposed for no less than eleven hours.

stopping day or night before we reached 24 billions!

Many of you no doubt have heard of the red corpuscles—tiny discs in our blood. They are so minute that if it were possible to pile one on top of another, as coins are sometimes seen piled in a bank, it would take about 15,000 corpuscles to form a pile 1 inch in height. If we allow one corpuscle to stand for each mile in the distance that separates us from Alpha Centauri, we should require a pile no less than 26,000 miles in height to represent the total distance! Sirius, the brightest star in the sky, is more than twice as far as Alpha Centauri.

These illustrations refer only to the distance of the nearest star, and would not serve to represent the distance of the majority of stars, in comparison with which Alpha Centauri and Sirius are comparatively close to us.

Meaning of "Light-year"

Astronomers have found that it is useless to express a star's distance in miles because the numbers are so large, and so they use another standard. We know that light takes time to travel through space, exactly as sound takes time to travel through air. If we watch a gun fired say a mile away, we first see a puff of smoke and then hear the report of the explosion, the interval between depending on our distance from the gun. Sound travels about 1,100 feet a second, but light is infinitely more swift, travelling some 186,000 *miles* a second. At this rate it takes but a second and a quarter to reach us from the Moon, and about eight minutes from the Sun. To cross the intervening gulf of space from Alpha Centauri, however, it requires four years and four months, during which time it is travelling at 186,000 miles each second! Thus, if Alpha Centauri were to be extinguished at the present moment it would continue to be visible to us as a star for four years and four months.

Astronomers use the rate that light takes to travel to express the distance of the stars. Alpha Centauri is said to be $4\frac{1}{3}$ light years distant: Sirius is $8\frac{1}{2}$ light years, and Procyon $10\frac{1}{2}$ light years distant. Vega, the bright blue star in the constellation of Lyra, is some 21 light years distant; and Polaris, the Pole Star, is 44 light years away from us. If you are interested in making calculations you can easily work out the distance in miles of any of these stars, by multiplying the number of seconds in the light years, and again multiplying your result by 186,000.

We must mention that it is not

MILLIONS OF STARS REVEALED

Part of the Milky Way in the constellation of Cygnus, the Swan. This is one of a series of remarkable photographs revealing the Milky Way to be composed literally of clouds of stars, each one of which is a sun.

necessarily the brightest stars that are nearest to us. Everyone knows that the stars are not all of the same brightness—indeed, it has been said that no two stars shine with exactly the same amount of light. Although the bright stars may seem to be nearer to us than the faint ones, it is more than likely that they are larger or more luminous suns at a great distance, while the faint stars may be smaller or less brilliant suns near at hand.

The stars are divided into constellations or groups, and it is believed that this was done ages ago by the Chaldean shepherds. They fancied the stars formed figures in the sky, just as we sometimes imagine we can see pictures in the fire. The Chaldeans gave these star figures names, and these same names have persisted to this day. The Chaldean shepherds also made up imaginary tales and legends about the deeds performed by their heroes in the skies, and although most of these stories have been lost a few of them have been handed down to us to-day.

Since the days of the Chaldeans much knowledge has been gained of the heavenly bodies by means of the telescope and the spectroscope. Yet the wonder remains that without these comparatively modern aids to the astronomer these wise men of ancient Babylon were able to learn so much and to pass on their knowledge to others.

Some of the brighter stars themselves are now known by special names, but the majority are known by prefixing a Greek letter to the name of the constellation in which they are situated.

STAR MAGNITUDES

WE have said that stars are not all of the same brightness. They are classed by magnitudes, which, however, do not take into account the actual size of the stars, but only deal with their brilliance as it appears to us. We must remember that although the bright stars seem to be nearer than the fainter stars, it by no means follows that this is actually the case. The astronomer takes all these facts into account when engaged on the long task of classifying the stars according to their different magnitudes.

It has been found that the number of the stars in each magnitude increases in a certain proportion down the scale. Roughly speaking, each magnitude has about three times as many more stars as the preceding one. Thus, there are 11 stars of the first magnitude, 39 of the second, 133 of the third, 446 of the fourth, and so on. Stars of the first magnitude give about 100 times as much light as those of the sixth, and about a million times as much as those of the sixteenth.

There are a few stars that are brighter than the average stars of the first magnitude, and these are specially classified. If we take Aldebaran (in the constellation of *Taurus*, the Bull) as a typical first magnitude star, Sirius (in *Canis major*, the Large Dog) is about nine times as bright and is said to be one and a half times above first magnitude. Sirius is the brightest star in the Northern hemisphere.

The Number of the Stars

People with fairly good sight can see stars of down to about the fourth magnitude, whilst those with keen sight can see stars down to the sixth magnitude. If we look up at the sky on a clear night we may think we can see tens of thousands of stars. As a matter of fact a person of average sight can see only about 500 stars with the naked eye. Those with keen sight can see about 4,500 stars without a telescope, whilst quite a small telescope will show stars down to the ninth magnitude, of which there are about 140,000 visible. The 40-inch telescope of the Yerkes Observatory will probably show 100,000,000 stars, whilst the 100-inch reflector of Mount Wilson can photograph stars of about the twenty-first magnitude, of which it is estimated there are at least a billion! The great 200-inch telescope

A STAR THAT SPLIT

Great interest was caused among astronomers when in 1925 a new star, called *Nova Pictoris*, was seen to flare up and (apparently) to split into two. This was the first recorded instance of a star becoming double "before our eyes," as it were, although there are many double stars to be seen in the heavens. Although this tremendous upheaval occurred some 500 years ago, it is only now that we are able to see it. It has taken all those centuries for light to bridge the tremendous gulf that separates our little planet from this giant cataclysm.

Topical Press.

LISTENING-IN TO THE STARS

This is the pioneer radio-telescope at the University of Manchester Experimental Station at Jodrell Bank, Cheshire. The huge bowl-shaped framework is a wireless receiving aerial, and it behaves like the concave mirror in a reflecting telescope, but gathering radio-waves instead of light-rays. Note that it is mounted on a turntable.

on Palomar Mountain is twice as powerful again.

Star catalogues have been made from time to time, and include the position of the stars measured as accurately as possible in the circumstances appertaining at the time the catalogue was made. The first star catalogue, made by Hipparchus, the Greek astronomer, contained the places of 1,080 stars, but unfortunately it is lost. The oldest star catalogue we possess, made about 137 A.D., is contained in Ptolemy's *Almagest*, and gives the position of 1,025 stars. In 1580, Tycho Brahe compiled a catalogue of 1,005 stars, which catalogue was the last to be completed before the invention of the telescope. In 1862, Argelander, at Bonn, in Germany, completed a more modern catalogue. Using a 2½-inch telescope, he catalogued over 324,000 stars.

The introduction of the photographic dry plate was of great importance to Astronomy, for photography enables accurate records to be made of star positions. In 1887 a great photographic catalogue was planned, the work being shared by eighteen observatories—Algiers, Bordeaux, Cape of Good Hope, Catania, Cordoba, Greenwich, Helsinki, Melbourne, Monte Video, Oxford, Paris, Perth (Western Australia), Potsdam, Rome, San Fernando, Sydney, Tacubaya, and Toulouse—each observatory undertaking to photograph a certain part of the heavens. The whole catalogue will necessitate the exposure of 100,000 plates. The work has already taken many years, but steady progress has been maintained. It is estimated that when the catalogue is finished the position of nearly 4,000,000 stars will be recorded. Not only will this catalogue be of the greatest value to

L.N.A.

THE WORLD'S LARGEST RADIO-TELESCOPE

When completed, this gigantic radio-telescope at Jodrell Bank will be used to study unknown objects in the sky which broadcast radio-waves though they cannot be seen. This picture is of a scale model, but the actual instrument will be 303 feet high and 250 feet in diameter. The model of Nelson's Column is on the same scale.

generations of astronomers who follow, but it will be a marvellous achievement—a triumph of accuracy, perseverance, and patience.

Since the building of the great 200-inch telescope on Palomar Mountain, and the establishment of the new Schmidt star cameras, other surveys of a more specialised nature have been embarked upon, such as the counting of the spiral nebulæ described below.

The Stars are Moving

Early star catalogues have been of great assistance to astronomers in helping them to find out what changes are taking place in the position of the stars—for the stars are not fixed

THE GREAT NEBULA IN ORION

One of the grandest objects in the heavens. The astronomers' telescopes reveal hundreds of thousands of these wonderful nebulæ of all sizes and shapes.

in space, as they are generally supposed to be. Their movement in space (called the " proper motion ") is quite distinct and separate from their movement across the sky each night, which, of course, is simply due to the Earth's rotation on its axis. Over 200 years ago Halley discovered that the two bright stars Sirius and Arcturus had changed their places since the days of Ptolemy. Sirius had moved southwards by about half a degree and Arcturus by a full degree.

Some of the stars have enormous proper motions—that is to say, they are moving at incredible speeds—but, owing to their enormous distances from us, their movements in the sky can only be detected over a comparatively long period of time. One of the swiftest moving stars is that known as Groombridge 1830. This star is of the sixth magnitude and is moving at a speed of about 528 miles a second. Another star with a high proper motion is an eighth magnitude star in the constellation of Pictor. As the star is at about the same distance from us as Sirius, it is therefore either much smaller or less brilliant than Sirius, for it is not visible to the naked eye. Its proper motion is such that in about 200 years its position will have altered by nearly as much as the diameter of the full Moon.

It is interesting to know that our star, the Sun, also has a proper motion. Accompanied by the planets and their satellites he moves at a speed of about thirteen miles a second.

Different Kinds of Stars

The visible stars vary enormously in size and colour, and they are classified accordingly. There are Red Giants, like Betelgeuse in the constellation of Orion, which is so big that if it were in the position of the Sun the orbits of the Earth and Mars would both lie right inside it! And there are the White Dwarfs, like the companion to Sirius, which is probably not much bigger than the Earth. Such very small stars, however, have much the same weight as ordinary stars, and the matter of which they are composed must be so dense that a lump of it the size of a matchbox might weigh a ton! Other types include the Blue stars, Yellow Dwarfs, and Collapsed Super-giants. Our Sun is a fairly average specimen of Yellow star.

Then there are double and multiple stars, which, like the Pole Star, consist of two or more stars circling round each other. Castor, one of the " Twins," consists of three stars revolving about each other, and each of these is itself a

A STRANGE OBJECT IN THE SKY

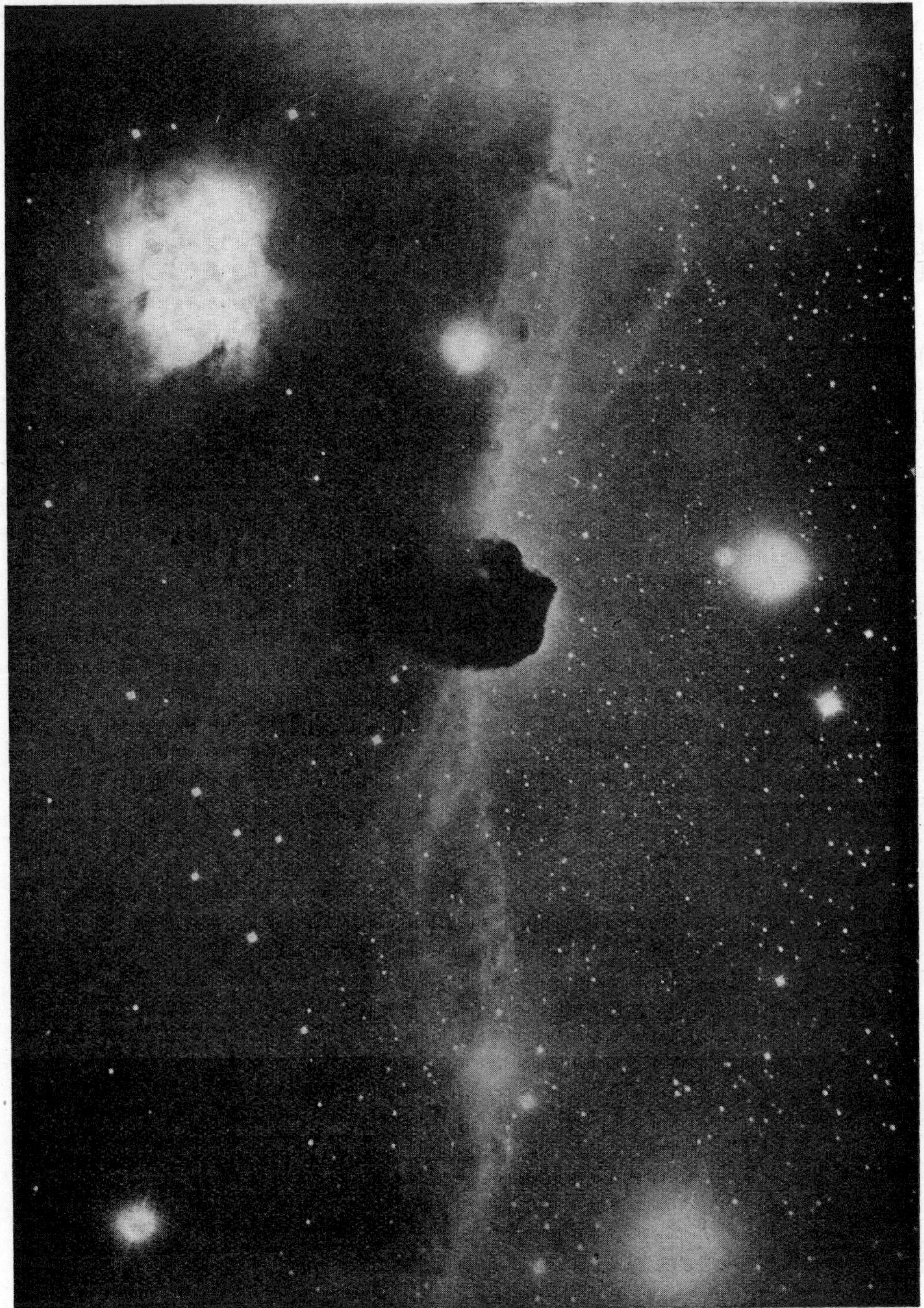

Royal Astronomical Society.

THE HORSE'S HEAD

This is an enlarged photograph of a small nebula in Orion near the one shown on the opposite page. Look at the dark object in the centre and see if you can discover its resemblance to a horse's head by turning the page round! It is believed to be a mass of dark matter blotting out the brilliance of the nebula behind. (The bright globes are large stars.)

double star, so that though Castor appears to the naked eye to be a single bright star, it is really a system of six separate stars! Double and multiple stars cannot be distinguished from single stars except through a telescope.

Sometimes one member of a double star passes right in front of its companion, so as to shut off its light, and then the whole double star appears to blink and is called a " variable " star. This blinking has nothing to do with " twinkling," which is an effect of the Earth's atmosphere on the light of all stars, but is a slow fluctuation in brightness occupying several days or even years. And some variable stars are not double stars at all, but single stars which periodically blow themselves up and then shrink again—which they may do in the course of a few hours! Very rarely a star may explode, and then a very bright star suddenly appears in the sky where before there was only a very faint one, or perhaps none visible to the naked eye at all. Such stars are called Novæ, and they usually become fainter again after some months have elapsed.

AN ISLAND UNIVERSE

This spiral nebula is to be seen in the constellation of *Canes Venatici*, the " Hunting Dogs." The nebula, which lies in the remotest depths of space, may be a universe in process of being formed. When you look at it your eyes are receiving light that left it thousands of years ago.

Radio-Stars

The stars we see or photograph are all luminous bodies. That is to say, they give out light-rays which can affect our eyes or the photographic plate. But there are also millions of dark stars which we can never see, but whose existence has been inferred by astronomers. Some of these dark stars send out radio-waves, and very delicate radio receivers have now been constructed which can detect them. These receivers are connected with enormous, bowl-shaped aerials, able to be directed to different parts of the sky like telescopes, and they are known as radio-telescopes. Some of these are shown in the accompanying pictures. A radio-star makes a faint hum or whistle when picked up by the telescope, and the radio-astronomer has to distinguish this from the continuous background noise broadcast by the whole Milky Way (which is described below).

The Nebulæ

Scattered about the heavens are a class of objects that in the telescope look like misty patches of light. These are the *nebulæ*, or " little clouds," some of which were seen by the ancient astronomers. Some were studied by Galileo, who came to the conclusion that they were clusters of stars so far away that the individual stars of the cluster could not be distinguished (or "resolved," as it is called) by the telescopes of that time.

The great astronomer Herschel was the first to suppose that the nebulæ were not all of a starry nature, and that some were gigantic clouds of glowing gas. This suggestion led to much discussion and argument, and in the attempt to settle the matter much attention was paid to these objects, observer after observer endeavouring to show that they were star clusters as Galileo had said. Nor were the efforts confined to observers, for every telescope maker tried to produce instruments of sufficient power and optical qualities that would resolve all the nebulæ into star clusters. It was left to Sir William Huggins to prove (in 1864), with a wonderful instrument called the spectroscope, that all the nebulæ could not be clusters of stars, and that some at any rate were composed of glowing gas as Herschel had said.

THE "BRIDAL VEIL" NEBULA

The "Bridal Veil" nebula in the constellation of Cygnus, the Swan. The bright star at the top does not belong to it.

The nebulæ have been called "the workshops of the Creator," for here, it is believed, new stars and new star systems are being formed.

As we have mentioned, a few of the brightest nebulæ are visible to the naked eye. Many more can be seen with a small telescope, but by far the greater number can be studied only by photography. The first photographs of nebulæ were taken by Henry Draper, of New York, in 1880. Since that time thousands of photographs have been taken and an immense number of these objects have been revealed. It has been estimated that with only an hour's exposure about 300,000 nebulæ could be photographed with the 60-inch reflector of Mount Wilson. There would be a much greater number within the range of the 200-inch telescope, and the number revealed by giving longer exposures is enormous. Most of the starry nebulæ are of a spiral form and they have been called "island universes." They are much farther away than the gaseous nebulæ and the visible stars.

It is now well established that there are also many dark nebulæ, which do not shine. These non-luminous clouds of gas are only detected because they obscure the stars that lie behind them. They make dark patches in the "star-dust" of the sky, and sailors have given them fanciful names—such as the "Coal-Sack" and the "Horse's Head."

The Milky Way

On a clear night we can see a faint

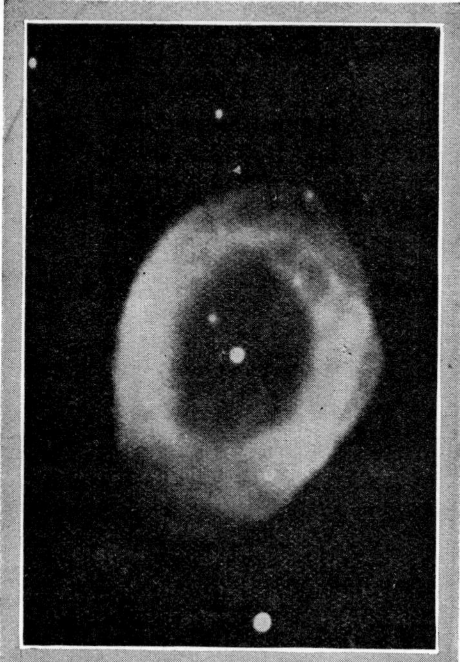

A RING NEBULA
This curious object is the annular or ring nebula in the constellation of *Lyra*. It may represent a star which has exploded.

band of misty light stretching overhead. It is of irregular width and outline and is called the Milky Way. Aristotle supposed it to be due to the atmospheric vapour, and Anaxagoras thought it was the shadow of the Earth in the sky. When Galileo observed it with his telescope he saw that it was of a different order altogether, and that it was composed of myriads of faint stars so far away from us as to be indistinguishable separately to the naked eye. Much of our present knowledge of the Milky Way is due to the late Professor E. E. Barnard, who first successfully photographed it at the Lick Observatory in 1889. He used a special lens that "covered" a large area of the sky, and that had a great "light grasp." He took hundreds of photographs, exposing his plates for over seven hours. These photographs showed the Milky Way in its true nature. It was found to consist literally of clouds of stars, grouped in the form of a flattened disc, something like a thin watch. In fact, the Milky Way turns out to be another spiral nebula, just like those which we see in our telescopes, and which appear so small only because they are so far away.

The Smallness of the Earth

Astronomy has taught us many things, not the least important of which is to realise our comparative insignificance. Some people are accustomed to think of their individual importance; others think of the importance of their city, or the importance of their country in the world's affairs. At one time the world's cleverest men thought the Earth was the centre of the Universe.

Astronomy has changed all this, however, and we have come to understand that the Earth is but one of nine planets circling round a comparatively huge Sun; that this Sun is but a star —one of hundreds of millions of other stars, many larger and brighter than it is—embedded in a huge star cloud, which itself is only one of many such clouds that are included in the Milky Way. We know that our Sun is no more favourably placed than any one of 10,000 other suns in the same star cloud, and that we do not occupy any particularly favourable position in the Universe.

Realising all these material facts, we cannot help our thoughts being led in another direction. We are moved to exclaim with the Psalmist—"the heavens declare the glory of God ; and the firmament sheweth His handiwork."

And again, with him we are tempted to ask—

"When I consider Thy heavens, the
work of Thy fingers,
"The Moon and the Stars which Thou
hast ordained;
"What is man that Thou art mindful of
him ?
"And the son of man, that Thou
visitest him ?"

A Guide to the Use of Our English Language

The Priceless Gift of the Written Word

Letter	Egyptian Hieroglyphic		Hieratic	Phoenician	Greek	Roman
a	eagle				A α	Adaa
b	crane				B β	B b
d	hand				Δ δ	D d
k	bowl				K k	K k
n	water				N ν	N n
r	mouth		4		P ρ	R r

HOW OUR ALPHABET BEGAN

As man progressed from his primitive state he had the desire to write down his thoughts and ideas. His first efforts to express himself in writing were by crude drawings and from these an alphabet gradually grew. This varied in different countries and with the various languages which slowly developed.

THE MAGIC ART OF WRITING

FLAG—MOON—DAISY—SEA: These are just words but you have only to read them once to get a vivid and clear meaning in your mind. Now the words are each composed of a few letters and the letters are merely marks made by printer's ink on paper. Yet they give you in a flash a whole picture: you can almost see the thing they stand for. That, in a nutshell, is the magic of writing or, in this case, of printing, which is, after all, just an artificial or mechanical way of writing.

The Second of the R's

We are going to consider how this magic works and what it can be made to do. The important thing is that any one of you can learn its secrets and use your knowledge to make your life a success. This does not mean that you will all wish to become writers or authors, but in the modern world you can't do any sort of business without some writing.

Even the smallest amount of writing can be done well or badly. The purpose of this book is to help young people to do things well because, to recall the old saying, if a thing is worth doing, it is worth doing well. This chapter will explain what writing is and show you why it is worth doing well. We will consider the magic art in two ways. Firstly, we must think of how to write, then of what to write.

When our Grandfathers and Grandmothers were at school they used to say that they began by learning the three R's; this was a sort of old-fashioned joke, for the three R's were meant to stand for Reading, Writing and Arithmetic, and they certainly all begin with the R sound, but our Grandparents hadn't learned much about writing if they thought it was spelt with an R. And they seem to have lost sight of the A in Arithmetic! But that famous phrase — the Three R's—is a useful reminder that education starts with learning to read, to write and to work with figures. You start by getting to know the shapes of the letters—by reading them; then you learn to make these shapes yourself—that is writing. It is the second of the Three R's which is our concern here, and is probably the greatest of the three.

What is Writing ?

Most young boys and girls can draw before they can write. Now the human race, when it was young and just beginning to become civilised, could draw before it could write. Men found that they wanted to say things to other men who were not present at the time, or that they wanted to leave what they thought behind them for others to think about. So they made simple drawings on the walls of their caves. These were rough and rather like your younger brother's drawings of animals and flowers. But they told a simple story carved there with flint on the rock. They were the beginnings of writing.

Men soon saw that if they had much to say they would have to improve these messages to make them express more ideas and at the same time to make them quicker and easier to record. So gradually they agreed that certain marks or signs would represent certain spoken sounds. From this came letters, and once an alphabet was formed, men could combine the letters in endless groups, or words, and could then convey all manner of thought on every kind of subject. They had evolved the written language.

Different Alphabets and Characters

Of course, mankind, scattered over all the world, in different countries, in different climates, and with different voices, naturally did not all work out an alphabet in the same way. But all the alphabets were worked out through the ages for the same purpose: to enable men to put their thoughts down in a lasting form, to write so that others might read. Here are some specimens of the letters and characters used in other lands.

關 須 給 大 肝 證 而 佳 充 以 骨 齒。

CHINESE

سي باچك رهتي حاصل ادهہ مخروم آن اهہ پرمد هہ.

HINDUSTANI

Говорили они мало и мало видили он.

RUSSIAN

Jeder schuf Gott sind zum macht, nichts ist.

GERMAN

Each character is part of an alphabet, or in Chinese may represent a word. And they all have to be *written*.

The Purpose of Writing

As we have already seen, the purpose of writing is to put thought in permanent and accessible (that is, easy to get at) form. That can be described as the basic principle of writing. But there are many different aspects of this desire of men to put their thoughts on paper, ranging from the rough pencil note which you make to remind yourself of something perhaps only a few hours later, to the very carefully polished words and phrases set down by an author or scholar after years of study, to be read by future generations as great literature. Let us consider a few of these purposes of writing.

Firstly, there are personal or private letters to be written. Most boys and girls, when they have with a great struggle at school learned to write a few simple words, probably begin by proudly sending a little note to Mother, Father, Grannie or Grandpa. They have begun something that will continue thoughout their lives. There will always be times when a friend or relation has to be told your news and a letter has to be written. There are still things that can be more easily said, even to a very close friend, in a letter than by telephone or even in conversation.

Letters and Diaries

Then there are business letters. Can you imagine the world of to-day, even with its telephones, if there were no business letters? You must learn to write, if only for these two reasons—private and business letters. It would be difficult to go through life without having at some time, and probably frequently, to compose either or both.

But you may want to write for other reasons. Do you keep a diary? Here you will make day-to-day entries of interesting things that happen, perhaps not very important things to-day, but things which in a year or two will recall pleasant occasions or events which may have led to greater and more important milestones in your career.

We cannot mention diaries without thinking of what is undoubtedly the most famous diary written in English. This was just such a diary as you might keep, but it was written faithfully and fully each day and no trivial event or observation was left out. It was written by Samuel Pepys three centuries ago and it has become a great piece of literature which the historians have studied to learn about England as it was in the days of Pepys. People who love good writing study this diary and enjoy the skill with which Pepys used his language to record his simplest thought. You may, however, get joy from keeping a diary without trying to become another Samuel Pepys and it is one very good way to practise the art of writing.

AN EARLY HORNBOOK

One of the earliest forms of school primers was the Horn Book. This consisted of a piece of paper or vellum, on which the alphabet was printed, covered by a sheet of transparent horn, and mounted on wood.

So far we have thought of writing as an art at the service of everybody. There are, however, people whose business it is to write. They are the journalists and the authors whose profession it is to chronicle or record events, to set down their own and other people's thoughts or to convey important messages from Governments to the people and sometimes from the people to the Governments. Writing for them is a business but it need never cease to be also an art. The most humble journalist on a little village paper who has to report a meeting in the Church Hall, can still, if he is a good writer, produce fine English prose.

Speaking broadly, journalists are those writers who fill the pages of our daily newspapers, our weekly reviews and periodicals, our magazines and quarterlies. They are in turn broadly divided into news journalists and periodical journalists, and you will naturally see that the first group have to write more quickly, have less time to consider how they write, and must arrange their thoughts before the events they are describing have ceased to be "fresh" news.

Journalists and Authors

To become this sort of writer requires special training and long and perhaps tedious practice until you can be quick and accurate and always interesting to read. The periodical journalists, on the other hand, have more time; we say their writing is more "leisurely." They have time to think and consider the effects and results of events; they are less concerned with telling their readers about the events themselves.

These journalists are more akin to the next group of writers—writers of books, or more simply, authors. Authors, in the fullest sense of the word, strive to produce literature rather than what the journalists call copy—that is the journalistic word for the stories and articles they write.

Other Fields for the Writer

It is well said "of the making of books, there is no end." There can be scarcely a home which does not have some books in it somewhere. Books have been written about everything under the sun. So by far the greatest field for the writer is the authorship of books. But you may immediately think of the man who stands out head and shoulders above all the others as the greatest writer in the English language, William Shakespeare. He was a playwright; although now his plays are published in book form he wrote lines for actors to speak on the stage. This is dramatic writing and of the making of plays too it is difficult to see the end. Men who have observed how their fellow men live, how they speak, what sort of characters they have, how now they laugh, how they weep, have put their observations in writing in the form of dialogue. They do not merely tell a story—they make characters, by talking to one another, tell the story.

One modern type of playwright does not have to consider that his audience is watching his characters. He is the radio dramatist, who writes his plays for performance on the wireless. The speech of his characters, with perhaps just a few sound effects, are all he has with which to hold the scattered audience who may be listening all over the world. This writer's play is usually called a "script."

Other modern writers, playwrights too, write the material which is made into films or televised. They have got back from the period of the wireless play which cannot be seen to the theatre play which the audience watches. But they have a scope which the theatre dramatist never had. Shakespeare, on the small Elizabethan stage, which did not even have the scenery and all the lighting of the theatre as we know it, had to convey to his audience the places in all corners of the world and in all times of history, where his characters lived. You will see that the magic art of his writing was the important thing.

The film writer, whose play is called a scenario, is not limited in this way.

He has merely to say to the producer who makes the film, "I wish my characters to appear next in the Sahara Desert, on a glacier on the Alps, or on board a four-masted grain ship on its way from Australia," and the film producer can do it. The cinema audience will see the people there. But do not think his art is easy. The scenario writer has much to learn about the great and complicated machinery of film making. To be this sort of writer you will have to study not only writing but the whole fascinating industry of the cinema. Similarly, the writer for television has a special technique to master.

What We Write On

It is almost impossible to think of a world without paper. This book you are reading, your morning news and the letters you write are all on paper; but just as modern writing is the result of long years of development from the early cave drawings, so paper is the result of progress through the ages in writing material. From the wall of the cave on which these first letters in the infancy of man were cut or scraped with flints, the next step probably was to tablets of stone.

One person must have thought it would be useful to take his writings or drawings with him, so he put them on a slab of stone that could be carried about or hidden away for others to see at some distant date. (You will remember from your Bible stories how Moses, the Great Law Maker of the Israelites, wrote the Ten Commandments he got from God on the mountain on tablets of stone.) But these early writers were also beginning to think of other suitable materials, blocks of wood rubbed smooth so that they gave a good writing surface, the inner bark of trees, the skin of animals, dried and made into leather and much later down the centuries when man had learnt to weave cloth from the fibres of plants, linen and paper (as we now know it).

As with the different alphabets, so in different parts of the world were different materials used. It is to ancient Egypt that you must return to see the beginning of the writing material

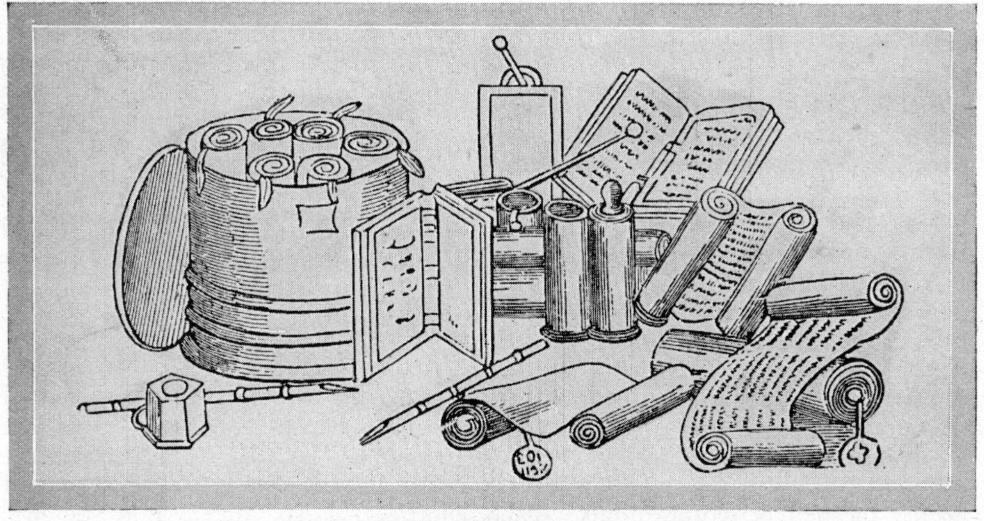

ANCIENT IMPLEMENTS OF WRITING

In this drawing is shown on the left a case containing six ancient books rolled up and labelled with their titles. A stylus and inkstand are in front, and to the right a reed pen. Waxed tablets, joined as with hinges, stand near the centre, while on the right are more volumes, some partly unrolled, written on papyrus, with title-labels attached.

that was to be paper—and, indeed, to see the beginning of the very word, paper. The Egyptians from first drawing their hieroglyphics on stone, developed a new art. Along the banks of the Nile in the warm moist atmosphere there grew a reed called the papyrus which was something like a bulrush. In the centre of these reeds was a yellowish white pith which the Egyptians removed. Side by side they laid dozens of these strips, then in the other direction another layer on top of them. They pressed the two together while they were still moist and they were moulded into a thin smooth surfaced sheet which took its name from the reed—papyrus. You will see how this idea began both the word and principle of modern paper. It is perhaps not surprising that since our alphabet came from this wonderful civilisation of the Nile the material on which it is used also developed there.

What We Write With

In every phase of this magic art of writing there is a long and romantic story. If you were asked to write your name you would probably write it on paper without even thinking, and you would write it with a pen or a pencil. Now these two tools of the writer are not things that have always been ; they also are the result of man's progress through the years. No doubt when tablets of stone or plaques of wood gave way to less hard materials, so the flints were thrown away and replaced by other " markers." Sticks or rough brushes may have been used first, dipped in the blood of animals or in the natural dyes of the trees of the forest. The Egyptians are believed to have used the sharpened end of a reed or feather to write on their papyrus, and we know that in our own British history the first pens were quills. You can make a quill pen for yourself to-day by simply making a slanting cut through the thick " stem " of a goose-feather.

Between Writing and Printing

From the quill developed the metal pen point in a holder. This lasted longer and was smoother to use, but it still had to be dipped in the inkwell. To-day we have fountain pens carrying their own well of ink in their holders.

Your pencil, generally called a " lead " pencil, is not, of course, made of the metal lead ; it is really a long thin rod of graphite, with a protective wood skin. The wood has nothing to do with the writing, it is merely for ease in handling and to prevent the brittle graphite from breaking as you work. It does not always do this, as you know to your cost. If you press too heavily your pencil breaks and the wood has to be sharpened away till you have a fine writing point of graphite again. Perhaps you are lucky enough to have a propelling pencil. It is really the first cousin of the fountain pen ; it requires no sharpening and carries its own supply of leads.

In the business world, however, letters to-day are mostly written neither with pen nor pencil, but by means of a typewriter. With this wonderful machine one can write at great speed and with great clarity. It is a mechanical writer and comes half-way between simple writing and printing—the process of mechanical writing which is enabling you to read these lines at this moment. Elsewhere in this work you will find all about printing presses, but remember that even the very biggest of them is doing nothing more or less than reproducing someone's writing.

Hand-writing a Guide to Character

Actual writing, that is, hand-writing, the making of marks with a pen or pencil on paper, is a thing we take for granted. To most educated people to-day it is indeed as natural and effortless as speaking. But you will remember your own early difficulties at school, when you first had to learn to write. No so many years ago there were many grown-up men and women even in this country who could scarcely write their own names. So we should not take hand-writing too much for granted, even although, like riding a bicycle or swimming, it is an art that once learnt, is never forgotten.

Most children first learn to form the capital letters, then go on to what is called " cursive " writing. This is the usual writing employed for letters, etc. The word " cursive " simply means " run together," one letter linked up to, flowing into, or running on to the next one with no breaks between. We will not go over what you learned at school here, except to say that you must always write clearly or legibly (legibly means able to be read). What you may not have learned in your early writing lessons is that your hand-writing is a guide to your character. Like your clothes or your speech, it gives some indication to others of the sort of person you are.

The Magic Art of Writing

The Magic Art of Writing

The Magic Art of Writing

STYLES OF HANDWRITING

In the present century handwriting has generally deteriorated and the " copperplate " (top) of the Victorian era has all but vanished. A straightforward and legible business hand is seen in the middle, while variations of the script style are becoming increasingly popular to-day.

In the field of business and business correspondence you will sooner or later discover yet another kind of writing—shorthand. There are several systems of shorthand writing, but they all have the same purpose, to enable words spoken or dictated to be taken down by the shorthand writer in signs which stand for the various sounds of the syllables instead of spelling the words in cursive writing. Because we have shorthand, cursive writing is indeed often referred to as " long hand " to distinguish the two. A shorthand writer is called a " stenographer " and many girls may begin their business careers by learning shorthand in order to become shorthand typists.

Typing, or typewriting, on a machine is the simplest and commonest form of mechanical writing; it is less elaborate, less expensive and more convenient than printing, and again it is much faster than writing with pen and ink. It is of course also much more legible, since the writer's character cannot creep into it—good or bad. When a business man says he writes a letter, he usually means that he has dictated the words he wanted to say to his stenographer or shorthand writer, who from the shorthand notes turns the symbols back into words on her typewriter, producing the finished letter for his signature. His signature is almost certainly the only bit of true writing in the letter.

LETTER WRITING

The Form of the Letter

Just as there are correct things to wear or correct manners at table, so there is an accepted way of setting out the letters you write whether to a member of your family or to an unknown business acquaintance. At the top of the letter comes the heading. This gives the address from which the letter is being sent. It is usually written or printed at the top right-hand corner of the notepaper in this form:—

5, Medway Avenue,
Tunbridge Wells.

The next thing to remember is to date your letter. This is placed immediately under the last line of your address in the top right-hand corner. Thus:—

The Thatched Cottage,
Bilberry Road,
Seaton,
Devon.
25th October, 1945.

You are now ready to start the letter proper. Beginning at the left-hand margin and a little lower on the paper than the date you have just put on the right, you commence with the salutation—*Dear Aunt Jane.*

The Salutation

These first few words of the letter—" Dear So and So," are worth a little thought. The word " dear," though it may be a loving greeting in the case of certain friends or relatives, is always used. Its use is a courtesy or convention and it is employed even if you do not know the person to whom you are writing. When " dear " is meant to be more than a convention and convey real love or friendship, it is usual to begin " My dear." The name of the person to whom you are writing then follows—if it is a close friend, of course, you use their Christian name; if a relative, dear Aunt, or Uncle, and so on; or just dear Mr., Mrs., or Miss, if the letter is a formal one.

If the letter is a business one, you would begin:—

Dear Sir, or *Dear Sirs*,

or, if writing to a woman,

Dear Madam.

The First Line

You have now come to the beginning of the letter proper.

As you know, at the beginning of every paragraph in any piece of writing, whether a letter or not, you indent, that is to say you commence a little further in than the normal margin of the paper. In the case of a letter the first line of the body of the letter under the salutation is indented a little further than the normal paragraph indentation. This will generally mean that it begins almost under the end of the salutation itself.

Avoid Unnecessary Tricks

For the sake of clarity and bearing in mind always that the primary purpose of writing anything is to convey a meaning to your reader, you should break up the matter into paragraphs. In a letter it is almost better to have too many than too few. Make sure your lines run straight across the paper and leave a reasonable space between the lines. You may remember when you were first at school that you could only achieve this by writing in a ruled copy book; even some adults find it an advantage to use a heavily ruled guide paper under their notepaper.

Elsewhere in this chapter we shall have something to say of punctuation marks; we will just mention here that it is as well to avoid if possible using punctuation tricks in your writing such as underlining a word two or three times, or suddenly spelling the whole of a word in capital letters. You should rely on the clear way in which you string your words together to give any particular word emphasis, or stress.

When you come to the end of the letter, there are definite forms and customs to be observed just as there were at the beginning.

Ending a Letter

The formal end of a letter is called the " subscription," which simply means the " writing under." Indeed, many years ago the subscription used to begin with the words, " I now subscribe myself " and so on. Now we simply begin the subscription " Yours sincerely " or whatever the appropriate word may be. It is occasionally permitted to insert the words " I remain," but such a subscription is now almost as old-fashioned as "I subscribe myself."

In writing to a member of the family the most strictly appropriate wording would be "Yours affectionately" or "most affectionately," but this is often varied to "Your loving daughter," "your affectionate niece," and so on. Sometimes if the mood of your letter is intended to be more than usually affectionate, you should use a subscription on these lines: "I am, dearest Aunt Jane, your affectionate nephew, Richard."

When writing to friends, other than family friends, you will normally subscribe yourself, "Yours sincerely," "Yours very sincerely," or "Yours most sincerely." To a person whom you know but slightly, and this would cover most business communications, you will put "Yours truly," or "Yours faithfully," this latter being more generally used nowadays. Then comes your signature.

Signature

You will, of course, sign yourself with your Christian name only to all your family and to your most intimate friends. To the rest, you will sign your full signature. This is not necessarily your name in full. Thus, *Alfred Walker Smith* may sign *A. W. Smith*, *Alfred W. Smith* or even *A. Walker Smith*, just as he prefers.

A signature is a distinctive thing, and your very own. You must do it your own way. You should not, however, in your desire to make it specially distinctive, allow it to become either illegible or ridiculous. You know your own name; perhaps the other person doesn't.

The Envelope

Always remember to check through your letter before finally folding it and placing in an envelope for posting. If you have said in the letter that you are enclosing something with it make sure that the enclosure is there. Fold your letter carefully and not too often—just often enough to enable it to fit neatly into the envelope. Every unnecessary fold makes it less easy to handle and read when it is received.

The address on the envelope follows very much the same form as the heading at the top of the right-hand corner of your letter. On the letter, of course, was your address, on the envelope is the name of the addressee—that is, the person to whom you are writing. It should take the following form:—

Mrs. F. Buck,
The Haven,
Westdene,
Dorset.

You will notice that the address is "staggered," that is to say, it goes down like stairs from top to bottom. This is not merely a custom; it is done to make each line as clear as possible to the Postal Authorities. Try the simple experiment for yourself, of writing an address straight down, one item directly under the other; you will see that it would be more difficult for the staff of sorters in the post office to pick out speedily the town, the road and finally the actual house.

For the same reasons of clarity the address should be written squarely in the middle of the envelope, bearing in mind that a stamp will go on the top right-hand corner, and in addition to the stamp the cancellation markings made by the Post Office. If you address the envelope too high and too much to the right the address will be obscured by these markings.

Your letter is now ready to post.

Postcards

Postcards in general use are of two types: plain postcards and picture postcards. The plain postcard is addressed exactly the same as a letter on one side; on the other it should bear the sender's address, but in practice the salutation may be dropped and the subscription omitted.

In the case of the picture postcard the reverse side is divided into two halves. On one side goes the address, on the other the message. Do not allow your desire to say more than you have room for tempt you to carry your message across into the address section. This is not fair to the postal authorities. If you have so much to say, you should write a letter.

Telegrams

A telegram is really a shortened, abbreviated or condensed form of letter. You may send a telegram in two ways. If you are a telephone subscriber, all you need do is to get on to the telephone exchange, ask for "Telegrams," then proceed to dispatch it. You will be required to give your own telephone number, then the telephone number or address of the person to whom you are sending it. You then dictate your short message clearly, spelling any unusual words. You finish by giving your "signature." A telegram is meant for speed, therefore the shorter it is the more quickly it will go because there is less delay in its transmission. Bear in mind that after you give it to the telephone exchange it is sent over the telegraph lines to the receiving office nearest to your friend's address. A telegram is of course more expensive than a letter.

In a telegram there is no need to write beautiful smooth-flowing or even strictly grammatical English; you merely wish to give the essentials in a way in which they cannot be misunderstood. For example, in a letter you might say "You will be extremely pleased to hear that as a result of all my careful studies this term, I have been placed head of the form in the examination and have therefore gained a scholarship to York University." In a telegram all you need say is "Gained first in term exam., and York scholarship."

Transmitted by Radio

The alternative method of sending your telegram is to go into a post or telegraph office and ask for a telegram form. You then write your message on the form which is clearly laid out so that you cannot mistake its purpose, and hand the form to the clerk or operator, who will count the number of words (including the address of the person to whom you are sending it) and calculate how much it is going to cost you. The actual rate has varied at different periods in the history of the Telegraph Service and may do so again. A minimum charge of 3*s.* for twelve words and 3*d.* for each word thereafter is the rate for inland telegrams at the time of writing. The minimum charge means that even if the address and message is less than a total of twelve words you still pay as though it were twelve words.

When a telegram, or as it is often called in ordinary conversation, "a wire," is sent to some place overseas, it is usually called "a cable." The word, of course, really refers to the under-sea cables or lines along which the message is transmitted. Although to-day most cables are really telegrams transmitted by radio, they are still generally referred to as cables.

When you have written a letter, put it in its envelope, addressed, sealed, and stamped the envelope, you have then to post it. The action of posting a letter, so far as you are concerned, is the end of the matter. It is a great tribute to our postal services that people everywhere take so much for granted the slipping of a letter into a letterbox. It never occurs to us that it will not reach the person for whom it is intended; and how rarely does it ever fail to get there. When it is lost in the post it may well be that it has been badly or carelessly addressed, that the envelope has not been properly closed or even that the mail bag containing that particular letter has been stolen or destroyed by accident.

A SCHOLAR OF THE MIDDLE AGES

Before the invention of printing between the years 1440 and 1450, all books were written and copied by hand. In the picture above a famous scholar and penman of the Middle Ages, Jean Mielot, is seen at work writing on parchment, then regarded as a great art as such books were not merely executed in beautiful lettering but were often illustrated with exquisite designs and drawings.

If your letter is particularly valuable and you cannot afford to have it lost, or if you want to have a proof that you posted it, you may "register" the letter. You must go to a post office to do this. You will receive a receipt for the letter and the post office will accept responsibility for its safe delivery. There are additional rates of postage for Registering a letter.

Problems of Spelling

Some people naturally find spelling easy. They have what is known as a photographic memory for written words. When they see a word written they are impressed not only with its meaning but with its very shape. They see it in their mind's eye.

Other people just as naturally have no visual or photographic memory of this sort, although they may have a wonderful memory for the sound of a spoken word and perhaps quick and fine perception of a word's inner meaning. To such people spelling errors will be all too easy. For them, alas, and there are many of them, English is a most unkind language. So many of its words are not written at all as they are spoken. So many of its letters are silent, so many have sounds that vary from one word to another, and there are so many rules continually broken, that unless you have a strong photographic memory you are almost certain to make some spelling errors in English.

In the following paragraphs we are going to mention some of the commoner spelling mistakes and indicate some short cuts, or rules, that may help you to write them correctly.

Double Consonants

Very often double consonants have the same sound as a single consonant. For instance, gh may have the same sound as g (ghastly), or c as ch (chaos), or t as th (thyme). And there is, of course, the famous double consonant, ph which is pronounced neither like a p nor an h, but like an f (Phyllis). But the kind of double consonant that gives most trouble should perhaps be called the twin consonant. This is brought about by the adding of suffixes, or endings, to words. For example—bit, bitten, although the consonant has been doubled, the sound has not really changed. Some words, of course, have twin consonants, although there is no suffix added. Compare paper with pepper. Here are some rules for dealing with the double, or twin, consonant.

1. If you are adding a suffix which begins with a vowel, for example, *-ing*, or *-ed* to a word of one syllable, which itself has a single vowel followed by a final consonant, this final consonant is doubled. For example, blot, blot*ted*, blot*ting*.

2. The final consonant is not doubled if the word ends in two consonants, or if it has a double vowel before the final consonant.

For example: roast, roast*ing*; bleed, bleed*ing*.

3. In the case of words of more than one syllable ending with a consonant, this consonant is doubled if preceded by a single vowel and if the accent is on the last syllable.

For example: rebut, rebut*ted*.

4. The consonant is not doubled when the last syllable is not accented or stressed.

For example: fillet, fillet*ed*; benefit, benefit*ed*.

5. After a final *l* when a suffix begins with a vowel, the *l* is usually doubled, even when the accent does not fall on the last syllable.

For example: marvel, marvel*led*.

6. If a final *l* is preceded by two vowels, the *l* is not normally doubled before a suffix beginning with a vowel.

For example: feel, feel*ing*.

Note.—Two well-known exceptions which simply must be learned and memorised: woollen and parallel*ed*.

7. Words ending in double *ll* are interesting when a suffix beginning with a consonant is added. Sometimes one of the *l*'s is dropped, sometimes it is retained. Ill retains the double *l* in illness, but loses one of its final *l*'s in wilful. The double *l* is nearly always kept before the suffix *ness*. Still, still*ness*, full, full*ness*, chill, chill*ness*. Single *l*'s are not doubled before the suffixes *-ish*, *-ism*, *-ist* and *-ment*.

For example: devil, devil*ish*; real, real*ism*; moral, moral*ist*; fulfil, fulfil*ment*.

8. When words end in *s* to which a suffix beginning with a vowel has to be added, there is no definite rule as to whether the *s* is doubled or not. Generally, however, the *s* tends to double. Such plurals as bus*es*, focus*es*, atlas*es*, are not really exceptions to this tendency as they are words which have become English.

Words ending in a double *s* retain the double *s* when a suffix is added, whether it begins with a vowel or a consonant.

For example: bless, bless*ing* or bless*ed*; remiss, remiss*ness*.

Perhaps the second greatest difficulty in spelling English words is that two vowels may have the same sound. For example, ton and run. The O and U sounds, you notice, are identical. There are really no short cuts to mastering this difficulty. If you have the visual memory you will remember which vowel is used in which word, when you have seen it once. If you have not this sort of memory one of the best ways to aid it is to write a new word of this sort when you come across it in your reading several times over until it becomes fully impressed on your mind. The word stomach, for example, has clearly a U-sound, yet it is spelt with an O. But there are, alas, confusing exceptions. For example, a B.B.C. announcer has pronounced the town Bromley, in Kent, Brumley. All of its natives would not agree to this, whereas, almost without exception, the town of Tonbridge in the same county, is pronounced as Tunbridge, not Ton-bridge.

Another common source of spelling errors is the fact that many of our words are not really English at all. They are borrowed from foreign languages which may not even use the same alphabet as English. Obviously, so far as English is concerned, their spelling is an artificial agreement. An excellent example of this is the Japanese word for suicide, "hara-kiri." This is usually pronounced harry-karry, and therefore it is often wrongly spelt "hari-kari" by people who have a half-knowledge of its origin. Such foreign importations, too, have just to be firmly and resolutely written and re-written until the correct spelling becomes a habit. But here are some other groups of spelling difficulties to which some sort of rule can be applied, although there are nearly always exceptions.

(*a*) A spelling rule which nearly everybody knows as well as they know the rhyme about the days of the month: "Thirty days hath September, etc.," is this:

"I before E except after C."

The ie or ei combination in words is fraught with difficulty. The rule is little more than a guide. Here, for example, is a list of common exceptions.

Ancient.	Sufficient.
Efficient.	Deficient.
Inveigh.	Weigh.
Neither.	Sleigh.
Reign.	Rein.
Foreign.	Height.
Deign.	Their.

There are, however, two sub-rules that can be applied to the exceptions.

(i) I before E except after C in words with the vowel sound double e. (Exceptions to this sub-rule are *seize*, *weird*, *counterfeit*.)

(ii) I before E except after C, unless the C has an sh sound. The word *fancied* is an exception to this sub-rule.

(*b*) Should a verb end in -ise or -ize? A great English authority on words, Fowler, whose works you will probably study when you are older, almost excuses the difficulty of knowing which is which. Generally, words with a Greek or classical origin from the Greek *izo*, should end *ize*—words like baptize and epitomize, but even they are frequently spelt even by good writers *-ise*. This is really copying the French manner. But here is a list of words, listed by Fowler, as correctly spelt *-ise*.

Advertise.	Advise.
Apprise.	Chastise.
Comprise.	Compromise.
Demise.	Despise.
Devise.	Defranchise.
Enfranchise.	Enterprise.
Excise.	Exercise.
Improvise.	Incise.
Premise.	Supervise.
Surmise.	Surprise.

It is interesting to note that in America the -ize spelling has become almost as universal as the -ise spelling has in this country. As we have noted, a universal rule is, strictly, wrong in either country. The root origin of the word is the correct guide.

Tricky Word Endings

We have noticed the rules and exceptions regarding the spelling of words ending in consonants, particularly double consonants. But there are other sources of difficulty at the end of a word when a suffix has to be added. For example: *-ly* is an adverbial ending. There is an immediate problem when it has to be added to an adjective already ending in *l* or *ll*. The rule to follow is simple. After the ending has been added, the resulting adverb should end in *-lly* whether the original word had one *l* or two. *Bountiful* gives *bountifully; full, fully; doleful, dolefully*, and so on.

A similar difficulty which can be remembered with the last one is the formation of a noun ending in *-ness* from an adjective which already ends in an *n*. The rule is that the word retains the *n*, resulting in a double *n*. *Thin*, gives *thinness; solemn, solemnness.*

Here is another tricky ending to watch. It applies to words which end in *e*, when a suffix beginning with a vowel has to be tagged on. The rule is that the single *e* is generally dropped. If the suffix begins with a consonant it is generally retained. *Rude*, gives *rudely* or *rudeness*. *Crude, crudity and crudeness.* There is one word in this connection which has been a puzzle to spelling authorities for years and the correct spelling is not yet fully settled by the experts. The word is *judgement* or *judgment*. You will notice it is formed by adding the suffix *-ment* to the word *judge*. According to the rule we have just quoted, since *-ment* begins with a consonant, the *e* should be retained. Most dictionaries give the form *judgment*, and consider it the exception that proves the rule. Some experts justify the dropping of the *e* on the grounds that the *e* is not necessary to help the correct pronunciation. It has even been suggested that the meaning of the word *judgment* is so important and so separate that it is well not to associate it too closely with the root word *judge*. In the case of a word like this, the great thing is to be consistent. Think about it, ask one or two people whose opinions you respect, then decide which version you will adopt. Having done so, you should always spell it that way and abide by your *judgment*.

There are, however, exceptions to the dropping-of-the-e-rule, about which there is no argument. *Singe* becomes *singeing* (singing obviously wouldn't do). *Notice* becomes *noticeable* to help the pronunciation (the c might otherwise become hard). For the same reason *gauge* becomes *gaugeable* and *whole, wholly*.

If the word ends in *ie* and the suffix *-ing* has to be added, the *ie* becomes *y* (exception, *hie* becomes *hieing*). Notice *die, dying; dye, dyeing*. Words ending *ye, oe, ee* retain the final *e* before *-ing; fleeing, shoeing, eyeing*. If a word ends in a *y*, the *y* becomes *i* unless the suffix begins with *i*. *Parry* becomes *parried* or *parrying*. If *y* ends the word, following a vowel, this change does not take place. *Enjoy* becomes *enjoyed* or *enjoying*. (Exceptions, *say, said; pay, paid; slay, slain.*)

Plurals

A Latin word like radius becomes rad*ii*, whereas the word bus (really the Latin word omnibus) has the plural bus*es*. These two examples suggest the general rule. If the word has never really ceased to be classical, it is given a classical plural in English. If the word has become to all intents and purposes a native English word, it forms its plural in the native English way, namely, by adding *s* or *es*. Words of foreign origin ending in *o*, like *ditto, commando, crescendo*, add *s* only, to form the plural. Otherwise, " native " words ending in *o*, like *cargo, potato, hero*, add *es*. Where, however, the particular word already ends in two vowels, such as *folio and cameo*, *s* only is added. This is less a matter of logic than to avoid three vowels coming together. *Photo, piano, dynamo*, which are really abbreviations, add *s* only. It is interesting to note that if you have to use a single word like *no*, or *go*, in the plural, *es* is added, probably to make the word more acceptable.

Note these plural endings. *Phenomenon* becomes *phenomena*. *Premise* becomes *premises*, *rotunda* becomes *rotundæ*, but *stanza stanzas*. Index becomes *indices*. Note also a host

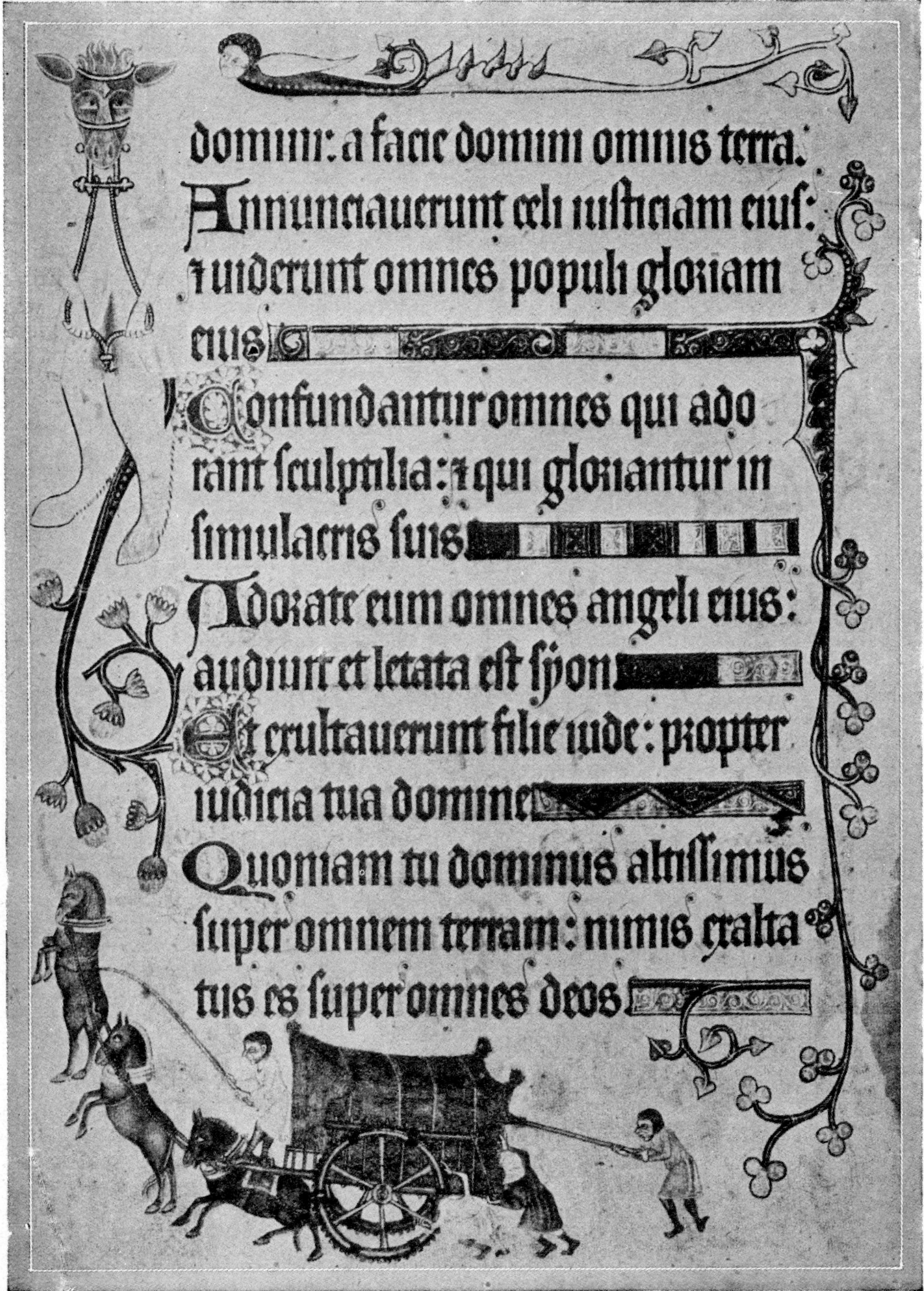

dominum: a facie domini omnis terra.
Annunciauerunt celi iusticiam eius:
et uiderunt omnes populi gloriam
eius
Confundantur omnes qui ado
rant sculptilia: et qui gloriantur in
simulacris suis
Adorate eum omnes angeli eius:
audiuit et letata est syon
Et exultauerunt filie iude: propter
iudicia tua domine
Quoniam tu dominus altissimus
super omnem terram: nimis exalta
tus es super omnes deos

By permission of the British Museum.

For the greater part of a thousand years, before William Caxton set up the first printing-press in England in 1476-77, the only books produced in this country were written by hand. Most of them were the work of monks, and a fine example of their craftsmanship is seen in the photograph above of a page of the Luttrell Psalter, written about 1340. The passage shown here is a portion of Psalm 97, from the end of verse 5 to end of verse 9.

of peculiar plurals which most people spell correctly because they are so common, *mouse, mice; house, houses; ox, oxen; hoof, hooves; loaf, loaves;* but *sheep, sheep.*

Care should be taken about the plural of nouns ending in y. The rule is that the *y* becomes *ies,* unless it is preceded by *e* when the *ey* simply has the *s* added to become *-eys.* Poppy becomes popp*ies,* but storey becomes storeys as distinguished from story, stor*ies.*

The Prefix Al

When the word " all " is prefixed to another word to make a compound word, one of the l's is usually dropped. For example, already, almost, altogether. All right should always be written as two words. " Altogether " and " all together " have rather different meanings.

When the word " full " is used as a suffix, although there is apparently nothing to influence the final l, it is dropped. Hope becomes hope*ful,* beauty, beauti*ful,* care becomes care*ful* and sorrow becomes sorrow*ful.*

When " All " is the Ending

Here is a common source of spelling mistakes. You may have to look twice to decide whether the following words are correctly or incorrectly spelt. Appal, enthrall, install, befall. According to that great authority, the Concise Oxford Dictionary, the double l is necessary following the a, whereas words like distil, annul, following other vowels, show single l's. However, some good writers spell enthral with one l and the Oxford Dictionary breaks its own rule by spelling appal with one.

Adjectives ending in -ed

If a word ends in a vowel and you wish to use it as an adjective, with the -ed ending, for example, halo, halo*ed,* there is always a problem. As a general rule, however, add a single *d* if the word ends in a single vowel sound, e. For example, pedigreed, filigreed; add *-ed* if it ends otherwise.

What is a Diphthong ?

Œ and Æ are diphthongs. They are really clumsy and unnecessary in modern English. Indeed, in the case of many words originally spelt with a diphthong it is now an affectation of writing to use the diphthong. Ether was originally Æther. Medieval was mediæval. There is some reason, however, for retaining the diphthong with such foreign arrivals to the language as hors d'œuvres.

Some Prefix Difficulties

The most frequently mis-spelt prefix is *un* or *in,* meaning not. If a rule can be given at all, it is this. Words of Latin origin, take *in.* Words of native English origin, *un.* But, alas, this rule is very frequently broken, and formations, even with the same root, are not consistent. Digest, for instance, gives you undigested, but indigestible. The best way here, as with so many of our spelling difficulties, is to try and photograph the correct form in your mind. Here is a short list of common words showing the correct *in* or *un* prefix.

*In*admissible.	*Un*acceptable.
*In*adaptability.	*Un*adaptable.
*In*applicable.	*Un*alterable.
*In*appropriate.	*Un*apparent.
*In*cautious.	*Un*charitable.
*In*civility.	*Un*congenial.
*In*conceivable.	*Un*considered.
*In*considerable.	*Un*controllable.
*In*consolable.	*Un*corrupted.
*In*distinct.	*Un*deniable.
*In*distinguishable.	*Un*distinguished.
*In*efficient.	*Un*expurgated.
*In*explicable.	*Un*grammatical.
*In*flexible.	*Un*grateful.
*In*gratitude.	*Un*objectionable.
*In*hospitable.	*Un*obliging.
*In*opportune.	*Un*quenchable.
*In*quietude.	*Un*scientific.

*In*sanitary.	*Un*sociable.
*In*soluble.	*Un*substantial.
*In*surmountable.	*Un*successful.

Notice particularly the prefix *in* when it means "in" rather than "not." It has variations, *im* (usually for reasons of sound, *im*merse) and *en* or *em*. Here are a few words to study. We give the spellings generally accepted as correct, though the alternative is not always wrong.

*In*quire.	*In*ure.
*In*grain.	*En*treat.
*En*trust.	*En*mesh.
*En*sure.	*In*sure (business).
*En*dorse.	*En*case.

A particularly difficult prefix to handle is *for* or *fore*. The trouble is that the prefix has a large number of different shades of meaning. It does not always imply going before in time or order or rank. When it does imply this sense of order it generally takes the form ending with the e. For example : forehead, forearm, foremast, forefather (ancestor). When the meaning is slightly away from the idea of priority, the *for* form is more general. But the *for* words are rare and are tending to fall out of use. Forgo means to go without rather than to go before, hence the absence of the e. Forbid suggests exclusion, not priority. Forbear suggests abstinence. Forget, forgive, forlorn, forsake, forsooth, forswear, likewise have no sense of priority.

Foreclose is an interesting exception with which to end this group of words. To follow our rule it should have been *forclose* because it suggests exclusion rather than priority.

Ante or Anti ?

The prefix *ante* means before, whereas *anti* means opposed to or against. If you bear these meanings in mind you will not readily mis-spell words like *anti*septic (opposed to or against sepsis or poison,) *ante*diluvian (before the flood, or ancient). The word *anti*-macassar might not immediately help you until you think of its fundamental meaning "against or opposed to macassar oil." Hence a covering over the back of the chair to protect it from hair-oil.

Some More Common Confusions

There are some word endings so much alike that they give rise to frequent spelling mistakes, all the more so because in many cases it is difficult to lay down a definite rule.

-xion or -ction. The tendency nowadays is to prefer the ending *ction* in words like conne*ction*, defle*ction*, infle*ction*, and refle*ction* although from the etymological point of view, that is having regard to the root of the word, the "x" spelling is more correct. Even the more important standard dictionaries are at variance in regard to these noun endings. You would not be wrong to use "x"—indeed, you might be more academically correct, but the *ct* form has the greatest support in common journalistic and literary usage.

-In or -Ine. Words like gelatine, margarine and insulin, all have a scientific origin, and the variation in spelling is based on a scientific rather than grammatical principle. Neutral substances are spelt *-in*, basic substances *-ine*. Ordinary people, with no special scientific knowledge will, perhaps, however, find little help in this rule ; as so often in English, they will just have to try and fix the correct form in their minds.

-Or or -Our. You may have noticed that English words like humour, odour, and clamour are spelt in American writing humor, odor, clamor. We are rather inclined to criticise the Americans for what we regard as a modern short-cut version, but we are on rather delicate ground here, for we ourselves consider we are correct in writing stup*or*, trem*or* or the very common horr*or*. The Americans are at least consistent. Some day we may imitate

their consistency without feeling that we are losing the dignity of our language. In the meantime we keep the "u" in such words as col*our*, and vap*our*, but we drop it when we make the noun coloration, the verb vaporise, or to revert to our earlier examples, the adjectives odor*ous*, humor*ous*, clamor*ous*.

-Ey or -Y. One of the first and simplest efforts at word-making which a child learns, is to make an adjective out of a noun by giving it a -y ending. You talk of a green-y colour when you mean it is slightly green. The -y not only forms an adjective but tends to minimise or reduce the force of the noun. The spelling problem comes with words like mouse, nose, stage, blue. A silent "e" at the end of a word is usually dropped when the "y" ending is added. Thus we get the adjectives mousy, nosy, stagy. With blue, however, the "e" is retained because it is really part of the "ue" and in that sense is not silent. By contrast the word plague becomes plag*uy*, because the *ue* is silent.

When the noun already ends in a y, *-ey* is added: clay giving clay*ey*.

Able or -ible

Able or -Ible. Unfortunately, no authority has yet provided a really good short-cut to good spelling so far as the adjectival endings *-ible or able* are concerned. We therefore are giving you a list of the commoner words in pairs, to provide a contrast that may help you to remember which are the "a"s and which are the "i"s.

-ABLE WORDS	-IBLE WORDS.
Accept*able*	Access*ible*
Account*able*	Adduc*ible*
Approach*able*	Admiss*ible*
Believ*able*	Comprehens*ible*
Blame*able*	Destruct*ible*
Convers*able*	Convert*ible*
Debat*able*	Deduc*ible*
Describ*able*	Discern*ible*
Dispens*able*	Divis*ible*
Excit*able*	Illeg*ible*
Excus*able*	Express*ible*
Govern*able*	Dirig*ible*
Indefatig*able*	Invinc*ible*
Insuper*able*	Incorrig*ible*
Lament*able*	Irasc*ible*
Limit*able*	Expans*ible*
Lov*able*	Leg*ible*
Manage*able*	Neglig*ible*
Notice*able*	Ostens*ible*
Pass*able*	Plaus*ible*
Penetr*able*	Percept*ible*
Presum*able*	Permiss*ible*
Reconcil*able*	Reduc*ible*
Respect*able*	Respons*ible*
Refut*able*	Resist*ible*
Return*able*	Revers*ible*
Reput*able*	Ris*ible*
Sale*able*	Sens*ible*
Service*able*	Suscept*ible*
Trace*able*	Tang*ible*
Vulner*able*	Vis*ible*

A Spelling "Dictionary"

Here follows a short list of words which have been proved by teachers and printers and writers to be easily mis-spelt. Some of them we have mentioned already in connection with particular rules or difficulties, but they are here given in alphabetical order for your quick reference. (If you are having a Spelling Bee or a Quiz with a spelling question, this list will give you a fine selection of test words.)

Abbot
Abbreviate
Abdicator
Abductor
Aberration
Abridgement
Abscess
Absence
Absinthe
Abstemious
Abundance
Abyss
Accelerate
Accessary (of persons)
Accessory (of things)
Acclimatize
Accommodate
Accompanist
Accordion
Accrue
Acetic (acid)
Acknowledgement
Acoustic
Acquiesce
Acquire
Actuary
Addressee
Adducible
Adieu
Adjectivally
Adjudgment (but *Adjudgement* permissible)
Adjudicator
Adjunct
Admissible
Adulatory
Adventitious
Advertisement
Advisable
Æolian
Æon
Aerial
Aesthete
Affiliation
Affright
Ageing
Agglomeration
Aggrandizement
Aggravate
Aggregate

Aggression
Aggrieve
Agitator
Agriculturist
Aileron
Ajar (door)
A-kimbo
Albatross
Albinos
Albumen
Albuminous
Alfresco
Alibi
Ailment
Alimentary
Allegeable
Alligator
Alliteration
Allocation
Allot
Allotted
Aluminium
Amanuensis
Ambidextrous
Amiable
Amphibious
Anæmia
Anæsthesia
Analogous
Analyse
Ancillary
Annul
Anoint
Anomalous
Anonymous
Antarctic
Antediluvian
Anteroom
Antimacassar
Antimony
Antirrhinum
Antiseptic
Aping
Apoplectic
Apostrophe
Appal
Apparatus
Apparel
Apparent
Appellant
Apposite
Aqueduct
Aqueous
Archipelago
Arctic
Armadillo
Ascendance
Ascertain
Ascetic (austere)
Asphalt
Assassin
Assess
Assurer
Asthma
Auger (tool)
Augur (prophet)
Aurora Borealis
Auxiliary
Avoirdupois
Awesome
Awful
Ayah

Bagatelle
Baksheesh
Balanceable
Balloted
Balustrade
Bandoleer
Banister
Banqueting
Barcarole
Baritone
Barrel
Battalion
Bayonet
Beatitude
Believable
Benzene (spirit distilled from coal gas)
Benzine (spirit obtained from petroleum)
Bevelling
Biannual (twice a year), dist. from Biennial (every two years)
Biasing
Bilberry
Binnacle (Compass stand)
Binocular
Bivouacked
Bizarre
Blancmange
Bogy (ghost)
Bogey (golf)
Bogie (truck)
Boycott
Brochure
Broccoli
Bucolic
Budgerigar
Bulldog
Bulrush
Bulwark
By and by
By the bye

Caddie (golf)
Caddy (tea)
Calendar (almanac)
Calender (to smooth)
Calibre
Camaraderie
Camellia
Cannonade
Canonical
Canvas (cloth)
Canvass (solicit)
Capercailzie (bird)
Carburetter
Carcass
Caress
Caste (class)
Castellated
Cataloguing
Catarrh
Catechism
Caterpillar
Cauliflower
Cemetery
Centenary
Centring
Chameleon
Chandelier
Changeable
Chauffeur
Chiaroscuro
Chilblain
Chord
Chrysalis
Chrysanthemum
Cider
Cinnamon
Cipher
Clangour
Clayey
Clientele
Clique
Colander
Collaborator
Colloquial
Colonnade
Colossal
Commemorate
Commingle
Committed
Committee
Commonalty
Communal
Complement (that which completes)
Compliment (flattery)
Condign
Confectionery
Connection
Connoisseur
Conscientious
Contagious
Corollary
Corroborate
Courageous
Crèche
Creosote
Courtesy
Crochet (knitting)
Crotchet (music)
Crustaceous
Curtsy

Daguerreotype
Dais
Dandelion
Debatable
Deceased (dead)
Deciduous
Defendant
Deflection
Deified
Demesne
Derogatory
Descendant
Desiccate
Dilapidated
Dinghy
Diphtheria
Dirigible
Disappear
Diseased (ill)
Dissimilar
Dissociate
Doggerel
Doily
Dullness

Ecclesiastical
Echelon
Ecstasy
Eczema
Edelweiss
Effervescence
Eisteddfod
Ellipsis
Embarrass
Embed
Emissary
Empanel
Enmesh
Ensconce
Ensure
Envelopment
Erasure
Erroneous
Erysipelas
Escutcheon
Etymology
Eulogize
Euphuistic
Exacerbation
Exaggerate
Excrescence
Exercise (practice)
Exorcize (drive away)
Exhibitor

Exhilarate
Exonerate
Exotic
Expense
Extempore
Extraordinarily

Facetious
Facsimile
Fakable
Fascinate
Fiasco
Fidgeting
Filleting
Fillip
Finicking
Flaccid
Flannelette
Flannelled
Fledgeling
Flexible
Florescence
Forbear (verb.)
Forebears (ancestors)
Foreclose
Forfeit
Foully
Frolicking
Fuchsia
Fugue
Fulfil
Fumigator
Furze
Fusilier

Galaxy
Gallivant
Gambolling
Gaol
Gaseous
Gasolene
Gauge
Genuflexion
Germane
Geyser
Ghastly
Gherkin
Ghetto
Ghoul
Gillie
Gladiolus
Gluey
Glutinous
Glycerine
Gnome
Grandeur
Gruesome
Guerrilla
Gorilla
Guillemot
Gymkhana

Gymnasium
Gypsy
Gyrate

Habiliment
Hæmorrhage
Halcyon
Half-caste
Halibut
Handkerchief
Hara-kiri
Harangue
Harass
Hare-brained
Headachy
Heifer
Heighten
Heinous
Herbaceous
Hereditary
Heterogeneous
Hiatus
Hiccup
Hieing
Hinging
Hirsute
Holocaust
Honorarium
Hoopoe
Hoping
Horoscope
Horsy
Hullabaloo
Humorist
Hyacinth
Hydrangea
Hygiene
Hypocrisy

Icicle
Idiosyncrasy
Immanent
Imminent
Impeccable
Impresario
Impromptu
Inaugurate
Incidentally
Indelible
Independent
Indictment
Infallible
Infinitesimal
Inflection
Inflexible
Ingenious (clever)
Ingenuous (innocent)
Inimical
Innocuous
Innuendo
Inoculate

Inquire
Install
Insular
Insure
Integer
Interrogate
Interstice
Intriguing
Inure
Inveigle
Ipecacuanha
Isosceles
Isthmus
Itinerary
Ivied
Ivory

Jeopardy
Jocose
Jocund
Jugglery
Juiciness

Kaleidoscope
Kedgeree
Kennel
Kernel
Khaki
Kudos

Labyrinth
Lackadaisical
Lacquer
Lager
Lagoon
Lama (Buddhist priest)
Llama (animal)
Languor
Laryngitis
Lassitude
Lassoing
Legerdemain
Leprechaun
Leprosy
Liaison
Librarian
Licence (a permit)
License (verb to permit)
Liege
Lieutenant
Lineage (ancestry)
Liniment (embrocation)
Linguistic
Linoleum
Liquefy
Liqueur
Liquorice
Lissom
Literal
Lodestar

Loggia
Longevity
Lorry
Lousy
Luscious
Lustre

Macaroon
Machinery
Mackerel
Maelstrom
Magenta
Magneto
Mahogany
Mahout
Manacle
Mandible
Mandolin
Maniac
Manikin
Mannequin
Manœuvre
Margarine
Marmalade
Mashie
Massacre
Mayonnaise
Mazy
Medicine
Medieval
Meerschaum
Meringue
Meter (measuring instrument)
Metre (rhythm)
Millinery (hats)
Millennium
Millepede
Millionaire
Mimicking
Miniature
Miscellaneous
Mischievous
Mis-spelt
Moccasin
Moiety
Monocle
Mosquito
Moustache
Mousy
Mulligatawny
Myopia

Naive
Nasturtium
Nausea
Necessarily
Negligible
Nicety
Niece
Nincompoop

Oasis
Obbligato
Obedient
Obese
Oboist
Obscene
Observatory
Obsession
Obsolete
Ochre
Odorous
Odyssey
Offence
Offensive
Offertory
Olfactory
Ominous
Omission
Omniscient
Oneself
Opossum
Opposite
Orangeade
Ordinance (rule)
Ordnance (cannon)
Orgy
Oscillate
Ossified

Paging
Palette
Palfrey
Palliasse
Panacea
Papyrus
Paraffin
Parallel
Parallelogram
Paralyse
Paraphernalia
Paroxysm
Parquet
Passable
Pebbly
Pedalling
Pedlar
Peewit
Pencilling
Peninsula
Penniless
Perceive
Perennial
Perfunctory
Permissible
Perquisite
Personnel
Petroleum

Petulance
Phenomenon
Phlegm
Phosphorescence
Phosphorus
Physicist
Physique
Pianoforte
Piccaninny
Piccolo
Picaresque
Plague
Plain-sailing (*fig.*)
Plane-sailing (*naut.*)
Plausible
Plebeian
Pleurisy
Poignancy
Pomegranate
Possess
Postilion
Potato
Practice (noun)
Practise (verb)
Precedent
Prestige
Pretence
Pretension

Primeval
Principal (chief)
Principle (law)
Prise (force open)
Privilege
Proffer
Propaganda
Propeller
Prophecy (noun)
Prophesy (verb)
Propitious
Proscribe (denounce)
Prescribe (set down)
Pseudonym
Psychology
Psychiatry
Ptarmigan
Pterodactyl
Ptomaine
Puerile
Pygmy
Pyjamas
Pyrotechnic

Quarrel
Quarreller
Quarrelsome
Quay

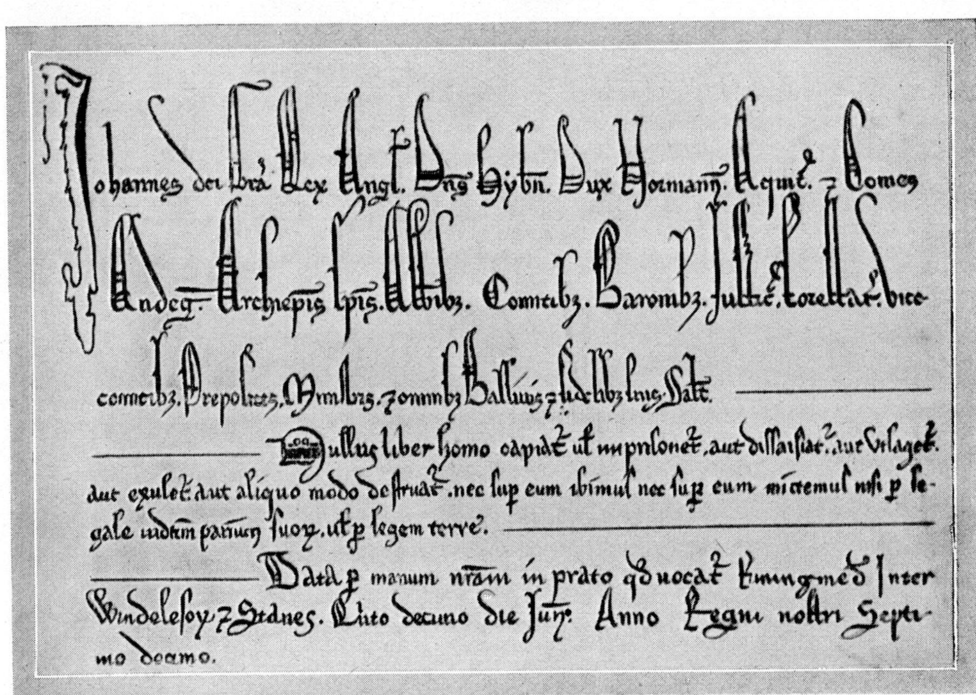

Johannes dei gratia Rex Angl. Dns Hybn. Dux Normann. Aquit. & Comes Andeg. Archiepis Epis. Abbatibz. Comitibz. Baronibz. Justic. Forestar. Vicecomitibz. Prepositis. Ministris. & omnibz Ballivis & fidelibz suis Salt.

Nullus liber homo capiatur vel imprisonetur, aut dissaisiatur, aut utlagetur, aut exuletur, aut aliquo modo destruatur, nec super eum ibimus nec super eum mittemus nisi per legale iudicium parium suorum, vel per legem terre.

Data per manum nostram in prato quod vocatur Runingmed Inter Windelesor & Stanes. Quinto decimo die Junii Anno Regni nostri Septimo decimo.

E. H. Gooch.

THE WRITING OF THE GREAT CHARTER

Handwriting has undergone various changes during the centuries, and in the illustration above are shown facsimiles of the writing in the original Magna Carta, to which King John set his seal at Runnymede on June 15th, 1215. Few written documents have been so important in establishing the rights of every man in this country to justice, no matter what his rank or position.

Querying
Queue
Quinsy
Quixotic
Quotient

Radiator
Radish
Raisin
Ransom
Ratio
Recognize
Reconnaissance
Reconnoitre
Reflection
Remembrance
Reminiscence
Renaissance
Reprieve
Resplendent
Resuscitate
Rhinoceros
Rhododendron
Rhubarb
Ricochetting
Rinse
Risible
Rissole
Rivalling
Rivalry
Rosiness
Rottenness
Rubicund

Saccharine
Sacrament
Sacrilege
Sacrosanct
Saddler
Sapphire
Satellite
Sceptic (scoffer)
Schottische
Sciatica
Scimitar
Scintillate
Scythe
Sedentary
Seize
Septic (infected)
Shako
Shallot
Shillelagh
Siege
Silhouette
Siphon
Siren
Sobriquet
Soliloquy
Somersault
Sootiness
Spongy
Spontaneous
Stationary (fixed)
Stationery (paper)
Stereotype
Stiletto
Stomachic
Stupefy
Stymie
Subpœna
Subterranean
Subtle
Succinct
Summary (short)
Summery (summer-like)
Supererogatory
Supersede
Suspicious
Sycamore
Sycophant
Symmetry
Synonymous
Syringe
Syringeing

Tangible
Tattoo
Teetotaler
Teetotum
Termagant
Terpsichorean
Thieving
Thraldom
Titillate
Tobogganing
Tonsillitis
Tragedian
Tremolo
Tunnelling

Ubiquitous
Umbrella
Unctuous
Underrate

Veld (S. Africa)
Velocipede
Venal (sordid)
Venial (pardonable)
Veranda
Vermilion
Veterinary
Vicarious
Vicissitude
Victualling
Vinegar
Violoncello
Virtuoso
Viscous
Voracity
Vying

Walrus
Wassail
Welsher
Whereabouts
Wherewithal
Whimsy
Wilful
Woebegone
Woollen
Wraith

Xylophone

Zigzagging

Punctuation

However well you form your sentences, however good your spelling, your grammar and your style, you cannot just write on and on, filling page after page without a stop.

Stops in your writing are known as punctuation, and while there are no hard and fast rules about punctuation that can be compared with grammatical or spelling rules, there are certain principles to be observed. If a piece of writing is meant to be read or spoken aloud, the main purpose of punctuation becomes clear. The insertion of punctuation marks indicates the natural pauses that the speaker will have to make in order to convey the sense most lucidly. But writing, even if it be meant to be read only—not aloud—should be punctuated as an aid to the better understanding of its context.

To-day, we tend to write short, crisp sentences, terminated by full stop, or period. Fifty years ago, even the masters of English prose tended to write extremely long sentences, which compelled the use of the lesser punctuation marks, the comma, the colon, semi-colon and marks of parenthesis. There is no mathematical formula for the use of punctuation marks. Punctuation varies, as we have shown, from one age to another, and from one writer to another. You will even find in the works of one first-class writer of English an inconsistency in punctuation.

Once again, as we cannot repeat too often, in any attempt to explain the magic art of writing, the best way to acquire it is to study the masters.

The Full-stop (.). This is the basic punctuation mark—the point. The word punctuation is derived itself from the Latin word for point and you will notice its kinship with the word puncture. The full-stop ends a sentence. The next sentence begins with a capital letter and you will remember that it is generally considered bad style to commence a sentence with a preposition. Even this old and respected rule is, however, frequently broken in good modern prose.

The full-stop is also used at the end of a word which has been abbreviated or shortened. Such abbreviations tend, however, to become words in their own right, and the full stop is dropped. When the word department is spelt dept. the full-stop persists, probably because no one attempts to consider the abbreviation a word on its own.

Making Your Meaning Clear

The Comma (,). This mark of punctuation is very much overworked to-day. It might be described as the mark which indicates the shortest or slightest pause. It should not be used when the formation of the sentence produces breaks naturally. On the other hand, it should not be omitted if its inclusion makes a meaning clearer. Where a more definite break occurs, this should be marked by a semi-colon.

The Semi-colon (;). The very nature of this punctuation mark is an excellent indication of its proper use. It is at one and the same time a comma and a full-stop. Its value lies somewhere between the two.

The Colon (:). This punctuation mark is not very popular in modern writing. It is generally used to indicate the beginning of a list or of a quotation rather than as a mere sign of pause or break. It is, however, a valuable punctuation mark for making out of two short opposed sentences one well-balanced contrast. For example—" Mary is good : Jane is not."

Be Sparing with the Dash

The Dash (—). In modern journalism, if not in more literary writings, the dash is used frequently, as an easy alternative to the correct punctuation mark. You should try to use the correct mark, not the dash, because the dash has some special purposes of its own for which it is really useful in writing. (1) To show hesitation. The dash is most valuable in such a sentence as this. " Shall I say adieu—or au revoir." (2) To indicate the interruption, or a sudden turn of thought. " No one in the class—except Tom—would be so stupid." (3) To insert an explanation, " This book—PICTORIAL KNOWLEDGE—is designed to bring you success." (4) To create a surprise at the end of a sentence. For example. " He cried for water—and they brought him wine." (5) To sum up a list. " She possessed gowns, furs, jewellery—finery of every kind." (6) For parentheses, that is, a word or words inserted in a sentence which is grammatically complete without them. For example—" The Prime Minister—I saw him—was not smoking a cigar."

The use of dashes for parentheses in this way is not advised. There is a better alternative. Brackets can be used when the above sentence would become " The Prime Minister (I saw him) was not smoking a cigar." If brackets are used exclusively for parenthesis there can be no confusion. As shown by (1), (2), (3), (4), and (5), the dash has other uses. When a reader comes upon a dash, he may assume that a parenthesis has begun, only to discover that the final dash never appeared and that he is not, in fact, reading a parenthetical clause at all.

When to Use Inverted Commas

Quotation Marks (" "). These marks are generally referred to as " inverted commas." Their primary use is to introduce the actual words of a speaker. For example : John said " I shall arrive at noon." They are, however, also used to mark a passage taken from another book. In this use they are strictly quotation marks. In written as distinct from printed English, inverted commas may also indicate the title of a book, or play, or a picture, piece of music, etc. Thus: They listened to the "Moonlight Sonata."

The printer can avoid the necessity of using inverted commas in this way by using italic type: They listened to the *Moonlight Sonata.* Both in printing and writing inverted commas are used when a word is being quoted and not being used for its meaning in the sentence. For example: There are too many "don'ts" in Jimmy's conversation. Quotation marks have yet another purpose: to show that a word is not being used in its literal or usual sense. They watched the "shadows" on the cornfield. Without quotation marks this would imply that the shadows of clouds or trees were visible on the corn. With the quotation marks it may indicate the light and shade of the growing corn when moved by the wind.

Remember when addressing letters that the name of your friend's house need not go in quotation marks. Nor in general writing need the names of ships, aeroplanes, railway trains and so on, unless there is any risk of confusion. He saw it in "The Sun" would immediately indicate that he saw it in a paper called The Sun. Without the quotation marks one might be tempted to suppose that he had been making observations in a solar observatory.

Note. Single inverted commas are used for a quotation within a quotation. Example: John said, "I could just hear Frank call 'Let us go home,' and I knew they had finished."

The Apostrophe ('). The apostrophe has two uses in English writing: to indicate that a letter has been omitted, or to indicate the possessive.

The Play's the Thing is a good example of (1). Here the apostrophe is inserted to indicate that the letter i has been omitted from the words "play is." The use of the apostrophe for this primary purpose in words like don't, can't, shan't, is particularly interesting. It is, of course, strictly correct to use the apostrophe. There is, however, a tendency nowadays to omit it from cant and dont, which of course stand for "cannot" and "do not" but have become to some extent words on their own. Some writers including George Bernard Shaw have favoured the omission of the apostrophe. Care should be taken in spelling the word "its." This may mean either it is, in which case it should have an apostrophe—it's, or it may be the possessive of the pronoun it, in which case it does not have an apostrophe. "Its name is chocolate and it's good to eat."

In a Possessive Sense

The use of apostrophe '*s* at the end of a word to indicate the possessive, is with most singular words a very easy rule to follow. Instead of "the cap of the boy" you say "the boy's cap." When the word is in the plural, however, the apostrophe comes after the *s*—the boys' caps.

Where a singular word already ends in *s*, it was previously the custom to make it possessive by adding an apostrophe without any further *s*. This still applies in English poetry, but in normal prose and current conversation we add the apostrophe '*s*. For example, St. James's Road.

The Question Mark (?). This punctuation mark explains itself. Its only proper use is at the end of a direct question. It has no other proper use in good written English. For example, you would not put a question mark at the end of the sentence "I asked him where he was going." You would, invariably, at the end of the direct question "Where are you going?" A question mark should never be used in the middle of a sentence to indicate a joke or make a doubting comment. For example, you would not write "Johnny has painted a picture (?) of a sunset." If you really wish to indicate that Johnny's effort isn't really much of a picture, you can say so in many better ways.

To be Used With Care

The Exclamation Mark (!). Perhaps the best guide to the use of the exclamation mark at the end of your sentences is to say that it expresses emotion. It is a mark of bad writing to use too many exclamation marks. The words themselves will express all the emotion that is necessary in most cases. Exclamation marks should be used after interjections such as ah, oh, or after short phrases used as interjections, such as "My goodness!" "By Jove!" Exclamation marks should also properly follow short emotional sentences such as "What a tragedy!" "How I love you!" The exclamation mark is also properly used when you apostrophise a person or thing, "My trusty sword!" "You darling!" There is yet another use of this interesting punctuation mark, and one which should be carefully considered. It is sometimes permissible to insert it at the end of a sentence which is not to be taken literally, or which has a surprise element in it. For example, "Mr. Jones is, of course, an extremely important person!" "They arrived at the deserted cottage only to find it inhabited!"

The use of exclamation marks after sentences like these can generally be allowed if the words themselves do not fully and effectively express the meaning and the tone you intend.

When Two Words are One

The Hyphen (-). The hyphen indicates that two or more words are to be regarded as one. You cannot go far wrong in your use of hyphens if you remember that they are used to form one word. All that prevents them being run together without a hyphen, is possibly the clumsiness of the word which would result. The tendency is for hyphenated words or phrases to drop their hyphens when the compound idea has become acceptable and familiar. A flying boat would be a miraculous ship that travelled through the air, a flying-boat is a special kind of flying machine which lands on and takes off from the water. It will probably become "flyingboat."

In your writing, of course, hyphens are used at the end of your line when you have not room to complete the word. You break it off where convenient (and this should be at the end of a syllable), insert a hyphen and put the remainder of the word at the beginning of the next line. (No second hyphen is necessary.)

General Note on Punctuation

Punctuation, commonly called "stops" in writing, has a real purpose in assisting meaning. It is not just a sort of decoration, or a way of enabling you to look clever. So use your punctuation carefully and sparingly. You will notice that throughout your reading and throughout this article, certain words are printed in *italic type*. This is a form of punctuation in order to stress or pick out a word or phrase. You cannot, of course, employ it in your handwriting, nor can you use it on the average typewriter. In writing or typing, therefore, when you wish to *italicise* a word, it is customary to underline it, but be extremely sparing with your underlining.

The Words You Use

Having got over the initial difficulty of English grammar and English spelling so that you compose your writing correctly as a purely mechanical process, you can begin to think of style or character in writing. If all proficient writers were merely masters of grammar and spelling, they would write in practically the same way, yet you know that there are differences in style of writing just as there are different tones of voice in speaking.

Broadly, style arises from two main causes. Firstly, the vocabulary or words at the disposal of the writer; secondly, the way in which he uses them. This of course is apart from the fact that he will use them grammatically. The average man in a job which does not involve writing, uses at the most two or three thousand different words in his daily speech and in the few letters he writes. The business man will use many more, and the professional writer or journalist will use most of all, perhaps 30,000 or 40,000 different words.

Acquiring a vocabulary in your own language is not a question of solemnly sitting down with a dictionary and memorising long lists of words. If you are learning a foreign language you may have to do this in a modified form; but you acquire your own vocabulary largely by observant reading and listening. To the intelligent person the building up of an extensive vocabulary is a natural process, and by reading most people bring about an improvement of their vocabularies, as well as by experimenting with words and their opposites.

The cross-word puzzles, which appear in nearly every daily paper, are to a very large extent a game of synonyms and antonyms. Crosswords are a first-class game for improving your fund of words.

By far the greatest number of words in the dictionary, however, have no synonyms or antonyms, but express one precise and specific idea. They name one thing. No other word will do. You can best add to your list of such words by observant reading of all kinds.

There are of course many words which are special or technical. It may be that they belong to a particular business, trade, science, or industry. Such words would not normally be required by persons other than those concerned in the particular field. But no word however specialised should be ignored. There may be a time when you would wish to use it, not necessarily to describe the thing to which it applies, but perhaps to make more clear your description of something else. You are now beginning to use what are known as "figures of speech." You are employing a word incorrectly, not so much for its strict definition, as for the clear suggestion it gives.

Synonyms and Antonyms

Hate is a crisp, simple English word with a very definite meaning; it is one which perhaps unfortunately a child learns almost as soon as he learns the word love. Now here are some synonyms of this short word hate. Dislike, detest, abhor, loathe, abominate. You can see that these words cover various degrees of hating, some express more, some less, intensity, and some express it more urgently. Dislike would seem to be the least intense; abominate the strongest. There is in the word abominate a sense that the hate has been carefully considered, endures for a long time, and is strong and unchangeable. If you are learning to be a stylist in your writing you will pick the one word that fits most closely to the sense, so that you make your reader appreciate the feeling as you feel it.

The opposite of a synonym is an antonym, a word which expresses the contrary or negative idea. Good is the antonym of bad. With a wide selection of synonyms and antonyms at your command you will see how easy it is to keep monotony out of your writing, to give it force and balance. Consider the word hate, you may write "I hate people who tell tales." You may use any of the synonyms of hate to improve the sentence and you may also employ the antonyms of hate by turning the sentence around—you can say simply "I do not like people who tell tales."

These are, of course, very easy words and ordinary examples, but you can acquire a wide and varied vocabulary if you are mentally alert both to new words you see in print and to new words you hear in conversation, on the radio, in the cinema, or at the theatre. Such alertness requires training.

When you hear a new word, or see it, you must not allow yourself to slide over it, merely picking up the general meaning of the sentence. You must allow your mind to focus on the word, study what it looks like, or consider how it sounds. You should then take the first opportunity of finding out its meaning. This you can do either by asking someone who is likely to know, a parent, a teacher, or an older friend, or by looking up the word in the dictionary. The last method is perhaps the best, but it requires, naturally, a little more effort. But whatever you do, don't let the chance of acquiring a new word slip by you.

Mondiale.

PAPYRUS ON WHICH THE ANCIENTS WROTE

For many centuries papyrus was used by the Egyptians as we now use paper for writing purposes. It was made from the pith of the papyrus plant's stems, moistened with water and compressed, often with the aid of gum, to form a sheet. Our photograph shows an ancient papyrus which is in process of being restored.

In this way you will gradually have, as it were at your finger tips, a word for each idea you wish to convey, and such is the variety and flexibility of the English language you will have not only a word for each idea, but several words. Your vocabulary will in fact include synonyms which will enable you very often to express more than the mere meaning. With them you can introduce mood, speed, light and shade, and you will select the particular synonym which best fits the general feeling as well as the meaning you are striving to convey. Here are some examples of synonyms to illustrate the selectivity of our mother tongue.

SOME USEFUL SYNONYMS

ABBREVIATE—abridge, curtail, condense, compress, epitomise, lessen, reduce, shorten.

ABHOR—abominate, detest, hate, loathe.

ABLE—capable, competent.

ABODE—dwelling, habitation, residence.

ABSORB—engross, engulf, imbibe, swallow.

ABUNDANT—ample, copious, plentiful.

ACCEPTABLE—agreeable, grateful, welcome.

ACCOMPLISH—complete, effect, achieve, fulfil, execute, realise, finish.

AGITATE—shake, disturb, move.

AID—assist, help, succour, relieve.

ANGRY—passionate, hot, irascible, hasty.

ARDUOUS—hard, difficult, laborious.

ARTFUL—crafty, artificial, deceitful, cunning, dexterous.

BACKWARD—loth, unwilling, reluctant, averse, undeveloped, slow.

BECOMING—suitable, graceful, decent, meet, fit.

BRIGHT—clear, shining, sparkling, brilliant, glistening, glittering, lucid, resplendent, clever.

BUSINESS—trade, calling, occupation, vocation, profession, employment, work.

CALL—exclaim, cry, invite, name, summons.

CLEVER—skilful, able, talented, gifted, ingenious, expert, proficient.

CLUMSY—awkward, uncouth, bungling, unhandy.

COURAGE—heroism, valour, bravery, firmness, fearlessness, daring.

DECLARE—announce, pronounce, testify, proclaim, assert, assure, affirm.

DIE—expire, depart, perish, wither, decay, languish.

EAGER—earnest, excited, ardent, impetuous, quick, vehement.

EXPLOIT—feat, accomplishment, achievement, deed, performance.

FALSEHOOD—fabrication, fiction, lie, untruth.

FAMOUS—celebrated, eminent, renowned, distinguished, illustrious.

GENEROUS—liberal, bounteous, beneficent, munificent, noble, kind.

GUARD—protect, defend, shield, watch.

HEALTHY—well, sound, wholesome, salutary, salubrious.

HUMBLE—meek, lowly, subdued, modest, unpretentious, unassuming.

IMPLY—mean, signify, denote, involve.

JOY—happiness, delight, rapture, ectasy, pleasure.

KEEP—detain, hold, support, retain, maintain, reserve.

LANGUAGE—tongue, speech, dialect, idiom.

LOVE—affection, fondness, devotion, liking, partiality, sympathy, infatuation.

LUXURY—profusion, abundance, excess, extravagance.

MAGNIFICENT—noble, grand, sublime, glorious, splendid, superb.

MYSTERIOUS—hidden, dim, dark, obscure, mystic, latent.

NAKED—exposed, rude, unclothed, uncovered, simple, plain.

NAME—cognomen, appellation, title, credit, reputation, denomination.

NOURISH—feed, uphold, maintain, cherish, nurture, support.

OBEDIENT—submissive, compliant, yielding, dutiful, obsequious, respectful.

OFFENSIVE—abusive, insulting, impertinent, insolent, rude, obnoxious, mean.

OVERWHELM—overpower, crush, upturn, subdue, overthrow.

PART—share, portion, division, piece, section.

PLAY—recreation, amusement, pastime, game, romp, relaxation, entertainment.

PLEASURE—satisfaction, delight, happiness, enjoyment, joy.

PUZZLE—confound, perplex, mystify, bewilder, entangle.

QUIET—calm, repose, tranquillity, rest, ease, peace, placidity, stillness.

RAVENOUS—voracious, rapacious, greedy, hungry.

REWARD—recompense, remuneration, compensation, satisfaction.

ROUGH—harsh, uncivil, rude, uncouth, unmannerly, unpolished, rugged, severe.

SARCASM—satire, irony, ridicule.

SECURE—safe, certain, confident, sure, procure, warrant.

SYMPATHY—compassion, condolence, agreement, commiseration.

TALK—conference, discourse, chat, conversation, sermon, communication, lecture, dialogue.

TEACH—instruct, direct, educate, enlighten, coach, expound, lecture, tutor.

TRUE—honest, candid, sincere, reliable, plain, upright.

ULTIMATE—last, final, end, latest.

USE—practice, custom, habit, service, usage, advantage, utility.

VALUE—price, worth, rate, account, regard, respect, appreciation.

VISIBLE—apparent, discernible, evident, distinct, manifest, obvious, plain.

WARMTH—fervour, ardour, cordiality, heat, fervency, glow, zeal, animation.

WONDERFUL—strange, curious, astonishing, surprising, marvellous, admirable.

YET—but, however, notwithstanding, nevertheless, still.

ZEALOUS—concerned, earnest, ardent, anxious, enthusiastic, warm.

There is of course one important factor in this magic art of writing, about which very little has been said in these pages, and that is Grammar. You will learn this at school and nowadays it is not made quite such a complicated, dry-as-dust subject as it was only a few years ago. Grammar is today regarded as the servant of the language, not its master.

It is something to be learned or understood when one is young so that there is no need to worry too much about it later, because by then its main rules have become almost an instinct. Correct speech and correct writing are less a matter of rules and regulations than of clear thinking, just as good manners depend less on strict rules than the simple instinct of showing consideration for others.

The Importance of Politeness And Courtesy

Manners Makyth Man

Specially drawn for this work.

IN THE DAYS OF CHIVALRY

Politeness and courtesy were regarded as essential qualities among the knights of the Middle Ages, and the word chivalry came from the French word meaning men on horseback. By their knightly behaviour, especially towards women, the knights gave the word chivalry the meaning it has to-day of bravery and courtesy.

A GUIDE TO GOOD MANNERS FOR BOYS AND GIRLS

HOW often have you heard people say—" It isn't done! " They mean that something which you *have* done or which you are just about to do is not the right thing to do. They may not mean that it is wrong or wicked, but they mean that it would be bad manners, that it would offend decent, well-behaved people and customs that have become almost laws. Remember that good manners are unwritten laws which control our behaviour. You cannot be fined or sent to prison if you break them, but you will be showing yourself to be a person who doesn't care about the way you live, and soon other people won't care about you. They won't respect you and your value in the world will go down. You may also have heard it said that people take you at your own valuation: that what you think of yourself is what they will begin to think of you. You can show respect for yourself and set your own valuation high by your good manners.

We Have Many Words for it

As all of you who have studied English know, there is usually more than one word in our language for each idea we want to express. Sometimes there are a lot of words meaning practically the same thing. You can tell to some extent by the number of different words for one idea, how important that idea is in our lives. It shows that people through the ages and in all kinds of homes, have thought a lot about it. For example, just think how many words there are for liking—loving, adoring, cherishing, treasuring, petting, caring, worshipping, and doubtless you can add many others. Now we can tell that good manners is an important idea in our existence. How many, slightly different, words and phrases there are to cover this idea!

The Strong Tide of Custom

Etiquette, politeness, good behaviour, chivalry, charm, polish, grace, decorum, civility, consideration, discipline, deportment, breeding. These are nouns meaning good manners, or courtesy. Now can you think of some adjectives meaning good-mannered. Try! (To help you, if you can't think of many, a few are printed at the foot of this column.)

Now can you make a list of words that mean just the opposite of good-mannered? For example, rude and vulgar. Look at the bottom of the column again if you can't think of many.

The idea must be a great and important one to have had such influence on our language. We need no finer proof that the idea is widespread and strong in our lives.

King Canute found that he could not order the sea to stop flowing in over the sand. You will find that you must accept the strong tide of custom and etiquette that runs through all civilised life. You will get more out of life if you accept that fact soon.

There is nothing "soft" about behaving well. Think of the knights who met great adventures with courage and strength. They are the symbol of chivalry and good manners.

Words that Tell a Story

We can learn a bit about manners by just studying the word itself and some of the other words connected with behaviour.

The word manners comes from an old Latin word *manuarua*, which meant "mode of handling." Are not your manners the way you handle things and events, the way you handle other people, and above all the way you handle yourself in society?

Etiquette is really a French word meaning ticket. There was a time in the court and select society of France when one could only attend an event by presenting a ticket. This was to make sure that only the right people would attend, the people who would behave in a courtly manner. So the word began to be used for the rules of courtly behaviour which are to-day a sort of ticket admitting one to the company of good society.

History in a Word

The word polite is really a first cousin of the word polish, in fact we can call a polite person polished. You are polite if your manners are smooth and if you avoid friction. You are impolite if you are behaving roughly or if you are unpolished.

But perhaps the word chivalry, which stands for a very special sort of good manners, is the most interesting word of all. It comes from the Latin word for a horse, *caballus*, and you may not think there is much connection between a horse and good manners. But briefly the connection is this.

The Latin word *caballus* became the Italian *cavallo*. This in turn gave the old French word *cavallerie*, meaning men who rode on horses. (This is almost the word cavalry, which we now use for horse soldiers.) It also gave the old French *chevalerie*, meaning

---

Words meaning good-mannered—obliging, refined, cultured, cultivated, well-bred, elegant, respectful, courteous, of good bearing, gentlemanly, ladylike, urbane.

Words meaning bad- or ill-mannered—coarse, primitive, rough, unimproved, insolent, impertinent, offensive, cheeky, impudent, churlish, boorish, ill-bred, uncivil, forward, disrespectful, barbarous, saucy, insulting.

first " men on horseback," then gallant men, then knights, and then knightly behaviour, or *chivalry*. There is a whole chapter of exciting history in that word!

What is Professional Etiquette?

We have considered what etiquette is generally in our lives, but you may hear people speak of professional etiquette, which is rather a different thing. It will be unlikely to affect young people until they have gone into their first job and begun to mix with others in a business rather than a social way. " Professional Etiquette " is the term applied to those customs and rules of conduct that hold good in certain businesses, especially in the profession of Medicine, that is amongst doctors, or in the Law, amongst lawyers and solicitors. Other professions, like teaching or journalism, have their etiquette too, of course, and in fact almost any business has its own " good manners." But etiquette in this sense is less a matter of politeness than a necessary code of behaviour. A breach of professional etiquette may mean that the doctor's or the lawyer's whole career is as good as ruined. Nothing quite so harsh or serious happens if you commit a breach of etiquette in the more ordinary sense.

Here are some examples of professional etiquette. A doctor never goes to another doctor's patient without telling the first doctor that he is doing so. Even if he has been called in by the patient this still applies. A doctor must never advertise himself. If he writes for the magazines or papers (except for medical papers), or if he broadcasts, you will find that he uses a pen-name or calls himself " The Doctor," or something of the kind. There are, of course, certain exceptions where a doctor is not in practice, or he may have special permission to broadcast or lecture. Otherwise such conduct is a breach of professional etiquette. Again, a doctor during his work will often be told all sorts of personal family secrets. Naturally, the etiquette of his profession says that he must not tell these things to other people or make use of the information he gets for his own benefit.

In the Legal Profession, the same sort of etiquette applies. A lawyer must, for instance, be loyal to his client. It would not do for him to change sides in a case simply because he thought his client was going to lose. At the same time he must be loyal to his profession, which exists to preserve law and justice. And the lawyer, like the doctor, will be told many intimate secrets which he must not disclose.

Your Voice Tells

One of the greatest of the gifts that distinguish Man from all the other animals is the gift of speech. Human beings can convey ideas to each other by the spoken word. The more cultivated the people are, the wider is the range of their language; or to put it simply, the more ideas you have the more words you need to express them. But whether you have many ideas or few, it is your duty to the people to whom you are talking to express your ideas as clearly as possible.

Now you can be hard to understand for two main reasons. First, you may speak badly—your voice may not be clear. Second, the words you use and the way you string them together may be careless. Let us consider these points in order to observe the Etiquette of Speech.

First, your voice: your voice is a speaking machine like a gramophone or a wireless set, and you must make sure that it is working smoothly and well to get perfect results. Here are some of the things to watch. Don't speak too quickly or people won't be able to follow what you are trying to say. Equally, don't speak too slowly, or they will become impatient waiting for you to get on with it. Practise talking at a good medium pace.

If you talk too quietly or softly you won't be heard properly. The very quiet voice puts your listeners to a strain which is not considerate, and what is more, it gives the impression that you are afraid of being heard. This could only mean that you are not very sure of what you are saying or that you are saying something you don't really want to be heard.

With a Country Accent

It is almost as bad to talk too loudly. This will suggest perhaps that you are a bit too sure of yourself and want to appear big and important. You will make the best impression if you talk at a medium "volume." Think of tuning the loud-speaker when you practise this.

Boys and girls should be specially careful in talking to elderly folks who may be rather deaf. In this case they must talk more loudly than usual, but they should try to do so *naturally*. People who are slightly deaf don't like to be reminded of it. Once more you see that to have good manners you must think of the feelings of others.

Although good manners in speech have nothing to do with accent, which is usually due to the part of the country you live in, they have much to do with tone. There is, in fact, a vulgar and a well-bred way of speaking the same accent.

We have no gramophone record of Shakespeare speaking, but it is almost certain he spoke in the rich country accent of his native Warwickshire and not the town accent of the London in which he made his fame. But we can be almost certain that he did not speak his accent vulgarly, or in a slip-shod way. His wonderful writing shows how much he enjoyed the sound or music of words.

To-day, of course, the accents in the different parts of the country are dying away to some extent. Television and the cinema, and the fact that people can travel about so quickly and easily make for a levelling up of all the accents. There is a "wireless" English, which in the main has little accent at all, and is understood everywhere. It may not be the best to you or me but it is clear and good, and with it we can speak easily and well in any sort of home in any part of the country.

It is every bit as bad to be affected in speech as to be careless. To put on airs and graces is bad manners. You know how a comedian on the stage sometimes puts on a very polite voice? He overdoes it to make you laugh. You will be just as funny in your everyday life if you overdo it and try to be "fearfully refined." Be natural, that is the great thing. Take note of good speakers and model your voice on theirs.

It is good to let your feelings be noticed in your voice as well as the mere meaning of the word you use. This prevents your voice becoming flat and monotonous. (The word monotonous means one-toned.) Your feelings, however, should not be the masters of either you or your voice. If they become the master you will be just making noises—not speaking.

Your Choice of Words

Now we must think of the second point about the Etiquette of Speech: the words you use. Apart from the way you say things, your vocabulary, or selection of words, and the order in which you place them are signs of your manners. Here, too, it is best to note carefully the good speakers: don't use long words because you think it will sound clever; don't use too many slang words. Using slang usually means that you cannot think of a good English word to use, and it often means that you have just picked up a word like a parrot and keep on using it.

It goes without saying that curses and swear words are the worst possible manners. Many young people use these words without even knowing their meaning, just because they feel it is "grown up." This is nonsense and grown-ups who use such words are just showing the world that their minds are undeveloped and that they are not grown up at all.

Meeting People and Saying Good-bye

When you meet someone you say "How do you do?" This is not a question which is meant to be answered by "Very well, thank you" or worse, "Oh, I'm not feeling so good to-day." The correct response is to return the remark, "How do you do?" If of course you are asked a definite question about your health, that is another matter.

If you are introduced to someone it is usual to extend your hand and say "How do you do? Mr. Smith (or Miss Jones)." It is polite to use the name in this way, so when you are introduced, listen carefully. If you have to do the introducing, remember these points:—

- A gentleman is introduced to a lady—not the other way round.
- A young person to an older person.
- An ordinary person to a famous or important person.

You lead the person to be introduced forward and say to the person to whom you are making the introduction, "May I introduce Jack Robinson?" Assent will be given by a nod or a smile; you then say "Mr. Jack Robinson—Lady Jones," or whoever it may be. The introduction will probably be followed by a handshake, but the person being introduced should wait for a hand to be extended.

Good-bye is perhaps the best and most customary thing to say when you are departing. Farewell is rather old-fashioned now, and any childish remark like "Ta-ta" or "Toodleoo," is of

Specially drawn for this work.

THE STRONG TIDE OF CUSTOM

The old story in history-books tells how King Canute despite his great power could not stop the sea from flowing inland with the tide. So, too, we all find that in our everyday life we must accept the rules made in accordance with the strong tide of custom.

course bad manners, as well as being ridiculous. Three French expressions are common and polite for good-bye on certain occasions. *Adieu* means I commend you to God, and implies that the good-bye may be for ever. It really means Good-bye and God bless you. *Au revoir* means good-bye until we meet again—probably soon. *Bon voyage* means literally good journey and is a good-bye message to those going long distances on boats or trains or by aeroplane.

Telephone Manners

Most boys and girls use the telephone now almost as much as their elders—at least at home, because, of course, most telephoning is done during working hours by people at business. So it is just as well to remember that there are good and bad manners on the telephone.

If you are using a public call box, don't go on talking if someone else is waiting. Say what you want to say and finish. You can easily explain to the person to whom you are speaking that someone is waiting. It is unfair to keep others waiting unnecessarily and it may be that they have a really urgent call to put through. Someone may be ill and they may be most anxious.

If you get a wrong number, don't be bad-tempered with the operator at the exchange. She is doing a very complicated job and the exchange is a highly complicated machine. No machine is foolproof, and no girl who has a long and tiring job can avoid making a mistake sometimes. Be polite. Don't make her difficult job more difficult.

If you are calling someone up, say who you are straight away. "This is James Smith." If the person you want to speak to has not answered the phone, say "May I speak to Mary (or Mary Jones) please." Don't say "Is that Mary," when you know very well it isn't. If you are answering a call, say your number at once, like this: "Putney 1234." There is no need to say "This is Putney 1234" or "Putney 1234 speaking." You are letting the caller know as simply and as quickly as possible that he has the right number. This is efficient as well as being good manners.

Another thing worth remembering in telephone conversations is this: don't ask questions which the person at the other end may find it awkward to answer. They may not be alone even if you are. So if you must ask personal questions, you should ask first if your friend is able to speak freely. Saving others embarrassment, when on the telephone, or anywhere else, is the simplest of good manners.

Lastly, don't shout. Speak clearly. Shouting sounds rude and unnatural. The telephone instrument will not work any better if you bellow. It is very carefully made to carry your softest words if they are well and clearly spoken. If you listen to any experienced telephone user you will notice he speaks in a quiet normal voice.

A Word about Wireless and Television.

It is vulgar to keep a wireless set blaring all day long if you have any near neighbours. And most selfish to tune it up loudly late at night.

Don't walk into a room and switch the radio or television off just because you are not interested in the programme. Others in the room may be. Ask them first. And don't put the wireless on, especially loudly, if others in the same room want to talk or read quietly without a background of noise. Ask first; they may have no objection, but it is good manners to give them the chance of saying so.

Because a wireless or television set can't speak back, some people think it fun to make remarks during a programme. This is all right if it is just fun and if no one else is listening seriously. If you are not interested, or think the programme stupid, don't spoil it for someone else who is listening intently.

With wireless as with everything else

good manners are so much a matter of thinking of other people.

We need hardly say that at the theatre or concert it is ill-mannered to speak during the performance. Even whispering is distracting to other people.

If you must leave an entertainment before the end to catch a train or for some other reason, at least wait till the end of a particular item, scene or turn. It is better not to take your seat at all after the interval unless you can remain all the time.

Don't arrive late for "a show." You may disturb dozens of people as you go to your seat and it is also unfair to the performers.

When you have taken your seat, stay in it and don't fidget or on any account stand up to get a better view. If you do, those behind you certainly will not.

Boys should always allow the ladies and girls to be seated first before sitting down themselves and they should, of course, pass the programme to the ladies before reading it themselves.

A cinema or picture house is a much less formal place than a theatre or a concert hall. Perhaps because there are no real actors on the stage, people are inclined to behave less politely. But although the actors cannot hear you making remarks about them or adding clever "wise-cracks" of your own, other people in the audience can. They may not feel that the film requires any extra help from you!

If you have a younger brother or sister with you who cannot quite follow the film, tell them not to ask questions, but wait till afterwards, and then you will tell them all about it.

Knights of the Road

Chivalry, which as we have seen is another term for good manners, was the special quality of the knights of old. As they rode along the highroads of England with their squires they became renowned not only for the great deeds they did, but for the politeness and courtesy with which they treated their fellow travellers. You can be a knight of the road to-day, although your charger has been exchanged for a motor car or motor cycle.

Good driving means the knowledge of the Highway Code—all the rules and laws which have been drawn up to make motoring safe. Most of these laws are just reminders to drivers that there are others on the road: other drivers, cyclists and walkers to be considered. If you fail to observe these rules it may bring serious injury or even death, so the law through the Courts can punish you severely by fines or imprisonment. But it all amounts to just another case of manners.

Rules to Remember

We give below some of the more important points from the driver's etiquette which young people, many of whom can already drive, or will soon be doing so, should think about. They are so full of the chivalry of good common sense that they scarcely have to be learnt.

Keep to the left. Don't hold selfishly to the crown of the road.

Don't stop or turn to right or left without giving the proper signal for those following to see.

Don't overtake or pass another vehicle without warning.

On hills give way to those coming up, if you are travelling down, even if in strict law they ought to wait for you.

Stop and let pedestrians go over first at the official crossings.

Always look out for old folks and young boys and girls as they are not so able as you are to avoid disaster.

Don't blow your horn just for the fun of it, but always sound it where a warning is necessary.

At night dim, or switch off, your headlights when meeting another vehicle.

At all times watch out for fellow

Specially drawn for this work.

ETIQUETTE AT THE COURT

Etiquette is a French word meaning ticket, and at one time, when the Royal Court of France set the fashion in Europe, only those who presented their ticket of invitation were admitted. Thus the word has come to be used for correct behaviour in society generally.

travellers in difficulty; perhaps quite a little thing that you can do will help, and all other matters apart, you never know when you may be in need of friendly aid yourself.

Rules of Conduct in the Street

Many of the points of etiquette to be observed when you are out walking are a relic of the days when the public highway was quite a dangerous place —at any rate for ladies out alone. There were footpads or thieves, pick-pockets and other undesirable characters, especially at night, when streets were only dimly lit by gas, or before that when there was no proper street lighting at all. It was indeed an adventure to walk abroad. Gentlemen, naturally, gave the ladies their protection. Think of these things as you study the present-day rules of conduct. They make clear many things that seem pointless now; but as in other aspects of manners, it shows good breeding to respect old traditions.

A gentleman will walk on the outside (next the street) when with a lady on the pavement. Two gentlemen allow a lady to walk in the middle. On entering a gate or door, a gentleman will open it for a lady, standing back to allow her to pass through first.

A gentleman will assist a lady to get on or off a public vehicle. He will also open the door of a private car for her when she is getting in or out.

Raising One's Hat

A gentleman may give his arm to an elderly lady when walking with her. Young people should not walk about arm-in-arm. Apart from looking rather cheap, it obviously takes more room on a crowded pavement. When going over a busy crossing, however, it is a different matter and an arm will be courteous and helpful.

If a gentleman meets a lady he will raise his hat. Boys should do this. It is not enough merely to touch the cap or salute. (In uniform, of course, saluting is correct.)

When a gentleman is walking with a lady and another gentleman recognises the lady by raising his hat, the first gentleman will raise his hat in response, thus acknowledging the courtesy on behalf of his companion.

Normally, in walking in a busy place, a gentleman will fall back slightly to allow a lady to go first. In the case of a very dense crowd, however, he would go ahead of her to clear the way.

Even when walking alone there are things to be remembered, and it is not only the gentleman or boy who must remember them. A lady or girl has to make her contribution as well to the good manners of the street. The following rules apply to both sexes:—

Walk smartly; don't dilly-dally, but equally don't rush along.

Don't swagger; walk naturally but equally walk as though you were sure of yourself, not just slinking along as though you were shy and ashamed.

Don't wave your arms about or shout and so make an exhibition of yourself.

Be on the lookout for those who need your help and give it promptly and gladly. Be specially ready to help the blind or elderly people.

Don't swing parcels or cases, umbrellas or walking sticks about so that they are a danger to others.

If it is raining and you have your umbrella up, be most careful not to let it bump into other people.

And at all times watch where you are going. (You must have heard that often enough, and it is a good motto in life as well as a rule of manners when walking in the street.)

Ladies should remember to acknowledge the " salute " of a gentleman. When he raises his hat they should smile slightly.

Shaking Hands and other Salutations

It is difficult to say how the custom of shaking hands originated. Perhaps it is just a natural expression of friendship, but it may date from savage days when men went about armed. When they met they gave each other their weapon hands to show that they were not going to use them.

The custom to-day is general throughout the world, though there are other forms of greeting (apart from words). For instance, the French used to kiss on both cheeks, a custom still kept on ceremonial occasions.

Hand-shaking is used for all sorts of occasions from a simple meeting to a formal gesture of congratulation from the Queen to one of her subjects. Just think of some of the uses to which we put this salutation. To meet a friend; to bid good-bye; to express love or friendship; to seal a business bargain; to express sympathy; to show joy; to indicate that a quarrel is forgotten; to promise to play fair before a game.

What a wealth of meaning can be put into this gesture, and how much you can convey your own character by your handshake.

The correct handshake to-day is a simple grip with the right hand, extended at the height of the waist. The actual " shake " is no longer fashionable, and any form of vigorous swinging up and down is absurd. The grip should never be one that would hurt a weaker person nor should it be limp and cold. Get into the habit of " shaking hands " warmly and definitely, and avoid appearing either too distant or too cordial.

This easy everyday fashion is like so many other points in etiquette. It is done best when it is done naturally, but this does not mean that you should not be on your guard against letting it become careless and meaningless.

In Trains and Buses

Two things are easy to remember about the etiquette of travelling in public conveyances.

A gentleman boards the vehicle last and alights first. A gentleman will assist ladies to get aboard and alight; he will assist ladies to place parcels on the rack, cases under seats, etc. A gentleman will never remain seated while an elderly lady or gentleman has to stand. He should rise and politely offer his seat.

Be on the look-out for mothers with small children; they are almost certain to need your help.

Do not take up more than your share of space and do not allow your luggage to occupy seats where others might be sitting. In fairness to other passengers you should leave heavy luggage in the luggage van, or, in the case of buses and trams, in the corner reserved for luggage (usually under the stairs).

Always offer a lady the choice of seats. She may prefer to face the engine or to have her back to it; she may like to be next to the window or away from it. Neither open the window on a cold day, nor close it on a warm day without consulting the other passengers. Be tidy; place tickets in the box provided or in the first waste-paper basket.

Avoid all travelling, if you possibly can, when you have a bad cold or cough. Besides being irritating, it spreads infection.

Some Don'ts are more than Manners

As you go about in public you will see signs and notices put up in various places that warn you not to do certain things. It is usually bad manners to do these things, but the notices are not put up for reasons of etiquette only. They have a very real or practical purpose as well.

For example, you may see in a train, bus or tram a notice " Do not spit." It is bad manners to spit, but even worse, spitting spreads disease. People who smoke in compartments marked " No smoking " are not only bad mannered, they are probably lazy as well, because unless the train is very crowded indeed, it should be easy to find a corner where smoking is permitted.

" Do not lean out of the window " is another instruction you may see in trains. This is for your safety. If you get nothing worse than a speck of coal in your eye by looking out, that can be bad enough, but more serious accidents have happened to people ignoring this notice.

In parks you will frequently see two notices. To obey them is good manners because if you ignore them you will spoil the beauty of the parks for others. One says " Keep off the grass." This is not meant to spoil your fun. It is meant to keep you and lots of others from wearing the grass down till there are ugly tracks and patches across it. The other says " Don't leave waste paper about." Wire baskets are usually provided. You should use them or the park will become untidy and so not such a pleasant place for you or anyone else.

Party Manners

In these days the tendency is to do away with much of the formality which was at one time regarded as necessary when inviting friends to a party. An informal little note, or even an invitation by telephone, has become usual. Even so, the old rules of courtesy remain and a prompt reply should be sent, accepting the invitation, or if, unfortunately, the invitation cannot be accepted, a brief explanation should be given.

Arrive punctually: on no account before the time stated, and not too late, either. When you get there, leave your outdoor things in the room which has been set aside for the purpose. Your host should be there to introduce you to other guests, but there is no need to be too formal about this. Be friendly, not shy, and get to know the others.

Be ready to join in whatever games are suggested. You can have fun without being rough or rowdy, and on no account have fun at someone else's expense. In most games someone has to be caught out. If it is you, take it in good part. If it is one of the others, don't make them uncomfortable by laughing or joking too long.

At the end of the party you should make a point of seeing your hostess, shaking hands with her, and thanking her for the grand time you have had. Never overstay your welcome. Go when the others go, and make sure you have got everything you brought with you. Leaving things behind is a nuisance to your hostess as well as to yourself.

Behaviour at Table

Etiquette at meal times is a most important subject. Above all, practise good table manners at home so that when you eat in other people's houses or in restaurants you do not feel uncomfortable or wonder awkwardly what to do. You should do the right thing naturally.

See that your chair is a comfortable distance from the table, neither so near that it is awkward nor so far away that you will drop things.

When you get to the table, wait for the ladies to be seated first.

If grace is the custom, do not start to eat until it has been said.

When you have finished wait till your hostess (or your mother or father, at home) has risen or says you may be excused. Don't just get up and go.

Throughout the meal, don't gobble, and don't be so slow that you hold everyone else up.

You can have pleasant conversation during a meal; but don't talk with your mouth full.

Don't reach across the table. If you want anything, ask or wait for it to be passed.

Now, these are all general rules for any meal anywhere; here are some special rules for particular dishes, etc., which you ought to know:—

Soup. Use the soup spoon from the right of your plate. Don't be noisy. Use the side, not the tip of the spoon. As the plate gets empty, tip it *away* from you.

Fish. Use the proper fish knife and fork. Ordinary steel knives and forks spoil the flavour. With fillets, or shell fish, you may not require the knife, but may use the fork only.

Game. This means pheasant, grouse and other fowl. Use the special knife and fork, smaller than the normal, and made so that you can easily remove the meat from the bones.

Joint or Entrée. This is what we would usually call the main meat course. Certain *entrées*, like minced steak, should be eaten with the fork alone, held in the right hand. It is rude to mop up gravy with bread. In the case of a joint, don't start eating until all the accompanying vegetables are served; but you need not wait for others to start before starting yourself.

Sweet. Dessert fork only for jellies, trifles, blancmanges, etc. Generally the fork only unless the sweet has a custard, or is served with cream, fruit juice, etc. If necessary to do so when the plate gets nearly empty, tip it *towards* you.

Small spoon is usually provided for ices, which can be helped on to the spoon with a wafer biscuit.

Cheese. Should be cut in small pieces with the knife provided and conveyed to the mouth on a biscuit or bread.

Bread is broken, not cut, at dinner, and is placed at your left hand.

There are, of course, many other small yet important points that you will want to know about for bigger dinners: for instance, you eat asparagus by lifting up the limp shoots with the left hand fingers and you eat sweet corn by nibbling it off the cob.

Paying a Visit

If you are invited to spend part of your holidays at a friend's house, first be sure you acknowledge the invitation. Find out when you are expected—perhaps your hostess will give a hint by saying "There is a good train at such-and-such a time on Wednesday." Make a point of catching that train.

When you get there settle in quickly and without fuss to the routine of the house. Do things their way, not yours. Unpack as soon as you can in your room, which you should always keep tidy.

In the morning turn your bedclothes down and fold up your pyjamas or nightdress. Girls can be helpful by making their own beds.

Get down punctually for breakfast and do not be late for other meals either. When you leave be sure and say "Thank you" to your hostess, and when you get back to your own home write to her and say how much you enjoyed your visit, thanking her again.

Playing the Game

You must often have heard people say "It isn't cricket." Do you know exactly what they mean and what they imply?

Cricket is a game with a long history and great traditions, and although you may think it could be improved, you must go on playing it according to the rules.

So in life, people remark "It isn't cricket" when someone does something which may be smart or clever but which is not fair according to the rules of decent living. They often say "It isn't playing the game," which is much the same thing. Games form an important part of our existence and have an etiquette of their own.

Firstly, you should play the game for the sake of the game. You should of course play as well as you can and play to win. If you lose, don't be depressed, or make excuses or become bad tempered. Be a sport! Admit that the other fellow was better than you, congratulate him and leave it at that.

If you win, don't brag about it. Thank your opponent for a good game and wish him better luck next time. You can show your sportsmanship just as much by the way you behave when a winner as by the way you can take a beating.

One more word about the Etiquette of Sport. At most games there is a crowd of spectators to watch the skill of the players. Spectators and players alike must remember one thing in any game if they are to show their good manners and sportsmanship. They must accept the decision of the referee or umpire or judge.

Finally, don't keep all your good manners for people outside your own home; good manners, like charity in the proverb, should begin at home. In fact, nowhere are they so necessary; when people are living at close quarters a lack of consideration for others causes irritation, quarrels, and unhappiness.

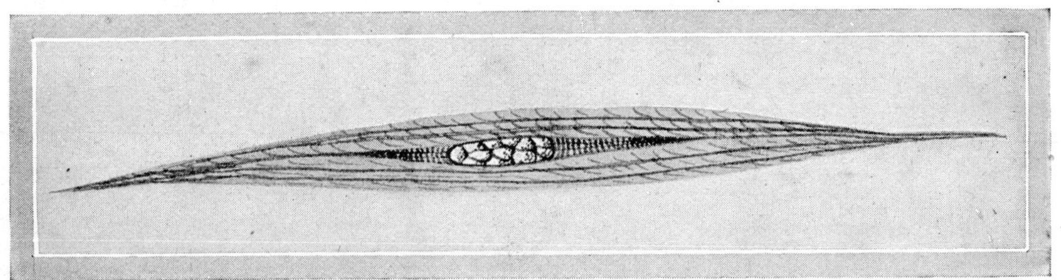

Specially drawn for this work.

A MUSCLE CELL

The body is made up of countless millions of tiny specks of living material called " cells." These cells are not all alike; they vary in appearance according to the special work they have to do. Muscle cells are packed closely, like sardines in a tin, and bundles of them are bound together in fibrous sheaths.

HOW THE BODY WORKS

PHYSIOLOGY tells you how your body " works." It would need several large books to tell you *all* about it; and you would need to spend several years using a microscope and doing experiments to help you to understand what was written in the books. Here it is only possible to give you a very simple and general idea.

A Wonderful Machine

The body is sometimes said to be like a machine or a motor car. In some few ways this is quite true; but your body is *much* more wonderful than a machine. A machine can " go," and after a time it wears out; but it cannot grow, it cannot produce young ones like itself, it cannot repair itself while it is still working, and—above all—it cannot *think.* Every living being, therefore, does some things that no sort of machine can be made to do; and many living things can think to some extent. No animal, however, can think so well as an adult human being, or even so well as a small child; so that the human brain is the most wonderful thing in the world.

In many ways the body is like a whole nation, consisting of millions of tiny citizens, each working steadily and contentedly at his own special job. Some are members of the government, and some of local committees in charge of certain jobs; some are members of a defence army; some are chemists, some scavengers, some messengers, some transport workers; some are actually little living machines, little living factories and living laboratories; some occasionally rebel, refuse to stick to their jobs, and attack their neighbours. In fact, nearly the whole work of a nation goes on within your body, except farming and fishing and mining; for your body has to " import " its food and other " raw materials "; but here again your body is unlike a machine, for it can decide what it needs, and plan how to supply its needs.

We call the stuff of which our bodies are made " tissue." Thus muscles are made of " muscle tissue," bones of "bone tissue," and so on. We can recognise the different sorts of tissue under the microscope; for, although they are all composed of cells, the cells of each sort of tissue are different from the cells of other sorts of tissue.

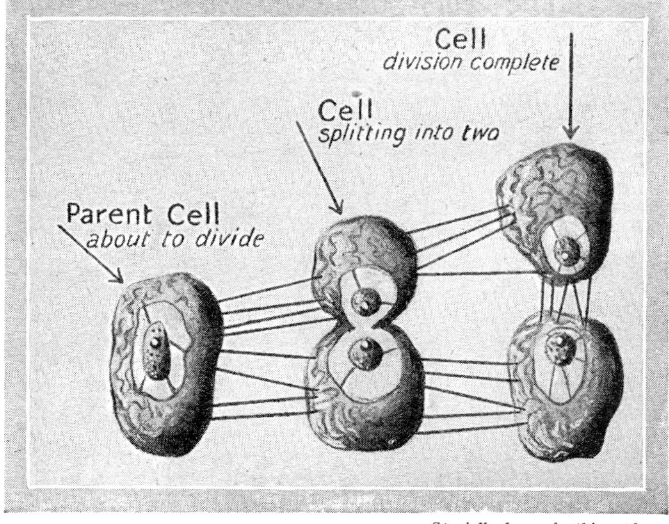

Specially drawn for this work.

MAKING NEW CELLS
In order to *grow*, you must make new tissue, so that your body can become taller and heavier. You also need new tissue to *repair* yourself, as when your flesh heals after cutting a piece out of your finger. Here you see a parent cell dividing into two daughter cells.

How You Grow

All living stuff—plant and animal—is composed of cells; and cells, or at least some of them, can exist separately as single cells, which absorb food material from their surroundings, keep what is useful to them, and get rid of the rest—together with their own waste material.

Cells increase by simply dividing into two cells—one cell *becomes* two cells, each exactly like the "parent" cell. *This is how you grow:* your cells divide and divide again, so long as extra tissue is needed—muscle cells divide and increase the number of muscle cells, bone cells divide and make new bone, and so on.

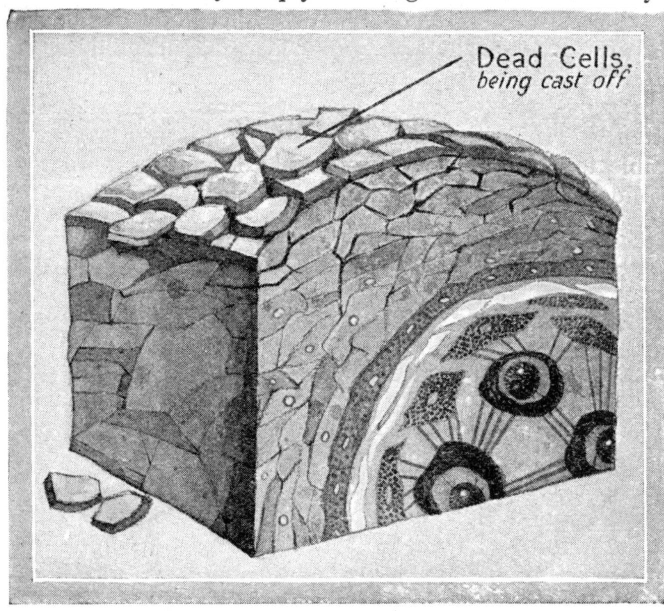

Specially drawn for this work.

WORN-OUT SKIN CELLS
Your skin wears, just like your shoes or clothes—but you repair it yourself by making new cells to replace those that are worn out. Here you see worn-out cells being shed from the surface of the skin.

Cells wear out, so that you have to provide material to make good the "wear and tear" as well as material for growth.

In doing its work a cell uses up fuel, just as a motor engine does. The burning up ("combustion") takes place without flame, of course; but it needs oxygen (one of the gases in the air we breathe) just as much as an ordinary fire does.

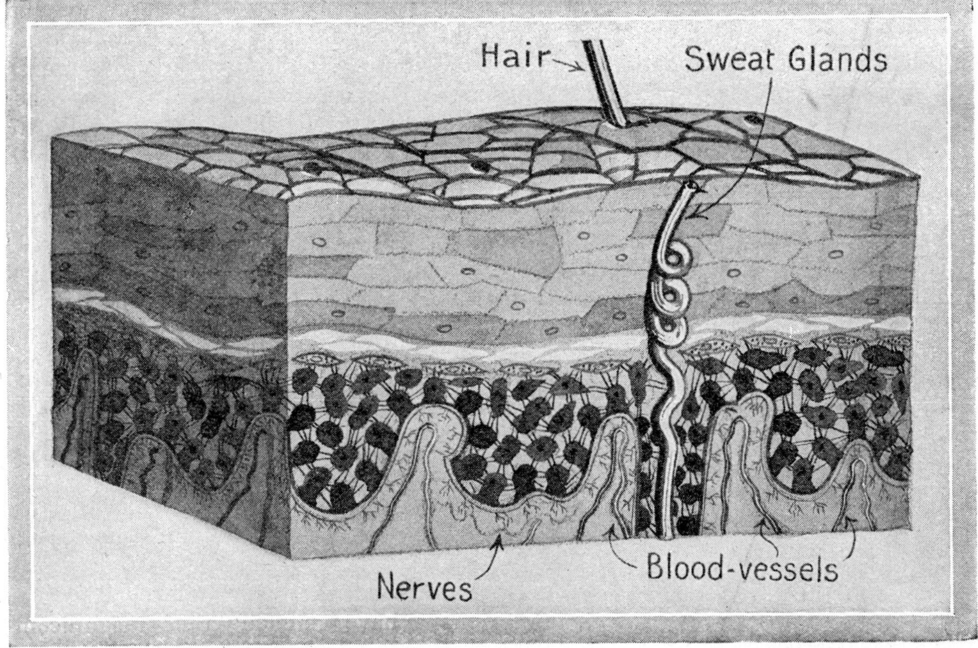

Specially drawn for this work.

WHAT THE SKIN IS MADE OF

The skin contains many different sorts of tissue. The flattened cells on top are called " pavement cells "; they protect the more delicate structures underneath. There are also muscle cells, fat cells, fibre cells, nerves and blood-vessels, hairs, and special glands with long coiled tubes (sweat glands) which open at the pores of the skin. The body gets rid of some of its waste matter in the sweat which comes from the millions of sweat glands in the skin.

The materials for growth and repair and the fuel for energy to do work all come from your food, and this food material is carried round the body by the blood; the oxygen for combustion is carried by the blood too; and all the waste material of wear and tear and of combustion are removed from the tissues by the blood.

The Framework of the Body

Steel and concrete, bricks and wood, provide a satisfactory framework for buildings; but the body needs a very special sort of framework. It must be such that it contains strong " houses " for some of the important organs, such as the brain; it must be flexible—capable of movement, and these movements of many different sorts, so that we can walk, use our arms, bend and twist our bodies, and raise, lower and turn our heads; it must be sufficiently strong to stand a good deal of rough usage; and yet it must not be too heavy; and it must, for many years, be able to *grow* and to grow *gradually*. So that it may fulfil all these requirements it is made of that remarkable substance *bone*.

Bone is nearly twice as strong as oak—a cubic inch of hard bone will support a weight of 2 tons. It is elastic, so that it springs back into shape after some degree of bending; in some parts of the world where suitable wood is scarce, the natives use animals' ribs for their bows. If bone is bent so far that it breaks, it can mend itself by growing fresh bone to join up the broken ends. With all this, bone is light in weight.

The bony framework is made up of over 200 separate bones, wonderfully jointed and held together by strong bands and muscles. There are joints which work very much like the hinges of a door, which can " open and shut "; your finger joints are examples of this sort. There are " ball-and-socket " joints (smooth rounded knobs fitting into hollows) like those of the shoulders which allow movement in almost any direction. There are pivot joints, and gliding joints. There is the backbone, which is something like a string of cotton reels separated by layers of india-rubber, and which can bend and twist and yet is sufficiently strong to enable you to drop from a height on to your feet without collapsing into a heap or injuring yourself in any way.

Just as each part of a bridge, designed by an expert engineer, is arranged so as to withstand all the strains and stresses which it will have to bear, so each bone and each joint of your body is so constructed that it can do all that it has to do.

What the Muscles Do

Over all this bony framework are the muscles. A muscle is able to alter its shape, as you realise when you bend your elbow to display your bulging " biceps " muscle. A muscle lies limp and inactive when it is not doing work; but when necessary it can increase its thickness and at the same time lessen its length. If the two ends of a muscle are attached to two bones, then when the muscle shortens itself it pulls the two bones towards one another. A muscle cannot push—it can only shorten itself and pull, and so you will find that muscles and groups of muscles often work in pairs; as an instance one group of muscles pulls and makes your fingers bend, and another group of muscles pulls and brings your fingers out straight again.

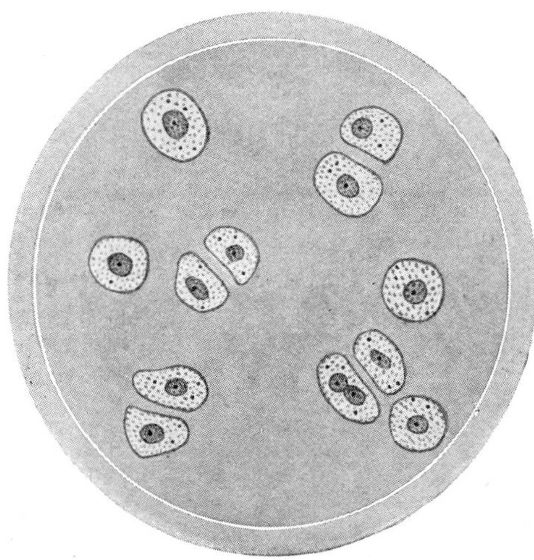

Specially drawn for this work.

CARTILAGE CELLS

The surfaces of bones which move against one another in a joint are covered with a smooth, glistening tissue called " cartilage." You can see this tissue on the knobs of the drumstick of a chicken before it is cooked.

When you use a machine, it wears out a little. When you use a muscle, it, too, wears out; but your body very soon makes good the wear, so that the muscle does not become smaller—in fact, the more often you make a muscle work hard, the bigger it becomes. You may have envied the magnificent-looking muscles of a blacksmith or a weight-lifter; but, unless you really need these heavy, bulging muscles for your work, it is certainly not worth while trying to develop them. Most of us need a reasonable amount of strength combined with activity and liveliness, and above all, we need general fitness; so that it is wiser to go in for outdoor games than to exercise with heavy dumb-bells.

Our Waterproof Covering

The whole of the body is protected by a living garment of skin; but the skin is something more than a waterproof covering—it is an organ which has most important work to do.

The skin has fine nerves, which take information to the brain. If you hold your hand too near the fire when you are making toast and are in danger of burning it, the nerves in the skin of your hand flash a message to the brain " We are being burnt! " Your brain at once flashes orders to the necessary muscles, and they snatch your hand away. There are actually separate nerve endings in your skin to receive sensations of heat, cold, and pain, as well as nerve endings which simply report " touch."

Keeping the Temperature in Order

The temperature of the body must remain nearly constant if we are to be in health. A great deal of *surplus* heat is produced in the tissues of the body, and unless this were got rid of we should soon be in a state of high fever and die of " heat-stroke." The skin has a great deal to do with the regulation of the temperature; it assists to keep the right balance between the amount of heat produced and the amount given off by means of its blood-vessels and its sweat glands. The blood which is circulating in the skin blood-vessels gives up a good deal of its heat to the air on the surface of the skin; and the skin can regulate the amount of blood in these vessels by narrowing or widening them. When moisture evaporates, heat is taken up from the surroundings, which become cooler in consequence.

When we are producing a lot of heat during a game, the skin pours out a great deal of sweat which evaporates; and during this evaporation much heat is taken up from the skin. At the same time, the blood-vessels of the skin widen, bringing more blood to the surface, and so the rate of cooling is increased.

Yet another very important work of the skin is helping to get rid of some of the waste products from the blood; this waste is dissolved in the sweat. In certain diseases, the kidneys—those great blood filters—are unable to work properly; and we can make the skin do extra work, and get rid of the waste which is usually removed by the kidneys.

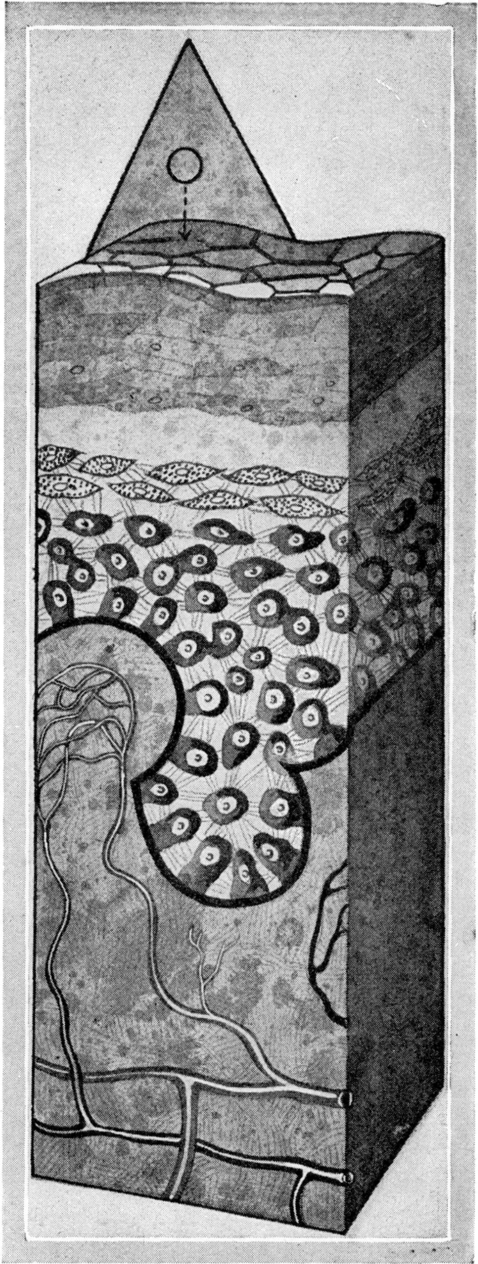

Specially drawn for this work.

THE TWO LAYERS OF THE SKIN

The triangle shows the smooth, naked-eye appearance of the skin; but when seen through a microscope, it looks like crazy paving, and the surface is uneven. The thick black line in the middle divides the upper skin (epidermis) from the true skin (dermis) which contains the sweat glands, blood vessels and nerves. You can see the capillaries joining the arteries and veins.

Why the Blood " Circulates "

" Circulation " means " going round and round." Blood has to keep on going round and round your body as long as you are alive, whether you are awake or asleep. It does not just wander about aimlessly—it is driven round along certain paths, collected up again, sent out to be "cleaned and renovated" (so to speak), collected up again, and then sent out on another journey. The "organ" which keeps the circulation going is the heart.

The heart is more than a single pump. It is a very powerful muscular organ, containing two separate receiving chambers and two separate pumping chambers. There are special names for all these chambers, but we need not bother about them here.

For No. 1 pumping chamber the blood is forced out in jerks into a great blood-pipe or "blood-vessel," which divides and subdivides into smaller and smaller pipes, which carry the blood all over the body. These blood-vessels which carry blood *from* the heart are called "arteries." The pipes become so small finally that they are called "capillaries" or hair-like blood-vessels; they form a complete network in every part of the body, but they can only be seen by means of a microscope.

The blood from the capillaries moves on, and the capillaries join up into larger and larger blood-vessels which at last return the blood to No. 1 receiving chamber of the heart. The pipes which carry blood *to* the heart are called "veins."

From No. 1 receiving chamber the blood is forced into No. 2 pumping chamber, and from there it is pumped into the lungs through an artery, which divides and then subdivides into capillaries; and these form a network throughout the lungs. The blood collects up again into veins, and finally into one vein, which takes it back to No. 2 receiving chamber of the heart. From No. 2 receiving chamber the blood is forced into No. 1 pumping chamber, and then the whole business is repeated.

You will notice that there are already *two* circulations—one from the heart, round the body, and back to the heart, and the other from the heart, to the lungs, and back to the heart. There is yet a third circulation, which will be mentioned later.

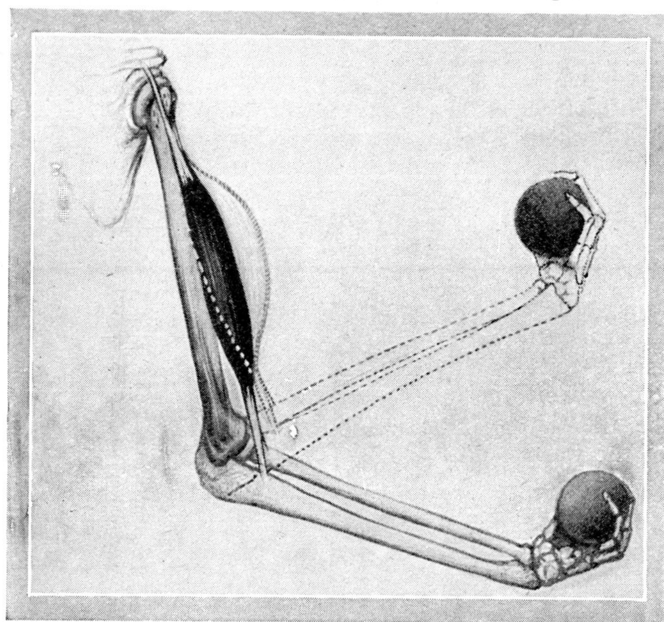

Specially drawn for this work.

HOW A MUSCLE MAKES YOU MOVE

When you contract your biceps, it pulls in its attachments. As it cannot pull your shoulder down towards your elbow, the resulting movement takes place at the other attached end of the muscle, and your forearm is raised.

Why Blood is Red

The blood does so many things, and so much happens to it, that it is really difficult to know where to begin. If it were just plain red stuff like paint, and we could imagine that we were watching a single drop of it for half an hour or so, it would be quite easy; but it is not just plain red stuff, and the parts of even a tiny drop probably do not remain the same for any length of time. Blood consists of a clear fluid containing fuel material, repair material, waste material and many other things; and floating along in this fluid are millions of tiny white cells, and many more millions of tiny disc-like red cells which give it its colour; and all the time the blood is doing things—giving up some of itself and receiving stuff into itself.

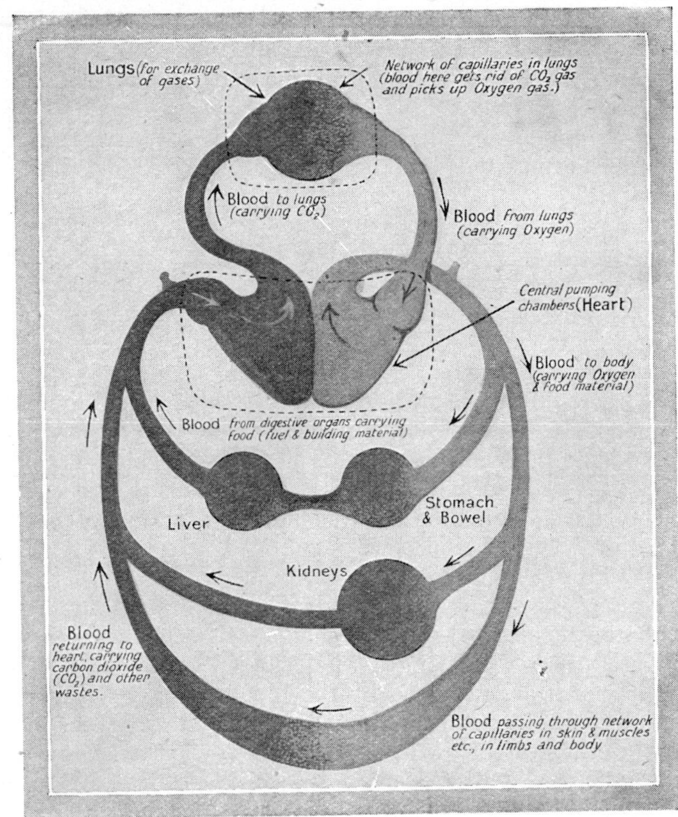

Specially drawn for this work.

THE CIRCULATION OF THE BLOOD

The blood makes two journeys; one to the lungs, to collect oxygen and get rid of carbon dioxide, and the other throughout all the body tissues and organs, to deliver food and oxygen and collect up carbon dioxide and other wastes—like the milkman who delivers milk and at the same time collects up the empty bottles.

Perhaps we could follow one red cell for a while. It was made in some part of the bone marrow, but we will begin following it from one of its visits to the No. 1 pumping chamber of the heart. With many millions of other red cells it is pumped out into a huge artery, and tumbled along jerkily into ever-narrowing blood-vessels until at last it is moving in a capillary which winds its way among the cells of a muscle which is being used. The capillary is so small that there is only just room for one red cell to pass along it at a time, and even then it is a close fit, so that the red cell touches the walls of the capillary. Each muscle cell is like a tiny motor engine, and it needs oxygen to enable it to burn up fuel material to provide it with the energy or power-to-work. Now the red cell is carrying oxygen—not in bubbles, but dissolved, so to speak; and it is able to give up this oxygen, which oozes through the walls of the capillary and is used by the muscle cell.

The muscle cell, like the motor engine, gives off "exhaust gas," which oozes through the walls of the capillary and is taken up by the red cell. Our red cell—no longer such a bright red as it was when it was carrying oxygen—is pushed along and passes into a tiny vein which in turn passes it into a larger vein, until at last it is tipped back into No. 1 receiving chamber of the heart. From the heart it will be sent off to the lungs; what happens to it there will be told later on. Here we will just say that when it returns from the lungs to the heart it will again be of a nice bright red colour, and all ready to be sent off to some part of the body to carry out some other task.

A Long Journey

Now let us follow a tiny drop of the

clear fluid in which this red cell was floating. It, too, reaches the capillary close to the muscle cell where the red cell carried out its task. Some of it oozes through the capillary wall, and round the muscle cell. The muscle cell needs some of the fuel material, just as the motor engine needs petrol; this fuel it absorbs from the clear fluid, together with a little repair material. The rest of the clear fluid moves on and is picked up into tiny tubes, which are very similar to the capillaries; and these tiny tubes join up into bigger and bigger tubes and finally into one large tube; and this empties the clear fluid back into a vein which is just taking blood back into the heart. This is the third " circulation " we mentioned. The clear fluid (which is called " lymph ") goes out from the heart with the blood as far as the capillaries, but it then travels along a whole lot of tubes which are not used by the blood. It joins the blood again just before it reaches the heart.

The White Soldier Cells

The journey of a white cell may be more exciting than that of a red cell; for this white cell may have to act as a soldier, and defend the body from dangerous invaders. When a thorn sticks into your fingers there may be harmful cells or germs on the thorn, or on your skin, or in the air, and these may enter through the hole in your skin. Now the white cell can change its shape; when it meets a hostile cell it tries to flow all round it and then consume it. If there are sufficient white cells on the spot to destroy all the invading germs, well and good, but sometimes the enemies are strong and numerous, and many white cells are killed by them. Your body, however, hurries along more and more white cells to the spot, until at last they gain the victory.

You will have noticed that sometimes when you have pricked your finger it becomes hot and red and " inflamed "; this is because of the increase in the amount of blood sent to the danger spot. You may also have noticed some yellowish " matter "; this consists of dead white cells which have been slain in doing their duty.

These three are simply examples of the many tasks which the blood has to perform. A complete list of them would take quite a time; but here is a short and incomplete list:

Some Tasks our Blood Performs

The blood has to collect up into itself the digested food from the digestive organs, and the red and white cells from the parts where they are made, and oxygen from the lungs, and it has to carry away waste materials from the tissues. It has to supply all the organs and glands, which act as little chemical factories and laboratories, with the material from which they make their special juices, and it has to take some of these juices round to the parts where they are needed.

It carries various protective substances (" anti-toxins," etc.) which are able to destroy the poisons with which harmful germs may be attacking us. It visits various cleansing and filtering organs, where it parts with harmful waste matter, and also with any substance of which there is too much, for the health of the body requires that only a certain amount of some substances should be present in the blood, and if there is too much the body suffers. It carries sugar and starch to be stored up in the liver and muscles, so that there is a supply ready for use when it is needed; and when necessary, it fetches these reserves and delivers them to the places where the body needs to use them.

It visits the heart frequently, and there it is all mixed up together, so that its contents remain very much the same all over the body.

Many of these things are going on all the time and some of them only sometimes; and, of course, the body

WHAT THE HEART DOES

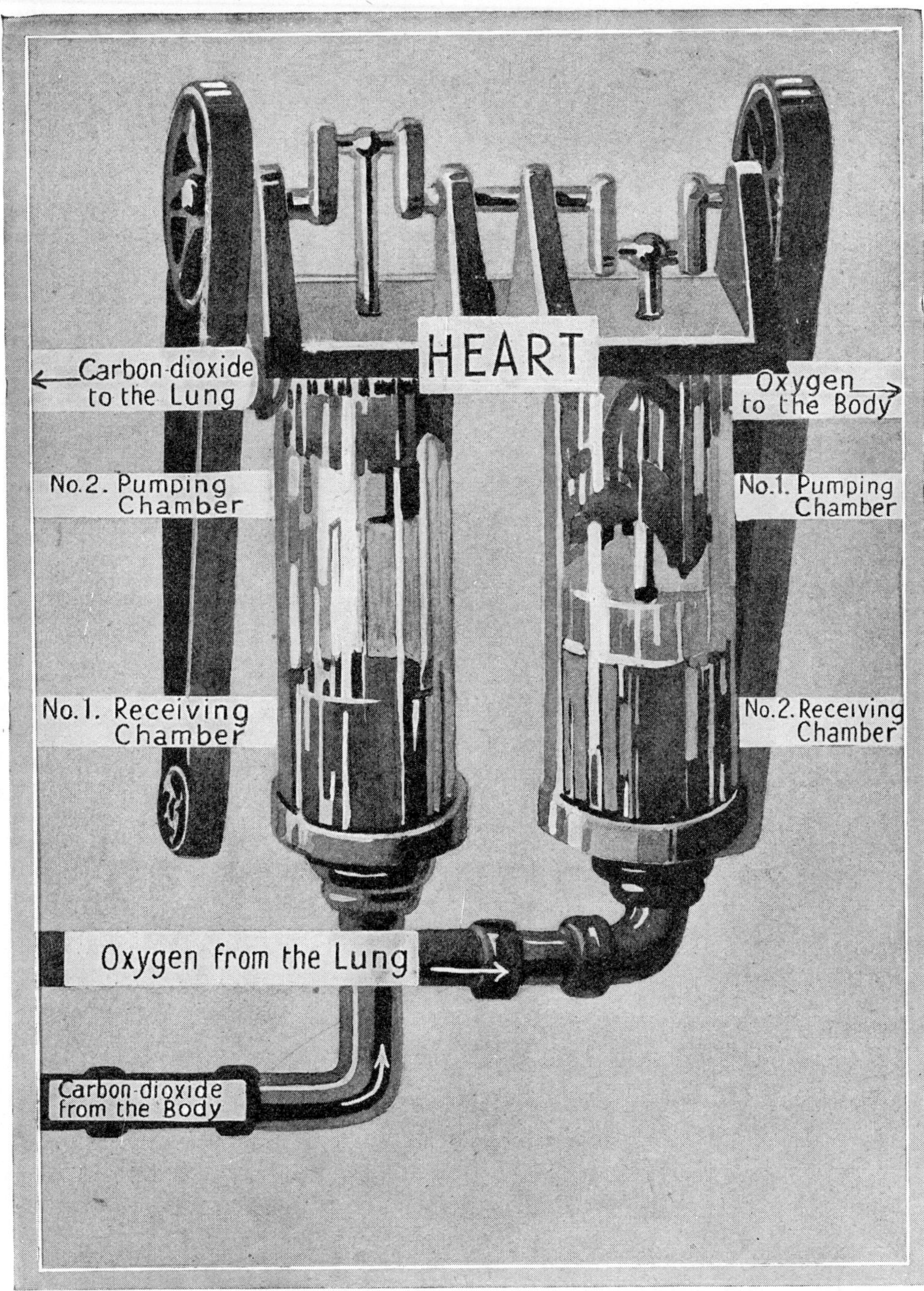

Specially drawn for this work.

If there were no means of keeping the blood circulating along its proper channels we should soon die for want of food and oxygen and from poisoning from our waste products. The heart is a powerful muscular organ which is specialised to form a central pumping station. One pump keeps the blood circulating through the lungs, and the other pump maintains the circulation through the body. The heart never ceases work during life, but it has much less work to do when you are sleeping than when you are taking vigorous muscular exercise.

can speed up things according to its needs. When you have just eaten a meal, for instance, there is a great bustle to supply digestive juices, and to supply fuel material for the organs which have to manufacture the juices and for the organs which have to churn up the digestive food. When you are running, much fuel has to be used up, so that a great deal of oxygen is needed; you must breathe quickly and deeply, and your heart must hurry up the circulation to the lungs. When you are asleep, on the other hand, both your breathing and your heart-beats slow down very much.

It is almost impossible to compare the blood with anything else in the world. In some ways it is like the water of a whole network of inland rivers and canals and streams, flowing past or through factories, carrying large loads of all sorts of things to these factories and taking away their waste; carrying messengers and troops and workmen; in fact, making possible the whole business of carrying on life; but even this does not give anything like a complete picture of *all* that the blood does.

Why You Breathe

Respiration is the breathing in of air into our chests and the breathing of it out again.

The air is composed almost entirely of two gases. About one-fifth is oxygen, which is a very *live* sort of gas; of course, a gas cannot itself be alive, but oxygen strikes us as being a very active sort of gas because of what it does. If you plunge a glowing splinter of wood into a jar of oxygen it at once kindles into a flame and burns brightly; if you plunge a thin, red-hot iron wire into oxygen it sparkles, splutters and burns like a firework. It is this gas which your tiny muscle cells must have so that they can burn up fuel material to make energy or power-to-work. Most of the other part of the air is a dead sort of gas which just thins out or dilutes the oxygen; for if we took too much oxygen, everything in the body would go on much too rapidly, and we should wear out too soon.

When fuel material of any sort burns, it combines or joins up with the oxygen; and the fuel and the oxygen together become another sort of gas, which is called " carbon dioxide "; (this is sometimes written CO_2 for short). It is this gas which we compared to the exhaust gas of a motor engine, when we were talking about the working of the tiny muscle cell. You will remember that the red cell gave up oxygen to the muscle cell and took away the " exhaust gas," which we can now call carbon dioxide.

How the Red Cells Work

We must now see how the red cell gets rid of the carbon dioxide and takes in a fresh supply of oxygen; for this is the whole aim and object of respiration, and the exchange must be carried on continuously or you will cease to live.

When you " breathe in," you take in air through your nose. You *can* breathe through your mouth; but this is unwise, because in your nose the air is warmed and moistened and the germs and dust are trapped. The air passes into a great pipe, which divides into two pipes, one of which goes to the right lung and the other to the left lung. These pipes divide up into smaller and smaller pipes, very much as the blood-vessels do; but, instead of becoming capillaries finally they end in tiny air-sacs.

The lungs are sometimes said to be like sponges; but they are much more like thick bushes with very tiny leaves, with pipes instead of stems, and air-sacs instead of leaves. If all these air-sacs could be spread out quite flat they would cover the floor of a small hall about 10 yards long and 10 yards wide; as they are all packed inside your chest it is plain that the walls of the air-sacs are extremely thin.

You will remember that the heart

pumps the blood into the lungs when it returns from a journey to some part of the body, carrying within its red cells the carbon dioxide. The arteries which carry this blood to the lungs split up into smaller and smaller blood-vessels until they become capillaries, and these capillaries run round all the little air sacs. The red cells give up their carbon dioxide, which oozes through the walls of the capillaries and through the walls of the air-sacs; at the same time the oxygen from the air-sacs oozes through into the red cells. The red cells, having exchanged their carbon dioxide for fresh oxygen, are gathered up again into blood-vessels and taken back to the heart, all ready to be sent off to some part of the body again.

Preparing the Air

When you " breathe out," the carbon dioxide passes out through your nose. The dead sort of gas we mentioned is just breathed in and breathed out again; it does nothing and nothing happens to it except that it becomes warmed. There is a good deal of moisture in the air you breathe out. If you think for a moment, you will find that nearly all living stuff is moist; moisture seems to be necessary to life, or at least to active life, and so the whole of the cells which compose your body are always moist. The air brings a lot of moisture with it when it comes away from the millions of tiny air-sacs.

You see that the organs which keep you supplied with oxygen and get rid of your " exhaust gas " are the *heart*—which sends the blood to the lungs and then receives it back again, and the *lungs*—there the actual exchange of gases takes place; but we must not forget the *nose*, which has important work to do in preparing the air to be taken into the lungs.

Quite probably you think that you " blow out your chest " by forcing air into it until it is full and hard; but this is not so. The muscles of your chest move the ribs and make the chest bigger round, while a great flat muscle which forms the base of the chest lowers itself and so makes the chest bigger from below. The lungs fit closely to the insides of the chest, although they are not actually attached; and so, when the chest becomes bigger, the lungs are sucked out, so to speak; and it is this that makes them suck air into the air-sacs. You *can* breathe without moving your ribs; but then you are only using the big flat muscle at the base of the chest, and you have to lower this and so push out your stomach.

The muscular movements by means of which you breathe must go on all the time you are alive; and as they work while you are asleep, they must be able to work without your " willing " them to work. You will read later on that quite a lot of the work of the body goes on without your having to " will " it; but the breathing muscles are interesting in that you can control them if you wish to do so; while if you take no interest in them they go on working just as well.

How the Body Deals with its Food

The material from which a machine is made and with which it is repaired has to be specially prepared before it can be used; and sometimes its fuel also is a manufactured article. Your body, the wonderful human machine, extracts and prepares its own fuel and building materials provided that we supply the " raw material " in the form of suitable food. Just as a builder needs special material in order to build a house, so our bodies need food which will supply the living bricks and mortar and tiles and window-glass and wooden beams for building up the living house which we occupy, and for repairing it when parts get broken or worn out, and for enlarging it as we grow.

The baby doubles its weight during the first six months of life, and by the end of the first year it should weigh three times as much as when it was born: afterwards, the rate of growth slows down considerably until, when we are adults, the only parts that continue to grow are the hair and nails. The baby, then, needs a good supply of the building foods; and these, together with its fuel food, it obtains from milk. You probably know that milk is a splendid body-building food for boys and girls and grown-ups as well as for babies; but people with teeth need solid foods, too, and they can extract the building materials from such foods as meat, fish, eggs, cheese, peas, beans and lentils. Then we need also " fuel foods " to supply heat energy and work energy, and these we get from the starches and sugars (carbohydrates) and fats.

I want you to realise that the food we eat is of no use to nourish the body until it has been digested and absorbed into the blood. You could actually starve to death in spite of large meals of unsuitable food—or even of suitable food if your digestion were unable to deal with it.

Let us see what will happen to the next dinner we eat. In order to make it quite clear to you, the pictures show the work being done by different kinds of machinery in charge of workmen; but you realise, of course, that your body machinery looks altogether different and that your " workmen " are cells and groups of cells.

Why we Chew our Food

In the mouth, your front teeth are the " cutters " which slice off portions of food. This food is then passed along by your tongue and cheek muscles to be crushed up by your back teeth, the " grinders "; and while you are chewing your food, it is being mixed with a digestive juice, the saliva or " spit," which acts on some of the starchy food; so you see digestion really begins in the mouth.

When the food has been chewed to a pulp and thoroughly mixed with saliva, it is ready for the next stage of digestion, which takes place in the stomach. The tongue pushes the food to the back of the throat and it is swallowed. Now the food has to make its way down the food pipe which passes through the neck and chest to the stomach. Certain muscles in the throat and a cleverly arranged little flap prevent the food from going the wrong way from the mouth when we swallow; otherwise, some of the food might pass into the air-pipe leading to the lungs. When, as occasionally happens, a crumb does accidentally get into the air-pipe, we make vigorous efforts to send it back again into the mouth by coughing.

What Happens to the Things We Eat

Now the food which has passed from your mouth does not just drop down into the stomach; as you know, you can swallow when you are lying down. It is pushed along by the muscular walls of the food tube, which widens out in front of the lump of food, so that it can pass along easily, and contracts itself immediately behind the food. You can imitate this by pushing an orange into a stocking and then squeezing the stocking behind it.

Your dinner will thus be collected into the stomach, which is really a part of your digestive tube enlarged so as to form a bag, with an upper opening leading to the food tube and a lower one leading to the small bowel. The lower door remains firmly closed while the meal is being well churned and mixed with other digestive juices which together are called " the gastric juice " and act on the body-building foods (" proteins ").

When the stomach part of digestion is finished, the door opening into the bowel tube allows the contents to pass through, and bowel digestion begins. Our picture shows a little man controlling this doorway. In the small bowel, more digestive juices are poured on food, some from the liver and some from the pancreas, and some from the lining of the tube itself. When we use the pancreas of an animal for food we call it sweetbread.

Here, in the bowel, digestion is completed; the food is quite dissolved, and you could no longer recognise portions of meat and cabbage and potato and pudding. The starches and sugars (bread, potatoes, jam, syrup, etc.) are changed into a special form of sugar; the fats (fat meat, suet, butter, cream, etc.) are changed into a kind of soap (the "soap" is changed back into fat as soon as it has passed through the bowel); and the building materials (meat, fish, egg white, etc.) are prepared into an acid substance. Now the food is ready for use, and it passes into the circulation. The remainder of the food we have eaten, which is not required for nourishment, is got rid of through the large bowel.

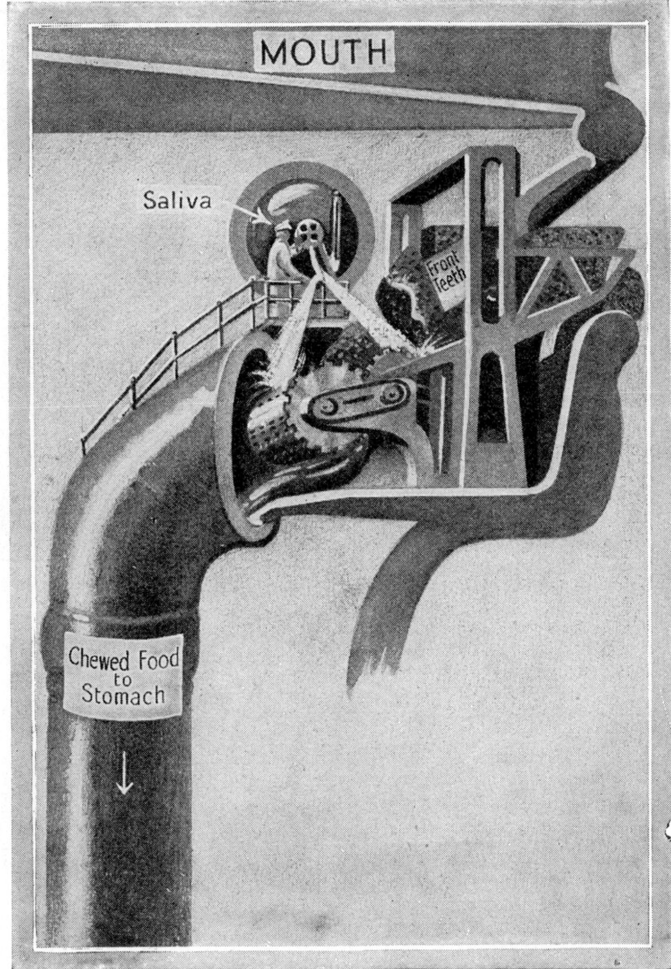

Specially drawn for this work.

DIGESTION BEGINS IN THE MOUTH

The front teeth are represented by the knife which is slicing off a portion of food. The food is then mixed with a digestive juice (saliva) and passed through the grinding rollers (back teeth). Thus food in the mouth is broken up, softened and moistened and partially digested during mastication. The saliva changes some of the starchy foods, such as bread, cereals and potatoes, into a form of sugar.

Why the Liver is Important

It is most important that the body should never be short of fuel, and so we are able to store sugar in the liver, to be released into the blood as we need it; some sugar is stored in the muscles also. The sugar is stored in the form of a special kind of starch, and it is changed back again into sugar before it is actually used. In the picture of the liver you will see the sugar being brought along from the bowel in the blood-pipe; and on the right of the picture you will see some of it taken out of store again and sent off to be used. We are also able to store fat in various parts of the body.

Other things happen in the liver, besides this storage of sugar. Worn-out red blood cells are extracted from the blood and pass out of the liver in the bile. Any excess of building materials is filtered out of the blood, and changed into a form in which it can be got rid of through the kidneys. Certain poisons

WHAT HAPPENS IN THE STOMACH

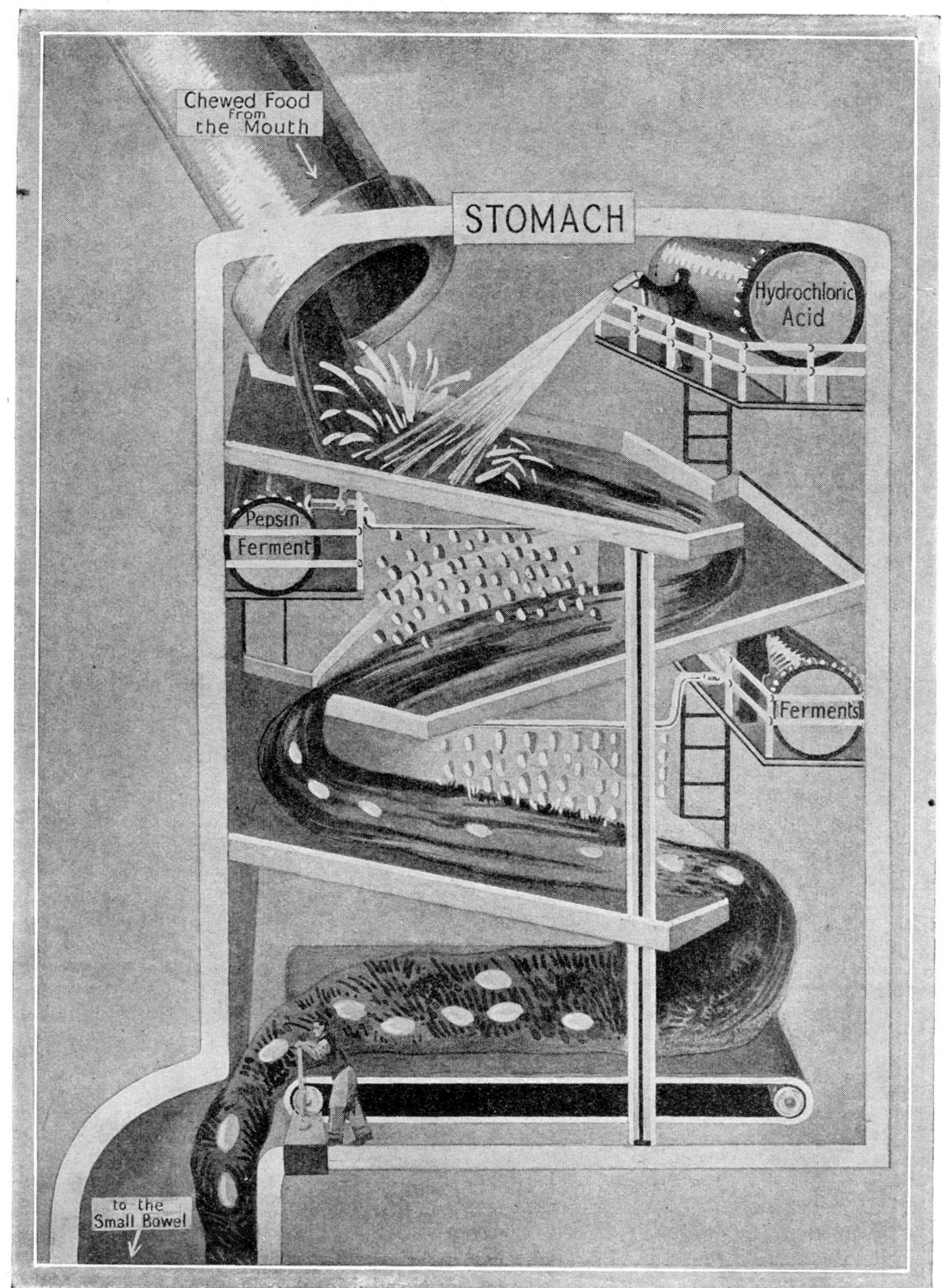

Specially drawn for this work.

You see food arriving from the food pipe into the stomach; and there it will remain until stomach digestion is completed. By movements of the muscular stomach wall, the food is thoroughly mixed with the gastric digestive juices, which include an acid (HCl), pepsin and other ferments. (1) Living germs swallowed with the food are killed by the acid. (2) Digestion of protein (body-building and repairing food) begins. (3) The outer coats of the fat cells are dissolved, setting free the fat. (4) Milk is curdled. The stomach should have emptied in three to four hours after an ordinary mixed meal.

DIGESTION COMPLETED IN THE SMALL BOWEL

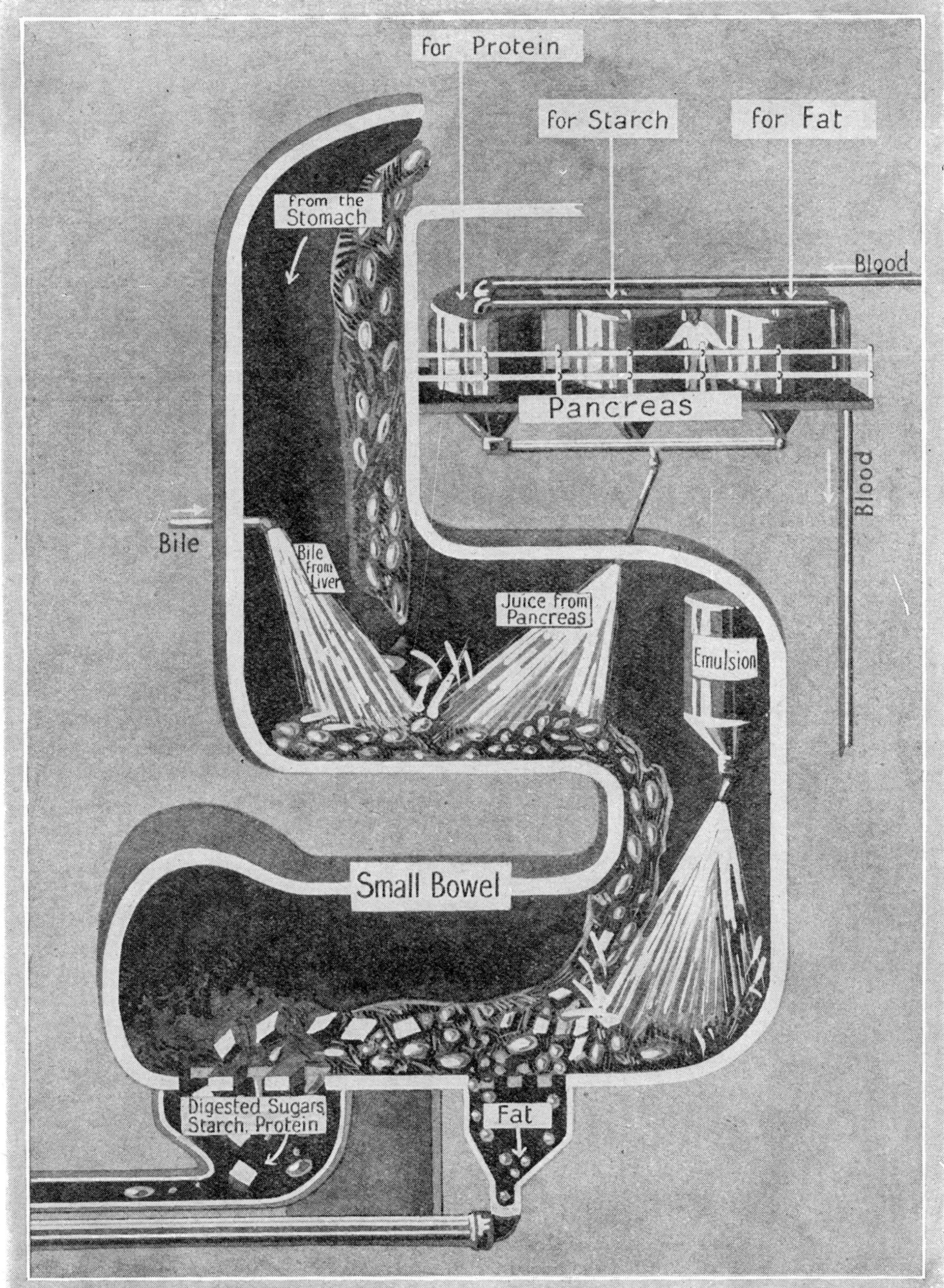

Specially drawn for this work.

On leaving the stomach, the food enters the small bowel, where bile from the liver makes fats more easily dealt with, the juice of the pancreas acts on all kinds of foods, and the juice from glands in the wall of the bowel completes digestion. While this is happening, the food is being churned up and pushed along towards the large bowel; and about five hours after a meal, the undigested waste of the food begins to enter the large bowel. The digested food is taken into the circulating blood, and is then carried to the liver for a thorough sorting out.

(which we call "toxins") are also removed from the blood as it passes through the liver, and are excreted, through the bile flow, into the bowel. The liver, then, has a great deal of important work to do; and you will understand why we feel "out of sorts" when the liver is not working well.

The blood passes on from the liver to the heart with its food supply (fuel and building material) ready to be used by the body cells; but the fuel part of it would be useless without oxygen, so the blood is pumped from the heart to the lungs, where the red cells may get a supply of oxygen from the air we have breathed in. Now everything is ready for the body to make use of the food, and the blood is taken back from the lungs to the heart to be pumped round, carrying its precious cargoes to all the parts of the body. When it reaches the tiny capillary blood-pipes, the red cells give up their oxygen and the fluid part of the blood oozes out to bathe the body cells. Thus the fuel and oxygen to supply heat and energy, and the building material to repair wear and tear, and material for growth, are finally delivered where they are needed.

All About Vitamins

We have talked of the fuel-foods and the building-material foods; but these alone are not sufficient to keep us alive. We need minute quantities of substances called vitamins. You can think of some of these as the lubricating oil necessary for the body machinery; without them the machinery would cease to work, no matter how much fuel-food was provided. Others are necessary to enable the body to use the building-material for growth.

Some vitamins are found in certain fatty foods, others in watery foods; the first kind we call "fat-soluble" vitamins, and the second "water-soluble" vitamins. The vitamin which prevents the disease rickets ("fat-soluble D") is found in most animal fats, and especially in cod and other fish liver oils, liver, fish roe, egg yolk (which contains a large proportion of fat) and in the butter and cream from the milk of pasture-fed cows. This vitamin is sometimes called "the sunshine vitamin," because it can be produced in the body by the action of sunlight on the skin. We can store this vitamin in our bodies; so that one advantage of sun-bathing during the summer is that we obtain a supply of vitamin D to help us over the winter.

Defence against Germs

The other fat-soluble vitamin is named "A"; it assists us in defending our bodies against infection with germs. If our food contains sufficient of this vitamin, we are less likely to develop diseases and better able to conquer them than if there is a shortage. Vitamin A is found in the fat foods which contain vitamin D, and also in green vegetables, carrots and tomatoes.

The water-soluble vitamins include vitamin B, which is necessary for the proper nutrition of the nerves and muscles. Lack of this vitamin causes the disease beri-beri, which is quite common in the East. Vitamin B is found in the seeds of plants, and in the eggs and internal organs of animals. Foods particularly rich in this vitamin are yeast, bran, peanuts, dried peas, beans and lentils, nuts, liver, heart and kidney, and whole-grain cereals, such as wholemeal flour and wholemeal bread.

Vitamin C is another water-soluble vitamin, and lack of this causes the disease scurvy, a disease which used to cause the deaths of a great many sailors in the Navy, before we discovered the cause and the cure. It is found in fresh fruits and vegetables.

On a good mixed diet, including milk and dairy produce, eggs, salads, oranges, tomatoes, nuts and whole-grain cereal foods (such as wholemeal bread, unpolished rice and whole barley), we are in no danger of suffering from shortage of vitamins. If, however, we eat mostly "refined" foods from which vitamins

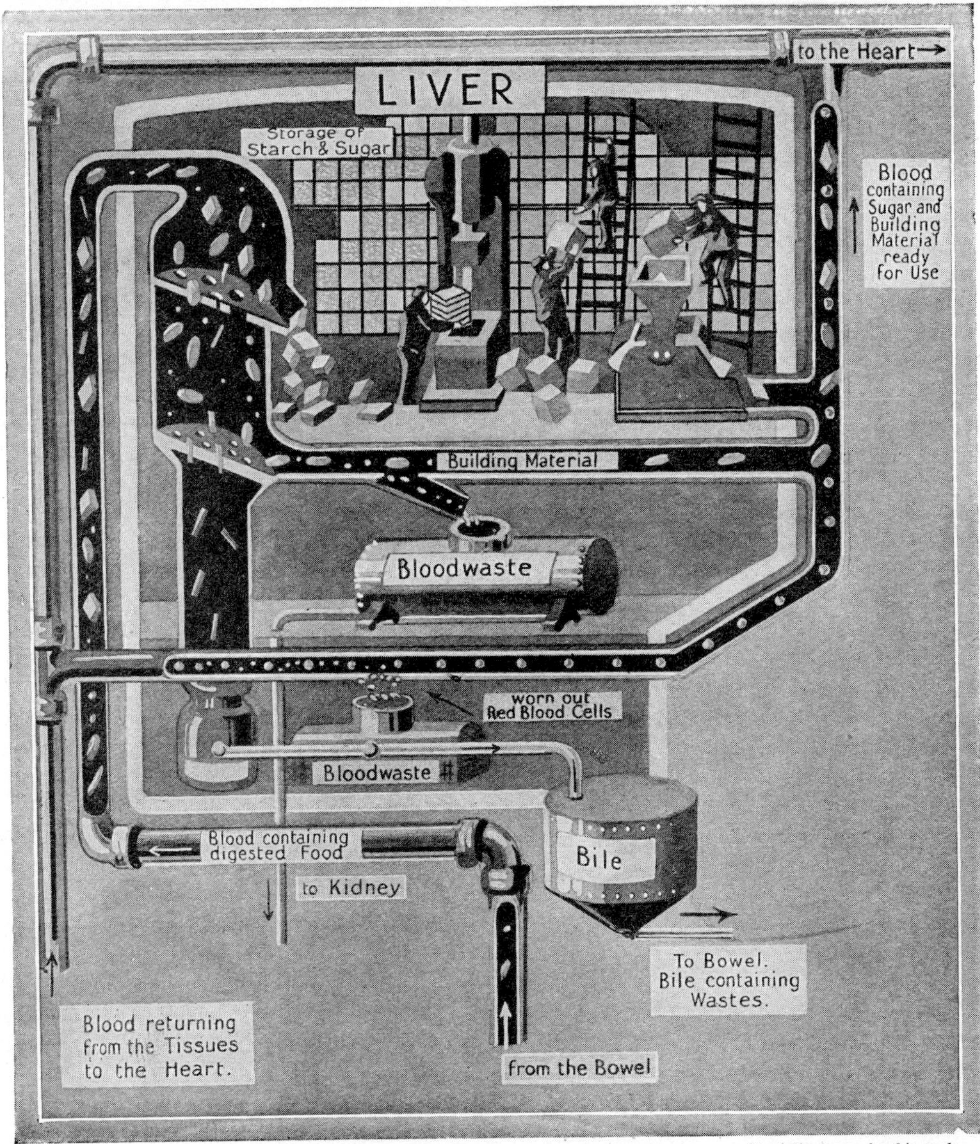

Specially drawn for this work.

THE WORK OF THE LIVER

The liver is a large gland which acts as a sort of clearing-house and store-house, where the digested food and any other material brought from the bowel is thoroughly sorted and dealt with. Some is passed on into the blood to supply the body with nourishment; some is stored, to be given out again as required; whilst some is rejected as poisonous, and sent out to be got rid of by the kidneys or in the bile. In addition, the liver filters off the worn-out red blood cells, which also pass out in the bile.

and minerals have been removed in the manufacturing processes, then the body machine will certainly be injured and we shall suffer from ill-health.

In order to maintain normal health and growth, we must eat food from which the body can get all that it needs—fuel, building material, minerals, vitamins and water. We cannot get all the water we need from food, although some foods contain up to 90 per cent. of water; we must drink water, too.

Now you can understand what is meant by a " balanced diet." There is no doubt that a great many of the common ailments are caused by not eating the right kind of food.

Removal of Waste

The body, like all living matter, produces waste; and if the waste matter is not got rid of regularly, poisons will accumulate in the blood. Our bodies have their own " health service " for getting rid of wastes, and the organs which are responsible for this function are called " excretory organs."

The living substance of which the body cells are composed (protoplasm) is in a continual state of activity, building up and breaking down. The waste products from this " wear and tear " are passed into the blood, which in due course flows through the excretory organs—the kidneys, lungs, skin and bowel wall. From the burning up of the fuel foods to produce heat-energy and work-energy, the waste gas, carbon dioxide, is formed, and this, too, finds its way into the blood, to be carried off and excreted through the lungs in the air we breathe out.

If you look at the picture of the liver, you will see that certain wastes are filtered off from the blood and drained into the bile, to be got rid of when the bile flows into the small bowel. The kidneys (there are two) are special filters, composed of masses of tiny tubes and specialised cells. They cleanse the blood which flows through them, and the waste products are excreted in the urine.

The waste matter which leaves the body through the bowel includes the undigested food, secretions from the bowel wall, large numbers of germs (mostly dead ones) and cells shed from the inner surface of the bowel.

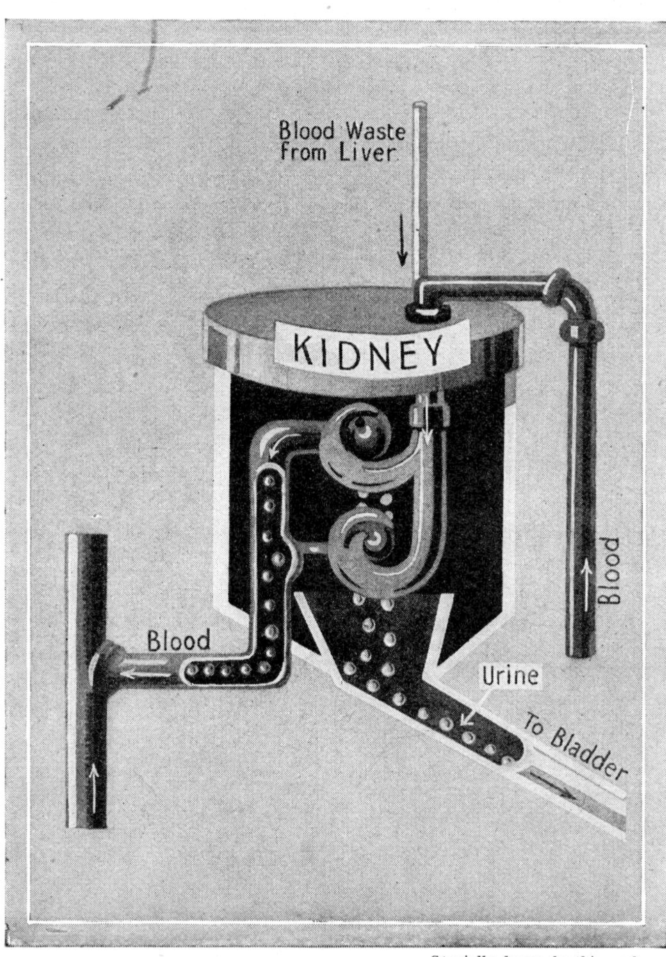

Specially drawn for this work.

THE KIDNEY

The kidney is a living filter. The tiny balls passing down to the bladder represent the waste material; the other balls passing along the blood-pipe which leaves the kidneys are materials the body needs. The kidney is able to sort out the things carried by the blood, rejecting what is harmful, and retaining what is useful. Actually, the kidney is packed with thousands of tiny coiled tubes.

YOUR NERVOUS SYSTEM

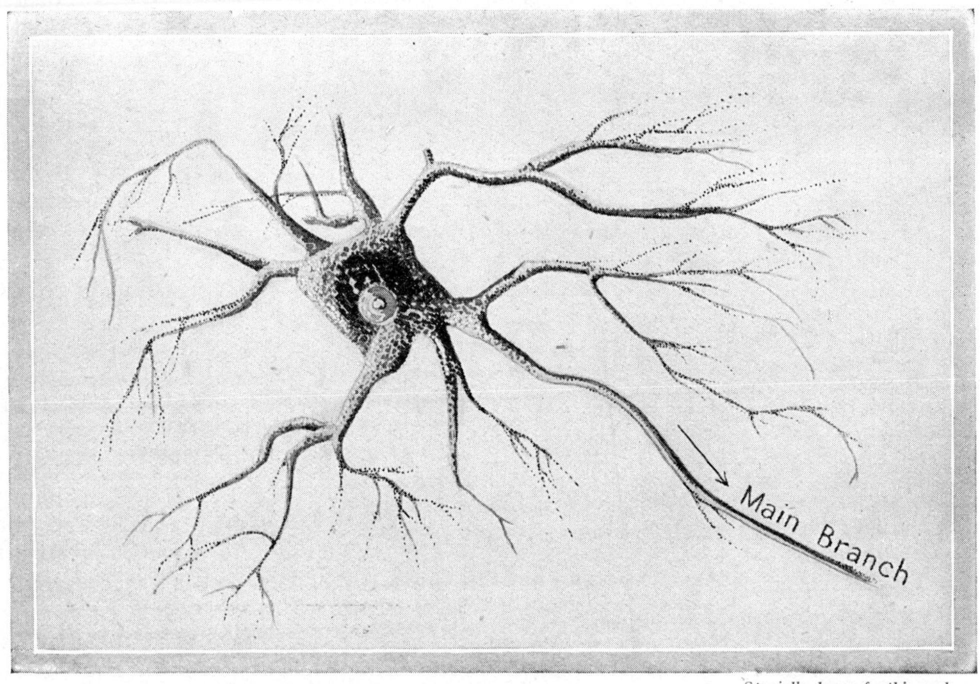

Specially drawn for this work.

A NERVE CELL

These are the cells which are found in your brain and spinal cord. You see how different they are from muscle or cartilage cells. The long main branches of nerve cells are bound together in bundles to form nerves. By means of these nerve cells and their branches, the brain and spinal cord, which form a sort of central government, are kept in touch with what is happening to the rest of your body.

YOU will by now agree that the body is in many ways like a great nation, with millions and millions of citizen cells, each one carrying on its work for the good of the whole, whether it is working as a single cell (like a red blood cell) or as one of a group (like a muscle cell or a gland cell). A nation needs some form of government, and such a well-run nation as your body needs a very efficient government indeed.

How your Body is Controlled

The work of governing is done by cells—*nerve* cells. These nerve cells vary a good deal in size and shape, but you can form a fair mental picture of one if you imagine a tiny white or grey cell, with no very regular sort of shape, and having many branching fibres and one long fibre; the long fibre may be very long, and bundles of fibres lying alongside one another are called "nerves." The whole of your bodily outfit of nerves and nerve cells together is your "nervous system"; and the great gathering of nerve cells in your skull, together with its continuation down inside your spine, is called the "central nervous system."

You may regard the central nervous system as being the government, with the brain as the thinking, knowing, remembering, considering, deciding and willing departments; while the spinal cord may be compared to county councils or some such subordinate controlling bodies. The great network of nerves and nerve cells throughout your body gathers information *from* every part, and takes instructions *to* every part.

You will readily understand that a

central government should not be troubled too much about routine affairs—jobs that have to be done in very much the same way, day after day. It is much better for some subordinate council or department or officials to look after such things; and so you find, in your body, that such things as breathing, digestion and the circulation, and other matters, are controlled and regulated without your having to " give your mind " to them.

It is, roughly, true to say that the whole of the actual " running " of the body, the *internal* affairs of the nation, so to speak, are carried out in this way. Your mind does not concern itself with them unless things are going wrong, and in some cases your mind cannot interfere with them, at least, to any great extent. Nevertheless, everything is conducted in a perfectly orderly and controlled manner—by means of nerves and nerve cells and groups of nerve cells; the needs of the body are noticed and reported, and the necessary instructions are given without your *knowing* anything about it.

Why Exercise makes us Breathe more Quickly

If you are exercising much, there is increased combustion in the muscle cells, and, because of this, a tendency for the carbon dioxide in the blood to increase; the increase in carbon dioxide causes the breathing control to send instructions to the breathing muscles to work extra hard; in consequence of this you breathe more quickly and more deeply, and the extra carbon dioxide is the more rapidly exchanged for fresh supplies of oxygen; and of course your heart has to work harder and faster too. All that you *know* about this is that you breathe faster, and that your heart beats more rapidly. The same hurrying-up of the breathing will take place when you are very high in the mountains where the air is rarefied and you are not getting as much oxygen as you want.

Many actions you have to think about at first—walking downstairs, guiding a pencil, playing on the piano; and some of them are so difficult that you have to give your whole mind to them. Yet, after a time and " with practice," as we say, these things become almost as easy and automatic as breathing. It is as though the mind has been able to say to some other part of the nervous system: " There you are! That's the way to do that. Just you carry on and see that it is done in the same way whenever I want it done—and don't bother me about it."

Why We Sneeze

We have not yet finished with the things that are done without your having to " give your mind " to them. If you happen to sniff pepper you will sneeze. Exactly what has happened? The nerve cells whose job it is to report have sent back a message, " Something here is upsetting us! " The message goes to some local control centre, and from this instructions are sent out to all the muscles which have to act to make a sneeze. " Get busy, and blow that stuff out of the nose—Sharp! " You don't have to *think* about this—in fact most people can't sneeze to order; you can, however, stop a sneeze sometimes, which shows that your mind *can* exercise some control.

Again, if someone puts a drawing pin on your chair you don't wait to think about it. Your whole body leaps up —*before you know what it is all about.* Perhaps we had better not imagine the messages which might be sent in this case. This leap of your whole body, because something has hurt some part of it, shows you how well the communications of the whole body are arranged; it is almost as though every part is always on the telephone to every other part, but only gives attention where and when there is need.

These actions in which some cause or " stimulus " leads to some effect or

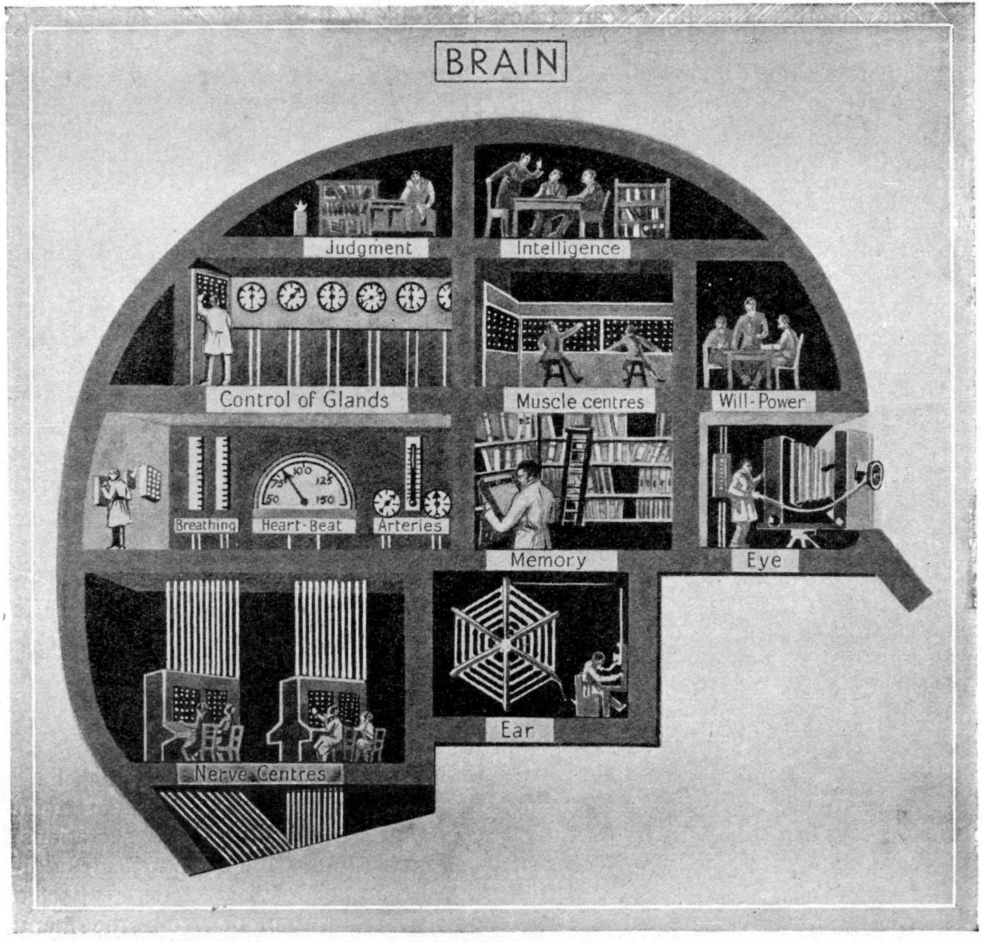

Specially drawn for this work.

THE BRAIN

The brain can be compared to the headquarters of the government, with its various departments, each with definite functions. It receives reports and sends out orders. It controls the muscles, the glands, the beating of the heart, the action of breathing. It registers what we see and what we hear. It is the seat of the higher functions of judgment, intelligence and will-power.

"response" without your having to think about it, are known as "reflex" actions. You will be able to think of a great many of them.

The Work of the Brain

We have left to the last that part of the government which has to feel, know, remember, consider, decide, and will. It is here that the human being is so superior to the other animals; these can breathe and digest, and have a whole outfit of reflex actions, and up to a point they can think; but none of them can compare for a moment with the human being in the qualities of the mind. The mind is not a bit of the brain; it is, rather, the word by which we describe some of the things the brain can *do*—we might almost describe the mind as a *property or quality of the brain.*

We have already shown that the *internal* affairs are carried on without your having to give your mind to them; and so we may now say that the mind concerns itself mainly with *external* affairs—the things that have to be done so that the body can take advantage of its surroundings; among these affairs we must include the seeking of food, the avoiding or warding off of danger, and so on. Of course, the mind goes far beyond this, and thinks of music, art, astronomy, right and wrong, and thousands of other things—but the more backward and uncivilised races still give most of *their* minds to their physical needs, and to the "struggle to survive."

Your mind must have information of all the surroundings, and this information it gains through special "sense organs." If you can imagine a human being who had never been able to see, hear, smell or feel, you can see that he would almost certainly be an idiot.

Your sense organs, then, gather information. Your eyes are like tiny cameras which take moving pictures and send them to your brain; your ears notice and report vibrations of the air; your nose detects and reports smells; your mouth tastes; while your skin reports heat, cold, touch and pain. All the information is actually picked up by nerve cells and their fibres, and it is understood and remembered by nerve cells in your brain. The pictures "taken" by your eyes are conveyed to the brain, and it is there that you really "see"—that is to say, it is there that you know what the picture is and what it means; the same is true of the other sense impressions—you see, hear, smell, feel, and taste *with* your brain, though you are enabled to do these things by means of your eyes and other sense organs.

Your Cells as Citizens

Our illustration of the government is not, of course, a true picture of the brain. There are definite "centres" within the brain which are concerned with special senses and organs and activities, but everything is so very complicated and so linked up with other things that it is impossible to give a true picture. The body has been likened to a nation, the cells to citizens, the central nervous system to the government, and so on—but this has been done in order to make it possible to tell simply about things which are very far from being simple.

The Influence of the Glands

Fifty years ago no one had any idea that certain little groups of cells, glands that send their secretions directly into the blood, had any great influence on our bodies and minds. To-day we know that these glands may determine whether we are normally intelligent people or idiots, peaceful or quarrelsome, highly-strung and nervous or calm and placid.

These special tissues used to be called "ductless glands" because the "chemical messengers" (secretions called *hormones*) are collected directly by the blood flowing through the tissue—they do not flow out from the gland through a special pipe or "duct" in the usual way. Now, however, we know that among the glands which have ducts to carry away some of their secretions (their *external* secretions) there are some which produce in addition secretions which are collected directly by the blood from the gland tissue; in order to include these, too, it is better to speak of *all* the glands which make "chemical messengers" as *the glands of internal secretion.* The word *hormones* means "things which set in action." They can be compared to little keys flowing along in the blood until they find the right lock; each lock has its own special key and no other will do, and they must unlock the right door before they can deliver their message.

Good health and normal growth and development of body and mind depend upon the proper working of these glands, which work together like the musicians playing in an orchestra. The violin cannot take the part of the piano, but each is necesary for the proper rendering of the music.

We do not yet know all about what

these glands can do, but what we do know is most interesting, and important, too, as we are able to use the knowledge in the treatment of certain diseases. Here we can mention only a few of the remarkable achievements of some of the glands.

What the Glands do

The thyroid, which is in front of your neck and can be felt moving up and down when you swallow, can be compared to the accelerator of a car, because its hormones regulate the rate at which the body engine works. If the thyroid produces too much secretion, the engine " races " and uses up its fuel and repair material too quickly, and the body fires burn wastefully. If there is too little of the thyroid hormone, the engine only just " ticks over " and it doesn't provide enough power for the body and mind to work properly; the body fires are sluggish and we become dull-witted and listless.

A baby whose thyroid did not produce enough hormone would not grow and develop normally, and would be quite unable to learn lessons like an ordinary child of the same age. One of the greatest triumphs of medical science is to be able to cure this form of mental deficiency in a child or adult by giving a medicine containing some of the precious hormone obtained from the healthy gland of an animal. Another gland (the pituitary) which is about the size of a pea, makes at least two powerful hormones. One of these controls the growth of your bones, determining whether you shall be a giant or a dwarf or just of normal size; another acts on certain muscle tissue, including the muscle in the walls of the blood pipes, causing it to contract or " tighten up," and this of course affects your " blood pressure."

Two other glands (the adrenals) make a hormone that prepares you to deal with emergencies, to protect yourself by fighting or running away. An extra supply of this hormone is poured into the blood during excitement or fear or any other emotion. It makes the heart beat more powerfully and releases extra fuel (sugar) into the circulation to provide for a greater output of energy; it makes you think and act more quickly and increases your muscular strength.

The pancreas is an example of a gland which has an external secretion (the digestive juice that flows through its duct into the small bowel), *and* an internal secretion or hormone. This pancreatic hormone controls the use of sugar by the body; and when the hormone is deficient or absent (as in certain diseases of the pancreas) there is too much sugar in the blood and some drains away through the kidneys. This is the condition known as diabetes and the new insulin treatment is the use of an extract of pancreas which contains this hormone.

Health and Disease

So far we have talked about the body in health; but the body has enemies—and, sad to say, we ourselves are often our bodies' *worst* enemies. We may neglect the body's needs of fresh air, exercise, proper food (well chewed and eaten at meal times only), rest, cleanliness inside and out, and we may poison it with too much alcohol or tea.

We are surrounded by enemy germs which will cause disease; they are everywhere, but the body has its defences. Your white cells are ever ready to slaughter off invaders, and they are a very formidable army; yet the body does not rely upon them alone. Many germs cause their damage by making poisons; your body is able to make antidotes—substances which will render the poisons quite harmless to you. In addition to this, the body is able to create other substances, which make the germs more easily conquerable by your white cells.

To keep yourself free from disease, keep your body fit, so that its three means of defence may be as effective as possible.

FIRST AID IN ACCIDENT OR ILLNESS

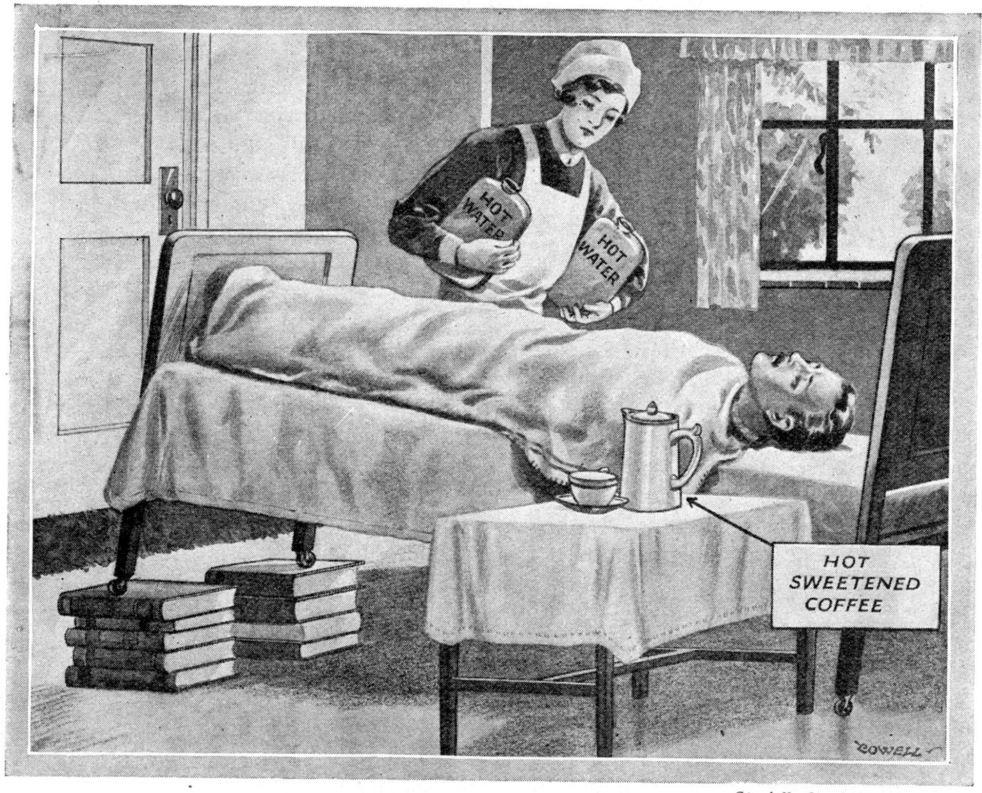

Specially drawn for this work.

TREATMENT FOR SHOCK

A condition of *shock* is a common effect of serious accidents, injuries and burns, and it is most important to know how to treat it, as a patient may die from shock. Here you see the essential *rest, warmth* and *stimulants* provided. The foot of the bed is raised to improve the circulation of blood to the vital centres of the brain.

To give "first aid" means to give immediate help to anyone suffering from injury or sudden illness, such as a broken arm or a burn or a fainting fit, until the arrival of a doctor. The right kind of help given at the right time is most valuable, but you cannot give this help unless you have learnt what the correct treatment should be. In serious cases, such as poisoning or a broken bone, or severe bleeding, send a message for the doctor without delay, stating the nature of the trouble if possible. Then do the best you can for the patient until the doctor arrives.

What to do for Shock

After an accident or poisoning, or even after great emotion, the patient may suffer from "shock." He will be very pale, his skin cold and clammy, his breathing irregular and quick, and his heart-beat weak and rapid. You can feel the heart-beat in the pulse at the wrist by placing your finger tips at the base of the thumb in front. The normal pulse rate in health is about 70, but in a condition of severe shock it may be as high as 140. A patient in this condition will be only half conscious, with pinched face and sunken eyes.

Anyone suffering from shock needs *absolute rest* (lying down with the legs and hips raised above the level of the head), *warmth* and *hot fluids* to drink. If you cannot get him into bed at once, cover with coats, rugs or any extra

PRESSURE POINTS FOR CONTROL OF BLEEDING

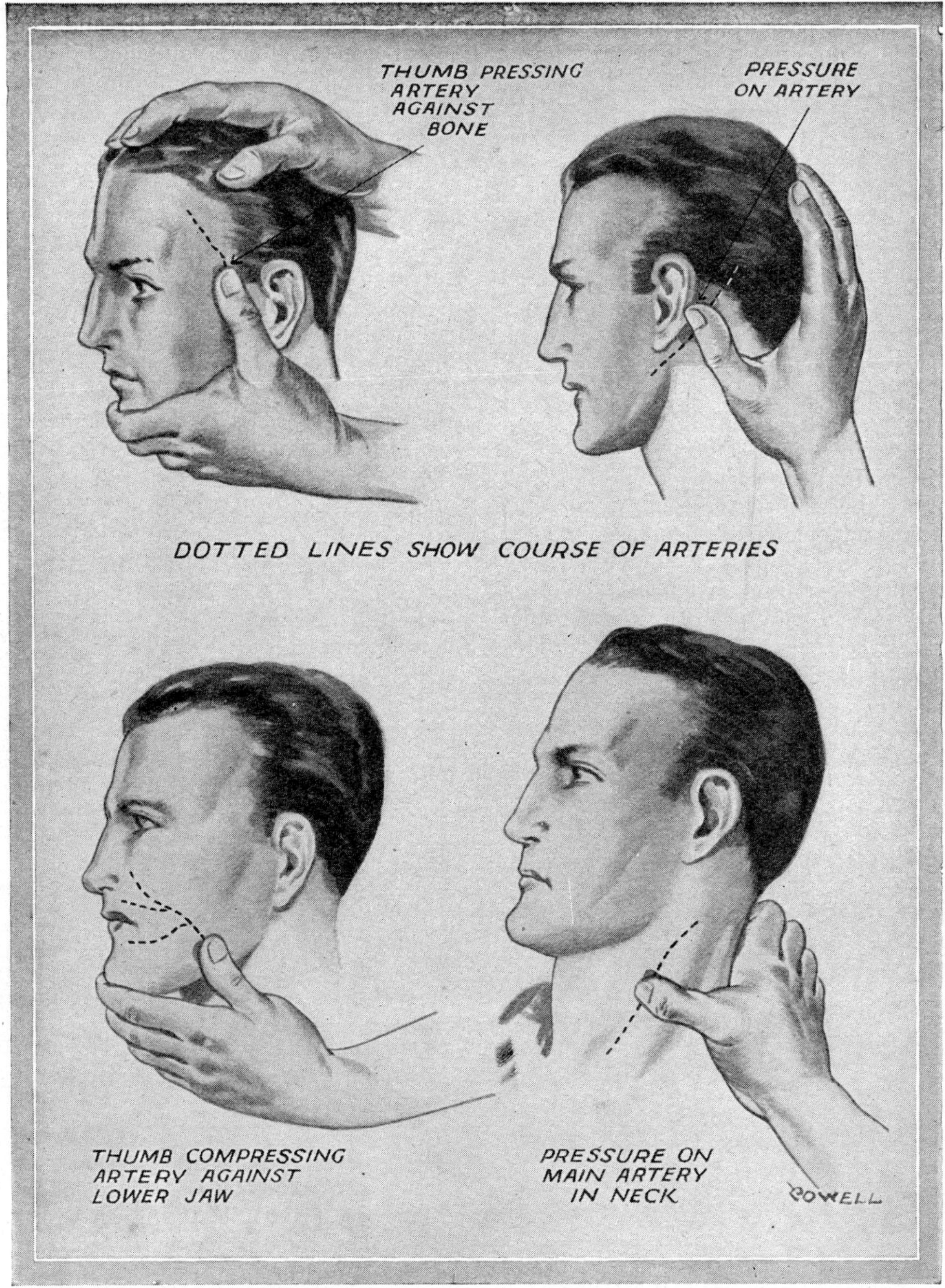

Specially drawn for this work.

To control bleeding effectively—whether you are using your thumb or a pad and bandage or a tourniquet—you should know the most suitable places to apply the pressure to the artery which is carrying blood to the bleeding point. Where arteries are lying deep, surrounded by soft structures, it would be most difficult if not impossible to apply sufficient pressure without injury. The best pressure points are where the artery lies near the surface and close to bone against which it can be compressed. Ambulance workers must know these points.

clothing available, and keep him lying flat, with pads (cushions or rolled clothing) to raise the hips and lower limbs. As soon as possible, he should be placed between warm blankets in bed, and the foot of the bed should be raised about a foot by supporting the ends of the bed on blocks of wood or piles of books. Provide hot-water bottles, and as soon as the patient can swallow, give hot fluids. Water alone is better than nothing, but if you can get hot sweetened tea or coffee, so much the better. Do not give brandy or whisky or wine.

Getting Rid of the Poison

In some cases of poisoning you must empty the stomach as soon as possible, to get rid of any of the poison that is still in the stomach. Sometimes you can cause vomiting by *tickling the back of the throat* with a finger or some other object, such as a feather or a piece of paper. If this method fails, and the patient can swallow, you should *give an emetic* (an emetic is something which causes vomiting).

Mustard dissolved in a tumbler of warm water—one teaspoonful for a small child up to a tablespoonful for a grown-up.

Salt dissolved in a tumbler of warm water—two teaspoonfuls for a child up to two tablespoonfuls for an adult.

Warning.—Never give an emetic when the person has taken some poison which leaves stains or burns on the lips, mouth or fingers.

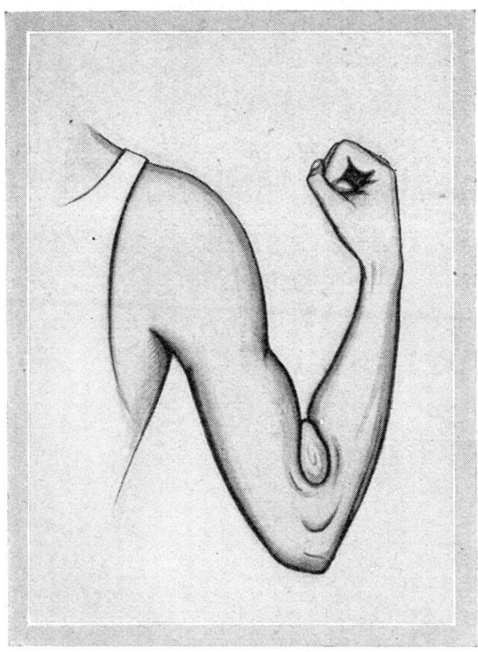

Specially drawn for this work.

BLEEDING ARRESTED BY PRESSURE AT A JOINT

Here you see compression of the blood-vessels at the elbow by a pad held in position by keeping the arm flexed. The pad must be pushed up close to the joint.

Stimulants

In some cases where the heart is feeble, you will be advised to give a stimulant, which is something that makes the heart work better. Any of the following will do:—

Strong tea or coffee with sugar; give a cupful.

Strong beef tea, a cupful.

Sal volatile, ten drops for a small child, up to a teaspoonful for an adult, in a tablespoonful of water.

Artificial Respiration (see Drowning)

Bites

For a *dog bite*, pour iodine on the wound or wash it in water containing an antiseptic such as Milton, Izal, Dettol, etc. If the dog is ill, or has a dirty mouth, the doctor may have to give special treatment ; so consult him without delay, and try to trace the dog.

For a *snake* (adder) *bite*, tie a handkerchief tightly round the limb between the bite and the heart; for instance, if the bite is on the foot, tie the handkerchief tightly round the leg. Keep the limb hanging down, and try to make the wound bleed by scraping or pricking it with a penknife or other sharp object. You can remove some of the poison by sucking the wound: the

BLEEDING FROM THE ARM OR HAND

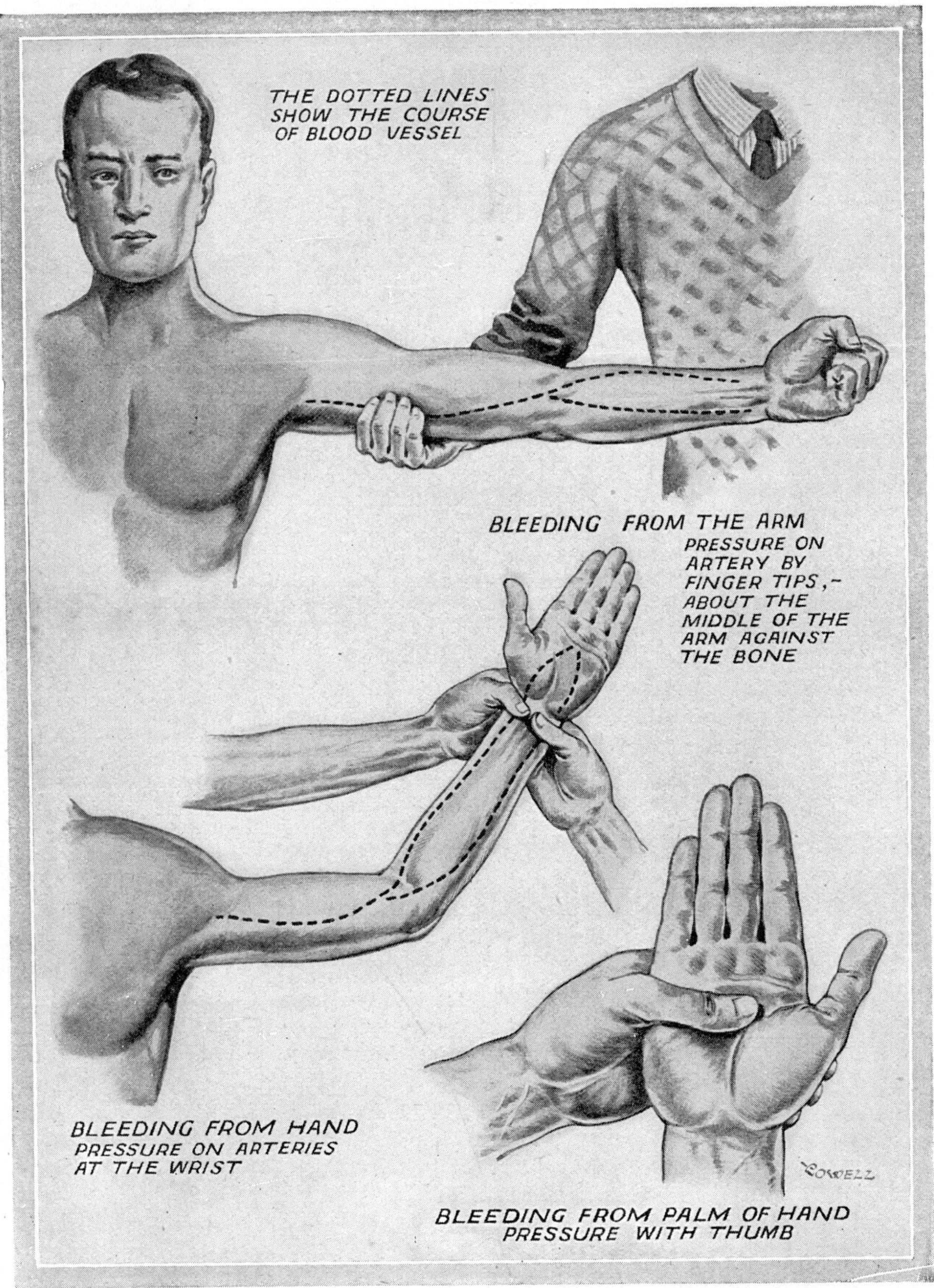

Specially drawn for this work.

Bleeding from the arm can be controlled by pressure on the pressure point, either with the fingers (as illustrated), or with pad and bandage, or with a tourniquet. Pressure at the wrist, to control bleeding from the hand, must be applied to both the wrist arteries, as shown in the diagram, since these arteries join to form an arch in the palm of the hand, and if one only were compressed, blood would still be carried to the wound by the other.

poison is harmless when taken into the mouth, provided you have no sore places through which it could get into your blood.

Give a stimulant (brandy, tea, or coffee), and, if breathing stops, do artificial respiration (see under " Drowning ").

Bleeding

A little bleeding, such as occurs from a slight cut on the finger or knee, will do no harm; it will be checked naturally in due course by the clotting of the blood. If, however, the blood is flowing freely, either in spurts from a cut artery or in a steady trickle from a cut vein, then you should try to check the bleeding without delay.

Bleeding can be stopped by pressure, either directly on the wound itself or on the main blood-vessel [artery] leading to the wound. You can exert pressure on the wound with the finger or thumb, preferably through a pad made from a clean handkerchief. If an antiseptic, such as Dettol, is available, dip your fingers or the pressure pad into it before touching the wound. You may be unable to keep up the pressure in this way long enough to stop the bleeding permanently. If possible, therefore, get the patient himself, or another helper, to check the bleeding temporarily in this way while you prepare a bandage. This may be used either to keep a thick pad in position over the wound or to tie round the limb so as to press on the blood-vessel carrying blood to the wound.

The pressure is needed at certain points between the heart and the injury, called " pressure points," where the blood-vessel can be squeezed flat against bone. The diagrams show you the main pressure points of the body. If you are using a bandage to check the bleeding, put some firm object, such as a smooth pebble or a flat cork, in a fold of the bandage immediately over the pressure point, and, having tied the bandage round the limb loosely, push a stick through the knot and tighten the bandage, just enough to check the bleeding, by twisting the stick. This type of bandage is called a *tourniquet*. The pressure must be released by untwisting the stick every quarter of an hour, if the tourniquet cannot be removed before that time.

Bleeding from the Nose

In most cases no treatment is necessary; but if the bleeding is profuse and keeps on, the bridge of the nose should be bathed with cold water (ice water if available), and a cold-water pad should be placed on the back of the neck. The patient should sit up with head thrown back and breathe through the mouth. If ice is available, give him a piece to suck.

Bleeding from the Socket of an Extracted Tooth

Plug the hole with cotton wool soaked in lemon juice or peroxide of hydrogen, or some other disinfectant, place a pad (a small folded handkerchief will do) over it, and tell the patient to bite on it, so as to press the plug firmly into the socket.

Burns and Scalds

If clothing catches fire, without a moment's delay smother the flames by wrapping over the burning part any clothes or rugs on which you can lay your hands; and prevent the person from running about. It is usually best to place him on the floor, with the burning clothes uppermost, and then roll him in rugs, blanket, shawl, tablecloth or anything else available, and keep him tightly wrapped until the flames are smothered.

If an acid or caustic fluid is spilled on the skin, drench the part immediately with water; then, in the case of acid, apply an alkali, such as milk of magnesia or washing soda solution, but for a burn from a caustic alkali put on weak vinegar and water, or lemon juice and

POINTS, BANDAGES AND REEF KNOT

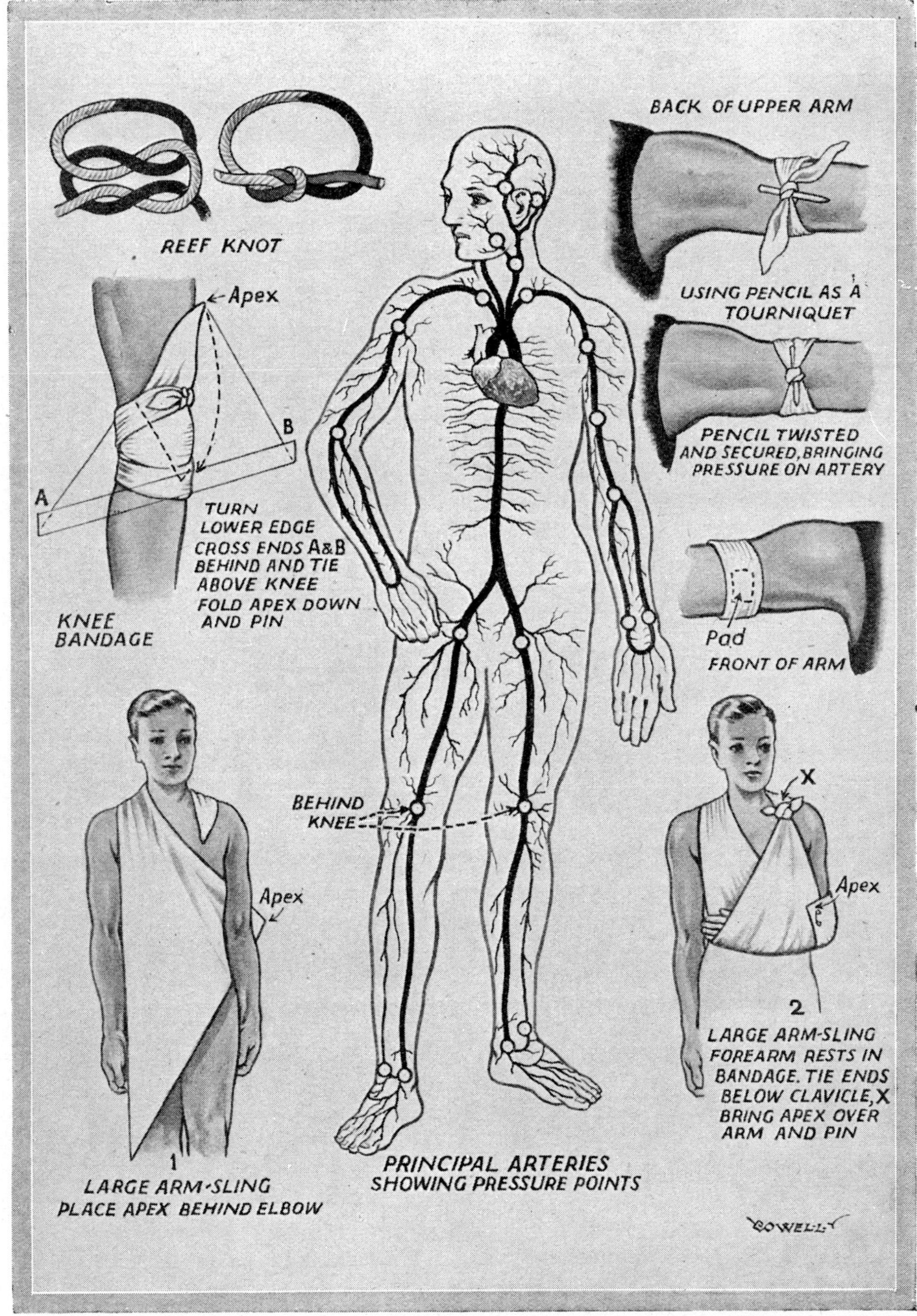

Specially drawn for this work.

In the drawing above the points where pressure should be applied to stop bleeding are shown by small circles on the main arteries. A tourniquet is used in the case of serious bleeding where digital pressure is insufficient. The tourniquet should never be left tightly applied for more than a quarter of an hour or the limb may be seriously affected. Bandages should always be tied with a reef knot, a simple rule for which is " right over left, then left over right," when the ends will lie in opposite directions.

water. Then dress the burn in the usual way.

To Dress a Burn.—If the skin is not broken, cover the burn with a dressing soaked in a solution of bicarbonate of soda (baking soda).

If the skin is broken, take care not to break any blisters, and do not pull off any pieces of clothing that may be stuck on the wound. Cut away clothing that cannot be removed easily, and cut round any parts that are stuck down. If the burn is on a part that can be immersed in a bowl of warm water containing a teaspoonful of bicarbonate of soda to each pint (temperature between 98° and 99° F.), soak the part in this warm bath; it will lessen the pain and shock, and will loosen the bits of clothing that are stuck down. Keep adding a little hot water to prevent the solution from cooling.

To dress the burn, cover the wound in strips of gauze or butter muslin soaked in solution of bicarbonate of soda. Let the doctor see the burn as soon as possible.

Shock from Burns.—The most serious effect of a bad burn, especially in babies and young children, is the condition of shock which is caused by the burn. Treat the shock (see p. 248).

Concussion (see **Head Injury**)

Drowning

Victims of drowning, suffocation, electrocution, gas poisoning, narcotic drugs, etc., may reach a condition known as asphyxia and immediate attempts at resuscitation must be made as soon as the patient has been removed

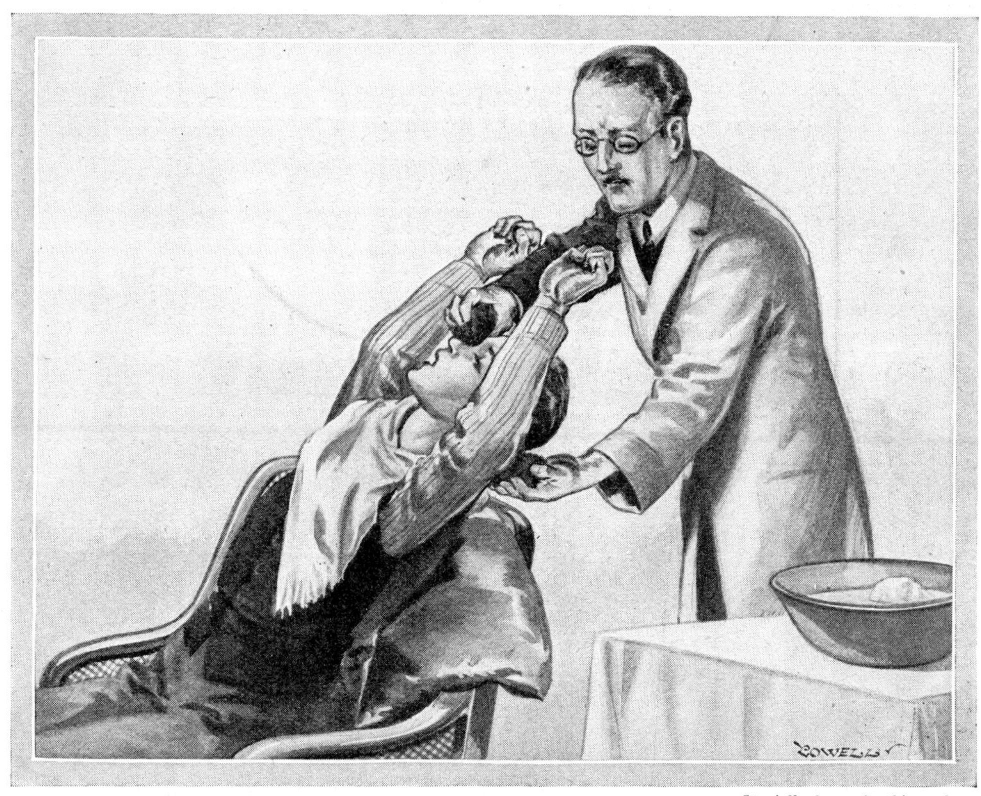

Specially drawn for this work.

NOSE BLEEDING

A little bleeding from the nose will do no harm whatever, and may actually do good. Only if the bleeding is very profuse and shows no tendency to diminish is treatment required. Here you see sponges soaked in ice-cold water being applied to the bridge of the nose and the nape of the neck, while the patient sits upright.

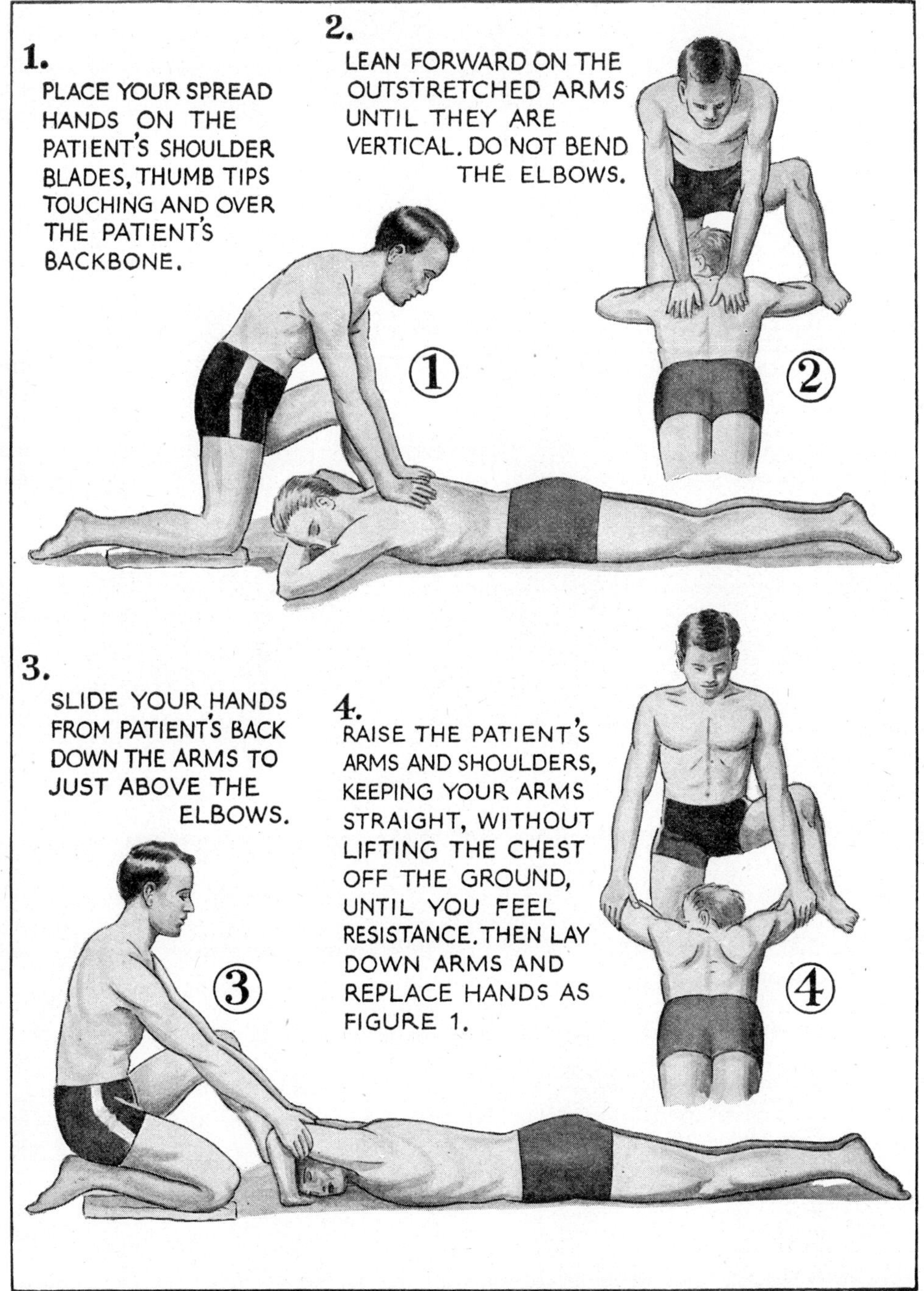

Specially drawn for this work.

The Holger Nielsen method has now been adopted by the Royal Life Saving Society as the most effective method of artificial respiration. The main points are: Begin immediately as every second counts. Place the patient in a prone position, face downwards, head turned to one side and resting on the back of one hand superimposed on the other. Then follow the treatment shown above. Pressure should be light and movements repeated 10 times per minute at a steady uniform rate.

to a safe place. In cases of drowning, clear the mouth of any obstruction such as weeds, etc., and, if necessary, loosen clothing at the neck and chest.

The Holger Nielsen method of artificial respiration is now regarded as the most effective, and a brief description is given here: (*a*) Place the patient in the prone position (face downwards) with head turned to one side, and the face resting on the back of one hand, which is superimposed on the other.

(*b*) Kneel a little in front of the patient's head so that the mid-line is in the same line as the patient's. Then place your spread hands on the shoulder blades of the patient, the tips of the thumbs touching and over the backbone of the patient. The wrists should be on an imaginary line drawn across the patient's armpits. (*c*) Rock forward on the outstretched arms until they are vertical. Do not bend your elbows. Pressure should be light—without force. This induces expiration. Time taken: 2 seconds.

(*d*) Remove the hands from the patient's back and grasp the patient's arms just above the elbows. Time taken: 1 second. (*e*) Lift the patient's arms until resistance or tension is felt at the patient's shoulders. Time taken: 2 seconds. (*f*) Lower the arms and return the hands to the shoulders, ready to resume pressure. Time taken: 1 second. Then repeat the movements already described in (*c*), (*d*), (*e*) and (*f*).

The compression and expansion cycle should be repeated ten times per minute at a steady uniform rate with two phases (compression and arm-lift) occupying approximately even time. If the patient shows no sign of revival, continue for five or six hours until unmistakable signs of death appear or until a doctor has pronounced life extinct. When the patient begins to show signs of life (slight movements, skin returns to normal colour), omit the pressure and continue with raising and lowering the arms at a rate of twelve times a minute. Give stimulants only after natural breathing has started.

Ear

Beads, peas, pencil ends, etc., are sometimes pushed into the ear by children. At the bottom of the ear passage there is a very delicate structure, the drum of the ear, which may easily be torn by unskilled attempts to remove the object. Therefore, unless the object is protruding so that you can get hold of it easily, do not try to remove it. Nor should you syringe the ear. Consult the doctor.

Eye

Bits of *dust or grit* may blow into the eye. *The eye should on no account be rubbed.* If you can see the speck lying under the lid or on the eyeball, very gently try to remove it with a wisp of cotton wool or the corner of a clean handkerchief, or a camel's hair brush. If it appears to be stuck in the surface put a drop of oil (castor or olive oil) into the eye, cover with a soft pad and bandage, and leave it for the doctor to attend to. Where the particle is embedded in the eye, there may be much less pain than when it is lying loosely on the surface, but there is a likelihood of germs getting into the eye and causing serious trouble. A doctor should be consulted as soon as possible.

If some *chemical irritant*, such as acid, ammonia or quicklime, splashes into the eye, without a moment's delay the lids should be opened and shut several times *under water*. The injured person can put his face into a basin of water to do this. After the eye has been thoroughly bathed, put in a drop of castor oil and cover with pad and bandage. Consult a doctor as soon as possible.

A "*black eye*" is really a bruise. It should be treated by cold bathing; and a pad of lint or a folded handkerchief soaked in cold water (ice water if available) should be bandaged over the eye.

Cuts or wounds about the eyelids may be bathed with plain warm water;

do not use an antiseptic unless the doctor orders this.

Fainting

A person who faints becomes unconscious because the brain is not getting enough blood, owing to the heart beating too feebly to pump sufficient blood up to the head.

Keep the patient lying down, with the head lower than the body if possible, so that blood can flow more easily into the brain. Give stimulants—smelling salts held to the nose and cold water sprinkled on the face, and sal volatile as soon as the patient can swallow. Don't let people crowd round, as the patient should have as much fresh air as possible. Loosen clothing at the neck and chest. A cup of hot sweetened tea or coffee should be given when the patient is recovering.

Fits

A *fit* ("*convulsion*") *in a baby* or young child may occur quite suddenly; the eyes become fixed, the face purple, and the limbs and body stiff, and the child becomes unconscious. Send for the doctor. Meanwhile, place the child on a couch or bed and loosen or remove the clothing. Apply cold cloths to the head, and as soon as possible put the child into a warm bath, continuing to bathe the head with cold water.

A "*stroke*" or apoplectic fit in elderly people may cause a sudden collapse in the street. The face becomes deeply flushed, and the patient breathes noisily or snores. There is loss of power [paralysis] in one or more limbs, and when the patient recovers consciousness, he may be unable to move his limbs. Send for a doctor at once. Keep the patient lying down, loosen the clothing and give plenty of air. *Do not give stimulants.*

An epileptic fit may occur during childhood, middle or old age. There is a sudden fall, often preceded by a shrill cry. There is gnashing of teeth and irregular movements of the arms and legs. The patient foams at the mouth and he may bite his tongue, causing bleeding.

The treatment of an epileptic fit is to protect the patient from injuring himself. Put something (a pencil, handle of teaspoon or piece of wood wrapped in a handkerchief) between the teeth to prevent biting of the tongue. Pull any furniture, etc., out of the way so that he shall not bruise himself during the convulsions, and protect him from fire. *Give nothing by the mouth.* Allow him to sleep when the fit is over, covering him with a rug or coat.

A hysterical fit is not serious, and the patient is not at all likely to hurt herself. She is very noisy, screaming or laughing or crying alternately, and she may throw her limbs about wildly, and even foam at the mouth. Do not show sympathy or appear particularly interested. Speak sharply to her, and throw cold water in the face if she does not control herself. The patient should see a doctor later, as hysteria is a sign of ill-health; it is not "just pretending." At the same time, the best way to help her during the fit is to appear unconcerned; any show of sympathy will make her more violent.

Fractures

If the limb appears bent or in an unnatural position, and there is loss of power and great pain on movement, or if you have heard the snap of the breaking bone, you must get a doctor as soon as possible; and, if the patient is away from home, arrange for an ambulance or other conveyance if he is unable to walk. If he must be removed before he is attended to by a doctor, gently move the affected limb into a natural position, and make a splint from walking-sticks, umbrellas, rolled newspapers, or any other suitable object which is sufficiently rigid to protect the broken bone. If there is no wound, the splint can be put on over the clothing; but if the skin is broken, you should cut the clothing if you cannot remove it easily, and dress the wound before putting on the splints. The splints should be well padded; they can be tied on with handkerchiefs.

Remember that if you have to straighten the limb to put on the splints, move the limb very gently and *never pull on it.*

Frost Bite

If your fingers, ears or nose become white and deadened with the cold, so that you have no feeling in them, *do not allow them to become warm suddenly.* Gently rub the parts with snow or cold water, and then *gradually* warm them with your hands or some part of your body. Do not go into a warm room until the parts have thawed and normal colour has returned.

Head Injury

A fall or a blow on the head may cause *concussion.* The patient looks very pale, and may vomit; he usually becomes drowsy, or he may be actually unconscious. The treatment is *quiet, rest and sleep.* Put him to bed in a darkened room, put cold cloths on his head, and send for the doctor.

If there is bleeding from the mouth, nose or ears, or if unconsciousness persists, there may be a fracture of the skull and serious *compression* of the brain. Treat as for concussion, but send an urgent message for a doctor. Until he arrives the patient should not be moved.

Heat Stroke

A patient who is exhausted by prolonged exposure to heat suffers from severe shock; he becomes pale and cold and may become unconscious. Treat as for shock.

Nose

Bleeding from the Nose.—See under "Bleeding."

Button, Bead, Pea, etc., in the Nose.—Children sometimes push objects up the nostrils and are unable to remove them. Let the child blow his nose vigorously, and let him smell pepper or snuff to make him sneeze; if you know which side is blocked, compress the free nostril with the finger. If this treatment fails to dislodge the object, *make no attempt to remove it yourself.* Take the child to a doctor.

If the object has been in the nose for some days before the child has confessed to putting it there, there may be a thick yellow blood-stained discharge.

Poisoning

Poisons act in different ways, and the treatment varies according to the type of poison which has been taken.

Corrosive poisons eat into and destroy the parts with which they come into contact, so that the lips and mouth are stained and burnt; and although we cannot see into the food-pipe and stomach, we know that they are similarly corroded. Therefore, in these cases, we must *never give anything to make the person sick,* because the injured lining of the food-pipe and stomach would probably tear with the movements of vomiting. Examples of corrosives are spirits of salt (hydrochloric), or of vitriol (sulphuric acid), carbolic acid, salts of lemon (oxalic acid), spirit of hartshorn (ammonia), quick-lime, caustic potash, caustic soda.

Irritant poisons cause inflammation of the stomach and bowel, but they are not so destructive as the corrosives. In cases of irritant poisons, we do give emetics to empty the stomach of the poison by making the patient vomit.

Narcotics act upon the nervous system, causing such symptoms as delirium, convulsions and unconsciousness.

Some poisons are both irritant and narcotic.

Treatment.—(1) *Send for the doctor* immediately, explaining that you suspect poisoning, and naming the poison if known.

Note.—Save any vomited matter, or motions passed from the bowel, or

FIRST AID FOR BROKEN BONES

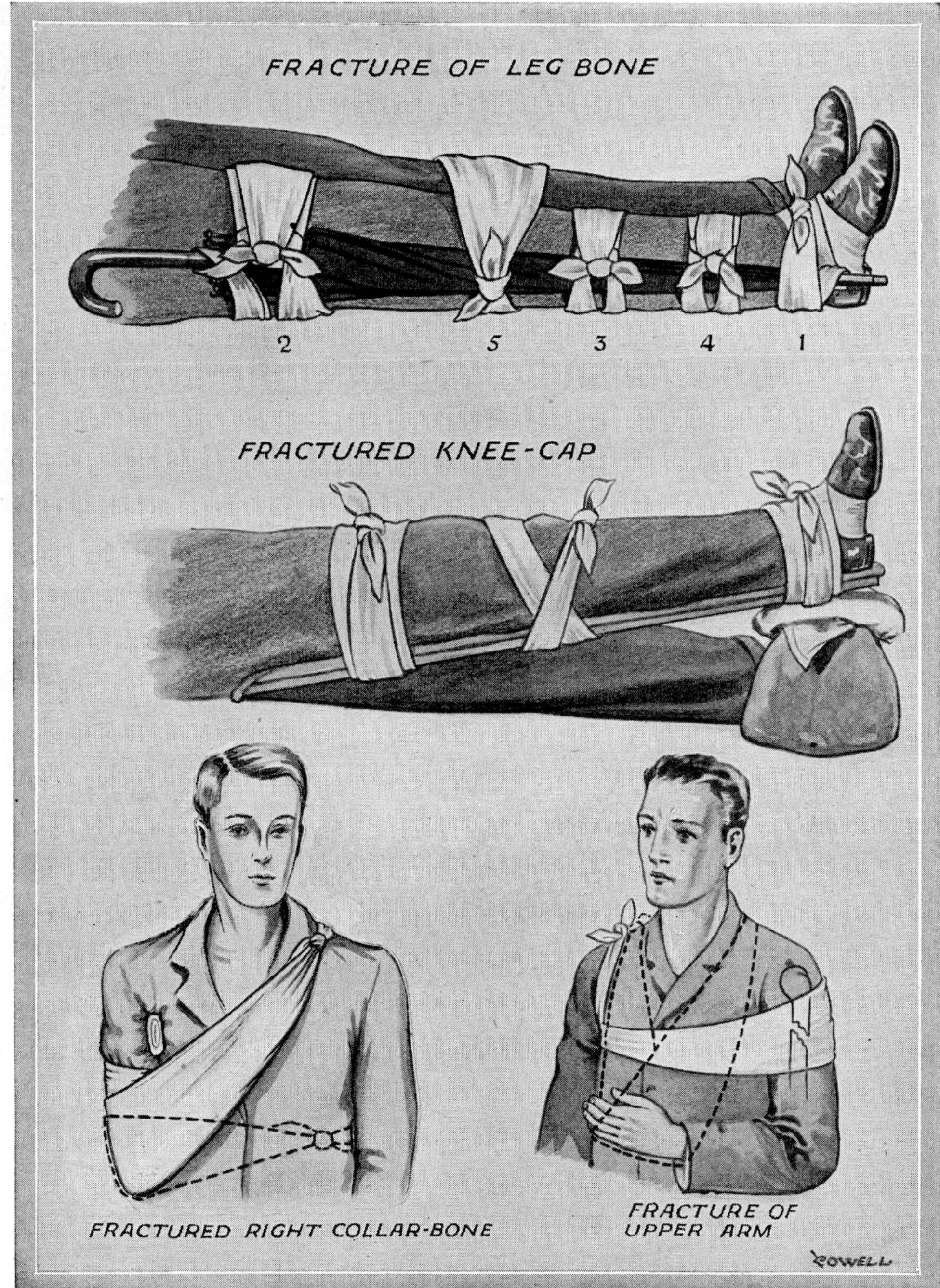

Specially drawn for this work.

Your aim is to keep the bone in a natural position with a bandage and sling, or by the use of a rigid support—a splint—which can be tied in place with handkerchiefs, mufflers, or any strips of material. The splint should be well padded so that it could not injure the soft parts. Splints can be made from walking sticks, umbrellas, the branch of a tree, or a cricket bat, hockey stick or golf stick. The numbers in the top picture show the order in which the bandages should be fixed.

bottles, glasses, etc., that have contained the poison.

(2) If the lips and mouth are not burnt, and you have no reason to suspect a corrosive poison, give the patient an emetic (see earlier paragraph on getting rid of the poison).

(3) If you know what poison has been taken, give something to make it harmless. We call this neutralising the poison, and the substance which does this is called the *antidote*.

Note.—The following list gives the antidotes for some common poisons:—

Poison.	*Antidote.*
Corrosive acids	Chalk or whitening, milk of magnesia, lime water.
Corrosive alkalis	Vinegar, lemon juice.
Carbolic acid, creosote, turpentine	Epsom salts.
Opium, morphia, laudanum	Condy's fluid, solution of potassium permanganate.
Strychnine, foxglove	Strong stewed tea.

(4) *Treat the Symptoms.*—Stimulants and warmth for shock.

Artificial respiration if breathing has ceased or is failing.

Keep the patient awake if he is very drowsy.

Soothe the sore throat, stomach and bowel by giving raw eggs beaten in milk, or plain milk, or flour and water.

For pain in the stomach, apply hot fomentations or hot poultices or a hot-water bottle to the stomach.

The following plants (berries, leaves) are poisonous:—

Deadly nightshade.	Henbane.
Privet.	Foxglove.
Holly.	Spotted hemlock.
Cuckoo pint.	Yellow vetchling.
Bryony.	Woody nightshade.
Laburnum.	

Laurel.

If a child shows signs of poisoning after eating unknown berries or leaves, give the child an emetic first of all, then give stimulants and warmth. Later, a purge (dose of castor oil) should be given. Artificial respiration may be necessary.

Sprains

Apply bandages soaked in cold water, and rest the injured joint, using splints or slings where necessary. Let a doctor see the injury as soon as possible in case there is also a broken bone.

Stings of Insects

It is generally accepted that the bee's sting is acid and that bicarbonate of soda or ammonia may help to neutralise the acid; the wasp's sting is alkaline and vinegar, lemon, or onion applied immediately may help. Bites from mosquitoes, midges, and other insects can be treated immediately by dabbing with iodine. A soothing ointment such as Ichthyol will relieve the swelling and irritation caused by any sting or bite.

Do not scratch any bite or sting, as this may cause it to become septic. If a bite or sting does become septic a doctor should be consulted.

Sunstroke

If the head and back of the neck are exposed to the sun's rays in hot weather, high temperature, giddiness, weakness and sickness may result and be followed by drowsiness or unconsciousness.

Treatment.—Take the patient to a cool, shady place, and remove his clothing. Douche the head, neck and spine with cold water or wrap him in sheets soaked in cold water, or put him into a cold bath.

When he has recovered consciousness, and the temperature has fallen to 102° F., put him to bed between blankets, and keep the room darkened. If he again becomes unconscious, renew the cold applications, and if breathing ceases, do artificial respiration. Give water to drink (*not stimulants*).

Favourite Hobbies: Pastimes at Home and Out of Doors

Fishing, Gardening, Photography, Stamps, Butterflies, and Moths

Topical Press.

FISHING FOR TROUT AT FLATFORD BRIDGE

Angling is an art, a sport, a science, or an amusement: a recreation for seekers after peace and quiet, or it may be an exciting pastime on occasion. As a sport its history is lost in antiquity, and to-day it has more followers than ever before. Something of its lure and the methods of the fisherman in fresh or salt waters is described below.

THE ANGLER'S ART

ANGLING, says the dictionary, is the art or practice of fishing with rod and line. The word is particularly used for the capture of fish as a sport and recreation as distinct from fishing as a business.

No doubt when angling first began primitive man was much more concerned with obtaining food, but even in the days of the ancient Egyptians, Greeks and Romans the sporting side and the arts and wiles required to lure the fish were properly appreciated. Studious men of bygone times found they could contemplate Nature and reflect on its wonders while trying to catch fish which would make a meal. Monks of medieval days were renowned as anglers.

In this country, as in others, a whole library of books has been written dealing with this "gentle art." So long ago as 1496 a "Treatyse" on Angling was written, and one of the most famous of our English classics is "The Compleat Angler," written by Izaak Walton, and published in 1653. "Most Anglers are quiet men and followers of peace," Izaak wrote, and added later: "God never did make a more calm, quiet, innocent recreation than Angling."

As a sport, Angling has several branches to-day, but they can be broadly separated into three main divisions : Coarse Fishing, Fly-fishing and Sea Angling. The first is probably the most largely practised, while fly-fishing is commonly regarded as even more sporting and more fascinating than any other form, though each will argue according to his tastes, and it is quite certain that each has its own particular charms.

Generally speaking there are two fish which are the object of the fly-fisher : Salmon and Trout. But there are a number of other fish which may be taken with the fly though they do not come into the category of "game fish," as salmon, trout and grayling are termed.

In this country salmon is rather outside the sphere of the average angler and for this reason when one speaks of fly-fishing it is generally assumed that trout is the object of the angler's wiles.

When Close Seasons Vary

All freshwater fish, except salmon, trout, char and grayling, are usually termed "coarse fish." The origin of this term is uncertain, but was quite probably applied because of the comparatively large scales which most of them have. Pike are fished for with small fish, dead or alive, or representations of them, but they can be classed with the coarse or general fish, the best-known of which are the Roach, Perch, Barbel, Chub, Dace, Gudgeon, Carp, Tench, Bream and Rudd. Most of these fish frequent rivers, lakes and ponds, but barbel are usually found only in running water, while dace rarely thrive in lakes. Chub, too, are usually found in flowing streams rather than in lakes or ponds.

There are close seasons for the different kinds of fishing, but the actual dates given in the calendar may be varied by the local authorities for good reasons. For coarse fish the close season is from March 14th to June 16th. Actually, any coarse fish caught during this period are worthless and afford very little sport. Generally speaking, September and October are the best two months of the year as it is usually about August when they begin to get into first-rate condition.

Trout cannot be fished for in England between October 1st and February 1st, but it is often mid-April before trout are in their best condition. The close season for salmon begins on September 1st for nets and at the beginning of November for the anglers with rods, both ending on February 1st. But all these dates may be varied by the responsible authorities in any area where it is considered advisable. Different dates apply in both Scotland and Ireland.

Tackle for Coarse Fishing

Leaving fly-fishing for a time and coming to the question of the implements required for coarse fishing, there is nowadays an almost bewildering variety of the first and most important article in the angler's outfit : the rod. Stories of boys making better catches with a long bamboo rod and a cheap line with a bent pin for a hook are probably true enough, since luck plays a big part in angling as in any other sport. So, too, do knowledge and experience !

Local conditions may influence the choice of tackle and the beginner will be wise to seek advice from some friendly angler in his own district. Generally speaking, however, the ordinary 3-jointed rod, 11 to 14 feet long, is right for the general angler. The main point about the rod should be that the balance feels just right to you. Before trying the rod you have in mind it is as well to choose your reel and have it fitted in its place on the butt as the reel naturally makes some difference to the general balance. The butt should have a cork handle as this gives a much better grip.

Your rod will be fitted with rings for the line to run through and the type known as bridge rings are better than the snake variety. If you can afford to have the porcelain-lined rings there is less chance of the line becoming fouled. In any case it is wise to have the top ring, right at the end of the rod, as well as the one next to the reel, lined with porcelain. It is a good plan to rub the joints of your rod occasionally with vaseline to prevent them from sticking.

Float, Hook and Sinker

The reel, or winch, is a matter of taste and the cost varies considerably. A 3-inch or 3½-inch reel is about the right size for a medium sized rod and it will hold 50 yards or so of fine line, which is ample for the average angler. A silk line is generally used and it is well to bear in mind that after being used the line should be properly dried. Coil it round a chair-back at home, or, better still, make a drier for yourself, and then when winding it on the reel again make sure there are no loops or kinks and that it is reeled quite tightly after drying.

This line needs two other fittings, a float and a hook. The hook is usually attached to a length of gut when bought and this gut has to be fastened to the silk fishing line. The tying-on must obviously be done securely, and if you can get a friend who is an expert in knot-tying, or has had experience of the task as an angler, so much the better.

As a general rule the line must be leaded with shot. This shot is usually bought ready split for the purpose. A pair of pincers will make it fit tightly on the line. As in the matter of knots, it is well to have advice from the dealer or a friend on the size of hooks you should buy. He will know the waters you are likely to fish and the kind of catch you may hope to get.

The object of the shot is, of course, to sink the line and partially submerge

Fox Photos.

YOUNG ANGLERS AT SEVEN ISLANDS POND

There is a story behind this picture which was taken at Mitcham in Surrey. High authority decided to use the pond in connection with some agricultural plan, but the youngsters appealed against a decision which would rob them of their fishing rights. They gained their point and official sanction was granted for the ancient pastime to continue at the pond.

Fox Photos.

YOUTHFUL COMPETITORS FOR ANGLING PRIZES

Fishing is sometimes regarded as a lonely recreation but there are times when it draws the crowd. Here is a picture, taken on the River Ouse amid the pleasant countryside outside Cambridge, in which we see a section of the 800 youthful competitors who took part in the Angling Society's annual juvenile competition.

the float in water. Just how many shot should be used depends on the size and type of float used and can really only be found by experiment, but an average of four or five is usually necessary. In very still waters some anglers will have no weight at all on their lines, but the float in this case is weighted at the lower end.

There are all sorts and sizes of floats: pretty ones made up of quill, or big ones of cork and wood, often used for pike-fishing. The porcupine quill with light, painted cork body is popular or a quill alone is often used. The float is usually kept in position on the line by a float cap, a quill ring or a small rubber ring.

With a good rod and line, properly fitted, the angler has practically everything that really matters except bait. There are a few other items that may be needed and are on occasion very necessary: a plummet which can be used for finding out the depth of the water in which one intends to fish, or a landing-net, which may be useful for lifting fish into the boat or on to the bank. A fishing-basket, known as a creel, or a bag, will be desirable for the big catch you hope to get when setting out.

Preparing the Bait

Having your tackle there remains one other important item, and that is the question of bait with which to lure the fish. Ground bait is food which is thrown in before and during the time when the angler is fishing and is intended to attract the fish to the particular part of the water selected by the man with the rod. Usually this ground bait is made with bran mixed with breadcrust, and perhaps cheese rind and similar odd scraps. These should be well broken and soaked in water to be made into stiff balls. For

BRITISH FRESH WATER FISHES—Plate 1

Specially painted for this work.

Life on this earth began in the waters long before the earliest man had appeared, and it was the fish that first developed a backbone. Other animal types developed on land and many of them have vanished in the struggle for existence, but in the seas and the rivers the fish has increased and multiplied. In this Plate we have some of the well-known fishes found in British rivers and lakes: 1. Pike; 2. Perch; 3. Carp; 4. Trout; 5. Roach; 6. Salmon.

BRITISH FRESH WATER FISHES—Plate 2

Specially painted for this work.

Fishes form the largest group of vertebrate animals in existence and are found in all waters, both marine and fresh, and at almost all temperatures. There are nearly twenty thousand species known to the Ichthyologist, as the scientist who studies them is called. In this Plate are seen seven other specimens of British fresh water fishes: 7. Stickleback; 8. Minnow; 9. Grayling; 10. Char; 11. Barbel; 12. Loach; 13. Miller's Thumb or Bullhead.

BRITISH FRESH WATER FISHES—Plate 3

Specially painted for this work.

Fishing for sport and recreation, commonly known as Angling, is broadly classified into two distinct types: " game fish " such as salmon and trout, usually taken with a fly, and " coarse fish," generally captured by what is known as bottom fishing as the bait to lure the fish lies near the bottom of the river or pool. Here we have five of the best-known coarse fish in our inland waters: 14. Gudgeon; 15. Tench; 16. Bream; 17. Dace; 18. Chub.

BRITISH SALT WATER FISHES

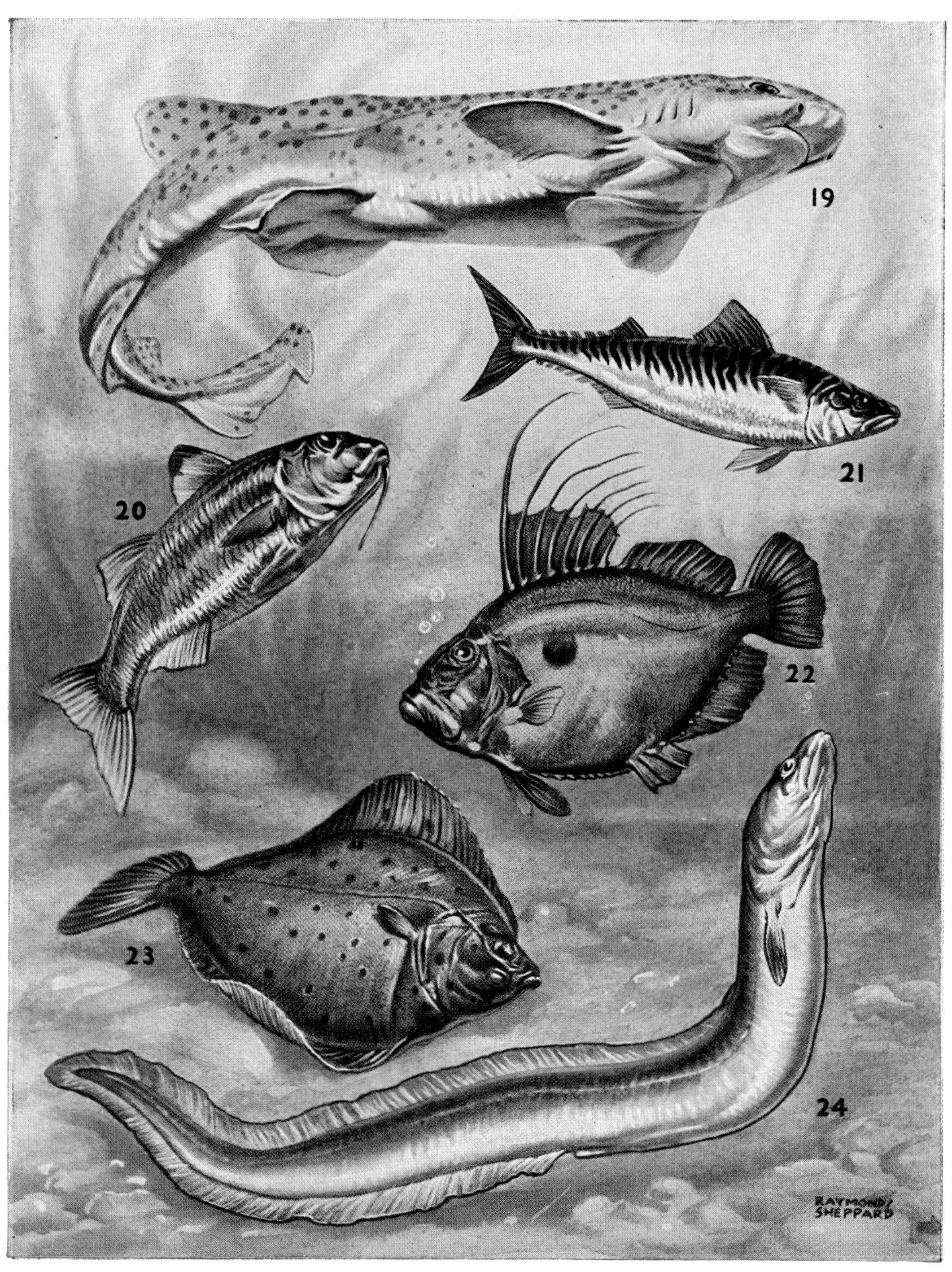

Specially painted for this work.

A wide variety of fish is found in the seas around our coast and some of them provide a welcome addition to our food supplies while others offer good sport to the sea angler. Fish are great travellers, and some of them, like certain birds, migrate to warmer climates when winter comes. In this Plate are shown six well-known British sea-water fishes: 19. Large Spotted Dogfish; 20. Red Mullet; 21. Mackerel; 22. John Dory; 23. Plaice; 24. Conger Eel.

the hook bait use gentles, worms of different kinds, or a paste made with $\frac{1}{2}$-pint wheat soaked in cold water and very gently stewed for four or five hours, adding more cold water about once an hour. Gentles can be bought and so can worms if one cannot easily obtain them otherwise. Local anglers will advise you on points such as these.

The ground bait is used first, one of the balls being broken in half ; then put in a little of the bait it is intended to use on the hook. This half-ball is made into another ball about the size of an egg. This ball can be gently thrown into the water or, better still, lowered into the water after squeezing the ball gently on to your fishing line at the hook end. A sharp jerk of the rod when the line is sufficiently far down will release the ball of bait and the line can then be withdrawn.

The place where the ground bait settles is where the fish will gather. Three or perhaps four balls of ground bait may be used before the hook is baited. Probably before then the angler will have tested the depth of the water with the plummet, fastened to the line, if he is in doubt about the depth. The float can then be adjusted so that the bait will rest a couple of inches or so off the bottom, allowing a little for the fact that the water will probably carry the line a little way. The line will be weighted with shot so that the float will remain an inch or so above the water.

The hook should be well covered with bait. If you are using a bait of wheat paste it should be firmly moulded round the hook. Now the line is cast by an underhand or round swing from the rod tip. Hold the rod in the right hand and the baited hook in the left, then swing the rod forward and release the hook at the same time. Let it settle and when the float is in its right place in the water see that there is the least possible amount of loose line between the end of the rod and the float.

Fox Photos.

ROD AND LINE IN LONDON'S SUBURBS

Our picture would scarcely be chosen for a London scene, yet it was taken at Grovelands Park in the suburb of Southgate. The lake is used for boating and fishing, and here we see young anglers taking part in a competition organised during their holiday time.

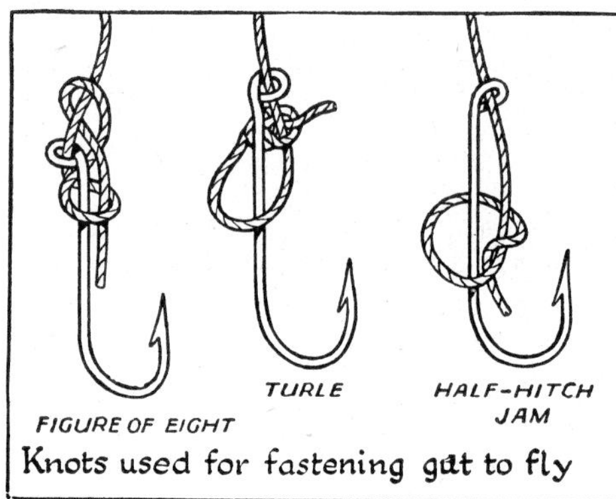

TYING THE HOOK

Artificial flies are usually bought tied to the hooks and here are shown three different ways of securing the eyed hook to the line.

Different Styles for Different Waters

Ground bait should be thrown in occasionally and further casts can be made with perhaps more line so that a fairly wide area is covered. When a fish bites, the float will dip or go under water ; sometimes a little preliminary nibbling by the fish will warn the angler, but as a general rule he must strike promptly, the point of the rod being brought up quickly without jerking it. Never let the fish have any slack line and try to keep it from coming to the surface until you are on the point of landing it.

There are different methods or styles of fishing adopted on different rivers, such as the Thames, Lea, Trent and the Midland rivers. One well-known style is known as Nottingham fishing and is no doubt specially suitable for some waters but not for others. About these different methods and particularly about the peculiarities of his own district, the beginner will learn as he progresses in the art.

In angling, as in most other arts and crafts, experience is the best of all teachers. If one can have the advantage of a few hints from an expert, especially about the waters in which one intends to fish, it will be a great help.

Roach is probably the most popular fish with the general angler. Nearly all rivers have a minimum size limit for the different fish, and all catches below that limit should be returned to the water at once, unless, of course, the angler is anxious to secure live bait for pike or for perch.

Fly-fishing

There are a number of fish which can be caught by dry or wet fly-fishing, and the main ideas on which all fly-casting is based are very much the same for all fish. Salmon fishing would perhaps be placed at the top of the list as the most exciting form of the sport, but the best salmon rivers in the United Kingdom are in Scotland and Ireland, though there are several rivers in England on which the sport is enjoyed.

Most of the salmon fishing in the British Isles is privately owned, and for this and other reasons it is unlikely to become a popular form of fishing. When one speaks of fly-fishing it is usually taken to mean for trout, though there are several other fish that can be taken with fly. Many anglers, once they have become victims to the fascinations of trout-fishing with wet or dry fly, have little interest for any other branch of the sport.

One curious point is that in trout

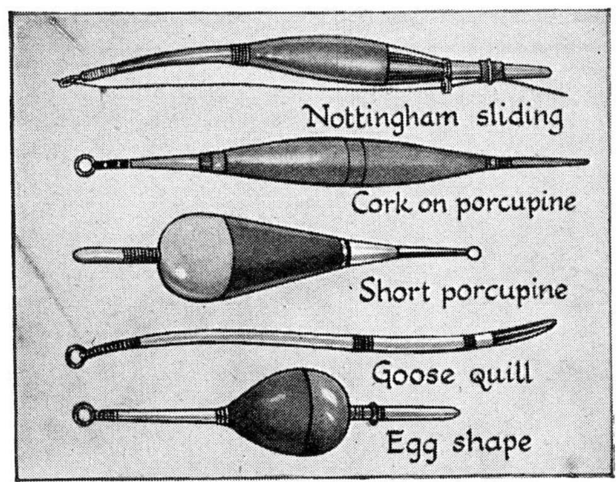

DIFFERENT TYPES OF FLOAT

There are various kinds of float used in general fishing from the small light quill to the heavier cork and wooden float used by the pike angler.

fishing the artificial flies used by the angler must resemble as closely as possible the insects which seem to be most popular with the fish as dainty morsels of food. In the case of the salmon there is no question of tempting the appetite of the fish ; the fly is merely used as an irritant. During its stay in fresh water the salmon is usually a bad-tempered creature, and amongst the things that annoy it are brightly coloured objects, especially gaudy insects. So the flies for salmon fishing are made as brilliant as possible. while trout flies are usually of sombre hues but tempting to the trout's taste.

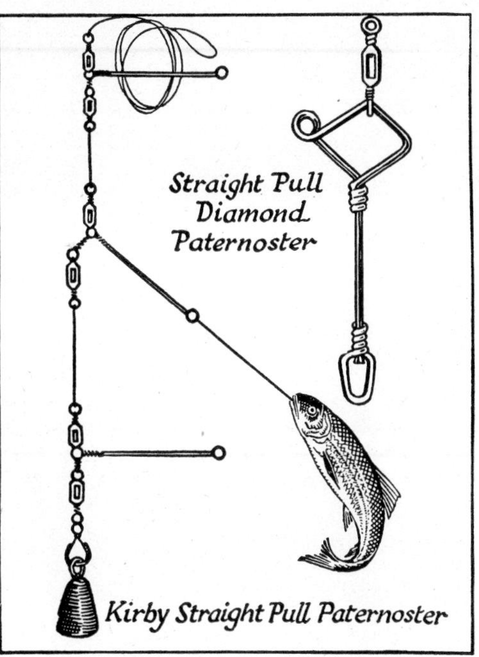

USED IN SEA ANGLING

Paternoster tackle is largely used in sea-angling, and in the drawing above two types of this particular kind of tackle are shown.

Tackle for Trout

Trout vary in size in different waters. Rapid streams tend to produce small fish and a half-pounder may be considered as one of reasonable size. In other waters such as the chalk streams of Hampshire, a 2 lb. fish would not be regarded as anything very wonderful and a half-pound fish scarcely worth mentioning. The record size is generally accorded to one of $39\frac{1}{2}$ lb. taken in Loch Awe in 1866, which is a long time ago, and may account for the fact that doubts have since been expressed by sceptics who do not question the weight of the fish but suggest it may have been a salmon.

HOW TO TIE SECURELY

Knots are important in all branches of fishing and in the diagram above three of the most useful knots for the angler are given.

So far as the indispensable tackle is concerned the list for fly-fishing is not unlike that used by the general angler : rod, line and reel come first as they do in most forms of angling. In addition, the silk-worm gut casts which will be tied to the line are necessary, and, one of the most important items of all, a selection of artificial flies. A landing-net, too, is a necessity, and a wicker creel or waterproof bag in which to take back the day's catch should be put on the list.

A box or waterproof pouch in which the casts can be safely kept and another

Specially drawn for this work.

HOW TO CAST WHEN BAIT-FISHING

Like every other interesting sport or recreation there is much to learn about the right and wrong methods in angling. In the sketches above our artist illustrates the way in which the young angler should manipulate his rod when throwing the line. After casting keep the rod-tip down till the float has settled then raise the rod until there is a minimum of loose line between float and rod-tip.

box or case to contain the flies will also be needed. These items are matters for individual choice, just as the various gadgets for the angler's convenience may appeal to one person and be despised by another.

A 3-piece, split-cane rod of about 9 feet in length and 6½ oz. in weight would be an appropriate kind to buy, though a greenheart rod is generally cheaper and by some people regarded as equally satisfactory. While it is good advice to say "Get the best rod possible," it may not be so wise in the case of the beginner, who will only find out by experience just what type of rod he really prefers. Probably the safe plan is to get a moderate-priced rod to begin with and this may, of course, serve for a long time.

As with most sporting implements, the great thing is to get one that feels right to you so far as balance is concerned. A friend may advise you in many ways, but you are the only one who can judge the feel of the rod in your own hands, after the reel has been fitted. It is worth buying a good reel for the simple fact that it may last you a lifetime. Make sure that the reel will suit the balance of the rod.

A Large Choice of Flies

Lines can be fairly expensive, but again the beginner will be fairly safe in buying a good standard make of double-tapered 30-yard line. The cast comes next, usually a 3-yards length of silkworm gut, generally looped at the thicker end for fastening to the line. Thickness is described as X or 1X down to 5X or finer lines; the higher the number the finer the line. "Fish fine" is good advice, but it can be carried too far, especially in the case of a beginner ; 2X is probably fine enough. The cast should be soaked in water before starting out. Sometimes an angler will soak the gut cast in luke-warm tea to stain it brown, thus rendering it less visible to the fish. General fishermen, too, sometimes adopt this device.

Artificial flies are usually tied upon eyed hooks so that they can be quite easily attached to the cast. A book might easily be written on this subject of flies which attract trout at the different seasons. The main point is that the angler should use one of the flies that appear about the time when he is fishing. At the end of May or beginning of June, for instance, the Mayfly arrives—a big fly which is taken greedily by trout during the few weeks of early summer. Other flies are made to imitate the nymphs or the immature stages of these flies.

There are many other flies from the March Brown and the Blue Dun or Greenwell's Glory of April to the Cinnamon Quill and Silver Sedge of August and September. But there is a big selection of flies which can be used in both dry fly-fishing and wet fly-fishing, and a knowledge of these, as well as the personal preferences of different anglers, is one of those matters on which experience alone is the road to knowledge.

Concerning the Different Methods

Here we are concerned only with a general outline of what is necessary. Actually there are broadly three main methods of trout-fishing with a fly : the Dry Fly ; the Wet Fly Upstream, and the Wet Fly Downstream. These

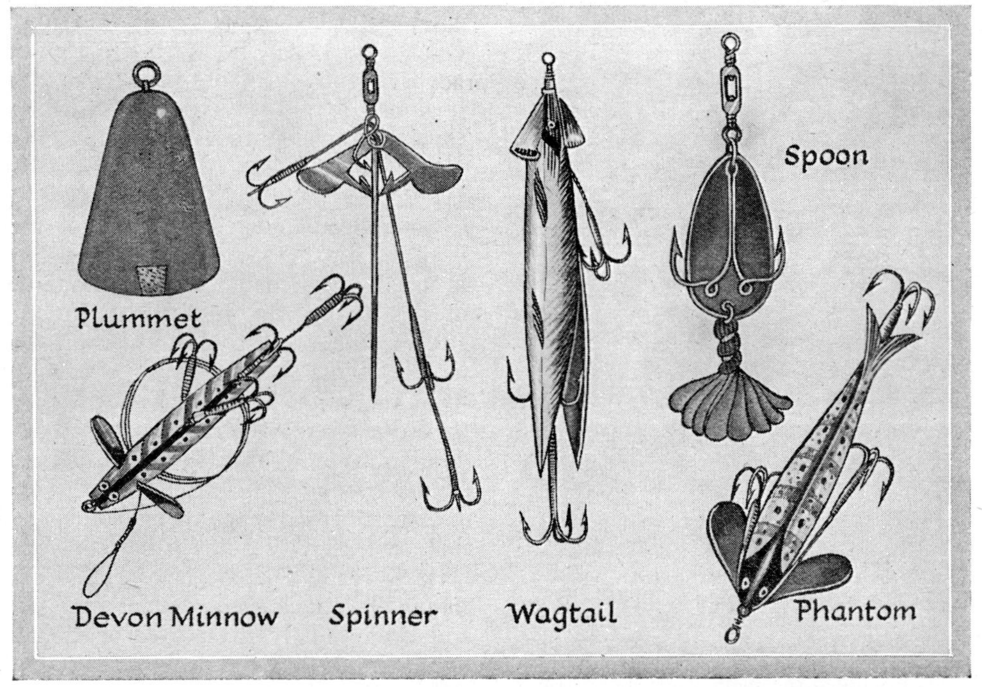

Specially drawn for this work.

SOME OF THE BAITS USED WHEN SPINNING

One form of fishing which has become increasingly popular is that known as "spinning." For pike it is probably the best and most sporting method, but it can be used for other fish as well, including salmon, trout and perch, according to circumstances. The bait is an artificial spinner of which the spoon type is probably the oldest, and, with the Devon minnow, among the most popular. In the top left-hand corner is the plummet, used in general fishing to ascertain the depth of the water.

THE ART OF CASTING
The first lesson the would-be fly-fisherman has to learn is the correct way to cast his line so that the bait will fall quietly on the water. In the above four sketches our artist has illustrated the method generally used.

terms largely explain themselves and the question of which is the best method or whether all are best in their turn, according to circumstances, is a matter of taste or possibly argument.

In the first the fly is cast just ahead of a rising fish. To make the fly alight naturally and gently on the water it is a good plan to cast at an imaginary spot about a foot above the spot on the water on which you wish your fly to alight.

Trout always lie in the water with head upstream ; the angler naturally stands behind the fish since it is important that he should not be seen. He casts his line in such a way that the dry fly, falling lightly and quietly on the surface of the water a foot or two in front of the fish, will float gently down quite naturally over the fish, and if he is the sort you expect him to be he will promptly take your fly.

The angler should not be in too big a hurry to strike ; in smooth water he gives the fish a reasonable chance to suck the fly fairly into its mouth. Then a twitch of the rod and the trout is safely hooked. It sounds simple enough on paper, but to become expert needs a good deal of practice and the beginner is apt to strike too quickly, especially on slow-moving streams.

For Wet Fly Fishing

Some elementary knowledge of flies is useful to the angler. Dry fly-fishing is usually carried out with an imitation of the mature fly, but in fast-running streams the trout feeds mostly on flies in the nymph stage as they struggle from the water to the air above where they can stretch their wings. Rather a different type of imitation fly is needed in these more turbulent streams, and instead of the wings being outspread they are tied close together to form what is really a single layer. The cast should be moistened with river mud and even the fly itself may be treated lightly in the same way so that it will sink under the water and not, as in dry fly-fishing, float on the surface of the stream. It is usually necessary to wade in the waters to be fished and suitable waders are another necessity.

Downstream fishing is often easier

for the beginner than is any other form. Casting the line is not so difficult as it is made across the water and the current does for the fly what the craft of the expert does in the other forms of fishing. But downstream fishing is only suitable in certain circumstances, when rivers are swollen, for instance, and unsuitable for either dry fly or for upstream fishing, though the trout may be plentiful enough.

Another kind of fishing for trout is known as spinning. In this case an imitation small live fish is used as bait. This is so made as to imitate the turning or wriggling movement of some of the commoner kinds of small freshwater fish. These man-made imitations have various names, among them being "Spoons," which revolve by their shape ; Devon minnows, shaped roughly like a fish ; Phantoms, which are more exact imitations of the real thing ; and Wagtails, which are made of pliable rubber.

The rod used in this kind of fishing is usually shorter and stiffer than one employed for fly-fishing, especially if the angling is being done from a boat. Reels, too, are rather more important as there are certain snags in spinning which can only be avoided by having a suitable automatic reel. Even the reel does not help in such matters as the avoidance of "kink" in the line, caused by twisting. For this reason the spinner usually has his line leaded, and the question of just where to put this weight is often a difficult one. In certain cases the lead can be attached to the swivel fitted to the artificial bait to enable it to do its spinning as it is drawn through the water.

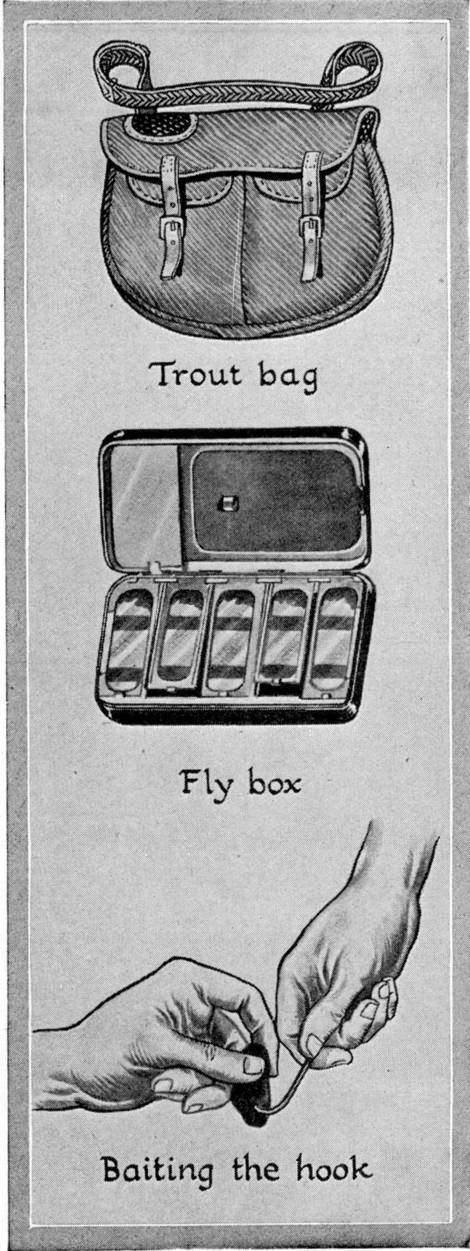

ANGLING ITEMS
Two articles of equipment necessary for the fly-fisherman are a bag for the catch and a box in which his artificial flies may be kept. The third drawing is for the general angler and shows how the hook should be baited.

A Good Eye for Water

Only certain types of water are suitable for spinning and generally speaking this particular form is not used except in cases where the more usual methods of fishing are unsuitable. Often enough on good fly-fishing water spinning is prohibited for the simple reason that it would make fishing with fly impossible or very nearly so.

Among trout anglers there will be

found many who have practised the art in all its forms, not excluding fishing with worms. Here again it can be said that in certain conditions this method may be the best, even though the fly-fisherman may consider that he is not treating the trout with the respect he has hitherto accorded the fish.

The best advice, of course, is to be gained from the experienced fisherman who knows the water where one hopes or intends to fish. No mere printed words can explain and illustrate the correct way of casting or landing or even tying. Only experience can give the angler "a good eye for water" or that instinct which tells one just where fish are lying in wait for the tempting fly skilfully cast by the quiet angler.

Sea-Angling

There are many holiday-makers who indulge in an occasional break at fishing when at the seaside, but it is usually of a very casual kind. A hand-line trailed over the back of a boat or the edge of the pier may yield catches and a certain amount of pleasurable amusement, but it scarcely comes in the category of first-class sport.

Rod, reel and line are the equipment of the true sea-angler, just as they are of the general and fly-fishing brothers of the Angle, as Izaak Walton called them. In choosing a rod it will depend on what kind of fish you are intending to lure. Usually the sea-angler's rods are short and stiff, probably 7 to 8 feet in length, made in two joints and generally of greenheart. If you have another top for this rod you will be equipped

Specially drawn for this work.

SEA-ANGLING FROM A BOAT

Both methods and tackle of the sea-angler differ from those of his brother sportsman who prefers the quiet streams and lakes inland. The sea-angler may indeed dispense with a rod and trail a handline on occasion, but rod, reel and line are usually employed. The rod is normally both shorter and stiffer and the line much longer and generally fitted with the paternoster tackle seen on an earlier page.

Fox Photos.

ALONG A SOUTH-COAST BEACH

Sea-angling differs in many ways from freshwater fishing and there is possibly more variety in the methods used to tempt the saltwater fish to take the bait. Here we see two anglers on the seashore casting their lines far out in the hope of a responsive tug to indicate that a fish has taken the bait and the thrill of landing a good catch is in store.

for bottom fishing as well as for pollack, mackerel and other fish caught near the surface.

A dressed waterproof line about 100 feet in length and made of gut substitute or gimp is generally suitable, though a fine silk line has been found best for a few fish. Among the fish to be caught off the British coast are Bass, Cod, Conger, Mackerel, Dab, Flounder, Plaice and Skate. Then there are Pollack and Coalfish, both members of the Cod family usually found in rocky waters, while other members of the Cod family include Whiting, Pouting, Haddock and Hake. The baits in general use are shrimps, mussels, crabs and various shellfish, lug and ragworms.

Grey Mullet is in its own class and the angler needs fine tackle and small hooks for this highly-prized fish. It can be understood that where there is such a variety of fish this question of tackle is a wide one. Often enough the paternoster and the leger are used. These curiously-named pieces of tackle are really a form of double or triple hooks. The paternoster is a long trace of gut or gimp to be attached to the line and with three "booms" of stiff wire ; a lead is at the bottom. The leger is usually so arranged that while the lead rests on the bottom the gut carries on beyond it and it is very useful in a strong tide and with the fish feeding just off the bottom.

Advice from the Old Hands

On rocky shores fishing can be done from the rocks, just as it can be done from a pier or jetty, but often it is better to go out in a boat a mile or more from the coast. As in all forms of angling the beginner will be wise to seek advice from one on the spot or from an angler who has had a fairly wide experience and knows what to expect on that particular stretch of the coast.

Obviously it is important to know what kind of fish can be taken in that part of the coast, what kind of bait has proved most profitable, the signs and portents which show that fish are there to be taken, and a good many lesser points which experience has brought forth. A knowledge of these may make all the difference between a dull wasted day and an exciting few hours of sport which will live in the memory.

There is one form of angling which the Americans have made popular in comparatively recent years and has now spread to other continents, and that is Big Game Fishing. The sport has also become very popular off the coast of New South Wales, Australia.

In Britain, Tunny has been the principal quarry, and off the Yorkshire coast in the neighbourhood of Scarborough has so far been the principal battle-ground. Fish weighing over 800 lb. have been caught here. It need scarcely be said that in this kind of fishing both angler and tackle must be strong enough to stand the strains on both when a huge fish finds itself on a hook at the end of a line.

But this kind of fishing, while having its own fascination as well as its exciting highlights, is scarcely the soothing, peaceful pastime of which Izaak Walton and a long line of enthusiasts through the years since his day have written their lyrical praises. It is the man or boy sitting by some quiet stream who captures his roach weighing a pound, or the fly-fisher casting his line over the waters of the Test or some other pleasant river far from the noise and bustle of the town, to whom the charm, the fascination and the joyous thrills of angling most surely come.

"We sit on cowslip banks, hear the birds sing, and possess ourselves in as much quietness as those silent silver streams which we now see glide so quietly by us," wrote old Izaak three centuries ago, and a writer of to-day, A. F. M. MacMahon, has summed it up in this way: "If you become one of us you will find that it is not only a hobby: it is a philosophy of life that may help you to find in yourself that happiness which, however hard to find there, cannot be found anywhere else."

Mirror Features.

MAKING THE MOST OF YOUR CAMERA

Copyright.

A GOOD STORY—AND A GOOD PICTURE

Obviously this fisherman on Brixham quay is telling an interesting tale of the sea. Note how cleverly the photographer has recorded the scene without the two young listeners being aware of the fact. Specially posed pictures are seldom as successful as this delightfully unconventional camera study.

THIS section is not intended for owners of super cameras who can afford the time and money to make a really serious study of the science of photography, but has been written especially for owners of the less expensive box and folding types of camera who are keen to get the best results from their modest kit.

Don't despair if yours is only a humble and ancient model, for the best camera in the world cannot of itself make anyone a successful photographer. It is camera-craft that counts in the long run—the wise preparation you make before you press the trigger. Many a prize-winning photograph has been taken with a simple box camera.

Cameras are like cars—you must know them thoroughly to get the best out of them. No two are exactly alike, although of the same make. Each has a " character " all of its own, so until we find out just how our camera behaves, what it can and cannot do, we must not expect every snapshot to be a success.

One of the first things we must realize is that the eye of a camera, the lens, is in many ways much less efficient than the human eye. It has not such an extensive field of view as we have ; it does not record the beauty of colour, but sees the world in terms of light and shade ; and not all it sees may be sharply in focus. What *we* may think a beautiful landscape to photograph, the camera lens may take (and make !) a very poor view of. So the sooner we get to know what the world looks like to our camera, the sooner we shall know the types of picture it can tackle most successfully. In fairness to the camera it must be stressed that it will often make a fine picture of a subject that appears drab or uninteresting

POPULAR MODERN CAMERAS

A. W. Kerr.

The Voigtlander Brilliant is typical of the good, inexpensive type of camera. It has a magnifying viewfinder and a lens which can be set to focus at approximately from 3 feet to infinity.

Kodak Ltd.

This Six-20 Folding " Brownie " is a useful camera of the folding kind. Notice the optical direct vision viewfinder mounted on the camera body enabling the camera to be used at eye level.

Kodak Ltd.

A box camera, such as this Six-20 " Brownie " E, for example, is ideal for beginners. It is not expensive and it is quite simple to operate.

Ensign.

The Ensign Ful-Vue Camera shown here has a super viewfinder which gives an extra large preview almost the size of the finished print.

HOW TO STORE YOUR PICTURES

Kodak Ltd.

This shows how the camera should be held. The sling strap, if there is one, should be round the neck, and the camera held against the body for steadiness.

L. Shaw.

Mount your photographs in albums like those used by these young enthusiasts. Small and inexpensive gummed corner-pieces, bought by the packet, hold the photographs in place.

L. Shaw.

Your negatives are worth keeping and the best way to do this is to put them in transparent envelopes which will protect them from damage. The negatives should be filed and numbered, and the details entered on an index card. This gives you an easy and quick way of finding any negative you need.

through our eyes. Once again we say : "Get to know your camera."

It may be helpful if we begin at the beginning and imagine that you have just come into possession of your first camera. It is not an expensive model ; it may be a box camera or a simple folding model. Both types are capable of taking fine pictures if you use them correctly. The lowest priced cameras have only one shutter speed (usually about 1/25 part of a second) which means they are not suited to the taking of "action" shots. A snap of an express train, an aeroplane landing, or the finish of a race, for example, would be just a streaky blur on the negative. With luck we might manage a picture of children playing a quiet game, a group of people talking, or a person walking slowly some distance away from the camera, but this is about the limit for action studies. To cut out movement, cameras with higher shutter speeds are required and we will refer to these later. Your camera is best suited to photographing landscapes, buildings and still objects generally.

The simple box camera has what is known as a fixed focus. This means that any object you photograph at less than a given distance (usually 6 feet to 10 feet) will be *out* of focus, but *in* focus for all distances above the minimum figure. Fortunately, some of the more modern box cameras are fitted with an extra lens (known as a portrait lens) which will enable you to get within 3 feet to 9 feet of your subject yet still have the picture in focus. So if you are thinking of buying a box camera, choose one that has a portrait lens incorporated. Readers who may have older box cameras can get round the problem of taking close-ups by buying a clip-on portrait attachment.

Even the cheapest box or folding camera has two or three "stops" or

Trevor Holloway.

WHERE TIME STANDS STILL

A quiet corner of one of the most photographed villages in Britain, Castle Combe, in Wiltshire. Old-world villages such as this, with their stone-tiled roofs, quaint gables and curious porches, offer great scope to the young photographer possessing only modest kit. Because the camera moved, or the shutter was opened, this otherwise well-composed picture is slightly blurred.

SOME CAMERA FAULTS

A yellow filter would have given greater contrast between grass and sky. The use of such a filter would have taken the drabness from this White Horse picture.

The chief fault here is the presence of a second Scout only partly in view. It distracts attention from the main figure and it would have been better to have left him out altogether.

Photos : Trevor Holloway.

Obviously a specially posed picture this, and too many activities going on in one scene. Bad grouping is another fault ; it looks as though the Scout with the axe is about to behead the fellow who is forward on the opposite side. A case of too many wood-choppers spoil the picture.

lens apertures. These "stops" are usually holes of decreasing diameter punched in a metal strip, and they enable us to control the amount of light that is allowed to pass through the lens and on to the sensitized film. On a dull day, or when taking a snap of a subject in the shade (such as under a tree) we need all the light we can get, so obviously the largest stop should be used. But on very sunny days (particularly at the seaside where the sea and sand intensifies the glare of the sun), the second or even the third (*i.e.* smallest) stop should be used.

An experienced photographic dealer told the writer that almost half the films he develops for his customers are over-exposed. He explained that the average camera-owner usually waits for a sunny day, or a trip to the seaside, to take his or her snaps. The majority just don't bother to alter the stops at all. They use the large stop for all their exposures and ignore the two smaller ones, no matter how bright the sun may be. A good tip to remember is that if your own eyes are affected by glare, it is a pretty sure guide that the second or third stop should be used.

Choice of Film

Before we start putting our camera through its paces, a word about the choice of film may be helpful. You probably know that great advances have been made in the manufacture of photographic film during recent years. The early films were "blind" to practically all colours and if you study old photographs you will notice that things like red bricks, fair hair or green grass look very unreal.

Nowadays we have a very wide range of films to choose from, but generally speaking they can be divided into three classes—orthochromatic, panchromatic and super-panchromatic. These are much faster than the old-time films and they are more sensitive to colour.

Trevor Holloway.

A GLIMPSE OF MEDIEVAL ENGLAND

Lacock, with its winding streets of medieval houses, is a happy hunting ground for the camera-owner. Here is just one example how your camera can record the beauty of wood and stone. It was at Lacock that Fox-Talbot made the first photographic negative and opened up the gates of photography for all.

Trevor Holloway.

A NOVEL VIEWPOINT

It is sometimes possible to add an artistic touch to your pictures by framing the subject with something in the foreground. An arched bridge made a pleasing frame for this picture of a village church. Overhanging branches or a gateway in a wall are other " viewpoints " worth trying.

Orthochromatic would be a good type of film for beginners as it can be used for all outdoor snapshot work and general photography, especially during the summer months. Panchromatic is a fast film giving good colour distinctions and, having a very fine grain, it is a good film to use from which to prepare enlargements. Superpanchromatic film is mainly intended for indoor and high-speed photography and would scarcely be suitable for new-comers to the art.

Closely tied up with the question of film is the subject of what is known as colour filters. Later on you will probably make much use of filters, but space does not allow us to make more than a brief reference to them here. Even the most sensitive of modern film does not " see " all colours in the same order of brightness as our eyes do. But by using filters (coloured discs of glass or gelatine) in front of the lens, this defect can be remedied to a great extent.

The filters are made in a variety of colours for different purposes. The pale yellow filter is perhaps the most useful. It allows most colours to pass through on to the film quite freely, but holds back part of the blue light. A landscape taken through a yellow filter makes a much more natural print than would otherwise be the case. But there is one point to be remembered—if you use a yellow filter you will need to double the exposure time.

Variable Shutter Speeds

So far we have dealt only with cameras having one shutter speed, generally referred to as " I " (short for instantaneous) on the box-type camera. Now, although cameras of this type are ideal to start off with, some readers may be interested in more advanced (and expensive !) models which have variable shutter speeds.

The ordinary box camera with its shutter speed of round about 1/25 second rules out almost all types of

Trevor Holloway.

A FINE SUBJECT FOR A SERIES

Keep an eye open for wayside oddities, such as this fine old market cross at Castle Combe. Some of these crosses date back to Norman times and many are of great beauty and historic interest. When photographing monuments such as these, try to include one or two people in the picture to add "human" interest.

action pictures; but with a camera having shorter speeds we can hope to get some snaps of the school's high-jump champion in action, the finish of a race or some good railway pictures and so forth. It also opens up the very wide field of nature photography—an exciting and fascinating hobby indeed.

In cameras of this type you will have noticed that the exposure time, or shutter speed, is controlled by moving a pointer over a scale graduated in fractions of a second—*e.g.*, 1/25, 1/50, 1/100 or even less. Suppose you wished to photograph the winner of a race breasting the tape. A box camera effort, owing to slow shutter speed, would result in a hopelessly blurred picture because the runner would have moved an appreciable distance during the time the shutter was open. For a sharp picture you would need to give a much shorter exposure, say 1/150 sec.

The following table will give you a general guide of exposure times when the subject is about 50 feet distant from the camera:

Street scenes with people walking slowly	1/25 sec.
The same, but with people walking more quickly	1/50 ,,
Farm animals grazing quietly	1/15 ,,
Horse trotting, man cycling or running	1/150 ,,
Horse galloping, fast-moving vehicles, etc..	1/200 or less

An important point to remember when using the higher shutter speeds is to use the correct stop, or aperture. If, for example, the shutter is only open for 1/100 sec., the light has only one quarter of the time to act on the negative that it has when an exposure of 1/25 sec. is given. To make up for this, it is necessary to use a larger aperture which will allow four times as much light to enter the camera.

If your camera has variable shutter

speeds you cannot hope to operate successfully without the aid of either an exposure meter or an exposure table. There are several simple and reasonably priced exposure meters on the market. By setting in the month, time of day, speed of film, nature of the subject, etc., you can read off the appropriate exposure (time and stop number) at a glance.

Knowing Your Camera

The best and quickest way of finding out how your camera behaves is to put it through a few practical tests. First of all, read what the makers say about the model. The well-known firms usually have some very sound advice to offer on getting the best out of the cameras they make. Next, buy two or three roll films of different makes or types, and use them solely for making experimental exposures. Concentrate on say a landscape, a building and perhaps an indoor subject.

Take the same subject in different lights, using different stops, exposure times and film. Keep a careful record of each exposure in a notebook and examine all the prints with a critical eye. You will probably be surprised how one print differs from the next, for better or for worse. Of course, these tests will not give you all the answers, but they will give useful guidance for future experiments.

Probably most of your first snaps will be of your friends and relations. These are always of interest and they become more interesting and treasured as the years go by. But a camera, wonderful instrument that it is, deserves much wider use than this.

Those of you who live in lovely or historic cities such as Bath, Chester or Edinburgh, have enough camera studies around you to keep you busy for a life-

Planet News.

WELLS CATHEDRAL

This is a fine Cathedral study with great pictorial value. The main interest centres on the Cathedral building and is not marred by the secondary interest of the swans on the lake in the foreground. This is a picture that helps us to understand why Wells Cathedral has been called " the most beautiful thing on earth."

time. And as for young London camera enthusiasts—well, they are in a photographer's paradise.

Why not specialize in a particular type of photograph ? You might keep an eye open for curious inn signs. Many of these signs are works of art and their origins and explanations are often most interesting. Old churches often contain wonderful examples of art in wood and stone, such as finely carved bench-ends and quaint gargoyles. Bridges make fine camera studies, so do windmills, old coaching inns, river and dockland scenes, old-world cottages, Tudor houses, gipsy camps and caravans, craftsmen at work—the scope is well-nigh limitless. Unusual angle shots of everyday subjects is another line you might like to try your hand at.

The writer's special interest is nature photography, concentrating on animals, birds and nests to be found in the countryside. Hunting with a camera is an exciting hobby indeed, full of adventure and unexpected experiences. One need not possess expensive kit, but infinite patience and a high standard of woodcraft is called for if one hopes to outwit the cunning of the wild folk. It only needs the alarm call of a moorhen or a blackbird to put every creature in the vicinity on guard. But what a thrill when you get a close-up picture of some animal or bird in its natural surroundings ! Nests and eggs of birds would make a fine series and there is no need to use a camera with high shutter speeds.

A very interesting series of pictures could be built up under the title of "Mother and Young". You might start off with a cat and her kittens. Next, perhaps, hen and chicks, duck and ducklings, swan and cygnets, mare and foal, cow and calf, ewe and lambs, and so on. If you live near a zoo you should be able to add considerably to the series. Actually, the zoo could be the subject for an almost limitless collection of "speciality" pictures.

Making a Good Picture

It is not only the subject of the picture that is important in making an interesting photograph. Background, setting, the amount of foreground or sky—all play their part. The following hints are worth remembering :—

Do not place the chief object of your picture right in the centre. That windmill, church or tower will look much better if nearer to one side of the picture. A horizon that comes halfway up the picture will spoil the general composition. Let it be well up or well down—but never halfway. Actually a low horizon is most effective.

Pictures can often be improved by framing the main subject with trees in the foreground or by taking the picture through an archway. If you stand about half-way under an arched bridge so as to include part of the sides and arch of the bridge in your picture, the effect can be very pleasing.

When photographing such objects as old bridges, curious monuments or buildings, try if possible to include people in the picture. An ancient stone bridge may be interesting architecturally, but it will make a much better picture if you can include children fishing from the parapet or show the oldest inhabitant of the village gazing down at the stream below. It adds what experienced photographers call "human interest" and also gives scale.

Most people look anything but their natural selves if they have to stand like soldiers in front of the camera. Far better let them be *doing* something—Mother knitting or Dad in the act of lighting his pipe. They'll feel more at ease and you'll get a one hundred per cent better camera study of them. Avoid stiff and formal pictures whenever it is possible. They seldom turn out a success. Perhaps the best way of photographing your friends is to "snap" them without their knowing it !

Landscapes often tempt us to use our camera, but, alas, results are frequently disappointing. Empty, uninteresting

PHOTOGRAPHING ANIMAL FRIENDS

This delightful picture of a young spring lamb is the kind of animal study that is always pleasing, though sometimes it is very difficult to take because one's pet will not remain still for long.

Photograph your dog, but be careful to avoid queer angles which distort. Such angles have been at work here making the dog's paws seem too large and out of proportion to its head.

Cats will often persist in following the photographer closely around. Kittens, too, move very suddenly : and you will have to be quick to get a charming study like this.

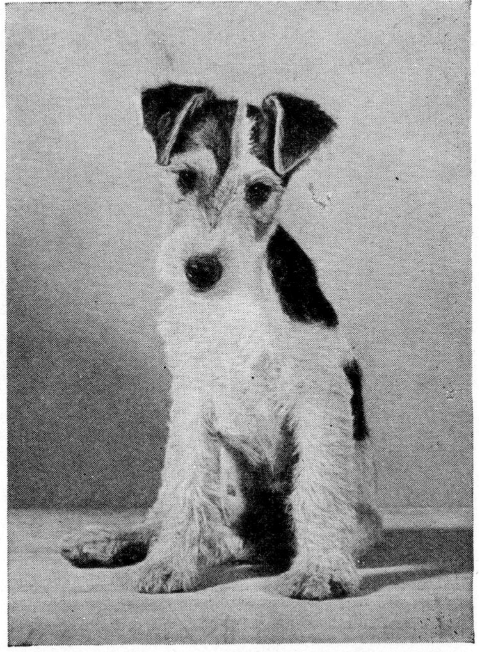

Photos : H. Armstrong Roberts.

Most pets cannot be made to pose and successful pictures—like this one of a rather forlorn wire-haired terrier—depend upon your being able to catch your pets in a quiet mood.

L. Shaw.

A SALISBURY GATEWAY

This beautiful entrance to the Cathedral Close makes another fine camera subject. Interest is increased by the figures walking towards the gateway, but those to the right are a distraction.

foreground spoils the more exciting parts of the picture. When taking a wide expanse of country it is often wise to have some object of interest in the foreground. The corner of a farmhouse or a few cows, for instance, would improve the composition of the picture as a whole. Try to make every photograph a *picture*, not just a " hit-or-miss " snapshot.

Some Common Faults

If you worked in a photographer's shop where customers' films were developed and printed, you would very soon be familiar with the most common faults that camera-owners make. It would soon be evident to you that many people just click the shutter and hope for the best. Alas for their hopes, for photography is not yet as simple as all that !

Let's imagine we are glancing through a batch of prints awaiting collection. Over and under-exposure has spoiled many otherwise good pictures. A great many other prints, even of still life subjects, are badly blurred. This fault could have been avoided if the photographer had held his or her camera firmly against the body and held breath when releasing the shutter. Better still, they might have improvised a support for the camera. At the seaside or in the garden, for example, one may rest the camera on the top bar of a deck-chair. A camera on a stand is worth two in the hand, so to speak !

It is usually wise to have the sun more or less behind you when taking a snap, but we notice that many snapshotters overlooked the fact that their own shadow was very much in the picture. Shadows can help to make fine pictures, but *not* in the way we have mentioned. Some prints seem to be about 90 per cent. foreground with what we presume to be the subject of the picture a mere speck in the distance. In other efforts, nine-tenths of the picture is sky, with not even a cloud to break the monotony.

Unsightly telephone posts and electricity cables mar many otherwise good prints, but sometimes it is difficult to get away from these things, especially in built-up areas.

Not a few prints are spoilt by unsightly backgrounds and pieces of litter lying around. The writer once saw a fine wedding group photograph, taken by a professional photographer, that included a battered old dustbin in the background, but nevertheless well in focus. The moral is : " Clear the deck " of anything that will spoil the artistic effect of your picture.

Seaside, camping and picnic snaps bring to light a common but amusing fault—feet of seemingly gigantic proportions ! The picture is usually that of a person sunbathing, taken, alas, from the feet end of the sunbather. The person's feet, being much nearer to the camera than anything else in the picture, appear enormous and usually

ON YOUR HOLIDAYS

H. Armstrong Roberts.

It's great fun taking a lovely picture like this of the family bathing in the sea ; but when you do take such pictures, take care to keep the salt water out of your camera.

H. Armstrong Roberts.

Plenty of good pictuies can be taken when the sea is calm and the sun is bright—especially if the photographer can wander into the sea after his subject.

A. W. Kerr.

At the seaside, it is not always necessary to have the family in the picture. Such simple things as a receding tide and sunlight on the wet sand make lovely studies.

A. W. Kerr.

Do not put your camera away when winter comes. When the snow has freshly fallen the fields and lanes will present such lovely studies as this for the photographer.

badly out of focus. Had such pictures been taken from the side, this ridiculous distortion effect would have been avoided.

Another very common fault is that many photographers try to get far too much in one picture. The result may be an uninteresting view of a fishing harbour full of craft, a vast expanse of country or coastline, or perhaps a general view of a crowded fairground—a lot of everything but nothing in particular. Far better single out an old salt repairing his boat, a picturesque country cottage, or a picture of your friend trying his skill at one of the fairground sideshows.

A picture which concentrates on a central idea is much better than one in which the interest is confused.

An All-the-Year-Round Hobby

Photography is not merely a hobby for the summer months. Frost and snow scenes can make exciting camera studies—skating, fun on a toboggan, the beauty and form of snow-drifts and so on. Indoors you might experiment with long-exposure pictures, or try your skill at table-top photography. Spring brings young lambs, fruit orchards in bloom and increasing activity in the world of animals and birds. Every season, in fact, brings its own special opportunities for the photographer.

One of these days, perhaps, you will become a member of your local camera club. These clubs are composed of camera enthusiasts who meet all the year round to talk over their problems, to compare their pictures and to plan excursions to all sorts of interesting places in quest of good subjects to photograph. They explore old castles and other interesting buildings, they visit beauty spots, prowl around docks and harbours, always on the look-out for good camera studies.

Photography is a fascinating hobby, even if one possesses only modest kit. Remember—it is camera-craft that counts in the long run. Make up your mind to give those super-camera owners a run for their money !

Trevor Holloway.

CURIOSITY DID NOT KILL THIS CAT

But it gave the photographer a chance to obtain a novel and amusing picture. A golden rule is: " Always have your camera handy." Very often the best opportunities crop up when least expected. Remember the Boy Scouts' motto, and " Be Prepared." The chance may never come your way again!

GARDENING FOR BOYS AND GIRLS

Studio Lisa.

THE YOUNG ENTHUSIASTS

As a healthful and fascinating hobby, gardening provides splendid exercise in the fresh air and there is plenty of scope for using our brains as well as our limbs because planning in advance is most essential. In gardening ground has to be skilfully prepared prior to sowing, and our attention must then be given to thinning, hoeing, weeding and watering before we can obtain our reward.

GARDENING is one of the most healthful occupations, for it is carried out in the fresh air and the work itself forms splendid muscular exercise for our bodies. As for the planning of a garden, there is abundant scope for careful thought, for imagination and individual ideas, so that our brains as well as our limbs can play their part.

Though there are sunny gardens and shady ones, each suitable for special subjects, the best all-round plot for girls and boys is one where there is a goodly amount of sun all the day through, with no large trees to cast shade, trees the spreading branches of which would cause constant drip in wet weather and whose hungry roots would impoverish the soil. In other words, an ideal garden is an open piece of ground, and if it faces south or possesses a southerly aspect, as we should say, so much the better. If yours is a shady, tree-flanked garden, perhaps looking into the north or east, you can only grow shade-loving plants successfully and may soon find you are robbed of a great deal of interest.

About the Soil

We speak of the earth or mould of which a garden is formed as the soil, and there are many distinct varieties. Stiff, reddish earth we term clay and some of the most productive gardens are those on well-worked clay soil. A sticky, yellowish soil is known as marl, and this is not a good staple for gardening purposes. When fine earth, sand and stones (especially waterworn pebbles) are mixed, we speak of a gravel

Reginald A. Malby.

CANDYTUFT

A lovely hardy annual, 12 inches high. Blooms: white, pink, purple, crimson, etc.

soil. Loam is a brownish soil, often charged with the fibres of decaying vegetation, and such fibrous loam is very suitable for flowers and vegetables. Sandy soil, as the name suggests, is a staple with a very large proportion of sand and you will at once understand that it dries out rapidly in hot weather. Chalk soil is light brown with bits of white chalk in it, being formed on the top of chalk rock. Peat soil is black, to a greater or lesser degree, apt to be very wet during the winter but excellent for an extensive range of plants that are peat-lovers.

You should get to know your soil because each type calls for slightly different treatment. Clay is good for roses, most of the vegetables and the majority of flowers. It needs deep digging in the autumn so that it may be thrown up in big unbroken clods for the frost to break down in wintry weather. Sifted ashes (especially bonfire and wood ashes), gritty sweepings from untarred roads and basic slag (to be bought from the garden stores) are all of benefit to clay. A gravel soil calls for decaying leaves and soft garden rubbish that has been rotted down in a compost heap or pit. Fibrous loam is improved by a little fine bone meal and some garden lime. Chalk soil is as a rule very thin, so that one cannot dig deeply, but it may gradually be improved if loam, leaves or material from the compost heap is added, hop manure also proving helpful.

Try to understand your soil so that you may know what to mix with it in order to obtain the best results. We speak of soil that has been well tended as being in good heart or perhaps in good tilth. It is from the soil that the roots of plants draw much of their nourishment, and you will never be very successful as a gardener unless you get your soil right before

C. W. Teager.

CLARKIA

This grows about 2 feet in height; rose, scarlet, pink and white flowers.

Reginald A. Malby.

CORNFLOWER

This hardy annual reaches a height of about 2 feet. Blue is the favourite, but there are pink and white varieties.

undertaking sowing and planting operations.

A Gardener's Tools

It is not possible to manage a garden properly without workmanlike tools. These tools and appliances should be strong and well-made and they call for constant care. They ought never to be left out-of-doors after use, for exposure to both sun and rain will quickly spoil them. Before being put away, the blades of spades and hoes, the tines (sometimes wrongly called prongs) of digging forks and the teeth of rakes should be cleaned by rubbing them with a piece of wood, bright metal parts being afterwards wiped over with an oily rag. Have a place for every tool and see that each one is kept in its place, all ready to hand when it is wanted. Just occasionally wipe the wooden parts with a rag dipped in linseed oil. Most garden tools have handles and hafts made of ash; linseed oil in moderation preserves this wood and makes it softer to one's hands.

Now, let us consider the tools we shall require:

A SPADE is, first of all, a most useful tool for autumn digging, for making holes in the ground for planting shrubs, for trenching, cutting edges and so forth. Obtain a spade that is not too heavy for your age and strength.

A FORK is an essential tool for general digging, both in the vegetable plot and in the flower borders. The tines may be flat or rounded, the latter being the more easy to use.

A RAKE in general gardening is used chiefly for making the soil surface smooth, for gathering together weeds after hoeing, raking up heaps of leaves or stones and so forth. Such a tool

Blanche Henrey.

HELICHRYSUM

A hardy annual bearing brightly-coloured flowers like double daisies; height, 3 feet. If stems are cut just before blossoms are fully open they may be dried for winter decoration.

having eight or ten teeth will serve your purpose best.

HOES are of various kinds and they are all most serviceable tools. A Dutch hoe is used with quick, pushing movements as one steps backwards over the ground and its purpose is to break the soil surface and keep it loose and crumbly so that plant-life may flourish; and, of course, to destroy seedling weeds. A draw-hoe is generally swan-necked and is used for drawing drills or furrows in which to sow seeds; for breaking the top crust of hard soil; and for chopping off weeds. One 4-inch Dutch hoe and one 3-inch draw-hoe are all you need obtain. They should be strongly fixed to stout handles.

A TROWEL is invaluable for setting out small plants, for use when potting up seedlings and for many other purposes.

A HANDFORK with four short tines has many uses. It is valuable for breaking the soil surface round plants, especially tiny seedlings; for planting bulbs, for weeding in the rockery, and also for transplanting.

A GARDEN LINE is essential. It may consist of a length of stout string; or, better still, of fine cord made specially for the purpose. Most gardeners attach one end of their line to a metal peg and the other to a reel with spike, but you can manage quite well with two pointed pieces of wood. You will want a line for forming a straight edge to a bed, border or lawn; for drawing even drills when sowing seeds, especially those of vegetables; for obtaining the correct course when planting out rows of seedlings, etc. Always wind up your line after use and store it in a dry place.

Getting the Garden Ready

We have already considered the fact that soils vary a good deal, so let us assume that you have been given a plot of ground for your very own and that you are going to get it ready, either for growing flowers or possibly a few vegetables. You may find that it has been neglected, so your first step must be to clear it entirely of weeds and unwanted plants.

In these days, when stable manure is almost unobtainable, good gardeners rely largely upon decaying vegetable matter for fertilising their ground. Grassy and other green weeds; tops and tails and outside leaves of vegetables; lawn mowings; tree leaves and all such refuse are built up into small tight stacks in the form of compost heaps. When once decayed, this garbage forms humus, one of the most valuable of all plant foods.

Hoe off the weeds from your plot, therefore, and let them serve as the foundation of your own compost heap. Then, once the surface has been cleared, you may commence digging in earnest, but you should understand that for plants to flourish the digging must be done deeply so that the roots do not encounter hard subsoil as they thrust downwards.

Probably the best start will be made if, with a spade, you dig out a barrow-load of soil from the top left-hand corner of the plot and deposit it at the bottom right-hand corner. You can now commence digging on the left at the top, working the soil to the left and forward as you dig in an even line across the ground. Whether using spade or fork, thrust the tool straight downwards as far as it will go. If you insert the blade or tines in the ground on a slope they will not penetrate nearly so far as if they go straight down. Now lift the spadeful or forkful of earth and throw it upside down in front of you and to the left. For spring digging, clods may be broken down with spade or fork: but in the autumn the rougher the surface is left the better. Roots of coarse perennial weeds, such as those of docks, dandelions, stinging nettles, bindweed and ground elder, should be picked out as you dig so that they may be dried off and burned on the bonfire.

SOME FLOWER GARDEN FAVOURITES

The Sweet Pea, " Queen of the Annuals," is a climbing plant and reaches a height of 6 feet or more. It does best when the ground is thoroughly trenched.

Snapdragons are excellent border plants for massing and best treated as half-hardy annuals. Various heights and almost all colours. Family name, Antirrhinum.

The Forget-Me-Not is a perennial, but best treated as a biennial and sown every year. Family name, Myosotis, or mouse's ear, from the shape of the leaves. Height, 6 inches.

Photos : Reginald A. Malby.

Sweet Williams are biennials. Seeds are sown in May or June, and the seedlings transplanted in September or October for blooming in the following summer. Height, 18 inches.

Let us say now that you have reached the end of the first row right across the plot. You will find in front of you a kind of little trench, and in this you may (with a fork) spread some stable or hop manure, if available; or a small quantity of the material from a thoroughly rotted compost heap. Proceed next with the digging of the second strip and so on until you have completed the task, when that barrow-load of soil you first dug out will help you to level off correctly. Do not hurry digging. Be sure to take your time and work methodically. At first the exercise may make you stiff, but the muscles will quickly become used to the calls made on them and then you will be neither stiff nor tired.

Planning a Flower Garden

Having dug over the plot deeply and well in order that sour soil underneath may be brought to the surface, sweetened by air and dried in the sun, we have next to decide what the garden is to contain and how its occupants shall be arranged for the best effect. The most satisfactory method is to take a piece of paper and set out a plan, more or less to scale, showing the actual area. Upon such a plan we can now write in notes of the subjects to be chosen and eventually draw up a list of plants or seeds required.

In the obtaining of a really effective floral border try to imagine for a moment that you are going to paint a picture, but that instead of using pigments you will depend upon bright flowers for the colours. Thus, you are sure to put your tallest subjects towards the rear to form an effective background. Plants a little less tall will be set next and then those of shorter stature until you come down to quite dwarf specimens well adapted to edging purposes.

So much for the planting of flowers of different heights. Bear in mind that plants coming near together should, so far as possible, blossom at the same time. In an autumn corner, for example, you may mass perennial sunflowers, rudbeckia, Michaelmas daisies, hardy border chrysanthemums and so forth.

The next point to consider is the correct arrangement of the plants; and, generally speaking, it is best to form bold groups. Thus, a mass of golden marigolds is placed next to a cluster of blue cornflowers with a third group, perhaps of clarkias, or candytuft, beyond. In any event, a draughtboard planting of single specimens dotted here and there is never so attractive as strong clumps. It is wiser, indeed, to grow only four, five or six of the best hardy annuals really effectively than to set a dozen sorts on such a small scale as to prove disappointing.

In this, your new little garden, you

Reginald A. Malby.

ANNUAL SUNFLOWER

Who does not know the tall single annual sunflower, which may attain to a height of 10 feet or even more? Helianthus is the family name and the variety "Russian Giant," with a big brazen face, is one of the largest.

may decide for the first season to grow nothing but annuals. Such plants are of annual duration, which means that seed is sown in the spring and the plants perish when they have produced their blooms. Seed of the annuals is obtainable everywhere in packets at very small cost and there is a particularly large choice of subjects, as the list below shows. To go further, there are two distinct types of annual, the hardy annual and the half-hardy annual. The former is *h.a.* in the lists and the latter *h.h.a.* The difference between the types is that one is liable to be destroyed by frost whilst the other is perfectly hardy. Actually, with some types of hardy annual, such as cornflowers, godetias, love-in-a-mist (nigella), eschscholtzias (the Californian poppy), candytuft and Shirley poppies, seed may be sown in the open garden in September and the seedlings left in the ground all the winter through. As a broad rule, however, hardy annuals are sown in March.

Reginald A. Malby.

BULBS IN FIBRE

Often called "indoor gardening," it is very fascinating to grow bulbs in fibre in undrained bowls, prepared fibre being readily obtainable where bulbs are sold. The miniature Roman hyacinths, daffodils and narcissi, scillas and crocuses are all excellent subjects for this interesting form of gardening.

Growing the Hardy Annuals

All the hardy annuals thrive in well-dug soil, but it is not advisable to make the surface too fine. When the earth is made unduly smooth by the use of a rake to excess, the top crust will bake very hard after heavy rain and then tiny seedlings cannot possibly get through. We must learn that the seed of hardy annuals varies a great deal in size, and deal with it accordingly, remembering that it is a good rule to cover seeds by two and a half times their height of soil. With big seeds like those of the nasturtium and annual sunflower we can make small holes with the sharp edge of a trowel at the proper distances and thus sowing becomes very easy. In the case of Shirley poppies we have seeds so small that they can hardly be singled out with a naked eye and they are best sown by mixing the seeds in a basin with many times their bulk of fine silver sand. The mixture may then be sprinkled thinly over the surface where the clump is to come and lightly covered with a little dry sifted soil you have laid by for the purpose.

Never forget that hardy annuals must be sown very thinly indeed. Again, when the tiny seedlings have appeared, they must be thinned out really hard. Most gardeners may attribute disappointment with these favourites to sowing too thickly and failing to thin promptly. Indeed, if each little plant has not a station to itself with sufficient space in which to develop overhead and to make a good root system it will not flourish. Further, the soil round the annuals ought always to have the surface kept loose and crumbly by use of the Dutch hoe, all big weeds being pulled out by hand.

Always carry out the sowing on a warm day when there is no strong wind and the soil is dry enough for the rake to be used effectively. An hour or two after a shower, when the earth is moist enough to receive seeds but dry enough on top for sowing, is ideal. If you are to grow annuals in a straight line, peg down the garden line first. For really tiny seeds you can make a very shallow drill or furrow by drawing a stick over the earth just close up to the line. For a deeper drill, as for larger seeds, you may use the corner of a hoe. After sowing, cover your seeds with very fine soil. In some cases you may be able to rake fine soil into the drill, using the back of the rake and not the teeth. In other cases you can perhaps pick up a lump of earth in your hand and crumble it along the row over the seeds. Do not attempt to water the seeds immediately they have been sown, but wait for spring showers. If no gentle rain has fallen by the time the seedlings are up give them a little water by means of a can with a rose having very small holes.

Reginald A. Malby.

HYACINTH

Hyacinth bulbs growing merely in water in cupped glasses produce splendid spikes of bloom. If tap water is used, a piece of charcoal should be placed at the bottom of the glass.

Annuals and Perennials

Among the Hardy Annuals are Alyssum, Candytuft, Clarkia, Coreopsis, Cornflowers, Godetia, Gypsophila, Larkspur, Mignonette, Nasturtium, Nigella, Poppy, Scabious, Sunflower, Sweet Peas, Sweet Sultan and Virginian Stock. All the Hardy Annuals thrive in well-dug soil, but, as mentioned earlier, it is not advisable to make the soil too fine or it may become hard when the sun shines after heavy rain.

The Half-hardy Annuals are so-called because the flowers are quickly destroyed if frost touches them. This means that the seeds must generally be sown in boxes of light, sandy soil under glass in March ; the seedlings are planted out about the last week in May, when, in most districts, there is little risk of further frost. In all other respects Half-hardy Annuals are treated in the same way as Hardy Annuals.

The Half-hardy Annuals include such flowers as Antirrhinum, Marigold, Petunia, Ten-week Stocks and Zinnias. Then there are the Biennials, the seeds of which are planted one year and the plants blossom about a year later. Most of the well-known biennials are Spring-flowering and include the Evening Primrose, Foxglove, Honesty, Sweet Williams and Wallflowers.

Plants which come up year after year and continue until their roots become worn out, are known as Perennials. Among these are Anchusa, Campanula, Delphinium, Hollyhock, Oriental Poppy and Polyanthus. There are also the tuberous Perennials, such as the Dahlia (which is only half-hardy and should be

DAFFODILS AND NARCISSI

A good example of the star-shaped, medium-crowned narcissus. This type is known as incomparabilis and the trumpets are usually prettily fluted.

This is the polyanthus or bunch-flowered narcissus, which is admirably suited for culture in fibre in undrained bowls. Many varieties have orange cups.

Here is the giant-flowered trumpet daffodil "King Alfred." The trumpet is the colour of old gold with the mouth turned back and strikingly frilled.

Photos : Reginald A. Malby.

The variety here illustrated is "Killigrew," which has a bright yellow perianth and an orange-red cup. Grouped in the Star Narcissus class, it grows strongly.

lifted and stored each year), Iris and Pæony.

Spring-flowering Bulbs

Some of the most beautiful flowers belong to the Spring-flowering bulb family. One of the most attractive ways of growing bulbs for decoration of the home is to plant them in fibre in ornamental bowls. The fibre, which should be well crumbled up before use and made moist, is usually bought already prepared with charcoal which keeps it sweet. The bowl is half-filled with moist, lightly-pressed fibre, then the bulbs are placed in position on the fibre at such a depth that the tops are level with the bowl brim. The bulbs should be spaced so that there is sufficient space between each for another bulb of the same size. Then cover the bulbs with more fibre, pressing it down fairly firmly. Just the tip of the bulb should be left showing above the fibre.

The bowls are now placed in a dark, but well-ventilated cupboard for at least three weeks, and for some kinds of bulbs even up to eight weeks. The object of this dark room treatment is to ensure that the root system gets well started before the green shoots are allowed to develop.

When the right time comes, the bulbs are brought out into daylight. Care should be taken to ensure that the fibre is always kept nicely moist. Even when in the cupboard the bulbs should be inspected occasionally, and, if the fibre appears to be too dry, it should be gently watered and kept just damp. After the bowls are brought out, the conditions in the living-room are entirely congenial for the bulbs, but avoid draughts or positions too near the fire.

The best month for planting spring-flowering bulbs in the garden is October, but if necessary they may be planted even as late as December. The bulb family includes Anemone, Bluebell, Crocus, Daffodil, Hyacinth, Iris and Tulip.

In the early years of your gardening hobby there will be little or no space in your small garden for vegetables. These will be a task for someone older, but it is in helping the older gardener that the beginner gains knowledge. In gardening, as in so many other worth-while hobbies, it is the enthusiast who is willing and anxious to learn from the experience of older followers of the craft who makes the best progress.

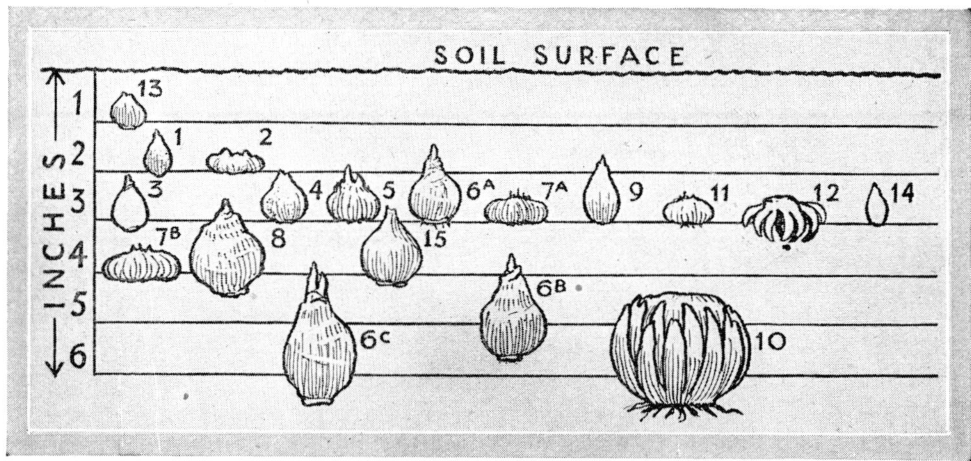

Specially drawn for this work.

A GUIDE TO BULB PLANTING

This diagram shows the approximate depths at which bulbs should be planted and here is the key: 1, Aconite. 2, Anemone. 3, Bluebell. 4, Chionodoxa. 5, Crocus. 6, Daffodil: (a) small, (b) medium, and (c) large. 7, Gladiolus: (a) small, (b) large. 8, Hyacinth. 9, Bulbous iris, 10, Lilies. 11, Montbretia. 12, Ranunculus. 13, Scilla. 14, Snowdrop. 15, Tulip.

The Hobby that is now a Science

Learning about Other Lands by Postage Stamps

A letter posted from the United Nations Post Office on the day the first U.N. stamps were issued. These stamps are only available at this one Post Office. All except the 20c. value have the inscription "United Nations" in various languages.

STAMP COLLECTING

STAMP collecting is, without doubt, the most popular of all indoor hobbies and there are many reasons for this. It can be enjoyed by girls and boys—and men and women too—all over the world because just as foreign stamps coming into this country are exciting to English collectors so our British stamps are "foreign" to those collectors who live in other countries. Through stamp designs, everybody can learn something about other lands. Very often there are delightful little pictures on the stamps showing views of famous beauty spots or recalling important events in the history of the country of issue. Even if there are no pictures there is something to learn for the postal value of the stamps helps the collector to understand something about the strange currencies throughout the world and the inscriptions show how a country's name is spelt differently in the "native" language compared with the English version. Again, it is only natural for the enquiring stamp collector to find out where the countries are when strange stamps come his way. Even the postmarks, or more correctly "cancellations," on a stamp are worth watching because the names of towns in different countries thus become familiar.

Too many young stamp collectors just stick their stamps in rows in albums and leave it at that. They are missing the best part of stamp collecting and perhaps this short article on the hobby will help them to get more out of their stamps.

For instance, if you are already a stamp collector do you read your stamp album, just as people read the newspaper

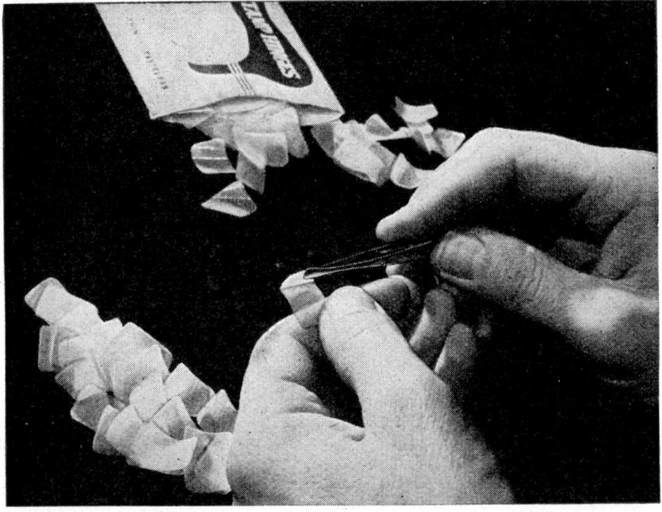

HOW STAMPS ARE MOUNTED (1)

Stamp mounts, or hinges, are indispensable to the collector. The "mount" is gummed on one side, and should be folded back by about one-third of the length, gummed side downwards.

concerned. This type of collection will interest friends who are not yet collectors and may well encourage them to take up this fascinating hobby.

How did it all begin? The first adhesive postage stamps to be used for prepaying letters—that is, to be stuck on before posting — were issued to the public in Great Britain on Wednesday, May 6th, 1840. They were the Penny Black and Twopenny Blue. Up to then anybody wishing to post a letter had to take it to a post office and pay cash over the counter, the amount varying according to the distance the letter had to travel (even if it was addressed to somewhere in Britain) and whether there were one or more sheets of paper. Some letters were handed in without payment

or a book? It is quite possible to do this and it brings your stamps to life in a very vivid way. Keep an eye on the newspapers each day and the chances are you will find a stamp design which fits into the news somewhere. It may be just the portrait of a prominent person, not necessarily a king or president; it may be the picture of a famous building where an important international conference is being held or the view of a town which is in the day's news or a picture of a volcano which has started erupting. There are many ways in which stamps issued before the event can be fitted into the news.

Where the stamps are quite common and it is easy to get a duplicate it is quite a good plan to mount them in a separate book together with the news-cutting

HOW STAMPS ARE MOUNTED (2)

The folded part of the mount should be damped and attached to the back of the stamp so that the fold is level with the top edge (but clear of the perforation) as shown above. The remainder of the gummed side is then damped and by it the stamp can be affixed to the album leaf. As the "fold" acts as a hinge the stamp can be lifted up and examined for watermark, etc., without being removed.

and the postage was collected on delivery.

Very early on, people were keeping the new stamps as curiosities and were using them to decorate plates, vases and other ornaments by sticking them down and then varnishing them over so that they would not peel off.

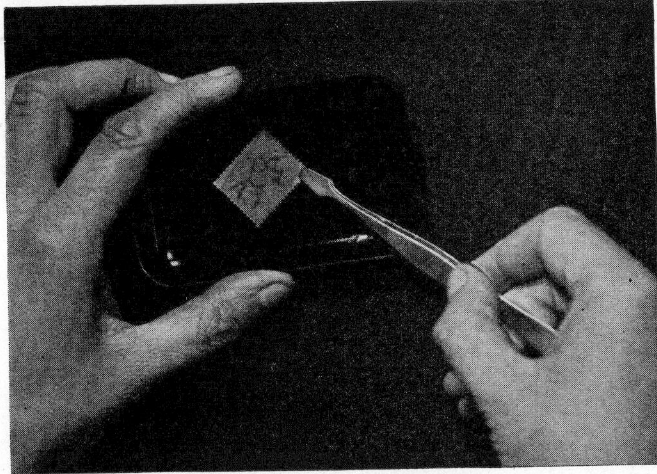

THE WATERMARK DETECTOR

One of philately's problems is to distinguish which watermark is on a particular stamp, where two similar stamps have different watermarks. Here the " Watermark Detector " helps. This is a small black tray on which the stamp is placed face downwards. Dip a small camel-hair brush into benzine, and apply it to the stamp. In most cases the watermark will appear clearly.

As other countries realized how useful the prepayment of letters by stamps could be, so they, too, issued stamps and gradually the idea spread all over the world. It was then that stamp collecting started to become interesting and collectors kept them in albums to show their friends. Stamp hinges had not been thought of and the stamps were stuck down with glue. This was unfortunate because many early stamps were ruined as the glue gradually perished the paper on which the stamps were printed. Another trouble was that stamps were damaged when collectors tried to move them into bigger albums as more and more new stamps came along.

In those early days, non-collectors used to look upon stamp collectors as being peculiar people, but to-day it is generally agreed that the hobby is educative and very worth while. Quite a number of schools encourage collecting and even run stamp clubs of their own.

The time has long since passed when there were scarcely enough stamps to go round. It is very different now, for new stamps are constantly being issued, not merely because they are necessary for postage purposes, but because stamps have become a form of advertisement for the country issuing them and because special sets commemorating important events of the moment or special anniversaries of great events of the past are keenly collected and provide many interesting pages in collections carefully " written-up " to tell the story behind the designs.

With such a great variety of stamps available it is impossible to keep up to date with a general collection of the whole world so most collectors, after a time at least, decide to confine their collections to the stamps of countries in which they have a special interest or whose stamps appeal particularly to them.

Beginning the Collection

However, at the start, every stamp collector should collect everything which comes his way for it is only by doing this that he will come to have that general knowledge about stamp collecting which will stand him in good stead when, a little later, he decides to be more selective. The more advanced collector will find it useful to know how to distinguish different sizes and types of perforation, how to tell various types of paper and methods of printing stamps. He will learn from handling everything which looks like a stamp and find out that some are not postage stamps at all but are labels, poster stamps (sold for charitable objects) and fiscal or revenue stamps. These are not listed in the standard postage stamp catalogues.

Apart from any gifts of stamps that come his way, the beginner is well advised to purchase as large a packet of different stamps as he can afford or a general mounted collection which he can re-arrange to his own liking in a new album. The larger the packet the very much more it will cost because, for example, 5,000 different stamps must include many which are beyond the "penny a time" class. To buy five different packets of 1,000 each may be cheaper, but duplication is bound to occur and much commoner stamps will be in each of the smaller packets.

Choice of an Album

No stamp collector should regard his hobby as a means of making money just because he has heard that stamps increase in value and, therefore, can eventually be sold—should he want to sell—for more than he gave for them. It is possible to build up a collection which will increase in value but only if it contains a number of rare stamps for which there is an increasing demand which forces the price up as the years go by. Far more collectors spend money on stamps which will always be easily obtainable and which increase in value so slowly that it will be a long time before they can be sold at a profit.

It is much better to regard money spent on stamps as money which would have to be paid out for any other form of pleasure, except that in the case of stamps at least part of the outlay can be recovered if required.

There are well over a hundred different stamp albums on the market. They are designed to suit every type of collection and the beginner is apt to be confused by the variety available. For the average collector there are two main types of album, a fast-bound illustrated book and a loose-leaf album with leaves ruled in tiny grey squares to guide the balanced mounting of stamps on the page.

For the younger beginner the fast-bound album is the most suitable. Each page has a printed heading, sometimes for more than one country where few stamps are likely to come the way of the collector. There are usually illustrations of typical stamps and a few notes of geographical and historical interest about each country. The drawback of the cheaper printed albums is that stamps are generally mounted on the front and back of each page and tend to catch one another when the pages are turned. Some of the more expensive albums are interleaved throughout to prevent this. To interleave a fast-bound book not made to take the extra pages is to invite trouble as the binding will break under the strain whenever the book is closed.

For the beginner in his teens, or for the adult beginner, the loose-leaf albums are preferable. The stamps are only mounted on one side of each leaf and the leaves in the less expensive of these albums are nearly always in a spring-back binder which has no mechanism to go wrong. Provided the binders are not over-loaded with extra leaves they last indefinitely. When one volume becomes full it is easy to split the collection into two volumes and let each volume, in turn, develop again into a full volume without disturbing the arrangement of the mounted leaves. The important thing is to buy one of the standard makes of albums so that there is no difficulty in matching the album when another becomes necessary or in purchasing spare leaves whenever wanted.

Most stamp album publishers issue illustrated lists of their products, and it is worth studying these before making a choice.

Other Accessories

Apart from an album, every stamp collector is advised to use the proper stamp hinges for mounting stamps—they only cost about 1*s.* per thousand—because these are made with a special gum which ensures the stamps remaining

EARLY BRITISH EMPIRE STAMPS

1. Newfoundland, 1866, 1c. (King Edward VII. when Prince of Wales). 2. India, 1902, 15 rupees. 3. Canada, 1868, 3c. 4. Malta, 1860, ½*d.* 5. Straits Settlements, 1867, 8c. 6. St. Lucia, 1860, 1*d.* 7. Gibraltar, 1886, ½*d.* 8. Cape of Good Hope, 1864, 2*d.* 9. St. Vincent, 1886, ½*d.* 10. Natal, 1862, 6*d.* 11. New South Wales, 1860, 3*d.* 12. Tasmania, 1870, 10*d.* 13. South Australia, 1902, 6*d.* 14. New Zealand, 1862, 2*d.*

NATIVE RULERS AND PEOPLES

1. Madagascar, 1930, 2c. 2. Mozambique Co., 1918, $\frac{1}{4}$c. 3. Transjordan, 1930, 5m. (H.H. the late Emir Abdullah). 4. Martinique, 1908, 15c. (Creole). 5. Tonga, 1920, 2*d*. (Queen Salote). 6. Kishengarh, 1899, 2 annas (Maharajah Sardul Singh). 7. Cochin, 1918, 10 pies (Maharajah). 8. Congo, 1923, 1·75 franc (Ubangi Man). 9. Somali Coast, 1915, 30c. (Native Woman). 10. Congo, 1923, 1 franc (Native Potter). 11. New Zealand, 1920, $1\frac{1}{2}$*d*. (Maori). 12. Johore, 1925, 3c. (Sultan Ibrahim). 13. U.S.A., 1898, 1c. (North American Indians).

HISTORICAL AND COMMEMORATIVE STAMPS

1. Australia, 2*d*. (Sydney Bridge). 2. Great Britain, 1*d*. (British Empire Exhibition). 3. Chile, 4c. (Fifth Pan-American Congress). 4. India, ½a. (New Delhi). 5. San Marino, 30c. (Exhibition). 6. Eire, 2*d*. (Shannon Barrage). 7. Canada, 3c. (Confederation, 50th Anniversary). 8. Switzerland, 7½c. (Peace Issue). 9. Japan, 10 sen (Crown Prince's Tour). 10. Japan, 3 sen (Imperial Silver Wedding). 11. Australia, 1½*d*. (Parliament House at Canberra). 12. Costa Rica, 20c. (Nicoya Centenary). 13. Australia, 1½*d*. (Sturt Centenary). 14. Canada, 13c. (Ottawa Conference).

in their places but at the same time permits the hinge to be peeled easily from the album page and the stamps without damaging either. Stamp hinges, too, are made on specially thin paper in order to prevent the bulging of the covers which would happen if thicker paper such as stamp edging or brown gummed tape were used.

The method of applying the hinges to the stamps is important. Place the stamp face downwards on a firm level surface. Fold the hinge so that about one-third of the gummed side is turned back. Moisten this very slightly and press it gently on to the stamp with the crease level with the top of the stamp and just below, and clear of, the perforations. Now moisten the longer remaining portion of the hinge and press the stamp gently into its place on the album leaf. If a mistake in placing has been made do not attempt to remove the stamp from the leaf until the hinge has had time to dry, as the surface of the leaf or the back of the stamp may become damaged.

Every collector should use tweezers for handling stamps. With very little practice it will be found that it is easier to pick up stamps with tweezers than with fingers, and it is much better for the stamps. However clean the fingers, they must transfer tiny spots of moisture to the stamps which then more easily collect dirt, and it cannot be too strongly stated that dirty stamps are worth a lot less than the same stamps in a clean condition. A good pair of stamp tweezers only cost 2*s.* 6*d.* at the most.

Another requirement in the fairly early stages is a perforation gauge. The majority of stamps are issued with perforations and it frequently happens that a change in the gauge of the perforation distinguishes a scarce, short-lived printing from an otherwise identical stamp with a different perforation. The gauge has on it a series of small dots or lines (sometimes both) arranged so that a given number occupy a distance of 2 centimetres. A stamp, on which the perforation holes exactly fit the row of dots spaced, for instance, fourteen to the 2 centimetres, is stated to be perf. 14. Most gauges are made with spacings ranging from about perf. 7 to perf. 18. Some stamps are perforated one gauge along the top and bottom and another along the sides. Taking the top first and a side next, the stamp is classified, for example, as perf. 14 × 15. More rarely, stamps have different perforations on three or even four sides.

Another useful accessory is the watermark detector. This consists of a black glazed tile with raised edges, or a shallow dish of some black composition in which the stamp to be examined is placed face downwards. The watermark, which is really a thinning in the paper, will usually show up (in reverse because it is put in the paper to be read from the front of the stamp) against the detector without any other help. If, however, the paper is thick a drop or two of benzine will make it semi-transparent and the watermark will show. Benzine can be applied without harm to mint or used stamps, but care must be taken to keep it away from a naked light. As with perforations, the watermark frequently determines the value of a stamp where there are two stamps otherwise alike, one quite common and the other rare.

Stamp Catalogues

Another necessity is a stamp catalogue. There are several published in Great Britain and elsewhere and with them the collector can arrange stamps in their proper order by denominations and sets.

Some of the catalogues are "simplified." This means that no differences of perforation, watermark or shade are listed nor are there any details of varieties of overprint. Such a catalogue is ideal for the beginner.

More detailed catalogues in which all the varieties of perforation, watermark, shade and overprint are listed are indispensable at a later stage. In Britain, the standard work of this kind is the Stanley

PICTORIAL STAMPS

1. S. Rhodesia, 2*d*. (Victoria Falls). 2. Japan, 2 sen (Fuji Mountain). 3. Papua, 4*d*. (" Lakatoi "). 4. Canada, 12c. (Quebec). 5. China, 13c. (Labourer). 6. Liberia, $1 (Steamer and Coast with Surf). 7. France, 10 francs (Port of La Rochelle). 8. Egypt, 1m. (Boats on Nile). 9. Montserrat, $1\frac{1}{2}$*d*. (View of Island). 10. Barbados, 1*d*. (" The Olive Blossom "). 11. Rarotonga, 4*d*. (The Harbour). 12. Iraq, 3 annas (Ruins of Ctesiphon). 13. U.S.A., 1893, 2c. (Landing of Columbus). 14. U.S.A., 1920, 1c. (" The Mayflower "). 15. Jamaica, 1900, 1*d*. (Llandovery Falls).

A MAP THEME

1. Costa Rica, 1924, 5c. 2. Paraguay, 1924, 1 peso. 3. Cyprus, 1928, $1\frac{1}{2}$ piastres, 4. Mexico, 1917, 40c. 5. Colombia, 1892, 1c. 6. Dominican Republic (and Haiti), 1900, 1c. 7. New Zealand, 1923, 1*d*. 8. Canada, 1898, 2c. (British Empire). 9. Eire, 1922, 2*d*. 10. Canada, 1927, 12c. 11. Mexico, 1926, 10c. (N. and C. and S. America). 12. Estonia, 1923, 100 marks.

ZOOLOGICAL STAMPS

1. Australia, 1½*d.* (The Black Swan of Western Australia). 2. Sudan, 1 mil. (Camel and Postman). 3. U.S.A., 4c. (Hunting the Bison). 4. Malay, 6c. (Tiger). 5. Paraguay, 5c. (Lion). 6. N. Rhodesia, 1½*d.* (Giraffe and Elephants). 7. Ethiopia, 8 guerche (Rhinoceros). 8. Australia, 6*d.* (Kangaroo). 9. Australia, 3*d.* (Kookaburra). 10. New Zealand, 6*d.* (Kiwi). 11. Peru, 10c. (Llamas). 12. North Borneo, 12c. (Crocodile). 13. South Africa, 1*s.* (Gnus). 14. Liberia, 75c. (Hippopotamus).

Gibbons stamp catalogue published in three volumes: British Empire; Europe (with colonies of European powers); Asia, Africa and the Americas.

All catalogues are basically the price lists of the firms which publish them and are not necessarily useful for the valuation of stamps, although some general idea of value can be obtained from the prices given.

Selective Collecting

Now that so many stamps have been issued since 1840, and so many more are being issued every month, it is impossible for any collector to keep up to date with a whole world collection. Since every collector likes to be as complete as possible, most decide, after a time, to confine the collection to some chosen countries or a group such as the West Indian colonies.

Collecting like this means that each country in the collection will be more complete than would be possible with a world collection, but it does not mean that the collector is "specialising." One advantage of this form of collecting is that it is possible to take a greater interest in the countries represented in the collection quite apart from the stamps they issue. It is possible to correspond with other collectors in those countries and to learn a great deal more about them.

The advanced philatelic specialist goes much deeper into the study of individual stamps of a single country. For instance, there are many common stamps of Australia and South Africa which to the non-collector look alike but which to the specialist are quite different from one another. Very tiny differences tell the specialist from which of the many printings made of a long-lived common stamp each individual specimen comes. Little flaws in the design enable him to say from where on the original sheet each stamp has come. The same kind of study applied to the English Penny Black enables the specialist to say which of the eleven printing plates used to produce these stamps was used for any particular stamp in the collection.

Thematic Collecting

For those who prefer not to attempt a general collection and feel that selective or specialised collecting is beyond them there is another alternative. Instead of regarding stamps as specimens coming from, say, France, Belgium, Canada or anywhere else, they arrange them according to the picture in the design.

Known as thematic collecting, it means that all stamps with ships are grouped together, or those with flowers, aeroplanes, animals, volcanoes, national costumes, churches and cathedrals all over the world, produce and industries, railway engines and an endless variety of other subjects.

The important thing in thematic collecting is to arrange them in a way which tells a story or teaches the collector something about the subject, or theme, of the collection.

This means that a collection of animal stamps would group all the members of one animal family, such as the gorillas, monkeys and baboons, together, with a note on the countries from which they come and how they differ from one another. Similarly, a thematic collection of birds could show how related species are scattered all over the world.

Naturally, collections like these must be mounted in a loose-leaf album and they give the collector plenty of scope for originality in arrangement and "writing-up."

Interesting Cancellations

Quite apart from the stamps themselves, there is a great deal of interest in the postmarks or cancellations. In a number of cases the stamp itself is worth very little but because of an unusual cancellation it is worth very much more.

Normally, of course, a cancellation merely gives the name of the town at which the letter bearing the stamp was posted. Sometimes that town may be

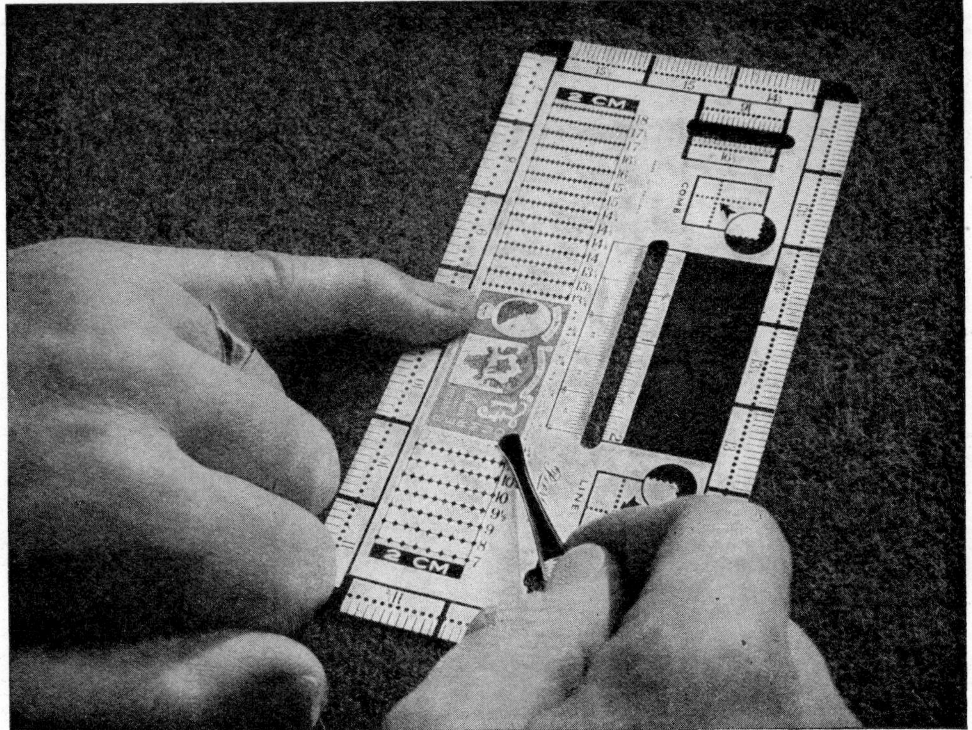

THE PERFORATION GAUGE

A very necessary portion of a collector's equipment is the "Perforation Gauge," as differences in perforation often determine to what particular issue a stamp belongs and its value. For instance, the first issue of the Gold Coast may have either 12½ or 14 perforations in a width of 2 centimetres. The method is to fit the perforations of the stamp to the little round dots, as shown in the picture. Upon this "gauge" gradations from 7 to 18 perforations to 2 centimetres are shown.

in a country other than that which issued the stamp. Where such use of a stamp has been officially authorised the stamp is said to have been "used abroad." This happened to many Victorian stamps of Great Britain. Several of the colonies did not at first have their own post office systems or their own stamps, and so agencies of the British Post Office were set up to deal with letters which were franked with ordinary British stamps. In each instance these colonial post office branches were supplied with specially numbered postmarking dies which collectors can identify. Some British stamps used abroad in this way are very rare indeed although the stamps themselves are quite common. Among the better-known examples are British stamps used in Malta and Gibraltar, where the numbers A25 and A26, respectively, cancelled the stamps.

In the same way, the stamps of Hong Kong were used in several Chinese ports where Britain had trading rights and operated a post for the benefit of the British merchants with businesses in them. Again, specially numbered cancellations were used.

There are other special services, such as travelling post offices on trains. Letters sorted on these trains have the stamps cancelled with special marks indicating which train they were carried by. Similarly, letters posted on board ships bear special cancellations. These are particularly interesting because the stamps are normally those of the nationality of the ship but the cancellations are those of the first port of call. In this way a British stamp may have a South African cancellation, or a French

STAMPS ON STAMPS

Courtesy H E. Wingfield & Co., London.

To commemorate the various anniversaries of their first issues of stamps, or special philatelic exhibitions, many countries have issued stamps reproducing early designs. Here are some of them from South Africa, Sudan, Barbados, Mexico, Liberia, Spain, Egypt, Mozambique, Bermuda, Germany, Mauritius, Australia and Pakistan.

Stamps provide a picture gallery of life in the colonies. Old forts, government buildings, native races and their ways of living are all illustrated in miniature on colonial issues. The selection shown here represents only a fraction of the interesting pictorial stamps available to all collectors. Many of them are nowadays printed in two or more colours and make a very attractive show in any stamp album.

NATURAL RESOURCES OF THE COMMONWEALTH

Courtesy H. E. Wingfield & Co., London.

Stamps depicting examples of the natural wealth of the British Commonwealth as follows: Oil (Canada), Tea (Ceylon), Wood Pulp for paper making (Canada), Cotton (Nyasaland), Coarse Flax for rope making (St. Helena), Turtles—for soup! (Cayman Islands), Limes (Dominica), Bananas (Jamaica), Cocoa (Gold Coast), Whales (Falkland Islands), Tobacco (Nyasaland), Butter (New Zealand), Tin Ore (Nigeria), Sugar (Mauritius) and Timber (Nigeria).

AUSTRALIA ON STAMPS

Courtesy H. E. Wingfield & Co., London.

Australian history, animal life and industries are well illustrated by stamp designs. *Top row:* Commemorative stamps for founding of New South Wales, Victoria and South Australia. *Second, third and fourth rows:* Some of the explorers who opened the country up, with native animals they found. *Fourth (centre) and fifth rows:* Industries of the country. *Sixth row:* King George V. (then Duke of York) opening the first Federal Parliament in 1901 ; Sir Edmund Barton and Sir Henry Parkes ; Federal Parliament House, Canberra.

STAMPS OF NEW ZEALAND

1. The " John Wickliffe and Philip Laing " (1848), 1*d*. 2. First Church, Dunedin, 3*d*. 3. Cromwell, Otago, 2*d*. 4. Tui or Parson Bird, 1*s*. 5. University of Otago, 6*d*. 6. Kea and Kaka, 1*s*. 7. Mount Cook, 2½*d*. 8, Tuatara Lizard, 8*d*. 9. Swordfish, 5*d*. 10. Lake Matheson, ½*d*. 11. Kiwi, 1*d*. 12. Mount Egmont, 3*s*. 13 and 14. Peace Issues, 6*d*. and 3*d*.

STAMPS OF THE SECOND WORLD WAR

Plate by courtesy of Messrs. Stanley Gibbons Ltd., Strand, London, W.C.2

1. Russia, 1943, 3r. 2. U.S.A., 1942, 3c. 3. Russia, 1943, 30k. 4. St. Pierre and Miquelon, 1942, 25c. 5. Polish Post Abroad, 1943, 1z. 50g. 6. Australia, 1940, 2*d*. 7. South Africa, 1941–42, 1*s*. (normal and "war economy" size). 8. Bulgaria, 1940, 2l. 9. U.S.A., 1943, 5c. 10. Norwegian Post Abroad, 1943, 20 ore. 11. Curaçao, 1941, 35c. 12. Canada, 1942, 20c. 13. Middle East Forces, 1942, 5*d*. 14. Netherlands Post Abroad, 1944, 3c.

stamp have an American one, and so on.

There are also slogan cancellations of many countries, some of them including little pictures in black and white. The slogan may advertise an exhibition, urge people to save more, advise them on road safety, ask them to keep their wireless sets quiet so as not to annoy the neighbours, seek support for a national charity, tempt tourists to visit the country or just wish them a Merry Christmas! The proper way to collect slogans postmarks is to cut the envelope to include the slogan, the circular town mark (which goes with it as a rule) and the stamp itself. Slogans can only be used at post offices where machines are used for cancelling stamps, and this means they occur on ordinary letters which bear common stamps.

All this will show that stamp collecting is much more than just " sticking little bits of coloured paper in rows on an album leaf " and helps to explain why millions of people throughout the world find entertainment and instruction in the thoughtful collection of these little labels which have so greatly helped to bring together the nations of the world. One of the greatest international organisations is the Universal Postal Union established in Berne, Switzerland, in 1874. Through it, the nations of the world have agreed to handle each other's letters. There is no finer example of international co-operation and it was all brought about by the postage stamp, which practically forced open the frontiers. No wonder it is thrilling taking part, as a stamp collector, in such a venture.

CURIOUS STAMPS

1. Mafeking, 1900, 3*d.* (portrait of General Baden-Powell). 2. Cape of Good Hope, 1853, 1*d.* (triangular). 3. Uganda, 1896, 4 annas (printed by the Missionaries at Usoga). 4. Jhind, 1882, 8a. Native issue. 5. Bamra, 1888. Native type set stamp. 6. Great Britain, 1870, $\frac{1}{2}$*d.* (" the little $\frac{1}{2}$*d.*"). 7. British Guiana, 1882, provisional 2c. (These stamps were perforated across with the word " SPECIMEN " to prevent fraud.) 8. Afghanistan, 1898, 2 abasi. 9. Kashmir, 1878, 2 annas.

Favourite Hobbies: Pastimes at Home and Out of Doors

Collections: How to Begin —and Afterwards

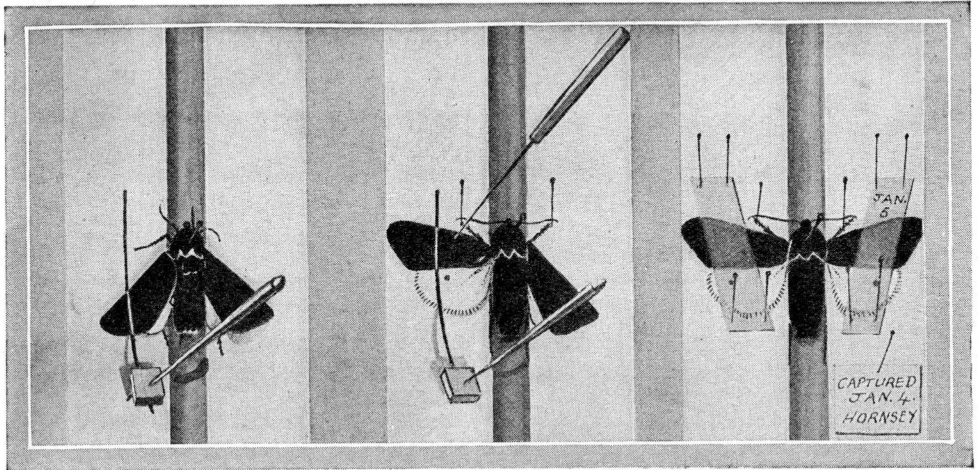

Photos and drawings specially prepared for this work by Bayne and Aris.

SETTING A SPECIMEN

In this picture we are shown how to set a butterfly or moth. This is the needle and bristle method and, beginning at the left of the picture, we see the three steps in this simple little operation, as described on p. 328.

BUTTERFLIES AND MOTHS

THE collecting of butterflies and moths has the advantage of being very inexpensive—except in personal effort, since one usually does not *buy* for one's collection—and of being done mostly in the open air.

A Full-time Hobby

The catching of the nimbler varieties of butterflies entails a good deal of healthy and strenuous exercise, as any seasoned collector will agree. Between them, during the warmer months of the year, butterflies and moths offer plenty of scope for devoting time to the pursuit of them; since one may hunt butterflies all day in suitable weather and, when dusk falls, transfer one's attention to moths, which get up about the time when butterflies go to bed—most of them, that is to say. During the summer holidays the enthusiastic entomologist —to give the collector of insects his rather formidable scientific title—will find plenty of work for his waking hours, however long they be.

Leaving the great rarities, such as the Purple Emperor, Camberwell Beauty and Swallowtail, out of account, anyone who perseveres can make a fairly complete collection of British butterflies, the species of which are not very numerous. They include, however, many beautiful insects—who could deny the adjective to the Purple Hairstreak, Orange Tip, Clouded Yellow, Red Admiral, Peacock, the Fritillaries, and the Blues, for example?—and, when assembled in the store-box or cabinet, make a fine display of colour.

What moths lack in the matter of

brilliant hues they more than atone for in variety, since British species number over 2,000. Not but what some of them—one thinks at once of the Tiger Moths, Burnets, and Underwings—are gay enough, and a great many very beautifully marked. No collector can expect to get together a complete collection of this order of insect ; but by way of consolation the field is so large that there are always species still to be captured.

CATERPILLARS AND PUPÆ.—Collecting does not necessarily begin with the capture of the insect, which, after all, is in the third of the three stages of its existence. For the collector will always have an eye wide open for caterpillars, which may be caged and fed till they turn into pupæ or chrysalises; and for chrysalises also. If things go right, a chrysalis will in due course present its finder with a perfect insect, and repay him for any trouble taken in the getting and keeping of it.

The Collector's Equipment

First, of course, we put the *net*, which should be shaped like a round-ended sack, and *not* like a jelly-bag, so that a " catch " may not be able to tuck itself away into a corner. The net can be made at home easily enough, out of a square yard of black gauze doubled and sewn up one of the long edges. One end is then rounded off to an arc of a circle, and stitched, while the other is hemmed firmly to a band of linen, doubled so as to form a tube for the ring of cane which keeps the mouth open. As for the ring itself, if a small extra expense can be faced, there is much to be said in favour of one subdivided into three pieces which fold or can be taken apart for packing into a small space.

MOTHS TO TAKE BY ASSEMBLING

This photograph shows three species of moth, the males of which can be taken by " assembling." The females are on the left and the males on the right. At the top is the Oak Eggar Moth, in the middle the Common Tiger Moth, and at the bottom the Black Arches Moth. From the collection of Ernest Aris, F.Z.S.

Butterflies used to be killed by pinching their bodies sideways, but this is a very crude method and almost invariably damages the specimen. For moths a *killing bottle* has always been necessary, and it is best that butterflies should be dealt with in this way also. The killing bottle had better be bought from a dealer. A supply of *glass-bottomed boxes* of different size which " nest " into one another should be taken on an expedition for holding live specimens which later on, after examination, may prove not to be wanted. Then, one must carry a cork-bottomed *collecting box* in which to place killed insects after they have been "pinned," and in order that they may be pinned one must have with one a stock of special entomological *pins* of various sizes, coated with black enamel to prevent corrosion. The collecting box is lined with cork. This cork should be kept damp in order to prevent the insects from becoming stiff before the collector is ready to set them.

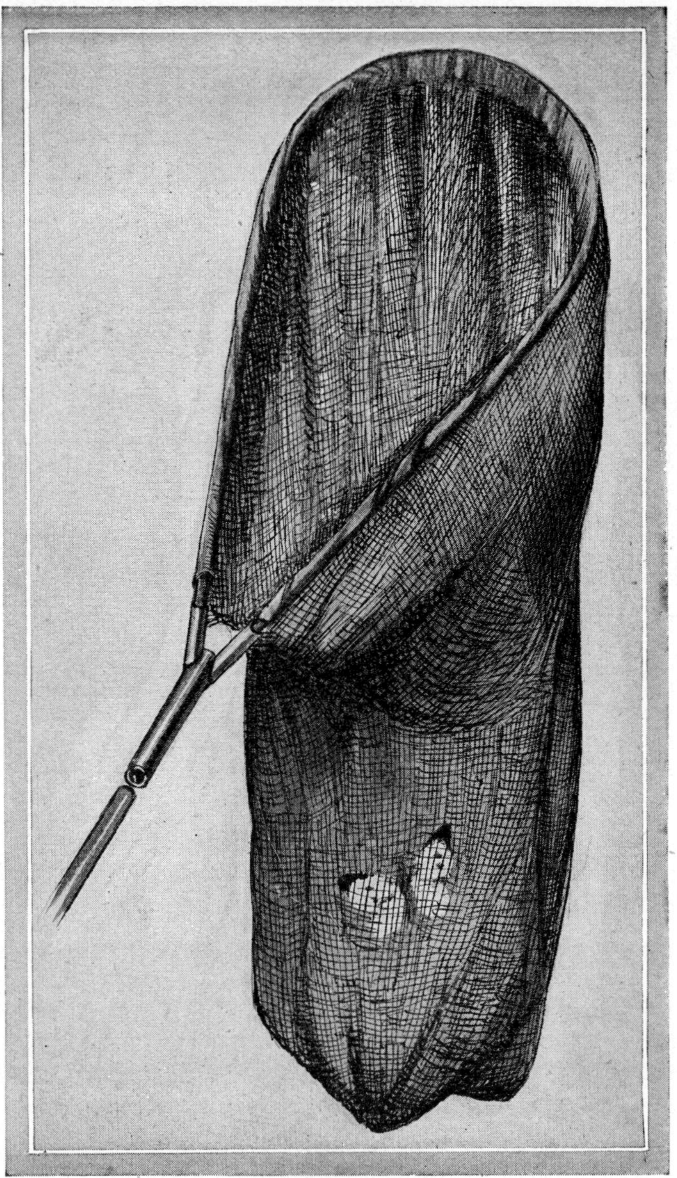

THE NET

The above illustration shows the construction of the net. A four-jointed cane is passed through the linen tube at the mouth of the net and its ends are inserted in the two arms of the Y-piece which is made of metal tubing. The handle is thrust into the base of the Y. Black gauze is best for the net, as it shows the captured insect clearly.

To hold all the items (except the net) named above—and perhaps some food as well—the list must include a *haversack*, preferably one with a strap of a wide webbing, which will not gall the shoulder.

So much for the field equipment. There remain the articles needed for dealing with the insects brought home. The most important of these is a series of *setting boards*, either flat or round topped, with a central groove for the insect's body. Several sizes will be needed. The best are of cork mounted on a wooden base, which has extended ends to slide into grooves of a setting case like shelves. The handy boy can easily make a setting case for himself. It stands upright like a cupboard, and should have a closely fitting door, in which there may be an opening covered with wire gauze. The equivalent of grooves may be made by nailing to the sides pairs of slips $\frac{3}{16}$ inch thick, set the proper distance apart. It need hardly be said that all the setting boards to go into a case must be of the

THE KILLING BOTTLE

This is an important item in the butterfly collector's equipment, and the best plan is to buy one from the naturalist's shop. The one seen above contains a small quantity of cyanide of potassium covered with a layer of plaster of Paris which allows the fumes to come through and asphyxiate the insect. There are other types which have become increasingly popular in recent years.

same length. A setting case is a most useful thing, as it prevents insects being damaged while on the boards.

Store Boxes

These are for housing the collection in, and their number must, of course, increase with the size of the collection. They can be made cheaply out of soap or similar boxes, a number of which of the same kind and size should be obtained, if possible, at one time, to make sure of their matching. Choose only those in good condition, and as well made as such things are. Soak off any adhering paper and fix the lids on firmly with fine brads. Then round off all corners with sandpaper, to present as neat an appearance as possible.

A mark is now run round the box exactly half-way between top and bottom with a gauge. The box is then slit very carefully along the line with a fine tenon saw. The raw edges of the halves are now smoothed down, and the inside of what were the top and bottom lined with sheet cork—or better still, cork lino, if odd pieces can be got from an upholsterer—firmly glued down. Next, thin slips are glued on the inside of one half all round, reaching from the bottom to $\frac{3}{8}$ or $\frac{1}{2}$ inch above the top, to make a lip round which the other half will fit snugly, and will be prevented from getting "out of register," while the box is rendered more or less dust-proof. The projecting edges are bevelled off slightly towards the inside to assist closing.

The last touches are to line the box inside with white paper, stain it or cover it with binding "cloth" outside, and fit hinges on one half, and hooks on the other. Of course, one cannot expect to turn out of such rough materials boxes which will compete in appearance with those sold by dealers: so before starting manufacture the collector might well consult a good catalogue and then decide whether to make or buy.

While on the subject of store-boxes, reference should be made to the importance of pinning into every one of them a piece of naphthalene, encased in paper well perforated with pinholes, to keep at bay the mites which attack set specimens if given the chance.

THE PILL BOX

Glass-topped pill boxes in various sizes are specially made for collectors of insects. They are useful when a collector wishes to examine a captive before deciding to kill it or let it go, or when he intends to take an insect home alive for breeding.

Hunting and Catching

The catching of butterflies is largely a matter of luck, the proper district for local varieties, fine weather, agility and dexterity. To capture moths on the wing in darkness is obviously impossible. So the collector has recourse to the fatal attraction that light and "treacle" have for these insects. A strong light near an open window will bring in many moths when the weather conditions are right, and one can have quite good sport on occasions round the street lamps of a town. Then there are illuminated moth-traps, to which entry is easy while escape from them is difficult, for setting up in selected places.

Also, one may take with one a net and a strong acetylene bicycle lamp and beat hedges. The insects "put up," as a sportsman would say, may often be netted while flying in the beam thrown by the lamp.

Another method is called "assembling." This is the best method for taking Oak Eggar, Tiger and Black Arches moths. A young female is enclosed in a lidless box, which is then covered with gauze and hung up on a branch or placed on a tree stump. The scent of the imprisoned moth will soon attract males of her own species from all quarters, and they can be caught as they flutter round the cage.

But the surest method of capturing many varieties is "sugaring" with a mixture of treacle and rum. Some collectors add a few drops of pear essence. Selecting a calm and warm evening, one smears the treacle with a

THE COLLECTING TIN

This is a tin box lined with cork. In it should always be carried a supply of assorted pins to suit various sizes of insect. The collector should be careful to keep the cork damp, otherwise his specimens will become rigid before he reaches home and he will then have all the trouble of relaxing them.

brush on the trunks and any easily reached branches of trees. The scent of the treacle attracts the moths as surely as the nectar of flowers, and the rum renders them—well, "incapable," so that they are easily boxed or transferred from their feast to the killing bottle. The light taken on one's rounds of inspection should be rather weak to avoid scaring the insects.

CABINET DRAWER, STORE-BOX AND SETTING BOARD
On the left is a drawer from a cabinet with various species of butterfly belonging to one family, set out in series. On the right is a store-box, which is so made that the insects can be displayed both above and below. The object in front is a setting board.

Blossoming shrubs are good hunting grounds when moths are in search of an evening meal and the light just suffices to betray them. Pay special attention to lavender, pinks, irises, tobacco plants, phloxes, sweet williams and laurustinus.

WHERE THE COLLECTION IS KEPT
This is an upright cabinet containing a number of shallow, glass-covered drawers. These drawers are very carefully fitted into grooves.

On Setting Moths and Butterflies

The "pinning" of an insect should be done carefully, through the centre of the thorax, the pin sloping slightly forward. The point should project sufficiently to allow the insect to clear the surface of the store-box easily when the pin is stuck well into the cork.

For setting, one needs a number of strips of paper, $\frac{1}{4}$ inch wide ; and small triangles of thin card, each transfixed by a pin at the centre. A setting needle made by inserting the eye end of a large sewing needle into a wooden handle must also be provided.

We will assume that a butterfly has been placed on the setting board, its body well down in the groove. The wings are parted carefully, and one pair pressed against the board. The front wing is then drawn into position—its most forward point well in front of the head—with the needle and clipped in position by a triangle, the pin of

BEATING THE SALLOWS

When the sallows are in bloom many moths of various species resort to them after dark to sip the nectar of their flowers. This juice is intoxicating and consequently when the branches are suddenly shaken or beaten with a stick the insects drop to the ground. If, therefore, the collector spreads a large white sheet under the tree before beating it he will have no difficulty in finding the moths with the aid of his lamp. The sallow is the " Goat Willow " tree.

ASSEMBLING AND LIGHT

A newly-hatched female is placed in a lidless box, which is then covered with gauze. It is now taken to a locality in which its species is found and the cage is hung on a bough or placed on a tree stump. The males, attracted by the scent of the decoy, assemble in numbers and are netted as they come.

In a woodland glade a sheet is hung up between two trees and illuminated by the light of an acetylene bicycle lamp. The moths are attracted by the light and settle on the sheet. They can be either caught with the net as they fly about in the dazzling rays of the lamp or taken from the sheet in a killing bottle or a pill box.

"SUGARING" FOR MOTHS

About half an hour before dusk the collector walks through the wood with treacle pot and brush and paints a patch on the trunk of a tree here and there along the rides. He then retires until darkness falls in order to give the moths time to sip enough of his bait to make them drowsy. When he revisits the sugared trees it is easy for him to select specimens from among the feasting insects and to take them in killing bottle or pill box.

which is tilted slightly to press a corner of the card against the wing. The rear wing is then treated in like manner, its front edge being of course arranged under the rear of the front wing. Finally, a paper strip is laid across the outer edges of both wings and pinned down firmly at the ends. The triangles can then be removed, and the process repeated with the other pair of wings. Each antenna should now be fixed in its natural position by means of pins.

The last, and by no means least important, operation is to pin opposite the insect a scrap of paper bearing dates of capture and of setting. For without this reminder it is easy to forget, and so remove the insect too soon; with the result that the wings may not have stiffened properly, so that they move backwards, spoiling the appearance of the insect and making re-setting necessary. The young collector should cultivate patience and allow at least a fortnight for small insects, and longer periods for the large. One specimen of each species of butterfly should be set *upside down*, to show the under markings.

Another Method

Another method of setting is shown in the picture on p. 281. In the first place the insect already pinned is taken from the collecting tin and placed in the groove of the setting board with wings lightly touching the surface of the board. The setting needle is then stuck in the board below it with the bristle resting on the wings as shown. Next the legs and antennæ should be set. Then the point of another needle should be inserted under a vein of the fore wing. By this means the wing can be swung up into the desired position without danger of being torn. The pressure of the bristle will hold it there. The hind wing should then be treated in a similar manner.

A piece of transparent paper should be placed over the two wings and pinned down securely. When this has been done, the bristle should be withdrawn and the wings on the other side dealt with similarly.

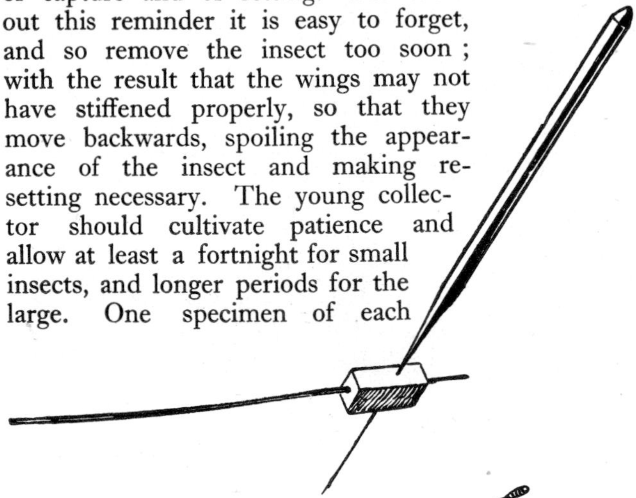

THE SETTING NEEDLE

This consists of a piece of cork, a bristle and a needle. The cork is cut to form a cube. The bristle is then passed through it lengthwise and it is pierced from side to side by a needle. By this means the bristle can be kept in position across the wings of the insect by being pinned firmly to the board.

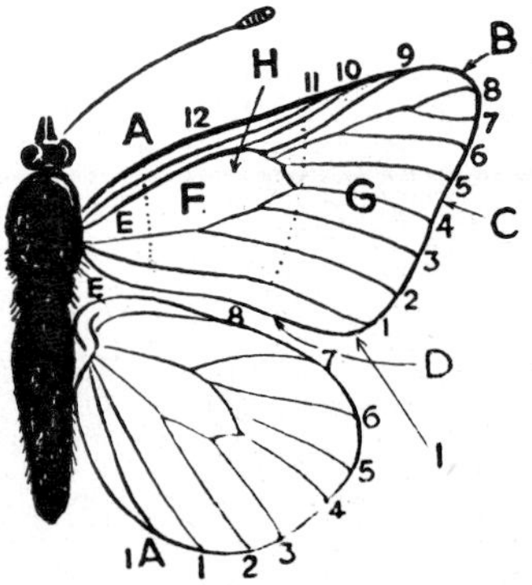

WING VENATION OF A BUTTERFLY

When setting the wings of butterfly or moth, the point of the needle should be put under one of the veins. The above diagram shows the various parts of the wings, as follows: A cortal margin, B apex, C outer margin, D inner margin, E base, F central shade, G outer shade, H discal cell, I inner angle, 1A internal vein, 1 submedian vein, 2, 3, 4 median veins, 5 lower radial, 6 upper radial, 7, 8, 9, 10, 11 subcortal veins, 12 cortal nerve or vein.

Relaxing

Any dead insects that have become stiff must be relaxed or softened before they are set. They should be stuck on a piece of cork, and placed in an airtight jar or tin containing a layer of damp sand. A few drops of carbolic acid on the sand will prevent mildew.

BRITISH BUTTERFLIES—Plate 1

Specially painted for this work.

All the butterflies shown on this and the following Plate are to be found within the British Isles. When sex is given it indicates that male and female are of different colouring: 1. Peacock. 2. Common Blue, m. 3. Red Admiral. 4. Small Copper. 5. The Swallowtail. 6. Orange Tip, m. 7. The Brimstone, m. 8. Marbled White. 9. Clouded Yellow, m. 10. Small Heath. 11. Painted Lady. 12. Large White, f. 13. Small Tortoiseshell.

BRITISH BUTTERFLIES—Plate 2

Specially painted for this work.

The numbered lists given on this and the previous Plate will enable you to identify the different species: 14. Brown Hairstreak, f. 15. Purple Emperor, m. 16. Purple Hairstreak, m. 17. Chalk Hill Blue, m. 18. Adonis Blue, m. 19. Pale Clouded Yellow, m. 20. Large Tortoiseshell, f. 21. Holly Blue, f. 22. Meadow Brown, m. 23. The Grayling, f. 24. Wall Butterfly, m. 25. Speckled Wood, f 26. The Comma, m. 27. High Brown Fritillary, m.

BRITISH MOTHS—Plate 1

Specially painted for this work

In the picture above are illustrated eighteen of our most common moths. 1. The Brimstone. 2. The Garden Tiger. 3. The Magpie. 4. The Plantain Tiger. 5. The Red Underwing. 6. The Cinnabar. 7. The Buff Ermine. 8. The Garden Carpet. 9. The Peach Blossom. 10. The White Ermine. 11. The Emperor, f. 12. The Dot. 13. The Burnished Brass. 14. The Cream-spot Tiger. 15. The Buff-tip, f. 16. The Angle Shades. 17. The Yellow Underwing. 18. The Humming-bird Hawk Moth.

BRITISH MOTHS—Plate 2

Specially painted for this work.

In this Plate a further fourteen British moths are seen. When sex is given it indicates that there is a difference in the colouring of male and female: 19. Death's Head Hawk Moth, m. 20. Red Twin-spot Carpet, f. 21. The Purple Bar, f. 22. Green Silver Lines, m. 23. Scarce Silver Lines, m. 24. Privet Hawk, f. 25. Purple Thorn, f. 26. Ruby Tiger, m. 27. Black Arches, m. 28. Eyed Hawk, f. 29. Alder Moth, f. 30. Scarlet Tiger, f. 31. Oak Beauty, f. 32. Large Thorn, f.

Central Press.

A FAMOUS ACTING SCHOOL

Many of our finest actors and actresses have started their careers with training at the Royal Academy of Dramatic Art in London. The Academy had its beginnings in the school founded by Sir Herbert Beerbohm Tree at His Majesty's Theatre. The picture shows senior students acting in a costume play.

THE PLAY'S THE THING

DO you like dressing-up and pretending that you are someone else? A knight in shining armour, perhaps, or a fairy-tale princess? At some time in our lives most of us enjoy this kind of "make-believe." It begins when we are very young, when we borrow old clothes from Father or Mother and invent our own stories and incidents to act. Later, at school, we may have the chance of acting in real plays, perhaps with the proper costumes, make-up, and something more like an actual stage than the room we play in at home. Amateur dramatics can be great fun, if you are prepared to put your heart into it. Although you will need both skill and luck to make a successful career on the professional stage, you can, like thousands of others who have neither the ability nor the wish to enter the acting profession, enjoy the thrills and pleasures of the stage by joining a local drama group or dramatic society.

There have been plays and theatres in one form or another for hundreds of years. Indeed, it is said that the great characters of Chinese drama date back to the eighteenth century before Christ. In ancient Greece, the poet Thespis, who lived in the sixth century B.C., was probably the founder of Greek drama. He is supposed to have been the first to employ "actors" to speak the *rhapsodes* or recitations at popular festivals; which is why actors and actresses to-day are sometimes referred to as "Thespians." In Roman Italy, the drama also played its part in local festivals and in its early form had a religious significance. The Etruscan performers, who were brought to Rome about 364 B.C., were at first only dancers and mimers performing in honour of the gods, but the name of *istriones* which was given to them has come down to us as the adjective "histrionic," meaning "relating to the stage, or to actors." Thus the art of acting is sometimes called "the histrionic art." But although Rome had her own popular players, her more serious drama had its origins in Greece.

Early Plays in Britain

Roman Britain had its theatrical entertainments. At Verulamium, which we now know as St. Albans, the remains of a fine third century theatre were discovered during excavations at this famous Roman centre, while Roman relics at Caerleon, on the river Usk, include traces of a large amphitheatre. But when the Romans left, the theatres became forgotten and acting did not become popular again until about the tenth century, when the Church found that the acting of stories from the Bible was a good way of teaching ordinary people the wonderful Christian message. The early "performances" took place in the churches and cathedrals, with the priests themselves as the "actors." Later, the *mystery-plays* and *miracle-plays* were performed in the market-squares and on the village greens, and often outside the church itself. Such plays were popular throughout western Europe during the Middle Ages, and came to be played by members of the trade guilds, especially at such times as the feast of Corpus Christi.

A stage would be built on the village green or outside the church. Unlike our modern stages, it consisted of three tiers. The uppermost tier represented Heaven; the lowest, Hell; and in between was Earth. Each guild often had its own special play. Can you guess who usually acted the story of Noah and the Ark?

Fox Photos.

THE THEATRE OF A ROMAN CITY IN BRITAIN

The theatre is a very old form of entertainment. Chinese drama is said to date back many centuries before Christ, and both Greeks and Romans had their theatres. At the Roman city of Verulamium, the modern St. Albans, you can see these excavated remains of a Roman theatre. Can you guess where the audience sat and where the stage was?

The Mansell Collection.

THE GLOBE THEATRE

The Globe Theatre, famous for its association with Shakespeare and his immortal plays, was built about the year 1598 by James Burbage and his brother. It stood in Bankside, Southwark, near a similar building which was used for " beere baytine " (bear baiting), which is seen in the background of this picture.

Naturally it was the guild of Fishermen and Sailors.

The early actors and audiences liked plenty of realism, and used both scenery and " effects." At Coventry, for example, smoke and flame were a necessary stage effect for the lowest of the three tiers, and a man was paid fourpence " for keeping fyer at Hell's mouth." Sometimes ropes and pulleys were used to permit angels to descend from " Heaven " to " Earth " and re-ascend. Trapdoors allowed Satan and his demons to appear or vanish quickly, which was sometimes a rather dangerous feat. At one performance of a French mystery-play in 1496 " he who took the part of Satan, as he was about to ascend from his below-stage trap, had his clothes catch fire so that he got badly burned; but he was speedily dragged out, stripped and re-clothed, and so was enabled, without any show of disturbance, to proceed with his role."

Among the many places noted for their plays were Chester, York and Coventry. In Cornwall, miracle-plays were often performed in specially-built open-air amphitheatres. The amphitheatre at St. Just, not far from Penzance, was restored some years ago.

In Shakespeare's Day

The miracle-plays were acted by guildsmen who were enthusiastic amateurs. What about professional actors?

They performed their simple plays on a cart or crude platform which, with a curtain as the backcloth, became whatever scene the play demanded, a forest clearing or the entrance to a castle. As the sixteenth century went on, the Renaissance brought about a revival of interest in the plays of ancient Greece and Rome and in time it became the custom for noblemen's servants to turn to acting or for actors to perform under the patronage of some rich lord. Often the plays were performed in the yards of

The Mansell Collection.

AN INN YARD WAS SOMETIMES A THEATRE

During the reign of Queen Elizabeth I, plays were often performed in the yards of London inns. A simple stage and backcloth were set up for the performance and the audience sat or stood in the open. In those days there were no actresses and female characters were played by boys.

inns and taverns. Not until 1576 was the first theatre built in London. Its site was a field near Shoreditch, just out-outside the boundaries of the city, and the building was called "The Theatre." Twenty-two years later, its beams were used by the Burbage brothers for building the famous Globe Theatre. Their partners in this theatre included William Shakespeare, in whose immortal plays Richard Burbage (the most popular actor of his day) often played the leading parts, with Shakespeare himself content with minor roles. Shakespeare wrote plays for the company for about fifteen years. You may know many of them, for they have become the most prized possession of the English theatre and have made Shakespeare our greatest national playwright.

The Use of Scenery

During the reigns of James I and Charles I the new Italian fashion of using scenery spread to England, where it made the Court *masques* (theatrical entertainments) quite lavish affairs. Among those who designed scenery for these costly productions was Inigo Jones, the famous architect. Theatres like The Globe, which were open-air buildings, gave way to indoor theatres, which permitted the use of quite ambitious scenery. The "Theatre Royal in Drury Lane," which was opened in 1674, was designed to use to the full the scenery and stage machines of the time. Charles II himself was a lover of the stage. He went regularly to the theatre and often suggested new plays himself. Among those who wrote for the theatre were John Dryden (1631–1700), William Congreve (1670–1729), Sir John Vanbrugh (1664–1726), Thomas Otway (1652–85) and Sir George Etherege (1634–91).

In Restoration times most of the playgoers were courtiers, but in time the habit spread to ordinary people with the result that many new theatres were built in London during the eighteenth century. Famous playwrights of the time included Oliver Goldsmith (1728–74), whose *She Stoops to Conquer* is a fine comedy of manners, and Richard Brinsley Sheridan (1751–1816), whose comedies — *The Rivals*, *The School for Scandal* and *The Critic*—were masterpieces of dialogue and wit. The most famous actor and theatrical manager of the century was David Garrick (1717–79), who reigned supreme at Drury Lane from 1747 until 1776. The many brilliant performers of the time included Mrs. Siddons, "the greatest tragic actress of the English theatre," and her brother, John Kemble. Later, there came such great artists as Edmund Kean, Sir Henry Irving and Sir Herbert Beerbohm Tree.

The Theatre To-day

Many fine playwrights were at work at the turn of the nineteenth century: Oscar Wilde, with his witty, if rather formal, comedies ; Sir Arthur Wing Pinero, whose serious plays portray English social life of his time so well; George Bernard Shaw, who used the stage to spread ideas and make people think; and Sir James Barrie, the writer of many delightful plays and creator of Peter Pan; you can read more of these and other notable playwrights in another section.

This great revival in drama was not confined to England, but occurred in many European countries. From Norway came the stark dramas of Henrik Ibsen; from Sweden, the dramas of Strindberg; from Russia, the comedies of Anton Tchekhov (also spelt Chekov and Tchechov); from the United States, the plays of Eugene O'Neill. In Ireland, the Abbey Theatre at Dublin became renowned as the home of a national

Fox Photos.

YOUNG ACTORS AT A DRESS REHEARSAL

These children from a London school are in a dress rehearsal of William Shakespeare's "Midsummer Night's Dream." Notice that their costumes are simple, but effective. If you know the story of this delightful play, you will also know why one of the actors is wearing the mask of an ass.

drama, whose great figures included J. M. Synge, a playwright of genius who specialised in dramas of Irish life.

To-day, despite the rival attractions of films, broadcasting and television, Britain has a strong and active theatre. It is always difficult to assess the work of contemporary writers and players and when we speak of the theatre to-day, a host of names spring to mind: T. S. Eliot, the great poet-playwright responsible for *The Cocktail Party* and *The Confidential Clerk*; Noel Coward, whose work embraces many types of stage production; Terence Rattigan, the writer of a number of delightful comedies; and Peter Ustinov, a highly original dramatist and producer, who is also known to the world as a successful film actor. We think, too, of the Old Vic theatre with its productions of plays by Shakespeare and other great English dramatists, its opera and its ballet; of the great theatre at Stratford-upon-Avon, famous for its Shakespeare festivals; and of actors of the standing of Sir Laurence Olivier and Donald Wolfit.

But the love of theatre extends across the whole country, through the repertory companies, whose actors have the hard task of producing a new play each week, to the amateur dramatic societies. For all of them " the play's the thing."

Producing a Play

How does one go about producing a play? Many qualities go to make the successful play producer, even if he or she is only concerned with the annual performance given by the school or village dramatic society. The producer must, of course, know the technical side of the theatre and have a command of the proper technical words and phrases; but he must also be a leader who knows how to handle people with tact and understanding so that they will accept his decisions without question and always give of their best. He must have, too, a feeling for the stage: a hidden sense that tells him the way in which a play should be interpreted and how he can make the most of its situations. In other words, there is much more to play production than getting your friends together, making sure that they know their lines and can speak them clearly enough for people at the back of the hall to hear, and seeing that they come on or go off the stage at the right points in the play.

Fox Photos.

MAKING UP FOR A SCHOOL PLAY

Make-up is a highly skilled art, but these young people evidently feel that they know sufficient to put their own finishing touches. If you are quite inexperienced, however, try to get advice from an expert or study one of the many books written on this subject.

Here are some hints for the young producer. Don't make the mistake of thinking that you can produce a play and act in it as well; production is a big enough task in itself. Remember that although the playwright may have included certain stage directions, it is best not to follow them slavishly. Sometimes the playwright's directions can be improved upon; often they only give the barest guide to what is required, leaving the producer to fill in the gaps. And they are usually written for the large stages of real theatres with very different "sets" (scenery, furniture, etc.) from those you will be using. Occasionally you may get the chance to see a professional production of your play before you start work on your own version. This can be helpful provided that you remember that the same play can be produced in many different ways, each of which will be successful. Copying a professional production does not necessarily give good results; it is certainly more satisfying if you can stage a production that is original.

Keystone.

THE FLOWER GIRL IS A BOY

Clever acting and make-up enable this boy to carry off successfully the role of a flower girl in his school's production of "Pygmalion," the famous play by George Bernard Shaw. The newspaper boy is certainly entering into the spirit of his part, too.

This does not mean that you should scorn the professional performance. See and study as many professional productions as you can. One can always learn from experts; and experience counts, especially in play-producing. If possible, start your training as a producer by acting as assistant to someone who is experienced.

What Shall We Act ?

If yours is a young society, be content with a modest start. There will be plenty of time later for those ambitious plays that you have always longed to produce. One society known to the writer began by holding winter play-reading evenings for its members. This gave the members a chance to try various types of play and part, and the producer a good opportunity for assessing the individual ability of each member. Then came the time when the society decided that it was ready to start on its first public performance. Three simple one-act plays were chosen, enough time for proper rehearsal was allowed, and the result brought enjoyment both to the audience and the society.

Choose a worthwhile play that you and the other members like and believe in. It should be a play which can be brought to life by your society or group. Plays which should obviously be avoided are those written for large stages and those demanding expensive costumes and scenery. Most societies have to be content with small stages, which means that plays with large casts must also be rejected.

Comedies are always difficult to choose and to act, because in comedy so much often depends on the "timing" of

Fox Photos.

A MORE AMBITIOUS AMATEUR PRODUCTION

This amateur production of "Peter and the Wolf" is of the more ambitious kind. Scenery is used against a plain background and the characters are carefully dressed. Many societies make their own scenery and costumes and get effects as good as, if not better than these.

experienced actors—for example, a carefully-timed pause can make all the difference between success and failure in raising a laugh from the audience. Again, comedies must be chosen with the audience in mind. A sophisticated, drawing-room comedy is not likely to find much favour with a country audience. A play that was a dismal failure in the West End of London because its humour was too straightforward, might be just the piece to delight the people who will come to see your show.

Remember that you cannot merely select a play and then go ahead with its production. Make sure that amateurs are permitted to act the play and arrange the payment of any royalties due to the author or publishers.

Casting

Telling your members what parts they are to play is known in the theatrical world as "casting." If you have a lot of members, auditions may help you to decide who is best qualified to play any particular part. But the producer often knows the abilities of his members from their work at play-readings or in past productions. He will know that so-and-so has much too harsh a voice to be cast in a sympathetic part, and that someone else is very good at speaking country dialects. Another member may be much too shy to put his whole heart into a part on the stage, but can make himself very useful back-stage. The producer will also know that his cast must work as a team, if the production is to be a success, and he will ensure that the members of the cast get on well with one another and can work together in harmony.

The Producer Prepares

The producer is now ready to plan his play. He must get to know the play really well, of course; and as he goes through it once again, he will have to decide the way in which each scene is to be played. He must also decide when and where on the stage the characters are to move.

To plan effective movement and grouping of characters, the producer should use a scale drawing of the stage. If scenery is to be used—and some societies get a lot of pleasure from building their own sets—the producer should see that it is planned to suit the play and the stage and to give the audience a clear view of everything that happens. Scenery, furniture, curtains and anything else that will be on the stage should be marked on his scale drawing so that the grouping of characters and all important movement can be planned intelligently.

Do not have movement for the sake of movement. If a character moves, there must be a good reason for it.

The producer will have to work with a number of other important people: the stage manager, who is responsible for setting the stage as the producer wants it; the wardrobe mistress, who is responsible for clothes for the play; the property man, who has to see that newspapers, cigarette cases, pistols, handcuffs and any other "props" needed in the play are in the right place, or with the right character, at the right time: and the prompter, who must be positioned where he can be heard by any actor who forgets his cue or lines.

Rehearsing

The first and obvious point about rehearsals is that your cast must know when and where each rehearsal is to take place, and which members of the cast will be needed. The cast must be prepared to work hard and it must be a point of honour with them that they do not let the producer down. The absence of a vital character can often ruin a rehearsal; everyone's time is wasted and the feeling of harmony and good teamwork, so essential to a good production, is undermined.

At the first rehearsal the producer will probably have the entire cast present and will explain to them exactly how he intends to handle the play. After this, the cast will go through the play, each actor reading his part aloud. This method ensures that everyone knows the general development of the whole play and how he fits into it, and enables the producer to start the broad lines on which the cast should work up their parts for the next rehearsal.

After this, the play should be taken stage by stage from the beginning. When rehearsal of the first act is well-advanced and the cast know their parts in this act, rehearsal of the second act begins. But the first act is not thereafter neglected.

Fox Photos.

SCENERY IN THE MAKING

Some amateur dramatic societies are lucky enough to have members who can build and paint scenery for the society's productions. Here, for example, is a young art student finishing a set he has built for his local Theatre Group.

It will be rehearsed again, at first by itself and later with the second act, and so on.

As the day of the final rehearsal draws near, the producer will probably concentrate on special scenes—those which, he feels, want a little extra polish. You cannot expect the cast to do everything the way you want it done from the first rehearsal onwards. They must be allowed time to master their lines and get into their parts. Do not try to put every fault right at once. Wait until your cast know their lines and basic movements before correcting the points of detail that make a finished production.

The last rehearsal of all is called the Dress Rehearsal, and for this the cast should wear their costumes and make-up. But the Dress Rehearsal is much more than an occasion for seeing that everyone is wearing the right clothes and is correctly made-up. Held on the stage which will be used for the public performance, with scenery and lighting exactly as they will be on the great night, the Dress Rehearsal tests the smooth-running of the whole production. Here is the producer's last chance of correcting that small point that may make so much difference when the play is acted before an audience.

So the great night comes, and the production is submitted for the judgment of the audience. The business of bringing the play to life has been hard, but enjoyable work for everyone in the society. Your production may be praised; it may be criticised. Praise is encouragement indeed, but never be downhearted through criticism; it may well help you immensely with your next production. The good producer is his own sternest critic and he reaches success by believing that each new production can be an improvement upon the last. Success or failure, he remains an enthusiast. For him, " the play's the thing."

Central Press.

LEARNING HOW TO MOVE

An important part of good acting is being able to move naturally and convincingly about the stage. For example, you may be called upon to faint or fall convincingly, and even if nothing quite so drastic is demanded you will probably require practice in using your hands—and in keeping them still. The group in this picture are receiving instruction from an expert at the Royal Academy of Dramatic Art in London.

Favourite Hobbies: Animals and Birds: How to Manage Them

Four-footed and other Friends in the Home

Studio Lisa.

QUINTUPLETS

Lively, alert and affectionate—what perfect pets these puppies of the wire-haired terrier breed are! If properly trained and cared for, they will grow up into strong and hardy little dogs, always ready for a romp or, if need be, a fight. A boy could not wish for a more loyal and amusing companion.

PETS FOR BOYS AND GIRLS

A WELL-KNOWN writer of stories for boys and girls has a very special picture above his desk. He tells his friends that, no matter what kind of day it is, sunny and bright as a summer day should be or dark and dreary as days so often are, the picture gives him a feeling of sunshine and happiness.

You will be wondering what sort of picture this can be and you will be surprised to learn that it shows a boy sitting on a hilltop looking straight before him, whilst beside him sits his dog—a perky terrier with its tongue hanging out as it recovers from the climb to the top of the hill.

Boy and dog are inseparable friends. You may be sure they have shared many adventures together, just as you can be certain that the boy has cared for his pet; he has fed him regularly with the right food; given him a comfortable place to sleep, free from draughts and damp.

Our friend the story writer likes the picture, not only because it is sunny but because it reminds him of the days when he was a boy and had a dog as a pet. He wrote many stories about the dog and made him quite famous.

Most boys and girls keep pets of one sort or another. There is quite a range of creatures to choose from but keeping pets brings with it a responsibility. They are creatures brought to play a part in home life and they cannot fend for themselves as do their cousins who live under natural conditions.

Owning a pet means that you must make a study of its special needs; the

L. E. A.

A LONG-HAIRED CAT

Persians and other pussies of this type need to have their coats brushed and groomed almost every day.

kind of food it requires and when and how often it should be fed; its special housing and sleeping requirements and so on.

Devoted care and attention for our lowly friends, whether they be four-footed or otherwise, teaches us to be thoughtful and thorough, gentle and considerate, and our pets respond by displaying their affection for us.

Don't keep a pet unless you are prepared to make some sacrifices for it. You must be willing to give up an occasional outing or a game when your duty calls you to attend to your pet. And it isn't much use going in for birds or animals as pets if you are likely to get tired of them and leave it to someone else to attend to their feeding or the cleaning of huts and cages.

Pets, like human beings, sometimes become sick or suffer from some complaint peculiar to them. We have to watch out for signs of sickness; a cat may want to sleep all the time and not care about its food; a dog may have a hot nose or a rough coat and have no wish to go romping with you; the eyes of your pet bird may be dull instead of bright and its plumage may be ruffled instead of smooth.

If you are in doubt about the health of your pet talk to your parents about it because prompt attention may save pain to the creature or prevent a serious illness.

In most towns nowadays there is a special clinic where children may take their animals and birds for skilled treatment in the case of sickness. No charge is made for this service but there is a collecting box into which you can put a few pennies if you can afford it. Your contributions will help to keep the clinic going and provide free treatment for the pets of those children who are not so well off for money.

A pet must never be allowed to suffer. It must be given treatment without delay.

If you are really keen on pet keeping you may like to join a club. It is quite possible that there is a fancier's society or a fur and feather club. In such societies and clubs you meet other boys and girls who keep the same animals or birds as you do and you can learn much about your pets from one another.

Many of these clubs hold shows and exhibitions, which are fascinating and interesting, and you will find that every encouragement is given to you to enter your pet in competitions.

Pets in A.B.C. Order

Now let's talk about some of the pets which are most suitable for young people to keep, and so that you can easily find the one in which you are most interested I have put them in alphabetical order. Let's start with:—

BANTAMS. These small fowls make excellent pets and, if kept properly, very profitable ones. There are many different varieties and the best way to choose is to ask the advice of an expert who keeps them. The cheapest way to start is to buy a setting of eggs and place them in the care of a broody hen who will bring up the chicks. April and May are the best months to hatch bantams and the period of incubation varies from eighteen to twenty-one days. If you have no means of hatching the eggs consult an expert about buying a batch of day-old chicks.

HOUSING. The more care you take about housing your bantams the better they will thrive. Get Dad to help you build a small poultry house. It must be securely covered with netting to prevent the birds from getting out or rats from getting in.

A run in front of the house is useful. It should be formed of wire netting on 2 inch by 2 inch wooden posts, with a door by which you can go in. Turn the soil over once a week with a garden fork so that it keeps sweet. Inside the roosting place provide a strong perch about 18 inches above floor level. In the run a drinking place will be necessary and a day perch is appreciated.

FEEDING. Mixed poultry corn is too large for bantams but they can take wheat and oats. The best food is small seeds, broken grain and dried insects which is sold ready-mixed by corn-chandlers. It is usually known as No. 2 Chick Food. In winter bantams like a well-mixed soft mash. The daily diet should be one mash feed, one grain feed and one helping of fresh, tender green-stuff.

BIRDS. It is not kind to keep birds, either British or foreign, unless you can give them a proper aviary. Remember also that it is breaking the law, as well as being very cruel, to cage wild birds. If you want to keep such birds as the Finches or some of the lovely foreign birds, you must buy those which have been bred in captivity.

You can keep them either in an out-door or indoor aviary. If outdoor the aviary must have a shelter shed, a covered run and an open flight. It should be placed against a south or south-west wall. A useful size would be about 12 feet by 6 feet, of which about 8 feet of the roof should be covered with board or felt and the remainder with netting. Board up the shelter shed completely at one side and in the front for about 3 feet. This will keep the rain out. The rest of the front can be a window, wire-covered to prevent the birds hurting themselves if they fly against the glass.

Studio Lisa.

THE SIAMESE CAT

Cats of the Siamese breed are particularly faithful to their owners and almost dog-like in their devotion. The body colour is creamy with mask, ears, feet and tail a dark seal brown. The eyes of these pussies are usually a decided blue.

H. Armstrong Roberts.

CAREFUL !

Parrots can not only be taught to speak some words and phrases : they may also repeat what they have heard when they are not meant to. At one time, the pet parrots of sailors had a reputation for swearing.

If you make an indoor aviary it should be as roomy and light as possible. Also make sure that the room is draughtproof.

Should you want to keep your pets in cages buy good ones of as large a size as possible. Give special thought to perching arrangements and feeding containers. Bear in mind that your birds must be kept warm, dry and snug and fed regularly.

FEEDING. Most of these birds will be happy on a staple diet of Canary seed, with linseed, hemp, dandelion and knapweed, but as their individual tastes and requirements vary and are too long to give here, it is best, if you want to keep such birds, to seek advice from a local Cage Bird Society.

BUDGERIGARS. As these are most popular among children we will deal with them in more detail. They are small members of the parrakeet family and are obtainable in many colours, blue, yellow, grey and so on. If you have only one you may keep it in a cage in a living room and it will be quite happy, but if you can manage to keep a pair they will be company for one another.

If you want to go in for breeding you will find that it can be done indoors if you have a large breeding-cage. Usually five eggs are laid and the incubation period is about eighteen days.

HOUSING. This has been dealt with under the section headed BIRDS and the same rules apply. There should be plenty of bird sand on the floor and cleanliness is most important.

FEEDING. The best food is millet seed and canary seed. Cuttlefish bone is also essential as it contains lime, which the birds need. Put a piece into the cage. You can buy it from any pet shop. Your pet will need green food, and will eat spinach, lettuce, groundsel, dandelion and seeding grass. Make sure it is quite fresh and never allow stale green food to lie in the cage. Slices of apple, carrot or turnip will also be appreciated. Fresh water must be placed in the cage daily. Never give meat. It is bad for the bird.

You will find the budgerigar a fascinating pet because you can tame it and teach it to talk. It will also fly happily about the room, but make sure windows are closed first or you may lose it.

CANARIES. This is another popular cage bird pet because of its lovely song,

BUDGERIGARS

Keystone.

These fine specimens from the collection of our Queen, then Princess Elizabeth, were exhibited at Olympia in 1950. The budgerigar is a small Australian parrakeet. Its original colour is grass-green, barred with black, and with touches of blue in the tail and wings; but many new colour varieties, including pure white and several shades of blue, have been evolved. In recent years these fascinating birds have become one of the most popular of family pets.

and as canaries have been bred as cage birds for so many years they live very happily. Buy your bird in the autumn when the new season's hatching is just on the market. If possible buy a cock bird for he is the best singer. If you want him only for a pet the Border Fancy is the best one to buy, for he is a good singer. If you want to exhibit then Norwich or Yorkshire are the best to purchase.

Housing. The canary is happy in a cage with a well-sanded bottom tray, but it must be kept clean. The cage should never hang above the level of any light in the room. Perches should be about half an inch in diameter or your pet may get sore feet.

Feeding. You can buy Canary seed at any cornchandler's or pet shop, and your pet will also like rape. Give two parts of seed to one of rape. He will also like green food and will prefer dandelion, watercress, chickweed, or spinach. He will also appreciate a bit of apple. Place a piece of cuttlefish in his cage, but never give lumps of sugar. Clean water should be provided every day.

H. Armstrong Roberts.

ANY TITBITS FOR ME?

It is difficult to resist the sweet appeal of his face, but remember that the Sealyham, like all terriers, is no lap-dog. Too much pampering will do him harm.

Don't hang your pet's cage in a window where it will get the full glare of the sun. The best place is facing the window, about 6 feet from the floor, and in a good light.

Offer your canary a bath two or three times a week but do not force him into it.

CATS. The cat is a most popular household pet and certainly earns its keep by ridding the house of mice. For that reason the cat must be thanked by being looked after and cared for. Your cat may be a long-haired Persian; a valuable Siamese, or just the ordinary short-haired common breed. Whichever it is it will appreciate a daily brushing, while the long-haired variety will need it if it is to be kept in good condition.

Your cat will need a bed and it must be placed in a warm place, free from draughts. An ordinary wooden box or a flat basket large enough for the animal to curl in comfort will do. Line the box or basket with brown paper or old newspaper, and then put an old blanket folded into several layers. It is a good plan to cover this with a piece of old sheet which can be washed frequently and so kept fresh and clean. Never allow your cat to sleep in your bedroom. If the animal must sleep outside the house make sure that it has a warm bed and good shelter available.

Feeding. If you take a kitten from its mother at the age of about eight weeks, which is the usual time, you will have to feed it four times a day. For the first week or two the feeds should be mainly milky ones—warm milk with a little bread soaked in it, or a little breakfast cereal soaked in milk. Then gradually change the mid-day feed to one of finely chopped cooked rabbit, a little boiled fish or minced meat. Occasionally add a pinch of bi-carbonate of soda to the meal. Take care to remove all bones.

When the cat is about five months old cut out one meal, and by the time he is eight or nine months old he should be on an adult diet. An adult cat needs only two meals a day—a mid-day one and a light supper, with a saucer of milk morning and evening. The cat can be fed on any sort of meat, fish and rabbit, remembering that a varied diet is as good for him as for you. He should also be encouraged to eat vegetables. Some cats will eat cabbage and lettuce leaves which have been boiled. Bread or potatoes should not be given as they are starchy foods and may set up skin trouble. Avoid giving the cat splintery bones.

Be sure to provide your cat with a sanitary box at night if he has no means of getting out. A shallow wooden box filled with a little garden soil or ashes will do, but it must be emptied and filled afresh each day.

Studio Lisa.

A CAT-AND-DOG LIFE

If kitten and puppy are adopted together in the family they will grow up to be as happy with each other as this pair of pets obviously are.

Never punish a cat by smacking or hitting it. A gentle tap with a lightly-folded newspaper will be enough if your cat does wrong.

Never allow a small child to hurt a cat by pulling it about, squeezing it, or " loving " it too much.

Never turn your cat out of doors at night to wander about all night without a bed. It is most cruel. The cat may get into a fight with a bigger cat or get wet through and catch a bad chill.

Treat your cat like one of the family and he will prove intelligent and a faithful friend.

DOGS. For hundreds of years the dog has been man's most faithful friend. To-day there are no fewer than ninety-four separate breeds, and if you want a thoroughbred dog for a pet you have a wide choice. But remember that the mongrel is often very intelligent and a loyal companion.

The choice of a dog depends on your tastes and where you live. If you have a house in the country, with plenty of fields and lanes for your dog to run in, and you have plenty of time to exercise it, then you can choose an Alsatian, a Great Dane or a Spaniel. But if you live in a small town house or a flat and your dog's outings must be limited to a run on pavements night and morning, then choose a small dog—one of the terrier breed will suit you, or possibly a Dachsund or a Corgi.

HOUSING. If your dog is to be kept outside in a kennel, then you must make sure that the kennel is large enough for him when he is full grown; that it is in a dry corner out of the draughts and that biting east or north winds do not blow right into it. The kennel must also be raised up slightly so that the floor does not get damp. Don't chain your dog unless you absolutely must. Then fix a stout wire along the wall and a ring on the dog's chain to slip on the

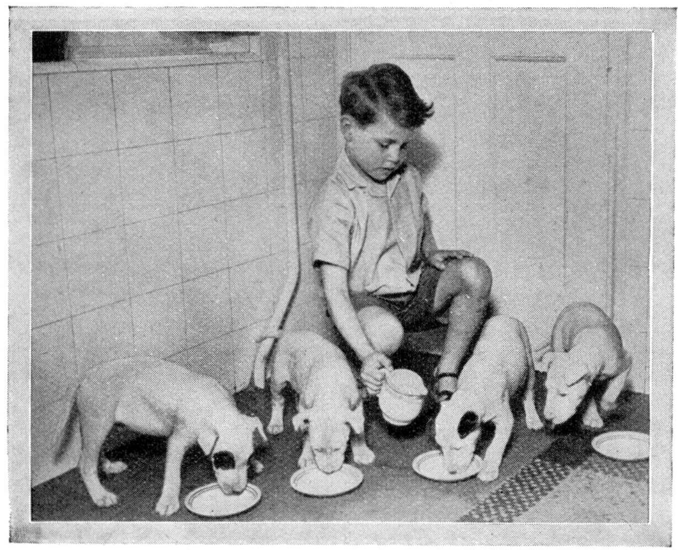

Studio Lisa.

BRINGING UP THE FAMILY

When first they leave their mother puppies must be fed every two hours, but be given only small helpings of food. These four puppies are thoroughly enjoying their ration of warm milk.

wire. The dog can then run up and down the length of the wire. If he must be chained then take him for a good run every day and let him off the chain whenever possible.

If your pet is a house dog then give him a comfortable basket or box, as we described for the cat. Never let dogs climb on to chairs and cushions and do not let them lie on the rug gazing into the fire. It harms a dog's eyes.

You must train your dog to obey so that he will come at your slightest whistle. You can do this by patience and kindness, and a little tit-bit as a reward when he learns to come at first call. But, however well trained he is, if you live in a busy town it is well to take him on a lead until you reach an open space where he can run.

The dog must have two regular runs, morning and evening, and if you are not prepared to do this, in all weathers, then don't have a dog as a pet. Don't let your dog roam the streets, where he will be in danger and perhaps a cause of accident to others.

The dog must be bathed regularly and brushed and groomed each day. His pads should be examined regularly to make sure they are not sore, nor his nails too long. Ears and teeth should also be examined.

FEEDING. Very young puppies must be fed every two hours, and given milk with one of the puppy foods, or groats, barley or arrowroot. After ten weeks reduce the feeds to four a day and give puppy biscuits or meal, followed by a drink for breakfast and tea; a mid-day meal of vegetables and gravy; and an evening meal of a little raw chopped meat, biscuit and gravy. The evening meal should be the principal meal of the day.

At six months reduce the meals to three a day by cutting out the mid-day meal, and at ten months give an adult diet of two meals, with plenty of hard biscuit and a variety of meat and vegetables at the evening meal.

Give your puppy bones (but not chicken or rabbit bones) and the grown dog a good hard bone. It is good for his teeth. Never give sweets or snacks from your own table between meals.

TRAINING. Be firm but kind with your pet. Don't scold him for a fault one day and laugh at him for the same thing next day. A well-trained dog knows by your voice if he has done wrong. There is no need to whip a dog but a smart pat with a newspaper will teach him he is wrong when he is young. Teach him not to foul pavements when he is out, but always to use the gutter.

Your Dog Licence

As soon as your dog is six months old you must take out a licence at your Post

Office. This will cost you 7s. 6d. a year and it is renewable each year on January 1st. It allows you to " keep one dog ".

GOATS. These animals make good pets and their milk is of value as it is specially good for babies and invalids. But if you decide to make the goat your pet you must realise that it will have to be milked twice a day without fail, and you will have to learn the correct way to do this.

The best goat for your purpose is the Nubian which has no horns.

HOUSING. In the summer a nannie can be tethered out of doors where there is rough pasture, either in a field or your garden. Give her a wide collar, a very long chain, and move her stake two or three times a day to give her fresh pasture.

During the winter months she will live in a stable or shed, which must be dry and free of draughts. A wooden bench raised an inch off the floor will be her bed and the floor must be covered with good clean straw, changed frequently, and there must be a window which opens or a door in two halves.

FEEDING. In addition to green herbage milking goats will need crushed oats, pieces of carrot, parsnip or swede, and they will appreciate rose hips, blackberries, shelled acorns and chestnuts, nettles and elm leaves. In winter give kale and a little cattle-cake. Three meals a day in winter should be sufficient.

GROOMING. Goats require daily grooming with a dandy brush. The udder must be carefully washed and dried before milking and the milker's hands must also be carefully washed before milking.

GOLDEN HAMSTER. This little creature has lately come into great favour as a pet and is a fascinating one to keep. He will become quite tame and playful.

HOUSING. A hutch made like a rabbit hutch will suit the Hamster excellently. You can give him a wooden box filled with straw for a nest. He is a great gnawer, and will soon gnaw his way out unless the hutch is very strong.

FEEDING. He eats very little. One meal a day is sufficient. Much of this

Studio Lisa.

BROUGHT UP ON THE BOTTLE

When nannies are kept for their milk it very often happens that the kids have to be brought up on the bottle, as is here depicted. An ordinary glass bottle is used with a special rubber teat, and one would generally depend upon cow's milk for the purpose. Dipping one's finger into milk and getting the kid to suck it soon teaches these little animals how to feed.

he will store in his hutch and it must be cleared out before it becomes stale and smells. He will eat wheat, oats, corn or cereals; all kinds of vegetables such as carrots, turnips, etc., cooked or raw; apples, pears, cherries, and so on, but no sour fruit or peelings. Dandelion leaves and chickweed are enjoyed and provide medicine. He likes a little milk to drink.

G.P.A.

MR. PRICKLES, THE HEDGEHOG

If you make a point of feeding a hedgehog at the same regular time each evening with a saucerful of bread and milk he will come for his meal and get to know you.

If you wish to breed from your pets you would be wise to consult an expert, or obtain a good book on the subject, so that you know the right way to set about it and the kind of preparations to make.

GUINEA PIGS. These little animals are good pets but they must be kept scrupulously clean.

HOUSING. Again a rabbit hutch does very well, but it must be absolutely damp-proof and away from draughts. It should have a sleeping compartment, and there must be plenty of room for the little animals to move about. Clean sawdust or peat moss should cover the floor of the " day " part of the hutch, while hay or straw should be in the sleeping side. On fine days make a covered wire run about 1 foot 6 inches high on the lawn and put the guinea pigs in it. They will crop the lawn for you and feed on clover and weeds at the same time.

G.P.A.

THE GUINEA-PIG OR CAVY

Guinea-pigs are quaint little pets, easy to manage and to feed when one has a large garden. They are quite defenceless and always gentle.

FEEDING. Guinea pigs are vegetarians and must not be given meat. Give a wet mash once or twice a day and leave a little dry food always in the hutch. Only give as much wet food or greenstuff as can be eaten at one time and give it in a little dish. Dry food is hay, bran, middlings, dry bread; while any of these, together with potatoes or other cooked vegetables, can be mixed with warm water for a mash. Don't make it sloppy. Green food must be given but not in large quantities. A little milk will be enjoyed, but they will drink water and some should always be in the hutch. Keep it clean and fresh.

HEDGEHOGS. These are really wild creatures but if one comes into your garden you can make a pet of it. He will enjoy bread and milk and if you put a saucer down each evening at the same time he will become a regular visitor. He will also eat insects. He will hibernate during the winter and may, in the spring, disappear as suddenly as he came.

MICE. These are fascinating little creatures and if you wish to breed them you will soon have a large stock.

HOUSING. You can buy mouse cages fitted up with revolving wheels and ladders, but you can just as easily make your own box. If you fit it with a glass front you will be able to watch your pets at play. Put plenty of clean sawdust on the floor of the cage and clean it out every day. About once a month wash the cage with disinfectant. Make sure it is dry before the mice are returned.

FEEDING. Mice will eat bread and milk; crusts of stale bread; pieces of carrot and apple; tender lettuce, and bird seed. No stale food must be left in the cage.

The way to pick up a mouse is to hold it firmly by the tail about half-way between the tip and the body. Never hold it by the tail tip.

PARROTS. Parrots are good company and entertaining and make excellent pets, but they must have plenty of human companionship or they become bored and miserable. If your pet is a

P.A.—Reuter Photo.

A NEWCOMER AMONG PETS—THE GOLDEN HAMSTER

Until 1945 the Golden Hamster, a small rodent about six or seven inches long, was almost unknown to the general public. Since then it has rapidly become a popular favourite. Hamsters have all the attractive qualities to be desired in small pets. When handled regularly they are very tame and full of harmless tricks and twists. They need no special food and thrive on dog biscuit, vegetables, fruit, dry bread and grass.

Fox Photos.

A COCONUT FOR THE TITS

Tom-tits and others of their clan are winter visitors to our gardens. They enjoy coconut, peanuts threaded on strings and pieces of suet or other fat, or even a meat bone.

new one leave him in his cage until he becomes accustomed to you, gently stroking him through the bars of the cage. Later he can be allowed to sit on a perch in the room and can be fondled and carried about.

FEEDING. It is best to feed on a special parrot-food mixture sold by a dealer, and not to give snacks and tit-bits from the table, but apples, carrot, turnip and a little lettuce should be given. No bones or meat must be given but special parrot grit should be given in a small container.

Your parrot will need fresh water for drinking and will occasionally appreciate a bath if water is put in his cage. Tie some twiggy bits of oak, lime or ash together and give them to your bird to nibble. It will be good exercise for his beak.

Patience and kindness will teach your bird to talk.

PIGEONS. These are interesting pets, whether you keep the purely ornamental kind or go in for homing pigeons and pigeon racing. If you want them just as pets then the Fantails are ideal and will be happy in a cote in the garden, but if you intend to go in for racing then your birds will need a proper house in a loft or attic at the top of the house.

If you want to breed then you can start with one pair at any time from March to June. Give them a large sugar box, with a front covered with wire netting, for a home; a nesting pan and straw can be provided and they will make their own nest. Two eggs will be laid and will incubate in about eighteen days. Perches and nesting boxes must be provided in the loft.

FEEDING. A corn mixture, consisting of tares, wheat, hard maize, lentils,

Fox Photos.

A TRIO OF "REX" MICE

These fancy mice were bred at a mouse farm in Essex and have a wonderful "wave" in their coats. They are very fond of brown bread and will make a home in the loaf after a meal.

Studio Lisa.

A DEVOTED COUPLE

Fantails are perhaps the prettiest of all domestic pigeons, and are an ideal choice if you want to have birds as pets in your garden. They are easy to keep in a cote, which should be divided into compartments if you have more than one pair. It is a pleasure to watch the domestic life of pigeons. Cock and hen stay loyally together for life, and share such duties as the hatching of eggs and the feeding of their young.

barley and oats should be given and a seed mixture of linseed, canary seed, hemp and rape. Feed in the evening so that you can attract your racing pigeons home with food. Grit must be available in a small container and clean drinking water. The birds will also enjoy lettuce, cabbage or dandelion leaves which can be hung where they can peck at them.

RABBITS. All boys and girls like keeping rabbits and if you go in for Angoras you will also have a source of profit from their long wool. Chinchillas and Havanas are kept for their pelts and skins, but if you do not want to kill your pets but merely to keep them for enjoyment then choose the ordinary domestic Flemish Giant or Belgian Hare.

HOUSING. The size of the hutch depends on the size of the breed and the number you have, but the animals must have room to turn round comfortably. Usually a hutch about 26 inches long, 18 inches deep and 18 inches wide will house one rabbit comfortably. There must be a separate hutch for each animal as grown-up rabbits rarely agree.

In the outer section place clean sawdust or peat moss on the floor, while the inner, sleeping compartment should be lined with hay. Both must be cleaned out regularly.

FEEDING. You can feed twice a day or once only, but whichever you decide must be regular. A mash made from flaky bran mixed with strained tea-leaves will be enjoyed, as will oats mixed with mashed potatoes, or chaff mixed with bran. Plenty of greenstuff such as lettuce, dandelions, outside leaves of cabbage, carrot and turnip thinnings, as well as many weeds, are all necessary to the rabbit's health. Never give greenstuff which is wet with frost. Rabbits are " bulk feeders " so give them plenty to nibble at.

WHAT AN AQUARIUM LOOKS LIKE

It is often cruel to keep goldfish in a small glass bowl, especially in the full sun. In a proper aquarium, however, these pets are perfectly happy and live for a great many years. Growing from the sandy bottom of the tank there should be selected water plants and a few ramshorn snails will act as scavengers. Read also " Keeping a Tropical Fish Tank."

There is a common idea in some places that rabbits do not need water. They do, and should be given a little each day. Wet greenstuff should not be given.

Young rabbits should be taken from their mother when about six weeks old but can be left a little longer in very cold weather.

Lift a rabbit by its ears if you must, but always support its body with your other hand while doing so.

RATS are very like mice in their needs and habits. They also can be kept in glass-fronted hutches, but they must be kept scrupulously clean. The young rats should be separated from their parents at six weeks and the bucks parted from the does.

FEEDING. Bread and milk can be the staple diet, but do not leave wet food in their hutches. Remove what is not eaten at once. Dry food, such as hard crusts of bread, pieces of carrot and apple, nuts, dandelion leaves, maize and dried peas can be given and left in the hutch. Clean water must be given each day.

SILKWORMS are fascinating to watch and you can usually buy eggs at a pet shop in early April. Place the eggs in a well-ventilated cardboard box and before long the caterpillars will hatch. Feed on fresh lettuce leaves and as soon as the Mulberry leaves appear on the trees give those.

If you cut a piece of white paper to fit the bottom of the box you can change this frequently to keep the box clean. If you wish to pick up a caterpillar do it with a camel-hair brush and not with your fingers.

The caterpillars will eventually spin silk and form cocoons. You may like to wind the silk but, of course, you will not get enough for any practical purpose.

TROPICAL AQUARIUM FISH—Plate 1

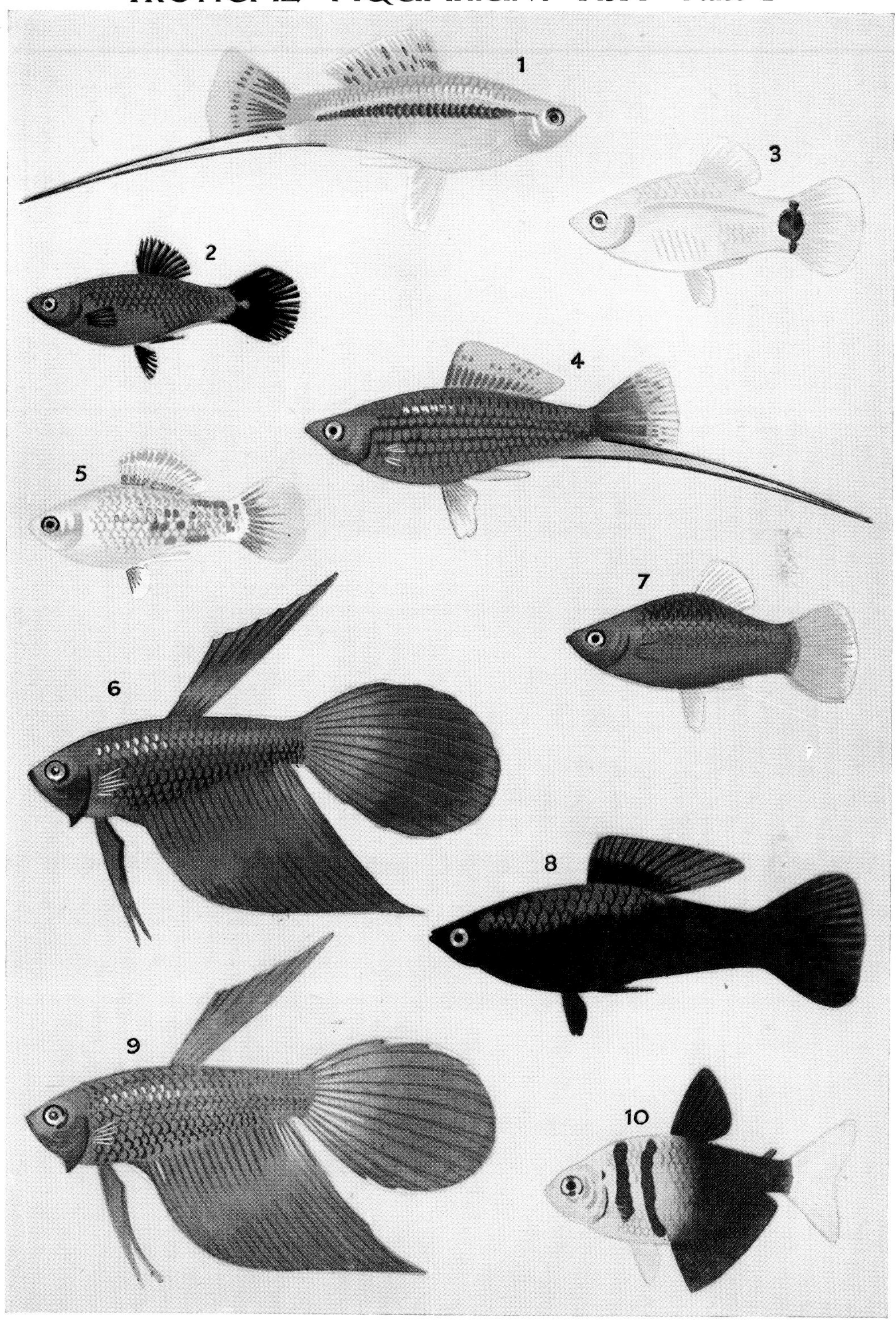

1. Green Swordtail. 2. Wagtail Platy. 3. Yellow Platy. 4. Red Swordtail. 5. Platy Variatus. 6. Red Siamese Fighter. 7. Red Platy. 8. Permablack Molliensia. 9. Blue Siamese Fighter. 10. Black Widow.

TROPICAL AQUARIUM FISH—Plate 2

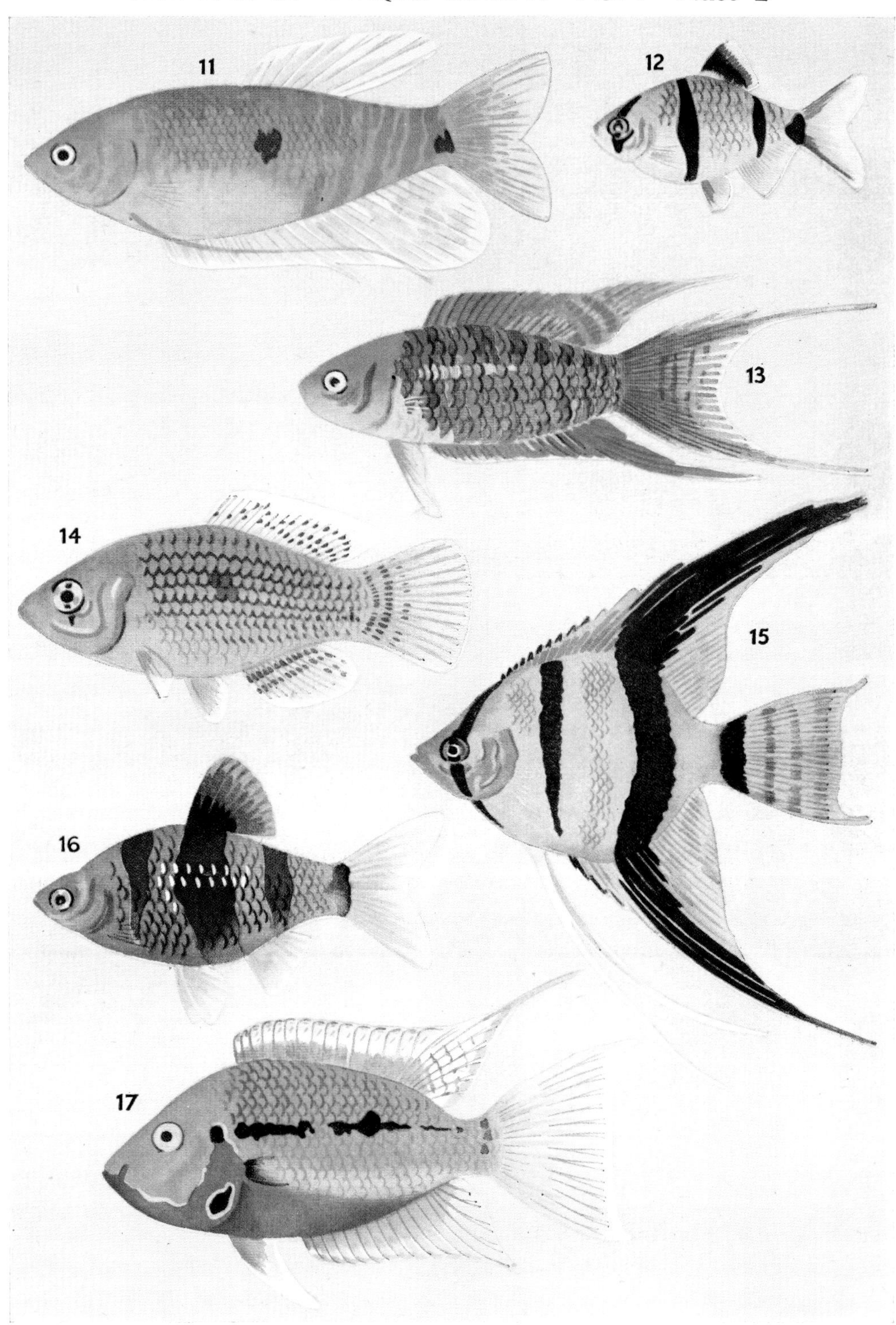

11. Three-spot Gourami. 12. Tiger Barb. 13. Paradise Fish. 14. Flag Fish. 15. Angel Fish. 16. Nigger Barb. 17. Firemouth.

RABBITS AND OTHERS

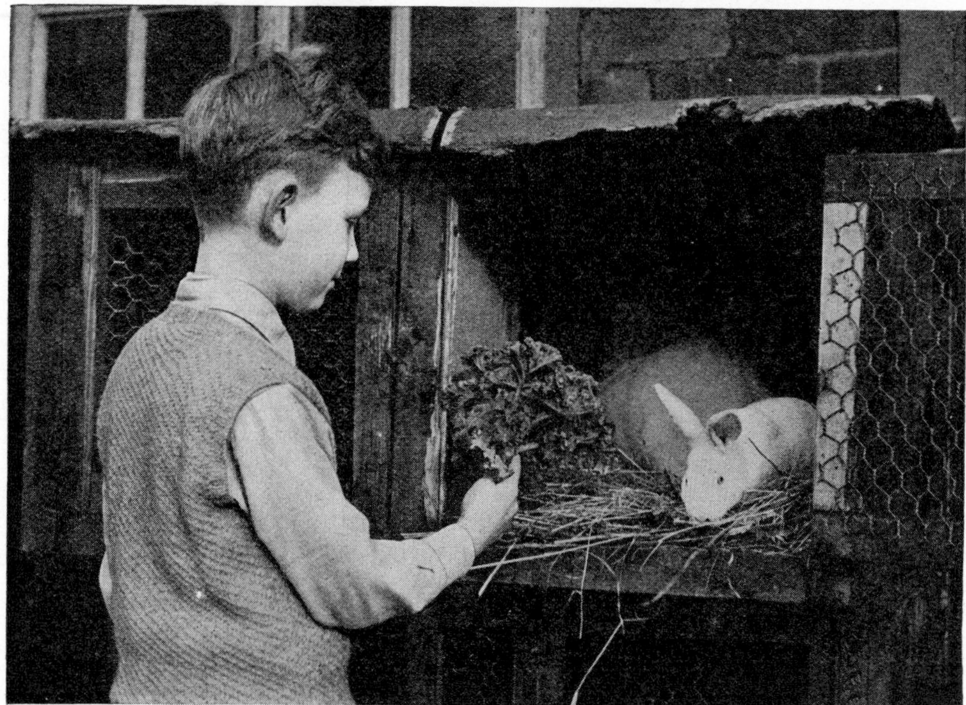

Easy to handle and requiring only a small amount of attention, rabbits have always been among the most popular pets for boys and girls. Plenty of greenstuff is an important part of their daily food.

Photos: Keystone.

Cats and rabbits are not usually good friends, but sometimes they become the best of companions. In this picture Wriggle-nose, the rabbit, and Ginger, the cat, are enjoying a meal together.

TORTOISES are reptiles but they make interesting pets and can be taught to come at a call from the owner. They have very keen eyesight but poor hearing.

There are two kinds—the Land or Iberian Tortoise and the Water Tortoise. Make sure which you are buying, for the Water Tortoise requires a pond or large aquarium. The Land Tortoise will live happily in your garden.

FEEDING. The tortoise will find his own food, and it will usually be the choicest row of young lettuces or tender pea plants. If your father grows vegetables then it is wise to make your pet a large wire-covered run on the lawn. Give him outside lettuce and cabbage leaves, dandelions, chickweed and so on. He will relish the petals from a fallen rose if they are fresh. Give him a shallow saucer of water. Feed him at the same spot each day.

A water tortoise needs worms, grubs, slugs, insects, and will eat bread and milk.

The one disadvantage of a tortoise as a pet is that it may, and very likely will, wander away and you will lose it.

In the winter it will hibernate. In a warm country it will find a sheltered spot and sleep all through the winter, but in this country the winter climate is too cold, for most of these tortoises come from abroad. So you must make your pet a proper shelter. When you find it creeping away and hiding in a clump of leaves towards the end of a September evening, then you know it is time to make a bed. Fill a box with leaves, hay and straw, put your pet in and put him away in a cool, dry and draught-proof shed or cellar. Open the box every day for a few days and if he seems very active put him out in the garden, bringing him in again as soon as the sun goes down. Soon he will sleep soundly all day and night.

When the spring comes you will hear a rustling in the straw on a sunny day. Put the box out in the garden and let your pet wake up and take a walk, but for a few weeks, while nights are cold, you will have to put him back to bed.

Most Water Tortoises are hardy enough to hibernate in the mud at the bottom of a pond, but if your pond is shallow, with a concrete bottom, then you would be wise to make an indoor bed for your pet.

Fox Photos.

TORTOISES WILL EAT FLOWERS

These tortoises have high-domed backs and are of the land variety. Though they enjoy warm bread and milk, they are by nature vegetarians, and their food usually consists of lettuce leaves, dandelion foliage and similar fare. At the same time, they are quite partial to flowers.

KEEPING A TROPICAL FISH TANK

Water Life.

A typical scene in a well laid-out fish tank. Note the carefully balanced arrangement of the rocks and the varied plant life, making the inmates feel at home in natural surroundings. An underwater picture like this is not made in a day, but you can get an equally lovely result with careful planning.

ANYONE can keep a humble goldfish in a bowl. This is an old Victorian idea and provided you remember to change the water and give him a few ants eggs he will survive his cramped life for quite a time. What a vast stride forward fish fanciers have taken today, and the principal secret of the new magic they have found lies in an instrument called a " Thermostat." The thermostat has enabled fish fanciers and aquarists and boys and girls in their own homes to keep the water in a tank at an even temperature and has thus enabled them to keep alive and healthy wonderful fishes from all over the world which naturally inhabit waters much warmer than the streams and lakes of this country. An average of 75° is generally regarded as suitable for most species.

The thermostat controls an electric heater in the tank; size according to the size of the tank and the amount of water it contains, so that whenever the temperature of the water falls below a certain level, on comes the heater and brings it up again.

The second great factor which has brought about the enchantment of the modern aquarium is selection and growth of tropical plants encouraged by top-lighting, because it is light—normally natural sunlight—which promotes plant growth.

You will see it is thus possible, with lights and heaters, to set up a miniature underwater jungle in which vegetation grows as it would, for example, in a backwater of the great Amazon River, and the fishes natural to South America live and breed and play continually under the artificial sunlight of an electric lamp. You should remember, when keeping a tropical aquarium, to make it as nearly possible a real corner of a natural underwater world, and not to clutter it up with grotesque coloured rocks, artificial arches and grottoes which belong to no natural country.

Although you can make your own fish tank with angle iron and glass, we do not advise the average boy or girl to attempt to do so. It is a rather specialised job, and in any case most large towns today have a well-stocked aquarist's shop where standard tanks can be bought at fairly modest prices. You can have fun, for example, with a tank no larger than 12in. × 6in. × 6in., which will hold eight medium sized tropical fish. But the ideal tank for a home, if you can afford it or get it for a Christmas or birthday present, is the standard 24in. × 12in. × 12in., enabling you to have no fewer than thirty medium sized fishes, or even up to forty of the small varieties.

Remember when making your original purchase that you require also a metal cover for the tank, provided with electric light socket; a heater, a thermostat and a small thermometer. As a modern fish tank will not be dependent on natural daylight you should avoid placing it in a window. In this position, in any case, the daylight will tend to develop green algae on the glass, which spoils the appearance of your underwater picture. You will also find it attractive to paint the outside of the back and side glasses of the tank a dark blue or black, to provide a contrasting background to your plants and fish and to exclude natural light.

You will find that when painting glass in this way it is better not to make it a uniform colour from top to bottom but rather to make it merge gradually from dark at the bottom to light at the top, or even light in the centre and dark towards the corners. This helps to give a sense of depth or what we know in the cinema as a 3D effect.

Other Useful Accessories

In the standard tank an aerator should not really be necessary but the use of an air pump gives you a continuous stream of bubbles through the water and enables you to keep more fish in the tank than you would otherwise do. This is due to the fact that the water absorbs oxygen from the air, thus replacing the oxygen breathed by the fish. Small air pumps are available, worked by electricity from your mains in the same way as your heater and thermostat and if you have an air pump, this also gives you an opportunity of using a filter if you wish. This forces the water up from the bottom of the tank through a glass tube and into a " trap " containing charcoal and other ingredients before it runs back into the tank again.

Naturally, these accessories help greatly in keeping the water clear but please note that no amount of aeration or filtering will ever make it completely unnecessary for you to siphon out the bottom of the tank approximately once a week.

The siphon is a very simple accessory and can, in fact, be merely a piece of

Laurence E. Perkins, F.Z.S.

This fairly rare fish is commonly known as a Headstander (*Chilodus punctatus*) because of the peculiar angle at which he swims in the water. The specimens above are not diving as one might think; they swim normally head down.

Laurence E. Perkins, F.Z.S.

Here is a very easy and extremely pleasant, hardy inmate for your Tropical Fish Tank—the popular Tiger Barb (*Barbus tetrazona*). The brilliant gold scales contrast with broad, black bands and red fins.

rubber tubing. You have, no doubt, learned about siphon action at school. No mechanism is necessary, all you have to do is suck a little water into the tube in order to start it flowing and then move the other end of the tube over the gravel at the bottom of the tank with a " vacuum cleaner " action.

Although a good community of snails will do much to keep the glass clean a very useful little gadget can be made with a rod of wood into the end of which an ordinary safety razor blade has been inserted at a slight angle. This can be rubbed or scraped up and down the glass to shave off the green algae. Do not worry if the algae floats about in the water. Some of your fish will very promptly eat it and enjoy it.

Even although you do not mean to breed tropical fish you should always try to have a spare tank available so that you may isolate a sick or wounded fish. This tank need not be an elaborate affair provided you have means of keeping the water at the required temperature—a large glass accumulator jar will do, or even the sort of jar your Mother may use for preserving fruit. If you are going to breed fish you may want glass or celophane panels to divide smaller tanks.

Do not be tempted to try unusual lighting effects in your tank. The ordinary clear or pearl lamp used for household lighting is the best. You may think it would be picturesque to try a coloured lamp—a red or green or blue one, to get weird effects. You are almost sure to be disappointed. The most lovely tanks are the most natural and the nearest approach to the natural tropical sunshine striking down through the green weeds is provided by the ordinary electric lamp.

Landscape in the Tank

Before planting anything in your aquarium you must lay out the rocks and gravel which are to form the landscape of your tank. Gravel can be bought from aquarists' shops and this is best.

Laurence E. Perkins, F.Z.S.

Two of the Cichlids family of fish (*Cichlasoma severum*), of which the commonest is the Kissing Gourami, indulging in the habit which gives them their name, but experts say they are *not* in love !

If you use natural gravel or river sand, it should be boiled before you put it in the tank. Similarly, natural rocks or stones should be sterilised by boiling, but these too can be bought ready for use. Remember that a lump of ordinary household coal does no harm to fish or plant life and can look very attractive. Try to place the rocks so that they form ledges high at the back and getting lower towards the front and so that they provide pockets of deep gravel for the plants to take root in.

SNAILS. It is a good idea to introduce a number of water snails, mainly to keep the glass free from green algae, and also to eat up unwanted scraps of food from the bottom. By far the best snail for the purpose is the Red Ramshorn which will breed and multiply in your tank. The Malayan Sand Snail can be disappointing because he remains buried in the gravel at the foot of your tank for days on end.

PLANTS. Since the growth of the tropical fish hobby quite a large number of interesting, varied and easily grown plants from many tropical waters are on sale in the aquarists' shops but you are best to begin with a few of the following which are easy to handle, hardy and sure to provide the bright natural surroundings which you want for your fish. On no account collect water-weeds from ponds or ditches.

Tape Grass or " Vallis ". This is probably the most popular of all aquarium plants. It grows vigorously like under-water grass, is bright green and helps to keep the water healthy. It spreads quite rapidly by runners like a strawberry plant and after a time you will actually have to thin it out of your tank. Its botanical name is *vallisneria spiralis*. An alternative and somewhat similar plant is *sagittaria* or arrowhead, and the third plant of the grassy type is *Hair Grass*, which is a perfect description of the plant.

Amazon Sword is the ambition of most aquarists and makes a lovely centre piece. It should only be used in the bigger tanks, but you can introduce " Water Sprite " or *Indian fern* in most aquaria, or *Hornwort*, *Spatterdock* or one of a number of plants called *Cryptocorynes* which are like blunt-leaved ferns. All these are in stock at most aquarists. Lastly, you may wish to have some floating plant, such as *Duckweed* or *Crystalwort* or *Bladderwort*, which forms a thick mass on the surface of the water and makes a wonderful hiding place for tiny baby fish. (This sort of plant is usually eaten by snails, which should be kept out of a tank containing it.)

Feeding. One of the great joys of tropical fish-keeping at home is that they are easily fed both summer and winter, and they take a surprisingly little amount of food. In fact, in a well planted and natural tank you can safely go away for as long as a fortnight on holiday, without making any special provision for feeding the fish.

All the tropical fish-shops sell little inexpensive packets and tins of various dried foods. Most fish can be kept healthy on these foods alone, but the most popular species of fish should have their meals varied with live food when you can get it. This, again, is obtainable from a shop and in some cases if you are lucky, you may be able to get a supply of certain of the live foods from a local pond, although you should not do this without some expert advice. The two main live foods available are:

(1) Daphnia
(2) Tubifex worms.

The daphnia (sometimes known as water fleas) are really tiny little crab-like creatures which pop about in the rather dirty water of certain ponds in almost solid masses feeding on the microscopic life in the water. (This microscopic life, on which the daphnia feed is the best food for many baby fish if you are interested in breeding. It is known as "infusoria", and to the naked eye is merely a slight cloudiness of the water. Under the microscope you will see that it is teeming with life.) Daphnia is sold in aquarists' shops.

Do not forget to change the water in the jar in which you are keeping the daphnia. These little creatures need oxygen as much as fish and use it up very quickly. They soon settle in a mass at the bottom of the jar and die if the water is not frequently changed.

The second popular live food is tubifex worms. These are tiny red thread-like worms about ½-inch in length which form into solid masses rather like some strange gorgon with a head of snakes. These masses should be broken up and the worms scattered in the tank, where the fish will very quickly gobble them up. Do not feed too many at a time or they will partly bury themselves in the gravel and the fish may have difficulty in pulling them out.

Laurence E. Perkins, F.Z.S.

A close-up view of two beautiful Pearl Gouramis (*Trichogaster leeri*), gliding over the rocks of the aquarium. Note the top of the electric heater and its cable, disappearing behind the rock.

Laurence E. Perkins, F.Z.S.

The famous Egyptian Mouthbreeder fish which, after it has laid eggs, gathers them in its mouth, where the young fry hatch, so that mother swims around with a mouthful of babies.

Feed just as much as can be eaten in a few minutes and feed again later. This is a first-class rule in fish-keeping—more trouble is caused by giving your fish too much than too little, and fish seem to have no sense about eating—they are always hungry. Both the fish and the water in which they live will be much better if there is no spare food around.

When live food is not available and you wish to vary the diet, most fish will enjoy an earth worm chopped up with a razor blade, or a little piece of red meat finely shredded. You can also get amusement and provide the fish with good exercise by dangling a little piece of meat or cooked fish or shrimp on a thread in the water.

Troubles and Diseases

If you stick to the popular and reasonably hardy species of fish recommended here and buy healthy stock from a good shop your fish should live for a long time in a healthy and lively condition, but unfortunately, as with human beings, they *can* suffer sudden ills. When in doubt consult an expert about it, but it is just as well to know some of the more ordinary diseases which can be dealt with without undue trouble and which can be cured.

White Spot. For some reason this is one of the troubles that an aquarist most fears, probably because it spreads so rapidly through the entire tank, affecting every fish if action is not taken very quickly. The disease is recognised by a rash of tiny pin-point white spots covering the body and fins. The fish is apparently irritated by the disease and will frequently rub itself against the plants or rocks to ease the irritation. Its fins will lie flat and not upright as in a healthy creature. At this stage, the whole tank should immediately be treated. It is no good just taking the first affected fish out and hoping that the rest are all right. Very effective white spot remedies are sold in small bottles and the contents are simply dropped into the water according to the directions and the entire tank darkened for two or three days. At the end of this period unless you are particularly unlucky, you will be delighted to see your fish free of spots and none the worse for the attack. It is sometimes advisable to raise the temperature of the water during this cure to approximately 85°.

Other diseases which may attack your fish more or less describe themselves. *Fungus* can appear in patches almost anywhere on the body and can sometimes be cured by removing the fish into a separate small container containing a teaspoonful of salt per half gallon of water.

Laurence E. Perkins, F.Z.S.

Though you may not at first wish to keep all these unusual examples, here is the famous Archer fish (*Toxotes jaculator*), which catches flies and insects above the water by squirting a jet of water at them.

A fish with *dropsy* takes on a bloated and puffed up appearance, and there is unfortunately no known cure. The disease, however, is not infectious. The kindest thing to do is simply to remove and destroy the affected fish.

Fin rot shows itself just as you would expect, by a fraying or splitting of the fins, but do not assume, however, that all frayed fins, are due to this disease—it may have been caused by a bit of rough behaviour on the part of one of the other fish. The cure for fin rot is a diet of live food after the affected parts of the fins have been cut away very carefully with a sharp pair of small scissors.

Unless you have a natural gift for looking after your pets, it is best to get expert advice when anything serious goes wrong, and in the case of tropical fish it is probably safer, and kinder, to remove and destroy any sick inhabitant, rather than risk complete disaster.

FISH TO KEEP. Although you may wish only occasionally to try the experiment of breeding tropical fish, the way in which they breed is the easiest everyday method of grouping or classifying the different species. In this sense there are two main groups: the live bearers which give birth to living babies or fry, which swim off the moment they are born, and egg layers which spawn, or lay eggs, from which the fry emerge, perhaps days later.

Laurence E. Perkins, F.Z.S.

Here is the bright and unusual yellow and black striped Bumble-Bee fish or Wasp Goby. Though attractive to look at he is sometimes a bully to other fish and should be introduced with care.

Laurence E. Perkins, F.Z.S.

Here is a gay and unusual aquarium inmate, usually known as a Scat (short for *Scatophagus argus*) and sometimes referred to as the Hundred-eyed Muckeater.

Popular live-bearers. Guppies or Rainbow fish. By far the easiest to keep, stand a considerable variation of temperature, and are prolific breeders. They are, however, cannibals and the fish eat their own young almost the moment they are born. It is therefore necessary to provide thick weeds in which the fry may hide.

Swordtails. These are probably the second simplest fish to handle. Green or red swordtails are the most popular, but there are black and albino varieties, also wagtail swords (red, with black tails). Only the males have the sword.

Platys. Very attractive colour variations and a hardy character, make this another extremely popular beginners' species. Blue, black, red, golden, wagtail and numerous hybrid varieties are available.

Mollies. The Black Molly—especially the true Perma-black—is a velvet or soot black all over, even to fins and eyes. It is surely one of the most engaging popular breeds, though not quite so hardy as the live-bearers already mentioned. Variations include Sail-fins and Speckled Mollies.

Egg Layers. Most fish are egg layers, so we shall divide them into smaller groups according to varying breeding habits and other characteristics.

Bubble nest builders. These fish

blow a nest of bubbles on the surface of the water into which the eggs are carefully deposited by the male fish as soon as the female has laid them. By far the most attractive and popular of this group is the Siamese Fighting Fish, with its wonderful spread of tail and fins and magnificent colouring.

Other popular bubble nesters are Gouramis (blue, striped, dwarf, pearl, thick-lipped, etc.) and the very attractive Paradise Fish.

Egyptian Mouth Breeder—surely one of the strangest creatures ever. When the eggs are laid they are picked up in the extremely large mouth of the female, and the baby fish are actually carried about in the mother's mouth.

Other popular and attractive Egg Layers include: The Zebra Danio; the Giant Danio and Spotted, Pearl, and White Danios; the Black Widow; the White Cloud Mountain Minnow; Harlequins; Tiger, Nigger, Chequer, Spanner, Clown and Rosy Barbs; the distinguished Angel Fish; Lyre tails, and Beacons, or Head and Tail Light fish, the Belgian Flag Fish; the Penguin; the Black Line Tetra; the Flame Fish; the Panchay; the Hatchet Fish; the Pencil Fish and, in fact, an endless variety of shape and colour, most of which are easily recognized by their very names. And perhaps the most beautiful of all the tropical fish you can keep, although it can only be bred in very special circumstances, the Neon Tetra.

Most of the fish we mention here can safely be kept all together in a community tank. You must of course, remember never to keep two male Siamese Fighters together, or they will live up to their name. And do not keep very small fish with very large ones ; the latter may be quite friendly by nature, but simply cannot resist snapping up the small fry.

We make no mention here of all the bright and wonderful tropical fish of the sea. This is not because they cannot be kept in indoor aquariums, but because only experts will have the time and apparatus necessary to keep the salt content as well as the temperature at a natural level.

Laurence E. Perkins, F.Z.S.

Popular hardy and attractive water plants for every home aquarist. 1. Cryptocoryne. 2. Cabomba, like a miniature feather boa. 3. Tape Grass or " Vallis," perhaps the commonest and most useful aquarium plant. 4. The light green and delicate Ludwigia. All of these plants look bright, grow easily in average temperatures and are good " oxygenators."

A fine model of a Vampire jet plane.

BUILDING A CABIN HIGH-WING MONOPLANE

THIS small, easily transportable lightweight rubber-driven model has been designed for really sound, stable flight. With this aim in view, the model was kept simple and on proven lines, with a reasonable-sized propeller and a deep fuselage forward, as will be seen from Fig. 1. The model is simple to fly, possesses great spiral stability when reasonably well trimmed according to the flying directions, and has a beautiful glide. Although it is a duration model, places where exceptional stresses occur, such as the nose and where the undercarriage is located, are adequately reinforced by sheet covering and plastic wood. A great deal of interesting and instructive general-purpose flying can be had with this model.

Figs. 2 and 3 show the stage-by-stage construction, and these instructions are augmented by this article. As a result, even a beginner should have little difficulty in making a successful model. Newcomers to aero-modelling should pay particular attention to accuracy of the fuselage outline, which will automatically give the correct angles of incidence to wing and tail. Care should also be taken with the paper-covering methods described, and to ensure that there are no warps in wing surfaces or twists in the fuselage. No model will fly with twisted or warped surfaces.

Let us now run through the constructional details, commenting on these stage by stage, with some notes on test flights at the end.

The Fuselage

A building board is advisable, but any flat surface, such as the top of a wooden box or table, will do if a board is not available. The advantages of a board are that no one will disturb the building operations in order to demand the table for other purposes. A half-finished operation can be left while the cement is setting, until the constructor can find an opportunity to do the next job on the model. Any thick wooden plank *with no twists* is suitable as a building board.

The plan has had to be produced with the fuselage and wings " cut in half " for economy of paper reasons. These " half components," shown half scale, should be enlarged and carefully cut out and joined accurately, being pasted down to a paper backing. Any piece of paper will do, provided the lines of the fuselage are kept accurate, for these lines give the correct trim of the model.

Place the plan on the board, and over the plan pin a sheet of greaseproof paper. This will prevent the balsa cement used for glueing joints sticking to the plan. Pins for construction are ordinary domestic ones. Pin the longerons down to the board. The fuselage side longerons are laid on top of each other, as the two fuselage sides are built together. This saves time and makes for accuracy. The pins are placed each side of the longerons in order not to weaken the wood by piercing. Where the uprights come, tiny pieces of greaseproof paper are interposed between the bottom and top longeron. This will prevent the longerons sticking to each other when the uprights are cemented in. Where a longeron has a sharp bend a little soaking in water is advisable before pinning into the lines of the fuselage. This applies to the bottom forward run of the fuselage (see Fig. 4).

Now cement in the uprights with plenty of cement at the joints. A quick-drying balsa cement should always be used.

FIG. 1
A three-quarter front view of the completed monoplane.

Another view of the plane. Not a wrinkle should be visible on the completed model.

When the cement is dry, separate the two sides of the fuselage carefully with a razor blade of the one-edge type. This blade is also used for all cutting of balsa wood. Clean up the joints and then place the two sides upright, having previously cemented in the side windows of very light sheet celluloid. These two sides must be absolutely vertical and at the right distance apart according to the plan, so that the four widest crosspieces can be cemented in. When the cement is quite dry, the nose and tail crosspieces can be cemented in, keeping these sprung in by temporary pins until the cement is dry. At this stage care should be taken not to pull the fuselage out of line or to twist it. This is the difficult period. When the cement is dry at nose and tail, the remaining crosspieces, of widths made according to the plan, can be cemented in at the correct stations, slightly springing out the longerons. If, as they should be, accuracy and ease of building are sought, it always pays to make a simple jig to get the fuselage true. This can be done as shown in Fig. 5.

Remember that a twisted fuselage or a lop-sided fuselage will never permit accurate flying, as wing and tail will be out of line with each other. It is quite possible to build without a jig, if one is reasonably skilled and is possessed of an accurate eye, but a jig ensures accuracy and is usually worth the time spent in making it. Furthermore, if a second fuselage is required at any time, a jig saves trouble.

The Fittings

Fittings such as wing-retaining dowels of hardwood, tail hook and undercarriage, etc., as shown in detail in Figs. 2 and 3, should now be made and fixed to the fuselage. When these items are fitted they should be reinforced by plastic wood smeared to the sheet balsa covering these points, which it will be observed are located mostly at nose and tail. The wing platform should also be reinforced in a similar manner. Plastic wood can be obtained at any model shop or ironmonger, and can be mixed with a little balsa cement. When dry, it "spreads the load" of highly stressed parts. This is an invaluable feature not seen on many models. It certainly adds very little to the weight, but adds tremendously to

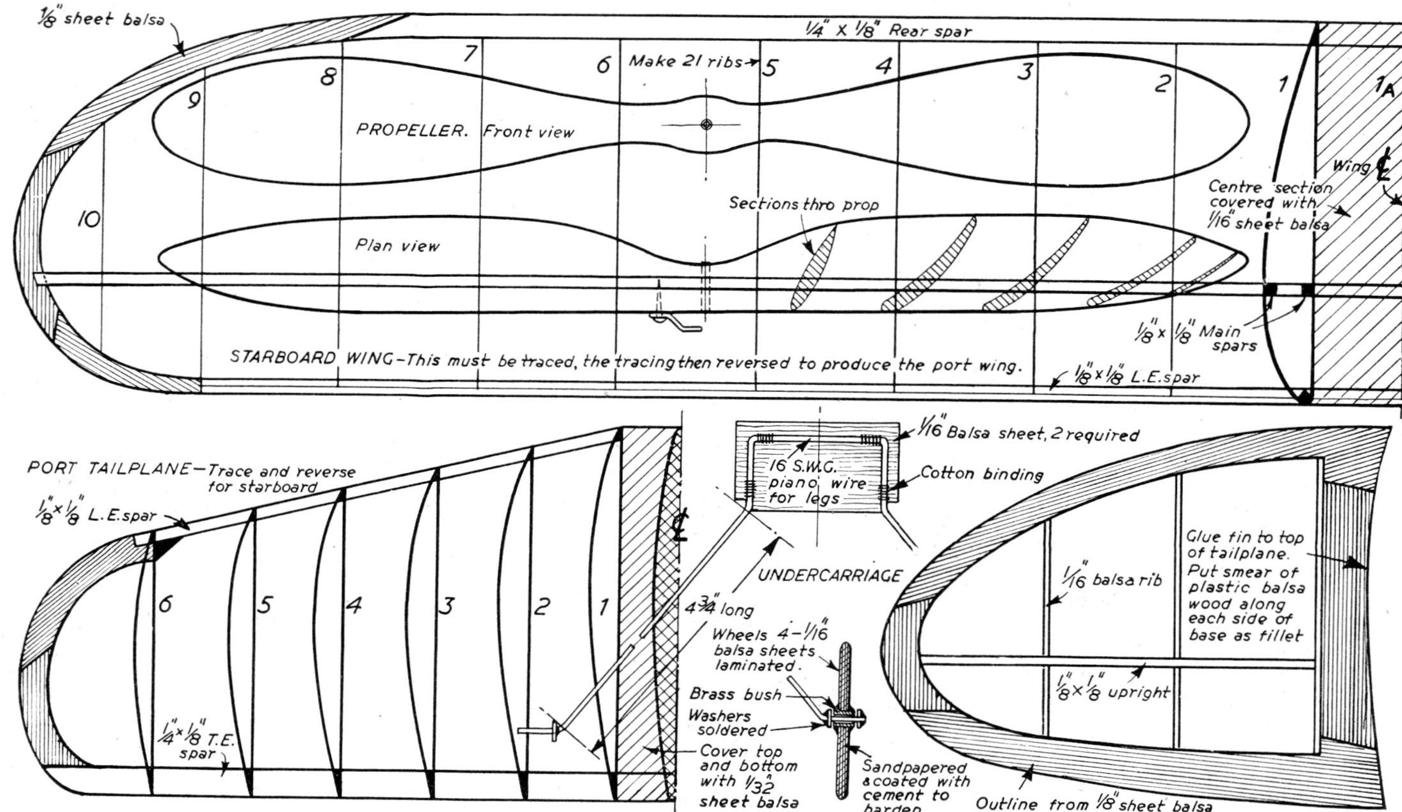

Fig. 2 (*above*) and Fig. 3 (*on the next page*) show stage-by-stage construction. The two halves of Fig. 3 should be separated and joined side by side. Both Figs. 2 and 3 should then be scaled up to the main dimensions given on Fig. 3.

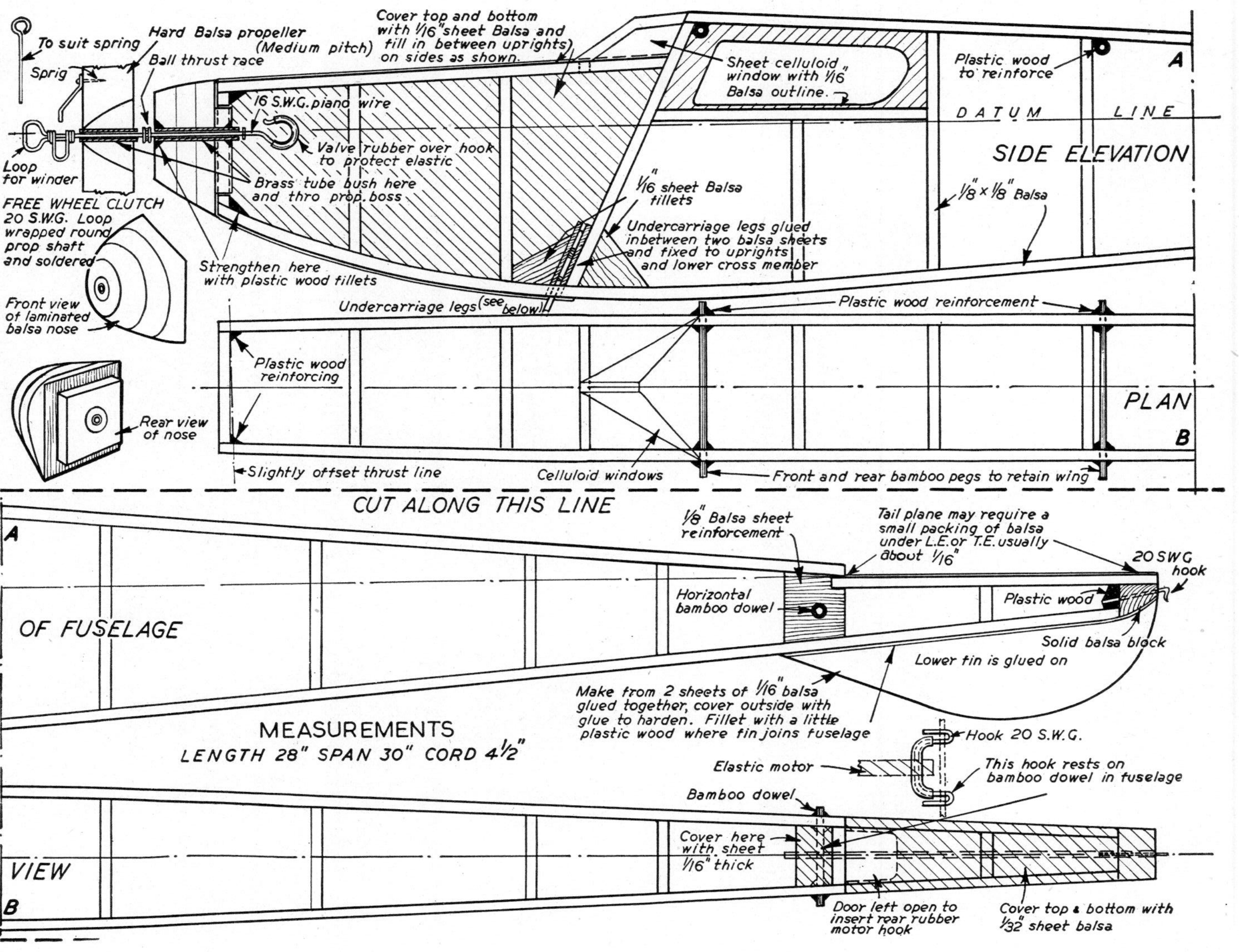
To suit spring
Sprig
Hard Balsa propeller (Medium pitch)
Ball thrust race
Cover top and bottom with 1/16" sheet Balsa and fill in between uprights on sides as shown.
Sheet celluloid window with 1/16" Balsa outline.
Plastic wood to reinforce
A
DATUM LINE
SIDE ELEVATION
16 S.W.G. piano wire
Valve rubber over hook to protect elastic
Loop for winder
Brass tube bush here and thro prop. boss
1/16" sheet Balsa fillets
1/8" x 1/8" Balsa
FREE WHEEL CLUTCH 20 S.W.G. Loop wrapped round prop shaft and soldered
Undercarriage legs glued inbetween two balsa sheets and fixed to uprights and lower cross member
Strengthen here with plastic wood fillets
Front view of laminated balsa nose
Undercarriage legs (see below)
Plastic wood reinforcement
Plastic wood reinforcing
PLAN
B
Rear view of nose
Slightly offset thrust line
Celluloid windows
Front and rear bamboo pegs to retain wing
CUT ALONG THIS LINE
A
1/8" Balsa sheet reinforcement
Tail plane may require a small packing of balsa under L.E. or T.E. usually about 1/16"
20 SWG hook
Horizontal bamboo dowel
Plastic wood
OF FUSELAGE
Solid balsa block
Lower fin is glued on
Make from 2 sheets of 1/16" balsa glued together, cover outside with glue to harden. Fillet with a little plastic wood where fin joins fuselage
MEASUREMENTS
LENGTH 28" SPAN 30" CORD 4½"
Hook 20 S.W.G.
Elastic motor
This hook rests on bamboo dowel in fuselage
Bamboo dowel
Cover here with sheet 1/16" thick
VIEW
B
Door left open to insert rear rubber motor hook
Cover top & bottom with 1/32" sheet balsa

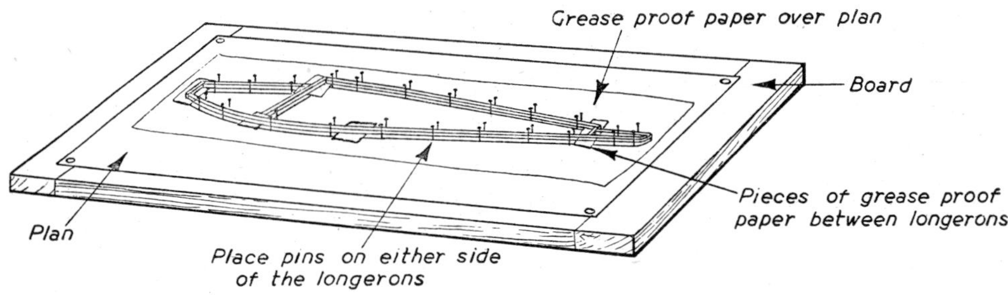

FIG. 4
Pinning down the fuselage outline to the building board

the strength, reliability and long flying life of the model.

The wing platform and tail platform are cemented on. The nosepiece is made from laminated pieces of balsa wood and then carved to the shape of the model's nose. The nose is drilled to take a bearing tube, and this drilling must be dead centre. Bearings and little ball-races to take the propeller thrust can be bought from model shops. The wire propeller shaft is carefully bent to shape by round-nosed pliers. The free-wheel mechanism makes for long glides and prevents a stopped propeller, which causes spiral dives when gliding. The free-wheel mechanism shown in Fig. 3 is therefore well worth the trouble of making, although for general-purpose flying it is possible to fly the model with a fixed propeller.

The Propeller

The propeller is a very vital component, for it provides the power. Propeller carving by a novice is not perhaps as easy as the rest of the model-building. If available, a piece of hard balsa should be used and a blank cut out to the outline shown on the plan by tracing on to the blank. The blades must be carved so that the sections as shown are incorporated and at the correct pitch angles. This matter of pitch and diameter of the propeller is always a very big secret of success in flying a light model. It is necessary to balance the propeller, as an unbalanced one will cause vibration and wobble, which will upset the model. To achieve balance, slowly spin the propeller on a shaft of wire. The blades should come to rest each time at different points. If one blade always stops at the bottom after rotation, it is too heavy and must be sand-papered down to match the other blade.

Wing, Tail and Fin

These flying surfaces are built up on the board over the plan with grease-proof paper interposed, after having cut the ribs to shape with a razor blade and sanded the outline smooth. The shape of the ribs must be accurately maintained by tracing the outline on to balsa sheet with a piece of carbon paper interposed between balsa sheet and plan. It is a good idea to make up one master rib for the wing, as this saves the plan. The rib can be made from three-ply and used to trace round. It can be saved for the future should another wing be wanted at any time.

The correct dihedral is obtained as shown in Fig. 7, p. 370. This is always important on any well-designed model, as the dihedral for lateral stability is " balanced " in design with the side area shown by the fin. If too big a dihedral is given, this may cause instability on turns. A small dihedral has a similar result and fails to recover the model in a gust. Blocks under the wing-tip ribs will ensure correct dihedral (see Fig. 7).

Covering the Flying Surfaces and the Fuselage

Rag tissue paper or " Silkspan "

STAMPS PAST AND PRESENT

These stamps show that the early issues were quite plain and without perforations; but later issues are more colourful and pictorial. The early stamps are a Ceylon 4*d.* (1859), the Penny Black of Great Britain (1840), a 2*d.* "Post Office" Mauritius (1847) worth about £4,000, a 4 anna Indian stamp (1854) and a Cape of Good Hope 4*d.* triangular (1853). The modern stamps are from Switzerland, Rumania, Austria, Hungary, Yugoslavia and Southern Rhodesia.

Cierva Autogiro

1 L-2 Stormovik

Victory Stamp

Douglas D.C.3.

Wellington & Hurricanes

Fictitious Airliner of U.S.A.

1939-45—Potez 63-11

Douglas Skymaster

Designed but not built
Fairey FC-1

AERONAUTICAL STAMPS

Top Row (reading from left to right): Spain, 1935, 2 pesetas; Russia, 1946, 15 kopeks; New Zealand, 1946, 3*d*. Centre Row: Switzerland, 1944, 1.50 francs; Poland, 1941, 1 zloty (for use on Polish Ships and Military Camps in Great Britain); U.S.A., 1944, 8 cents. Bottom Row: France, 1942, 1.50 francs plus 3.50 francs (for benefit of French airmen and their families); U.S.A., 1946, 5 cents; Réunion (French), 1944, 10 francs.

paper, obtainable from model shops, is used for covering. As mentioned at the beginning of this article, covering is a very important feature, for there should be a good surface free from drag-making wrinkles and the surfaces must not be warped by the doped covering. So many modellers make a nice air frame and then produce a poor-looking completed model because the covering is bad. Covering is really not difficult, but it requires a little practice and knowledge of the correct way to do it.

First cut the paper to the rough outline of the fuselage sides, allowing a reasonable overlap. Now smear the side to be covered with photo-paste. Lay on the paper evenly, but do not overwork or stretch. It may look a trifle loose, but, provided this is not excessive, it will not matter for we shall get it taut in a moment. The great mistake is to *overstretch* the paper over the framework when dry. Now trim around the edges, allowing approximately $\frac{1}{8}$ inch overlap. First stick this overlap down around the longerons with photo-paste, then cover the opposite fuselage side and then the top and the bottom, in that order.

Now borrow a scent spray and spray water over the covered structure evenly. When nicely wet allow to dry, but *not in front of a fire*. The paper, if reasonably well put on, will now shrink up evenly and not a wrinkle will be left when dry. When absolutely dry, dope the fuselage with two or three coats of good-quality model dope. This may appear temporarily to slack off the paper between coats, but as each coat is allowed to dry the paper will become taut and gain strength. Doping must be in a warm room free from moisture, but should not be done in front of a fire. It is important to see that the fuselage is kept true so that it does not twist as the drying takes place on each occasion.

If by any mischance a twist does develop or a wing becomes warped, it is usually possible carefully to twist these out by holding it in front of a hot fire until the doped surfaces soften. They should then be taken away to cool and the surface released when cool. Whilst cooling it should not be moved.

The nose block requires several coats of dope to harden. If the dope "blushes," it has either been applied in a damp atmosphere or is of a cheap and nasty kind. A good dope made by a reputable firm is well worth buying. "Cellon" or "Titanine" are full-size aircraft dope made by firms of world-wide repute, who also make model dope that gives every satisfaction. The wing should have two or three coats, but the tail and the fin only one coat, after the usual water shrinking. The tail unit is built lighter and may warp in hot weather if too much dope is used. Dope should be "flowed" on with a soft brush and never "worked" in like paints. Flow it on thickly without actually allowing it to run. It soon becomes tacky and dries very quickly so that any working back and forth with a brush will ruin the result.

When covering the wing, start with

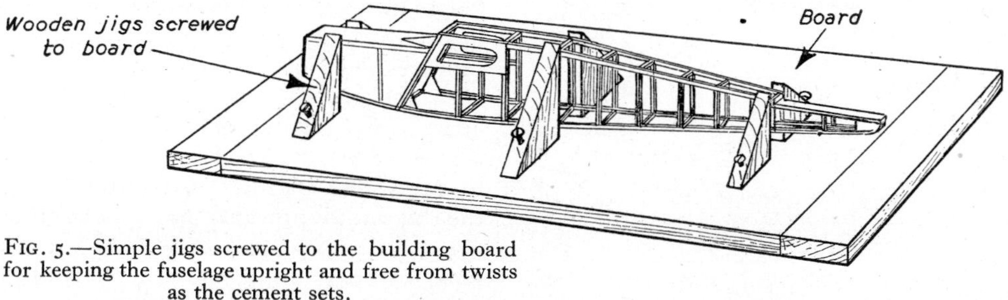

FIG. 5.—Simple jigs screwed to the building board for keeping the fuselage upright and free from twists as the cement sets.

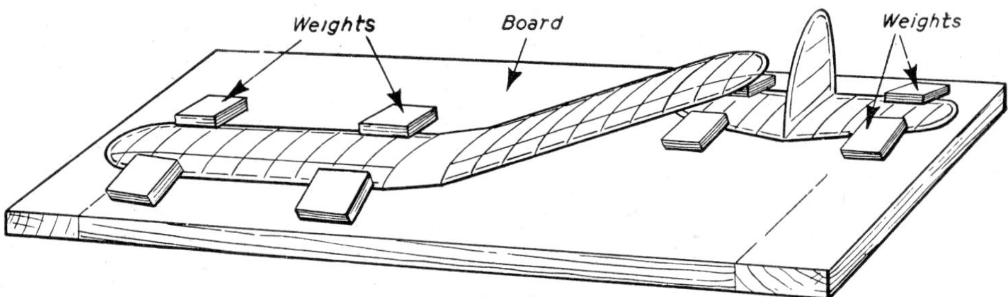

FIG. 6.—Weighting wing surfaces to prevent warping while the dope dries. Dope each wing separately and add weights carefully. Do not apply weights until uneven dope is sufficiently dry to prevent sticking to board.

the bottom and then cover the top by the same methods as used for the fuselage. Smear the outline with photo-paste, and include the bottom runs of the ribs to keep the slight under-camber. This is unnecessary for the tail, which has a flat bottom to its ribs. Whilst water or dope is drying on the wings, make sure that they are weighted down gently on to a flat board. This prevents warping, as the medium shrinks the covering material. Do one wing at a time to allow for the dihedral. Do not weight until the dope dries sufficiently not to stick to the board. It needs watching. If care is not taken, warped wings and tail will result and flying will be hopeless. One of the secrets of the expert flyers is obtaining unwarped flying surfaces, which enable proper trim to be made.

Remember, do not stretch the covering too much. Just lay it on *evenly* and the water spray will do the stretching efficiently. Of course, if you do put it on unevenly with vast wrinkles, no

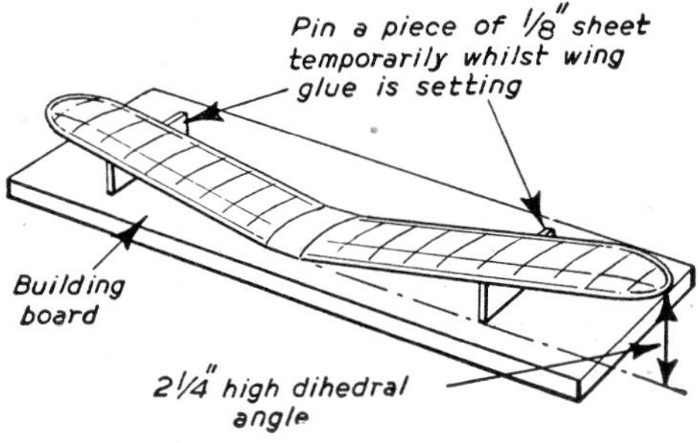

FIG. 7.—Setting the wings to the correct dihedral on a building board.

amount of water shrinking will do the job. Not a wrinkle should be visible on the finished monoplane.

The Rubber Motor

One of the troubles of a rubber-driven model is bunching of the un-wound rubber motor, which, when the model is on the glide, has to be longer than the fuselage. This may cause a shift of centre of gravity and the model dives or stalls on the glide. This is best overcome by making up the motor by the " corded method " as shown in Fig. 8. The cording allows the slack of the motor to be evenly spaced when unwound. It is a little more difficult for the novice at first and means that the motor must be " stretch wound," using a " winder " made up from a geared drill brace with a hook in the chuck. If an uncorded motor is used, it is best to fit one that is not too long and when winding up to restrict the number of turns, thus keeping the length of flights short. Even so this model should get " upstairs " well and have quite a long glide home when properly trimmed for a good glide. The beginner may feel that this is the best method to gain flying experience and indulge later in the " corded method " with the geared winder. In any case, apart from buying only the very best rubber, three things are vital. Firstly, to fit rubber bicycle valve tubing over the hooks to prevent the wire cutting the rubber strip. Secondly, use a really good rubber lubricant. Dry rubber always gives trouble and will incur extra expense for replacement. Last of all, never overwind rubber motors. Fig. 9 gives details for stretch winding.

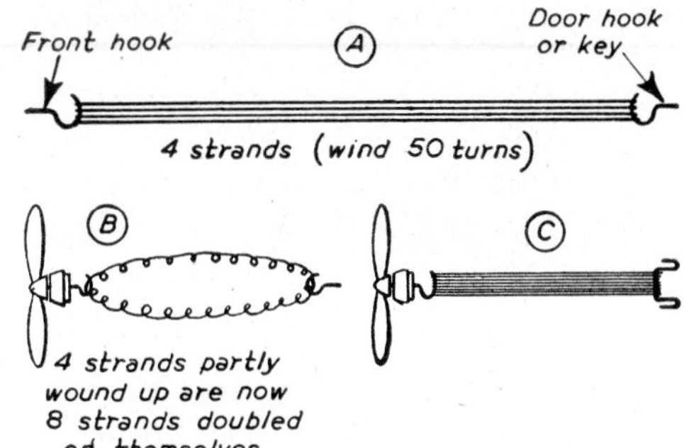

FIG. 8.—Make up the motor as at A; double the 4 strand skein over the propeller hook as at B, so that the motor becomes 8 strands. Allow the motor to go slack as at C.

Flying the Model

Now comes the important moment. The secret of success in flying is obtaining *careful gliding trim first and then controlling the power flight to prevent stalling by alteration to the thrust line.* It is advisable for the newcomer to commence by controlling his model through stable flight trim. The finer shades of trim come with experience.

To this end the glide trim will be dealt with first. It must be quite beyond reproach before we even try a power flight. If it is not obtained and adhered to, the model will stall or dive when the power ends and will probably crash.

First balance the model on the fingers with rubber in position and ready to fly. This should be done indoors in still air. The model should balance about the halfway back position from the wing's leading edge to the trailing edge. If not, add a tiny piece of lead to nose or tail. If the model is built properly this will be very small, as the design has allowed for the correct balance position. However, people build differently and balsa wood weight is variable, so there may be slight discrepancies.

Now choose a light and steady wind and, if possible, take the model out to a field with longish grass, where the effect of possible bad glide trim will be softened until we have got the trim absolutely correct, when the model will glide down to perfect landings.

Launch dead into the wind with fin set straight and throw the model like a dart at only a medium speed along a *level line*, and not upwards or downwards. If the speed of throw is approximately correct, the wind light, and the model's balance correct, it will glide flat and long, landing like a feather. The wing surfaces and tail must be square to the fuselage (see Fig. 10).

If the nose is heavy the model will dive slightly. Should this happen, put a piece of lead in the tail (temporarily retain it there under the tail rubber band) and try gliding again. If this corrects the plane the nose will now come up and the glide will be good. If it is still a trifle nose down, it may be helped by a $\frac{1}{16}$-inch slip of balsa under the tail trailing edge.

If, on the other hand, the nose has risen on the glide and the model balloons up in a stall, or even looks stallish, put a tiny bit of lead in the nose, and if the

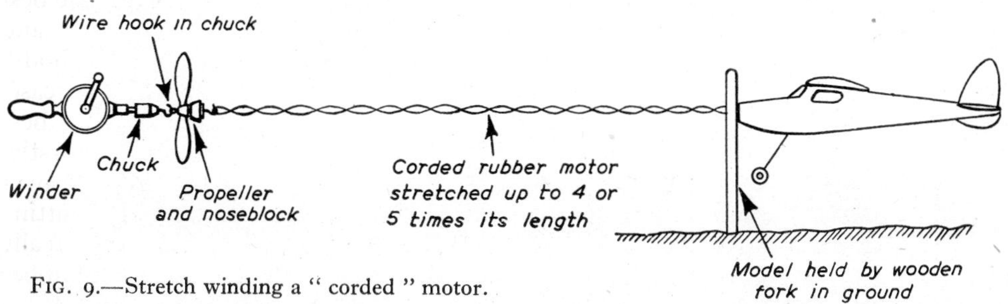

FIG. 9.—Stretch winding a "corded" motor.

subsequent glide is better but not quite right pack a $\frac{1}{16}$-inch sliver of balsa under the front (leading edge) of the tailplane.

Having achieved this long, flat glide, build in the pieces of lead or the bits of balsa packing (if any have been found necessary) by cementing into or on to the fuselage with a little plastic wood, to prevent movement in a rough landing. *Your model is now a good glider when the power ends*, provided you now trim it so that it does not end in a stall during power flight, which is what so many modellers permit. The best climb of a model aircraft, unless it is grossly over-powered, is in an even climb and not at some impossible angle like a helicopter.

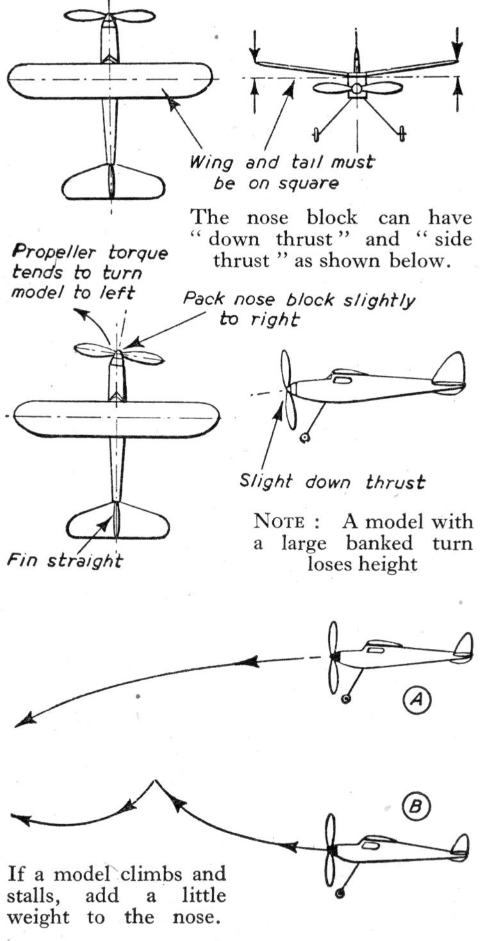

FIG. 10.—Flying the model.

At this stage power flights in easy stages can be tried. First wind about 50 turns and have a $\frac{1}{8}$-inch slip of balsa between the *top* of the nosepiece and the fuselage former. Try a launch as for a glide, *with all glide settings untouched*; NEVER TOUCH THESE SETTINGS for general purpose flying.

If the model flies at low altitude, take away the packing and try again with about 50 turns. If it now slowly gains height try 80 or 100 turns and gradually increase turns in subsequent flights, using down thrust by the packing strip if necessary. It will be observed that a certain amount of down thrust has been built into the nose in the design. It may not be necessary to give more. During these test flights we must keep control of the turn by alteration to side thrust by strips of balsa if necessary. It must be realised that a sharply-turning model will put its nose down on a banked turn, and a turn will prevent climbing. If excessive it will even nose the model into a spiral dive, which may end its life! In progressing with the tests it is necessary to keep the model TURNING UNDER POWER WITH A SLIGHT LEFT TURN. The natural propeller torque reaction will tend to turn it in left circles. Therefore it is usual to try the first flights with a slip of balsa of up to $\frac{1}{8}$ inch thick wedged between nosepiece and front; the former on the left side, that is, looking at the model from the top and to the front. This will counteract the left turn. Gradually reduce this thickness of packing until the torque reaction carries the model round in slow-climbing circles to the left under power with up to threequarters full wind, which is all that should normally be attempted if you want to preserve your rubber motor. Remember that after a few flights a rubber motor should be rested, when it will regain its natural elasticity. Never keep a rubber motor wound up for long periods.

Keep the fin straight and all surfaces true, unwarped, and placed on "square."

MODEL RAILWAYS

Keystone.

REPAIRS TO THE ROLLING STOCK

Here we have some youthful experts at work on their model railway at Dr. Barnardo's Home at Kingston-on-Thames. They are carrying out minor repairs to the rolling stock used on the track of the system seen on the next page. Altogether the model has 120 ft. of track and covers an area 16 ft. by 4 ft.

MODELS have always held a fascination for boys and the variety in existence gives us an enormous choice and field. There are those to be seen at great exhibitions and in museums or shop-windows before which thousands linger, and there are the practical hobbies for enthusiasts, running one's own railway, constructing a model 'plane or sailing a model ship.

These hobbies are not merely amusements for the young: they belong to that class of hobby in which the interest lasts a lifetime. The young boy of seven and the old boy of seventy meet on common ground when both share the same fascination in models and model making.

About the Gauges

For those of you who favour railways I cannot do better than give a brief review of the different model gauges in use in this country to-day and their special features.

When I first took an interest in model railways, wide gauges were in use, but as in those days model locomotive design bore little relation to the real thing, the size of gauge was not of vital importance. Lately a demand for more realism in models has grown up, which has resulted in the production of smaller gauges. You will see the necessity for this if you study the long type of express locomotive and realise the need for larger radius curves to run a model successfully.

For some years now, gauge "oo" (which is $\frac{5}{8}$ inch between the rails) has been making headway. The novelty of a comparatively inexpensive line, of a size which could accommodate a really comprehensive layout on a medium-sized table, meets with great enthusiasm. In the case of the Trix table railway, the locomotives are fitted with A.C. motors, either operated from A.C. mains through a transformer or worked from accumulators. In the Hornby " Dublo " system the engines are fitted with a permanent magnet motor working off direct current.

" oo " is the gauge for the man who prefers operation rather than construction. In the smallest gauges the building of locomotives and rolling stock is hardly a task for the amateur. He can get his fun from the running of his layout to a timetable schedule ; and, if he has an artistic tendency, in preparing railside features and a scenic background for the railway. " oo " gauge is too small for a clockwork mechanism and hardly possible in steam, so electricity is the only prime mover left. The small locomotives are easily controlled by a switch, which enables them to run forward or in reverse. There are other types of electric locomotives, and the model enthusiast will decide which suits him best.

Choice of Motive Power

Next on our list is gauge " o ", or 1¼ inches between the rails, probably the most popular gauge both in Europe and in America. It is a standard in all

Keystone.

A REMARKABLE MODEL RAILWAY SYSTEM

Helped and advised by their masters some 14 boys at Dr. Barnardo's Home constructed a complex Gauge oo electric double track, complete with fly-overs, tunnels, crossings and six stations. Operating the system is a matter of teamwork and each boy has his job on the line. The boys also run their own repairs workshop.

YOUTHFUL MODEL MAKERS

Coventry Evening Telegraph.

A branch of young model-makers has been formed at the Barkers Butts Senior School for Boys in Coventry. Our photograph shows a group of club members watching with keen interest the running of a model locomotive at a branch exhibition.

Leicester Mercury.

Young model-makers, members of the Belgrave Union branch, are seen here with their Leader at one of the club's exhibitions of model trains in Leicester.

No. 1 GAUGE

Mr. Victor B. Harrison's $1\frac{3}{4}$-inch lay-out at Bishop's Stortford—one of the finest gauge 1 railways ever built. The steam loco. "City of Truro" receives the all-clear as she passes through Lone Pine Station.

countries, and here I think we might discuss the prime movers available to the model railway hobbyist, clockwork, electricity and steam, for gauge "o" is

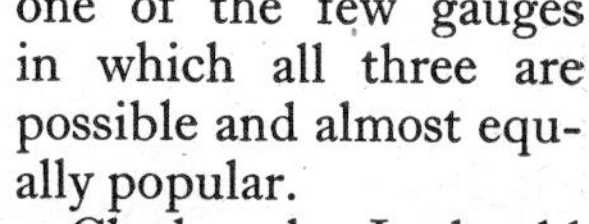

one of the few gauges in which all three are possible and almost equally popular.

Clockwork, I should say, is the most suitable choice for youth. One simply winds up a spring and there is no mess or smell or risk to a small child. Also it can be used with equal success indoors or out-of-doors in a gale of wind. The cheapest models are obtainable in clockwork, although most elaborate models can be built with clockwork mechanisms as prime movers.

A GAUGE "O" LINE

Mr. Cecil J. Allen sponsors an "o" gauge clockwork railway out of doors. In the garden for speed and healthy exercise or indoors for all-the-year-round working and super-detail production.

Steam always seems to make the greatest appeal and is the "senior" prime mover. There is with it the realism that

ELECTRICITY FOR GAUGE 1

Another view of Mr. Harrison's railway, showing the six-arch viaduct in the foreground. It is being crossed by a three-coach "Southern Electric" set.

corresponds to the work of the actual locomotive, and, given common sense, a model steam engine can be both clean and safe in its working.

The third power unit is electricity, the most popular prime mover of all. Electric trains take different forms—firstly models of existing electric trains and secondly replicas of steam locomotives with a specially designed motor concealed in the steam outline body. The most universal method is by means of track fitted with a conductor or third rail through which the motor picks up the current.

UNDER COVER

An enthusiast at the controls of his gauge "o" electric railway. The line has been built in a garage.

ANOTHER VIEW

This is a different aspect of the model railway above. Garages, attics, basements, etc., all prove good spots in which to set up a system.

The permanent magnet motor is the type which most model railwaymen consider the best prime mover when it comes to refinement of control. These motors have a current supply of about 8–10 volts D.C., supplied by storage batteries or from the A.C. house mains through a rectifier.

AWAITING THE RIGHT-AWAY

Here the train on a model railway is waiting with steam up for the right-away. This line is gauge 1.

TEACHING THE YOUNG IDEA

A group of Sea Cadets is included among those watching this demonstration by the owner of this realistic model steam trawler.

Electric locomotives are also fitted with alternating current motors working off 20 volts A.C. (but in general this is used on the less intricate kind of electric railway), operated from the house mains through a transformer.

Returning to gauge "o," the portable type of track is usually pressed tinned steel plate, but for more permanent structures scale model permanent way is used. To the average hobbyist gauge "o" presents perhaps the greatest scope. He can lay his own track, build his own wagons and coaches, and even construct his own locomotives. Signalling a line also presents another interesting phase of the hobby.

For the Expert

Gauge 1 (or $1\frac{3}{4}$ inches between the rails) is the next standard gauge, which is particularly popular with those who like an outdoor railway. As the scale grows, clockwork gradually becomes less suitable as a motive power and steam begins to come into its own. Gauge 1 is the commercial "limit" for clockwork traction, but electric power is also used quite frequently, and the size of the gauge 1 steam locomotive is big enough to house an efficient internally fired boiler. This gauge is a proposition for the serious amateur with both time and money to spend.

It is a big jump to the next gauge—$2\frac{1}{2}$ inches—which represents a scale of $\frac{1}{2}$ inch to the foot. This is the size beloved of amateurs with engineering knowledge, who build their own working steam models, either fed by methylated spirit or with proper fire-box using solid fuel.

Ships of All Kinds

Whether you own a model, build one or make a study of them, this hobby makes a strong appeal, for being a seafaring nation, the ocean and the ships which sail the Seven Seas are uppermost in a British boys' mind.

Model boats can be inexpensive ones made from pressed tinplate and driven by a clockwork motor, or with carved wooden hulls powered by either an electric motor or steam engine. This more elaborate type can be built in varied forms such as steam-yachts, tramp steamers, cargo boats, lifeboats—even modern liners or warships.

The most popular means of propulsion among amateurs is electricity. Where high speed is required, however, steam, diesel or petrol propulsion is far and away the most satisfactory.

Some very simple boats may be propelled by means of a twisted elastic skein, as is used for propelling some types of model aircraft. Another method is by means of a simple reaction motor of the type described on p. 364.

A PAGE OF MODEL SHIPS

This is a beautiful scale model of a Training Ship, the *Juan Sebastian del Cano*. It is one-fiftieth actual size.

Here is a model of a famous British battleship, one-sixty-fourth actual size. Vessels of the Royal Navy make splendid models.

Here is a working model of a private steam yacht, and it can be seen how perfect the vessel is down to the smallest detail. The construction of ship models is a clever combination of science and art forming one of the most fascinating of pastimes.

BOATS AND BOAT BUILDING

MODEL BOATS ON A LONDON POND

Sailing model yachts is a splendid hobby. Safe as well as interesting, the handling of one of these small craft calls for a good deal of skill. In gaining the knowledge necessary to get the best out of a boat, its skipper will soon acquire a sound working knowledge of the principles governing wind and sail.

BUILDING model boats is one of the most fascinating hobbies that any boy can take up. No great skill is required beyond the ability to handle tools moderately well ; whereas the pleasure and sport derived from the completed models will well repay all the care and trouble expended.

A Model Sailing Boat

Here is an easily made boat which will sail well if care is taken in building it (see Fig. 1).

The hull is made from a piece of wood 9 inches long, $2\frac{1}{2}$ inches wide, and 1 inch thick. Mark a centre line along the top and bottom of the wood and then carefully outline the shape of the hull as shown at B (Fig. 2). With a tenon saw, roughly cut away the parts C, C, and also the corners at the back. Now proceed to carve the hull to shape with a chisel. You will see, by looking at diagrams A and D, what the front and side of the hull should look like when finished. Give the hull a good rubbing all over with glasspaper. To represent planking, the parallel lines along the deck can be scored on with a bradawl, using a ruler as a guide.

For the keel, take a piece of $\frac{3}{8}$-inch wood $5\frac{1}{4}$ inches long and 2 inches wide and saw it to the size given at E. Taper the front part at F so that it forms a narrow edge. On each side of the bottom of the keel, nail a strip of sheet lead about $\frac{1}{2}$ inch wide and file this to a round shape. To fix the keel in place, cut a slot $\frac{3}{8}$ inch wide along the centre of the bottom of the hull, and after glueing the keel in place, drive in a couple of long fine nails as shown in diagram D.

The Mast, Spars and Sails

Wooden knitting needles, about $\frac{3}{16}$ inch diameter, can be used for the mast and spars, the lengths of which are given in the sketch of the finished boat. The bowsprit is fixed to the deck by two wire staples, and the bottom of the mast is pushed into a hole about $\frac{3}{4}$ inch deep in the hull.

The sails can be cut out of fine white linen to the sizes given, allowing about $\frac{1}{4}$ inch extra all round for hemming. Use very thin twine for the rigging and attach the ends of the shrouds to small screw eyes fixed in the deck.

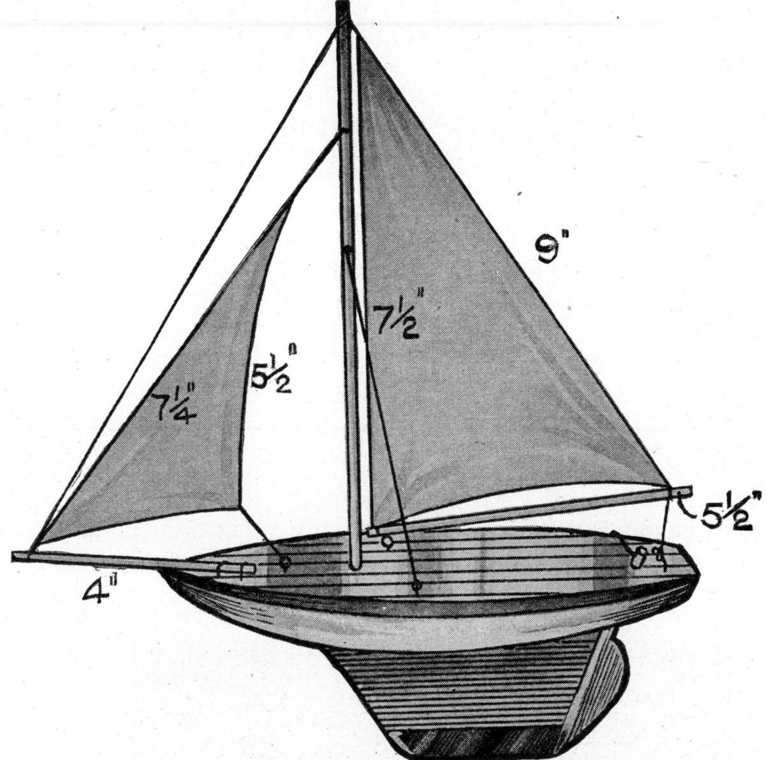

FIG. 1.—The model yacht as it appears when the construction is completed.

The Rudder

To complete the boat, a rudder can be fitted, fashioned out of a piece of $\frac{3}{16}$-inch fretwood to the dimensions given at G, the top part working in a hole in the hull, while the bottom part is held by two wire staples.

Give the hull two coats of white enamel and paint a $\frac{1}{4}$-inch band of bright red or blue all round the hull. When quite dry, your smart little craft will be ready for its trial trip.

A Model Racing Yacht

The model yacht illustrated in Fig. 3 is of very simple design, only two pieces of wood being used in the construction of the hull, details

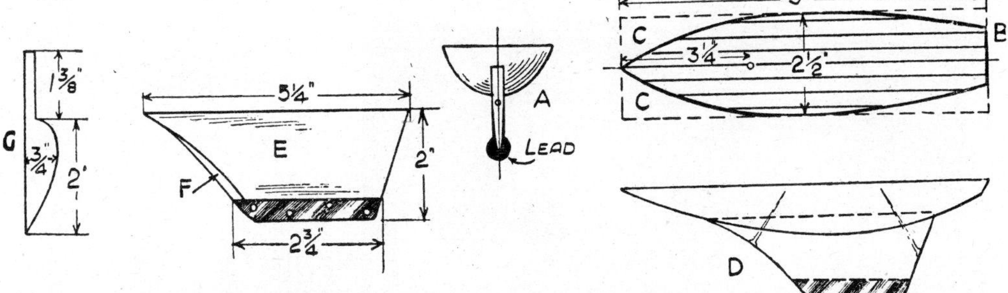

FIG. 2.—Diagrams A and D show the front and side views of the hull. Diagram B illustrates the shaping of the hull, while Diagrams E and G show the keel and rudder.

of which are shown in Fig. 4. Begin by cutting a cardboard template to the measurements given in Fig. 5. Then select a piece of straight-grained wood 15 inches by 5 inches, and at least $\frac{3}{4}$ inch thick. Thicker wood may be used, but will mean more trouble in cutting and shaping. Draw a centre line longitudinally upon this piece of wood. Place the straight side of the template against it and run a pencil round the curve ; then turn the template over and draw the other curve, thus ensuring balance. Cut round the outline with a fretsaw, and the hull is ready for shaping.

The best tool for this purpose is a small metal plane. Work lengthwise, first rounding the edges, and continuing until the hull is shaped like the cross section in Fig. 4, but leaving flat a portion along the centre for the attachment of the keel-fin. Shape the bows and the stern with a sharp penknife, and finish off the hull with sandpaper. The keel-fin is cut from $\frac{3}{8}$-inch wood to the measurements given in Fig. 4, the front and back edges being rounded as indicated by the shading. It is secured to the hull by three $1\frac{1}{2}$-inch brass screws, the heads of which are sunk flush with the deck. Cast a lead keel slightly larger than required and screw it to the bottom edge of the keel-fin, afterwards trimming it down with a file. The rudder and rudder-post are cut in one piece of $\frac{1}{4}$-inch wood, the post being rounded and a hole bored through the hull to receive it. The lower end is pivoted upon a right-angled brass wire staple as shown by the dotted line (see Fig. 4).

FIG. 3.—Here is an actual photograph of a workmanlike model yacht. Cheap and simple to make, this model will give excellent results.

The Mast and Sails

The mast is 16 inches high from the deck level but is cut $\frac{1}{2}$ inch longer to allow for stepping. Cut it $\frac{3}{8}$ inch square, then plane and sandpaper it until perfectly round and smooth. It fits tightly into a hole made at a point on the centre line 5 inches from the bows. The bowsprit is 5 inches long and is secured by two small nails. The mainsail boom is 9 inches long and is attached to the mast by means of a small brass screw-eye and a brass wire staple as shown in Fig. 4 ; the other end being rounded and a saw-cut made in it for securing the sail. The jib-boom is 6 inches long and is similar in construction to the mainsail-boom.

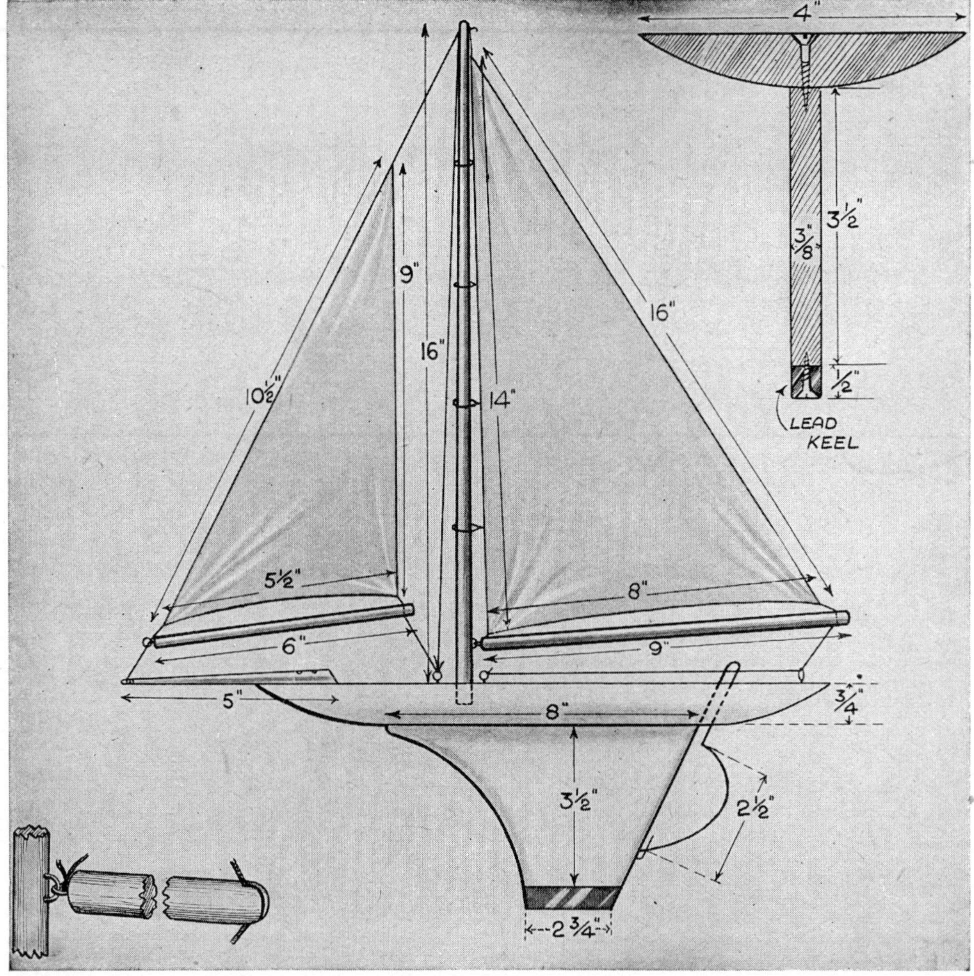

FIG. 4.—These diagrams show the constructional details of a model racing yacht. In the centre is the side elevation of the boat, whilst top right is a cross-section of the hull. At the bottom left-hand corner you are shown how to attach the mainsail boom.

The sails may be made from any convenient white material, or the special fabric sold for the purpose may be used. Cut a paper pattern before cutting the material, and allow an extra $\frac{1}{2}$ inch all round for hemming. If you mistrust your powers with the needle, get a female member of the household to do this part of the job for you. Four rings made from brass wire are sewn at equidistant points along one edge of the mainsail, and a length of thin cord is fastened to each of the corners of the sails for attaching them to the spars. The top of the mast has a saw-cut made in it where the cord passes over it, and three brass screw-eyes screwed to the deck at the positions shown complete the yacht.

1" 1⅝" 1⅞" 2" 1⅞" 1¾" 2" MAST 14"

FIG. 5.—Cardboard template for the hull.

A MODEL MOTOR-BOAT

FIG. 1.—A general view of the finished motor-boat.

FIG. 1 shows a motor-boat which is driven by the most elementary form of reaction propulsion, and it will be seen that the boat is of the cabin cruiser type.

Constructional Details

The hull is made from a single piece of thin tinplate, cut to the shape shown in Fig. 2. The metal is bent along the dotted lines, and the bottom of the hull at the forward end is bent slightly to conform to the curvature of the sides. All the joints are then soft soldered.

All the tinplate for making the boat described was obtained from two 2-lb. jam tins, which were cut up with the aid of a fine hacksaw and small pair of tin-shears.

The next part to prepare is the boiler tube, and for this an 18-inch length of $\frac{1}{8}$-inch outside diameter light-gauge copper tubing will be required. The middle part of this tubing is gradually bent round a wooden mandrel about $1\frac{1}{8}$ inches diameter (a tool handle will answer the purpose) to form a double coil, as shown in Figs. 3 and 4. One end of the tubing is passed through a hole made in the stern of the boat, the other end passing through a hole made in the bottom of the hull $\frac{5}{8}$ inch from the rear end, so that the projecting ends of the tube are one above the other when finally soldered in place. To enable this to be done the lower end of the tube is bent as shown in Fig. 3.

Before soldering the ends of the copper tubing in place, put a small block of wood, $\frac{3}{8}$ inch thick, underneath the coiled part of the tubing in order to provide sufficient space for the burner. The wood block is afterwards removed, leaving the copper tubing in the position indicated in Fig. 3, which also shows the methylated spirit holder in position.

Superstructures

The "turtle" deck is cut out to shape and to the dimensions given in Fig. 5, and then carefully bent till it fits snugly in the bows of the boat. It is then soldered in place.

The cabin is made from a single piece of tinplate cut out as indicated in Fig. 6, and bent on the dotted lines after drilling the hole for the funnel and the portholes. After soldering the four corner joints, place the cabin in position, and on the front of it mark a line coinciding with the curved back edge of the turtle deck. With the aid of a small metal saw, cut a curved slot as shown in the illustration, Fig. 4. The edge of the turtle deck, by projecting slightly into this slot, supports the front of the cabin. The rear of the cabin is

THE BOY THROUGH THE AGES

In this picture we see Marcus, a Roman boy in the days when Britain was part of the great Roman Empire. Many Roman officials and their families lived in the cities they built in this country. Marcus went regularly to school and learnt to count on the abacus, seen in the picture. There was no glass in the window, though the art of glass-making was well known to the Romans. Writing was done with a stylus on parchments which were later rolled and placed in a case.

TAKING TRIBUTE TO THE TITHE BARN

Leofric was a boy who lived in England during the Saxon period and in this picture we see him with the other villagers taking the tribute or tithe which was paid to the Church. From about the time of Bede this payment of tithes, the tenth part of the produce of the land or of other work, became part of the established customs of the country, and continued through the centuries. Leofric is carrying a little pig as his parents' contribution.

The boy who is the central figure in this picture was named Roger. He is making his way to Parliament with his master. At this period, in the days of Henry V, Henry VI, and Edward IV, wheels were used only on rough tumbrils for the carrying of farm produce. The majority of people travelled on horseback, and the goods of the country were mainly transported by pack-horse. Only the very elderly or infirm used litters such as the one seen on the left of the picture.

AN APPRENTICE WORKS AT THE LOOM

Giles, who lived in the fifteenth century, was happy to become an apprentice to a weaver in order to be taught how to make cloth on a loom, taking the crosswise threads with a shuttle in and out among those that ran the long way of the piece. His master belonged to the guild of his trade, which had made this country famous for its cloth-making. These guilds and their system of apprenticeship produced the most highly-skilled craftsmen in the world.

HUMPHREY VISITS THE THEATRE

Humphrey belonged to the spacious days of Good Queen Bess—the time of Walter Raleigh, Martin Frobisher, Francis Drake, and other great sailors whose names have come down to us in history. One of Humphrey's chief delights was to be allowed to pay a visit to the Globe Theatre in London to see performed the plays of Master William Shakespeare. Here, for example, he is most thoroughly enjoying the presentation of *A Midsummer Night's Dream.*

SAILING FOR LIFE IN A NEW LAND

Here we see Jabez, who was a member of a Puritan family. The Puritans rose in the sixteenth century, but were oppressed by the Stuarts, with the result that many of them left for America, there to establish new homes. In the picture we see Jabez with his father and mother, brother and sister, setting off from the quay for the galleon in which they were to brave the perils of the Atlantic and whatever unknown dangers might await them in the new lands beyond the ocean.

HOMEWARD BOUND FOR CHRISTMAS

Travel by stage coach became more general in the 18th century as the surface of the roads between the towns was improved. Here we see John in the year 1720; it had been arranged that he should travel from London to spend Christmas with his family at Cambridge. Snow lay deep on the country roads and every seat on the coach was booked. John had to ride uncomfortably in a basket at the back—a receptacle which came to be known as a "boot."

THE FIRST PASSENGER STEAM TRAIN

Tom was brought up in Manchester, and it was his good fortune, in 1830, to see the first passenger-carrying train on the railway-line between his home town and Liverpool. Here he is standing beside the track, waving excitedly as the engine clangs its way along. At the rear important people are riding in their own carriage, which has been placed on a flat-topped truck. The earliest third-class carriages were not covered in and it was not till after 1844 that passengers were entitled to have a roof over their heads.

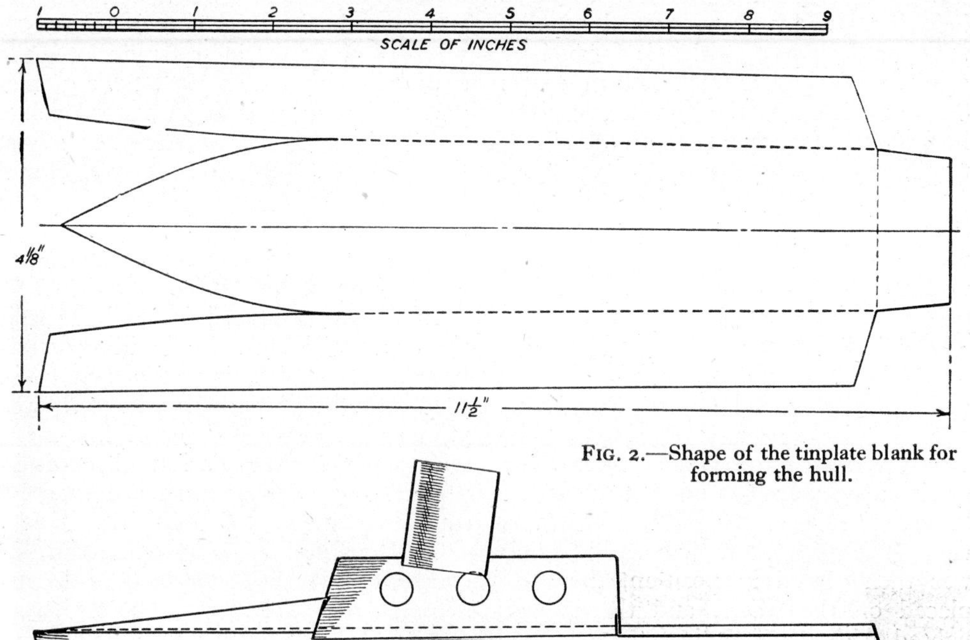

FIG. 2.—Shape of the tinplate blank for forming the hull.

FIG. 3.—(*above*) Sectional elevation and (*below*) plan, showing the arrangement of the propulsion unit.

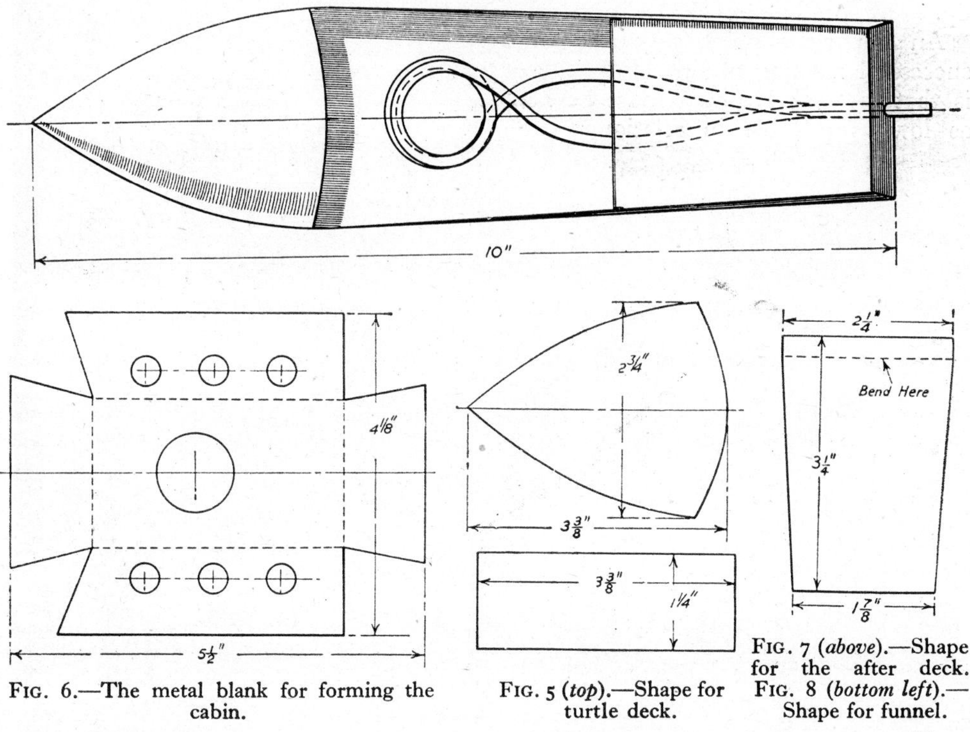

FIG. 6.—The metal blank for forming the cabin.

FIG. 5 (*top*).—Shape for turtle deck.

FIG. 7 (*above*).—Shape for the after deck. FIG. 8 (*bottom left*).—Shape for funnel.

held in place by the upturned edge of the rear deck part, which is formed by a piece of tinplate soldered in place. This part is cut to the dimensions given in Fig. 7. For the funnel, a strip of tinplate is cut out (see Fig. 8) and bent round a wooden former 1 inch diameter. The butt joint is soldered on the inside, after which the funnel is soldered on the inside of the hole in the cabin roof.

The Burner

In the boat illustrated, the burner consisted of a metal screwed cap about 1 inch diameter and $\frac{5}{16}$ inch deep. This was filled with solidified methylated spirit and placed under the coiled "boiler" tube each time the boat was run. The cabin, complete with funnel, was then placed in position, the boat placed on the water, and the burner lighted with a match inserted through one of the portholes.

As soon as the coils were hot the boat began to "chug" away in quite a realistic manner, and travelled along fussily until the burner spirit was used up.

An important point concerning the successful running of this kind of boat is that the coiled tubing must be kept as low as possible in relation to the water level when the boat is afloat. It will be noticed, in reference to the sectional view in Fig. 3, that the greater part of the tubing is below water level.

It may be found necessary to adjust the distance between the water level and the top end of the propulsion tube, and this can easily be done by placing a small weight on about the middle of the after deck.

Finally, with regard to the burner, if there is any difficulty in obtaining solidified methylated spirit, the small tin holder can be packed with asbestos yarn and a circular cover of fine-mesh wire gauze fitted over it to keep it in place. The asbestos yarn can then be saturated with methylated spirit.

This method of propulsion can, of course, only be used for small and light models requiring a tiny amount of power.

Additional speed can be obtained by fitting two or more of these reaction units to the boat. They should be mounted, of course, side by side. The speed of the boat can be increased if the projecting ends of tubes are slightly flattened.

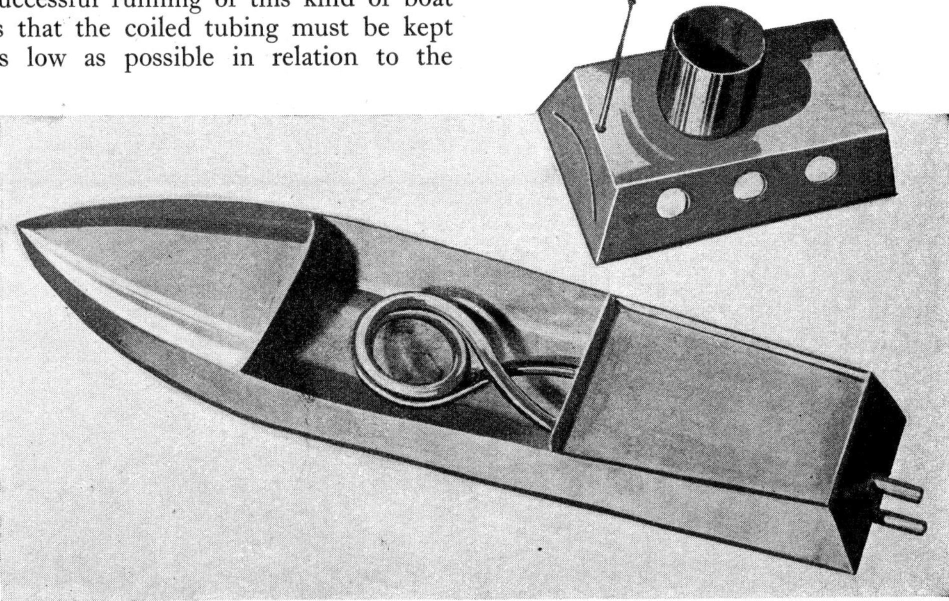

FIG. 4.—View of the boat with superstructure removed. Note the curved slot in the front of the cabin.

MODEL SHIPS IN BOTTLES

An artist's impression of a ship in a bottle.

A MODEL of a ship in a bottle often puzzles yet always appeals to everyone. It takes very little time to make and costs but a few pence and makes an attractive ornament. The materials required are as follow: several lengths of stout wire, some odd scraps of wood, putty, quick-drying enamel or paint, and a bottle either of the round or square variety. If possible, a square bottle should be used owing to the shorter neck. The parts are passed into the bottle by means of a length of wire with a needle firmly attached to it. Another length of wire with a bend of ½ inch at the end is used to form the rake which pulls the parts into position when they are in the bottle. At least two lengths are required for the paint brushes; tufts from an old clothes-brush answer very well, being secured firmly with thread. The ship consists of the following parts: the hull, the body, the top and the masts.

The length of the hull is 5¾ inches by ½ inch square. The raised fo'c'sle and stern are shaped from the solid hull. A glance at Fig. 1 should make its construction quite clear. Holes are drilled through for the rigging, and two holes are bored from the top to the bottom so that the foot of the mast can be secured with wire.

A hole is also bored at the bows to take the mast stay. Two masts are now required, each being 1¾ inches by ⅛ inch diameter. Two holes are then bored in each, the upper being for the rigging and the lower for securing them to the hull. Secure the masts to the hull as shown in Fig. 2 and pass a length of cotton through the left-hand hole of the hull, through the mast from the back to the front, down through the right-hand hole in the hull, up again, through the mast from the front to the back, down to the starting place, and draw taut with a knot.

The Mast Stay

Having wired on and rigged the masts, the next step is to put on the mast stay, which consists of thread or silk cotton. This is done as shown in Fig. 1, so that the masts can be raised or lowered with the rigging remaining taut. Care must be taken that the mast stay is sufficiently long to grip on the outside of the bottle. If the masts do not lie flat a piece can be cut from the hull, which can afterwards be covered by a thin piece of wood.

The body is made from three strips of wood 3 inches by $\frac{5}{16}$ inch by $\frac{3}{16}$ inch and four strips of very thin cardboard 3 inches by ½ inch; these are glued together with the cardboard at the top and bottom, with the remaining pieces of cardboard dividing the wood as shown (Fig. 3). (The edges of the cardboard overlapping the piece of wood may be sewn if desired, though this is not essential.) If sewn, the cotton becomes stiff after painting and will appear like rails. Dots may be added to give the effect of port-holes.

The Top and Funnels

The top is made from a strip of cardboard the same size as the body, and to this is fitted the bridge, boats, ventilators and funnels (see Fig. 4). These are all glued on to the top, except the funnels, which are placed separately in position in the bottle. Match sticks are suitable for the boats, while pieces of dowel rod ¼ inch long should be used for the funnels.

Small hatches, etc., may be added if desired.

Preparing the Bottle

Obtain a square bottle if possible, thoroughly clean and dry, and paint the bottom and end blue. The land is painted green, great care being taken that the brush does not touch the front of the bottle nor the front half of the top, as the whole view is obtained here, the remainder being the background. Unless the bottle is painted the putty will show white underneath when the bottle is turned over. When dry, the putty should be put in piece by piece and spread over the bottom with the rake, spreading out very thinly and making a sloping design to represent the land. As soon as the putty is in, paint the sea blue; a few dabs of white added give a good effect. The land can then be painted green. After painting, a few red-topped houses about a ¼ inch square may be added; these show up well and look quite large from the outside of the bottle. As each part of the ship is finished it should be painted, as it is impossible to paint the ship once it is inside the bottle.

The hull of the ship should be painted black except ⅛ inch. from the bottom, which should be painted red. The body, edges of pieces and top are painted white, the funnels red, with black tops.

Inserting the Model

With the ship and the bottle ready it is quite easy to fit the ship up inside. Lay the masts down towards the stern and push the hull into the bottle stern first. As soon as the bow is clear of the neck, hold it down with the rake and pull gently on the mast stay. As soon as the masts are upright, push the hull further in and then press down firmly with the rake. A spot of glue placed on the end of a wire dropped into the hole at the bows will secure the mast stay. Allow a few minutes to dry and then cut

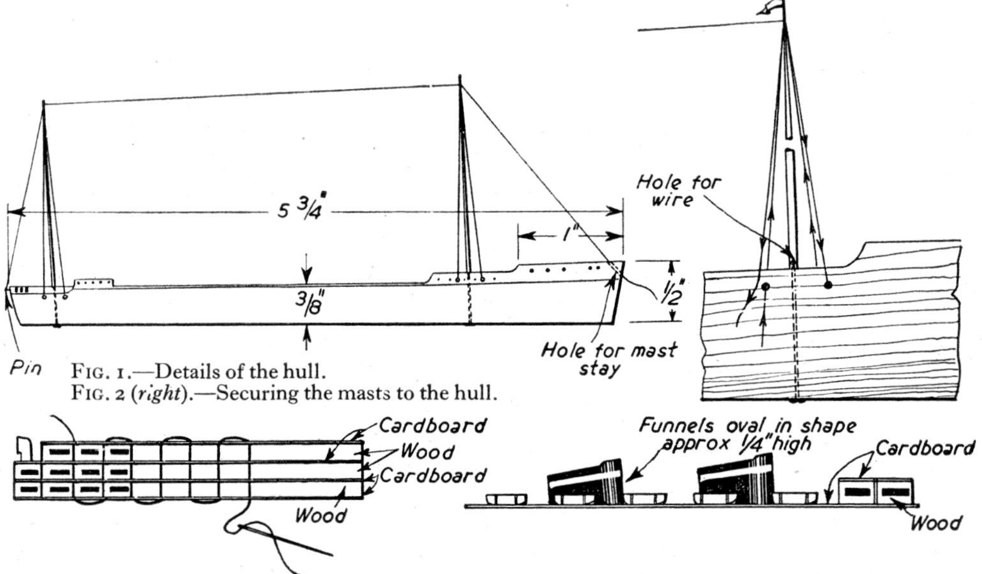

FIG. 1.—Details of the hull.
FIG. 2 (*right*).—Securing the masts to the hull.

FIG. 3.—How the body of the ship is formed.

FIG. 4.—Details of the bridge, funnels and boats.

off as close as possible to the end of stay, twirling the remainder round with a wire and burying it out of sight on the land side of the ship.

The next piece to be passed in is the body, which is glued in place. The same operation applies to the top, funnels and bridge piece.

The general methods of inserting model ships in bottles described in this section can be applied to more elaborate ships such as three-masters and full-rig ships, but these are tedious to make and require more skill.

It is possible to insert models other than ships, such as models of lathes, motor cars and aeroplanes. Even working models may be inserted in bottles. In this case they are usually powered by a small electric motor with the leads to the source of power such as the mains or battery passing through the bottle cap and being secreted under whatever material is used as a base for the model. Such models attract much attention at exhibitions and bazaars; in fact, considerable sums have been raised for charity by this means.

Kits of parts for small model boats are on the market and these save considerable time, since most of the parts come ready shaped.

A DIVING DOLL

THE uncanny and apparently automatic diving action of this doll makes it a most interesting toy. The doll should be a small celluloid one, about an inch or 2 inches high. They are obtainable at almost all toy-shops and cost only a few pence each. The dolls are hollow and ordinarily float on their backs. To make your doll into a diver, however, it is necessary that the feet should be weighted so that it will float upright. The best way to do this is to screw a wood-screw into the sole of the feet (they are usually moulded in one). Choose a screw sufficiently heavy that the doll just floats in the water, and the slightest extra weight would make it sink. By experimenting with different-sized screws you will find one which makes the doll float in a state of equilibrium.

A diving doll.

The best kind of " deep sea " for this diver to work in is a wide-mouthed glass jar, which should be as tall as possible. A pickle jar is a good type to use. Fill it up with water, put the doll in and tie a piece of thin rubber sheet (half an old balloon) tightly over the mouth. You will now find that a slight touch with your finger on the rubber cap will cause the diver to lower itself to the bottom, where it will stay until the pressure is removed. The explanation of the phenomenon is that the pressure created inside the jar acts on all sides of the doll, causing it to compress a little; the result is that the displacement of water by the compressed doll is less than what it was when it floated, and hence, being comparatively heavier, the doll sinks. As soon as the pressure is released the doll regains its original size and, thus becoming lighter, rises.

Such a slight movement of the hand is necessary to make the doll move that to the onlooker it appears to be acting of its own free will. Much amusement may be had by announcing that the doll will obey orders to dive or rise.

MAKING A SCOOTER

THIS strong toy can be made very simply.

Choice of Materials

A scooter has to stand a considerable amount of rough usage, and because of this a hard wood, such as ash or oak, should be used. The present scooter has a running board (see Fig. 1), and on the front of this is fitted a neck-piece, both of these parts being lettered A and B respectively in the illustration.

The steering handle and front fork are made with a centre shaft (C). The fork for the front wheel is formed by bolting two extension pieces (D), one on each side of the centre shaft at the bottom end, and the steering handle (E) is mortised to the top end. The steering handle and fork is pivoted to the neck-piece by means of an iron jaw-piece and long bolt, the jaw-piece being bolted to the handle and fork, with the long bolt passing through the neck-piece. The back wheel has a slot cut for it in the running board, and the front wheel fits between the forks, both being fixed with bolts.

The Running Board

The running board is shown in Fig. 2. It is 1 foot 11 inches long by 4 inches wide, with a slot $4\frac{1}{2}$ inches long by 1 inch wide, cut at the front end for the neck-piece, and a slot 5 inches long by $1\frac{1}{4}$ inch wide at the back end for the back wheel. The neck-piece will require a piece of wood 7 inches long by 8 inches wide, the method of setting out being shown in Fig. 3. First mark off the bottom $4\frac{1}{2}$ inches long, then mark the depth of 3 inches from the front top end for the portion over which the iron jaw-piece will fit. Set the top edge of this back $\frac{3}{4}$ inch and mark the width of $1\frac{1}{2}$ inches at the bottom. Join up these points to form the outline of the neck-piece and mark out the shape at the back with a pair of compasses set at the point x.

The Neck-piece

Cut out the neck-piece with a keyhole saw and bore a $\frac{1}{4}$-inch hole for the long bolt at the front end. The neck-piece is now fitted in the slot at the front end of the running board, to which it is fixed with two $\frac{1}{4}$-inch bolts.

The Handle

The centre shaft of the handle is 1 foot 11 inches long by $1\frac{1}{4}$ inches wide and 1 inch deep, and the two extension pieces, which are bolted one on each side of the centre shaft, are 11 inches long by 1 inch square. The steering handle is

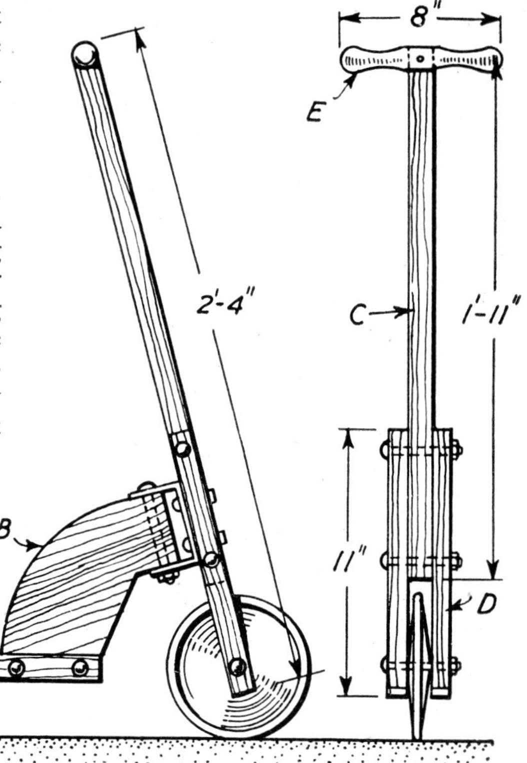

FIG. 1.—Side and front elevation of the scooter.

8 inches long by 1 inch square, with the ends rounded down with a spokeshave to give a good grip to the hands. A tenon is cut at the top end of the centre shaft, and a corresponding mortise is cut in the handle for fitting the two together as shown in Fig. 4. The joint is fixed by boring a small wood pin through it.

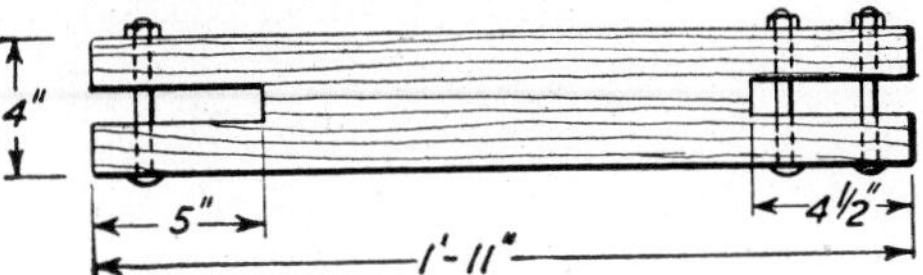

FIG. 2.—The running board.

The Steering Gear

The iron jaw-piece is formed from a piece of 1-inch by ¼-inch iron 7 inches long, and the ends of the iron should be rounded ¼ inch. Holes to receive the long bolt are bored or punched ½ inch from the ends, and two other ¼-inch bolt holes are also necessary for bolting the iron to the steering handle. When the holes have been bored, the iron should be heated and bent to the shape shown in Fig. 5. This may be easily done if the iron is held in a vice with 2 inches of the end projecting above the vice jaws, the projecting end being hammered to bend over at right-angles. The iron jaw is now bolted to the steering handle, after which the jaw is fitted over the neck-piece and the long bolt is fitted as shown in Fig. 1.

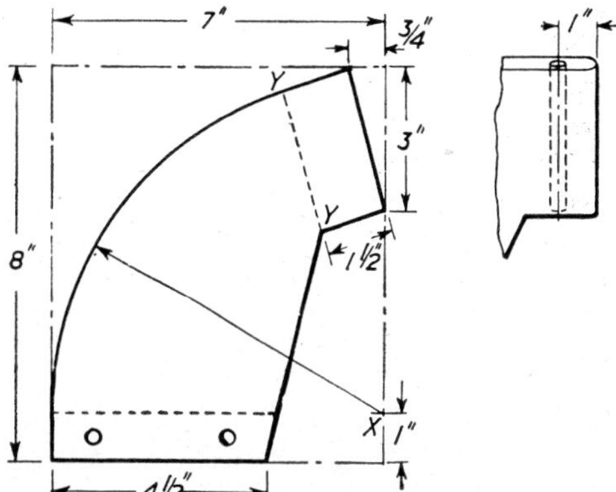

FIG. 3.—Details of the neck piece.

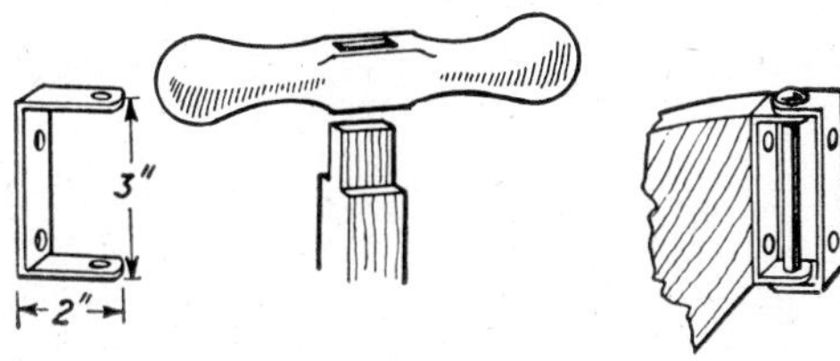

FIG. 4 (*centre*).— How to fit the handle. FIG. 5 (*left*).—Steering gear. FIG. 6 (*right*).—Fixing the steering brackets.

Another method of fitting the steering gear is to provide two iron jaw-pieces, one fitting within the other as shown in Fig. 6, and pivoted with a long bolt. The front jaw-piece is bolted through the steering handle and the back jaw is screwed to the neck-piece, which if this method is adopted will be shaped at the front as shown by the dotted line (Y . . . . Y) in Fig. 3, so that the grain of the wood will run perpendicularly instead of horizontally.

The Wheels

The wheels should be 4 inches diameter by 1 inch thick to enable spacing washers to be placed either side, and they may be of the solid wood kind or, better still, wooden wheels fitted with rubber tyres. Bolts and nuts are used to fit the wheels, and both the wheels and steering gear should be well greased or lubricated to make easy working.

On completion the scooter should be either painted or varnished.

For extra long coasting, ball-bearing wheels may be used. If you have an old pair of roller skates, wheels may be built around the skate wheels, when it will be found that far less effort is required to propel the scooter.

Do not forget the occasional drop of oil, which not only makes the wheels run freely, but also keeps away rust.

A minor improvement is to cover the footboard with rubber, which should be secured by means of rubber solution. Strips cut from the tread of an old bicycle tyre are useful for this purpose, but any suitable covering which provides a good grip can be used.

A TOY ELECTRIC MOTOR

MANY of the simpler types of home-made electric motor have a fair turn of speed, but not much power. The motor we are about to describe, however, is quite powerful enough to work models and at the same time quite easy to construct. The finished machine is shown in Fig. 1. It will be noticed that it has a three-pole armature revolving between a two-pole magnet.

The materials required are some 20-gauge sheet-iron, a few turns of insulated wire, a wooden base, a small steel spindle, some brass strips and one or two odds and ends.

The Field Magnets and Armature

First of all, carefully mark on the sheet-iron the shape for the field magnet and armature, as shown in Fig. 2. Cut these out very carefully with a pair of shears, using a file, if necessary, for the corners. The next job is to shape these "blanks," and this should be done with care. It will be noticed that little triangular pieces are cut away where the blanks are bent to form the pole pieces (see Fig. 3). This is necessary if the pole pieces are to be properly shaped. To strengthen this part, a little solder is run along the inside edge. Should you be unfortunate enough to break off one of the poles, do not solder it on again, as this will offer a high resistance to the lines of force; cut out another blank. The best way to shape the poles is to model them round a piece of 2-inch piping or anything similar of the right diameter, using a hammer, as shown in Figs. 3 and 4. The whole performance of the motor depends on how well this part of the work is done. The idea is to have the smallest possible space between the magnet and armature poles. It is for this reason that the boring of the holes for the spindle should be left until the blanks have been shaped, otherwise, if bored before the shaping, it may be found they are not quite central.

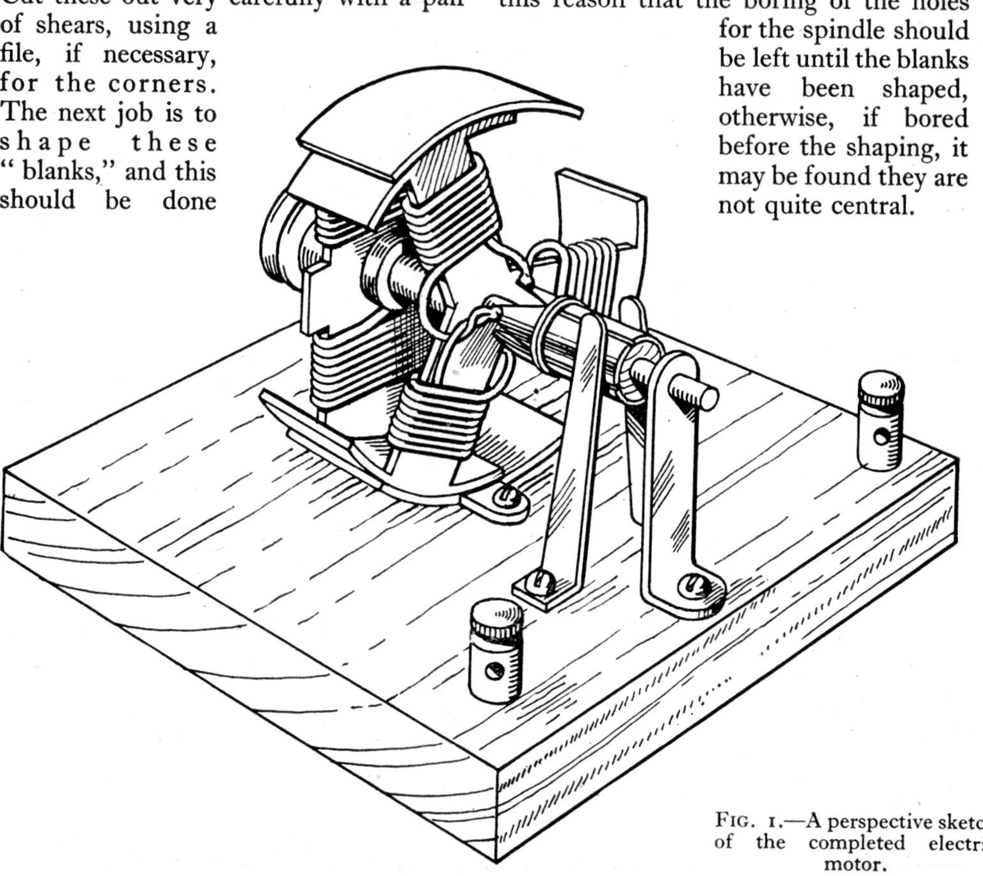

FIG. 1.—A perspective sketch of the completed electric motor.

Mounting the Armature Core

The next step is to mount the armature core on the spindle. It should be soldered to the centre of a $\frac{1}{8}$-inch steel rod $2\frac{1}{2}$ inches long. A brass collar, sweated on, will give added support and help to square the armature on the shaft (see Fig. 5). A similar collar should be sweated to the field magnet concentric with the hole for the spindle to give increased bearing surface. A small brass bracket is sweated on the back of the field magnet to enable it to be mounted on the base.

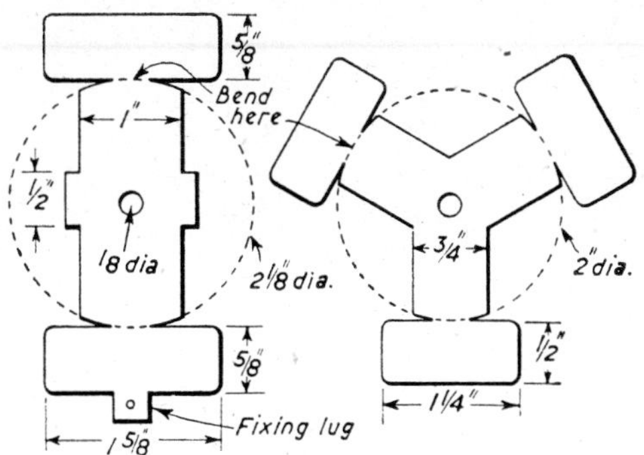

FIG. 2.—The pole-pieces and armature cut out and ready for bending.

Winding the Coils

Now comes the winding of the coils (Fig. 6). First bind the magnet and armature core with "Empire" tape, so as to prevent chafing of the insulation, then wind three layers of 22-gauge D.C.C. wire on to the field magnet and each of the armature poles. The magnet coils are really one coil in two sections, and the same direction of winding must be observed when passing from the one section to the other. To prevent the finished coil unravelling, the last turn should be bound to the next with a needle and thread. The armature coils are each wound separately and in the same direction. The inner end of each coil is bared and twisted together with the outer end of the next; thus there are three pairs of wires ready to be connected to the three segments of the commutator.

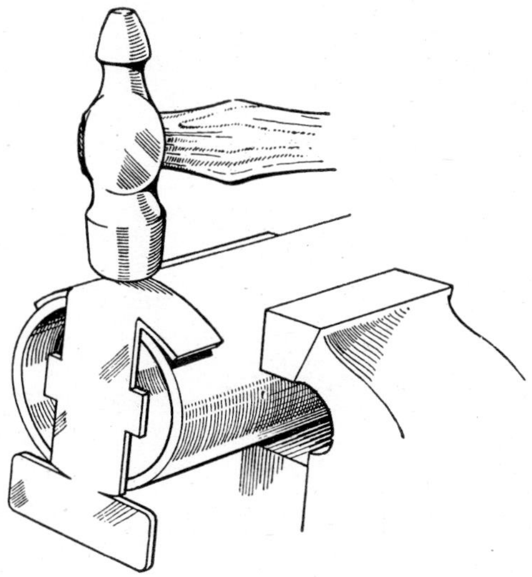

FIG. 3.—How to shape the pole-pieces.

The Commutator

The commutator is made from a piece of brass tubing $\frac{3}{4}$ inch long and about $\frac{3}{8}$ inch diameter, cut longitudinally into three segments. Each segment is tapered at one end to make a tag, to which is soldered the ends of the armature windings. A fibre or wooden collar, $\frac{1}{2}$ inch long by about $\frac{3}{8}$ inch diameter, is pushed on the spindle and the three segments glued to it with a small space between each. Each end of the commutator is also bound round with strong thread and glued. Fig. 7 will

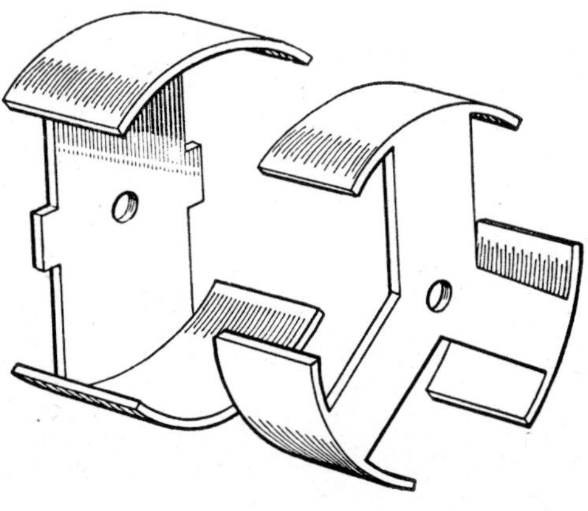

FIG. 4.—The finished pole-pieces and armature

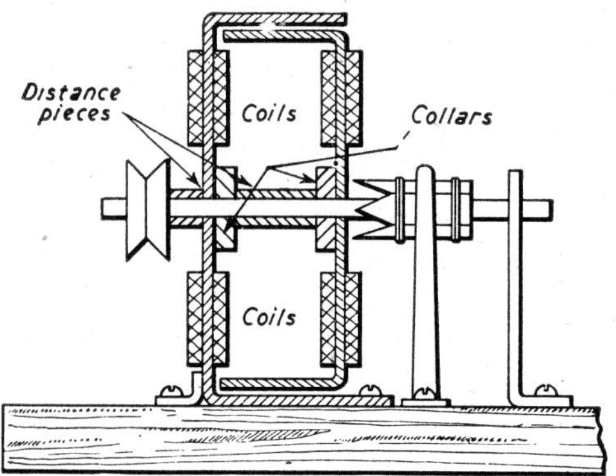

FIG. 5.—Details of the brackets supporting the field magnet and armature shaft.

make the construction of the commutator quite clear. The spaces between the commutator segments should be opposite the armature poles, but slight adjustment can be made, if necessary, when testing the motor by rotating the commutator on the spindle.

Mounting the Motor

The motor should now be mounted on the base. This is made from a piece of wood $3\frac{1}{2}$ inches by $3\frac{1}{2}$ inches by $\frac{1}{2}$ inch. The field magnet is fixed in position first by means of three small screws. The hole in the centre of the field magnet forms the main bearing. The other is made from a strip of the same sheet-iron as was used for the magnet and armature. Two distance pieces made from a narrow brass tube are used to prevent lateral play, and a small pulley is soldered to the shaft to take the drive (see Fig. 5). The brushes consist of two strips of springy brass taken from a flash-lamp battery.

The Connections

Two terminals are mounted on the base, the connecting wires being carried in grooves cut with a chisel in the underside of the base. A wire passes from one terminal to one end of the field magnet coil. The other end of the coil is connected to one of the brushes, and a wire taken from the other brush to the second terminal.

Testing

The motor is now complete and may be tested. If it is sluggish in starting or excessive sparking occurs at the brushes, it means that the position of the commutator is not quite right. A little experimenting will soon determine the best position. Should the commutator work loose on the spindle through twisting, a small " blob " of liquid glue will secure it. The brushes should not press too heavily on the commutator, but nevertheless should be firm enough to make good contact. A two-volt or four-volt accumulator will be found suitable as the source of power.

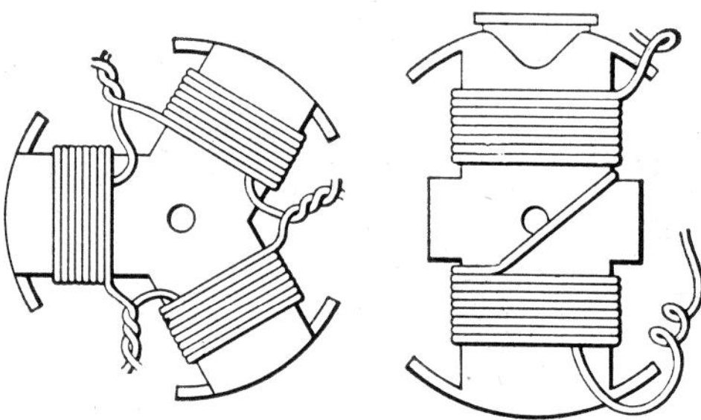

FIG. 6.—How to wind the armature and field magnet.

Dry batteries may be used to drive the motor but, of course, they will not last for so long as the wet type of accumulator. They will also prove more expensive. Having built the motor, you will find it fascinating to construct simple working models for the motor to drive. Of course, such models must be very lightly constructed and all their working parts must be quite free and kept oiled. One such model which may be simply constructed is that of a jointed man, cut out in wood and suitably painted, turning a grindstone.

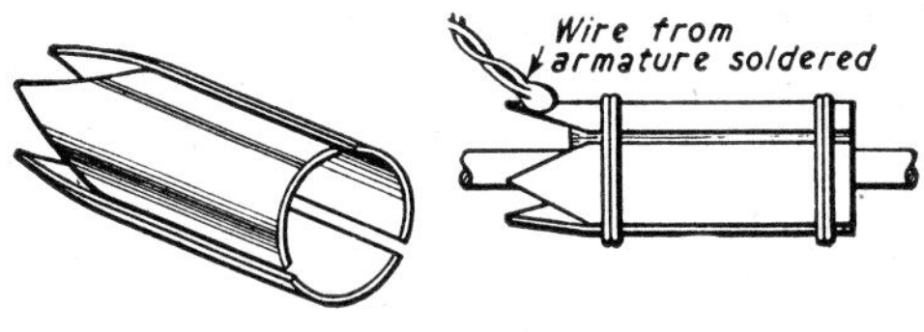

FIG. 7.—How the commutator is made.

A MODEL THEATRE STAGE

The stage front.

THE materials for making this miniature stage are cheap and easy to obtain, and most handymen have the necessary tools. If all the parts are made accurately to the measurements given, the model will be quite strong and steady.

The first part to be made is the stage front, which may be made from a piece of $\frac{3}{16}$ inch plywood. This must be cut 24 inches long and 20 inches high. Rule out the stage opening 14 inches long and 9 inches high, the bottom being 2 inches from the long edge of the wood, and the sides 5 inches from the shorter edges. The opening may be cut out with a fretsaw. The next section is the stage itself, for which another piece of plywood must be cut, 24 inches long and 18 inches wide. The slots must now be cut out for the framework to be added later. Mark two oblongs, 1 inch high and $\frac{1}{2}$ inch wide, on the stage front, 4 inches from the top and 1 inch from the sides.

These should be cut out with a fretsaw. At the same time cut two similar holes in the stage at the back corners, 1 inch from each side and with their long sides parallel to the sides of the stage. The stage must now be hinged to the stage front so that it opens on a level with the bottom of the stage opening, the hinges being screwed on at the ends and recessed.

The Stage Supports

Having carefully measured the thickness of the stage plywood, cut four blocks of wood 2 inches long, 1 inch

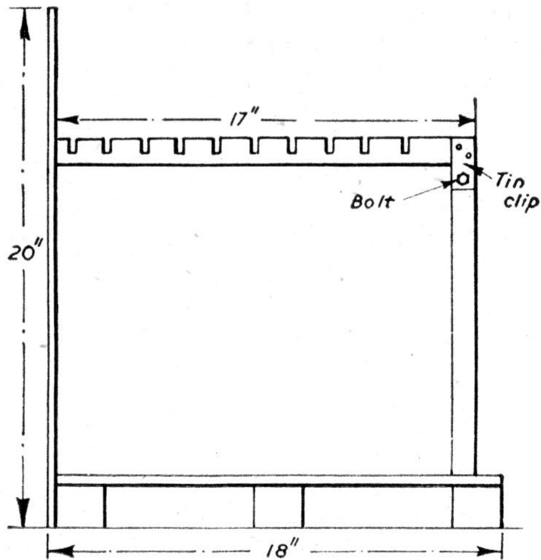

FIG. 1.—A side view of the model stage.

wide and 2 inches in height minus the stage thickness. These blocks must then be fixed with glue and nails at the corners of the stage and flush with the sides, to act as supports for the stage. Next obtain some wooden laths, ½ inch thick and 1 inch in width. From these cut two pieces 17 inches long and two pieces 15 inches long. On the longer pieces notches should be cut ¼ inch wide, ½ inch deep and 1 inch apart. Rule these out first in pencil; they must be exactly opposite on both sides.

Cut four pieces of thick tinplate, 1 inch wide and 2 inches long, and scratch a line across the centre of each, dividing it into two squares. In the centre of one square bore a hole large enough to take a very short bolt, about ¼ inch in diameter. In each of the other squares bore two small screw-holes diagonally opposite (see Fig. 2). Two pieces of tinplate are now screwed to the end of each of the notched strips, projecting downwards to form a slot with a hole at each side. Now fix the other end of the notched strips in the slots of the stage front, and the 15-inch strips in the slots in the stage. These should fit exactly into the slots and remain quite firm. The upper ends of the upright strips will now fit into the tinplate slots, and holes are bored in each for a short bolt, which goes right through both tin and wood, and a nut is screwed on the other end.

Decorating the Stage Front

The stage is now fitted up for giving a show and may be taken to pieces again in a few seconds. There are, however, several things to attend to first. There is the decoration of the stage front, which may be done in any way which appeals to the individual. Plastic wood, cut-out designs, modelling plaster, transfers, enamels and many other methods may be employed.

The next step is the construction of the scenery (see Fig. 4), which will be found quite easy and interesting to those who have some artistic ability. The best type of scenery is made with good white cardboard. This should be cut to about 28 inches long and 14 inches high and the scenes painted in matt surface or poster colours, small jars of which are sold by artists' colourmen. The properties and all other scenic pieces will for the present be left to the reader's own judgment, and for further guidance he should consult a

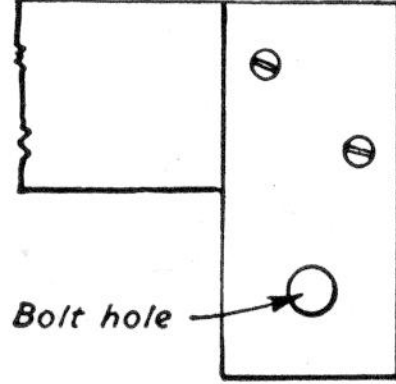

FIG. 2.—Method of fixing tin clips.

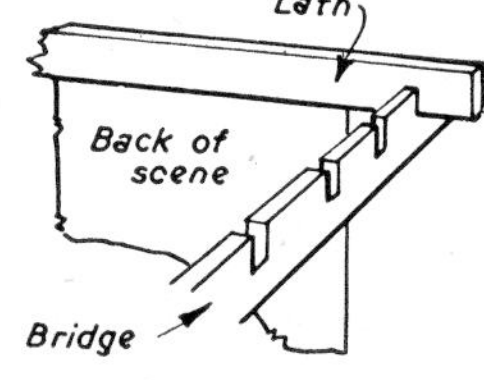

FIG. 3.—How the scenery is supported in the notches.

FIG. 4 —The scenery.

FIG. 5.—How the characters are operated by strings from above.

book on theatrical production, which may be found in any public library. The "actors" can be modelled in plaster or carved in wood, and if they are to be jointed the parts should be connected with strings and should work very loosely, as shown in Fig. 5. They may be operated by strings from above or by wires from the sides.

Lighting Effects

For lighting the stage, small pocket-lamp bulbs and batteries may be used. Four bulbs will be found sufficient; two should be fixed inside just above the top corners of the stage opening, and one should be fixed inside a tin footlight screen in front along the bottom of the stage opening. The outside of this screen should be enamelled black. The fourth bulb may be used as a movable light or fixed in a cylindrical gas-mantle box with a circular hole in one end for use as a spotlight, as shown in Fig. 6.

For plays you may select any of the well-known fairy stories, such as Babes in the Wood or Jack and the Beanstalk, suitably adjusting the dialogue to suit the characters. A large number of such fairy stories are published in cheap editions, and they include illustrations from which you can draw the characters.

For the best effect, the person reading the dialogue should not be seen, and those operating the characters should have copies of the script so that they work in unison with the dialogue.

This little stage may also be adapted for shadow shows, or for hand puppets. It is possible to rig up an imitation acrobatic act, and to combine the use of a gramophone so that the characters can simulate music.

FIG. 6.—Details of the spotlight.

KITES AND HOW TO MAKE THEM

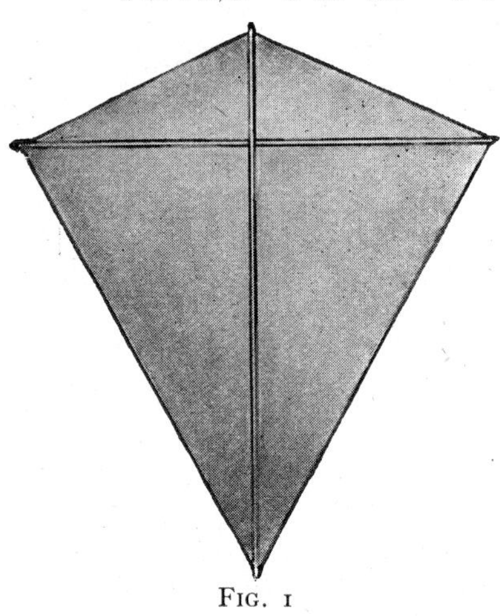

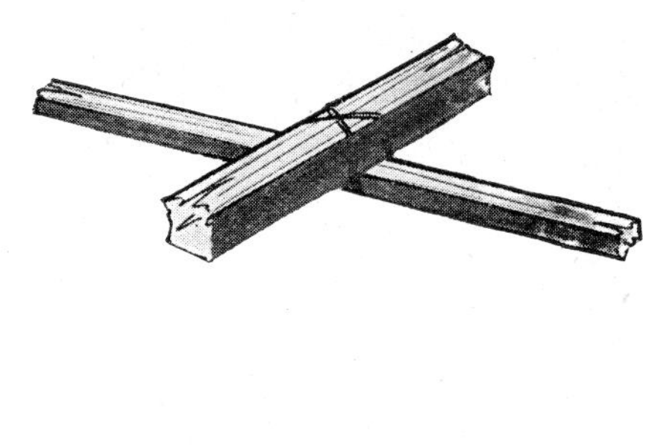

FIG. 1 FIG. 2

These two illustrations show the first steps in making the kite described here. Fig. 1 represents the frame of the kite, whilst in Fig. 2 you can see just how the bow is glued and lashed to the backbone.

HERE is a design for a kite that is very easy to fly, if carefully made and balanced. For the backbone cut a strip of straight-grained spruce, deal, or any light wood. This strip should be planed down to ¼ inch section, and cut 30 inches long. A strip of cane is needed for the bow; this should be slightly less in section.

The bow must be glued and lashed with strong thread to the backbone at a distance of 6 inches from the upper end; and, when the glue has set hard, cut to a length of 30 inches. To preserve the balance, measure 15 inches each way from the centre.

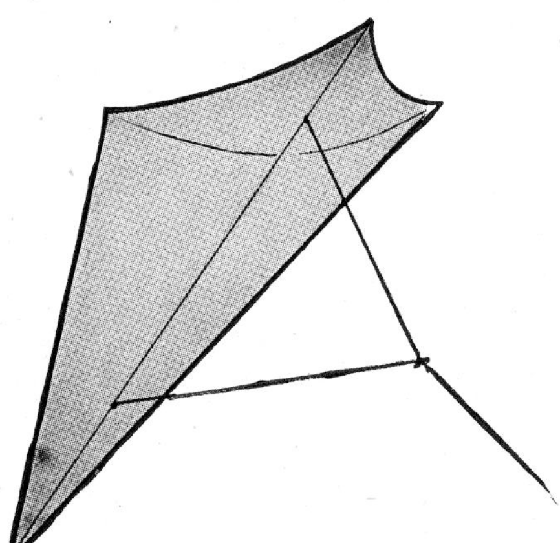

FIG. 3.—The kite when completed.

A length of strong thread, or fine twine, is tied at its centre to the tip of the backbone and tied right and left to the tips of the bow; see that both are the same length so as to keep the bow at right angles to the backbone.

The frame will now present the appearance shown at Fig. 1. For the covering use strong, brightly-coloured tissue paper, in one piece if possible. Lay the paper flat on the table, smear the face of backbone and bow with paste or liquid glue, press down on the paper, then turn the whole over and rub the paper well into contact. When set, trim the paper, with about ½ inch of margin, to the shape of the frame, paste the edges and turn them over the thread, then press well down.

Making the Bridle

Strengthen the four corners by pasting over a small triangular piece of paper. For the bridle, cut a length of twine about 4 feet and attach it to the backbone about 4 inches from the top and 6 inches from the bottom.

Cut a tiny notch in each end of the bow about ¼ inch from the tips. Into the notch, at one end, tie a length of twine, then slip the twine round the other notch, and draw the ends of the bow together until the depth of curvature is a trifle over 3 inches.

The kite line is attached to the bridle, so that the upper portion of the bridle is shorter than the lower. When flying the kite, vary the position of the line to get the best results.

How to make a fine Box Kite

To make a box kite you will require, first of all, four straight strips of light wood, each 2 feet 2 inches long and $\frac{1}{4}$ inch square, and two pieces of thin coloured paper measuring 4 feet 2 inches long and 9 inches wide. Take the strips of coloured paper, turn over the edges 1 inch and glue down the folds after inserting a length of fine, strong string in each fold.

When this is completed, glue the ends of each paper strip with a 2-inch overlap so as to form continuous bands 7 inches wide. Now fold each band to divide it into four equal parts, and at each crease glue one of the long sticks. The outer edge of each band should be 1 inch from the ends of the sticks, and there should be a space of 10 inches between the bands, as indicated in the first diagram. Before gluing the sticks in place, slightly notch each one at a distance of 5 inches from each end to receive the notched ends of the cross-pieces A (Fig. 4).

For the cross-pieces, take two pieces of $\frac{3}{16}$-inch by $\frac{5}{16}$-inch stripwood, each $16\frac{1}{2}$ inches long, place them together and drive a fine wire nail through the centre, turning the end of the nail up underneath. Treat two more pieces of the same length in the same way. Notch the ends as at B, open out the cross-pieces, and fit them inside the kite.

These should not fit too tightly, or they will split the paper. If they are too long, shorten them slightly and deepen the notches.

The flying line is tied on to one of the long strips in the position indicated at C. To fly the kite, let out about 20 yards of line, and get someone to throw up the kite a short distance in the usual fashion.

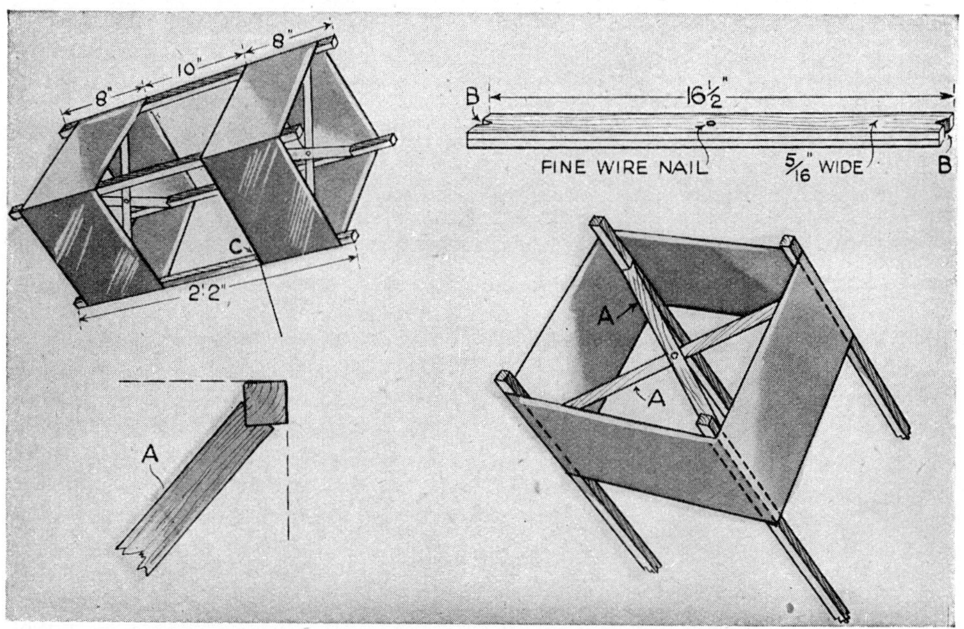

Fig. 4.—The top left-hand view shows the completed kite ; the top right view one of the stretchers ; the bottom left how the stretchers lock diagonally against the main members ; and the bottom right one of the cellules with the stretchers A in position.

A TOY GUN

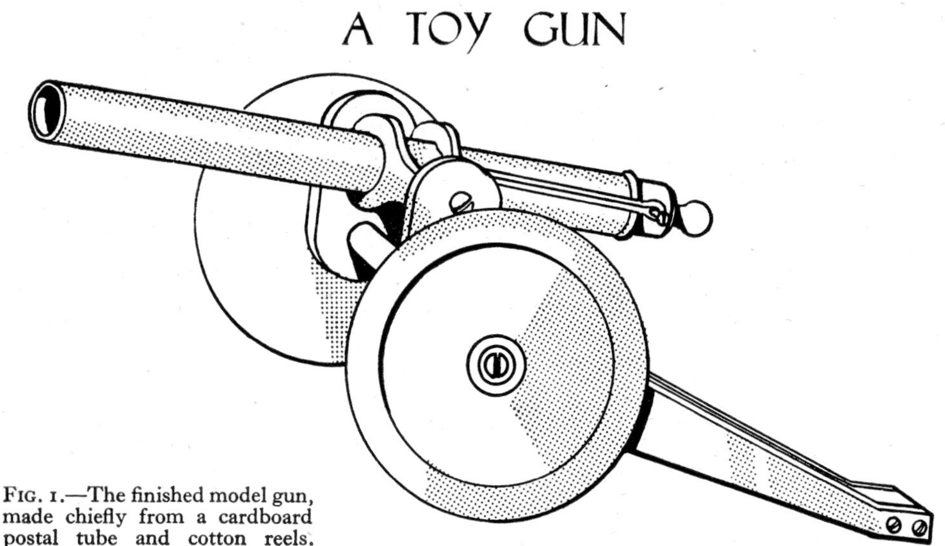

FIG. 1.—The finished model gun, made chiefly from a cardboard postal tube and cotton reels.

ALL that is required to make this toy gun is a piece of cardboard postal tube, some cotton reels, pieces of dowel rod and odd bits of fretwood. To provide the power for firing, rubber bands are used, while the ammunition may consist of small india-rubber balls. The completed gun is shown in Fig. 1.

First of all, obtain three empty cotton reels and saw an end off one as indicated at B, Fig. 2. Now obtain a cardboard postal tube, 9 inches long, into the end of which the body of the cotton reel just fits, as shown at B, Fig. 2. The plunger rod is a piece of dowel rod, $5\frac{1}{2}$ inches long, which should be an easy fit in the hole in the cotton reel. If it fits too tightly, rub it well with glass-paper. The part C consists of the body of another cotton reel, both ends being sawn off. The part D is a similar piece of another cotton reel. These parts are glued on to the end of the rod after passing it through the part B, which is then glued into the end of the gun tube. Into the part D screw two screws opposite each other as shown, and then screw a small wooden drawer knob into the end of the plunger rod.

The Trunnion Block

The next part to make is the trunnion block (F). Cut two pieces of ordinary fretwood to the shape shown, with a hole in the middle of each to give a good fit to the gun tube. Between the ends of each piece glue two blocks of wood (GG) and, when the glue has set hard, screw in two little hooks as shown. Slip the trunnion block on the tube and glue it in place $2\frac{1}{4}$ inches from the rear end of the tube.

For the trail, cut two pieces of fretwood to the shape and sizes given at H. Make two holes in each, the top one for the pivot screw and the bottom one to fit a piece of $\frac{1}{2}$-inch dowel rod, which forms the axle. This is $4\frac{1}{2}$ inches long. Cut a piece of wood (J) and screw it between the ends of the trail, as shown at K, Fig. 3. Another piece (L), also $2\frac{1}{2}$ inches wide, is screwed in place in the position indicated.

Assembling the Gun

Now fix the gun tube and trunnion in position by means of a screw through each side of the trail. Push the axle through the holes in the trail and glue it in place. Obtain two wooden wheels, about $4\frac{1}{2}$ inches in diameter, and fix these to the ends of the axles with round-headed screws, placing a washer under the head of each screw before screwing them in.

Lastly, obtain two strong rubber

bands, about 2 inches long, and loop them over the hooks and screws as shown at MM, Fig. 3. The finished toy, with the exception of the rubber bands, can be given a coating of grey enamel.

To work the gun, simply put a small rubber ball down the gun tube, pull the knob back and then let go. Plenty of amusement can be had by shooting at toy wooden soldiers.

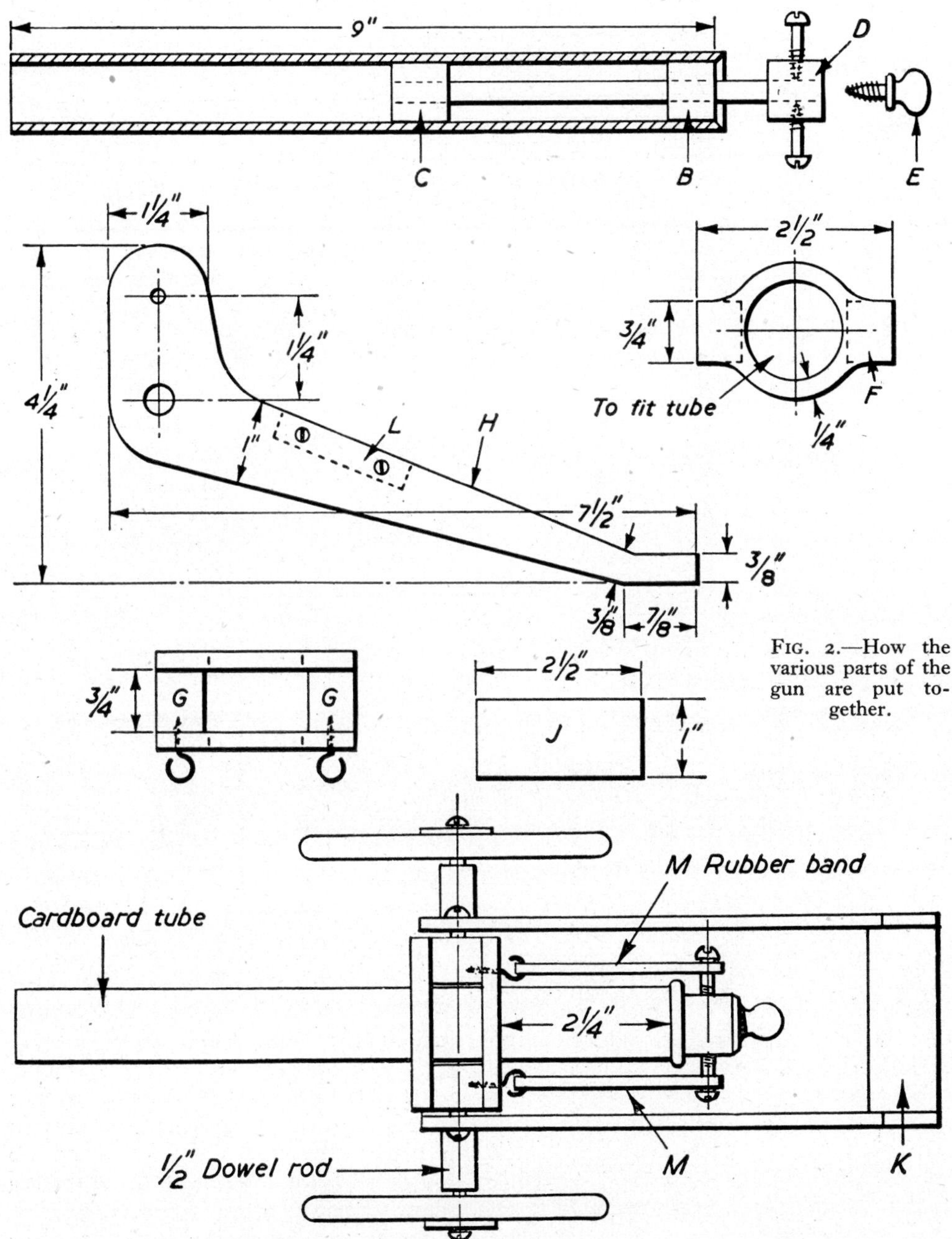

FIG. 2.—How the various parts of the gun are put together.

FIG. 3.—A plan view. The gun is worked by two elastic bands as shown.

A PANTOGRAPH

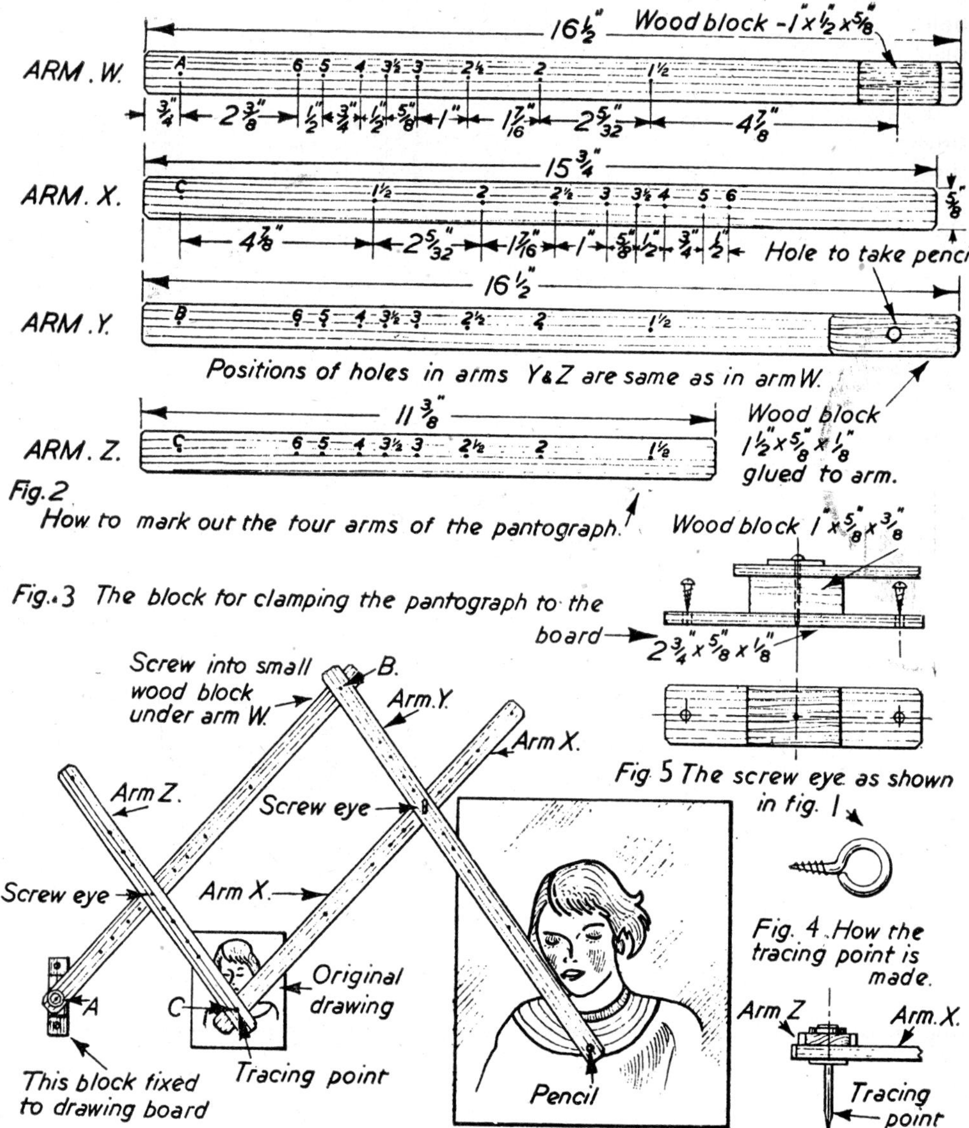

Fig. 2 How to mark out the four arms of the pantograph.

Fig. 3 The block for clamping the pantograph to the board

Fig. 1 — The pantograph completed. The assembling of parts is clearly shown.

A PANTOGRAPH is a simple tool by means of which you may copy, enlarge or reduce drawings and illustrations. The device shown in Fig. 1 consists of the various parts shown in Figs. 2 to 5. Use strips of oak $\frac{5}{8}$ inch wide and $\frac{1}{8}$ inch thick for the four arms, and carefully mark off the distances shown in Fig. 2. Drill the holes shown to accommodate the screw-eye illustrated in Fig. 5.

At the point A a little bar of wood is attached, as shown in Fig. 3, so that the end of the pantograph can be screwed down to the drawing-board. The tracing point C consists of a nail with a washer soldered beneath the arm X to keep it in place; the nail should be filed up to a sharp point and serves as the tracing point. See Fig. 4.

To accommodate the pencil a piece of wood is glued over the end of the arm Y, as indicated in Fig. 2, and a hole is drilled in it of a size to suit the diameter of the pencil. The other joints are made clear from the drawings.

To enlarge a drawing to, say, three times its size insert the screw-eyes into the holes marked 3, and upon tracing over the drawing with the tracing point the pencil will trace out the drawing three times the original size.

When it is required to reduce the size of a drawing, the positions of the pencil and tracing point must be reversed, and for this purpose a short, stumpy piece of pencil should be pushed over the tracing point and a piece of round iron pointed at one end, the same size as the pencil, should be pushed in the pencil hole. The various letters in Fig. 1 correspond to those shown in Fig. 2.

If accurate scale copying is to be done, it is very important that the distances of the holes from the points A, C and B (Fig. 2) should be carefully marked out. To ensure this, place the arms W, Y and Z together and scribe the three off together with a square. Having done this, place the point 6 on arm X level with the point 6 on arm W, and, by means of the square, scribe off the positions on arm W on to arm X. This will ensure that the positions are correct.

Operation

In using the instrument let the left hand press on the tracing point and the right hand grasp the pencil. Now guide the tracing point over the drawing to be copied and at the same time exert a slight pressure on the pencil. As the tracing point is moved over the drawing the pencil will make an enlarged copy of the original. It will probably be found at first that the pencil lines are wavy. This is because the pencil magnifies any false movement of the tracer.

MAKING A TOBOGGAN

EVEN if there are, in the course of a winter, only a few days on which tobogganing is possible it is well worth while being ready for them. The most useful type of toboggan consists of two rigid runners, with curved prows, supporting a level platform along which the rider sits or lies. Strength and lightness are the essential qualities, the former because of the strain imposed when the toboggan is racing downhill with a heavy load, and the latter because when you have made your run you must haul your sled to the top of the hill before you start again.

Choose, therefore, a strong, light wood. Straight-grained ash of $\frac{5}{8}$ inch thickness is very suitable.

FIG. 1.—The position of the three crosspieces.

The Sides

The finished size of these is 3 feet 6 inches by 5 inches. It is an advantage to make the sides together so that they may exactly correspond. Having planed and smoothed all four surfaces, therefore, you may fasten them together with a few thin nails and set about shaping the edges. Get the top and bottom edges straight and square first, and then

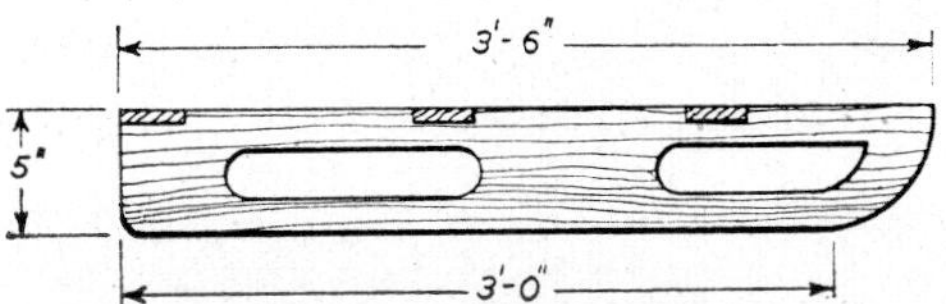

FIG. 2.—A side view, showing the notches for the crosspieces.

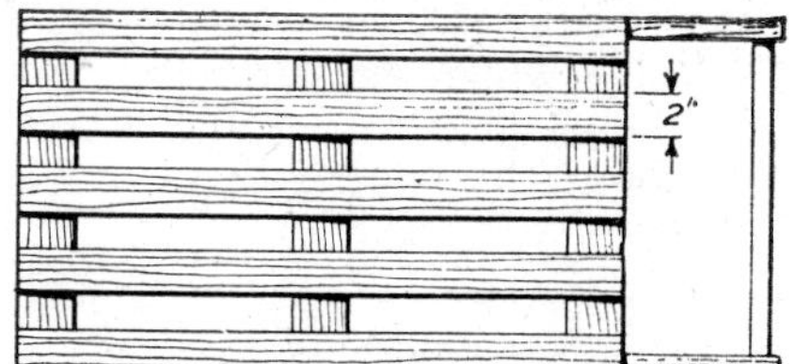

FIG. 3.—The completed toboggan.

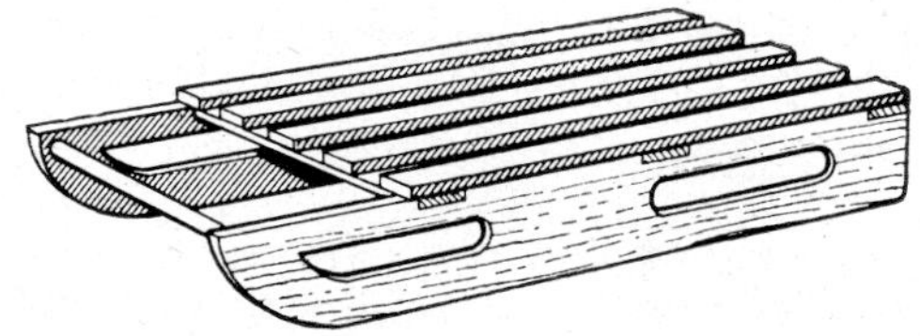
FIG. 4.—A perspective view of the completed toboggan.

make the curve of your prows. The curve should begin on the bottom edge 6 inches from the front. The rounding of the bottom rear corner should be slight and is merely for appearance.

The notches along the top which are to take the crosspieces should next be cut, each $\frac{5}{8}$ inch deep and $2\frac{1}{2}$ inches wide. This is shown in Fig. 1. Do not make the small round hole in the front corner at this stage, as it only goes part-way through each side. The size of the large holes depends largely on the strength of your wood—they must be sufficient to lessen the weight of the sides and yet not enough to materially weaken them. The front hole also serves the important purpose of a hand-grip, so that at least its top edge should be rounded.

The Three Crosspieces

Next prepare the three crosspieces from the same $\frac{5}{8}$-inch wood. Each should be 15 inches long and $2\frac{1}{2}$ inches wide. Before fastening them to the runners, which you will now have taken apart, you must get your front bar ready. This is best formed of round iron rod about $\frac{1}{2}$ inch in diameter; or you may use a rather thicker wood dowel. In either case a hole of the necessary size will have to be bored halfway through each side, so that the bar will be held firmly. Next, screw the crosspieces into the notches already prepared for them, as shown in Fig. 2, and smooth off the top so that it is all flush and rigid.

The framework is now complete and the lengthways spars have now to be added. They can be made of strong three-ply or a rather stouter wood. Each strip is 2 feet $7\frac{1}{2}$ inches long and 2 inches wide. There are five of them and they should be made very smooth, with well-rounded edges and ends, and then screwed to the crosspieces and spaced evenly apart (see Fig. 3).

Your toboggan is now practically complete. It remains only to stain or polish it to taste and to shoe the bottoms of the runners with iron. Ordinary narrow hoop-iron serves quite well when nailed on flat. If you can get a length of half-round metal, so much the better, for this, of course, will give a narrower running surface and so make for increased speed. Be careful to run the metal right up the front and part-way up the back of the blades so that there are no rough ends left in inconvenient places.

How to Use the Toboggan

There are three ways in which you may ride on it: (1) by sitting astride, gripping some "reins" fastened to your front bar and with legs jutting forward on either side of the curled prows, or with your hands gripping down at either side of you; (2) lying the full length of your chest, your head to the front, and keeping your place by holding the hand-grips cut in the sides of the sled; (3) lying on one side so that the lower hand grips the front bar and the other clutches a convenient spar. In this last style, too, the under-leg is curled beneath the body while the other juts out behind the toboggan; thus you travel head-first, as in method (2), though you are on your side instead of your chest.

Only one person can travel comfortably on the toboggan shown in Fig. 4, but if the dimensions are extended room can be made for from two to four people. You may, for instance, make your sled 6 inches high, 18 inches wide and 5 feet long, but remember the increased weight that you will have to handle, and which will probably make it impracticable for such a sled to be used unless you have the necessary companions.

A KALEIDOSCOPE

APART from the changing beauties of the kaleidoscope, which so please the eye, this instrument may be made to render a real service to those who are interested in the evolution of conventional designs for various decorative purposes.

The instrument to be described is convenient for that purpose, because once a suitable design has shown itself it can be retained in view for as long as is necessary for the operator to copy it on paper.

It will be seen that the instrument is built on the lines of a microscope, with a jointed limb, thus enabling it to be used upright or at any desirable angle (see Fig. 1).

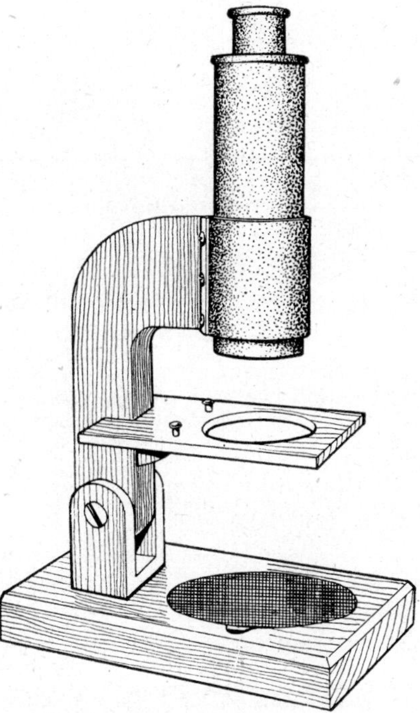

FIG. 1.—A side view of the finished kaleidoscope.

The Tube

The tube may be made of paper pasted and rolled round a ruler to the requisite thickness. Fig. 2 shows the tube in sectional view. The bottom is left open, and the top closed with a disc of stout cardboard perforated with a central hole, in which is fitted the smaller tube that carries the eyepiece with its lens. The latter may be bought quite cheaply and should focus clearly an object placed upon the stage of the instrument. The tube should have a length of 5 inches and an internal diameter of $1\frac{1}{4}$ inches. It will be seen that a small hole is made in the disc covering the eyepiece, and that the lens is placed immediately below it, being held in place with a cardboard ring. The whole of the inside of the tube should be blackened. French polish diluted with methylated spirit to which some lampblack has been added makes a good dull black that dries quickly.

The Reflectors

The reflectors are tapering strips of plain plate glass, say, $\frac{1}{2}$ inch wide at the small end and of a width at the large end which will just fit the tube when the two strips are set at an angle of 60 degrees with each other (see Fig. 2). These strips should be blackened on one side, for which purpose the mixture mentioned above would serve.

This makes a better reflecting surface than that of a silvered mirror because the reflections are from the front surface of the glass.

Fix the glass strips securely in the tube, which may best be done with cork wedges glued in place.

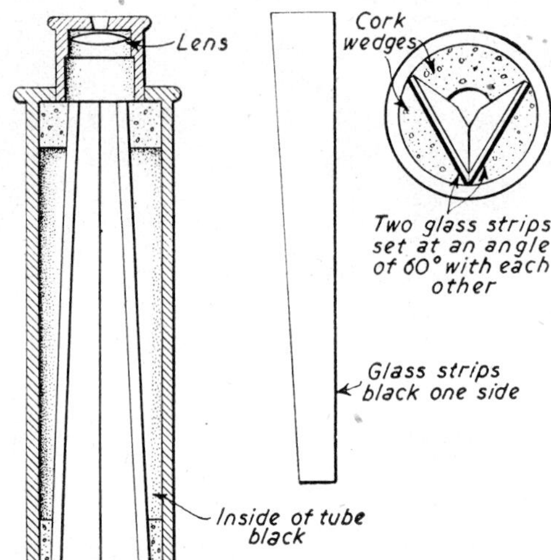

FIG. 2.—Sectional view of the tube (*left*), and details of the reflection mirrors.

The Stand

The stand, it will be seen, is built of wood, and its construction is clear from Fig. 1. The base should be hollowed and fitted with a slab of lead to give stability to the stand. The two short uprights are mortised into it. The limb, cut from ½-inch wood, will give the necessary distance apart to fix the uprights.

The stage may be ¼ inch thick, and should have a hole of the same diameter as the tube. Two small brass screws should be fixed as shown, and should stand up high enough to permit the container (shown in Fig. 3) to pass under their heads.

The head of the limb carries a short paper tube, through which the main tube can slide friction-tight.

Covering the Tubes

Both tubes can be covered with grained black leather cloth, which gives them a nice finish. The short tube may be lined with fine cloth, which is best applied when making the tube, using the main tube as a mandrel.

The short tube is joined to the limb with a strip of brass sheet bent to the curve of the former. It should first be screwed to the limb and then to the tube. The thickness of the short tube must be sufficient to give a good hold for the screws.

The upper surface of the base is recessed to hold a disc of opal glass, so that a white or black background may be had as desired.

The Container

The container consists of a disc of clear glass, as shown in Fig. 3, to which is attached a rim of cardboard, and is easily rotated with the finger until an attractive design appears.

Fig. 3 shows designs obtained by the use of opaque objects.

Certain coloured beads obtainable quite cheaply from popular stores may be used in the kaleidoscope, and will be found to provide an infinite variety of most beautiful patterns. Coloured Perspex may be used, cutting the pieces to the shape mentioned on p. 405.

The number of patterns which a kaleidoscope will provide is limitless, and it is unfortunately impossible to repeat a particular design.

Should you find any difficulty in obtaining coloured glass, you should go to your local chemist and ask him to obtain some pieces for you.

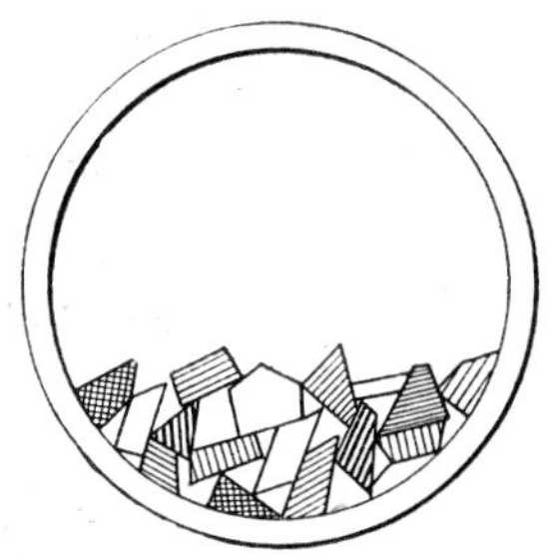

FIG. 3.—The container (*top*), and designs obtained by the use of opaque objects.

Favourite Hobbies : Things To Make and Do

Handcrafts of Many Kinds

Photos specially prepared for this work.

TWO FAITHFUL SERVANTS—YOUR HANDS

Some boys and girls hope that one day they will drive a powerful car, an aeroplane or a motor-boat. It is the ambition of others to ride a horse or excel in playing a musical instrument. You may have the opportunity in the future to do one or more of these fascinating things; but, if you are to become proficient, it is as well to remember that you must spend the waiting time in training your hands. A clever pair of hands is a priceless possession, and in the following pages you are shown many delightful methods of training your fingers to be sensitive and dexterous and useful to you in many ways.

HANDCRAFTS

LONG ago it was extremely necessary that everybody's hands should be trained to be useful. People who could not use their hands in those days could not have kept themselves alive at all.

Before a child could have clothes, for instance, it was necessary that the father should go out and shoot an animal to get its skin (and before he did that he had to make the bow and arrows).

In some countries it is still necessary for the inhabitants to supply most of their own needs, but even if they spend all their life in a country where it is possible to live without doing so, people who learned when they were young to use their hands are indeed fortunate.

Not only are things made by hand more worth while than those made by machinery, but when a person is interested in handcrafts, visits to museums and art galleries, and travelling in our own and foreign lands, all become means whereby new ideas may be found, and reading and the whole of life thus become more interesting.

A very important thing to remember is that if a child allows his hands to grow up useless he will never be able to train them afterwards. It is only when hands are young that they can learn.

Age 3 Years

BEAD THREADING

Materials :—

Large, Coloured Beads.
Thick Embroidery Cotton.
No needle.

Method

This is begun by tying a bead on to one end of the thread. The child should be encouraged to do it himself. He can never have skilful fingers if bigger people are constantly helping him.

The beads should be threaded in any of the designs on this page (Fig. 1), or the child can make up his own designs. Great care should be taken to make them correctly.

When the string of beads is long enough, the two ends should be joined. Bracelets and necklaces can be made as presents.

There is another method, suitable only for older children, as a needle is required.

Thread several beads on to the middle of a cord with a needle at either end.

Add the same number of beads, putting the thread through the row first from right to left, then through the row from left to right. Many good designs may be worked out.

RAFFIA WINDING

Materials :—

Cardboard Ring.
Plain and Coloured Raffia.

Method

Soak some thick strands of raffia in water for several hours. Take one strand and smooth it out flat. Hold one end of this strand on the front of the cardboard ring with the left thumb (Fig. 2), then wind it over the ring, covering the end with the first wrapping, and making each wrapping overlap the one before it.

When the ring is all covered, the other end should be tucked inside several wrapping strands and the whole kept in place with a strand of coloured raffia tied in a bow (Fig. 3).

Picture frames may be made for the doll's house in raffia. Take a circle of cardboard the size of a saucer, with a smaller circle cut out of the centre. Cover this in the same way as the ring.

A round box may be made by covering a ring and a circle the same size (with a very small hole in the centre) and sewing the ring on to the circle. Another covered circle may be used for the lid.

FIG 1

Here are three ways in which beads may be strung by a small child. If the child prefers to make other number combinations he should do so.

FIG. 2 FIG. 3

Above can be seen the method of starting to cover a ring with raffia. Fig. 3 shows the ring completed. Other things which can be done with raffia are described above.

Age 4 Years

WOOL WEAVING ON CANVAS

Materials :—

A piece of Rug Canvas.
Thick, Coloured Wool.
A Raffia Needle.

Method

Cut the canvas four squares larger in both directions than is needed for the finished article. Fold over two squares all round to make a neat edge.

Using the wool double, darn it at one square and out at the next all the way across, going through the double thickness at the ends. The second row of darning should cover the alternate squares (Fig. 1).

The darning can be done all in one colour or in stripes, or coloured borders (using the tacking stitch designs) can be worked by older children.

Mats, dolls' carpets, covers for blotters, kettle holders and other useful things can be made.

WOOLLY BALLS

Materials :—

Cardboard.
Scissors with rounded points.
Coloured Wool.

Method

Draw a circle about 3 inches across on the cardboard, using a cup or the lid of a tin. Draw another circle with a halfpenny in the centre of this. Cut these pencil lines with scissors. Make two of these cardboard circles.

Take several strands of wool. Hold the ends in front of the cardboard with the left thumb and wrap the wool through the hole and over the edges (Fig. 2). Work all round the circle, joining on new wool when necessary. When the hole is nearly filled up, cut the wool as in Fig. 3 on the next page. When the wool is cut, put a piece of strong string round between the two pieces of cardboard and tie it tightly. Pull off the cardboards and trim the ball neatly with scissors.

FIG. 1

Above a part of a doll's rug is seen in process of being woven. Thick wool is used, doubled, and a large-eyed blunt needle. The four-year-old should choose his colours himself. He should also have a definite idea of what he is making, and its use, before he begins.

HOW TO MAKE A WOOLLY BALL

Fig. 2 shows clearly how to start making a woolly ball. One colour, or several different colours, may be used. Older children can get good effects by making each round a different colour, so that the finished ball is striped. If the child makes the ball for a young brother or sister, let him tie it with elastic, leaving a long end which can be fastened to baby's pram. This makes a splendid plaything.

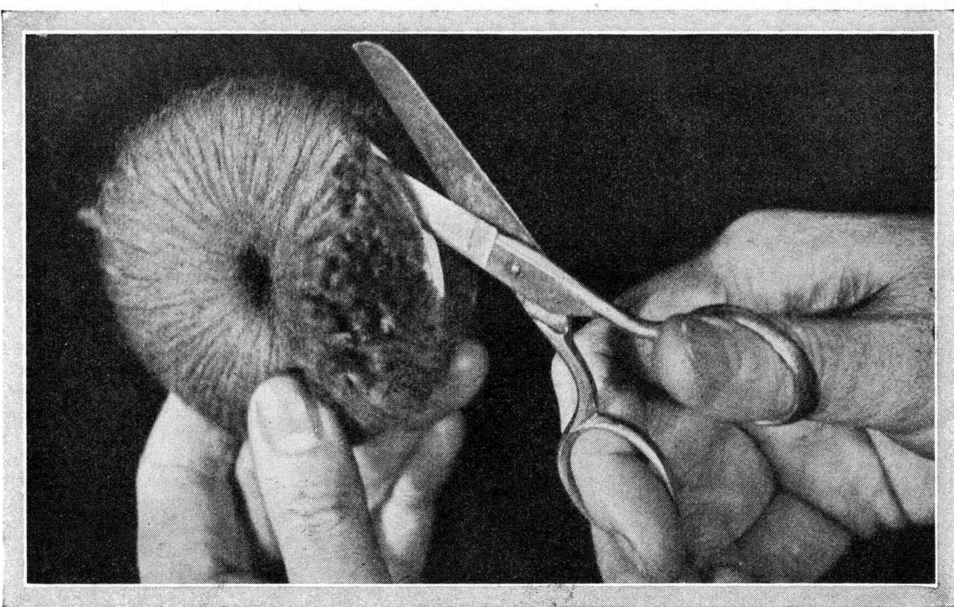

In Fig. 3 it can be seen how the woolly ball is cut. The space between the cardboard, where the string to tie the ball goes, is also seen. Two yellow balls make a chicken. The legs (a piece of millinery wire, bound with yellow wool, with the toes separate) are inserted through the hole in the larger ball before the wool is cut, and the smaller ball is attached for the head. A match and ink spots form beak and eyes.

Age 5 Years

PLAITED RAFFIA

Materials :—

Raffia.
Raffia Needle.

Method

Take three strands of raffia. Knot them together at the top and pin them down securely with a drawing pin to a table. Take the strand on the right, pass it over in front of the middle strand. It is the middle strand now. Take the strand on the left and pass it over in front of the middle strand. Then the one on the right, then the one on the left.

When the plait is about 2 inches long add another strand to each of the three, and after another 2 inches add a third strand to each to make a thick plait.

When a new strand is added leave the end sticking out (Fig. 1). When each strand is finished, add a new one in the same way. Make a plait several yards long, tie the end and clip off all the loose ends along its length.

Thread a thin strand of raffia on a needle. Wind the end of this round the thin end of the plait and secure it with a stitch. Cut off the knot, and coil the plait round on a table to make a mat. Sew each coil through from the side as in Fig. 2. Do not let the stitches show. Cut the strands off at the other end to make the plait narrow gradually. Finish off by sewing the end down securely and cut off the knot.

Coloured raffia can be plaited in with the other to form a border on the last row or two.

Useful mats may be made in this way, and can be either oval or round in shape.

A simple basket may be made by sewing two mats of equal size together, half-way round, at their edge. The handle can be a raffia plait with the ends knotted and fringed out to form a tassel.

Another shape of basket may be made by sewing the plait round as for a mat until the base is the right size, then raising the side in the method described in Indian Basketry (see p. 419, Fig. 3).

Dolls' hats, and furniture for the doll's house can all be made when the method has been mastered.

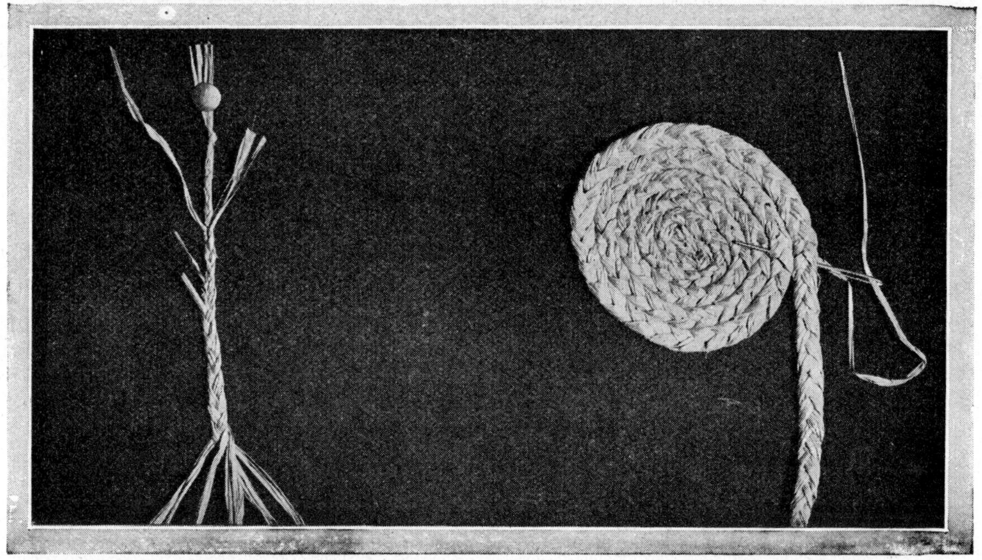

FIG. 1 FIG. 2

Fig. 1 shows the start of a raffia plait, with each new piece left sticking out, to be trimmed off afterwards. Fig. 2 shows how the plaited raffia is sewn together. Sew through only two rounds at one time.

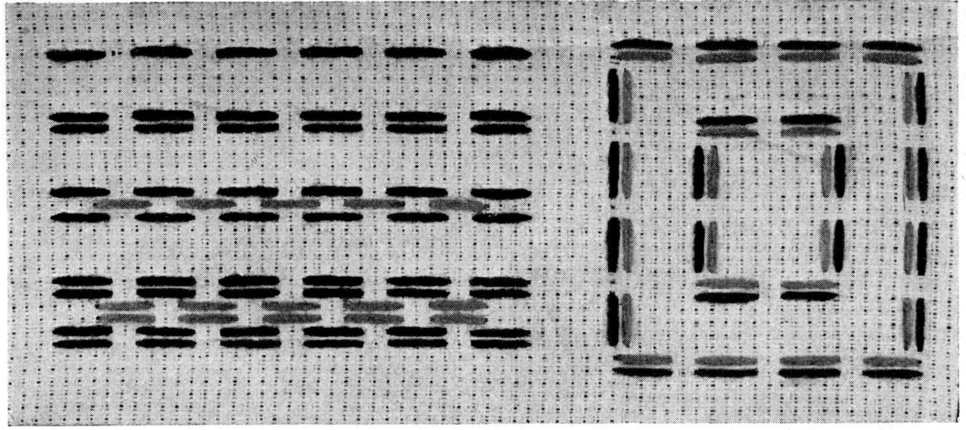

FIG. 3 FIG. 4

FIG. 3. Four examples of simple tacking stitch. FIG. 4. A square in tacking stitch to show how corners are worked. A useful article to make and decorate with this stitch is a small mat to go under a glass or vase. For small children very thick cotton is desirable.

SEWING

Materials :—

Crash or any other strong material with a loose weave.
Thick Sewing Cotton in two Colours.
Crewel Needle.

Method

Thread the needle and make a knot in the other end of the thread. A knot can be made by winding the end of the thread twice round the forefinger of the left hand and taking a stitch through this, pulling it up tightly. For small children thick thread is desirable.

Now start sewing along the edge of the material, making the stitches all the same length, and keeping the space between them the same length each time. This is the tacking or darning stitch shown at the top of Fig. 3. Under this in the diagram is a double row; then a double row with a different colour stitch between. The last example shows two double rows with a contrast double row between. Fig. 4 shows how to work corners in the stitch.

Handkerchief cases, nursery table cloths, hems of dolls' dresses and table mats can be ornamented in this way.

A mat to go under a glass or vase is a favourite article on which to begin.

If the child finds it difficult to sew on cloth at first, brown paper may be used.

FRAME KNITTING

Materials :—

A Knitting Frame.
Thick Wool or Twine.

Method

A small frame for making reins can be made from an empty cotton reel. Knock six tin tacks round one hole leaving most of each tack standing up. Larger frames can be made on the same principle, provided there is a space in the middle for the knitting, or the frames can be bought ready made, with wooden pegs instead of tacks.

Make a loop on the end of the wool. Slip this over one of the pegs. Now wind the wool round each peg in turn, taking it round the back, across the front, round to the back again and on round the back of the next peg. Wind it all round twice. Slip the lower stitch over the top of the other and off the peg on the last peg to be wound. This keeps the work from unravelling. Now slip the lower stitch off on each peg all round. Wind another row of stitches and slip off as before. Continue until the knitting is as long as required (Fig. 5).

Break the wool off about half a yard from the last stitch. Thread it on a needle and take each stitch off the frame in turn with the needle, pulling the wool through.

The end can either be finished by pulling the thread up tightly and fastening the wool, or it can be left flat and the two sides sewn together. If a bag is to be made, make a cord with which to pull it up.

Scarves, caps and tea cosies can be made in wool.

Bags for tennis balls or golf balls can be made in twine.

To Make Cord

If one yard of cord is wanted, cut four strands (more for a thicker, fewer for a thinner cord) $2\frac{1}{4}$ yards long. The cord is more even if one person twists at each end, but it can be made by one person alone if the end is securely fastened to a fixture.

Knot the strands at both ends. Twist the strands between the finger and thumb, twisting always away from the body, until they are quite tight (Fig. 6).

Double the strands, holding the twist midway between the two knots (Fig. 7), and knot the cord under the two knots, which should then be cut off.

Cord made in this way is useful for a variety of purposes.

If it is to be used for twine bags it is best made of twine.

Woollen cord is used on a great many knitted garments, with the ends finished with small woolly balls or tassels.

Silk cord is useful for finishing cushion covers, tea cosies, work bags and many other articles. A tassel is the best finish for a silk cord.

To make a tassel, take a firm piece of cardboard the same length as the finished tassel is to be. Wind the wool, silk or twine round this until the tassel seems fat enough. Bind the strands together at the top of the cardboard with the loose end of wool, and cut the strands through at the other end of the cardboard.

Gather the strands in one hand and bind them together again a little below the top. Sew the tassel to the end of the cord, and trim the other end with scissors.

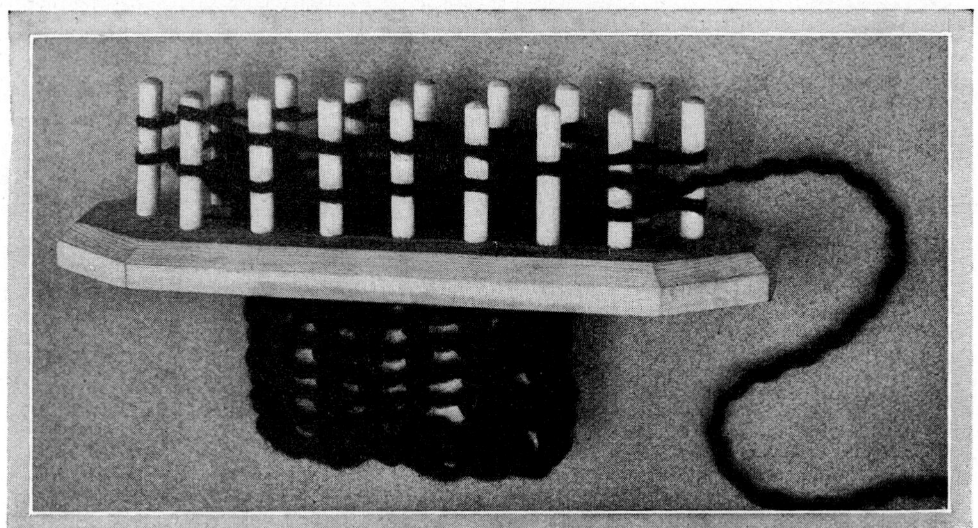

FIG. 5

This is how knitting is done on a frame. The peg that has only one stitch on it was the one that was wound last, so the bottom stitch was taken over the top one to keep the wool from unravelling. The finished part is seen coming out from the space in the middle of the frame. Only thick wool or string should be used on a large frame.

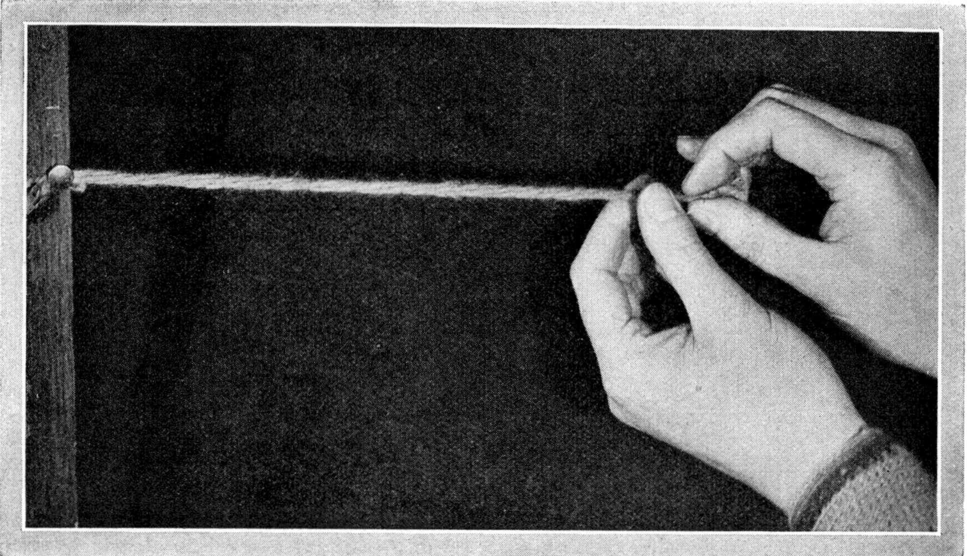

In Fig. 6 a cord is being made by one person. After the end has been firmly fixed the strands are twisted to the right. Cords of any thickness may be made, from quite thin ones of sewing cotton or silk to thick ones in wool. The thin cords, sewn along an edge of material, make very good button-holes if little spaces are left free at equal distances between the sewn-down parts.

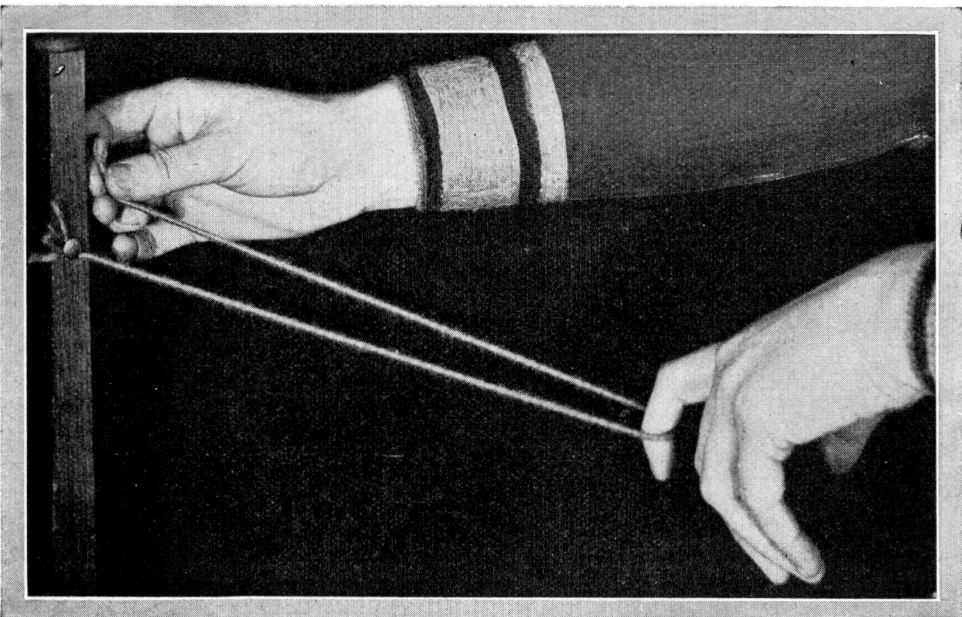

Fig. 7 shows the strands twisted and doubled, ready to be tied. Great care must be taken to hold the twist with the left hand mid-way between the ends, as is shown in the picture, otherwise the cord begins to twist in the wrong place and is never quite so even afterwards. Different colours may be used in one cord, or strands of silk and wool, or silk and cotton look well.

Age 6 Years

SEWING

Materials :—

Cotton or Woollen Material.
Thick Wool or Cotton Thread.
Crewel Needle.

Method

This is the same as before, but now stitches that go up and down as well as those that go across can be learned. The designs in the illustration (Fig. 1, p. 416) are not meant to be copied. It is more interesting for the worker to make up her own designs.

When the article to be made has been decided on, choose the material and the colours of silk and wool to be used, then draw several designs in coloured chalks on paper and choose the one most suitable for the purpose intended. The designs in Fig. 1 will give some ideas.

These paper designs may be used as friezes for the doll's house, for covering cardboard boxes or for other decorative purposes.

Practice will thus be gained in making designs to fit corners.

It will also be a good way to gain ideas of colour harmony.

Even after the selection of colour has been made, the choice of which is to be used as background and which as decoration is still important. A safe rule is that the brighter the colour, the smaller should be the space it occupies. If we look at the world out of doors we find that the large spaces are filled with browns and greens, whilst the scarlets, bright yellows and purples have only a small place.

Shoe bags, tray cloths, curtain ends, chair-backs and cushions can all be ornamented in this way.

WEAVING ON A FRAME

Materials :—

Stiff Cardboard.
Ruler.
Pencil.
Scissors with rounded ends.
Thick Wool in two Colours.
Crewel Needle.

Method

First make the Loom on which to Weave

Cut a firm piece of cardboard 7½ by 9 inches. Lay a ruler along the top (short end).

Put a mark at 1 inch and another mark at each ½ inch until 6½ inches is reached (12 marks in all).

Now measure ¼ inch down from the top on each side and make a mark. Draw a line to join these marks.

On this second line put the first mark at 1¼ inches and another at each ½ inch until 6¼ inches is reached.

Draw a line from the first mark on the top line to the first mark on the second line and another from it to the second mark in the first line. Do this until all the marks are joined.

Turn the cardboard top to bottom and mark the second end in the same way.

With scissors, cut the marked notches out of both ends of the cardboard.

This is the loom. (See Fig. 2, p. 417.)

To Make the Shuttle

Take a piece of cardboard 8 by 1 inches.

Cut a notch 1 inch deep at each end, and a little slit in the side of one of these notches.

To Thread the Loom

Take a ball of wool. Leave about ½ yard of wool at the back of the loom. Bring the wool forward at A. Pass the wool down the front of the loom, round the first point at the bottom, back across the front and round the second point at the top. Continue this until all the notches are full. There should be eleven strands across the front of the loom and no wool at the back except the loops round the points between the notches, and the end to tie.

Take the wool to the back at B. Leave ½ yard and tie to the piece left at A.

The strands across the front are called the warp.

DESIGNS FOR TACKING STITCH

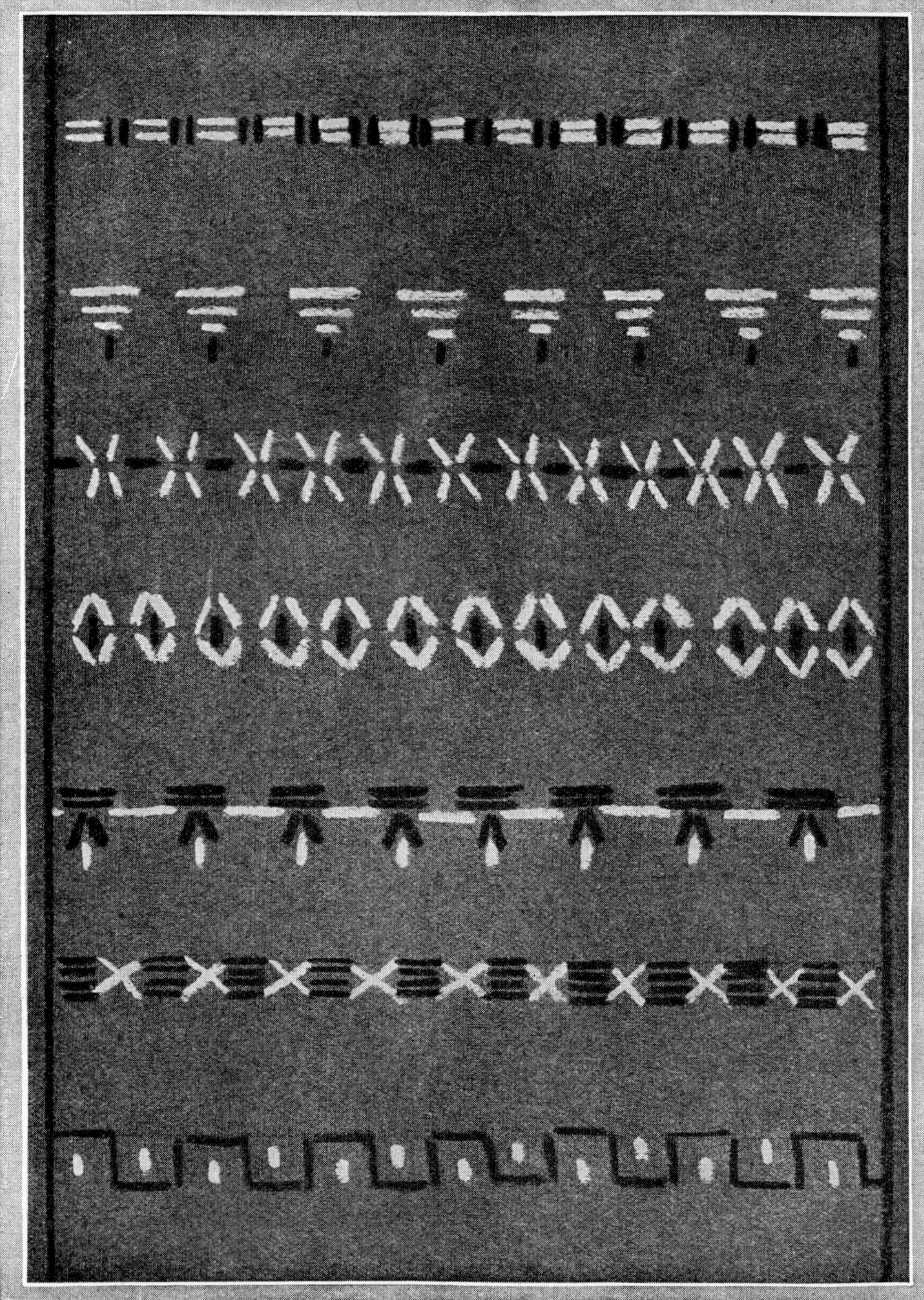

Fig. 1.—These designs for the use of two colours on a third coloured background may be used for other purposes besides tacking stitch. Pottery may be decorated with lines instead of stitches. Wooden boxes, trays, etc., can be painted thus in strong colours, or the designs may be used in weaving and basketry. Some colour combinations that were found good were: black and white on blue, black and yellow on grey, blue and green on grey, and green and coral on a natural-coloured linen.

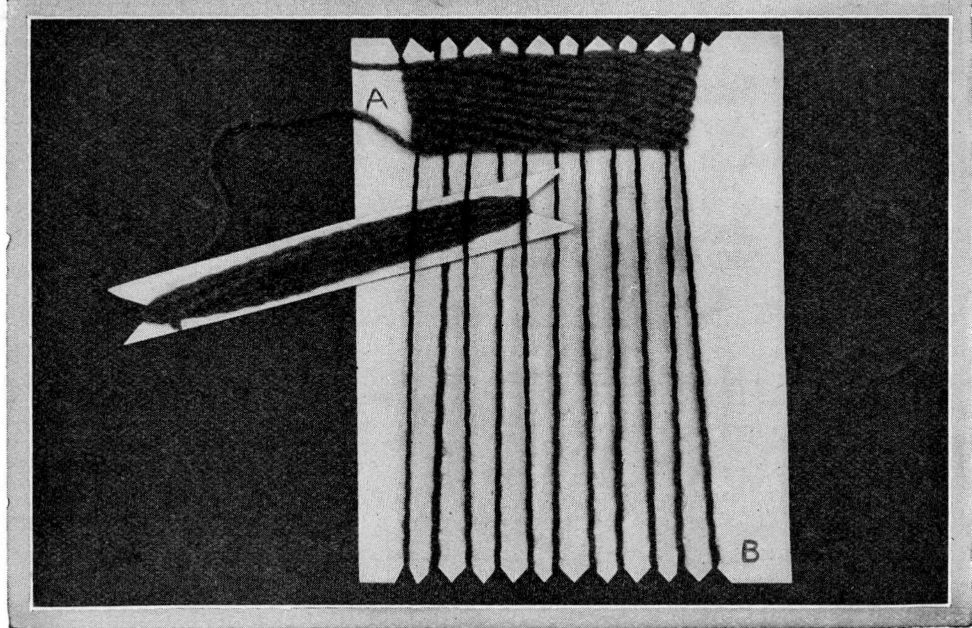

FIG. 2

In Fig. 2 can be seen a loom and shuttle which any child could make in cardboard. On it can be woven dolls' carpets in wool, mats in raffia, tea-cosies in wool, and other useful things. When the process of weaving has been mastered, the child will probably feel a desire to make a larger loom in wood on which more ambitious articles embodying interesting designs can be woven.

To Thread the Shuttle

Take the other colour of wool.

Secure the end of it in the small slit on the shuttle, and wind as much on to the shuttle as it will hold.

Tie the free end from the shuttle to the piece of wool left at the back of the loom. Now start weaving by passing the shuttle under and over the warp threads as in darning (Fig. 2). Care must be taken not to pull in the end threads of the warp. If this cannot be avoided put a knitting needle down each side and weave it in with the end thread. It can easily be pulled out when the weaving is finished. Continue until the warp is all covered.

The weaving threads that go across are called the weft, or the woof, and the whole fabric is called the web.

Untie the wool at the back and slip the web off the loom. Darn in the short end of weft thread at each end and fill in the loops at the ends either by darning with the long ends of warp wool, or, if a rug is being made, with a fringe.

If a fringe is to be used, cut a number of pieces of wool 3 inches long. Double one piece. Put the looped end through a loop in the rug and pull the two loose ends through the loop (as string is put in a luggage label). Knot one 3-inch piece of wool into each loop.

The web can be woven in patterns by going over or under more than one warp thread, or by using another colour of wool to weave stripes. If the tacking stitch borders have been done it will be found that the patterns in those can nearly all be worked in weaving.

Many things besides dolls' rugs can be woven, such as egg cosies (on a smaller loom), mats or pochettes. Raffia, twine and silk can all be used. Wool woven on a twine or silk warp gives good results.

Age 7 Years

INDIAN BASKETRY

Materials :—

Raffia.
Raffia Needles.

Method

Take three strands of raffia by one end. Make a loop round the first finger on the left hand with these and tie the strands together, where they cross, with a fourth strand (Fig. 1). Pull the ends until the loop almost closes up. Thread the fourth strand of raffia on to a needle and take four tight over-sewing stitches into the loop. Pull the ends again so that the loop quite closes (Fig. 2).

The long ends from the loop are called the tail. The strand with the needle is called the working thread.

After the loop is closed, take the tail in the left hand and the working thread in the right. Wind the working thread once round the tail, towards the body, then take it over the top and forward again and pass the needle through the centre of the loop. Repeat thus until six stitches have been taken into the centre and the work has again reached the knot.

Now cut the short threads off close to the knot and continue as before, once round the tail, but, instead of inserting the needle into the centre, put it into the space left by the twist round the tail on the first round.

It will be necessary to increase a stitch or two on each round on the base of the basket. This is done by taking two stitches into the same space, winding the thread once round the tail between these two stitches. The extra stitches should be spaced at equal distances on the round.

Add another strand of raffia to the tail once in every round until there are eight strands. (If a very large basket or a tray is being made, add strands until the tail is of the desired thickness.) When one strand in the tail is finished a new one must be added, as the tail must be kept at a uniform thickness.

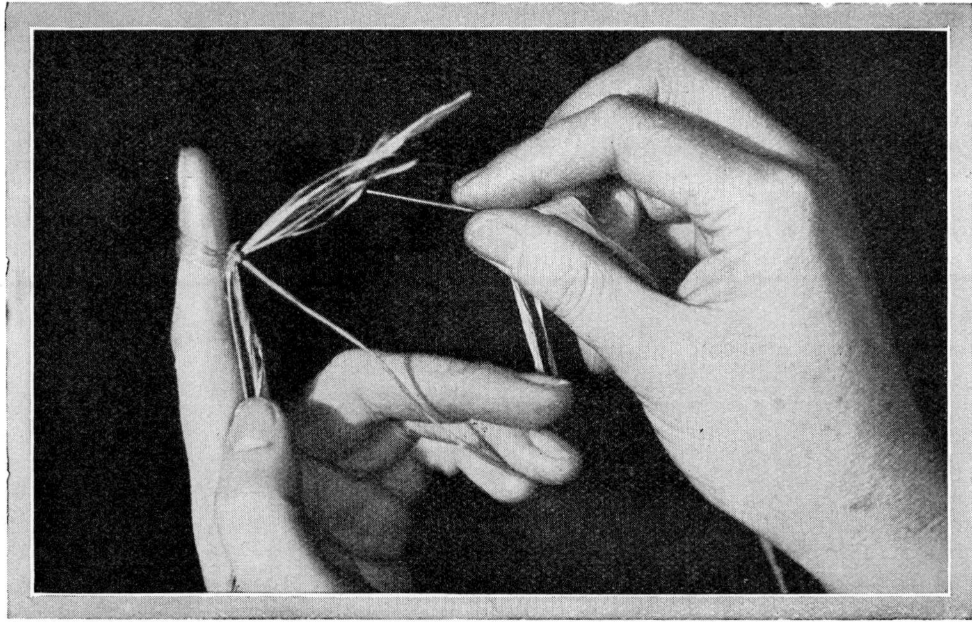

FIG. 1

This shows the first step in making the base of a coiled Indian basket in raffia. It is of importance that this step should be learned thoroughly, as all round baskets are begun in the same way, whatever stitch may be used later, and no basket can be successful without a satisfactory centre.

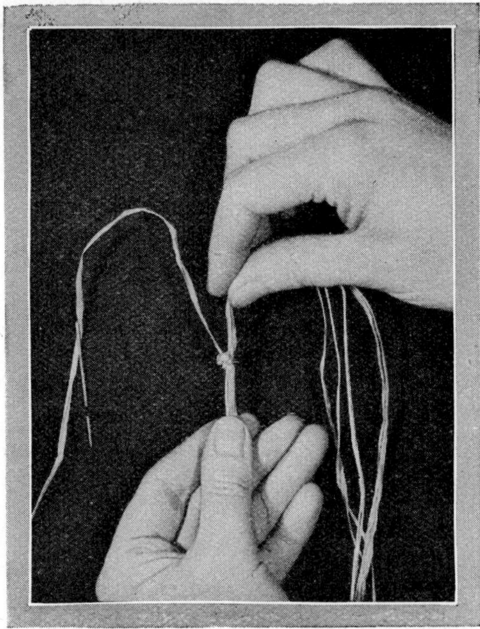

FIG. 2

In Fig. 2 four stitches have been taken into the loop seen on the finger in Fig. 1, and the ends are being pulled to close the loop.

FIG. 3

This shows how the tail is placed when the sides are to be raised. The tail should be pulled rather tightly while the first round is being worked.

When the working thread is nearly finished, let it be added to the tail and take a new thread. Hold the end of this, with the tail in the left hand, close to the basket and wind it round the tail in the ordinary way.

When the base is sufficiently large, start the sides by laying the tail on top of the last round instead of outside it (Fig. 3).

Continue without adding any stitches until the sides are of the height desired.

On the last round taper the tail by cutting off the strands at intervals until there is only one left. Fasten this down securely and run the working thread back inside the last round for about an inch, and cut both it and the tail strand off so that they do not show.

This method is known as LAZY SQUAW stitch, and is illustrated in Fig. 6.

Another method, which is known as coiled Indian stitch, is illustrated in Fig. 4. In this the working thread is brought forward over the tail and a stitch is then taken through from the back. Now pass the working thread up over the last sewn-down coil, behind and over the tail, and through from the back again. The centre is the same whatever method be used.

One of these two methods should always be employed for the base of the basket, as they are very strong and firm.

Two varieties which may be used for mats, or for the sides of baskets, may be seen in Fig. 5. The light part here is done in coiled Indian stitch, with four twists round the tail between the stitches. The border is done in Lazy Squaw stitch with four twists instead of one round the tail between the stitches.

In working coloured borders like those in Figs. 6 and 7, a coloured strand is introduced into the tail and this is used instead of the working thread for the coloured stitches, the working

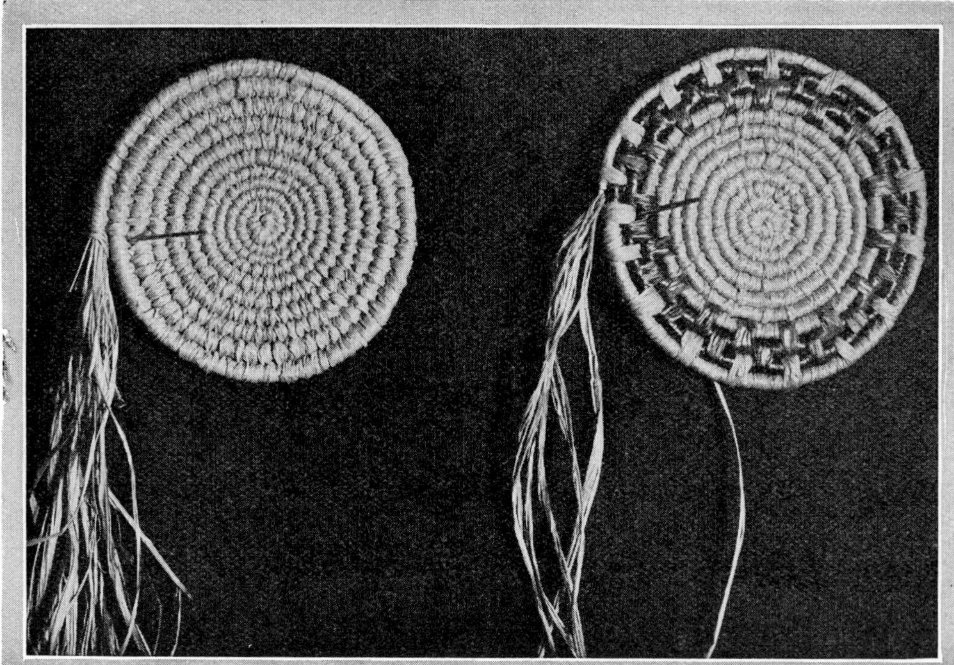

FIG. 4 shows a base in coiled Indian stitch, which is perhaps the favourite stitch of most people. The working thread is wound about the tail and brought through the last-completed round. This makes a firm base.

FIG. 5.—The light part has been worked in coiled Indian stitch with the thread wrapped four times round the tail, and the border is in Lazy Squaw with the thread wrapped four times round the tail.

FIG. 6 shows a basket done in Lazy Squaw stitch, with a coloured border introduced. In this stitch the coloured part shows clearly, as the long stitches stand out from the others.

FIG. 7.—Care must be taken to make the spacing even in working a basket of this kind. The stitches on the last row should be counted and the design worked out on squared paper before the side is started.

thread taking its place meanwhile in the tail.

Very interesting designs can be worked out in one or more colours. Ideas for these can be obtained by studying Indian baskets in museums. The Indians dye the materials for these with the bark and roots of various trees, and such natural dyes give the best colours. Boiling raffia with onion skins, old tea leaves, or coffee grounds, and rinsing well afterwards, will give good colours. Walnuts will give green in summer and brown in autumn. Lichens may be gathered on country walks and used to dye raffia. Some give green and some give a lovely yellow. Logwood, used alone, or with alum, with iron or with ammonia, produces excellent colours. Oxblood and cudbear are also useful. These can be had from the chemist, but it is more interesting to find one's own dyeing materials in the woods.

FIG. 8

This is the completed shopping bag described on this and the next page. Strong material that is not too stiff for the passage of the needle should be used—hessian or cross-stitch canvas are good materials for this purpose.

The Indians of North America make a great many of their household possessions in this basketry. They make cradles, trays and quite large chests with lids; and some of their baskets are so finely woven that they will hold water.

SEWING

Cross-stitch and over-sewing can be done now that tacking stitch has been learned. A shopping bag is a good article to make.

Materials :—

- $\frac{3}{4}$ yard Crash, 12 inches wide, with selvedge at both sides.
- A piece of Wide-meshed Canvas.
- Coloured Wools.
- Crewel Needle.

Method

Cut two strips of crash, each 3 inches wide, across the width of the material. Turn a $\frac{1}{2}$-inch hem to the same side on both edges of each piece. Now fold each strip lengthwise with the raw edges turned in, and tack.

Turn a double hem of 1 inch at each end of the other piece of crash. Tack these down to the right side and sew them on the right side, using coloured wool and any tacking stitches desired.

Fold the large piece of crash in two, with the sewn hems together.

Now take a piece of canvas the size of the folded bag. Tack it firmly to one-half of the bag on the right side.

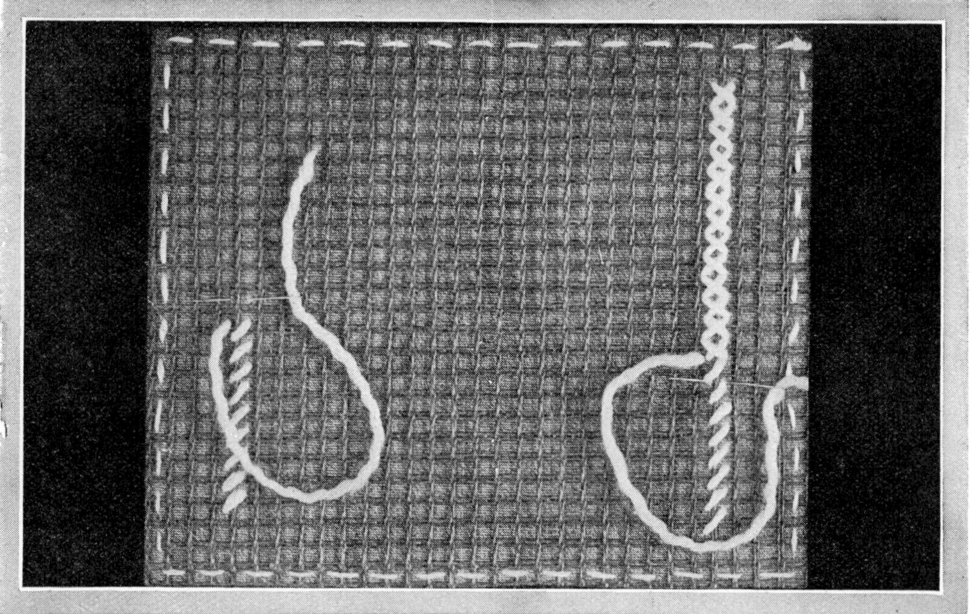

FIG. 9

Here you see the first row of stitches in position. It is most important that all the stitches should slant in the same direction. This applies to all cross-stitch work.

FIG. 10

Above the covering stitches are seen. This illustration shows also how the canvas is tacked on the front part of the bag before the work is begun. It must be firm and quite flat.

In working cross-stitch, bring the needle through from the back in a square near the lower left-hand corner of the canvas, working through both canvas and crash, which is now opened up flat. Count one square up and one to the right and put the needle in again here. Bring it out in the square to the left of the one where it was inserted, count one square up and one to the right, put the needle in, and bring it out at the next square on the left. Continue this until the hem is reached (Fig. 9). All the stitches must slant from right to left.

Now work down from the top and cover all the stitches already made with others slanting in the opposite direction, *i.e.*, from left to right (Fig. 10).

Another row can now be worked in the next spaces on the right, using another colour of wool. Begin one square up from the end of the first row and stop one square from the top. A third row in the first colour and the same length as the first row should now be worked on the right of the second row (Fig. 8). The pattern is next worked at the right-hand side of the bag. Some little cross-stitch trees can be worked for extra decoration, if wished. Children like to draw such patterns as these trees on squared graph paper. They are easily copied, stitch for stitch, on to canvas.

Then the threads of the canvas are all pulled out, leaving only the sewing on the crash (Fig. 8).

Tack and over-sew the sides of the bag (for over-sewing, see Plain Needlework section) in one of the colours already used. Over-sew the two strips and sew them securely to the two sides of the bag as in Fig. 8.

Cross-stitch can also be done on loosely woven material, where the threads of the material can be counted and act as a guide. The shopping bag in the photograph is made of this material.

Cross-stitch is used in working tapestry. In this the design is stamped on the canvas or it can be copied stitch by stitch from a chart. The background is filled in afterwards.

Long ago women were fond of commemorating events in this way. They were not taught to draw or paint and this was their only means of pictorial expression. Queen Matilda worked a tapestry representing fifty-eight scenes in the life of her husband William the Conqueror. Mary Queen of Scots and her Maries worked many tapestries of this sort. They were used as wall hangings and may be seen in historical buildings to this day.

Age 8 Years

CANE BASKET WEAVING

Pulp cane is the most suitable material for beginners to use, as long lengths of uniform thickness may be obtained.

For a first basket a very simple shape should be made, so that the whole thing can be done without help.

Materials :—

- Pulp Cane No. 6 and No. 3.
- A pair of Scissors with rounded ends.

Method

Soak the cane for one hour. Cut eight stakes 20 inches long in No. 6 cane.

Lay four of these on the table from left to right and the other four on top of them to form a cross, with all arms of the cross the same length. Cut another stake 12 inches long and put it with the stakes at the left hand arm of the cross, with the ends level. Now turn the cross so that the five stakes are at the top.

Take a piece of No. 3 cane. This is called a weaver. Lay the end of it on top and across the four stakes that go from right to left. Weave it under the five at the top, from the left, over the four at the right, under the four at the bottom and over the four at the left. In the second round take it under the odd stake (Fig. 1), over the other four at the top, under the four at the right side, over the four at the bottom and under the four at the left side. Third round, over the odd stake and so on until the weaver comes back to the odd stake again; weaving is always done from left to right.

Pull the stakes away from each other in twos and weave under and over these for three rounds. Now pull them away from each other again so that they are all separate. Be sure that the space between them is the same width.

When the base measures 6 inches across put it to soak again and cut seventeen stakes of No. 6 cane 10 inches long. Soak these also.

Insert one of these stakes at the right side of each of the base stakes, pushing it into the base weaving as far as it will go.

Gently bend all the stakes at right angles to the base, taking care not to crack the canes. Tie all the ends together with string at the top and leave for half an hour.

There is still a weaver attached to the base. Add another weaver by putting it between the two pairs of stakes in front of the weaver already there.

Bring the back weaver over one pair of stakes, behind the next pair and out to the front. Leave it there. Take the other weaver. Bring it over one pair of stakes, behind the next pair and out to the front. This is called pairing (Fig. 2), because it is done with a pair of weavers.

Do three rounds of pairing, then, using the two weavers as though they were one, and keeping the stakes still in pairs, weave nine rounds over one and under one. Working with two or more weavers in this way is called slewing.

Still using the same pair of weavers, do three more rows of pairing and cut both the weavers off inside.

Soak the basket upside down for half an hour.

Take any pair of stakes, and, weaving to the right, pass it behind one pair, in front of the next, behind the third and leave it inside. Do this until all the stakes are woven in, weaving the last pairs so that no join shows.

Cut the ends off close inside.

Fig. 3 shows this basket completed.

TO MAKE A STRONGER BASKET

Materials :—

No. 12 Cane.
No. 8 Cane.
No 4 Cane.
A Knife and a Bodkin.

Method

Cut eight base stakes, 7 inches long, in No. 12 cane. Make a split 1 inch long in the middle of each of four of these, using the bodkin (Fig. 4).

Take one of the unsplit stakes and pass it through the cut in each of the four split canes. Put the other three in the remaining space, making a cross.

Take a long length of well-soaked No. 4 cane and bend it, not quite half-way along its length. Hold the base stakes between the thumb and fingers of the left hand, with the split canes pointing up and down. Put the loop in the No. 4 cane over the top arm of the cross, twist the ends once (Fig. 5) and work two rows of pairing.

Open the stakes up into twos and work two more rows of pairing, then open the stakes again so that all are separate and work another two rows in pairing.

Cane weaving is a craft in which great accuracy and attention to detail are necessary. Each stake should point in its proper direction from the start, and care must be taken to maintain that direction throughout.

In weaving, the fingers of the left hand should always be inserted between the stakes, holding the weaver that has just been placed by the right hand. When a new weaver is needed it should be crossed above the end of the old weaver behind a stake, on the inside. It is only by giving great care to such details as these that good, even work can be produced.

The rest of the base is to be done in randing. Randing consists in taking the weaver over one stake and under the next. As the number of stakes in this basket is even, two weavers must be used. These follow each other round, but do not cross as in pairing.

Take the two weavers already in use. Take the one which finished the last row of pairing all round, over one and under one, until the second weaver is reached. Now take the second weaver all round, over one and under one, stopping just short of the first weaver. Continue this until the base measures 6 inches across. The last row must be done in pairing. Cut the weavers off and cross them.

Cut the base-stakes close to the weaving.

Cut thirty-two side-stakes, each 14 inches long, in No. 8 cane. These must be slyped, as in Fig. 6, and then the cut ends put to soak for half an hour.

With the bodkin make a little passage at both sides of each base-stake in turn, inserting the slyped end of the side-stake as soon as the bodkin is withdrawn. Gently bend the side-stakes until they are at right angles to the base. Tie them up and leave them for half an hour.

Upsetting the sides is done with three rows of triple weaving (sometimes called three-rod waling). The principle is the same as in pairing, but three weavers are used.

Insert three well-soaked No. 4 canes. Take the one on the left in front of two stakes, behind one, and out to the front. Always using the cane on the left, continue to do this until the three rounds are completed, taking great care that the stakes are equidistant and that each points in its proper direction.

Work the sides in randing, using two weavers. The basket in Fig. 7 has five rows of three-rod waling to strengthen

CANE BASKET WEAVING (1)

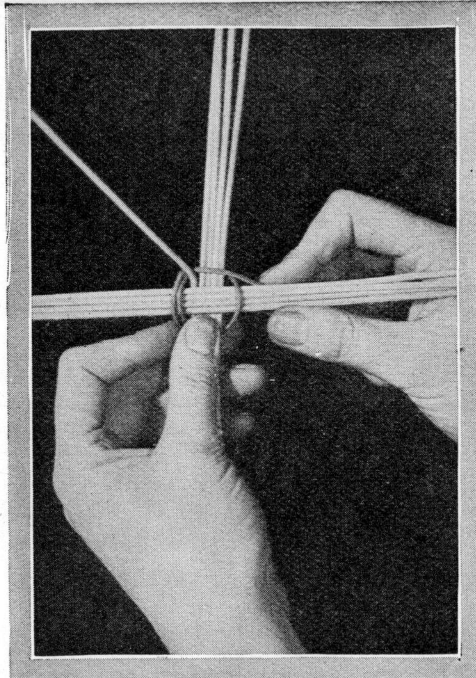

FIG. 1 shows the beginning of a basket in cane weaving. Note the position of the odd stake. It remains separate from the rest until the base of the basket is finished.

FIG. 2 shows the upsetting of the sides after the side stakes have been inserted. The weave shown is called pairing. It is stronger than single weaving.

FIG. 3.—The finished basket. It would make a good waste-paper basket. A work-basket could be made in the same way, with a wider base and shorter sides.

FIG. 4.—The canes are being split to start a strong base. The split must be exactly in the middle of the cane, and just long enough to take the other four canes.

CANE BASKET WEAVING (2)

FIG. 5 shows how the weaver is started in pairing. The loop must be not quite in the middle of the weaver, so that when the new weavers are joined on they come at different places.

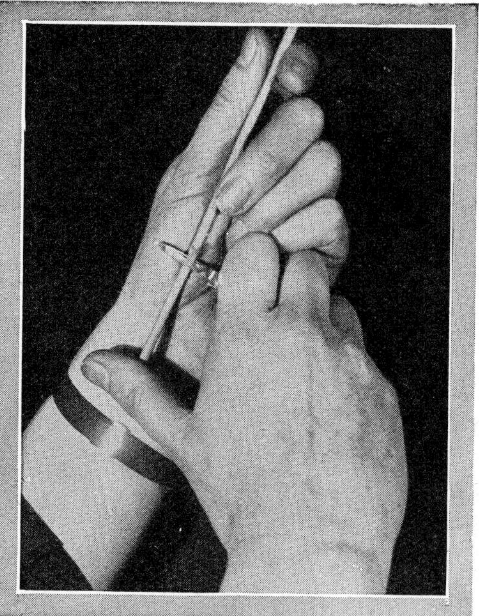

FIG. 6.—Here the method of slyping cane is shown. Make a gradual cut, leaving half the thickness of the cane at the end. Cane is slyped before being inserted for stakes or handles.

FIG. 7.—The upsetting of the side of this basket is done in three-rod waling. There is a strengthening band of this before the border is reached. The rest is done in randing.

FIG. 8.—Note how the handle is inserted and bound down with the split cane. The piece that made the cross is bound in all the way across, so that the handle cannot be pulled out.

it, then four rows of randing, before the final five rows of three-rod waling which make a firm foundation for the border.

The border is worked, after the canes have been soaked for half an hour, by bending any cane in front of the one to the right, behind the second, in front of the third, and behind the fourth, where it is left. The first two or three stakes to be bent for the border must not be pressed too close to the side, as the last stakes have to be woven under them. All the rest must be pressed down as closely as possible.

To Insert a Handle

A basket which is to be given a handle should have an even number of side stakes. Cut one very thick cane (or two thinner ones) to the length of the handle, plus twice the measurement of the side of the basket. Thus, if a 17-inch handle is wanted on a basket having sides 5 inches in depth, a cane 27 inches long must be cut (in Fig. 8 two lengths of No. 12 used).

The two ends must be slyped and pushed down beside two side-stakes on opposite sides of the basket, until they reach the base.

Call the two points where the handle enters the sides A and B respectively.

Take a piece of well-soaked split cane. Insert one end of it (at A) from the front, under the waling, and to the right of the handle-stake. Leave 10 inches on the inside. Take the other end of the split cane, carry it across the waling and the handle-stake and insert it under the border. Bring it to the front again under the waling, but still on the left of the handle. Cross to the other side of the handle and insert it under the border on the right side.

Now carry this long piece over the handle to B and bind the handle down on that side in the same way. When this is done, continue with the same cane (which must be sufficiently long to reach the other side) and wrap it firmly round the handle and the piece of split cane until A is reached (Fig. 8).

Push the end of the wrapping cane well down the side of the basket and fasten it down with the first end, which must then be pushed down the side also, behind the handle.

SEWING

Blanket stitch and Daisy stitch can now be learned.

A pram or cot cover would be a good article to make. Tea cosies or hot-water bottle covers would also be suitable.

Materials :—

A piece of soft Woollen Material 36 inches by 20 inches.
Coloured Wools.
Crewel Needles.

Method

Turn a single $\frac{1}{2}$-inch hem all round to the wrong side and tack.

Choose a thick wool in a colour to harmonise with that of the material. Hide the starting knot under the hem and work all round in blanket stitch. This is done by holding the thread down with the left hand and lifting a stitch with the needle pointing downwards. Put the needle through (Fig. 9). Work the corner as shown.

Ornament the cover with daisy stitch (see Embroidery Stitches), using one colour for the flowers and green for the leaves, making a suitable design.

KNITTING

The easiest way to learn to knit is to study the pictures, which show each step as it is done.

Some things which it is useful to know cannot be shown in pictures, but they are very important and, as knitting is one of the most useful crafts known, they should be carefully noted from the start.

Keep the work clean when not being done by wrapping it in a cloth, as wool catches dust very easily.

Always join wool by darning one end into another for about 2 inches.

When knitting a plain row, slip the first stitch purlwise.

FIG. 9

Shown above is the corner of a pram cover; the edge is worked all round with blanket stitch. The decoration is in daisy stitch. When plain blanket stitch has been learned, it is interesting to work alternate long and short stitches, and many different arrangements may be made.

When knitting a purl row, slip the first stitch plainwise. These make neat edges.

If the knitting seems too loose, use smaller pins. This will produce more even knitting.

If the casting off is too loose, use a smaller pin than that used for the rest of the work.

A cover for a doll's bed is suggested as a start. With 5-ply wool and No. 6 pins cast on fifty stitches. Work as long as desired in garter stitch and cast off.

Fig. 1, To Cast On

Hold the wool between the second and third fingers of the left hand, leaving 2 yards of wool at the back of the hand for every 100 stitches to be cast on. Twist the wool round the left thumb. Put the needle into this and knit it with the long end of wool attached to the ball, as if it were a stitch. Make another loop with the other end of wool and knit it in the same way. Cast on as many stitches as desired. This makes a very firm edge which will not stretch.

Fig. 2, Garter Stitch

In this stitch every row is a plain row, and is knitted by putting the needle into the stitch from the left side of the stitch, bringing the wool from the back and putting it between the needles, pulling the wool through with the right-hand needle and then slipping the stitch off the left-hand needle. There are four movements in each stitch, in, over, out and off.

Fig. 3, Stocking Stitch

(Alternate rows of plain and purl.)

The right side of stocking stitch is knitted in the same way as garter stitch.

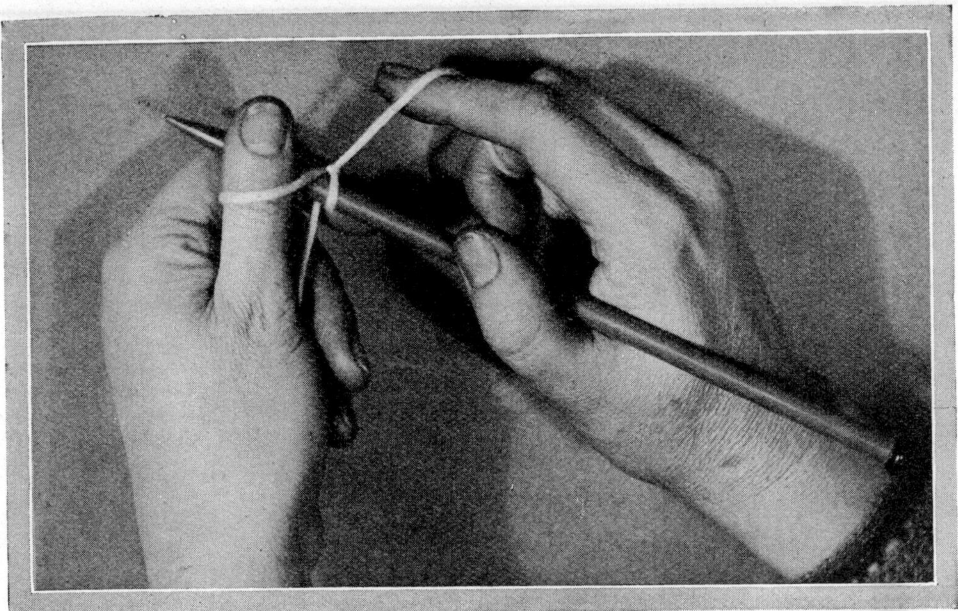

FIG. 1 shows how to cast on stitches for knitting. There are several different methods for this, but the one illustrated above is most generally useful, as it gives a good firm edge. Care must be taken to leave sufficient wool in the left hand to cast on the required number of stitches. The casting on of stitches for garments must not be too tight, or the strain will break the wool.

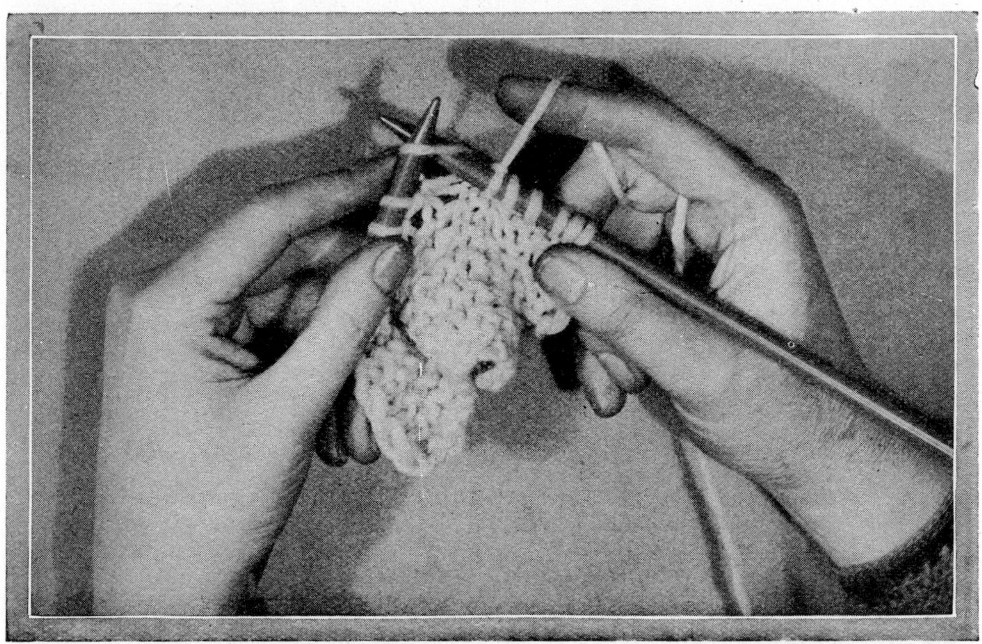

FIG. 2.—Here the method of working garter stitch is seen. The position of the hands is important. It will be noted that the wool is twisted round the middle finger of the right hand. This regulates the tension and keeps the work from becoming too loose. This is a useful stitch for pram or cot covers, babies' clothes, jumpers and many other things. Both sides are alike.

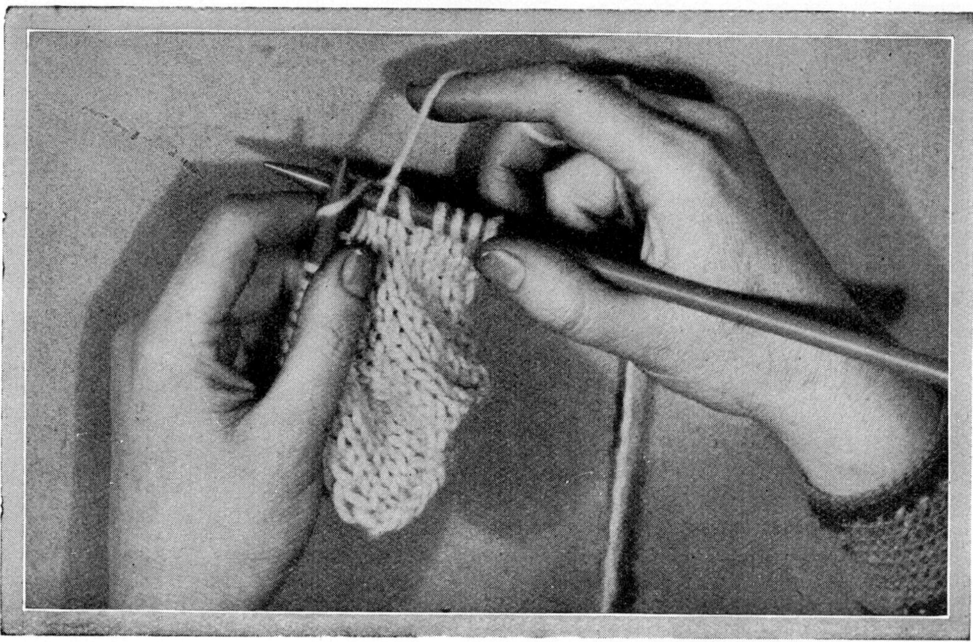

FIG. 3.—This shows the plain side of stocking stitch. This stitch is used for articles that are to be seen only on one side. For jumpers, dresses, hot-water bottle covers, caps, etc., it is useful. It gives a lighter web and stretches more easily than garter stitch and it takes less wool to work than the other. The finished surface is smooth instead of ribbed.

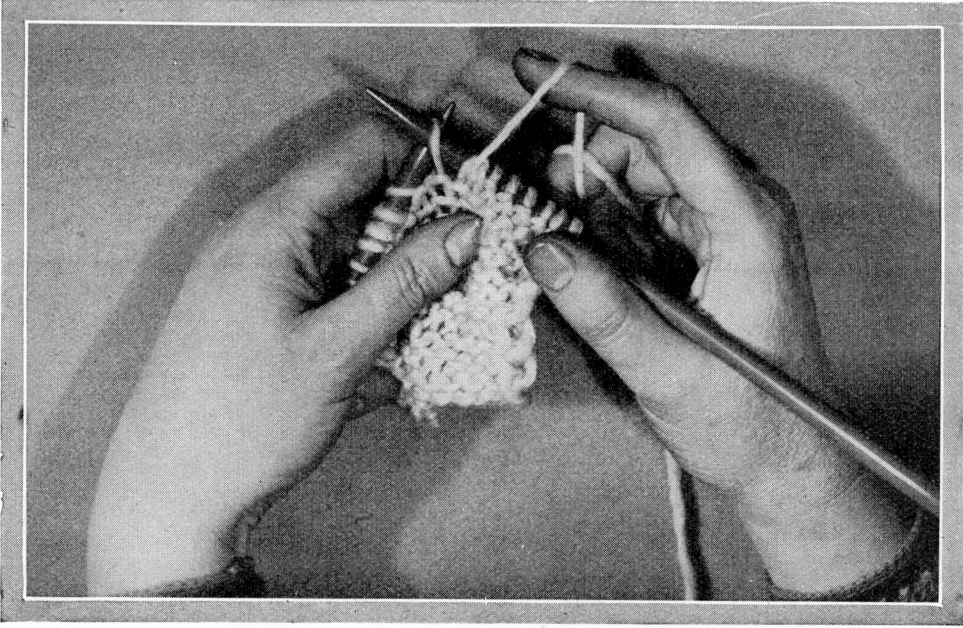

FIG. 4.—When stocking stitch is done on two needles only the reverse side must be purled. As will be seen above, the needle is put into the front of the stitch from the right and the wool brought forward over it. In making socks and stockings the work is done on four needles continuously, so that it is all done from the front, and there is no purl row. The wrong side looks like garter stitch.

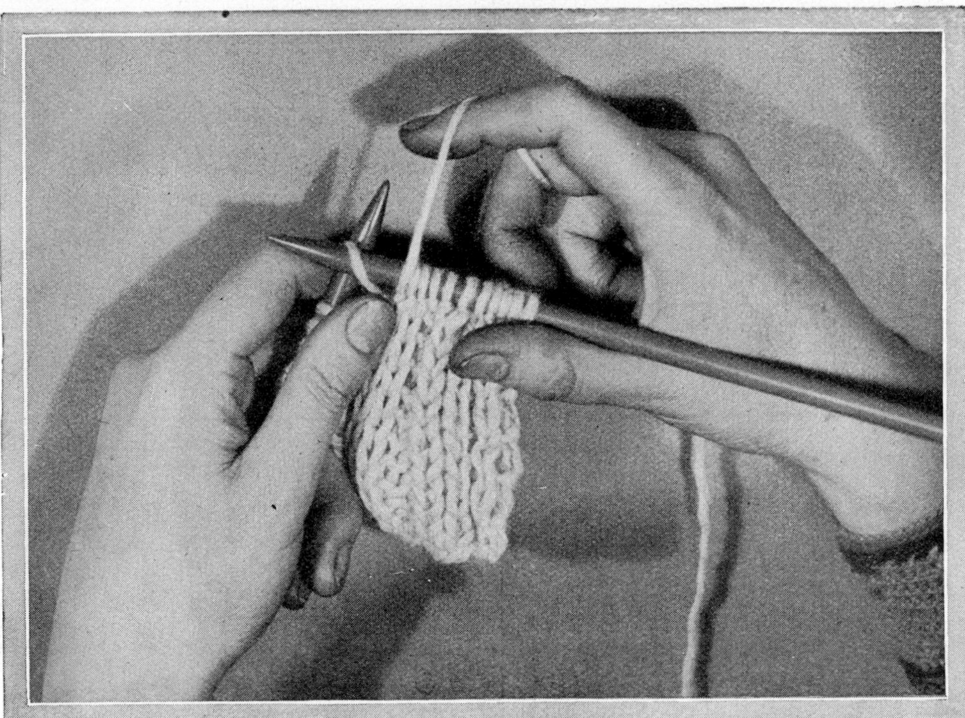

FIG. 5.—Ribbing is used when an elastic web is required. It is done by working a certain number of stitches plain and a certain number purl. On the other side the order of purl and plain is reversed.

FIG. 6.—Here the work is being cast off. Two stitches are knitted, and the first lifted over the second and slipped off the needle. Care must be taken not to make the casting off too tight.

Fig. 4

This shows the wrong side of stocking stitch. Put the needle into the right of the stitch from the back, put the wool between the needles, pull it through and slip the stitch off.

Fig. 5, Ribbing

This is done by knitting so many stitches plain and so many purl. Any number may be used, but the smaller the rib the tighter the web. Two and two is useful. Knit two stitches plain, bring the wool forward from the back to the front, purl two stitches, take the wool through from the front to the back. Repeat to the end of the row. In knitting a two and two rib the number of stitches must be divisible by four. In knitting three and three rib the number must be divisible by six, and so on.

Fig. 6, Casting Off

Knit two stitches. Insert the left-hand needle at the left-hand side of the first knitted stitch and slip it over the second knitted stitch and off the needle. Knit another stitch. Lift the second knitted stitch over the third and so on to the end of the row. When only one stitch is left, break off about 4 inches of wool, draw it through the last stitch and pull it up, then darn the end up the side of the knitting where it will not show.

CROCHET

Crochet also can best be learned from pictures. Use a bone crochet hook for wool or thick silk and a steel one for cotton or thin silk.

Fig. 6 shows a scarf that could be made by a beginner.

With a No. 8 bone crochet hook make a chain, with 5-ply wool, 1 yard long. Work a row of double crochet all round on both sides of this, back to the starting point.

Now work a row of treble crochet all round the double crochet, working only into the backs of the loops.

Continue this, using two or more colours and either double or treble crochet, until the scarf is the desired width, then break off 4 inches of wool, pull it through the last loop and darn it in.

Shawls, tea-cosies, chair-backs, caps and many other things can be made in crochet.

Fig. 1

Chain, which is the beginning of all crochet. Make a loop in the end of the wool. Pull the wool through this loop. Continue to pull the wool through each loop until the chain is sufficiently long.

Fig. 2

Single Crochet consists in putting the hook into a stitch in the chain or into the back loop of another stitch, putting the wool over the hook and pulling it through both loops at once. (Pull through once.)

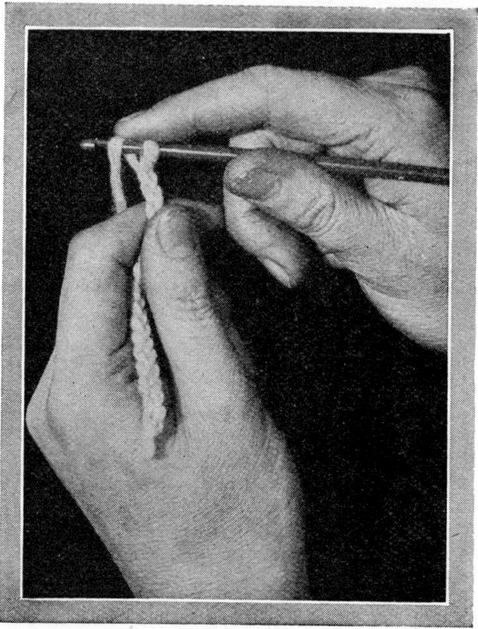

Fig. 1

This shows the method of making chain, which is the beginning of all crochet. Chain may also be used as a draw-string for knitted or crochet garments.

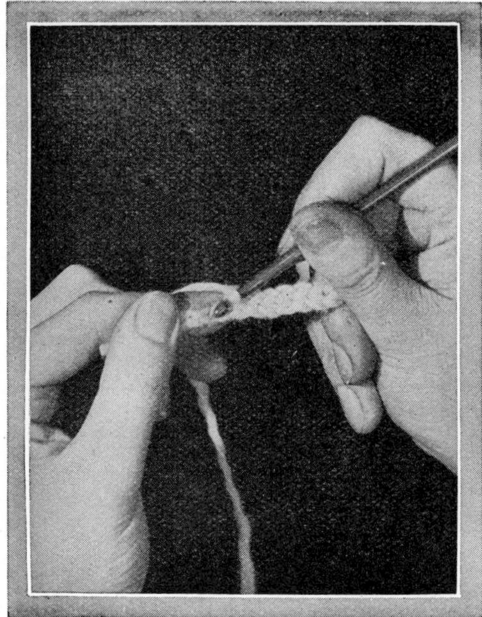

FIG. 2.—In single crochet, which is shown above, the wool is pulled through the loop only once, as the name implies. This stitch is used to neaten edges, as the work is very firm and close.

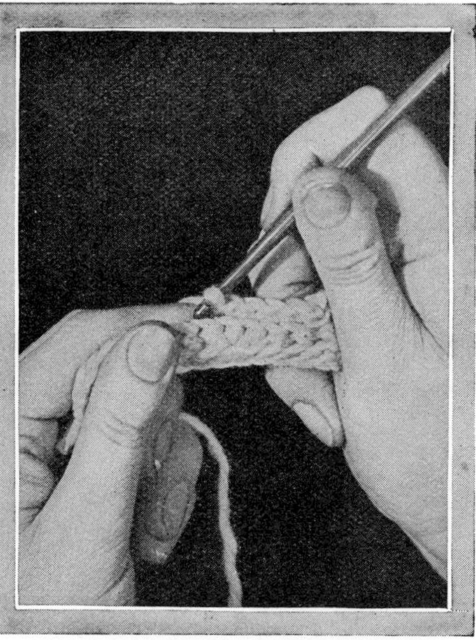

FIG. 3.—Double crochet, in which the wool is pulled twice through the loop, gives a very firm unyielding fabric. For yokes and cuffs of dresses and jumpers it is most suitable. It also may be used to neaten edges.

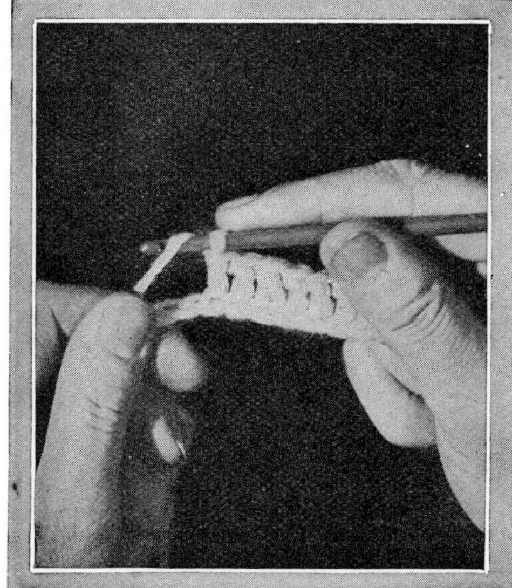

FIG. 4.—In treble crochet the wool is pulled three times through the loop. This gives a long, cord-like stitch. In wool it makes a light and fleecy texture, but it is mostly used in making fancy borders for trimming household linens, in cotton.

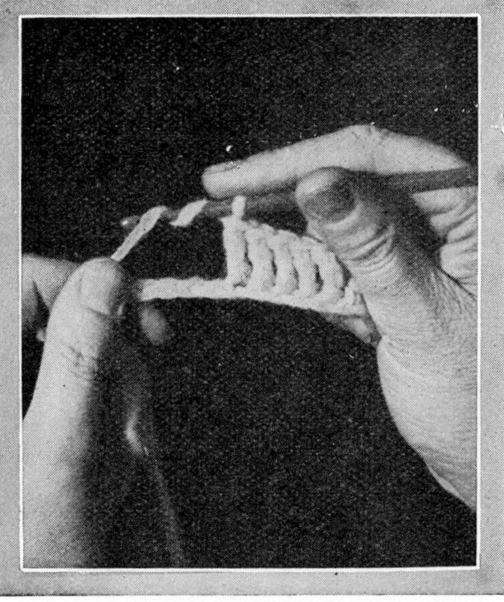

FIG. 5.—In double treble crochet the wool is pulled four times through the loop. This gives an even lacier texture than treble crochet, in wool. The stitch is useful in making slots through which ribbon is to be threaded.

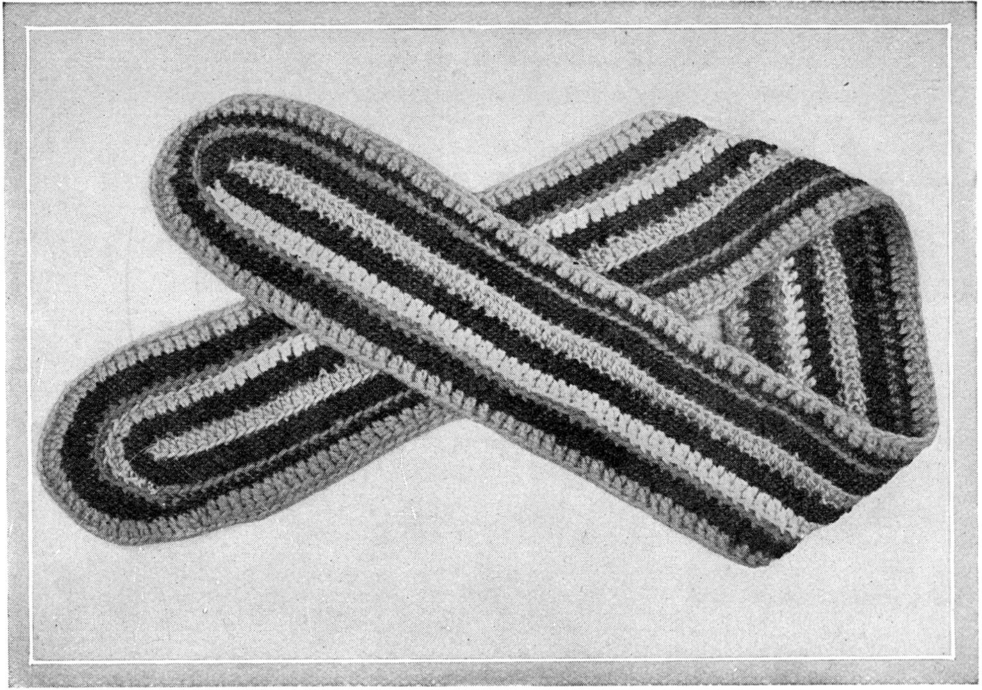

FIG. 6

The scarf above could be made by quite a small child. Very many useful things may be made in crochet in wool, and it is a craft which children much enjoy. They must be allowed free choice of wools, and must also be permitted to determine the shape of the article themselves, as otherwise this craft gives little scope for the creative instinct.

Fig. 3

Double Crochet starts in the same way as single crochet, but instead of the wool being pulled through two loops it is pulled through one, then the wool is put over the hook again and pulled through the remaining loops. (Pull through twice.)

Fig. 4

Treble Crochet. In this stitch the wool is put over before the hook is inserted. It is then pulled through one loop, the wool put over again and pulled through two loops, the wool put over a third time and pulled through the last two loops. (Pull through three times.)

Fig. 5

Double Treble Crochet. In working this the wool is put over the hook twice. The hook is then inserted and pulled through one loop, the wool is put over and pulled through two loops, the wool is put over a third time and pulled through two loops, and then it is put over a fourth time and pulled through the remaining two loops. (Pull through four times.)

POTTERY

Nowadays potters shape the clay on a potter's wheel. Long ago, before people lived in houses, they had nothing of that sort to use and had to make their pots by hand. The method they used was very much the same as that employed by the North American Indians to make baskets, and the only tools they had were their own hands and pieces of stone, stick or bone.

Take some clay just damp enough to be workable. Throw it down very hard on a table, pick it up and throw it down again. Do this a great many times. It is to drive all the air bubbles out of the clay and to distribute the moisture

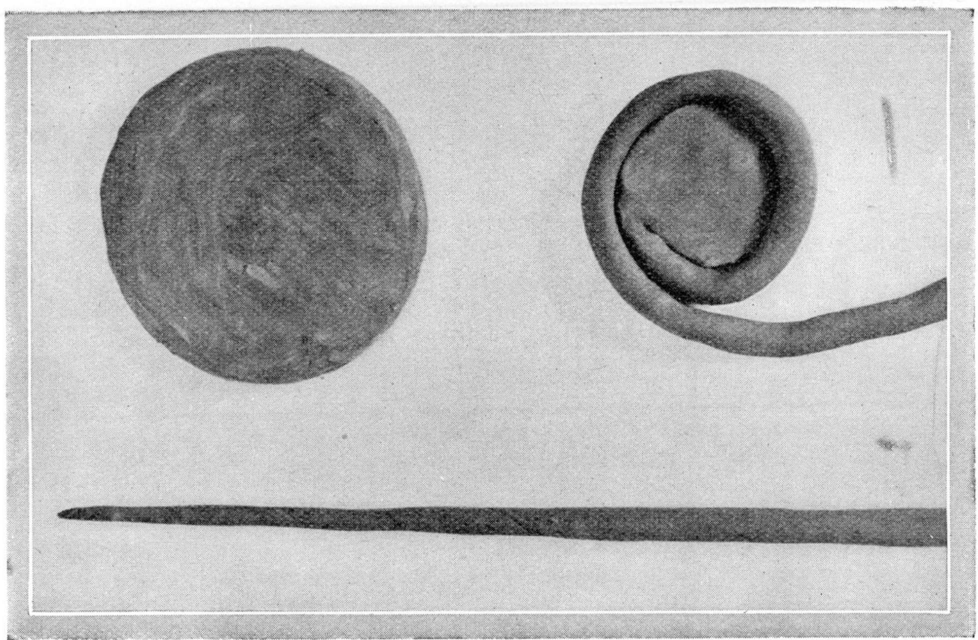

FIG. 1.—At the bottom of this illustration can be seen the beginning of the coil, with its tapering end. On the right the coil has been smoothed out in the centre. Each round must be smoothed as completed. On the left the completed base is seen, smoothed on both sides, trimmed to an exact round and ready for the first coil forming the side to be added.

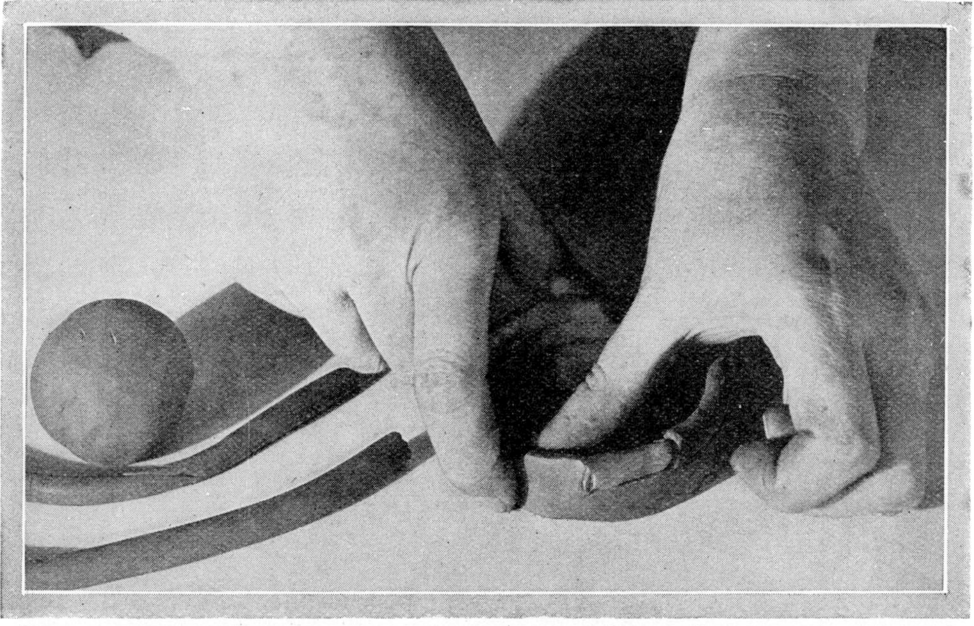

FIG. 2 shows the raising of the sides on the base. Note that each coil is joined at a different point. The position of the hands whilst smoothing the sides is very important. The thumb of the one hand should always be inside the pot to keep the clay from being pressed out of shape, while the forefinger of the other hand smooths the outside.

Fig. 3
This shows a pot made entirely by hand in coiled pottery, with the decoration put on with a piece of stick. The smoothing of the sides must be done with a very gentle movement, so that the pressure does not make the clay thinner in some parts than in others.

evenly. Cut it through with a wire and see that the clay is tightly packed together and stick the two pieces together again. Cover with a damp cloth. Repeat this every day for two or three days. It is called wedging the clay.

The clay should now be in a fit condition for use. Make a long roll of clay, slightly thicker than the pot is to be, by rolling the clay with the hand on a table or board. The end should taper to a point. When a long roll with no breaks has been made, start coiling it round as in the coiled basket work, pressing the coils close together and smoothing out the grooves with the thumb (Fig. 1).

When the base is large enough and quite flat, turn it over and smooth the other side. See that it is quite round. Lay the next coil on top of the edge instead of alongside and break off the coil when the round is completed. Start each coil in a different place, so that the joins do not come above each other (Fig. 2). The pot must now be smoothed outside and inside as the work is done. Continue until the pot is the right size.

A pattern can be made with a small piece of stick on the outside, taking great care not to press heavily or the pot will be thrown out of shape (Fig. 3).

The pot must be left alone for several days to dry.

The old way of firing pottery was to make a wood fire, then to rake it out, put the pot in the middle, and cover it with the hot ashes, leaving it there until it was cold. This can be tried, or the pot can be fired in a kiln in a pottery.

The use of the wedging will now be seen, for, if any water or air was left in it, the clay would sink in the firing at that place and the pot would be warped.

If the pot is to hold water it must be glazed and fired again. This second firing must be done at a pottery, as the heat to fire glaze must be much greater than any that can be maintained elsewhere.

SEWING

Some of the plain needlework stitches should now be learned. Using these (see Plain Needlework section) and tacking or other embroidery stitches make the child's apron illustrated in Fig. 4.

Materials :—

½ yard Linen.
Sewing Cotton.
Embroidery Cottons in several colours.
Sewing Needles and Embroidery Needles.
One Button.

Method

Cut a strip 3½ inches wide across the width of the material long enough to fit round the waist.

Taking the large piece of material, turn a ½-inch hem down each side, then fold over again, making a hem 1 inch wide. Tack both sides with sewing cotton.

Turn up ½ inch along the bottom and fold over again to make a hem 2 inches wide. Tack with sewing cotton. All these hems are to be turned to the right side.

Choose which colours of embroidery cotton are to be used and work a simple border on all hems, on the right side of the material.

Measure 2 inches up from the bottom hem. A crease may be made as a guide for the first row of tacking stitches, but no other guides may be used in working this border as the eye must be trained to judge the spacing without a guide.

Any tacking or embroidery stitches may be used in this border. Chain stitch is very effective used with tacking stitch. Blanket stitch, couching and herring-bone stitch also are good. Several colours may be used. The design must balance, *i.e.*, the top and bottom lines should be the same. The lines inside those should correspond, and so on into the middle line (see Fig. 6).

The top of the apron may be pleated as in the illustration, or it may be gathered and set into the band (instructions for setting gathers into a band are given in Plain Needlework).

The ends of the band which come beyond the apron on both sides should be over-sewn in colour and finished with a button and a loop to fasten.

Felt and linen, embroidered in an easy lazy daisy stitch, make an attractive breakfast set of tea cosy, egg cosy and napkin holder.

Materials :—

About ½ a yard of cream linen (according to width).
Coloured felt.
Embroidery Cotton in different colours.

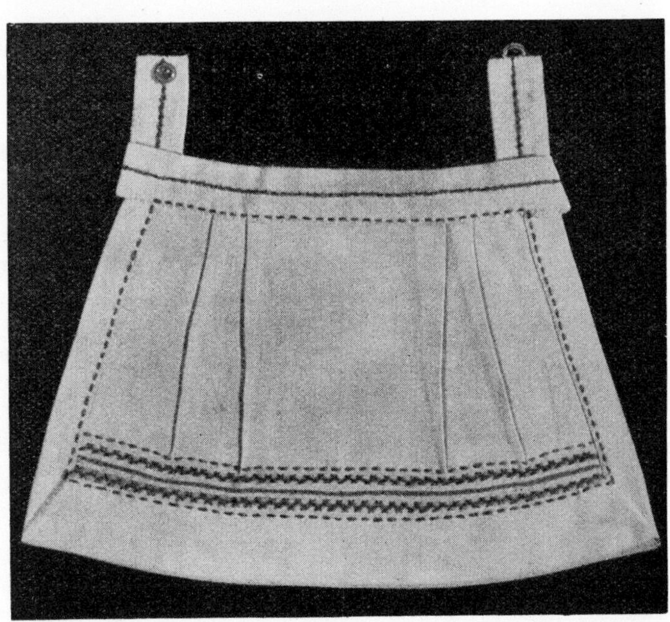

FIG. 4
The first article the child makes in finer needlework should be simple. An apron is a good choice; the seams are short and the decoration keeps the work from becoming monotonous.

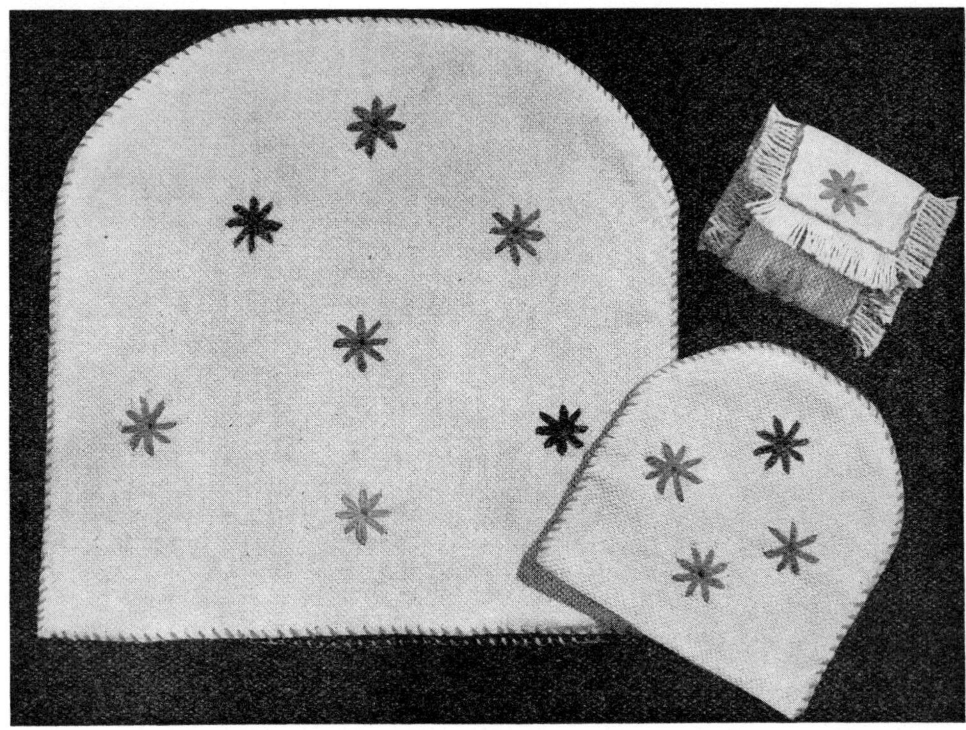

Fig. 5
This breakfast set of tea cosy, egg cosy and napkin holder in linen and felt is easy to make. Lazy daisies in different colours provide the decoration. The napkin holder is fringed.

Method

For the tea cosy, cut out two pieces of linen 11 inches square, then curve off the tops. Two pieces 5 inches square with curved tops make the egg cosy, and a strip $7\frac{1}{2}$ by $3\frac{1}{2}$ inches makes the napkin holder. Cut pieces of felt to correspond, making them $\frac{1}{2}$ an inch less in size than the linen. Embroider your lazy daisies on the linen, first marking positions with a pencil dot, taking the needle into the same centre hole each time. Then place the four pieces of felt for the cosies on the wrong side of the work, turn the linen over the edges, and tack all round. Sew the felt linings to the linen covers, then join the two large sections together with oversewing stitch at two sides and over curved top to make the tea cosy; the two smaller sections are joined in the same way for the egg cosy. Finish off the lower edges also with oversewing stitch. A row of tacking stitch joins the linen cover to the felt lining of the napkin holder, and then the $\frac{1}{2}$-inch all round is fringed by drawing out the threads. The "ring" is fastened with a press stud, or a button and worked loop.

PLAIN NEEDLEWORK

There are certain seams and stitches that are used on all garments and household linens. These are described and illustrated here. It is important that the correct way of doing each stitch and seam should be learned at the beginning, and these few general directions carefully noted.

Use as fine a needle as is suitable for the material. Its point should be very sharp and its eye just large enough to take the cotton or silk. A blunt point or a large eye would pucker the material.

For plain needlework use as fine a cotton or silk as is suitable for the material.

Knots should never be used, except

to start tacking or gathering. All other seams should be begun by taking several small stitches backwards. These will be covered by the seam. In hemming they should be hidden under the hem.

Take only a short length of cotton or silk in the needle. A long one twists and becomes knotted.

Tacking (Fig. 1)

This is used to keep two pieces of material in place while they are being sewn together. Take small stitches through, with a long stitch between, near, but not over the place to be sewn. It is best to tack with cotton or silk of a different colour from the material as it shows up better and can be more easily removed.

Hemming (Fig. 2)

This is the most usual way of finishing an edge. The hem must be even and should be tacked down before the sewing is begun. The needle is inserted in a slanting direction up and under the hem. It comes out just above the edge of the hem and is inserted again a little in front of the place where it came out. The thread must not be pulled tightly or it will pucker the material.

Back-Stitching (Fig. 3)

Back-stitching is the firmest method of joining two pieces of material. It consists in taking small stitches in a straight line, inserting the needle for each stitch at the point where it came out in the previous stitch.

Over-sewing (Fig. 4)

This method is most often used when two selvedges have to be sewn together. Tack them firmly in place. Take small stitches through both pieces of material, inserting the needle at the back and bringing it out straight through to the front. Insert it again for the next

Fig. 6

The border above is worked largely in tacking stitch, used horizontally, vertically and diagonally, but there are two lines of herring bone, two of chain stitch and four of outline stitch. Care and judgment must be exercised in the placing of the colours. Those that differ most from the background should form the smaller stitches.

PLAIN NEEDLEWORK (1)

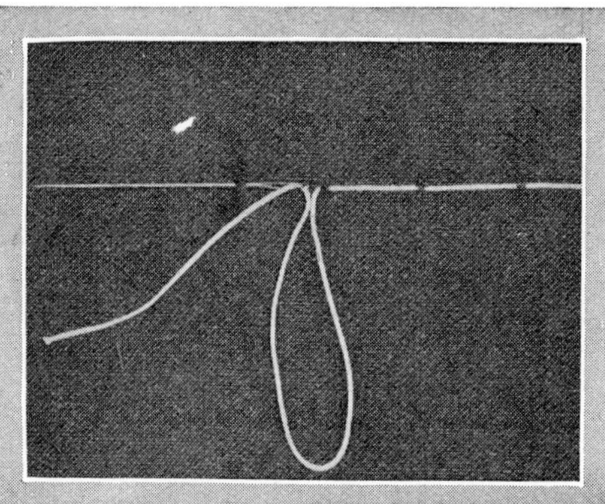

FIG. 1 shows how to tack two pieces of material together. Only a small stitch must be taken through, or the two pieces will pull apart.

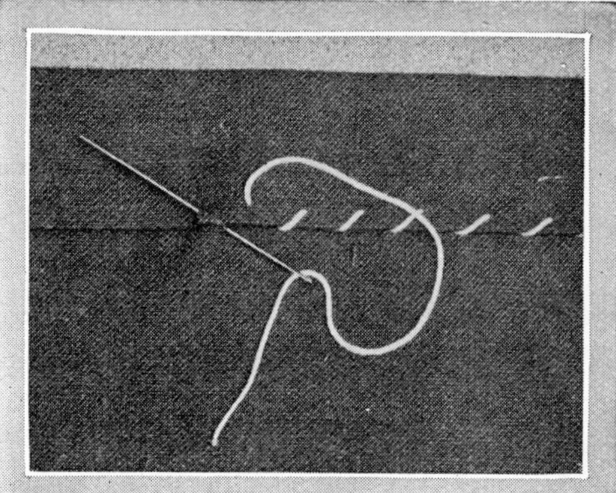

FIG. 2.—In hemming, the direction of the needle is all-important. It must slant, as in the picture, and be inserted again in front of where it came out.

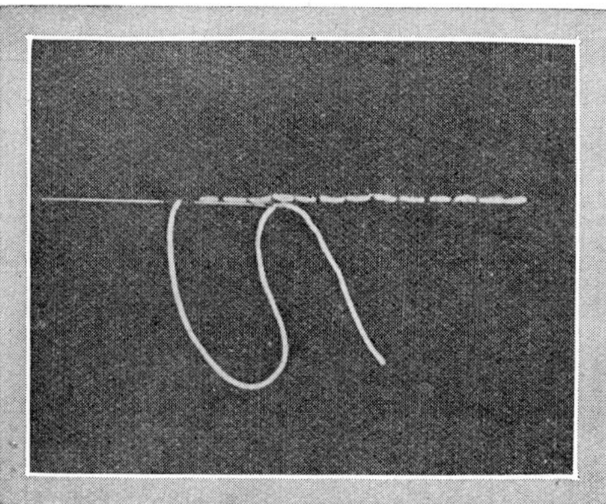

FIG. 3.—In back-stitching the needle is put in where the thread from the previous stitch came out. It is important to make all the stitches the same length.

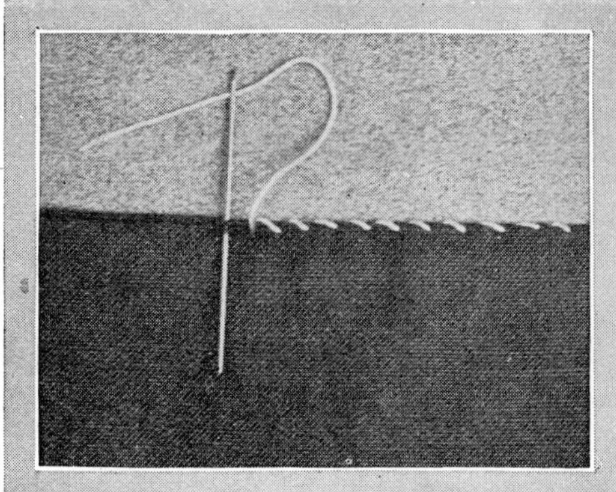

FIG. 4.—The direction of the needle is important in over-sewing. It should point straight towards the body as it comes through. Note how the stitches slant.

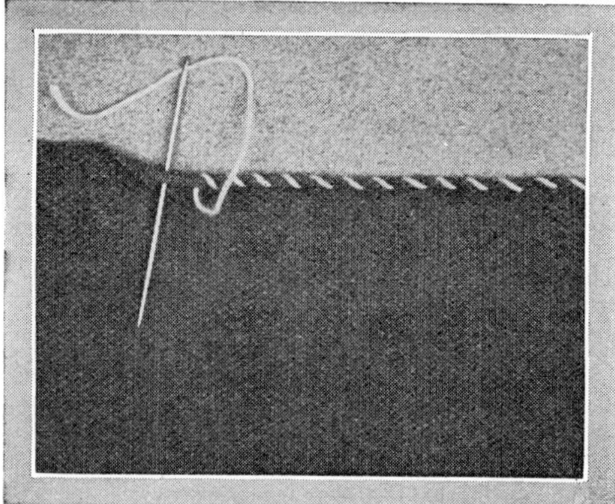

FIG. 5.—Whipping is the same stitch as over-sewing, but it is done over only one thickness of material, the edge of which is rolled over by the left thumb.

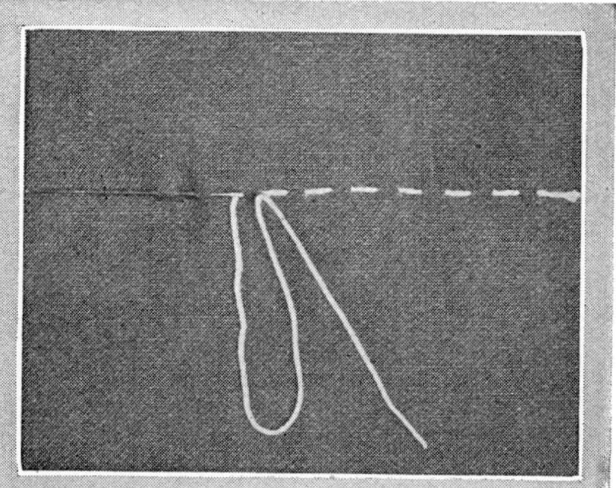

FIG. 6.—A knot is used to begin a gathering thread. The stitches must be of equal length, and of the same length as the space between.

PLAIN NEEDLEWORK (2)

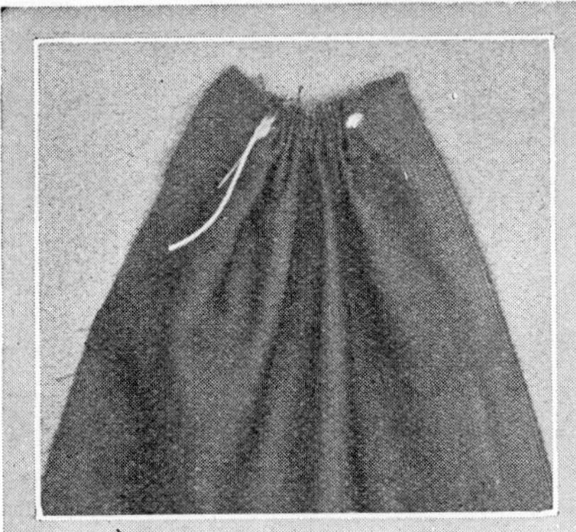

FIG. 7 shows the gathers pulled up for stroking. The eye end of the needle should be used for this, for fear of tearing the material.

FIG. 8.—Here the stroked gathers are ready to be set into the band. They must be tacked into position and then stitched down to the band on the wrong side, one stitch being taken over each pleat.

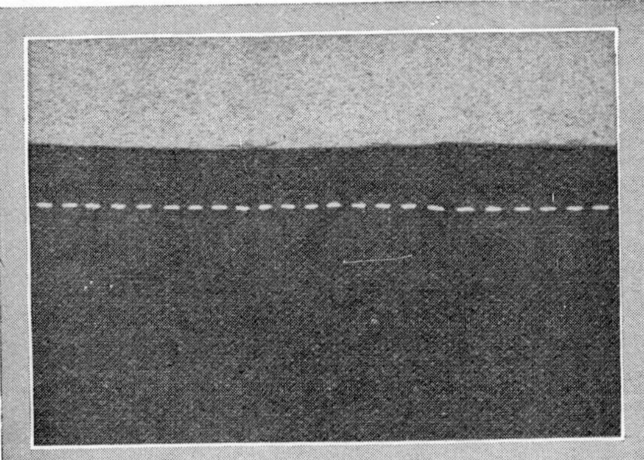

FIG. 9 shows the first part of a run-and-fell seam. The work must next be opened up flat and a small hem turned down on the back piece of material and tacked in position.

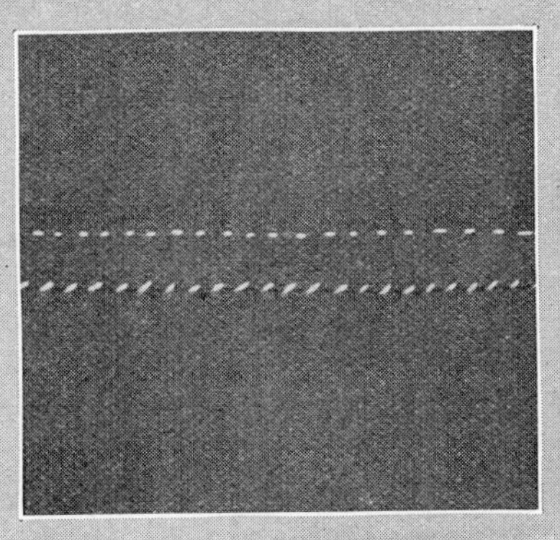

FIG. 10.—Here the hem has been sewn down and the finished seam is seen. It makes a flat join, and is useful in making underclothing.

FIG. 11 shows the first part of a French seam. This is done on the right side of the material. The raw edges are then trimmed as close to the seam as possible.

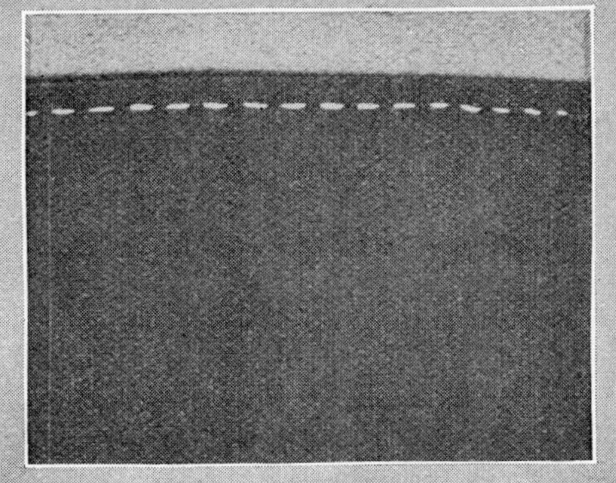

FIG. 12.—In this the finished French seam is seen. This second part is done on the wrong side of the material. The seam is used on dresses, blouses and children's clothes.

stitch a little in front of the place where it came out in the previous stitch.

Whipping (Fig. 5)

The stitch in this case is the same as in over-sewing. It is used to finish an edge where a hem is not desired, and sometimes lace is sewn on at the same time. Roll a small portion of the raw edge of the material towards the body between the moistened finger and thumb of the left hand. Sew this down as in over-sewing, then roll the next part. Never roll more than 1 inch at a time, as it comes unrolled and is apt to fray with too much handling. If lace is to be joined by this method it should have its straight edge laid at the back of the material and the stitch taken through both lace and material.

Gatherings (Figs. 6, 7, and 8)

This must be started with a knot which should be fairly large and should be on the right side of the material. Small even stitches are picked up, keeping the line parallel with the edge of the material (Fig. 6). When the end is reached, take off the needle and make a knot at the end of the thread. Put in a pin at right angles to the line of gathering thread, just beyond the last stitch, which should be ½ inch from the end of the material. Pull the gathering thread up tightly and wind the cotton round the pin, first round the head then round the point (Fig. 7).

To Stroke the Gathers. Hold the material with the gathered part over the first finger of the left hand. Take the needle in the other hand and pull it gently down between each fold of the material, using the eye end so as not to tear the material.

To Set the Gathers. When the gathers have all been stroked into position, take out the pin, attach the right-hand end to the band, ½ inch from the head of the band with a pin, attach the other end in the same way to the other end of the band, regulate the fullness and again wind the cotton round the pin. Tack the seam in position.

The gathering must now be stitched to the band, which is placed behind the gathers with the two right sides together and the raw edges at the top. Take one stitch through each fold.

Turn the ½-inch ends of the band to the inside, turning also a ½-inch hem on the wrong side of the band itself (Fig. 8). Tack this down over the gathering thread. Over-sew the ends, and hem the rest of the band, taking one stitch between each gather.

Run-and-Fell Seam (Figs. 9 and 10)

Tack two pieces of material so that the front piece is ½ inch lower than the back one (Fig. 9). The right side of the material is inside. Run all along the edge of this lower piece (running is the same stitch as gathering, but is not pulled up). When this is done, trim the lower piece as narrow as possible, open up the seam, and run a finger or thimble along the seam on the right side. Now fold over a very narrow hem on the back piece of material. Tack it and hem it down neatly. This is called felling (Fig. 10). It makes a neat flat seam.

French Seam (Figs. 11 and 12)

Put the pieces of material to be joined with their edges meeting. Tack them firmly. If a thick material is to be sewn this should be stitched a ¼ inch from the edge. If the material is thin a fine running stitch is better. This first seam should be done on the right side of the material (Fig. 11).

Now turn the garment inside out and make another seam, similar to the first, on the wrong side of the material (Fig. 12).

For flannel the first seam is stitched as for the first seam described above. Then the two raw edges are opened out and each is herring-boned down to the material (see Herring-bone).

Sewing on Buttons (Figs. 13 and 14)

Linen buttons may be sewn on in either of two ways. First by making a

PLAIN NEEDLEWORK (3)

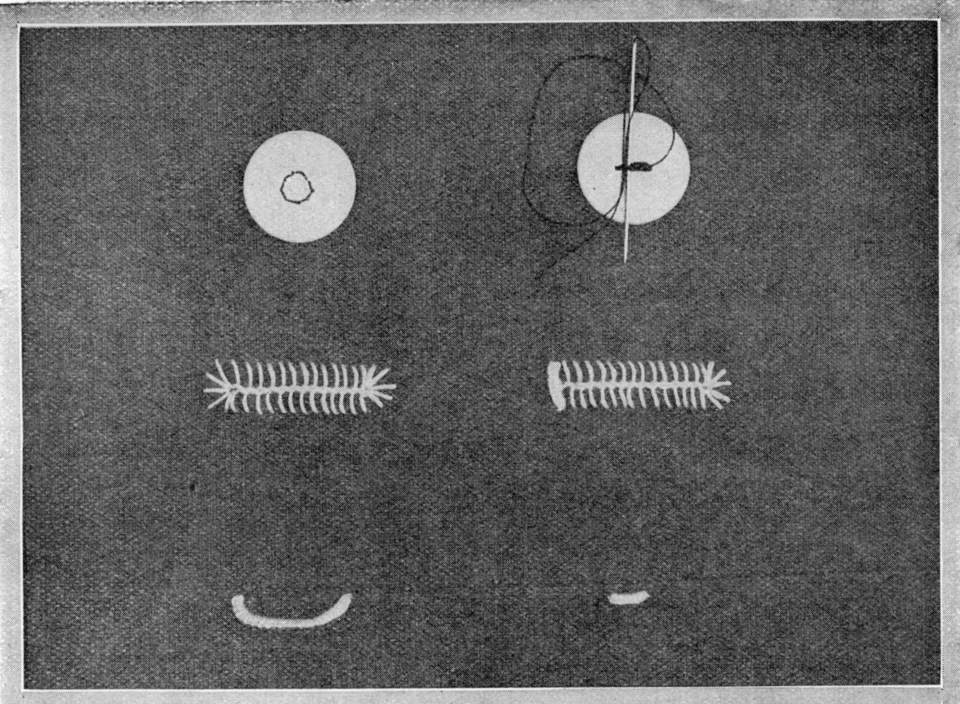

FIG. 13.—Linen button attached with a ring of stitching.

FIG. 14.—Linen button attached with a buttonholed loop.

FIG. 15 shows how to make an ordinary buttonhole.

FIG. 16.—A buttonhole that will stand a strain.

FIG. 17.—Large buttonholed loop, to take a button.

FIG. 18.—Small buttonholed loop to take a hook.

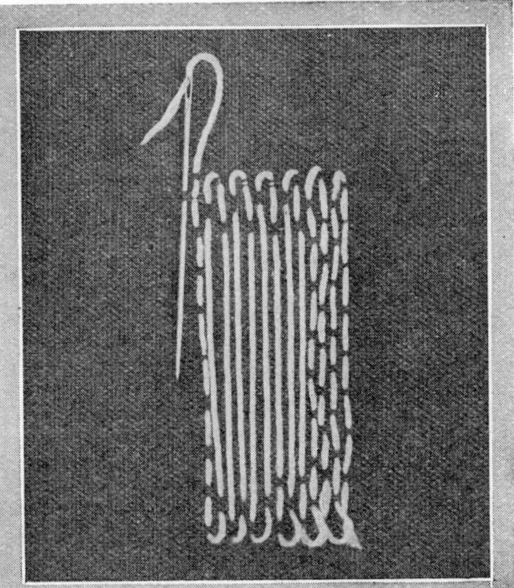

FIG. 19.—This shows how the right side of a darn should look before the cross-threads are darned in. Note the loops which allow for shrinkage.

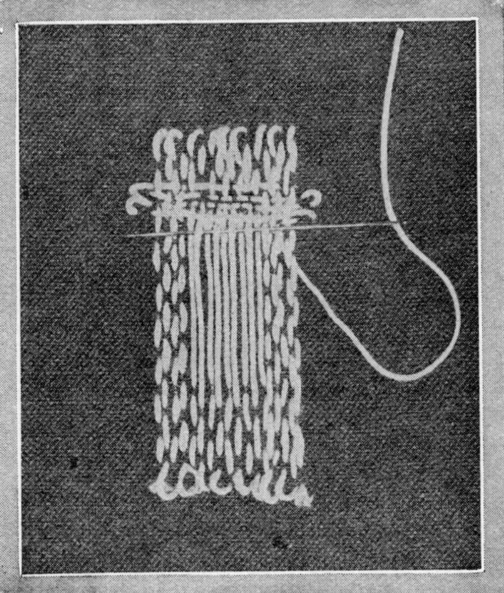

FIG. 20 shows the method of filling in the hole in darning. Thick wools or cottons should never be used for this work, as they tear the material in working.

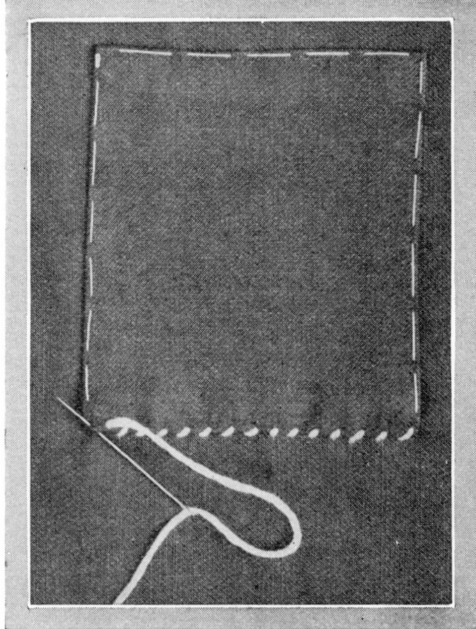

FIG. 21

A patch applied over the worn part. This must be tacked firmly in position and hemmed down with small stitches.

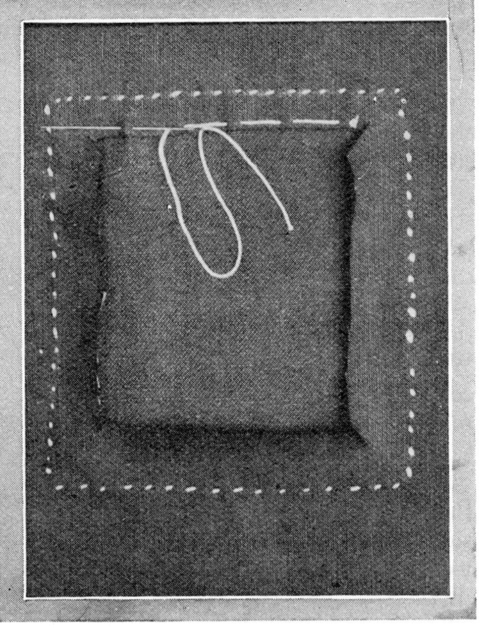

FIG. 22

Here is shown the worn part of the material cut away. The part that is left must be mitred, tacked and hemmed down.

ring of stitching as in Fig. 13, or by taking three or four long stitches across the top and covering these with buttonhole stitch as in Fig. 14, using the eye of the needle.

Buttonholes (Figs. 15 and 16)

Buttonholes must be cut on the straight of the material and should preferably lie across, not up and down, a garment. They must be worked as soon as cut, or the edges will fray.

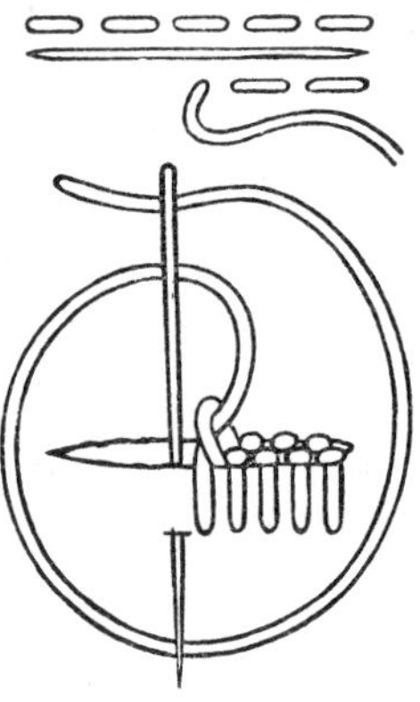

Tacking round the slit (*top*) and buttonhole stitch.

First mark the position of the buttonhole, then cut a small slit and test for size with the button to be used. Lightly tack round the cut at the edges. The small diagram shows you how the stitch is done—it is rather like blanket stitch worked the other way round, and from right to left. Work fanwise at the end where the strain comes, and work a blanket stitch bar at the other end. Fasten off at the back by running the thread under the stitches.

Loops (Figs. 17 and 18)

Where material is too thick to make a buttonhole a loop is often used. A pencil should be laid on the material and two or three stitches taken over this. Take the pencil out and test whether the stitches are the right length by passing the button through them. The button should go through easily, as the loop tightens when it is being covered. Cover these stitches with blanket stitch, being careful to see before starting that enough thread is in the needle to finish the work, as it is not possible to join it in the middle (Fig. 17).

A smaller loop for a hook is made without the pencil (Fig. 18).

Darning (Figs. 19 and 20)

Use fine wool or silk for darning, and work with the smallest-eyed needle that will take the thread. Use silk on silk and wool on wool. Work on the right side of the material.

Run two or three rows of darning stitch up and down the material by the side of the hole, leaving a small loop at the turning. Darning always shrinks in washing, and if these loops are left the darn will not pucker when it shrinks. When the hole is reached the thread to cover it must be on the right side of the material, and the needle should be inserted on the right side of the material on the other side of the hole (Fig. 19). Pick up two or three stitches on each side of the hole at top and bottom as well as at the sides. When the first threads are laid, cut off the wool or silk, and start darning from side to side, filling in the hole by going alternately over and under the laid threads as well as over and under the stitches at the sides of the hole. The thread is not fastened either at the beginning or end of the work (Fig. 20).

Patching (Figs. 21 and 22)

Take a piece of material to match the piece to be patched. Cut a square that will cover the hole and leave 1 inch to spare at all four sides. If the material is patterned, match the patterns on the patch. Turn in a ½-inch hem all round this square, tack it firmly and hem down on the right side (Fig. 21).

Turn over to the wrong side, cut away the worn material, slit up the corners to a depth of ½ inch, turn in a hem and sew it down (Fig. 22).

EMBROIDERY STITCHES

Blanket Stitch **(see p. 395)**

Chain Stitch (Fig. 1)

Hold the thread down with the left thumb. Take a stitch downwards from the place where the thread started. Pull the needle through. Take the next stitch from inside the previous one. This stitch may be worked in strands of silk, wool or cotton.

Couching (Fig. 2)

Place one or more thick threads in position and sew them down with one strand of a thinner thread, taking regularly spaced stitches. This looks best when the couching thread is in another colour from the threads which are to be sewn down.

Cross Stitch **(see p. 442)**

Daisy Stitch (Figs. 3 and 4)

Hold the thread down with the left thumb and take a stitch like a chain stitch (Fig. 3). Now insert the needle under the loop and bring out near the beginning of the previous stitch (Fig. 4). Use strands of silk, wool or cotton for this stitch.

Embroidery Darning (Fig. 5)

This is used in embroidery to fill up backgrounds. It may be worked in silk, wool or cotton. Lift a very small stitch and keep the work regular.

Feather Stitching (Fig. 6)

Hold the thread down with the left thumb. Pick up a slanting stitch to the left of the thread, with the needle pointing towards the body, pull the needle through. Hold the thread down and take the next stitch to the right of it, slanting towards the middle. This is generally worked in cotton thread, but can be done in silk.

Fly Stitch (Fig. 7)

Take a stitch as for feather stitching, but insert the needle in a line with the starting place of the thread. Catch the thread down with a small stitch as in daisy stitch taking the needle back to the right of the stitch just completed. This is suitable for thick threads only.

French Knots (Fig. 8)

Work this with double thread. Take

EMBROIDERY STITCHES (1)

FIG. 1.—*Chain Stitch.* — The needle goes back each time into the last loop.

FIG. 2.—*Couching.*—One or more thick strands sewn down with a thinner strand.

FIG. 3. — *Daisy Stitch.*—The first part resembles one chain stitch.

FIG. 4.—The needle taken back to the centre for the next petal.

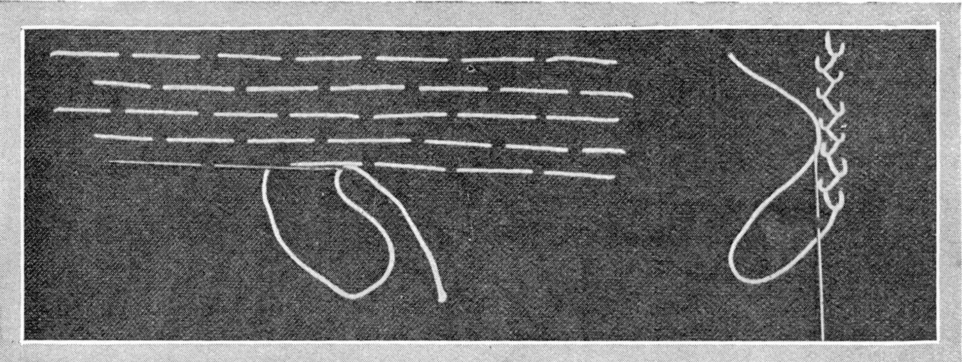

FIG. 5.—*Embroidery Darning.*—This consists of rows of tacking stitch, in which the stitches of one row alternate with the spaces in the previous row. It is used to fill in backgrounds.

FIG. 6.—*Feather Stitching.*—Notice the slant of the needle. It must be inserted each time below the end of the previous stitch.

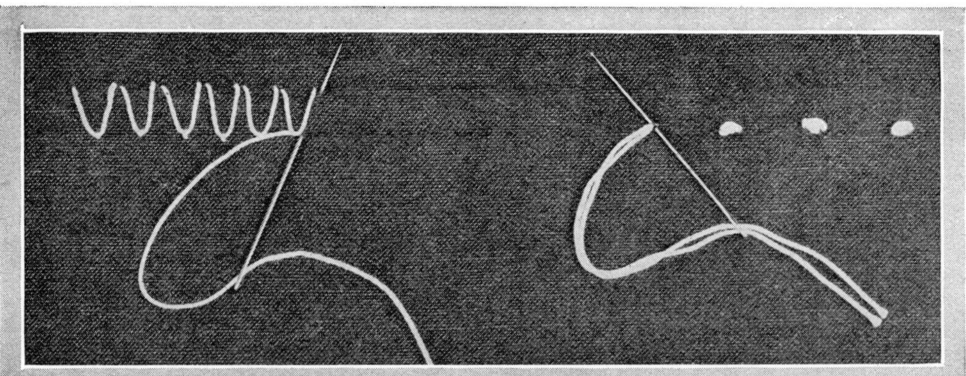

FIG. 7.—*Fly Stitch* is like daisy stitch with the top end open, and the stitches in a row instead of a circle. Two creases may be made in the material to keep the edges parallel.

FIG. 8.—*French Knots.*—These are often used to fasten down a hem. They are also used as centres for flowers, for small flowers, such as forget-me-nots, or to form a fruit.

EMBROIDERY STITCHES (2)

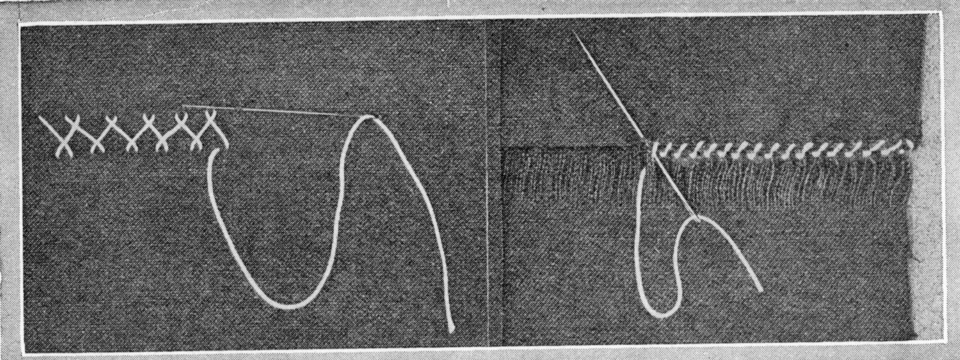

FIG. 9.—*Herring-boning.*—This is a useful stitch in embroidery. It may be worked solid in colour on the wrong side of transparent white material to form a design.

FIG. 10.—*Hem-stitching.*—This is very effective if the other edge of the drawn threads is also worked, keeping the threads in the same bunches (see p. 416).

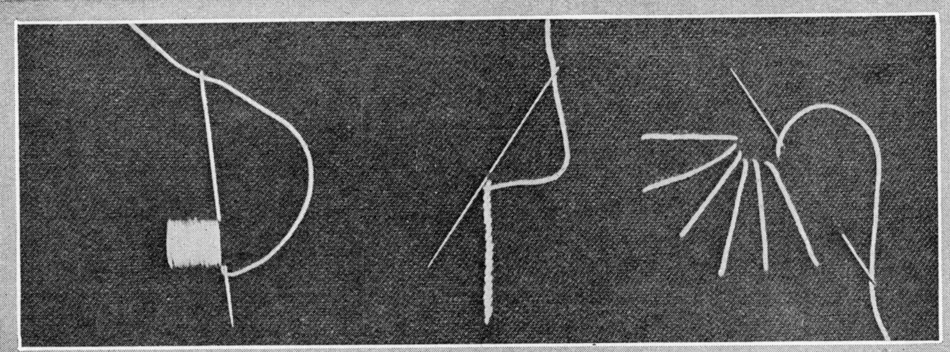

FIG. 11.—*Satin Stitch.*—This is a useful stitch for solid embroidery in either natural or conventional design. Padding underneath improves it.

FIG. 12.—*Stem Stitch.*—This is sometimes called outline stitch. It is used for outline embroidery, and also for stems and veins.

FIG. 13.—*Stroke Stitch* is very effective worked in thick wools or raffia on canvas. It is especially good for geometrical designs.

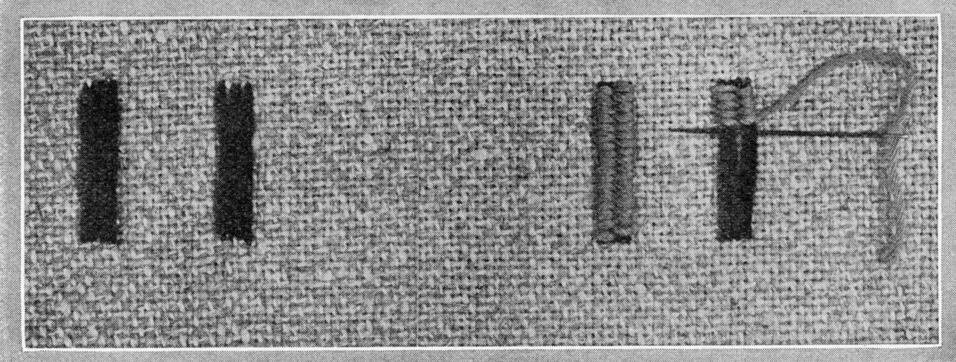

FIG. 14.—*Weaving Stitch.*—Laid threads are seen above. Instead of laying these, threads may be pulled out of any coarse-meshed material as for hemstitching.

FIG. 15 shows the method of weaving the threads shown in Fig. 14. The weaving may be done over any number of groups. There are only two groups in the illustrations.

a very small stitch with the needle, twist the double thread once round the needle, and, holding the twist with the thumb, pull needle through and insert it under the knot. This looks best in silk and cotton threads.

Herring-boning (Fig. 9)

This is worked from left to right on two parallel lines. Bring the needle to the front on the top line, then, keeping the needle under the thread, take a small stitch on the lower line, then one on the top line. This stitch is often used on flannel where a double folded hem is not desired. It should be worked in sewing silk. If a closed herring-bone stitch is worked, with no space between the stitches, a neat double row of stitches will result on the right side. It can also be used for decorative purposes in cotton or wool.

Hem-stitching (Fig. 10)

Below the hem pull out as many threads as desired. The number will vary according to the material used, more being pulled out in finely woven and fewer in a thick material.

Tack the hem down. Pass the needle under three, four or five threads, pull it through, then, bringing it back to the space it started from, take a hemming-stitch through the hem, bringing the needle out above the little cluster of threads thus pulled together. Silk thread should be used on a silk material and linen on linen.

Satin Stitch (Fig. 11)

This stitch is used to cover a space, the needle being inserted close to the previous stitch. It can be worked either from right to left or left to right. It is best worked in silk or cotton.

Stem Stitch (Fig. 12)

This should be worked in firm and fairly fine thread, as it is used for definite lines. Pick up a small stitch, always keeping the needle on the left of the thread and on the left of the previous stitch.

Stroke Stitch (Fig. 13)

This consists of single stitches taken in any direction the pattern may require. It is best worked in thick threads.

Weaving Stitch (Figs. 14 and 15)

Strands of thread may be worked for a foundation, as in Fig. 14, or threads may be drawn from the material. Divide the strands into equal numbers and darn them as in Fig. 15, using a tapestry needle.

Borders can be worked in this way in blocks of alternate colours, with drawn threads as a foundation, or darned strands may be used as slots for cord in drawing up bags. Thick silk, cotton or wool should be used for working.

Now that we have heard about all these different materials and what we can do with them, let us consider, what is rarely thought of, but much more important, the effect that the work has on the worker.

A piece of work may be well executed and beautiful, but unless it is the unaided expression of the worker (in choice of suitable material, choice of design and the method and means of working it out, as well as the work itself) it is of little value, as it has done nothing to strengthen the worker's individual powers.

And again, no matter how beautiful the result is, if the work is not the very best that the worker can produce it cannot be regarded as satisfactory. Remember the proverb, "The good is the enemy of the best," which means that a person who is content to do less than his best will be satisfied with second-best all his life, making no effort to improve. A child should not compare his work with that of other children, but with what he could previously do.

It is only if he trains his hands in this way to be the servants of his brain, and uses his intelligence, judgment, patience, perseverance and powers of observation in all his work that he will one day understand what is meant by "The joy of creation."